The Antitrust Revolution

The Antitrust Revolution

Economics, Competition, and Policy

Fourth Edition

John E. Kwoka, Jr.
Lawrence J. White

New York   Oxford
OXFORD UNIVERSITY PRESS
2004

Oxford University Press

Oxford   New York
Auckland   Bangkok   Buenos Aires   Cape Town   Chennai
Dar es Salaam   Delhi   Hong Kong   Istanbul   Karachi   Kolkata
Kuala Lumpur   Madrid   Melbourne   Mexico City   Mumbai
Nairobi   São Paulo   Shanghai   Taipei   Tokyo   Toronto

Copyright © 2004 by Oxford University Press, Inc.

Published by Oxford University Press, Inc.
198 Madison Avenue, New York, New York, 10016
http://www.oup-usa.org

Oxford is a registered trademark of Oxford University Press

Library of Congress Cataloging-in-Publication Data
The antitrust revolution : economics, competition, and policy/[edited by] John E. Kwoka,
Jr., Lawrence J. White.—4th ed.
p. cm.
Includes bibliographical references.
ISBN-13 978-0-19-516117-5; 978-0-19-516118-2 (pbk.)
ISBN   0-19-516117-3; 0-19-516118-1 (pbk.)
1. Trusts, Industrial—Government policy—United States—Case
studies.   2. Antitrust law—Economic aspects—United States—Case
studies.   I. Kwoka, John E. II. White, Lawrence J.
HD2795 .A64 2003
338.8′5—dc21   2002042551

Printing number: 9   8   7   6   5   4

Printed in the United States of America
on acid-free paper

To Margaret, the best of all daughters.
J. E. K.

To the two most important people in my life:
Martha and David.
L. J. W.

Contents

PART II. Horizontal Practices

PART III. Vertical and Related Market Issues

PART IV. Network Issues

The Economic and Legal Context

Preface

This book consists of reports from the front lines of a revolution. The revolution in question involves the critical role of economics in the antitrust process, and the reports in this book are descriptions of recent antitrust cases written by economists who were involved in them. These case studies provide insight into how economists think about antitrust issues, how economic evidence is treated in courts of law, and how economics increasingly influences the entire antitrust process. Each case provides a detailed description of key issues, arguments, and evidence. Each provides an evaluation of the economic and legal significance of the proceeding. And each sets out an economic perspective on an interesting industry and the policy questions that it raises.

The first edition of *The Antitrust Revolution* was gratifyingly well received. Many reported to us the enthusiasm of students, instructors, and practitioners of antitrust for the type of economics-oriented case studies that comprise this volume. That reception encouraged us to pursue a subsequent edition, then another, and now this, the fourth. In one sense our motivation has been unchanged throughout: to capture and convey the ever-greater role of industrial organization economics in the antitrust process. But over time this purpose has taken on other dimensions.

For example, it has become apparent that the "antitrust revolution" is an ongoing phenomenon. There is no universally agreed-upon target toward which antitrust analysis and policy are moving. Rather, the underlying industrial organization economics is an evolving body of understanding, so new ways of looking at issues are constantly emerging. Each new edition of *The Antitrust Revolution* reflects these changing perspectives, as it should. In addition, however, these four editions collectively make clear that economics plays a central role in a growing number of cases, and certainly in all major antitrust cases of our time. This is the revolution that we seek to chronicle.

This edition is much changed from its predecessors. The collection has grown to twenty cases, of which fourteen are entirely new. The large number of new cases reflects the increased frequency with which economically important issues are being raised and decided. These newly written cases include several from technology-based industries, including the Intel, Microsoft, and AOL-Time Warner cases; major mergers such as Heinz–Beech-Nut, MCI WorldCom-Sprint, and GE-Honeywell that raise significant policy questions; and cases alleging collusion, predation, and other anticompetitive practices, such as ADM, American Airlines, and prescription drug pricing.

As before, while most of the cases in this volume involve antitrust issues raised before the Federal Trade Commission or the Justice Department's Antitrust Division, they also concern cases brought by private parties, as well as others pursued by the states' attorneys general, or raised before regulatory bodies in their competition-protection role. The authors represent in some cases the sides that prevailed, and in others the sides whose arguments fell short. And while most of these cases are resolved, at least a couple remain in the courts or are subject to further appeal.

This edition also has a new organization of the cases. In addition to sections on Horizontal Structure, Horizontal Practices, and Vertical and Related Market Issues, all of which appeared in the past, there is a new section on Network Issues. This contains mostly new cases where the network properties of the industry—operating systems, information networks, etc.—play an important role in the central antitrust issues. This new section also reflects the increasing attention that antitrust is paying to network industries. Readers will undoubtedly note that there are other cases in the book that also involve network industries, but where the central issues are not their networks, we have located them under the otherwise most appropriate heading.

We have kept several cases from the last edition where those cases continue to illustrate important issues and applications of industrial organization economics. As always, we regret not being able to retain more previous cases, but with this edition that problem has been substantially alleviated. Oxford University Press has posted all previous cases not in this edition—back through the first edition—on its website, so that instructors, students, and practitioners can access them conveniently. These can now be found at www.oup.com/us/antitrustrevolution.

For this fourth edition we would like to express out gratitude to the many people who have provided assistance. These include Paul Donnelly and Stephen McGroarty, our editors at Oxford University Press, for their support for this project, and Suzanne Robblee, our editorial assistant at Northeastern University, for managing the flow of work and ensuring the completion of this undertaking. In addition, we want to thank our numerous authors—now twenty-six in number, apart from ourselves—for their interest in participating in this project, for their willingness to write balanced accounts of cases about which they invariably feel strongly, and for responding to all our suggestions and deadlines. We are genuinely excited by their reports from the front lines of the revolution.

Most of all, however, we want again to thank our own students, students everywhere, instructors, and practitioners who have read *The Antitrust Revolution.* Your enthusiastic reactions and your helpful comments have contributed much to making this fourth edition a reality. We hope that this volume meets your expectations.

J. E. K.
L. J. W.

Contributors

Jonathan B. Baker is a professor at the Washington College of Law, American University, and Editorial Chair of *Antitrust Law Journal.* He has served as Director of the Bureau of Economics of the Federal Trade Commission, Senior Economist at the Council of Economic Advisers, and Special Assistant to the Deputy Assistant Attorney General for Economics in the Antitrust Division of the U.S. Department of Justice.

Gustavo E. Bamberger is a Senior Vice President of Lexecon, Inc. He has provided expert antitrust testimony to U.S. federal courts, the Canadian Competition Tribunal, and a variety of regulatory agencies, including the U.S. Federal Energy Regulatory Commission, the U.S. Federal Communications Commission, and the U.S. Department of Transportation.

Severin Borenstein is E.T. Grether Professor of Business and Public Policy in the Economic Analysis and Policy Group of the Haas School of Business at the University of California at Berkeley. He is also Director of the University of California Energy Institute and a Research Associate of the National Bureau of Economic Research.

Steven R. Brenner is a Vice President in the Washington, D.C., office of Charles River Associates. Previously, he was a consultant to the OECD, Senior Economist at the Federal Communications Commission, and on the faculty of Grinnell College.

Jeremy Bulow is the Richard Stepp Professor of Economics at Stanford Business School. He has served as the Director of the Bureau of Economics of the Federal Trade Commission.

Dennis W. Carlton is a professor in the Graduate School of Business at the University of Chicago, an NBER Research Associate, and a consultant with Lexecon, Inc. He has been a member of the Economics Departments of MIT and the University of Chicago, as well as the Law School and Graduate School of Business at the University of Chicago.

John M. Connor is Professor of Agricultural Economics at Purdue University. He formerly taught at the University of Wisconsin at Madison and headed the

Food Manufacturing Research Section of the U.S. Department of Agriculture's Economic Research Service.

Serdar Dalkir is a Ph.D. Economist at Microeconomic Consulting and Research Associates.

Aaron S. Edlin is Professor of Economics and Law at the University of California, Berkeley, teaching industrial organization and antitrust law. He served as Senior Economist to the President's Council of Economic Advisers from 1997 to 1998.

Kenneth G. Elzinga is Robert C. Taylor Professor of Economics at the University of Virginia. He was one of the first Special Economic Assistants at the Antitrust Division of the Department of Justice and more recently was Thomas Jefferson Visiting Scholar at Cambridge University.

Joseph Farrell is Professor of Economics and Chair of the Competition Policy Center at the University of California, Berkeley. From 1996 to 1997, he was Chief Economist at the Federal Communications Commission and from 2000 to 2001, he was Deputy Assistant Attorney General at the U.S. Department of Justice.

Gerald R. Faulhaber is Professor of Business and Public Policy at the Wharton School, University of Pennsylvania. He served as Chief Economist at the Federal Communications Commission from 2000 to 2001.

Franklin M. Fisher is the Jane Berkowitz Carlton and Dennis William Carlton Professor of Economics at the Massachusetts Institute of Technology, where he has taught for more than forty years.

John E. Kwoka, Jr., is Neal F. Finnegan Distinguished Professor of Economics at Northeastern University, Research Professor of Economics at George Washington University, Research Fellow of the American Antitrust Institute, and Editor of the *Review of Industrial Organization.*

Jeffrey K. MacKie-Mason is the Arthur W. Burks Collegiate Professor of Information and Computer Science at the University of Michigan, where he is also a Professor of Economics and Public Policy. He is the senior partner of ApplEcon LLC, and has been a National Fellow at the Hoover Institute of Stanford University.

Christopher Maxwell is a Vice President with Charles River Associates. He has previously been an Assistant Professor of Economics at Boston College.

John Metzler is a Principal at ApplEcon LLC.

David E. Mills is Professor of Economics at the University of Virginia.

Barry Nalebuff is the Milton Steinbach Professor of Economics and Management at Yale School of Management.

Michael D. Pelcovits is a Principal at Microeconomic Consulting and Research Associates and was formerly Vice President and Chief Economist of WorldCom, Inc. He has worked at the Federal Communications Commission and taught at the University of Maryland.

Robert Porter is William R. Kenan Jr. Professor of Economics at Northwestern University. He is also an editor of the *RAND Journal of Economics,* and a research associate of the National Bureau of Economic Research.

Daniel L. Rubinfeld is Robert L. Bridges Professor of Law and Professor of Economics at the University of California, Berkeley. He served as Deputy Assistant Attorney General for Antitrust in the U.S. Department of Justice during 1997 and 1998.

F. M. Scherer is Aetna Professor Emeritus in the John F. Kennedy School of Government, Harvard University, and Lecturer in the Woodrow Wilson School, Princeton University. Between 1974 and 1976 he was Director of the Federal Trade Commission's Bureau of Economics.

Evan Sue Schouten is a Vice President with Charles River Associates.

Carl Shapiro is the Transamerica Professor of Business Strategy at the Haas School of Business, University of California, Berkeley. He served as Deputy Assistant Attorney General for Economics in the Antitrust Division of the U.S. Department of Justice from 1995 to 1996.

Frederick R. Warren-Boulton is a Principal of Microeconomic Consulting and Research Associates. He served as Chief Economist and Deputy Assistant Attorney General in the Department of Justice, and has been a Resident Scholar at the American Enterprise Institute, and Associate Professor of Economics at Washington University, and a Research Associate Professor of Psychology at American University.

Lawrence J. White is Arthur E. Imperatore Professor of Economics at the Stern School of Business, New York University. He has served as a Board Member on the Federal Home Loan Bank Board, as the Chief Economist in the Antitrust Division of the U.S. Department of Justice, and on the Senior Staff of the Council of Economic Advisers.

J. Douglas Zona is Vice President in the New York City office of Cornerstone Research, where he also heads the firm's antitrust practice. He has consulted on antitrust and econometric issues for the Antitrust Division, U.S. Department of Justice, and the Federal Trade Commission.

Introduction

Antitrust policy in the United States now spans three different centuries and many epochs in this nation's economic history. The first law to be enacted—the Sherman Act of 1890—was a reaction to widespread discontent with business during the Industrial Revolution. The Clayton Act and the Federal Trade Commission Act of 1914 were directed at anticompetitive mergers and other conduct as the nation moved toward the Great Depression and two world wars. Most recently, this country has found itself in the midst of an equally profound Information Revolution. Each of these periods has raised questions concerning the effects of dominant firms, mergers, collusive behavior, vertical integration, predatory pricing, tying, and other matters. And each of these periods has answered these questions with an antitrust policy that has reflected the objectives and the understanding of its time.

But over the past thirty years another revolution has taken place—a revolution in antitrust policy itself. This revolution has involved the ascendance of industrial organization economics in antitrust policymaking, with profound effects on the institutions, interpretation, and enforcement of antitrust. The concept of antitrust has had broad political and popular support throughout its history, but there never has been an equivalent consensus about what actual policy should be. One reason is that the language of the original laws left many of the important details unresolved, so that policy came into focus slowly as the courts provided interpretations of such terms as *monopolization, substantial lessening of competition,* and *conspiracy.* That process in turn tended to produce a formalistic interpretation of the law without much regard for the growing body of knowledge about the economics of companies and industries. Another reason for the lack of consensus was the tension between populism—which gave rise to the antitrust laws—and the equally strong belief that private enterprise ought to be left alone. This tension has run through the entire history of antitrust, periodi-

1

cally resulting in policy shifts reflecting then-current sentiment or changing views about certain business practices.

Some of this started to change in the late 1960s. The Antitrust Division of the Justice Department promulgated *Merger Guidelines* in 1968, which were developed by a panel of economic and policy experts alongside the staff lawyers of the Division and embodied an industrial organization framework for analysis. The courts issued some notable opinions that made clear their unease with aspects of their previous approaches to antitrust issues and their receptivity to economic arguments. The Federal Trade Commission and the Justice Department both began having prominent academics as their chief economists or economic advisors. That practice, in turn, brought other economists to the agency staffs, strengthening their economic expertise and ensuring more sophisticated analysis within the agencies.

Over the past thirty years this revolution has progressed to the point that industrial organization economics now plays a crucial role in virtually all phases of antitrust policymaking. Economics helps determine what cases the Justice Department and the Federal Trade Commission pursue. Economics frames the central issues for investigation and, based on data analysis and theory, evaluates the likely competitive effects of various practices by companies or of structural changes in industries. And the courts themselves have embraced economic reasoning in their own analyses, a change made possible by the increased economic sophistication of the judiciary. All of this has progressed to the point that a prominent antitrust scholar has declared that while "antitrust is, first and most obviously, law," it "is also a set of continually evolving theories about the economics of industrial organization" (Bork 1978, p. 10).

The first salvo in this economic revolution in antitrust was represented by the so-called "structure-conduct-performance" school of economics, often associated with the work of Edward Mason, Joe Bain, and others trained at Harvard University. This perspective emphasized the structural roots of competition, a view that found support in path-breaking empirical work relating industry concentration to profits and price-cost margins. By extension it looked askance at many mergers, much conduct of dominant firms, vertical integration, and even conglomerate mergers. It is worth emphasizing that the structure-conduct-performance school enjoyed wide support in the profession at the time, finding expression in the first *Merger Guidelines* of 1968 and in the first appointments of leading economists to the antitrust agencies. The influence of this school on the agencies, the courts, and antitrust policy was a tremendously significant event.

The second wave of the antitrust revolution was "Chicago School" economics, so named for its place of origin, the University of Chicago, where its most prominent advocates taught, notably, Aaron Director and George Stigler. Beginning in the 1970s, that school emphasized the use of basic microeconomic theory for evaluating the effects of industry structure and conduct on economic performance. It argued, for example, that mergers should be analyzed in terms of both their likely price effects and the plausible cost savings achieved by the merged company. It further claimed that price increases are not so easy to achieve, either because of the inherent difficulty of tacit cooperation or because of ease of entry by new competitors. For these reasons mergers were said to be generally pro-competitive, and not properly evaluated with such indicia as market shares and industry concentration. On other issues, the Chicago School was equally adamant. Price cuts almost invariably reflect lower costs and legitimate competitive behavior rather than predation. Efforts by manufacturers to establish retail prices or to constrain the behavior of independent retailers almost always represent efforts to control certain aspects of the sale in which the manufacturers have a legitimate interest.

The different perspective of the Chicago School extended to its view of the very purposes of antitrust. It argued that antitrust should be guided solely by economic efficiency. Efficiency, this school maintained, is what the plain language of the law implies, and in any event is the only objective that can sensibly be pursued. And it has documented numerous instances in which the pursuit of other objectives has actually imposed costs on consumers rather than enhancing the competitiveness of markets.

This was—and is—by no means the consensus view either of the original purposes of antitrust or of what antitrust should now pursue, but the challenge represented by the Chicago School both sharpened the focus of antitrust and helped to discredit some of its more dubious past pursuits. For example, most students of antitrust are at some time led through cases of the 1960s that endorsed the populist objective of protecting small business and that prohibited mergers between companies with small market shares. By the 1980s and 1990s, by contrast, mergers of huge petroleum companies were approved with only minor modification, and mergers in the steel and airline industries won approval despite large market shares.

Similar changes in antitrust policy are apparent with respect to firm conduct. Whereas earlier Supreme Court cases held that virtually any tampering with market price was illegal per se, by the late 1970s the Court admitted the possibility of pro-competitive justifications even for price fixing by horizontal competitors. In the area of predatory pricing, the traditional view seemed to be that price cuts injuring competitors were evidence of predation, but more recent cases have adopted a permissive view of what is considered acceptable pricing behavior on the part of an incumbent firm. And in contrast to earlier hostility toward most vertical mergers and price agreements, the antitrust agencies now challenge few such arrangements. Also gone from the agenda of the agencies are cases involving price discrimination, with its generally ambivalent economic effects; potential competition, partly because the judicial standard of proof is so high and partly because of the view that potential entrants are numerous; and conglomerate mergers, previously challenged on potential competition grounds or simply on the basis of their sheer size.

These changes have not resulted from the Chicago School critique alone, since many economists of all persuasions had long pressed for antitrust policy that better reflected evolving economic understanding. That said, many believed the Chicago School approach to be too simplistic and dangerously close to repealing much of antitrust. These economists argued that market shares and concentration were informative—if not dispositive—about competitive conditions, and that entry was rarely so quick, cheap, and easy as to obviate concerns about cooperative behavior among existing companies. They raised serious reservations about permissive policies with respect to price cutting and other dominant firm practices, arguing that predatory or disciplining behavior does indeed occur. A significant number of economists were unwilling to go so far as to absolve vertical relationships of all anticompetitive potential. And many rejected the contention that strict economic efficiency was or should be the essential purpose of antitrust.

Over the past fifteen or twenty years, this counter to the Chicago School approach has been advanced through the infusion of more advanced theory and empirical work into antitrust economics. More powerful theory, better adapted to specific issues, has proven capable of identifying specific conditions under which various practices may have anticompetitive effects, even if they are generally benign. Careful consideration of information imperfections, sunk costs, reputation effects, and strategic behavior have improved our understanding of many matters, including predatory pricing, vertical restraints, tying and bundling, and raising rivals' costs. In addition, techniques of empirical analysis have become much more sophisticated, with data better suited to the task, models well grounded in theory, and superior econometric tools. Empirical evidence, for example, has given new support to the proposition that concentration affects competition and pricing within industries, a contention eroded by earlier critiques.

There has been, in short, a reconsideration of the entire range of antitrust issues. This more nuanced "post-Chicago economics" argues that many formulations of the preceding twenty years were reliant on overly simplistic theory, with the result that important distinctions were overlooked and excessively sweeping conclusions were drawn. It contends that many practices must be evaluated in light of facts specific to the case rather than being pigeonholed into theoretical boxes. And it is more skeptical of the ability of the market automatically to discipline firms and thereby negate the anticompetitive potential of mergers and various practices.

Post-Chicago economics is not—or at least not yet—a unified alternative paradigm. It has not displaced the Chicago approach in many quarters. And some have expressed concern that its more fact-based approach will make determinations of antitrust violations more difficult. But it has gained acceptance as an intellectually rigorous alternative approach to antitrust. And, of course, it is very much a part of the economic revolution in antitrust. Economics constitutes its foundation just as much as the economics of their times guided the structure-conduct-performance school and the Chicago School. These new views simply represent another step in that revolution. There no doubt will be many more such steps, as economics strives to clarify the effects of structural changes and various business practices on market performance.

While the outcome of that process cannot be foretold, two predictions can safely be made. The first is that the paramount importance of economics in the antitrust process is firmly established. Enforcement policy and court decisions will be grounded in economic analysis to an ever-greater degree. Supporters and critics of policy issues all now debate them in terms of competition and efficiency, clearly conceding the central role that economics plays.

In addition, these advances in economic understanding continually improve the rationality and consistency of antitrust policy. As these advances gain acceptance, they progressively narrow the range within which policy decisions are made. That is, by demonstrating that some propositions are incorrect, lack generality, or suffer from other defects, the advances limit the degree to which future policy can ever revert to those defective propositions.

That does not imply complete agreement about the proper course of antitrust. A considerable range of acceptable policy remains, and there is—and will be—legitimate disagreement over goals and strategies within that range. But to an increasing extent that range is bounded by economics and will shrink as our economic understanding grows. The antitrust revolution is secure.

REFERENCES

Bork, Robert H. *The Antitrust Paradox.* New York: Basic Books, 1978.

Letwin, William. *Law and Economic Policy in America.* New York: Random House, 1965.

PART I

Horizontal Structure

The Economic
and Legal Context

Markets may be structured in a wide variety of ways, but purely structural concerns in antitrust arise in the cases of monopolies and oligopolies. Since the monopoly model is at the heart of almost all antitrust analysis, we will begin with a discussion of monopoly and then move on to oligopoly.

MONOPOLY

Economics

The microeconomic theory of monopoly is straightforward: A single seller of a good or service, for which (at a price that would just yield normal profits) there are no good substitutes and for which entry is difficult, will be able to take advantage of its market power. If the seller can sell only at a single price to all buyers (i.e., it cannot practice price discrimination), then its pursuit of maximum profits will lead it to sell a smaller output and maintain a higher price than would an otherwise similar competitive industry.[1]

Figure I-1 portrays this outcome. As the figure indicates, the maximizing price will not be at "the sky's the limit" levels but instead will be related to the demand curve (via the derived marginal revenue) for the monopolist's output and the monopolist's marginal costs.[2] An immediately important point is that the demand curve—which expresses the empirical reality that at higher prices customers generally buy less—does limit the extent to which the monopolist's price can exceed competitive levels.

This monopoly outcome is *socially* less efficient than the competitive outcome, because of *allocative* inefficiency: The monopolist produces too

---

[1]A similar argument applies to monopsony: a single buyer in a market, who can gain by buying less and at a lower price than if competition among buyers prevailed.

[2]The familiar formula for profit maximization is $P_M = MC/(1 + 1/E_D)$, where E_D is the (negative) elasticity of demand. Once P_M has been determined, the monopolist's output (Q_M) can be derived from the demand relationship.

FIGURE I-1 A Comparison of Monopoly and Competition

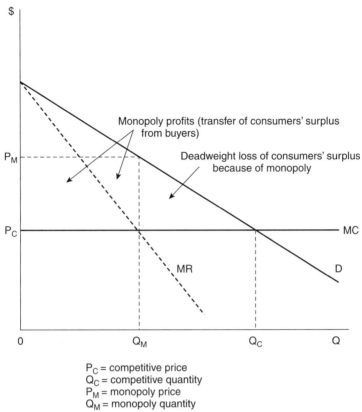

P_C = competitive price
Q_C = competitive quantity
P_M = monopoly price
Q_M = monopoly quantity

little; equivalently, there are buyers who are willing to buy at prices that are above marginal costs (and who would be able to buy from a competitive industry) but who are not willing to buy at the higher monopoly price (and who buy other, less desirable things instead). The lost consumer surplus of the buyers, portrayed in Figure I-1, is frequently described as a "deadweight loss triangle."

The higher price (which is the cause of the allocative inefficiency) also yields the higher profits or "overcharge" of the monopolist (which is sometimes described as "monopoly rents"). This overcharge is largely a *transfer* from buyers to the monopolist and is represented by a rectangle in Figure I-1.[3]

---

[3]Since the monopolist should be willing to spend an amount up to the size of the rectangle to defend its monopoly, some of this rectangle may be "burned up" in costly efforts (e.g., political lobbying, raising barriers to entry) to protect its position. Such efforts represent a socially wasteful use of resources and thus add to the deadweight loss of monopoly. See Posner (1975). Also, the absence of competitive pressures may induce less than fully efficient production processes ("X-inefficiency") and thereby add to deadweight loss. See Leibenstein (1966).

Any monopoly seller would like to be able to practice price discrimination, thereby segmenting the firm's market on the basis of the buyers' willingness to pay. In order for price discrimination successfully to occur, (a) there must be buyers with different willingnesses to pay;[4] (b) the firm must be able to identify who they are (or have some mechanism that will cause them to reveal themselves); and (c) the firm must be able to prevent arbitrage (i.e., prevent the buyers who receive low prices from reselling to the buyers who would otherwise receive high prices). If the seller could identify each buyer and make an all-or-nothing offer to that buyer at the latter's maximum willingness to pay, this would constitute "perfect" price discrimination (frequently described as "first-degree" price discrimination).[5] Other forms of price discrimination can involve block pricing ("second-degree" price discrimination), segmenting buyers by geography or by customer type ("third-degree" price discrimination), bundling (Adams and Yellen 1976), and tying (Burstein 1960).

Instances of true monopoly can be found in the U.S. economy, although they collectively account for only a small fraction of U.S. GDP. Examples include local residential telephone service (in some geographic areas), local electricity distribution, local natural gas distribution, postal service for first-class and bulk mail, the single hardware store (or gasoline station, or pharmacy) in an isolated crossroads town, and firms producing unique products that are protected by patents (e.g., those patented pharmaceuticals for which there are no good substitutes). Over time, technological advances tend to erode existing monopolies (e.g., by producing substitutes and by expanding market boundaries through reduced telecommunications and transportation costs), but also to create new ones.

It is a short conceptual leap from the single seller to the dominant firm—a firm of uniquely large size but one that also faces a "fringe" of smaller competitors. Though technically not a monopoly, the dominant firm will still be able to enjoy the fruits of its market power. The extent of its enjoyment will be determined by its costs relative to those of smaller firms, the elasticity of the demand for the product, the elasticity of supply by the fringe, and the ease or difficulty of entry.[6] Historical examples of such market structures include U.S. Steel in steel, Alcoa in aluminum, IBM in mainframe computers, Xerox in photocopying, and Kodak in cameras and film, at least for some time periods. More recent examples include Microsoft in

---

[4]This condition is clearly satisfied by a monopoly; it is also satisfied by any firm that faces a negatively sloped demand curve (i.e., that sells a differentiated product), so price discrimination can arise under monopolistic competition or differentiated oligopoly as well.

[5]One paradoxical consequence of such perfect price discrimination is that the allocative inefficiency of the monopolist disappears, even while the transfer to the monopolist increases.

[6]See Stigler (1965) and Landes and Posner (1981). Though the dominant firm model is usually presented in terms of a commodity product, where the fringe firms' disadvantages lie in their inferior production technology, the model readily extends to the case of a differentiated product, where the fringe firms' disadvantages lie in their inferior brand acceptance.

personal computer operating systems,[7] Intel in microprocessors,[8] and United Parcel Service for small package delivery services.

Monopoly can arise in four ways. First, economies of scale may indicate that a single firm is the most efficient structure for serving the entire market. In essence, the technology of production may be such that unit costs decline over the relevant range of production. It is important to note that this "natural" monopoly outcome is dependent on both the nature of the technology *and* the size of the market. Thus, where markets are small, monopoly may be more likely, whereas larger markets may be able to accommodate multiple efficient producers (if unit costs do not continue to fall at relatively high volumes, or if product differentiation is important to buyers). Also, although engineering relationships often indicate unlimited economies of scale, the difficulties of managing a larger enterprise may yield higher rather than lower unit costs at higher volumes.

Second, incumbent firms may merge to create a monopoly or a dominant firm. Historically, the merger wave of 1887–1904 yielded a large number of such consolidations, including U.S. Steel (steel), Standard Oil (petroleum), American Tobacco (cigarettes), American Can (tin cans), Kodak (cameras and films), DuPont (explosives), and more than sixty other monopolies or dominant firms (Markham 1955; Nelson 1959; Scherer and Ross 1990, ch. 5). As will be discussed below, an important goal of modern antitrust policy is to prevent the creation of market power through mergers (of which a merger-to-monopoly would be the limiting case).

Third, a firm may own a unique and advantageous input into production. For example, market power may arise from the ownership of a unique natural resource (e.g., metallic ores) or the ownership of some patents—e.g., Polaroid's early patents on self-developing film, Xerox's early patents on photocopying, pharmaceutical companies' patents on unique drugs, and Intel's patents on its microprocessors. However, most patents convey little or no market power. All are intended to encourage investment in new ideas and their implementation by creating property rights that prevent quick and easy free-riding on the efforts of innovators. It is this aspect of patents that leads to their description as "intellectual property."

Fourth, government policy can be the source of monopoly. Historically, exclusive government franchises—for rail, air, and trucking service (between some city pairs); local and long-distance telephone service; local cable television service; local banking; and postal service—have yielded monopolies, along with government regulation to deal with them. With the advent of the deregulation movement of the mid-1970s and after, such government-protected monopolies have become more rare, though not wholly extinct.

---

[7]See Gilbert (1999) and Case 19 by Daniel Rubinfeld in Part IV of this book.

[8]See Case 14 by Carl Shapiro in Part III of this book.

A monopoly or a dominant firm may be able to entrench or enhance its position by raising barriers to entry or raising the costs of its rivals (Salop and Scheffman 1983, 1987). Such efforts will be the subject of discussion in many of the cases in Parts II, III, and IV of this book.

Antitrust

The primary efforts of government to deal with monopoly have been through explicit regulation—e.g., through formal regulatory commission or boards—or through government ownership. But from its beginnings in 1890, antitrust law has tried to address monopoly issues. Section 2 of the Sherman Act creates a felony offense for "every person who shall monopolize, or attempt to monopolize, or combine or conspire with any other person or persons, to monopolize . . ."

The antitrust approach to horizontal *structural* issues, however, has not been especially potent, at least since 1920. Two important Supreme Court cases in 1911—*Standard Oil*[9] and *American Tobacco*[10]—yielded government victories and the structural dissolution of dominant firms in the petroleum and tobacco industries, and similar government victories followed for the next nine years. The Court's reasoning in those cases, however, established a "rule of reason" that applies to monopolization cases: Courts should consider behavior and intent and efficiencies, as well as just monopoly structure.[11] This approach led to the government's loss in 1920 in *U.S. Steel*,[12] after which the government became wary of bringing such cases.

A renewed vigor in antitrust enforcement in the late 1930s led to a suit against Alcoa, yielding a final appellate decision (*U.S. v. Aluminum Company of America,* 148 F.2d 416 [1945]) that was perhaps the high-water mark in emphasis on structure—but also the turning point. Declaring that Alcoa's 90 percent market share of aluminum clearly represented monopoly, the court appeared to stand ready to infer monopoly from its high share. Yet the court also went on to state other reasons why Alcoa should be convicted, and those reasons were in essence its bad acts. The ambiguity over whether structure or conduct was key was not resolved until the *Grinnell* case (*U.S. v. Grinnell Corp.,* 384 U.S. 563 [1966]), in which the Supreme Court stated that a violation of Section 2 required two factors: possession of monopoly power, and willful acts to acquire or maintain such power.

The effect of this language was to require detailed examination of acts and practices of monopoly firms for their effects, perhaps for intent, and for alternative explanations. All of these have rendered most such proceedings

---

[9]*U.S. v. Standard Oil Co. of New Jersey et al.,* 221 U.S. 1 (1911).

[10]*U.S. v. American Tobacco Co.,* 221 U.S. 106 (1911).

[11]Sec. 2, after all, condemns the effort to "monopolize," not the structure of monopoly.

[12]*U.S. v. United States Steel Corp.,* 251 U.S. 417 (1920).

extremely long, complex, and too often unclear. Together with judicial reluctance to tamper with firm structures, this has resulted in few subsequent cases where the government has sought structural relief, and still fewer successes.[13] Government-initiated monopolization cases have usually focused on behavioral remedies, as have privately initiated monopolization cases.[14]

In sum, antitrust (at least since 1920) has not played a large role in dealing with monopoly market structures through horizontal structural relief. Absent a major change in the legal environment, this will likely continue to hold true.

OLIGOPOLY

Economics

The essence of oligopoly is that the number of sellers is few enough so that each seller is aware of the identity of its rivals and aware that its own actions affect their decisions (and that the others probably have similar perceptions). This condition is sometimes described as "conjectural interdependence."

A wide range of price-quantity outcomes is theoretically possible. At one extreme, a tightly disciplined cartel may be able to maintain prices and quantities that approximate those of a monopoly; at the other extreme, if sellers myopically focus on price competition in a commodity industry, only two sellers are necessary to approximate the competitive outcome.[15] Accordingly, there is no definitive price-quantity "solution" or outcome for an oligopoly market structure (unlike the specific outcomes that can be predicted for a monopoly structure and for perfect competition).

As will be discussed more thoroughly in Part II, economic theory argues that market structure characteristics (e.g., the number and size-distribution of sellers, conditions of entry, the characteristics of the sellers and of their products, and the characteristics of buyers) are likely to influence the ease or difficulty with which sellers can come to a mutually beneficial understanding with respect to prices or other important dimensions of conduct. In turn, this will imply differences in market outcomes.[16] Thus, there are im-

---

[13]A survey can be found in Scherer and Ross (1990, ch. 12). The government's success in achieving a 1982 consent decree that broke up AT&T involved vertical structural relief; see Noll and Owen (1994). Similarly, the government's short-lived remedy in its victory over Microsoft involved vertical structural relief; see Case 19 by Daniel Rubinfeld in Part IV.

[14]See the case discussions in Parts II, III, and IV of this book. Also, private plaintiffs legally cannot obtain structural relief from the courts; see *International Telephone & Telegraph Corp.* v. *General Telephone & Electronics Corp. et al.,* 518 F.2d 913 (1975).

[15]However, product differentiation "softens" the competition and results in a less competitive outcome.

[16]In addition to the discussion in Part II, see the overviews provided by Shapiro (1989) and, especially with respect to horizontal mergers, Jacquemin and Slade (1989).

portant links between oligopoly structure and conduct; oligopoly structure matters—which brings us naturally to the consideration of antitrust.

Antitrust

The primary vehicle for a structural approach to oligopoly[17] is Section 7 of the Clayton Act, which instructs the Department of Justice (DOJ) and the Federal Trade Commission (FTC) to prevent mergers "where in any line of commerce or in any activity affecting commerce in any section of the country, the effect of such acquisition may be to substantially lessen competition, or to tend to create a monopoly." Though the Act was passed in 1914, Section 7 was largely a dead letter until 1950 because of an unintended loophole.[18] The Celler-Kefauver Act of 1950 closed that loophole, and Section 7 gained life.

A series of government challenges to mergers in the 1950s and 1960s led to a set of important Supreme Court decisions, beginning with *Brown Shoe*[19] in 1962. In those decisions the Court indicated that it was ready to prohibit both horizontal mergers between competitors and vertical mergers between customers and suppliers, even in markets where the merging parties' shares were relatively small and entry was easy. The Court expressed concerns about competition but also opined that Congress had intended to halt mergers so as to preserve market structures with large numbers of firms, even at the sacrifice of some efficiency that might be achieved by a merger. However, the Court backed off from this tough, semipopulist position in two merger decisions in 1974.[20] The Supreme Court has not rendered a decision on a government challenge to a merger since then.

Flushed by the favorable Supreme Court decisions of the 1960s, the DOJ's Antitrust Division developed a set of *Merger Guidelines* in 1968. The *Guidelines* indicated the circumstances (described in terms of industry four-firm concentration ratios and the sales shares of the merging firms) in which the DOJ would be likely to challenge mergers, so that the private antitrust bar could provide better guidance to its clients. While those *Guidelines* reflected the economic and policy understanding of the time, it soon became apparent that they were too restrictive and too rigid. As a result they fell into disuse during the 1970s, awaiting an effort to revise them in accordance with advances in economics and different views about appropriate policy.

---

[17]Parts II, III, and IV of this book will address behavioral approaches to addressing oligopoly issues.

[18]The 1914 act forbade mergers that were effected through one company's purchase of another company's equity shares. Merger candidates quickly realized that they could easily evade this restriction by simply having one company buy all of the underlying assets of the other company.

[19]*Brown Shoe Co. v. U.S.,* 370 U.S. 294 (1962).

[20]See *U.S. v. General Dynamics Corp. et al.,* 415 U.S. 486 (1974) and *U.S. v. Marine Bancorporation et al.,* 418 U.S. 602 (1974).

The 1968 *Guidelines* were largely scrapped, and a new set was issued in 1982. Economists played a large role in the development of the new *Guidelines* and in subsequent revisions in 1984, 1992 (when the FTC joined as an author),[21] and 1997. These *Guidelines* have proved influential in shaping antitrust lawyers', economists', and eventually judges' approaches to mergers (Werden 2002). They certainly shaped many of the economic arguments that were developed in the cases discussed in this part. Accordingly, we next turn to a more detailed discussion of the *Guidelines*.[22]

THE HORIZONTAL MERGER GUIDELINES

The *Horizontal Merger Guidelines* start from the fundamental premise that the antimerger provisions of the Clayton Act are intended to prevent the exercise or enhancement of market power that might arise as a consequence of a merger. They thus reject the populist position that the pure sizes of the merging entities should be a consideration in the evaluation of a merger.

Using the analytical base of the microeconomics of monopoly and oligopoly discussed above and in Part II, the *Guidelines* address six crucial issues:

- the delineation of the market for merger analysis, so as to determine whether the merger partners compete with each other and the sizes of their (and other relevant sellers') market shares;
- the level of seller concentration in a relevant market that should raise antitrust concern about a merger;
- the potential adverse effects of mergers, either through coordinated behavior among sellers or through the possibility that the merging firms might unilaterally, postmerger, be able to affect prices and output;
- the extent and role of entry into the market;
- other characteristics of market structure that might make the postmerger exercise of market power easier or more difficult; and
- the extent to which merger-related cost savings and efficiencies that are promised should be allowed as a defense of a merger that appears to increase the likelihood of the exercise of market power, and the types of efficiency evidence that should be considered.

Each will be discussed in turn.

---

[21]Also, the 1992 revision modified the title to *Horizontal Merger Guidelines.*

[22]The *Guidelines* can be found at www.usdoj.gov/atr/public/guidelines/hmg.htm. A recent compendium of discussions of the *Guidelines* is embodied in Baker (2002), Kolasky and Dick (2002), Scheffman et al. (2002), Werden (2002), and Williamson (2002).

Market Definition

The *Guidelines* define a relevant market for antitrust merger analysis as a product (or group of products) sold by a group of sellers who, if they acted in concert (i.e., as a "hypothetical monopolist"), could bring about "a small but significant and nontransitory increase in price" (SSNIP). This is equivalent to defining a relevant market as one in which market power can be exercised (or one in which existing market power can be enhanced). The *Guidelines* indicate that a 5 percent price increase sustained for one year is the likely SSNIP value that the enforcement agencies will use. The smallest group of sellers that satisfies the SSNIP test is usually selected as the relevant market. These principles apply to the determination of both product markets and geographic markets. Under this definition, markets might be as small as a neighborhood or as large as the entire global economy; the determining factor is simply whether buyers would switch in sufficient numbers to undermine the price increase.

The logic of this approach follows from the goal of preventing mergers that create or enhance market power as measured by such a price increase. The SSNIP test identifies the smallest group of sellers who could exercise such market power. With one exception, the market definition paradigm focuses on sellers (since it is sellers who exercise market power). That exception arises when a group of sellers could practice price discrimination and raise prices significantly for an identifiable group of customers (defined by a geographic area or a business function). In such a case, that group of customers may also be considered to be a relevant market.

A stylized graphical example, using geographic differentiation, can further illustrate these points concerning market definition. In Figure I-2, imagine a set of, say, shoe stores (A, B, C, . . .) stretched along a highway, with one mile between each store.[23] Customers are located continuously along the highway in between the stores. Initially, let us assume that any customer will buy only from the lowest-price store location that is immediately to her right or left;[24] i.e., she will not "skip over" a store to get to the next one. (Let us call this a strong preference for adjacency.) Each store effectively competes with the stores on each side of it and gets a roughly equal share of the potential customers on each side of it.

If stores D and E merge, then the customers located between them are "trapped"; if the merged D–E firm can identify which of its customers are from the "trapped" region and can price discriminate, it will likely raise its prices to them. If the price increase satisfies the SSNIP criterion, the merger will be anticompetitive, and the trapped customers between any two adjacent stores will thus constitute a relevant market. Even if the merged D-E

---

[23]The example uses geographic space and one dimension; but the insights apply equally well to product space and to multiple dimensions.

[24]For the sake of simplicity, we abstract from transportation costs.

FIGURE I-2 An Illustration of Market Definition Concepts

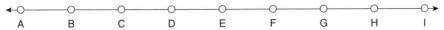

firm could not identify the trapped customers (or devise a means whereby they revealed themselves), it might still find that it could raise its overall prices to considerable heights and earn sufficiently huge profits from its trapped customers (if they had quite inelastic demands for shoes) to offset its lost profits on the lost sales to the non-trapped (former) customers (its former share of customers between C and D and between E and F).[25] In this case the merger would be anticompetitive, and any two adjacent firms would constitute a relevant market.

Now let us suppose that the buyers' preferences for adjacency are less strong, and customers are willing to skip over one store in their pursuit of cheaper shoes. Effectively, each store competes with the three stores to its right and the three stores to its left. The merger between stores D and E would no longer pose a competitive problem, because none of their customers are trapped.

Further, in this case the minimum number of adjacent stores that could possibly constitute a relevant market would be four. (Two stores clearly do not, and even three do not, since there are still no trapped customers.) If a hypothetical monopolist were to control stores C, D, E, and F, customers between D and E would be trapped. If the monopolist could practice price discrimination, it could profitably raise the price to them, and the customers in the middle of the four stores constitute a relevant market. If price discrimination is not possible, then it seems unlikely that the gains from charging high prices to the trapped D-E customers would offset the lost profits on the lost sales to the (former) non-trapped customers (all of the customers between C and D and between E and F, and its share of the customers between B and C and between F and G). So, the relevant market would have to include a larger number of adjacent stores (such that the hypothetical monopolist's gains from enough trapped customers more than offset its loss of profits from the lost non-trapped customers). Further analysis (of the type described below) would be necessary to determine whether a merger between any two sellers within this market (of, say, any adjacent seven stores) would create an anticompetitive problem.[26]

---

[25]This might also be considered an instance of "unilateral effects," which is discussed below.

[26]This example also points out an interesting paradox. Suppose that the seven sellers B, C, D, E, F, G, and H were found to constitute a market when customers were willing to skip over one store. A conspiracy among the seven sellers to raise prices would be unlikely to stick, since the flanking firms (B and H) would lose customers and receive no gains and thus would likely leave the conspiracy, thereby exposing C and F, etc. But if E owned B and H, then the flanks would be protected. Thus, a three-way merger of E with B and H might be more conducive to a coordinated price increase by the seven than would the merger of E with D and F.

17

As this example illustrates, the strength of buyers' preferences for individual companies' products vis-à-vis other individual companies' products is key to the delineation of the market.

Seller Concentration

With the market boundaries determined, the analysis turns to the postmerger level of seller concentration and the merger-induced change in that concentration that would trigger enforcement attention. The conventional basis for this approach is the belief that cooperative conduct is more likely at higher seller concentration levels (see, for example, Stigler 1964), although an alternative theory of anticompetitive harm—the "unilateral effects" approach (which will be discussed below)—is also considered.

The *Guidelines* use the Herfindahl-Hirschman Index (HHI) for this measurement. The HHI for a market is computed by summing the squared market shares (expressed as percentages) of all of the sellers in the market. Thus, an atomistic market would have an HHI very close to zero; a pure monopoly would have an HHI of 10,000 ($100^2 = 10,000$); and a duopoly consisting of two firms with, for example, 70 percent and 30 percent market shares, respectively, would have an HHI of 5800 ($70^2 + 30^2 = 5800$).

The *Guidelines* specify two nominal decision points: For an "unconcentrated" market with a postmerger HHI below 1000, the merger will rarely, if ever, be challenged. For a "highly concentrated" market with a postmerger HHI above 1800, if the merger itself causes an increase in the HHI of 100 or more,[27] there is a presumption that the merger is anticompetitive; whereas, if the increase in HHI is between 50 and 100, there is heightened scrutiny of the merger. In either event, other factors (e.g., ease of entry, strong buyer power) could overcome this presumption. For a "moderately concentrated" market with a postmerger HHI between 1000 and 1800 and a merger-based increase of 100, the presumption of competitive concern is weaker.[28]

In practice, the enforcement agencies have been considerably more lenient than the nominal HHI thresholds would indicate. Rarely have mergers in postmerger markets with an HHI of less than 2000 been challenged, and mergers in markets with substantially higher postmerger HHIs have also escaped challenge. In essence, the merging parties in such instances have been able to convince the enforcement agencies that other characteristics of

---

[27]A quick method of determining the change in the HHI that is due to the merger of two firms is to multiply their premerger shares and then double the result.

[28]There are two ways of translating the HHI threshold points into more familiar terms. An HHI of 1000 would be yielded by a market with ten equal-size firms (each with a 10 percent market share); an HHI of 1800 would be yielded by a market of between five and six equal-size firms. Alternatively (since most markets do not have equal-size firms), the two decision points translate empirically (on the basis of simple correlations) to four-firm concentration ratios of approximately 50 percent and 70 percent, respectively (Kwoka 1985).

the market and/or the merger make the postmerger exercise of market power unlikely.

Adverse Effects

The *Guidelines* present two theories concerning the adverse effects of mergers. The first and more traditional approach holds that a heightened probability of coordinated behavior would arise as a consequence of an industry structure with fewer sellers and with the merged firm having a larger market share. The *Guidelines* recognize that characteristics other than seller concentration can affect the likelihood of coordinated behavior, including entry (which is discussed in the following section) and other features of the market that could facilitate monitoring and policing of any seller understandings (which are discussed in other market characteristics).

Alongside the traditional concern that postmerger oligopolistic sellers might coordinate their behavior, the *Guidelines* (since 1992) mention a second mechanism that could result in competitive harm: unilateral effects.[29] Unilateral effects arise in markets where, even in the absence of cooperation with other sellers, the merged firm could find a unilateral price increase profitable. The most obvious circumstance in which this might occur is when the two merging sellers are each other's major competitors in a differentiated product market, so that the elimination of competition between the two as a result of the merger significantly relaxes the prior pricing constraint that each felt. Other products are simply too imperfect as substitutes to prevent price increases, and for the same reason other sellers' cooperation in the price increase is not necessary.[30]

Ordover and Willig (1993) provide a stylized example of unilateral effects, which we adapt for this discussion. Suppose that all frozen beets are produced by a single company, B. Another single company, C, produces all frozen carrots, and all frozen spinach is produced by company S. Each company has set its own prices so as to maximize its own profits. An important constraint on each company's pricing is whatever elasticities of substitution among the different vegetables exist among consumers.

Now suppose that beet producer B merges with carrot company C. Two things now occur. First, the merged company BC would now find that a higher price for beets would be profitable, because some of the lost customers switch to carrots, and so the merged company BC gains (internalizes) some profits from those customers, which the stand-alone company B would not have gained; similarly, a higher price for carrots is profitable for

---

[29]Enforcement procedures now almost invariably set forth one of these two possible concerns as part of agency challenges to a merger.

[30]The *Guidelines* highlight a postmerger market share of 35 percent for the merging firm, along with strong customer preferences for the two premerger firms' products, as worthy of special concern.

BC where it was not profitable for the stand-alone company C. Second, the merged company BC can do better than this outcome because it is now able to set the price of both products simultaneously so as to maximize joint profits.[31]

Note that the competitive harm from this merger does not result from collusion or cooperation; rather, it results from the ability of the merged company to internalize more of the benefits of the price increase. Clearly, this result depends heavily upon the pattern of elasticities and cross-elasticities among all products in the differentiated product setting.[32] While these are not always easy to estimate or specify, antitrust enforcement has made some progress in this area over the past decade. Aided by detailed scanner data (data recorded at point of purchase in supermarkets, drug stores, and the like), the FTC and DOJ have begun estimating models of differentiated product competition in the context of actual mergers.[33]

Entry

Since easy entry by new firms could thwart sellers' efforts to exercise market power even in highly concentrated markets, the *Guidelines* recognize entry as an important component of merger analysis. They recognize that, for entry to obviate concerns about the potential for postmerger exercise of market power, it must be "timely, likely, and sufficient in magnitude, character, and scope." Timeliness requires entry to occur within a period of two years. The criterion of likelihood is satisfied if the entrant would be profitable in the post-entry market. Sufficiency in magnitude, character, and scope requires that the entrant be capable of restoring the degree of competition that is lost as a result of the merger—that is, that the entrant be as capable and vigorous an entity as the one eliminated by the merger.[34]

The *Guidelines* acknowledge that high levels of "sunk costs" can be a significant barrier to entry; "sunk costs" are the acquisition costs of tangible and intangible assets that are "uniquely incurred to serve the relevant . . . market" and that cannot be completely recouped by redeploying them elsewhere. (Examples include specialized production equipment, marketing

---

[31]Ordover and Willig's example has more subtleties in that they allow for multiple producers of beets and of carrots, and hypothesize a merger between leading producers of each. While perhaps more realistic, the issues are much the same as those set forth here.

[32]An illuminating merger simulation based on elasticities and cross-elasticities can be found at www.antitrust.org.

[33]For discussions of these techniques, see, for example, Werden and Froeb (1994) and Shapiro (1995). This kind of approach was used in the analysis of the MCI WorldCom-Sprint proposed merger, which is discussed in Case 4 by Michael Pelcovits in this part.

[34]It is interesting to note that the current *Guidelines* do not set out an explicit method for analyzing "potential entrants": firms that are poised to enter the market quickly. Such firms can exercise significant constraint on existing sellers, making a market more competitive than is apparent from a consideration of existing sellers alone, but also raising significant competitive issues if the potential entrant is itself a party to the merger. For further discussion, see Kwoka (2001).

costs, training costs, research and development, advertising, etc.) The *Guidelines* specifically ask whether, despite the presence of sunk costs, sufficient entry would be likely to occur within two years in response to a merger-induced price increase.[35]

Other Market Characteristics

As mentioned earlier, the traditional theory of postmerger seller coordination recognizes that other market characteristics can influence the market outcome. Sellers always have an incentive to "cheat" on any implicit (or explicit) understanding among themselves that tempers their competition, especially if they believe that such cheating (e.g., price cutting) can go undetected for a considerable period. Accordingly, the ability of sellers to detect and "punish" (through, e.g., severe price cutting) deviations from any understanding is important for the success of any sustained period of noncompetitive behavior.

The *Guidelines* discuss the major market characteristics that oligopoly theory recognizes as important determinants of sellers' abilities to detect and punish deviations and thus to coordinate their behavior:

- the availability to all sellers of key information about market conditions and individual transactions;
- typical pricing or marketing practices by firms in the market;
- the level of concentration on the buyers' side of the market;
- the degree of complexity in the quality and service dimensions of the product or products at issue; and
- the antitrust history of the sellers in the relevant market.

Cost Savings and Efficiencies

In principle, the cost efficiencies achieved by a merger could yield social savings that would more than compensate for the social loss created by the exercise of market power. Figure I-3, drawn from Williamson (1968), illustrates the trade-off. Suppose that a merger converts a competitive industry into a monopoly but also achieves cost efficiencies. The social gain is represented by the rectangle of reduced costs; the social (deadweight) loss is the triangle. If the area of the rectangle exceeds the area of the triangle, the merger yields a net social gain. The overcharge rectangle (which is a transfer from buyers to sellers) may still be an obstacle to a merger if the goal of antitrust is considered to be solely to help consumers or if, as seems to be the case, consumers matter more than do producers.

---

[35]Firms that could enter easily (i.e., without the expenditure of significant sunk costs) within one year are considered to be in the market, as part of the market delineation process.

FIGURE I-3 The Efficiencies/Market-Power Tradeoff

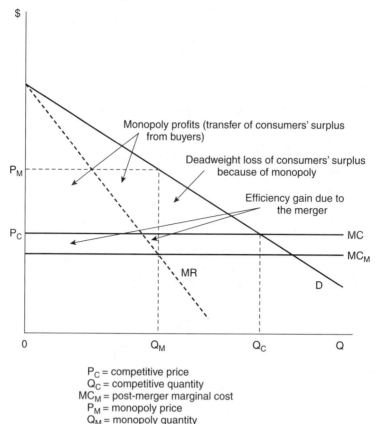

P_C = competitive price
Q_C = competitive quantity
MC_M = post-merger marginal cost
P_M = monopoly price
Q_M = monopoly quantity

If, however, the cost reduction is great enough, the postmerger price could be lower than the premerger price, even taking into account the postmerger exercise of market power. Or, as is sometimes argued,[36] the postmerger efficiencies may change the dynamic within a sluggish oligopolistic industry and allow the merged firm to challenge the industry leader aggressively. More often, however, some modest efficiencies may result from a merger, leaving the enforcement agencies and/or the courts with the task of making a judgment about the extent of the possible price increase that might be risked in order to achieve cost savings.

An important practical problem is that efficiencies are easy to promise before a merger, but often difficult to deliver after the fact, especially in the context of the difficulties of the postmerger firm's efforts to integrate per-

---

[36]See, for example, the discussion of the Heinz–Beech-Nut proposed merger in Case 6 by Jonathan Baker in this part.

sonnel, equipment, systems, and cultures from the two premerger firms.[37] The *Guidelines* recognize the trade-off and the dilemma and try to strike a compromise, stating that the agencies "will not challenge a merger if cognizable [i.e., merger-specific and verifiable] efficiencies are of a character and a magnitude such that the merger is not likely to be anti-competitive in any market."

MERGER ENFORCEMENT PROCEDURES

Under the provisions of the Hart-Scott-Rodino Act of 1976 (as amended in 2001), the parties to all prospective mergers that exceed specified thresholds[38] must notify the FTC and DOJ of their intentions to merge and provide basic information about the companies involved.[39] Within a few days the FTC and the DOJ decide which agency will be responsible for reviewing the merger. The basis for this allocation is usually the presence of expertise about the industry within the agency (although political "horsetrading" between the agencies when prominent cases arise is not unknown). Most mergers receive a quick screening and are found to be innocuous. In instances where there is potential for anticompetitive effects, a group of lawyers and economists within the relevant agency are assigned to undertake further analysis.

The agency has thirty days (fifteen days if the merger involves a hostile takeover) from the initial notification during which the merger cannot be consummated (unless the agency's quick screening reveals an absence of problems and the agency so notifies the parties involved). At the end of that period the parties can consummate their merger unless the agency makes a "second request" for more information. In this event, after the parties deliver the requested information,[40] the agency has an additional thirty days (ten days for a hostile takeover) to reach a decision. In complex and controversial mergers, however, the elapsed time from the initial notification to the agency's decision can be considerably longer than the sixty days, partly

---

[37]See the discussion of the UP-SP merger in Case 1 by John Kwoka and Lawrence White in this part.

[38]The thresholds for notification involve the sizes of the parties and of the transaction. Basically, the acquiring firm must have at least $100 million in sales or assets and the acquired firm must have at least $10 million in sales or assets. Also, the transaction must be valued above $50 million; if it is valued above $200 million, the size-of-parties test is eliminated. Beginning in 2005 the dollar thresholds will be adjusted annually by the percentage changes in U.S. GDP. The enforcement agencies are still free to challenge a merger involving smaller parties.

[39]The act was the response to complaints by the enforcement agencies that they sometimes found out about mergers late or even only after the event and that legally "unscrambling the eggs" of a completed merger created an unnecessary extra burden on merger enforcement.

[40]The parties' lawyers often request meetings with agency officials to present their case for the absence of competitive harm, to which they typically bring company executives and economics consultants/experts.

because of the parties' delays in delivering requested information and partly because of the agency's requests for delays.

If the agency concludes that a merger does pose a potential problem, the parties and the agency will try to determine if there is an acceptable remedy, or "fix," that would alleviate the agency's competitive concerns and still allow the merger partners to gain the efficiencies or other advantages that they seek from the merger.[41] Typically, solutions can be found whereby the merger partners sell off facilities (for some product lines and/or in some geographic areas) to smaller rivals or to entrants, so as to reduce the relevant HHIs to acceptable levels. For example, in mergers between large banks with overlapping branch networks in multiple metropolitan areas, a standard remedy is to require the merging banks to sell sufficient branches to smaller rivals so as to decrease the HHI levels in each metropolitan area to acceptable levels.[42]

If an acceptable remedy cannot be found, the agency will indicate its intention to challenge the merger in court. Often, this announcement alone will cause parties that are unwilling to endure the additional delays, costs, and uncertainties of a court challenge to abandon the merger.[43] If they choose to contest the agency's action, the agency will typically seek and quickly obtain a temporary restraining order from a Federal District Court judge.

The agency then asks for a preliminary injunction (PI). Usually, within a few weeks the judge conducts a small-scale trial, lasting a week or two, that is nominally about the fairness of granting a PI but is really a mini-trial on the merits of the two sides' arguments about the potential anticompetitiveness of the proposed merger.

The judge's decision on the motion for the PI is often determinative: If the agency wins, the parties are unwilling to appeal and simply cancel the merger;[44] if the parties win, the agency drops the case. But appeals to a federal circuit court of appeals by either side are possible.[45] Or the losing party can (but only rarely does) request a full-scale trial on the merits of the case, which can take many months or even years of pretrial maneuvering, extensive document requests and depositions, and a lengthy trial itself.[46]

---

[41]This was true of the BP-ARCO merger discussed in Case 5 by Jeremy Bulow and Carl Shapiro in this part.

[42]An interesting recent analysis of these remedies can be found in FTC (1999).

[43]This happened in the MCI WorldCom-Sprint proposed merger discussed in Case 4 by Michael Pelcovitz in this part.

[44]This happened in the Staples-Office Depot proposed merger discussed in Case 2 by Serdar Dalkir and Frederick Warren-Boulton in this part.

[45]This happened in the Heinz–Beech-Nut proposed merger discussed in Case 6 by Jonathan Baker in this part.

[46]If the DOJ is the prosecuting agency, the trial takes place in federal district court, and the losing party can then appeal to a circuit court of appeals and then to the Supreme Court. If the FTC is involved, the case is adjudicated by an administrative law judge (ALJ), who then reaches a decision and writes an opinion. The losing party can then appeal to the full Commission for a final agency

It should be noted that not all mergers are reviewed by the DOJ or FTC, or even subject to the *Merger Guidelines* standards. In regulated industries, primary antitrust authority often rests with the regulatory agency,[47] or authority is shared with the DOJ or FTC.[48] The regulatory agencies usually evaluate mergers under a broader "public interest" standard, of which antitrust concerns constitute only one part.

REFERENCES

Adams, W. James, and Janet L. Yellen. "Commodity Bundling and the Burden of Monopoly." *Quarterly Journal of Economics* 90 (August 1976): 475–498.

Baker, Jonathan B. "Responding to Developments in Economics and the Courts: Entry in the Merger Guidelines." Accessible at http://www.usdoj.gov/atr/hmerger/11252.htm.

Burstein, Meyer L. "The Economics of Tie In Sales." *Review of Economics and Statistics* 42 (February 1960): 48–73.

Federal Trade Commission, Bureau of Competition. "A Study of the Commission's Divestiture Process." Washington, D.C., August 1999; available at http://www.ftc.gov/os/1999/9908/divestiture.pdf.

Gilbert, Richard J. "Networks, Standards, and the Use of Market Dominance: Microsoft (1995)." In *The Antitrust Revolution: Economics, Competition, and Policy,* 3d edn., edited by John E. Kwoka, Jr., and Lawrence J. White, 409–429. New York: Oxford University Press, 1999.

Jacquemin, Alexis, and Margaret E. Slade. "Cartels, Collusion, and Horizontal Merger." In *Handbook of Industrial Organization,* vol. 1, edited by Richard Schmalensee and Robert H. Willig, 415–473. Amsterdam: North Holland, 1989.

Kolasky, William J., and Andrew R. Dick. "The Merger Guidelines and the Integration of Efficiencies into Antitrust Review of Horizontal Mergers." Accessible at http://www.usdoj.gov/atr/hmerger/11254.htm.

Kwoka, John E., Jr., "The Herfindahl Index in Theory and Practice." *Antitrust Bulletin* 30 (Winter 1985): 915–947.

Kwoka, John E., Jr., "Non-Incumbent Competition: Mergers Involving Constraining and Prospective Competitors." *Case Western Reserve Law Review* 52 (Fall 2001): 173–211.

Landes, William M., and Richard A. Posner. "Market Power in Antitrust Cases." *Harvard Law Review* 94 (1981): 937–996.

---

decision. If the merging parties are unhappy with the Commission's decision, they can appeal to a circuit court of appeals.

[47]This was true of the UP-SP merger discussed in Case 1 by John Kwoka and Lawrence White in this part.

[48]This was true of the Bell Atlantic-NYNEX Merger discussed in Case 3 by Steven Brenner in this part, the MCI WorldCom-Sprint merger discussed in Case 4 by Michael Pelcovits in this part, and the AOL-Time Warner merger discussed in Case 18 by Gerald Faulhaber in Part IV.

Leibenstein, Harvey. "Allocative Efficiency vs. X-Efficiency." *American Economic Review* 56 (June 1966): 392–415.

Markham, Jesse W. "Summary Evidence and Findings on Mergers." In *Business Concentration and Price Policy,* 141–212. Princeton: Princeton University Press, 1955.

Nelson, Ralph L. *Merger Movements in American Industry, 1895–1956.* Princeton: Princeton University Press, 1959.

Noll, Roger G., and Bruce M. Owen. "The Anticompetitive Uses of Regulation: *United States* v. *AT&T* (1982)." In *The Antitrust Revolution: The Role of Economics,* 2nd edn., edited by John E. Kwoka, Jr., and Lawrence J. White, 328–375. New York: HarperCollins, 1994.

Ordover, Janusz, and Robert Willig. "Economics and the 1992 Merger Guidelines: A Brief Survey." *Review of Industrial Organization 8,* no. 2(1993): 139–150.

Posner, Richard A. "The Social Costs of Monopoly and Regulation." *Journal of Political Economy* 83 (August 1975): 807–827.

Salop, Steven C., and David T. Scheffman. "Raising Rivals' Costs." *American Economic Review* 73 (May 1983): 267–271.

Salop, Steven C., and David T. Scheffman. "Cost-Raising Strategies." *Journal of Industrial Economics* 36 (September 1987): 19–34.

Scheffman, David, Malcolm Coate, and Louis Silva. "20 Years of Merger Guidelines Enforcement at the FTC: An Economic Perspective." Accessible at http://www.usdoj.gov/atr/hmerger/11255.htm.

Scherer, F. M., and David Ross. *Industrial Market Structure and Economic Performance.* 3rd ed. Boston: Houghton-Mifflin, 1990.

Shapiro, Carl, "Theories of Oligopoly Behavior." In *Handbook of Industrial Organization,* vol. 1, edited by Richard Schmalensee and Robert D. Willig, 329–414. Amsterdam: North Holland, 1989.

Shapiro, Carl. "Mergers with Differentiated Products." Address to ABA International Bar Association, Nov. 9, 1995, Washington, D.C.

Stigler, George J. "A Theory of Oligopoly." *Journal of Political Economy* 72 (February 1964): 55–69.

Stigler, George J. "The Dominant Firm and the Inverted Price Umbrella." *Journal of Law & Economics* 8 (October 1965): 167–172.

Werden, Gregory J. "The 1982 Merger Guidelines and the Ascent of the Hypothetical Monopolist Paradigm." Accessible at http://www.usdoj.gov/atr/hmerger/11256.htm.

Werden, Gregory J., and Luke Froeb. "The Effects of Mergers in Differentiated Products Industries: Logit Demand and Merger Policy." *Journal of Law, Economics, and Organization* 10 (October 1994): 407–426.

Williamson, Oliver E. "Economies as an Antitrust Defense: The Welfare Tradeoffs." *American Economic Review* 58 (March 1968): 18–36.

Williamson, Oliver E. "The Merger Guidelines of the U.S. Department of Justice—In Perspective." Accessible at http://www.usdoj.gov/atr/hmerger/11254.htm.

CASE 1

Manifest Destiny? The Union Pacific and Southern Pacific Railroad Merger (1996)

John E. Kwoka, Jr., and
Lawrence J. White

INTRODUCTION

The Union Pacific (UP) and the Southern Pacific (SP) railroads have had long and intertwined histories. The UP and the Central Pacific (a predecessor to the SP) were the two railroads commissioned by President Abraham Lincoln in 1862 to construct a transcontinental rail system. The UP laid rail westward from Kansas while the CP began construction in Sacramento. The driving of the Golden Spike into the rail that joined the two at Promontory, Utah, in 1869 helped realize the country's "manifest destiny" of integrating from coast to coast.

Over the next century the UP and the SP (in various corporate guises) provided rail transportation services throughout the western United States. They expanded and in the early 1900s even sought to combine, though they were rebuffed by the courts.[1] In 1995 they tried again, this time successfully. In August of that year the managements of the UP and SP announced their intentions to merge into a single integrated railroad. The proposed

The authors filed comments in this case on behalf of the Dow Chemical Company and the Kansas City Southern Railway Company, respectively. The authors wish to thank Nicholas DiMichael, Gregory Bereskin, William Mullins, and John Spychelski for helpful comments on an earlier draft, which was presented at the Transportation and Public Utilities Group session at the American Economic Association meetings, January 4, 1998. Gratitude is also owed to Kamen Masjasov for research assistance.

[1]In 1901 the UP purchased 38% of the SP's stock and gained effective control of the company, but in 1913 the UP was ordered by the courts on antitrust grounds to relinquish its ownership interest and control.

combination immediately sparked controversy, which persisted well after its approval and implementation.

Though U.S. railroads were deregulated extensively in 1980, vestiges of regulation have remained, including a special regime for dealing with mergers. Instead of being subject to the Department of Justice's or Federal Trade Commission's merger review and enforcement procedures that apply to most other companies, railroad mergers were reviewed by the Interstate Commerce Commission (ICC) until the end of 1995 and since then by the ICC's successor, the Surface Transportation Board (STB).

The ICC/STB's legislative mandate in assessing mergers is broader than that of Section 7 of the Clayton Act. Rather than focusing just on the competition and efficiency issues and the trade-offs (if any) between them, the ICC/STB is instructed by legislation also to consider a railroad merger's effects on "the adequacy of transportation to the public" and "the interest of carrier employees," among other things. But a major focus of the agency has been on the same antitrust issues—market power versus efficiencies—that have held the attention of traditional antitrust merger enforcement.

On the other hand, while the issues are in principle the same, the ICC/STB has been more accommodating toward railroad mergers. This posture is evident in two ways. First, the agency has tended to accept claims of efficiencies by merger advocates without substantial proof[2] and without inquiring whether the efficiencies are uniquely attributable to the merger. Second, where there are competitive concerns with a merger, the ICC/STB has usually sought to remedy them with modest requirements, such as trackage rights for other railroads.[3] The result has been a strong presumption in favor of railroad mergers.[4]

After the UP-SP merger proposal was formally filed with the ICC, dozens of interested and affected parties—eleven other railroads; thirty-eight individual shippers and nineteen trade associations representing shippers (the largest of which represented 1400 individual shippers); five federal agencies; twelve state governments (as well as many individual communities within those states); and five labor unions—offered comments to the ICC/STB on the proposed merger.

In July 1996, eleven months after the initial announcement of the proposed merger, the STB announced its decision: approval of the merger largely as proposed by the UP and SP. The combined UPSP became the

---

[2]By contrast, the antitrust agencies have traditionally been more skeptical with respect to efficiency claims.

[3]As discussed below, trackage rights permit a second railroad access to otherwise captive shippers over the first railroad's tracks. The adequacy of such remedial conditions is a matter of continuing controversy.

[4]Railroad managements understood this presumption quite well. When the ICC was abolished, they lobbied strenuously and successfully to transfer antitrust authority to the STB rather than allow it to go to the Justice Department's Antitrust Division. The chief proponent of the STB plan was the CEO of the UP (Machalaba and Nomani, 1996; Wilner, 1997, p. 306).

largest railroad in the United States in terms of trackage, freight haulage, and revenues. Whether it thereby gained efficiency and/or achieved market power were the hotly disputed questions before the STB.

BACKGROUND

Rail Transportation in the Twentieth Century

For much of the twentieth century railroads have fought a losing competitive battle against the other surface modes of freight transportation: trucking, pipelines, and water (ship and barge) transport. Though railroads continue to play a major role in U.S. intercity freight transportation, the industry's share—41 percent in 1995—is substantially lower than was the case in the early decades of the century. To some extent rail's defeats have been the natural consequences of the technological gains of the other modes, especially trucks. But rail's competitive position was clearly impeded by the ICC's all-encompassing rate and service regulatory structure, in which the industry had been enmeshed since 1887.[5] Even the inclusion of interstate trucking into the ICC's regulatory regime in 1935 failed to stem the tide.

This losing competitive battle was first reflected by rail's declining share of intercity freight hauled and then by widespread financial losses and bankruptcies. At least partly in response to the railroads' competitive and financial losses, the industry engaged in a long series of mergers, which reduced the number of Class I railroads[6] from 186 in 1920 to 39 by 1980. The mergers enlarged railroads' traditional regional scope, but no railroad gained direct national, or even coast-to-coast, coverage.[7]

The Congress in 1980 passed the Staggers Act, which substantially deregulated the industry and gave railroads wide discretion for pricing flexibility, up as well as down. The industry quickly made use of its newly acquired flexibility. Prices (freight rates) adjusted to new levels, reflecting in some instances competitive influences and in others railroads' exercise of market power. With greater flexibility generally, the railroad industry's share of freight haulage stabilized and actually increased by a few percentage points.

---

[5]Standard critiques of the ICC's general discouragement of competition and creation of inefficiencies can be found in Meyer et al. (1959), Friedlaender (1969), Friedlaender and Spady (1981), and Keeler (1983). Some specifics can be found in MacAvoy and Sloss (1967).

[6]Class I railroads refer to those above a specific size criterion set by the ICC. As of 1950, a Class I railroad had to have at least $1 million in revenues; as of 1996, the minimum size was $255 million.

[7]Because of interchange arrangements, all railroads are connected to each other (their freight cars run on each others' tracks), and freight shippers that are at or close to a rail terminal can reach any other place that is close to a rail terminal.

TABLE 1-1
Class I Railroads in the Western U.S.

	Route Structures (mi)	Revenues ($ million)	Employees
Burlington Northern (BN)	22,189	4,995	30,711
Union Pacific (UP)	18,759	5,167	29,946
Southern Pacific (SP)	17,499	2,942	18,251
Santa Fe (SF)	8,352	2,681	15,020

Source: *Railroad Fact Book 1995.*

And mergers proceeded apace. The thirty-nine Class I railroads of 1980 had diminished to only eleven by early 1995. As shown in Table 1-1, only four major railroads remained in the western United States. The Union Pacific and the Burlington Northern (BN) were roughly comparable in route structure, revenues, and employees, followed by the Southern Pacific and the Santa Fe (SF). Within a span of just twelve months in 1995–1996, the BN and the UP each had merged with one of the other two large railroads, leaving western railroading in the hands of just two carriers.

The first of these huge mergers was Burlington Northern's acquisition of the Santa Fe, proposed in August 1994. That combination had 33,000 miles of track and $7.1 billion in revenue and became, by a substantial margin, the largest railroad. The parties promised cost reductions and improved service, such as new single-line service to the Pacific Northwest to SF customers and access to California markets for Burlington shippers. Concerns over reduction in competition were addressed by providing other railroads (including the UP and the SP) with trackage rights in key areas. This merger was approved by the ICC in August 1995.[8]

The Proposed Merger

Two weeks before the BN-SF merger secured final approval, the UP announced its intention to acquire the SP. This would create a railroad with 35,000 miles of track and $9.5 billion in revenue, vaulting it into first place. The companies claimed that the combination would be able to offer new and improved services to shippers, to relieve capacity constraints that the UP and SP faced on certain routes, and to save $500 million in annual expenses, an estimate that was later increased to $750 million.

As shown in Figure 1-1, the UP's route structure connected three West Coast areas—the Pacific Northwest, northern California, and southern California—with Utah, from which its high-capacity double track extended

---

[8]A key opponent of this merger before the ICC was the UP itself. When later the UP unexpectedly withdrew its opposition, some speculated that this represented an implied agreement between UP and BN not to oppose each others' mergers (Gruley and Machalaba, 1996). No evidence to this effect was found. The UP also entered its own bid for the SF, driving up the BN purchase price from $2.7 billion to $4 billion.

FIGURE 1-1 The Merging Railroads.

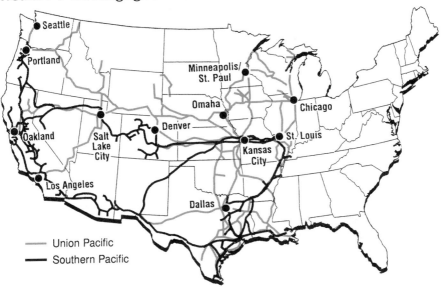

Reprinted by permission of *The Wall Street Journal* © 1996 Dow Jones & Company, Inc. All Rights Reserved Worldwide.

east to Iowa and Kansas through what is known as the "central corridor." Previous acquisitions plus trackage rights with other railroads gave the UP access to Chicago, Milwaukee, and points in Minnesota to the north, as well as to Memphis, New Orleans, and the Texas Gulf Coast to the south. The UP enjoyed a reputation for strong management, attention to service, and cost efficiency.[9]

The SP and its related companies had major lines from Portland to Los Angeles—the so-called "I-5 corridor"—and then to San Antonio, Houston, and New Orleans, together with important gateways to Mexico. Its central corridor route ran from northern California to Utah and Kansas and then to St. Louis. From there, SP lines branched south to Louisiana and Texas and north to Chicago. Despite a strong route structure, the SP was widely perceived as having inadequate terminals and outdated locomotives and providing poor service.

Even a quick review of the UP and SP routes highlighted certain competitive problems with this merger. The combined UPSP would reduce to two or sometimes one the number of railroads serving hundreds, perhaps thousands, of shippers throughout the west. In addition, it would dominate all the major gateways to Mexico and control access to the huge petrochemical shippers along the Texas Gulf Coast.

[9]The UP had been encountering some difficulties, however, as a result of its recent acquisition of the Chicago & Northwestern Railroad.

The principal substantive response by the UP and SP to these concerns was to allow their major competitor, the newly formed BNSF, to run its trains over some of their tracks. Nearly 4000 miles of the combined UPSP track would be subject to track-use agreements, by far the largest reliance on this technique ever attempted. By contrast, UPSP would divest only a minimal 335 miles of routes, also to BNSF, for about $150 million. Though these remedies left many shippers with fewer alternatives, the applicants appealed to the prospect of stronger competition and cost efficiencies as a solution. The adequacy of this response was a central issue in the competitive analysis.

Analyzing Railroad Competition

Railroad competition has some unique properties that bear examination. To begin, the basic output or service provided by railroads is the transportation of commodities from suppliers (shippers) to their customers. Since the locations of both the shipper and its customer are fixed (at least in the short run), rail service must connect the point of origin with the destination in an efficient manner. But the technology and costs of rail service drastically limit the number of viable connections; any rail connection involves huge fixed and (literally) sunk costs in the form of rights-of-way, bridges, tunnels, the track itself, and the maintenance of all of these facilities. Such a cost structure implies that a substantial range of declining long-run unit costs is likely and that relatively high volumes of freight are necessary for break-even operation.

Direct "door-to-door" service is feasible for some large-volume shippers and recipients—for example, large-volume shipments of coal in lengthy "unit trains" from mines to electric utilities. But much more typically, the commodities (in freight cars) of many shippers are collected and assembled at a marshalling yard into a larger-volume, multiple-car train in order to achieve economies. At the terminating rail center, the trains must be disassembled and the freight cars sent to their respective customers.

In such a network competitive restraints on freight rates can occur in a number of ways, including intramodal and intermodal competition, source competition, and destination competition.

Intramodal Competition

Despite the cost structure described above, major city-pair connections that generate sufficient freight shipments often have more than one railroad providing freight service.[10] Where such direct competition exists, shippers might expect the most vigorous rivalry and most favorable rates.

---

[10]At least part of the reason for the multiple-line service is the legacy of railroad construction in the nineteenth century, when the fixed costs loomed relatively less large.

Yet even in these circumstances, there may be limits on competition. One rail carrier may have a cost advantage because of superior equipment, superior management, or a superior route. Or oligopolistic interactions may arise between the railroads, resulting in higher freight rates anyway. Also, if the same railroads provide rail service over many routes, these multi-market contacts serve to convey signals and implicit reassurances that can provide the basis for oligopolistic coordination.

Oligopoly coordination may be restrained by other transport modes, but it is unlikely to be deterred by the threat of entry, since the cost structure of railroads makes entry prohibitively expensive.[11] A different possible constraint takes the form of a threat of potential entry. Even where a shipper/recipient is served by only a single railroad, a second railroad may be close enough that it can realistically threaten to build a short spur line to connect to the shipper.[12]

One other special form of intramodal competition is important to note: Sometimes a railroad will extend "trackage rights" to a second railroad, so that the latter can run its trains over the former's track (typically for a relatively short distance) and thereby connect shippers/recipients to the second railroad's track network. In principle this can result in competition between the two carriers despite the single track. However, the relationship between the two railroads is that of landlord and renter, and there are many ways that the landlord can use its position to mute the competitive threat from the tenant. For example, the fee for use of the tracks may be set so high that the second railroad has to price its service noncompetitively. In addition, the landlord railroad can use its train scheduling ("dispatching") prerogatives, track maintenance routines, and longer-run investments affecting the route to favor itself and raise its rival's costs or degrade the latter's service. And the extensive and close contact between the two railroads, especially on routes where they are the only providers of rail service, may provide the basis for oligopolistic coordination.

Intermodal Competition

Some types of rail freight, for some distances, and at some locations can be economically hauled by alternative modes: truck, barge, or pipeline. Truck is most competitive for shipments over shorter distances (usually less than 500 miles), for shipments that are not in large volumes, and for "high-value" goods (i.e., goods that have a high sales value per weight or cubic measure).[13] Barge is best suited for "low-value" commodities and is rele-

---

[11]Even the construction of extensive new branch or feeder lines by incumbent railroads is a rare event.

[12]This is usually described as a "build in"; if the shipper pays for the spur line, it is called a "build out."

[13]Truck transport is often faster than rail, which usually involves delays because of the assembling/disassembling process described in the text. The inventory-holding costs for high-value goods are greater, and truck's speed thus gives it an important advantage vis-à-vis rail.

vant only where the shipper and recipient are both on or near navigable waterways.[14] Pipeline is limited to a few commodities (primarily petroleum, petroleum products, and natural gas) and to shippers and recipients that are at or near pipeline connections.

Source Competition

A shipper often must compete for customers at a particular destination with other suppliers located at different points of origin. If the other origin points connect to the recipient's location via *other* railroads, then the railroad serving the first shipper is in indirect competition with the other railroads.[15] The extent to which this indirect competition among railroads is effective depends on whether the competing shippers themselves have similar costs and the rail distances are not too dissimilar.

Destination Competition

In some cases a shipper may have alternative destinations, with direct connections via different railroads, to which it might ship its goods. One example is the inland shipper that is sending goods overseas and could use any of a number of seaports, served by different railroads, as its point of export.[16] Again, the railroads are in indirect competition with each other, and the effectiveness of this competition will depend on ocean shipping charges from the various ports, the ports' charges themselves, and the rail distances from the shipper to the ports.

THE UP-SP'S CASE FOR THE MERGER

The Union Pacific and Southern Pacific filed extensive documentation with the ICC/STB in support of their proposed merger. They claimed that the combined UP and SP would strengthen competition throughout the western United States in several specific ways. They expected to achieve substantial cost reductions and significant improvements in the quality of rail service. Service improvements for SP customers would be especially noticeable given the recent inadequacies in the SP's operations. In addition, the merged system would become a more effective rival to the larger, just-formed BNSF. And finally, to address possible competitive concerns, the UP and SP had

---

[14]Barge tends to be slower than rail or truck, so high-value goods are not suitable for this mode.

[15]This point is clearest in the instance where the shipper has a second branch location, served by a second railroad, from which it can serve the recipient. Equivalently, an overseas shipper that is sending goods to a U.S. recipient at an inland location is likely to have a choice of ports and possibly of railroads that connect to the recipient.

[16]It can also arise when the shipper can send its goods to alternative domestic customers; e.g., a coal mine may have a choice of electric utilities, to which it is connected by different railroads, to which it might ship its coal.

prearranged an extensive trackage rights agreement with the BNSF. Over-all, therefore, the merger would result in "a pervasive, dramatic intensi-fication of transportation competition throughout the West" (Peterson, 1995, p. 6).

Efficiencies

The UP and SP provided detailed projections of the various types of com-petitive benefits that would occur. Several of these involved direct opera-tional matters, such as route length, single-line versus joint-line service, and alleviation of capacity constraints. Since costs—both explicit transport costs and implicit time costs to shippers—are a direct function of route length, the UP and SP documented the mileage reductions that the integra-tion of their track networks would make possible along major routes. For example, the shortest mileage between Oakland and Chicago would de-crease by 189 miles for shippers who previously were served only on UP track, and by 388 miles for SP's customers. Between Portland and Houston there would be savings of 262 miles for SP customers and 249 for the UP's. Numerous other instances of significant mileage savings were noted. In most cases the UP and SP focused on how their integrated route mileage would compare with that of the merged BNSF, underscoring their belief that they needed to shorten traffic distances to remain competitive.

A companion benefit of the merger would be far more extensive sin-gle-line service. In contrast to joint-line service in which shippers' products are handled by two railroads along a continuous route, single-line service eliminates delays, reduces loss and damage, simplifies rate determination, and avoids incompatibilities in operating procedures and priorities between carriers.[17] One important example concerned the I-5 corridor from the Pa-cific Northwest to Los Angeles and continuing to points in the southwest, which previously lacked single-line service and lost much traffic to truck or water transport. The applicants anticipated gaining substantial portions of that traffic once they offered single-line service. Numerous other examples were provided.

The applicants also noted that capacity constraints impinging on the UP and even more seriously on the SP would be alleviated by the merger. On many single-line routes, growing traffic had caused substantial in-creases in congestion costs. With more trains operating at different speeds or needing to move in both directions, rail system efficiency declined. Inte-grated management of alternative or parallel routes would permit flexibility in asset utilization, concentration of trains by speed or direction on single lines, and ultimately lower costs. Similar considerations were raised in the case of yards and other facilities.

---

[17]In essence, the replacement of joint-line with single-line service is a form of vertical integration, since a supplier-customer transaction between two carriers (the freight hand-off in a joint-line movement) is being replaced by single ownership.

All of these improvements in operations would result in faster, more frequent, more reliable, and cheaper service to shippers throughout the western United States. Other benefits involved improved access to terminal facilities together with improvements to those facilities.[18] Combining the best of the UP and SP terminal facilities would strengthen the merged entity's ability to provide shippers with such services. In addition, the applicants promised to upgrade some facilities, build one new intermodal facility in Colton, California, and improve coordination among others in the merged system.

Further benefits would accrue from improved deployment and utilization of equipment. Freight cars could be used more frequently, especially specialized equipment such as refrigeration cars. These savings alone were estimated to produce the equivalent of 3000 additional rail cars' becoming available. Equipment could be positioned to minimize downtime and empty backhauls. For example, the UP's routes west of Utah spread like three fingers to the Pacific Northwest, the Bay area, and the Los Angeles basin, but lacked connections up and down the West Coast. That meant that UP equipment in, say, Seattle could not assist in relieving a bottleneck in Oakland without repositioning through an out-of-the-way third point. The addition of the SP's I-5 corridor lines would enable the UP to move equipment directly from Seattle to Oakland. In addition, this route structure would permit "triangulation" of traffic movements; for example, refrigeration cars with citrus from Florida to Los Angeles could next go to Idaho and return with potatoes to Florida. These movements would have required added cars or costly repositioning in the absence of an I-5 corridor link. All of these factors would provide shippers with better and cheaper service.

Lastly, the applicants listed other ways in which they could achieve efficiencies, including the reduction of corporate overhead, consolidation of computer systems, and more economical purchasing. Planned layoffs totaled 4900 employees out of a combined work force of 53,000.

The applicants sought to quantify the annual cost savings that they anticipated from the merger. From voluminous materials about individual routes, facilities, equipment, and operations, the parties stated that the savings would amount to $290 million in the first year of the merger and grow to a total of $750 million per year at the point in time when the process was completed. As shown in Table 1-2, more than one-third of the total would come in the form of labor savings, and roughly an additional one-fifth each would come from operations and from general and administrative. Although the one-time costs of integration would total nearly $1.5 billion, these costs would cease after four years whereas the annual savings would persist indefinitely.

---

[18]Terminals include intermodal facilities for truck-rail or barge-rail transport, auto ramps for off-loading automobiles, storage-in-transit yards in which customers use their own rail cars for temporary storage, transloading facilities for shippers that truck their product to the terminal, etc.

TABLE 1-2
Summary of Benefits ($ thousands)

	YEAR 1		YEAR 5	
	Annual	**One-Time**	**Annual**	**One-Time**
Net revenue gains	22,814		76,045	
Operating benefits				
Labor savings	90,585		261,150	
Nonlabor savings				
Car utilization	3,803		12,677	
Communications/computers	(11,861)	(82,479)	14,214	
Operations	46,501	(529,947)	157,756	9,905
General/administrative	<u>110,797</u>	<u>139,805</u>	<u>137,970</u>	<u> </u>
Total operating benefits	239,825	(472,621)	583,767	9,905
Employee relocation		(26,594)		
Labor protection/separation		(107,411)		
Shipper logistics savings	27,251		90,836	
Total benefits	289,890	(606,626)	750,648	9,905

Sources: UP and SP, *Railway Merger Application,* vol. 1, p. 93.

Other Motivations: Weakness of the SP; the BN-SF Merger

Apart from these claims concerning cost savings, the applicants made two other significant arguments for the merger. First, the Southern Pacific was very much an ailing firm with diminishing competitive vigor. It needed new equipment, upgrading of yards, improvements in rights of way, and installation of advanced operating systems for planning, routing, tracing, and billing purposes. The BN-SF merger had heightened competitive pressure on the SP and cast doubt on the latter's future capabilities. In its SEC filing for the third quarter of 1995, the SP declared that without the proposed merger it lacked the resources to compete with the BNSF and with an independent UP and suggested that it would have to reduce its service.

As a consequence the UP and SP argued, "The only certain solution for SP is a merger with UP" (Peterson, 1995, p. 83). Part of the merger proposal, in fact, was a promise to invest $1.3 billion within four years in upgrading some SP facilities, building additional terminals, and so forth. The greatest beneficiaries of the merger would be the SP's customers, who would no longer experience the service problems that had been plaguing its operations. A considerable number of SP shippers submitted comments favoring the merger.

The applicants' final reason for their merger was the BN-SF merger itself. Throughout their filing, they repeatedly stated that the BN-SF merger precipitated—indeed, necessitated—their own combination, although the logical connection was often not made explicit. The BNSF was said to be "far larger" than the UP or the SP, whether measured by mileage, employees, tons of freight hauled, freight revenues, or operating income. In addition, the BNSF was described as leading in various technologies and moving rapidly to consolidate its gains from the BN-SF merger.

Thus, the applicants claimed, a UP-SP merger was required in order to create an entity capable of competing on even terms with the BNSF. Leaving the UP and the SP separate, by contrast, would handicap the UP and actually imperil the SP, with significant adverse effects on shippers. For competitive reasons, too, the UP and SP concluded, they must be allowed to merge.

Dealing with Competitive Concerns

An important element in their case for the merger was the applicants' concession that on some routes competitive questions needed to be addressed. For numerous shippers, the UP and the SP represented the only two railroads to which the shippers had access. The merger would, of course, reduce this number to just one. Many more shippers had the UP, SP, and a third railroad—typically, the BNSF—as alternatives. They, too, would face a reduction in their choices. These so-called "2-to-1" and "3-to-2" shippers were the focus of much attention from the outset.

Trackage Rights

The merger applicants sought to preempt competitive concerns over 2-to-1 shippers through a trackage rights agreement with BNSF. The guiding principle of this agreement was that the BNSF—the strongest possible alternative railroad, but also the primary, even sole, competitor on most routes—would be granted access to all 2-to-1 shippers on the merged UPSP lines.[19] Every such shipper was identified, and trackage rights were granted in a manner designed to preserve their competitive options. This was done even where shippers previously made little use of one of their rail alternatives, where other railroads existed but with somewhat circuitous routes, and where the BNSF already had a good competitive route.

The result of the trackage agreement would be that all 2-to-1 shippers would have as many railroad alternatives as before. Moreover, since the alternatives would be more efficient than previously, shippers would in fact be better off. The merger application cited a number of shippers that approved of these trackage rights agreements.

The applicants calculated that the traffic covered by trackage rights totaled over $900 million for 2-to-1 shippers. Even more striking was the extent of the track miles subject to this agreement—about 4000 track miles, or

---

[19]In return for trackage rights, BNSF agreed not to oppose the UP-SP merger.

about 11 percent of the entire UP-SP system. Whereas trackage rights had previously been used selectively to address competitive problems, the UP-SP proposal made such rights a centerpiece of their merger proposal.

Vigorous Competition

Another key consideration involved 3-to-2 shippers. The applicants contended that all such shippers would be better off as a result of the merger, since they would have access to two financially sound railroads with comprehensive networks throughout the west. This would be better than their existing alternatives, namely, the "powerful BNSF, a smaller UP, and a weak SP that will become even weaker."[20]

The applicants went on to assert that, despite the presence of only two railroads, the UPSP and BNSF would compete vigorously. As proof, they cited current examples: duopoly competition for coal traffic in the Powder River Basin in Wyoming and for Seattle-Chicago intermodal traffic. They also noted that rail rates had decreased on routes in Texas, Oklahoma, and Kansas after the UP had acquired the Missouri-Kansas-Texas line in 1988.

Furthermore, the applicants argued that there was "no valid economic empirical evidence . . . showing that a 3-to-2 merger of rail carriers would lead to price increases" (Willig, 1995, p. 550). Existing studies were said to suffer from data inadequacies, incorrect specifications, statistical biases, and other problems that made them unreliable and irrelevant to the present merger. More relevant, in this analysis, was a number of factors that made competition between UPSP and BNSF overwhelmingly likely. The applicants argued that monitoring and policing among even two sellers in rail markets would be difficult, since the railroads' service offerings could be extensively differentiated (in terms of speed of delivery, extent of damage to shipments, information provided to customers, billing systems, etc.) and this differentiation could easily mask secret price cutting.

Also, many freight shippers were large and capable entities who could shop around and play the rail carriers off against each other. The opportunity to obtain the freight business of a large shipper (through a price cut) would be tempting enough to cause the carriers to engage in secret price cutting and thus undermine any "cooperative" or "noncooperative" price discipline. In essence, a large shipper could hold an "auction" for the right to carry its freight, and this auction environment would yield competitive outcomes. In sum, the "Bertrand" model of unfettered price competition among sellers was a reasonable approximation to rail markets with even as few as two carriers.

For all these reasons, the applicants contended that no remedial action was required to protect 3-to-2 shippers. In taking this position they knew that they were "preaching to the choir": Past ICC rulings had specifically

---

[20]UP and SP Railroad Merger Application, vol. 1, p. 19.

found that going from three to two railroads would increase competition, so long as the merger entailed superior "character of competition," "more competitive routes," "more diverse geographic competition," and stabilizing a weak competitor.[21] The UP-SP anticipated a similar judgment in this case.

THE ARGUMENTS AGAINST THE MERGER

The opponents[22] of the merger offered three basic arguments: (1) The merged entity would be able to exercise market power, individually or in concert with one or more other railroads, on a large number of routes involving billions of dollars of shipments; (2) The UP-SP's proposed solution to part of the market power problem—the offering of trackage rights to the BNSF—was wholly inadequate; and (3) the promised efficiencies were highly speculative, especially given the difficulties that the UP had recently experienced in absorbing the Chicago & North Western Railroad (CNW). The opponents recommended that the ICC/STB either reject the merger outright or condition its approval on the UP-SP's divesting (that is, selling) substantial amounts of its postmerger duplicative track to rival railroads where the merger threatened to create market power.

The Exercise of Market Power

The UP-SP merger, by the applicants' own admission, would reduce the number of rail carriers in hundreds of (city-pair) rail markets for thousands of categories of goods. But the applicants had substantially underestimated the extent of the problem.

2-to-1 Markets

The instances where the merger would create effective monopolies— reducing the number of rail carriers from two (the UP and the SP) to one (the new, combined railroad)—were numerous. They accounted for as much as $2 billion of rail freight revenues out of about $18 billion in total western freight revenues in 1994. This was substantially above the applicants' estimate of $900 million. The difference was largely due to the applicants' counting as "2-to-1" only those instances where both the shipper and the recipient were directly connected to the UP and the SP (and only the UP and SP). This neglected instances where either the UP or the SP might be close enough to the shipper or the recipient (or both) so that the threat or

---

[21]*Norfolk Southern Corp.—Norfolk & Western Ry. and Southern Ry.*, 366 ICC 171, 223 (1982). *Guilford Transportation Industries—Delaware & Hudson Ry.*, 366 ICC 396, 411 (1982).

[22]The opponents included many (but not all) shippers, other railroads (but not the BNSF), and the U.S. Departments of Justice, Transportation, and Agriculture.

actuality of using truck or barge for short trans-shipments or the possibilities of build-ins/build-outs effectively kept the two lines in competition with each other.[23] The applicants counted such instances as pre-merger monopoly that would not experience any reduction in competition.

The applicants also ignored instances where the UP or SP might have a monopoly at one end of the shipment but the other carrier was one of two different carriers that were competing at the other end and thus interline shipments were currently necessary[24]; the merger would effectively create a single-line service monopoly. And finally they overlooked instances of source competition and destination competition where the UP was the sole carrier on the one route and the SP was the sole carrier on the other.

In short, even if the granting of trackage rights to BNSF was an adequate solution where it was proposed, it did not address the creation of effective monopolies in markets that were about as quantitatively important. Freight-rate increases of about 20 percent were estimated[25] to be the likely result of the reduction in the number of carriers from two to one.

3-to-2 Markets

In hundreds of markets the merger would reduce the number of effective rail carriers from three to two and thus create or exacerbate problems of oligopolistic behavior among the remaining two carriers.[26] These instances were estimated to involve about $5 billion in rail freight revenues. Further, in a large fraction of these markets the second carrier would be the BNSF, so the merged UPSP and the BNSF would experience a multitude of multi-market contacts, threatening to exacerbate the potential oligopoly problems. The applicants' claims that competition would remain vigorous in these markets was supported neither by theory nor by the evidence.

Most strands of oligopoly theory indicate that a market with only two sellers and high barriers to entry would be likely to result in a noncompetitive outcome: a higher price and lower output than would be true if complete price competition were to prevail. Theories of "cooperative" behavior would predict that the two would be aware of each other's presence and of

---

[23]One of the largest shippers affected by the merger, Dow Chemical, was in this situation. Its huge petrochemical complex in Freeport, Texas, was exclusively served by the UP, but both the SP and the BNSF operated lines that passed within about 35 miles. For various reasons the BNSF was not interested in building in, but the SP had engaged in extensive discussions with Dow about such a possibility. The UP-SP merger would eliminate this competitive threat, and Dow anticipated price increases.

[24]Recent research (Winston et al., 1990; Grimm et al., 1992) has shown that in such instances the monopoly carrier did not capture all of the potential rents.

[25]On the basis of cross-section regression models that compared rates on routes with one, two, three, etc., rail carriers, holding constant the other important features of the routes (e.g., distance, type of goods being shipped, etc.). See Majure (1996) and Grimm (1996). Industry views are that captive shippers pay a 20–30 percent premium, consistent with these estimates (D'Amico 2001b).

[26]Similar concerns were raised, though with less potency, with respect to the $265 million in markets where the merger would cause the number of rail carriers to be reduced from four to three.

the consequences of aggressive actions and would mutually try to monitor and police each other's actions, resulting in a non-competitive outcome. The "Cournot" theory of "noncooperative" behavior—each seller uses quantity as its strategic tool and assumes that its rival will not change its quantity in response to any strategic move—would predict a noncompetitive outcome. A "dominant firm" model, where one firm dominates a market (in terms of market share) and has a cost or product differentiation advantage over its rivals, would predict a noncompetitive outcome.[27] Only the "Bertrand" theory of noncooperative behavior—that each seller uses its price as its strategic instrument and assumes that its rival will hold its price unchanged in the face of price reductions—would lead to the prediction of a competitive outcome in a market with only two firms.

The applicants had claimed that coordinated or cooperative behavior, even among as few as two railroads, would be difficult because of the differentiated nature of rail service and the opportunities for secret price cutting that thereby were present and that the Bertrand model was the best approximation for rail service. But, the critics replied, with only two carriers and a service (freight haulage) that is readily observed, monitoring and policing would still be feasible and would be strengthened by the multitude of markets in which the UPSP and the BNSF would repeatedly be in contact with each other. Also, the applicants' reliance on the differentiated nature of rail markets and on the Bertrand model to support their claims concerning the competitiveness of rail markets implied a logical inconsistency: The Bertrand model's prediction of a competitive outcome applies only for sellers with uniform products. Extensions of the Bertrand theory to sellers with differentiated products (the existence of which appeared to be crucial to the applicants' claim that monitoring and policing of each other's behavior would be difficult) indicate that the product differentiation "softens" competition between them, leading to a noncompetitive outcome. In addition, though the applicants had likened rail competition for large customers to auctions, standard auction theory (McAfee and McMillan, 1987) predicts that the fewer are the bidders in a sealed-bid (secret) auction, the less favorable will be the prices from the perspective of the auctioneer.

Equally important, a huge body of empirical literature supported the application of oligopoly theory predictions to real-world markets. Higher seller concentration (a reduction from three sellers to two sellers in a market would represent a sharp increase in seller concentration) is generally associated with higher prices and higher profits (Bresnahan, 1989; Schmalensee, 1989; Weiss, 1989). Especially relevant was research (Kwoka, 1979) indicating that the shares of the leading two firms are crucial in this relationship and that the presence of a sizable third firm could cause price-cost margins to decline. Further, recent empirical research on railroad freight

---

[27]On $2 billion of the 3-to-2 routes, the combined UPSP would have market shares of 70% or greater.

markets, as well as specific econometric studies conducted by the critics to buttress their arguments, showed that the number of carriers on a route influenced freight rates in the expected ways.[28] A reduction from three carriers on a route to two would be expected to cause freight rates to rise by about 10 percent. And research on airline markets (Evans and Kessides, 1994) showed that increases in multimarket contacts led to higher prices. Also, empirical research on auction markets showed that the theoretical predictions as to the consequences of numbers of bidders were borne out in real-world auction markets. And an analysis of the bids that the Department of Defense (DOD) received for rail freight movements of military equipment showed that the number of bidders mattered (Ploth, 1996).

The SP as a Weak Carrier

Though, as the applicants claimed, the SP was a financially weak carrier, it was not in danger of failing; it had successfully raised capital in recent years, and its recent operations had shown some improvements. Further, its presence in many rail markets clearly made a difference in terms of the competitive vigor of those markets. Empirical analysis using regression techniques showed this to be the case; an analysis of the DOD bid results showed that the presence of the SP as a bidder caused the winning bids to be lower (i.e., more favorable to the DOD as customer) (Ploth, 1996).

The Trackage Rights Agreement

The UP-SP's trackage rights agreement, critics argued, was wholly inadequate as a remedy for the likely competitive problems that would be created by the merger. First, the agreement did not cover half (about $900 million) of the markets where 2-to-1 problems would effectively arise and was not applicable to any of the 3-to-2 markets (about $5 billion).

Second, the agreement raised all of the landlord-tenant problems discussed above and more: The UP-SP had structured the arrangement so as to disadvantage the BNSF and mute the vigor of the latter's competition. The pricing arrangement converted the UP-SP's *fixed* costs of track ownership and maintenance into *variable* (per-ton-mile) charges on the BNSF's traffic, clearly pushing BNSF's prices upward. In addition, numerous instances were cited of the BNSF's being given inferior track routings or inadequate access to complementary facilities. And, finally, trackage rights for long-hauls might require crew changes, switching, and other matters that were vastly more complicated than for the typical trackage-right runs of fifty to hundred miles.

Third, the fact that it was the BNSF that was the "tenant" in virtually all of the trackage rights agreements meant that the number of multimarket

---

[28]See Grimm (1985, 1996); MacDonald (1987, 1989a, 1989b); Winston et al. (1990); Grimm et al. (1992); Burton (1993); Wilson (1994); and Majure (1996).

contacts, with their risks of heightened oligopolistic coordination, was increased substantially.

The Promised Efficiencies Were Highly Speculative

The primary justification for the merger was the very large efficiency improvements that the merged entity would achieve. But, the critics argued, these projected gains greatly overstated the likely actual gains that could be attributed to the merger:

First, the merger would mean a larger organization, which would be harder to manage. And the melding of the two corporations could yield the same problems of *inefficiencies* that the UP had recently experienced in its absorption of the CNW.[29]

Second, some of the applicants' estimates of cost savings involved the inclusion of trends in productivity improvements that would likely occur anyway, even in the absence of the merger.

Third, some of the cost savings involved transfers from other parties, which meant no real social gains.

Fourth, some of the single-line integration efficiencies could instead be achieved by better coordination between the independent UP and SP. For example, as a means of providing better service to each carrier's customers, each line might grant trackage rights to the other for through service on a cooperative basis.[30] Indeed, many railroads already engaged in mutually advantageous trackage rights or reciprocal switching arrangements whereby, on a mutual basis, one carrier would locally transfer rail cars from a shipper's siding to another carrier's tracks or deliver the cars from another carrier's tracks to a recipient's siding.[31]

One especially skeptical critic estimated that, after all of these adjustments were made, the applicants' claimed cost savings of $750 million per year might actually be as little as $73 million annually (Christensen, 1996).

A Summing Up

The merger's opponents argued that the risks of new or enhanced market power in hundreds of rail freight markets were quite high, that the trackage agreement with BNSF was woefully inadequate as a remedy, and that the

---

[29]The *Wall Street Journal* began a news report on that experience as follows: "Union Pacific Corp., plagued by widespread delays and service disruptions, is rushing to correct the problems caused by surging grain traffic, locomotive and crew shortages and troubles digesting its takeover of Chicago & North Western Transportation Co. earlier this year" (Machalaba, 1995).

[30]Such cooperative granting of trackage rights would introduce new and improved service where there had been less attractive (joint-line) service and would be less likely to encounter the problems enumerated for the BNSF trackage rights arrangement.

[31]But, a critic of the critics might ask, if the coordination was so easy to do, why hadn't the UP and SP already done it? One response might be that the BN-SF merger had awakened them to new possibilities—like the merger itself—that had not seemed relevant before.

promised efficiencies were speculative at best. They urged outright rejection of the merger or alternatively conditioning its approval on the divestiture of duplicative tracks. In the hands of rival carriers, trackage would be less likely to create oligopolistic problems.

THE STB'S DECISION

The UP and SP filed their merger application with the ICC in November 1995. Over the next several months the ICC and then the STB reviewed a voluminous record and conducted public hearings on the major issues. In arriving at its decision, the STB heard both protests against the merger and testimony urging its approval, generally conditional on the BNSF trackage agreement. The BNSF itself took no position. Rather, it emphasized that it was the sole railroad that would be able to provide strong competition to the now-larger UPSP and could do so if and only if the trackage agreement were fully implemented.

On July 3, 1996, the STB announced its decision to approve the merger subject to a slightly modified BNSF trackage agreement together with other requirements affecting individual routes and shippers. Overall, its decision reflected the UP-SP position on all the major issues. The Board concluded that the merger would result in superior service, substantial cost savings, enhanced competition, and by virtue of the trackage rights agreement full protection to captive shippers.

With respect to cost savings, the STB endorsed the UP-SP list of "non-quantifiable benefits" such as shorter routes and more reliable service. It assessed the quantifiable annual benefits from the merger at $627 million, excluding only two items from the list advanced by the applicants. These were $76 million in revenues from diverted traffic (since this was not a cost savings to the UP-SP), and about $48 million in trackage rights proceeds from BNSF (which were transfers rather than real resource savings).

The far more conservative evaluation of cost savings advocated by the critics was characterized as "largely theoretical concerns" (Surface Transportation Board, 1996, p. 110) and essentially rejected. The argument that the parties could achieve major efficiencies by greater interfirm coordination was dismissed as unrealistic and inconsistent with the companies' past behavior, which after all did not do so. Moreover, the critics' belief that considerable productivity gains would occur anyway did not undermine the validity of the efficiencies identified as specifically flowing from this merger. Only with respect to the two relatively minor cost items noted above did the Board concur with the critics' position.

The Board went on to address the many competitive concerns that had been raised. The critics' claim that the merger would cause 2-to-1 shippers substantial harm was rejected on the grounds that it was based on the premise that BNSF, through its trackage rights agreement, would have no effect on rates. The Board asserted that the latter "will effectively replace the competition that would otherwise be lost" so that competitive harm, if any, would be "negligible" (Surface Transportation Board, 1996, p. 103).

While the circumstance of 3-to-2 shippers was not addressed in the merger agreement, the Board was adamant that the evidence did not support the view that they would be significantly harmed. Shipper statements favoring the merger were cited; empirical studies based on particular commodities were declared unrepresentative; studies of nonrailroad markets were dismissed; the applicants' criticisms of these studies were cited without qualification. On the basis of such reasoning, the Board concluded what it had concluded in earlier merger applications: that two railroads were sufficient to bring about competition. And if there was any possibility of competitive harm, it would be outweighed by the very large efficiency benefits of the merger (Surface Transportation Board, 1996, p. 121).

The STB cited approvingly the prearranged trackage rights agreement with the BNSF. It modified the agreement slightly to provide more extensive coverage to the BNSF and greater protection to certain shippers. In particular, for those shippers that were currently captive to (say) the UP but had opportunities for build-ins/build-outs or transloading to the SP, the Board extended BNSF's trackage rights to points that preserved those build-in/build-out and transloading possibilities.

Concerns that the trackage agreement might not result in effective competition because of the rates charged by the UPSP or because of the terms under which the BNSF would operate were rejected. The Board's response was to assert that the full mileage charge inclusive of fixed costs was consistent with past practice and "well within a reasonable level" (Surface Transportation Board, 1996, p. 140). It stated that any concerns over discrimination in dispatch and other constraints on the BNSF's operations were addressed by the detailed trackage rights protocol that the UP-SP had entered into with BNSF. The Board rejected arguments in favor of more divestiture, asserting that this would be more burdensome than monitoring the trackage agreement.

Finally, the STB addressed the allegation that the merger would result in an overall western railroad duopoly that would likely collude rather than compete. It cited its experience with other mergers and the lack of a specific example of two-railroad collusion as a basis for summary rejection of such concerns.

Having thus disposed of all contrary arguments, the Board concluded:

> [T]he merger as conditioned [by the trackage rights agreement] clearly will be pro-competitive in the sense that it will stimulate price and service competition in markets served by the merged carriers. The merger will create a more efficient and competitive UP/SP system competing head-to-head throughout the West with BNSF. UP/SP customers will benefit from tremendous service improvements brought about by reductions in route

mileage, extended single-line service, enhanced equipment supply, better service reliability, and new operating efficiencies. [Surface Transportation Board, 1996, p. 108]

THE AFTERMATH

"We learned a lot [about] how to do it right next time. . . . I guarantee there won't be a repeat of service problems in the future with or without the Southern Pacific."

RONALD J. BURNS,
President and CEO, Union Pacific Railroad (Machalaba, 1995)

For the first few years after the UP-SP merger, the warnings of the critics as to the difficulties of merging the two organizations and managing a larger railroad were disastrously prescient. The UP executive's assurances (quoted above)—that the railroad had learned from its problems in absorbing the CNW—proved ill founded.

The merger was implemented in September 1996, and the UP began its integration efforts. By the summer of 1997, however, these efforts were unraveling. One harbinger was a deterioration in safety. The UP experienced three major train crashes that resulted in seven deaths. The Federal Railway Administration, which is responsible for enforcing safety standards, launched an unprecedented investigation of the UP's entire network.

Simultaneously, the UP began experiencing congestion and service problems, as trains and shipments began slowing down and backing up and shippers and recipients began complaining about lost shipments and long delays. Despite the UP management's assurances in August 1997 that the problems were being solved, the carrier's service worsened. Newspaper articles (Machalaba 1997; Mathews and Machalaba 1997) described the UP's rail system as "near gridlock" in many places and recounted many instances of losses and delays.

Analysts focused on the managerial and logistics problems that the railroad had experienced in implementing the merger. For example, the UP and SP had different computer systems and dispatching methods, and workers from the one system were unable to adapt readily to the other's computers and operations. Cutbacks in management, crews, and equipment—part of the projected efficiencies of the merger—made the problems worse.

In September 1997, under pressure from the STB, the UP proposed measures that were both extreme and embarrassing to a major railroad, but necessary given the extent of its problems. First it announced a plan to charter a large container ship on the West Coast, load it with the backed-up containers stored in its western rail yards, and send it through the Panama Canal for delivery at the Texas Gulf Coast. That plan was scrapped within a few days in favor of a proposal to send its freight on competing truck and rail carriers, including the BNSF. That plan proved to be of limited help.

It is still too early to tell whether the long-run effects of the merger will meet the rosy predictions of the merger applicants and the STB—substantial efficiencies and no increase in market power—or will be closer to the dire warnings of the merger's critics—heightened market power and few net efficiencies. But the short-run consequences of the merger were all too clear: The costs to rail freight shippers and recipients, especially in the southwestern United States were substantial.[32] Bringing these problems under control simply took time. It was not until 2000 that the UP seemed to have gotten control of its organization and system, although even then critics remained (Schmeltzer 2000). Some shippers who suffered losses sued the railroad; others began the costly process of building alternative routings; and a few even succeeded in encouraging new small railroads to start up on specific routes (D'Amico 2000).

As for the rail industry as a whole, consolidation continued to unfold. Three months after the STB approved the UP-SP merger, the managements of the CSX railroad (one of the two major railroads in the southeast) and of Conrail (the sole major railroad in the northeast) announced an agreement to merge Conrail into CSX. A week later the other major southeastern railroad, the Norfolk Southern (NS), made a higher offer for Conrail. After a few months of financial and legal wrangling, the three parties agreed that CSX and the NS would jointly buy Conrail and split its route structure and equipment between themselves. This transaction was approved by the STB in June 1998. Despite extensive planning, so as to avoid the absorption problems experienced in the UP-SP merger, both acquirers experienced significant service disruption problems, which lasted for more than a year, in absorbing their respective Conrail pieces.

The next shoe to drop was the decision of the Canadian National Railway Co. (CN) to purchase the Illinois Central (IC), a major U.S. carrier with north-south routes from New Orleans to Chicago and surrounding communities in the Mississippi Valley. Since these two carriers had few overlapping routes—it was a true "end-to-end" merger—it raised little controversy, and the CN-IC merger was approved by the STB in June 1999.

The next merger proposal, however, proved to be the straw that broke the (STB) camel's back. In late December 1999 the BNSF and the CN proposed a merger that would make the BNSF the first transcontinental U.S. railroad (although its Atlantic terminus would be solely in Canada). The STB, concerned about the service disruptions that had followed the UP-SP merger and the CSX-NS-Conrail transaction and also concerned about what other merger proposals might soon follow, never seriously considered the merger. Instead, the agency proposed and then approved (in March

---

[32]Weinstein and Clower (1998) estimate that the losses to Texas shippers in the last half of 1997 alone were over $1 billion.

2000) an unprecedented fifteen-month moratorium on all Class I railroad mergers.

During that moratorium, the STB reconsidered its policy approach to mergers and issued a new policy statement in June 2001.[33] That new statement retained the public interest balancing approach that had traditionally guided the agency but added explicit requirements on merger applicants to provide assurances as to the pro-competitive nature of their proposed transactions, to provide backup plans in the event of service disruptions following a merger, and to inform the agency as to the likely consequences of the transaction on the future course of rail industry mergers.

The new policy statement did not indicate, however, a change in philosophy of the STB with respect to crucial competitive issues, such as market delineation and oligopoly behavior (such as 3 to 2 concerns), although future mergers might not present such issues in the profusion that was presented in the UP-SP merger.[34] Also, whether the requirements placed on applicants will actually be greater remains to be seen, since applicants already provide extensive (but, as we have seen in the case of UP-SP, not necessarily accurate) documentation and assurances as to why their merger will be pro-competitive and not create service problems. Underscoring these concerns about the policy statement, shippers were widely critical of it, while railroads mostly expressed satisfaction (D'Amico 2001a).

In sum, rather than adopting something akin to the stance of the DOJ and the FTC—a positive attitude toward competition, a concern about oligopoly behavior, and a skepticism toward claimed efficiencies—the STB seems (despite its rhetoric to the contrary in its new policy statement) to be continuing along its traditional path. The test of this proposition will occur when, as will inevitably be the case, one of the two remaining eastern rail lines proposes to merge with one of the two remaining western lines.

REFERENCES

Bresnahan, Timothy F. "Empirical Studies of Industries with Market Power." In *Handbook of Industrial Organization,* vol. 2, edited by Richard Schmalensee and Robert Willig, 1011–1057. Amsterdam: North-Holland, 1989.

Burton, Mark L. "Railroad Deregulation, Carrier Behavior, and Shipper Response: A Disaggregated Analysis." *Journal of Regulatory Economics* 5 (December 1993): 417–434.

Christensen, Laurits R. "Verified Statement," on behalf of the U.S. Department of Justice, April 9, 1996.

D'Amico, Esther. "Holdups on the Rails." *ChemWeek,* Sept. 20, 2000: 27.

---

[33]STB Ex Parte No. 582 (Sub-No. 1), "Major Rail Consolidation Procedures," June 11, 2001.

[34]See Kwoka and White (2000a, 2000b) for a more complete critique.

D'Amico, Esther. "STB's Final Rail Merger Rules 'Disappoint' Shippers." *ChemWeek,* June 20, 2001a: 15.

D'Amico, Esther. "BNSF and Chemical Shippers Set up against Union Pacific in Texas." *ChemWeek,* Aug. 29/Sept. 5, 2001b: 9.

Evans, William N., and Ioannis N. Kessides. "Living by the 'Golden Rule': Multi-Market Contact in the U.S. Airline Industry." *Quarterly Journal of Economics* 109 (May 1994): 341–366.

Friedlaender, Ann F. *The Dilemma of Freight Transport Regulation.* Washington, D.C.: Brookings Institution, 1969.

Friedlaender, Ann F., and Richard H. Spady. *Freight Transport Regulation: Equity, Efficiency, and Competition in the Rail and Trucking Industries.* Cambridge, Mass.: MIT Press, 1981.

Grimm, Curtis M. "Horizontal Competitive Effects in Railroad Mergers." *Research in Transportation Economics* 2 (1985).

Grimm, Curtis M. "Verified Statement," on behalf of the Kansas City Southern Railroad, March 26, 1996.

Grimm, Curtis M., Clifford Winston, and Carol A. Evans. "Foreclosure of Railroad Markets: A Test of Chicago Leverage Theory." *Journal of Law & Economics* 35 (October 1992): 295–310.

Gruley, Bryan, and Daniel Machalaba. "Proposed Big Railway Merger Draws Criticism from the Justice Department." *Wall Street Journal,* April 15, 1996, p. A6.

Keeler, Theodore E. *Railroads, Freight, and Public Policy.* Washington, D.C.: Brookings, 1983.

Kwoka, John E., Jr., "The Effect of Market Share and Share Distribution on Industry Performance." *Review of Economics and Statistics* 41 (February 1979): 101.

Kwoka, John E., Jr., "Does the Choice of Concentration Measure Really Matter?" *Review of Industrial Organization* 39 (June 1981): 445–453.

Kwoka, John E., Jr., and Lawrence J. White. "Letter to Linda Morgan, Chairman, Surface Transportation Board." November 17, 2000a. See www.antitrustinstitute.org/recent/89.cfm.

Kwoka, John E., Jr., and Lawrence J. White. "Railroad Merger Rules Should Be Analytical, Objective, Transparent; So Far They're Not." December 6, 2000b. See www.antitrustinstitute.org/recent/91.cfm.

MacAvoy, Paul W., and James Sloss. *Regulation of Transport Innovation: The ICC and Unit Coal Trains to the East Coast.* New York: Random House, 1967.

MacDonald, James M. "Competition and Rail Rates for the Shipment of Corn, Soybeans, and Wheat."*Rand Journal of Economics* 18 (Spring 1987): 151–163.

MacDonald, James M. "Railroad Deregulation, Innovation, and Competitive Effects of the Staggers Act on Grain Transportation." *Journal of Law & Economics* 32 (April 1989a): 63–96.

MacDonald, James M. "Concentration and Railroad Pricing." In *Concentration and Price,* edited by Leonard W. Weiss, 205–212. Cambridge, Mass.: MIT Press, 1989b.

Machalaba, Daniel. "Union Pacific Struggles to Clear Up Delayed Shipments." *Wall Street Journal,* November 30, 1995, p. B4.

Machalaba, Daniel. "A Big Railroad Merger Goes Terribly Awry in a Very Short Time." *Wall Street Journal,* October 2, 1997, p. A1.

Machalaba, Daniel, and Asra Q. Nomani. "More Rail Deals May Be Down the Track." *Wall Street Journal,* July 5, 1996, p. A2.

Majure, W. Robert. "Verified Statement," on behalf of the U.S. Department of Justice, April 11, 1996.

Mathews, Anne W., and Daniel Machalaba. "An Unsolved Mystery: Where Are Shippers' Rail Cars?" *Wall Street Journal,* October 13, 1997, p. B1.

McAfee, R. Preston, and John McMillan. "Auctions and Bidding." *Journal of Economic Literature,* 25 (June 1987): 699–738.

Meyer, John R., Merton J. Peck, John Stenason, and Charles Zwick. *The Economics of Competition in the Transportation Industries.* Cambridge, Mass.: Harvard University Press, 1959.

Peterson, Richard B. "Verified Statement," on behalf of the Union Pacific and Southern Pacific Railroads, November 17, 1995.

Ploth, I. William. "Verified Statement," on behalf of the Kansas City Southern Railroad, March 25, 1996.

Schmalensee, Richard. "Inter-industry Studies of Structure and Performance." In *Handbook of Industrial Organization,* vol. 2, edited by Richard Schmalensee and Robert Willig, 951–1009. Amsterdam: North-Holland, 1989.

Schmeltzer, John. "Merger Doubters Still Stalk Union Pacific Deal." *Chicago Tribune,* October 2, 2000.

Surface Transportation Board. "Decision No. 44, Finance Docket No. 32760," concerning the Union Pacific and Southern Pacific Railroads, August 6, 1996.

Weinstein, Bernard L., and Terry L. Clower. "The Impacts of the Union Pacific Service Disruptions on the Texas and National Economies: An Unfinished Story." prepared for the Railroad Commission of Texas, February 9, 1998, mimeo.

Weiss, Leonard W. *Concentration and Price.* Cambridge, Mass.: MIT Press, 1989.

Willig, Robert. "Verified Statement," on behalf of the Union Pacific and Southern Pacific Railroads, November 20, 1995.

Wilner, Frank N. *Railroad Mergers: History, Analysis, Insight.* Omaha, Neb.: Simmons-Boardman, 1997.

Wilson, Wesley W. "Market-specific Effects of Rail Deregulation." *Journal of Industrial Economics* 42 (March 1994): 1–22.

Winston, Clifford, Thomas M. Corsi, Curtis M. Grimm, and Carol A. Evans. *The Economic Effects of Surface Freight Deregulation.* Washington, D.C.: Brookings, 1990.

Prices, Market Definition, and the Effects of Merger: Staples-Office Depot (1997)

Serdar Dalkir and
Frederick R. Warren-Boulton

INTRODUCTION

On September 4, 1996, the two largest office superstore chains in the United States, Office Depot and Staples, announced their agreement to merge. Seven months later, the Federal Trade Commission voted 4 to 1 to oppose the merger on the grounds that it was likely to harm competition and lead to higher prices in "the market for the sale of consumable office supplies sold through office superstores." The merging parties chose to contest the FTC's actions in court. On June 30, 1997, after a seven-day trial, Judge Thomas F. Hogan of the U.S. District Court for the District of Columbia agreed with the FTC and granted a preliminary injunction, effectively dooming the merger.

Staples broke new ground in terms of both the economic theory and the type of evidence presented at trial in an antitrust case. The antitrust enforcement agencies had traditionally focused on the increased probability of collusion following a merger as the primary theoretical underpinning for merger policy. In contrast, *Staples* spotlighted the potential for a merger to have "unilateral effects," a shift in focus first signaled by the 1992 revision

Frederick R. Warren-Boulton served as an expert witness for the FTC in this case. Serdar Dalkir contributed to the economic analysis and the preparation of the expert testimony. Thanks are also due to Stephen Silberman, Robert Levinson, Melvin Orlans, James Fishlein, and Daniel Hoskin for helpful comments on earlier drafts.

of the Department of Justice and FTC *Merger Guidelines.*[1] Focusing on the characteristics of individual suppliers, the FTC argued that Staples, Office Depot, and OfficeMax were sufficiently different from other suppliers of office products, and sufficiently close competitors to each other, that the "sale of office supplies through office superstores" could be defined as a market separate from the sale of office supplies in general. In another departure, for evidence of the likely anticompetitive effect of the merger, the FTC relied primarily on direct estimates of the merger's effect on prices, rather than just predicting that an increase in seller concentration would cause significant (but vaguely specified) price increases. In addition to internal documents describing pricing policies and simple (but powerful) price comparisons between cities where Office Depot and Staples currently competed and those where they did not, the FTC's evidence on price effects included a large-scale econometric model that predicted the effect of the merger on prices. It also included an "event study" that used stock market data to calculate both the effect of the merger on shareholders and the financial market's implicit estimate of the effect of the merger on the prices charged by office superstores.

BACKGROUND

Office Depot and Staples are, respectively, the first- and the second-largest office superstore (OSS) chains in the United States. Staples pioneered the office superstore concept in 1986. In 1997, Staples operated approximately 550 stores in twenty-eight states. It had 1996 revenues of some $4 billion and a stock market valuation of approximately $3 billion at the end of 1996. Office Depot, which adopted the concept of superstores within months after Staples invented it, operated more than 500 stores in thirty-eight states, had 1996 sales of approximately $6.1 billion, and had a stock market value of about $2.2 billion at the end of 1996. The rationale for the superstore concept was simple: While large businesses were able to purchase office supplies through high-volume contract stationers, small businesses and individuals had no comparably convenient, low-cost source of office supplies and other business-related products. The office superstore was to do for office supplies what the supermarket had done for home groceries.

The typical superstore is approximately 23,000 to 30,000 square feet in area, stocks 5000 to 6000 items, is located in an urban business area, and looks like a warehouse. Approximately half of Staples' and Office Depot's revenues are derived from sales of office supplies, with the rest coming from the sale of computers, office furniture, and other business-related

---

[1]U.S. Department of Justice and Federal Trade Commission, "Horizontal Merger Guidelines," reprinted in 4 *Trade Reg. Rep.* (CCH) p. 13,104 (1992, revised 1997). Also see http://www.ftc.gov/bc/docs/horizmer.htm.

items. Both chains purchase virtually all of their inventory directly from manufacturers in large quantities, enabling them to receive volume discounts that are unavailable to small and medium-sized retailers. These lower costs have led to dramatically lower prices: office supplies are typically sold by superstores at discounts of 30 to 70 percent below manufacturer-suggested retail prices.

At one time, twenty-three competing OSS chains slugged it out in the market. By the time of the proposed merger, however, OfficeMax was the only remaining close rival to Staples and Office Depot. Spun off from K-Mart in 1994, OfficeMax operated 575 superstores and seventeen delivery centers in over 220 areas in forty-eight states. Like Staples and Office Depot, each OfficeMax superstore offered an extensive selection of over 7000 items at discount prices, selling primarily to small and medium-sized businesses, home office customers, and individuals. OfficeMax's total revenues for fiscal year 1997 were $3.2 billion, with office supplies making up about 40 percent of total revenues.

The success of the OSS concept had redefined the retailing of office supplies in the United States, driving thousands of independent stationers out of business, just as the growth of supermarkets had driven out thousands of small "Mom and Pop" grocery stores. The competitive rivalry between the superstores had, however, benefited consumers substantially. Each OSS chain slashed prices; drove down costs; developed innovative approaches to marketing, distribution, and store layout; and expanded rapidly, bringing to increasing numbers of consumers the convenience of one-stop shopping at low prices. Office Depot had, at least in recent years, been the most aggressive and lowest-price competitor.

On September 4, 1996, Staples and Office Depot announced an agreement under which Staples would acquire Office Depot by exchanging 1.14 Staples shares for each outstanding Office Depot share, a roughly $4 billion deal. After a seven-month investigation, the FTC decided to challenge the merger.[2]

THE FTC'S CASE

The FTC argued that this merger could be expected to lead to a significant decrease in competition in the market for consumable office supplies sold

---

[2]After the Commission's initial vote, the FTC staff negotiated a tentative agreement (subject to the Commission's approval) with Staples and Office Depot that would have authorized the merger to proceed unchallenged if the two companies agreed to divest a sufficient number of stores to OfficeMax to preserve two competitors in cities where Office Depot and Staples were currently the only two superstores. On March 26, 1997, OfficeMax signed an agreement to buy sixty-three Staples and Office Depot stores for the fire-sale price of $108.75 million, subject to the consent of the FTC. But on April 4, 1997, the Commission voted to reject the proposed settlement and thus to challenge the merger.

through office superstores, and that the resulting price increases could be expected to be substantial. To prove its case, the FTC used a number of sources of data and analytical approaches to predict the price effects of the proposed merger. It argued that all of the evidence indicated that there would be large and long-lasting price increases, and therefore considerable harm to consumers.

The FTC was careful to compare the expected merger-related changes in prices and costs with the prices and costs that would have prevailed in the absence of the merger. Specifically, the FTC recognized that OSS prices might continue to fall after the merger, but argued that because prices would fall significantly further without the merger, the merger would still harm competition. Likewise, the FTC stressed that the efficiencies claimed by the defendants must be merger specific.

Concentration and the Competitive Effects of a Merger

The underlying theme of merger policy is that mergers or acquisitions should not be permitted to create, enhance, or facilitate the exercise of market power, defined as the ability profitably to maintain prices above competitive levels for a significant period of time. The *Merger Guidelines* emphasize two ways in which mergers can lead to higher prices: coordinated interaction and unilateral effects.

When only a few firms account for most of the sales of a product, those firms can sometimes exercise market power by either explicitly or implicitly coordinating their actions. Coordinated interaction is of particular concern in homogeneous product markets, where all firms must charge very similar prices. Circumstances may also permit a single firm, not a monopolist, to exercise market power through unilateral or noncoordinated conduct, that is, without the concurrence of other firms in the market or in the absence of coordinated responses by those firms. Unilateral price effects are of particular concern if the products or services are differentiated, but those supplied by the merging firms are much closer substitutes for each other than for those of other suppliers. In any case, the exercise of market power causes a transfer of wealth from buyers to sellers and a mis-allocation of resources.

Defining the Relevant Market:
"Consumable Office Supplies Sold
Through Office Superstores"

The FTC argued that the relevant product market was "the sale of consumable office supplies through office superstores." The FTC supported its market its market definition, in part, by introducing evidence showing that: (1) OSSs offer a distinct set of products and services; (2) OSSs regard each other as their primary competitors; (3) non-OSS retailers do not tightly constrain OSS pricing; and (4) a hypothetical merger to monopoly among all three

OSSs could be expected to result in a significant increase in their prices for consumable office supplies—an outcome that would not occur if OSSs and other stores selling office supplies were in the same product market.

1. *Office superstores offer a distinct set of products and services.* The FTC argued that OSS firms were different from other vendors of office products because they carried a broad range of consumables and maintained large amounts of stock on hand. These attributes of office superstores created a one-stop-shopping opportunity for consumers that was not provided by other retailers or mail-order suppliers of office products.

Like customers of supermarkets and department stores, customers of office supply superstores benefit from being able to buy a large number and variety of products on a single visit. The full "price" to an office superstore customer of acquiring these products is the amount paid to the store, plus the customer's noncash costs of shopping. These noncash costs include the value of the time required to visit the store, gather information about products and prices, and shop. Since each visit to a store involves a fixed cost, customers prefer to purchase a bundle of items on each visit, especially low-cost "consumable" items that need to be purchased regularly.

Customers who purchase a bundle or basket of items need to decide: (1) which store to go to and (2) what products to buy on each visit. The first decision is relevant if one is analyzing a merger among a particular class of retailers (e.g., office superstores, department stores, or supermarkets) and needs to define a market for a particular type of retailing service. The second decision is relevant if one is analyzing a merger among manufacturers of particular products sold by those retailers (e.g., binders, women's dresses, or canned tuna).

OSSs devote significant shelf space to consumable office products and maintain a large inventory to ensure the convenience of one-stop shopping for customers. Superstores carry up to 7500 items of consumable office supplies, computers and computer-related products, and office furniture. While certain non-OSS retailers (mass merchandisers, warehouse club stores, computer stores, and consumer electronics outlets) sell a number of the same products that OSSs sell, they typically stock far fewer office supply items[3] and/or carry a very limited assortment of consumable office supplies.

In court, both sides presented witnesses, exhibits, and affidavits that addressed the extent to which OSS retailers differ from non-OSS retailers of office supplies. Faced with a mass of conflicting evidence, the FTC strongly recommended that the judge visit several sellers of office supplies to see for himself how superstores differ from other office supply retailers. As one FTC expert witness put it, "One visit would be worth a thousand affidavits."

---

[3]Estimates of office supply items carried by the warehouse club stores range from 100 to 289. Mass merchandisers like K-Mart and Target typically carry fewer than 570 office supply items. Even Wal-Mart, which carries a relatively broad range of office supply items (between 1067 and 2400), nonetheless did not appear to be a significant competitor of the OSS firms.

2. *OSSs regard each other as their primary competitors.* The parties' internal documents (at least those predating the merger announcement) showed that each was concerned primarily or exclusively with competition from other office superstores. Indeed, Staples defined "competitive" and "noncompetitive" markets solely in terms of the presence or absence of OSS competitors,[4] and referred to its participation in an "office superstore industry."[5] Office Depot's documents similarly focused primarily on other OSS firms as competitors. The FTC argued that such evidence demonstrated that Staples and Office Depot recognized that other OSS firms were their main competitors.

3. *Non-OSS retailers have little effect on OSSs' price changes.* The FTC argued that the presence of non-OSS retailers could be expected to have little effect on the prices charged by OSS, especially in markets where more than one OSS was present. This implied that the presence of non-OSS retailers in an area would not prevent the merged office superstore from raising prices and that such non-OSS retailers should not thus be included in the relevant market.

The FTC did not dispute the fact that, in markets defined by Staples as "noncompetitive markets" (i.e., in markets where only one OSS was present), retailers like warehouse clubs and computer stores would be the closest competitors of the OSS. But the FTC argued that one could not infer from this that non-OSS retailers would provide effective competition for OSS firms in "competitive" markets, those where two or more OSSs already were present. A monopolist maintains a price so high that any further increase would cause a sufficient loss of customers to be unprofitable. Thus, a monopolist is distinguished not by the fact that it faces no competition, but by the fact that its closest competitors are too distant to prevent it from maintaining its price at a level significantly above cost. Ultimately, however, every monopolist "creates" its own "competitors" by maintaining its own price sufficiently high.[6]

---

[4]For example, Staples' FY95 Marketing Plan defined competitive markets as markets with another office superstore (i.e., Office Depot or OfficeMax or both), and noncompetitive markets as those with only local stationers or warehouse clubs.

[5]Staples's internal documents further established that it viewed OSS firms to be its primary competitive constraint. A March 1996 memorandum discussing possible price increases if Staples bought OfficeMax specifically referenced only one competitor, Office Depot, as a possible price-constraining influence. In a document analyzing new store openings, under the heading "Competitive Store Additions in Staples Markets," only Office Depot and OfficeMax store openings were listed. No other entity was listed as a competitor. In a similar vein, it is clear that Staples did not view mail-order firms, independent stationers, or other nonsuperstore-format vendors of office supplies as price-constraining influences.

[6]This point has come to be known as the "cellophane fallacy" after the Supreme Court's decision in *U.S. v. E.I. du Pont de Nemours & Co.,* 351 U.S. 377 (1956). In that case, du Pont was accused of monopolizing the cellophane market. The Court reasoned that cellophane had many substitutes and the company's share of flexible wrapping materials did not warrant a monopoly ruling. In so doing, the Court failed to recognize that had du Pont sold cellophane at a competitive price (instead of the monopoly price) there would not have been many similarly priced substitutes.

Thus, in a market with two OSS firms, each OSS could overwhelmingly be the other's primary "competition" and provide the only effective force holding the other OSSs pricing at present levels. If these two OSSs merged, the new firm would find it profitable to raise its prices until competition from non-OSS retailers eventually made further price increases unprofitable. The post-merger OSS monopoly would then be constrained by the prices charged by these new, non-OSS "competitors." In short, even though warehouse price clubs or Wal-Mart might be important competitors to Staples in geographic markets that have no other OSS rivals, such non-OSS suppliers are not significant competitors to Staples in geographic markets where Staples faces other OSS competitors, that is, in the markets that the FTC thought were relevant to analyzing this merger.

The FTC's econometric analysis supported the conclusion that non-OSS competitors do not constrain OSS pricing in geographic markets where two or three OSS chains are present. Indeed, simulations of the effects of eliminating individual non-OSS retailers from such markets showed that none of those retailers (except Best Buy, which had tried and failed to implement an OSS-type format, and had effectively exited by the time of the merger) had any statistically significant effect on Staples' prices.

Further evidence of differences between OSS firms and other office supplies retailers involved price differences. In general, suppliers that compete in the same market have similar prices for the same products. If consumers can easily switch among suppliers, higher prices, adjusted for quality, will not be sustainable.[7] The FTC presented evidence that office superstores in the same geographic market tend to price office products at the same level, just as warehouse clubs in the same geographic market tend to price office products at the same level. However, prices for office products in the same geographic market often differ significantly between OSS firms as a group and warehouse clubs as a group.[8]

4. *Econometric evidence supported an OSS product market.* Under the *Merger Guidelines,* the relevant product market in this case turned on the following question: Would a merger to monopoly among the OSS chains in a city allow the merged entity to raise the prices of consumable office supplies by 5 percent or more? If the answer is yes, then "office supplies sold through office superstores" is a relevant market under the *Guidelines.*

The FTC addressed this question by constructing a large-scale econometric model of prices for office supplies. The analysis was designed to de-

---

[7]When consumers are deciding among stores where they can purchase a group or bundle of products, competing stores in the same market would be expected to show a very similar price index for a representative basket of products, without necessarily showing very similar prices on individual items.

[8]A Prudential Securities survey reported that in Detroit all three OSS firms had virtually identical prices for the basket of office supplies sampled (total prices differed by from 0.4% to 2.0%). In contrast, the price of a basket of items common to any of the three OSS firms and to Best Buy was 18% to 19% higher at Best Buy (Prudential Securities, 1995, pp. 64, 67).

termine how Staples' prices varied from one store to another as a function of the number of nearby Office Depot or OfficeMax stores, the number and identity of potential nonsuperstore rivals such as discount mass merchandisers or warehouse club stores, and differences in costs and demand conditions across local markets. The FTC had weekly data from the parties, for over eighteen months, covering more than 400 Staples stores in more than forty cities. The data included prices for a large number of individual stock-keeping units (SKUs) as well as a price index for consumable office supplies.

The FTC's analysis predicted that a merger to monopoly in markets where all three OSS firms were present would raise the price for office supplies sold through OSSs in those markets by 8.49 percent. Such an increase would not be possible if OSS firms were constrained by other retailers. These results confirmed that "consumable office supplies sold through office superstores" was a relevant market under the *Guidelines* criteria.

The Merger's Likely Anticompetitive Consequences

The FTC argued that voluminous evidence—structural, documentary, and statistical—all supported the conclusion that the combined Staples/Office Depot entity would raise prices for office supplies. As to the structural evidence, a merger between the OSS firms in a hypothetical market with many OSS chains would not necessarily have any anticompetitive effect, because the merged firm would still have many close competitors. As we have seen, however, only three OSS chains compete anywhere in the United States. Therefore, OSS market concentration would increase significantly in all local markets in which both Staples and Office Depot were present as the number of OSS competitors fell from either three to two or from two to one. The companies' own documents indicated that Office Depot was the main constraint on Staples' prices[9] and that, but for the merger, Staples planned to cut prices significantly over the next few years in response to current and future competitive pressures from Office Depot. The proposed merger would eliminate these pressures.[10] Finally, statistical analyses of the potential effects of this transaction predicted that, absent efficiencies, the merger could be expected to lead to large price increases. In addition, data from financial markets indicated that investors implicitly believed the merger would lead to significantly higher prices even after allowing for the effects of any efficiencies.

---

[9]The CEO of Staples, Tom Stemberg, testified to this point by arguing that, "Office Depot is our best competitor" and "our biggest competitor." Stemberg described that this "best" and "biggest" competitor posed a more severe pricing constraint upon Staples than did the third office supply superstore chain, OfficeMax.

[10]In fact, in anticipation of the merger, Staples canceled a 3% price cut on nonpaper supply items.

Structural Evidence:
The Change in Concentration and Market Power

The structural effect of the proposed merger would have been to reduce from three to two the number of suppliers in markets where all three OSS firms would otherwise have competed and to create a monopoly in markets where only Staples and Office Depot currently competed, at least until entry by OfficeMax could reasonably be expected.

Table 2-1 shows Staples management's estimate for the percentage of Staples stores located in "Staples-only," "Staples and Office Depot," and "Staples, Office Depot, and OfficeMax" markets in 1995 and their projection for the year 2000. Absent the merger, Staples management anticipated a significant increase in competition from Office Depot and OfficeMax, as indicated by its projection that by 2000 markets with all three chains would account for 69 percent of Staples stores, up from 17 percent in 1995.

Therefore, the eventual effect of the merger would be to reduce the number of competitors from three to two in most geographic markets and from two to one in all but a few of the remaining geographic markets. (A small number of markets still would have only one OSS by 2000 even in the absence of the merger.)

Empirical Evidence Pointing to Likely Price Increases

In almost all merger cases before *Staples,* the DOJ or FTC relied primarily, if not exclusively, on indirect structural evidence of the kind presented above to infer that a significant price increase could be expected from that merger. *Staples* is unique, however, in terms of the large number of independent sources of strong, consistent, and direct evidence that were introduced at trial to show that prices would likely increase as a result of their merger. Five of these sources are discussed below.

Predictions of Staples' Management: Staples' own documents showed that, absent this merger, Staples' management expected that wider competition would force it to lower prices and/or raise quality. Its *1996 Strategy Update,* part of the FTC's trial evidence, forecasted that the per-

TABLE 2-1

Percentage of Staples Stores in Staples-Only Markets, Two-OSS Markets, and Three-OSS Markets

Year	Staples Only	Staples & Office Depot	Staples & OfficeMax	All Three	Total
1995	17%	29%	37%	17%	100%
2000	12%	7%	12%	69%	100%

Source: Plaintiff's Exhibit 15, p. 32.

centage of three-player markets would increase to nearly 70 percent by the year 2000. It went on to predict that this could intensify the pressure on Staples' prices and also lead to greater operating expenses as a result of a higher service quality and higher marketing expenditures.

Staples also predicted that, absent the merger, its retail margins, averaged over its entire sales (i.e., arranged not just over consumable office supplies and not just over markets where it faced competition from Office Depot) would decline by 150 basis points ("bps"), or 1.50 percentage points, by the year 2000 as a result of increased competitive pressure (ibid., p. 66). Of that margin fall, 60 bps would come from markets where Staples competed only with Office Depot and reflected Staples goal (absent the merger) to eliminate the price differences on nonpaper supply items between Staples and Office Depot.

Direct Comparisons of Prices Across Local Markets: Statistical data generated during the ordinary course of business by the companies showed that, on average, both Staples and Office Depot priced significantly lower when they confronted each other in local markets.[11] As shown in Table 2-2, Staples' office supplies prices were 11.6 percent lower in markets occupied by Staples and Office Depot than in Staples-only markets; they were 4.9 percent lower in markets with all three OSSs than in markets where Staples faced only OfficeMax. Competition between Staples and Office Depot also had a significant restraining effect on Office Depot prices. These data could be used to infer the likely increases in prices after the merger (on the assumption that Staples' price patterns would dominate): +11.6 percent for the markets where premerger there was a Staples-Office Depot duopoly (accounting for 29% of Staples' stores); and +4.9 percent for the markets where premerger all three OSSs were present (accounting for 17% of Staples' stores).

Estimates from Econometric Analysis: The FTC performed an econometric analysis using store-level price data to estimate how prices differed across markets depending on the number and identity of firms in a market.[12] In essence, this econometric analysis was a more formal and

---

[11]In court, the FTC presented a particularly striking example of these price differentials: matching full-page color advertisements that appeared on the same day in two Florida cities, Orlando and Leesburg. Every detail was identical except the prices, which were 30 percent to 114 percent higher in Leesburg (with Office Depot only) than in Orlando (with three OSSs). This natural experiment provided the clearest evidence of both the existence of an OSS market and the likely effect of the merger on prices. To see a copy of the exhibit, go to http://dalkir.tripod.com/depotad/index.html.

[12]The statistical analysis was based on a large sample of store-level price data, drawn from 428 Staples stores in the United States over the twenty-three-month period from February 1995 to December 1996. The model examined statistically how Staples' prices varied with the extent of OSS competition, the presence of non-OSS firms (such as Wal-Mart, K-Mart, Target, and Best Buy), and potentially location-specific cost and demographic variables. See Baker (1999) and Ashenfelter et al. (2002) for an extensive discussion of the econometric studies that examined the extent of localized competition between the merging firms. For on-line articles discussing econometric as well as other aspects of *Staples,* go to http://www.antitrust.org/cases/merger.htm.

TABLE 2-2
Average Price Differentials for Office Superstore Products, Differing Market Structures

Benchmark OSS Market Structure	Comparison OSS Market Structure	Price Reduction
Staples only	Staples + Office Depot	11.6%
Staples + OfficeMax	Staples + OfficeMax + Office Depot	4.9%
Office Depot only	Office Depot + Staples	8.6%
Office Depot + OfficeMax	Office Depot + OfficeMax + Staples	2.5%

complete analysis of the kind of data just discussed. Using these estimates, the FTC calculated the overall price effects of the proposed merger: an average of 7.3 percent for the two- and three-firm markets where the merger partners were both present.

Estimates from the Prudential Study: A Prudential Securities (1996) study reported the results of a pricing survey that compared prices for office supplies at office superstores in Totowa, New Jersey, a three-player market, and in Paramus, New Jersey, a nearby (25-minute drive) two-player market (Staples and OfficeMax). The survey showed that prices, especially on visible general office supply products, were more competitive in three-player markets than in two-player markets. In particular, the survey found that Staples' prices on a basket of general office supplies that included the most visible items on which the office supply superstores typically offer attractive prices were 5.8 percent lower in three-player Totowa than in two-player Paramus.

Estimates from a Stock-Market Event-Probability Study: Financial market investors vote with their dollars (or bet) on whether a merger will raise or lower prices. A merger that raises market prices will benefit both the merging parties and their rivals and thus raise the prices for all their shares. Conversely, suppose the financial community expects the efficiencies from a merger to be so large that the merged firm will drive down market prices. In this case, the share values of the merging firms' rivals would fall when the probability of the merger goes up. Thus, evidence from financial markets can be used to predict market price effects when significant merger-related efficiencies are alleged.

The authors analyzed the effect of the proposed merger on share prices and concluded that, if consummated, the merger would raise the value of OfficeMax's shares by 12 percent (or $200 million) but would have little or no effect on the share values of other retailers of office supplies; see Warren-Boulton and Dalkir (2001). These findings confirmed both that the

merger would have anticompetitive price effects and that the OSSs constituted a relevant market.

Entry

Potential Entry of Other OSS Firms
Did not Constrain the Incumbents

The FTC argued that the threat of entry by a new OSS supplier would
not prevent the merger from raising prices until such entry actually occurred. A potential entrant would assess the profitability of entry on the
basis of what it expected prices to be after its entry, not before. Therefore,
as long as incumbents could adjust their prices rapidly in response to entry,
pre-entry prices would be irrelevant to the entry decision. And, since incumbents could not deter entry by keeping prices below the pre-entry
profit-maximizing level, the best pricing strategy would be to "make hay
while the sun shines." In other words, "investing" in entry deterrence by
maintaining low prices was not a profitable strategy for incumbents.

Under certain conditions, however, potential competition can affect
the prices of the incumbents. Usually, this requires both low sunk costs of
entry and an inability on the part of incumbents to reduce their prices rapidly in response to entry.[13] These conditions, however, were not present in
the OSS industry. To the contrary, a significant share of entry costs into a
local area was sunk costs, and incumbents could adjust their prices quite
rapidly in response to entry. Therefore, prices of office superstore products
could not be affected by potential entry.

This conclusion was supported by evidence in the documents. (For example, according to Thomas Stemberg, the CEO of Staples, Staples had not
changed its prices in anticipation of entry by rivals.) The documents also
showed that, when Staples considered entering a local market, it did not
look at the prices in that market, but rather at the number of competitors.

Significant Barriers to Entry

While an individual office superstore could take advantage of store-
level economies of scale and scope, a chain of superstores could also take
advantage of economies of multistore operation. The latter economies appeared at different levels for different functions. Economies of scale in advertising, for example, clearly appeared at the local and regional levels.
Thus, Staples' strategy for entry into a large urban market consisted of first
establishing a number of stores in the periphery and advertising only in

---

[13]If sunk costs are low (or firms are able to enter into long-term contracts with customers before actually entering) and incumbent suppliers are not able to change their prices quickly in response to
entry, then the incumbents may not wish to encourage entry or to risk a significant loss of market
share if entry occurs by maintaining high pre-entry prices.

local suburban papers until a critical mass was reached sufficient to make advertising in the large metropolitan newspaper or on television economical. For major markets, this implied a critical, minimum efficient scale of operation (a minimum number of stores) at the local level, with economies of scale for multistore operation that could extend into the regional level. The effect of such economies of scale on entry was described by Stemberg (1996, p. 59):

> By building these networks [of stores] in these big markets like New York and Boston, we have kept competitors out for a very, very long period of time. Office Depot only came to metro New York in late 1995. They're not in New York with any meaningful presence, they're not in Boston, and they're not in Philadelphia or anywhere in between. One of the reasons is that we have a very, very good network and it's really tough to steal the customer from a direct competitor when you don't have the economies of advertising leverage.

Stemberg's description of Staples' strategy to deter entry in its home base was similar: "Staples was trying to build a critical mass of stores in the Northeast to shut out competitors and make it cost-effective to advertise in the region's high-cost media" (p. 61).

Some economies of scale in advertising even extend to the national level, perhaps due to a better ability to use network television advertising. Such economies give Staples a stronger incentive to enter markets where Office Depot and OfficeMax are already present, since this reduces advertising costs per dollar of revenues for Staples by increasing the total number of stores and the sales over which such costs can be spread.

All three OSS chains assess prospective new markets in terms of the existing numbers of OSS firms and the demand for additional OSS locations. Markets that have little or no "room" for additional stores are said to be "saturated."[14] Because multiple-store entry is typically necessary to enter a given metropolitan market, markets that are already saturated or nearly saturated are difficult to enter. An Office Depot document listed every market (as defined by Office Depot) in the United States and gave the total number of existing Office Depot, Staples, and OfficeMax stores, as well as estimates of the total number of OSS locations each area could support. The Office Depot estimates implied that, in many major markets in the United States today, there is insufficient demand for new office supply superstores to allow an entrant to achieve competitive-scale economies. In short, the time has passed for a new chain to enter by building a significant number of stores in a new market without creating a glut of superstore ca-

---

[14]The parties defined "store potential" as the maximum number of OSS firms that can be supported in a given market, given existing market conditions, and defined the ratio of the number of OSS firms in a market to store potential as the degree of "market saturation."

pacity or locations. Thus, a firm currently attempting to enter cannot do so under the profitable conditions that the three incumbents faced in the past.

Efficiencies Were Not Sufficient to Offset Price Increases

The FTC argued that the efficiency claims made by the merger parties were exaggerated for several reasons. First, only efficiencies that are merger specific should be credited; that is, efficiencies likely to be achieved absent a proposed merger are irrelevant to the analysis of that merger. In this case, much of the anticipated efficiency gains were the result of the merged firm's increased scale. This in turn raised several questions: (1) Given the rate at which the parties were growing independently, many scale-related efficiencies could be expected in a short time through internal growth. (2) Achieving economies of scale in procurement does not require the expansion in retail operations that a merger would bring. Procurement cost reductions can be achieved by expanding sales through mail order or contract stationer operations, and both Office Depot and Staples had expanded such operations before their merger announcement. Thus, even if the parties had presented evidence to show that past expansions had lowered procurement costs, this would not have established that the claimed efficiencies were merger-specific. (3) Scale economies seldom continue indefinitely. Thus, particularly in the case of procurement costs, Staples and Office Depot may already be large enough to achieve the maximum sustainable price discounts that their suppliers can offer.

The second reason for the FTC's skepticism as to the parties' efficiency claims was the lack of support by reliable evidence. In particular, the efficiency claims made by the parties increased dramatically between the time that the deal was first approved by the Staples' board and the time that the parties submitted an efficiencies analysis to the FTC. Because it was not clear what new information or insights the parties gained in that time period, there was a strong presumption that the substantially lower cost-saving estimates first presented to the Staples board were more reliable.

Third, under the *Guidelines,* efficiency gains are relevant only insofar as they result in a lower price to consumers. The share of any cost reductions that is passed on by a profit-maximizing firm increases with the proportion of those cost reductions that is attributable to variable (rather than fixed) costs; with the competitiveness of the industry; and with the share of firms in the market to which the cost reductions apply. In this case, the proposed merger would have substantially reduced competition. Further, any cost savings would have been limited to the merged firm. Therefore, historical estimates of the share of cost savings that the parties had passed on to consumers would significantly overstate the share of any merger-specific cost savings that would be passed on.

Specifically, the FTC's analysis showed that the merger would bring true efficiencies that were the equivalent of only 1.4 percent of sales and that only a seventh of these cost savings would be passed through to consumers. Thus, the net price effect of the merger would be substantial: the 7.3-percent price increase predicted by the FTC's econometric model of pricing, less an efficiency pass-through of 0.2 percent (= $1.4\% \times 0.15$), for a net increase of 7.1 percent.

THE DEFENDANTS' ARGUMENTS

Staples and Office Depot argued that the merger would not have anticompetitive consequences. Their defense focused on two main arguments: (1) the FTC's product market definition was erroneous; and (2) regardless of the market definition, the efficiencies from the merger, ease of entry into OSS retailing, and the defendants' track record of lowering prices after their past acquisitions of other OSS firms all indicated that the merger would not raise prices.[15] Either of these two arguments, if accepted, would have disproved the FTC's argument that the proposed merger would lead to a substantial lessening of competition in the relevant antitrust market.

Market Definition

The defense vigorously challenged the FTC's claim that OSS firms constituted a relevant market for antitrust purposes. Staples and Office Depot argued that the FTC's market definition was based exclusively on the *identity* of the seller and not on the *characteristics* of the product or service supplied by sellers. The respondents claimed that OSS firms were part of a broad market for retailing office supplies in which they held a low share. An OSS firm was constrained in its pricing not just by other OSS firms, but by all office product retailers.

The defendants argued that a retail product market is defined by the nature of the product being retailed; since office supplies sold by an OSS are not different from those sold by other retailers, both types of retailers are in the same market. The fact that OSS chains use different retail formats implies that they have found a particularly good way of competing with other retailers and does not imply that other retailers are in a different market. Thus, the defendants rejected the notion that office superstores supply a distinct bundle of goods and retail services that would enable a monopoly OSS to raise OSS prices.

The defendants also rejected the FTC's argument that Staples' and Office Depot's own documents define OSS firms as "the competition" and

---

[15]The defense cited two past acquisitions as examples of the two companies' record of lowering their prices after a merger. According to the defense, the price of office supplies had fallen in each of the respective areas after Office Depot's acquisition of Office Club in Dallas, Texas, and Staples' acquisition of HQ Office Supplies Warehouse in Los Angeles, California (both in 1991).

"the market." Citing a previous court decision, they argued that the term "market" does not necessarily mean the same thing to a company and to an antitrust agency. Further, they contested the FTC's use of selected passages in Staples and Office Depot documents as evidence in this regard: they claimed that other passages in the same documents used the term "market" also to include non-OSS firms. The defendants submitted exhibits showing that each regularly checked the prices of non-OSS firms, such as Wal-Mart, Viking, Best Buy, and Comp USA, along with the prices of other OSS firms. According to the defense, this illustrated the intense competition between OSS and non-OSS firms. As another illustration, the defense submitted a study that showed that the sales of a Staples store would fall by 1.4 percent with the opening of a new computer superstore, 2.4 percent with a new Wal-Mart, 3.7 percent with a new warehouse club, and 7.2 percent with a new Best Buy.

Efficiencies and the Net Price Effect

The defense claimed that OSS firms were founded on the principle of providing low prices through large sales volume. Thus, the defendants argued, the merger would increase the total volume of their (combined) purchases and lower the prices that they paid to manufacturers of office supplies. They also claimed that the merger would lower administrative, marketing, advertising, and distribution costs. Under the defense's assumption that the merged entity would pass on to consumers two-thirds of the cost reductions, Staples and Office Depot would be able to cut prices significantly after the merger.

The defendants disputed the FTC's argument that much of their claimed efficiencies could be achieved absent the merger. Moreover, they argued, even if some of those efficiencies could eventually be achieved through internal expansion, a merger would allow those efficiencies to be achieved much faster.

The defendants submitted an econometric study that suggested that Office Depot had a relatively small effect on Staples' pricing and that a merger between the two would (absent efficiencies) increase prices for consumable office supplies by only 2.4 percent (compared with the FTC's estimate of 7.3 percent) at Staples stores in markets with both Staples and Office Depot present, by 1.3 percent when averaged over office supplies at all Staples stores, or by 0.8 percent when averaged over all products and all Staples stores. The defendants also argued that, based on their estimate of cost savings and of the proportion that would be passed through to consumers (0.67 versus the FTC's estimate of 0.15), the efficiency gains alone would cause prices to be lower by 3 percent over all Staples' products and stores. Thus, the net effect of the merger would be to *reduce* the prices faced by the average Staples customer by 2.2 percent ($0.8 - 3.0\% = -2.2\%$).

No Barriers to Entry and Ease of Expansion

The defendants argued that entry into the office supplies business was easy. Stores could be constructed within months, and sunk costs were low because the product did not decay and there were no fashion crazes.[16] In addition, OfficeMax had increased its planned new store openings in 1997, demonstrating ease of expansion by existing competitors. Finally, entry or expansion did not necessarily entail costly new store openings: existing multiproduct retailers could enter, or expand into, the office supplies business by increasing the share of the shelf space they allocated to office supply items.[17]

Public and Private Equities

The defense argued that blocking the merger would impose losses on both consumers and shareholders. The main consumer benefits from the merger that would be lost were the claimed efficiencies and lower prices discussed above; in addition, the combined company would be able to expand faster than either could individually, creating value for customers and for the U.S. economy. Any cost savings not passed on to consumers would benefit the shareholders of Staples and Office Depot. Finally, the defense argued that there was no need for a temporary restraining order or a preliminary injunction to stop the merger because the merger was reversible. If postmerger evidence demonstrated an anticompetitive effect, the merged entity could always be split back into two separate companies.

JUDGE HOGAN'S DECISION

The court agreed with the FTC and granted a preliminary injunction. Judge Thomas F. Hogan first noted that the law required the FTC to show only a reasonable probability of harm to competition to obtain a preliminary injunction. In his decision, Judge Hogan defined the relevant product market as the OSS submarket and found that Staples and Office Depot would have a "dominant market share" (between 45 percent and 100 percent) in many geographic markets after the merger. He also concluded that FTC's pricing evidence demonstrated a reasonable likelihood of anticompetitive effects.

The judge noted that neither the public nor the private equities claimed by the defendants were sufficient to offset the likely anticompetitive effects.[18]

---

[16]Two examples offered to demonstrate the ease of entry were U.S. Office Products Co. and Corporate Express. Office Products had been founded recently (in 1994); both firms had expanded rapidly by acquiring small local dealers; their sales had also increased fast within the past few years.

[17]The defense's example was that Wal-Mart had already started expanding the shelf space it allocates to office products.

[18]The court stated that unscrambling the eggs, that is, undoing the merger if definitive anticompet-

The Product Market

The court found that the sale of consumable office supplies by office super-stores was a submarket within a larger market of all office supply retail-ers.[19] Baker (1997) discusses the judge's opinion on the product market in light of the April 8, 1997, revised *Merger Guidelines* and concludes that the court's "hidden opinion" treats the submarket argument as "a legal hook for reaching unilateral competitive effects from a merger among the sellers of close substitutes."

Judge Hogan recognized that it was difficult to overcome the "initial gut reaction" to the definition of the product market as the sale of consum-able office supplies through office superstores. Since the products sold by OSS firms are the same as the products sold by non-OSS retailers, "it is log-ical" to conclude that all these retailers compete. However, he noted, a firm could be a competitor in the "overall marketplace" without also being in-cluded in the relevant antitrust market.[20] He found plausible the FTC's ar-gument that a small but significant increase in one superstore's prices would not cause a large number of its customers to switch to non-OSS re-tailers; instead, those customers would turn primarily to another OSS.[21]

The judge observed that office superstores were very different from other office supply retailers in terms of appearance, size, format, the num-ber and variety of items offered, and the type of customers targeted. While it was "difficult fully to articulate and explain all of the ways in which su-perstores are unique," he found that: "No one entering a Wal-Mart would mistake it for an office superstore. No one entering Staples or Office Depot

---

itive effects were to be found in the future, was not a realistic option in this case. In addition to the difficulties involved in subsequently separating the merger partners, consumers would face the risk of being harmed if the merger was to be let through, and that damage could never be repaired by undoing the merger. *Federal Trade Commission* v. *Staples, Inc.,* No. 97-701 (1997).

[19]In reference to submarkets within a market, the court decision cited the Supreme Court in *Brown Shoe:* Well-defined submarkets may exist that, in themselves, constitute product markets for an-titrust purposes, and it is necessary to examine the effects of a merger in each such economically significant submarket to determine if there is a reasonable probability that the merger will substan-tially lessen competition. *Brown Shoe* defined several practical indicia to determine the presence of a submarket within a broader market, which Judge Hogan used to determine whether OSS chains constitute a submarket. See *Brown Shoe* v. *United States,* 370 U.S. 294 (1962).

[20]The court cited the notion of functional interchangeability in *Du Pont* (referring to interchange-ability between cellophane and other wrapping materials) and *Archer-Daniels-Midland* (referring to interchangeability between sugar and corn syrup) cases. Noting that the *Staples* case is an ex-ample of perfect functional interchangeability in the sense that a legal pad sold by Staples or Office Depot is functionally interchangeable with a legal pad sold by Wal-Mart, it recognized that the analysis should go further and look at the cross-elasticity of demand between products, again cit-ing the *Du Pont* case. See *U.S.* v. *E. I. Du Pont de Nemours and Co.,* 351 U.S., 377 (1956); and *U.S.* v. *Archer-Daniels-Midland Co.,* 866 F.2d 242 (1988).

[21]The court did note some limitations of the data underlying the FTC's individual analyses, and it further noted that the FTC could be criticized for looking at only brief snapshots in time or for con-sidering only a limited number of items, but it concluded that taken together, there was sufficient evidence for a low cross-elasticity of demand between the consumable office supplies sold by the superstores and those sold by other retailers.

would mistakenly think he or she was in Best Buy or CompUSA. You certainly know an office superstore when you see one."[22] He argued that this is one practical indication for the OSS firms' constituting a submarket within a larger market.

Another practical indication for determining the presence of a submarket was "the industry or public recognition of the submarket as a separate economic entity." The judge found that the FTC had offered "abundant evidence" from the merging companies' internal documents that they evaluated their competition as other OSS firms and interacted with other OSS firms in making long-term plans. While Staples and Office Depot did not completely ignore non-OSS retailers, there was sufficient evidence that showed that Staples and Office Depot consider other OSS firms as their main competition.

Likely Effect on Competition

The judge was convinced that the proposed merger would likely have anticompetitive effects. He reached this conclusion from two pieces of evidence. First, having accepted the FTC's product market definition, he found the concentration statistics to be a source of serious concern.[23] After the merger, a combined Staples-Office Depot entity would have a dominant market share in many local geographic markets.[24]

Second, the pricing evidence showed that an OSS was likely to raise its prices when it faced less competition from other OSS firms. Furthermore, without the merger, Staples and Office Depot would probably enter into each other's markets and reduce prices. The merger would mean that these future benefits from increased competition would never be realized.

Entry

In a market defined as office supplies sold through superstores, the court focused on the entry of new OSS firms, not just any office products retailer. To achieve economies of scale and be profitable, a new OSS would have to open many stores and incur high sunk costs. Further, an entrant could not easily achieve economies of scale at the local level because many of the OSS markets were already saturated by existing OSS firms. The judge

---

[22]*Federal Trade Commission* v. *Staples, Inc.*, No. 97-701 (1997).

[23]The pre-merger Herfindahl-Hirschman Index for the least concentrated market, Grand Rapids-Muskegon-Holland, Michigan, was close to 3600, whereas for the most concentrated market, Washington, D.C., the pre-merger HHI was about 7000.

[24]The combined market share would be 100% in fifteen metropolitan areas. In addition, in twenty-seven other metropolitan areas where the number of OSS firms would drop from three to two, the combined Staples-Office Depot market share would be above 45%. The HHI would rise on average by 2715 points because of the merger.

found it extremely unlikely that a new OSS would enter the market and counterbalance the anticompetitive effects of the merger.[25]

Efficiencies

The judge noted that under the law it is unclear whether efficiencies constitute a viable defense. He stated that even if efficiencies can provide a legal defense in principle, in this case the defendants had not shown efficiencies sufficient to refute the FTC's presumption of anticompetitive effects from the merger. He found that the defense's estimates of the efficiencies were unreliable, unverified, and unrealistic. Among other problems, the defendants did not distinguish between merger-specific and other kinds of efficiencies, and given Staples' historical pass-through rates their assumption that two-thirds of the cost savings would be passed through to the customers was unrealistic.[26]

CONCLUSION AND AFTERMATH

The FTC's victory in *Staples* came as a surprise to many observers. The casual empirical facts—there were many retailers of office supplies, and Staples and Office Depot together accounted for only a small percentage of the aggregate sales of such products—seemed determinative.

But the FTC's careful marshalling of the data—especially, its use of the price data to show that the office superstores were a separate market—proved important in convincing the Commission itself and then Judge Hogan that the merger would be anticompetitive. It seems likely that these kinds of data, which have become readily available from the scanner technology that has become common in retailing, will become increasingly important in the legal judgments related to mergers involving retailers or manufacturers of goods that are sold primarily at retail.

Since *Staples,* both the agencies and merger applicants have routinely used direct evidence on the closeness of merging competitors and the expected size of a merger's price effects, in defining the relevant product market and/or predicting the effect of the merger on consumers' welfare.[27]

---

[25]As for the expansion of non-OSS suppliers into the OSS markets, the judge noted that it was unlikely that they would undo the merger's anticompetitive effects. Specifically, the expansions by U.S. Office Products and Wal-Mart would be unlikely to constrain a potential increase in the prices of the merged entity. In relation to the defense's argument that existing retailers could simply expand into the office products business by reallocating shelf space, the judge reasoned that while these retailers certainly had the power to do so, there was no evidence that they in fact would, following a 5% (small but significant) increase in the prices of the merged entity.

[26]Historically, Staples passed through 15–17% of its cost savings to customers, as estimated by the FTC's econometric analysis. For a discussion of the FTC's estimation of the extent to which the merged firm would pass on cost savings from the acquisition to buyers, see Baker (1999).

[27]One such case, *FTC v. H.J. Heinz Co. and Milnot Holding Co.* ("baby food case"), is the subject of Case 6 by Jonathan B. Baker in this part. The FTC has also used scanner data in a similar way to

In *Staples,* much of the efficiencies argument of the defendants was based on scale economies. Within three years following the merger's abandonment, Staples and Office Depot each achieved the size (about 1000 stores) that they would have achieved as a single firm had the merger been approved (Balto 1999). As the parties' premerger strategy documents had forecast, many of the new stores were in the overlap markets.[28] Thus, most of the efficiencies that the parties could have expected from the merger were achieved without much delay and without the detrimental price effects from a merger.

REFERENCES

Ashenfelter, Orley, David Ashmore, Jonathan B. Baker, Suzanne Gleason, and Daniel S. Hosken. "Econometric Methods in *Staples.*" Mimeo (2002).

Baker, Jonathan B. "Econometric Analysis in *FTC* v. *Staples.*" *Journal of Public Policy & Marketing* 18 (Spring 1999):11–21.

Balto, David A. "Supermarket Merger Enforcement." (1999) http://www.ers.usda.gov/briefing/foodmarketstructures/conferencepapers/balto.pdf.

Federal Trade Commission v. *Staples, Inc.,* 970 F. Supp. 1066 (1997).

Muris, Timothy J. "Antitrust Enforcement at the Federal Trade Commission: In a Word—Continuity." Prepared remarks before American Bar Association's Antitrust Section Annual Meeting, Chicago, Illinois, August 7, 2001; http://www.ftc.gov/speeches/muris/murisaba.htm.

Prudential Securities. *Office Supply Superstores: Industry Update,* October 3, 1995.

Prudential Securities. *Office Supply Superstores: Industry Update,* March 28, 1996.

Stemberg, Thomas G., ed. *Staples for Success: From Business Plan to Billion-Dollar Business in Just a Decade.* Santa Monica, Calif.: Knowledge Exchange, 1996.

Warren-Boulton, Frederick R., and Serdar Dalkir. "Staples and Office Depot: An Event-Probability Case Study." *Review of Industrial Organization* 19 (December 2001): 467–479.

Werden, Gregory J. "A Perspective on the Use of Econometrics in Merger Investigations and Litigation." *Antitrust* 6 (Spring 2002): 55–58.

---

evaluate supermarket mergers (see "A Blue Light Special for Mergers?" *The Deal,* October 5, 1999). The availability of scanner data has created a virtual "cottage industry" for econometricians predicting merger effects, either by estimating reduced-form equations as in *Staples,* or by a two-step process where demand elasticities are first estimated and then become inputs into a merger simulation model (see Werden 2002 and more generally http://www.antitrust.org/simulation/simulation.html); this is an approach that has become so successful that it has created its own backlash (see Muris 2001).

[28]Staples Annual Report 2000.

CASE 3

Potential Competition and Local Telephone Service: The Bell Atlantic-NYNEX Merger (1997)

Steven R. Brenner

INTRODUCTION

On April 21, 1996, Bell Atlantic Corporation and NYNEX Corporation announced that they had reached an agreement to merge. Nearly sixteen months later, after the Department of Justice (DOJ), the Federal Communications Commission (FCC), and many state public utility commissions had cleared the transaction, the two companies completed their merger, one of the largest in U.S. history. Bell Atlantic was the local telephone company for most customers in six eastern states from Virginia through New Jersey, and NYNEX provided local telephone service for most customers in seven states from New York to Maine. Together, the two companies had assets of $51.3 billion and operating revenues of $27.8 billion. Much public attention focused on the size of the merging companies, but the combination also raised serious competitive issues.

The authorities reviewing the merger were most concerned about the merger's effects on potential competition, although other competitive issues were raised. The two firms were not head-to-head competitors in any relevant antitrust market when they announced their merger. Each supplied essentially the same range of telecommunications services, but to different consumers in adjacent East Coast regions. The Telecommunications Act of

Steven Brenner consulted with and filed testimony for MCI Telecommunications Corporation with the New York Public Service Commission analyzing this merger. The author would like to thank David Rivers and Guillermo Petrei for research assistance and to acknowledge the contributions of Professor Franklin M. Fisher of M.I.T. to the analysis of this merger for MCI, but the author alone is responsible for the views expressed here.

1996, signed into law only months before the merger was announced, was intended to open the way for competition in markets for local telephone service. Local telephone providers—such as Bell Atlantic and NYNEX—were expected to face entry and competition from new suppliers. A key issue was whether, if the two did not merge, one or both of the companies would enter the other's market and compete with its neighbor. If so, would elimination of that entry harm competition?

Analysis of competitive issues in a merger always involves predicting behavior in future, postmerger market conditions. In this case, however, the analysis had to deal with the impact of important market changes other than the merger. Analysis of potential competition had to consider the effects not only of possible entry by one of the merging firms, but also of entry by other firms as a result of the 1996 Telecommunications Act. If enough other firms were going to be successful entrants, eliminating entry by one of the merging firms would have little effect on competition. The difficulty of projecting future market conditions made it harder than usual to find clear evidence to establish the presence or absence of anticompetitive effects.

Changes in both regulation and technology meant that some changes in industry structure were likely to promote efficiency. At the same time, the prospect of enhanced efficiency justified an argument for preserving the opportunity for competition to develop where before there was regulated monopoly. Were the two firms merging in order to supply services more efficiently in the new market environment, or because they hoped to shore up their old, dominant position when regulatory barriers that had protected them were lowered? It was difficult to be comfortable with the argument that the merger should be approved if one could not see into the future clearly enough to be certain that competition would be harmed. At stake might be whether and how fast competition would develop for local telecommunications services for which incumbent suppliers, such as Bell Atlantic and NYNEX, had been nearly the only providers.

BACKGROUND

Regulatory Changes

From the early decades of the twentieth century into the 1960s, telecommunications service was essentially a regulated monopoly.[1] Only one local telephone company was authorized to provide service in each area; regulation erected absolute barriers to entry. For most areas and customers, the local telephone company was part of the AT&T Bell System.[2] AT&T's

---

[1]For more complete summaries of the movement from regulated monopoly toward competition, see Brock (1981) and Temin (1987).

[2]Companies other than AT&T supplied telephone service to some areas, but each company served only its own territory and customers. GTE was the largest of the non-Bell companies.

Long Lines Division also provided the great bulk of long-distance services throughout the country.

Cracks began to appear in this edifice of regulated monopoly in the 1950s. MCI was one of the companies that drove a competitive wedge into this structure when, in the late 1960s and early 1970s, it sought authorization for, first, a competing private line service to businesses, and then a competing switched long-distance service. In both cases, the company wanted to interconnect and use facilities of the local telephone company to give its customers access to MCI's facilities, and AT&T resisted. This resistance, among other actions, led to a government antitrust case filed against AT&T in 1974.[3] The case went to trial in January 1981, and one year later, after its motion for summary judgment was denied, AT&T settled the case.[4]

As part of the settlement, AT&T divested itself of its local operating companies, while retaining its long-distance and equipment manufacturing operations. The divested local operations were turned over to seven newly created holding companies, each providing local service in a different region of the country. Bell Atlantic and NYNEX were two of the new regional Bell operating companies (RBOCs). The new RBOCs would provide interconnection and access services to long-distance companies—such as MCI, Sprint, and a newly separate AT&T—but would not compete with those companies. The MFJ settlement prohibited RBOCs from providing any services that crossed the boundaries of newly created regions called LATAs.[5]

The MFJ framework was designed to encourage competition for services that crossed LATA boundaries, but made little direct provision for competition within LATAs. As time passed, however, firms also began to be interested in competing with RBOC and non-RBOC local exchange companies. Firms that became known as competitive access providers (CAPs) installed fiber optic cable in large metropolitan areas to provide businesses with competing sources of supply for dedicated circuit (point-to-point) service within local or regional areas. Later they sought to offer other local services. Throughout the latter part of the 1980s and into the 1990s, state commissions and the FCC grappled with questions about which local services competing firms should be allowed to supply and what kinds of interconnection the established carrier should provide.

---

[3]The government case also considered AT&T's actions involving other forms of interconnection. In particular, it covered AT&T's attempts to limit the connection to its phone system of so-called "customer premises equipment" supplied by competitors—the phone instrument itself and switching equipment used by businesses. The discussion here summarizes selected issues of the case and its settlement; for a more complete review see Noll and Owen (1994).

[4]This settlement was known as the *Modification of Final Judgment,* or MFJ, so named because formally it modified a 1956 consent decree that settled an earlier antitrust case that the government had brought against AT&T.

[5]LATA is an acronym for "local access and transport area." Individual LATAs varied in size from a few counties in more populous areas to entire states with lower population densities.

These developments put pressure on the MFJ framework. Proponents of local telephone competition argued for eliminating all remaining regulatory barriers that hindered competing firms from entering and providing local services. The RBOCs argued for eliminating the MFJ restriction that prevented them from providing inter-LATA service, a restriction they claimed was obsolete at a time when they faced increased competition for local service. These and other pressures for change culminated in the Telecommunications Act of 1996.

The 1996 Act prohibited state or local laws or regulations that directly or indirectly prevented competing firms from providing any local telecommunications service. Local companies were required to interconnect with each other at cost-based rates so that customers of different companies could call each other. Incumbent local telephone companies also were required to sell or rent so-called "unbundled network elements" (UNEs) at cost-based rates. For example, the incumbent telephone company had to allow new local carriers to lease the use of the "local loop," or line, that connects each customer to the local network and the use of the incumbent's local switches. Local telephone companies also had to allow other firms to purchase their local service at a wholesale rate and then re-brand and resell that service.

These provisions were intended to reduce the sunk costs that a competing firm had to commit to begin service; purchased network elements offered an alternative to capital expenditures on network facilities, and resold services allowed a new carrier to market service to customers without building facilities to serve them. Resale also allowed firms to market a bundle of services—for example, long-distance and local service—without committing investments in both local and long-distance network facilities.

The 1996 Act also set conditions under which the RBOCs could be released from the MFJ restriction on offering inter-LATA service. Once they satisfied a checklist of conditions related to opening local markets to competition, RBOCs could apply to the FCC for authority to offer inter-LATA service.

The 1996 Act therefore presaged significant changes in the market conditions faced by Bell Atlantic and NYNEX, with or without their merger: competition from other companies for the local services they provided, and the prospect that each could begin providing inter-LATA long-distance services in competition with AT&T, MCI, Sprint, and other firms to which they also would be selling access services.

The Merging Companies

Bell Atlantic and NYNEX each offered a wide range of local and regional telephone services to a wide range of customers. Understanding the range of both services and customers is important for defining antitrust markets and analyzing competitive conditions in those markets.

The basic and largest local service is plain old telephone service (POTS). POTS allows a customer to call and receive calls from any other telephone customer in a local area. Bell Atlantic provided POTS to about 18 million people via 17.7 million access lines in six states—Maryland, Pennsylvania, Virginia, New Jersey, West Virginia, and Delaware—and the District of Columbia. NYNEX provided local service to about 20 million people via 20.6 million access lines in New York, parts of Connecticut, and the five New England states (FCC 1997, pp. 17–18).

Providing switched local service is very capital-intensive. First, the telephone company must run a local wire loop to connect each customer to the first or end office switch of the telephone network. Multiple electronic switches route calls to the local loop of the person being called over circuits or trunks that carry traffic between the switches. Sophisticated signaling networks and computers help direct calls, monitor information for billing, and signal network conditions (such as a "busy signal"). Local network facilities also deliver calls to long-distance companies and receive calls from them for delivery to customers. This "access" service allows the long-distance companies to complete their calls without also providing the local portion of the call.

Local telephone companies such as Bell Atlantic and NYNEX also provide other services used by business customers. They supply dedicated circuits that carry traffic between two specific locations in a local area and are used by businesses with high volumes of traffic on that route. They also supply switched data services that route and carry "packets" of data among multiple locations using technology similar to that of the Internet. As long as the locations for these services were within a single LATA, Bell Atlantic and NYNEX could provide the service.

Review by Authorities

The DOJ's Antitrust Division carried out the required Hart-Scott-Rodino review of this proposed merger. The DOJ issued a second request for extensive additional documents and information, with which the companies complied by July 1996. In April 1997, the DOJ announced it had completed its review and concluded that the proposed transaction did not violate antitrust laws. The Department did not seek modification of the proposed transactions or commitments from the merging parties in a consent decree. As is usual in such cases, the Department provided no further information on the analysis by which it reached its conclusions or on the evidence on which it relied. The transaction also was reviewed and cleared by thirteen state commissions (of which only three presented their own discussion of the effects of the merger on competition).

The FCC also reviewed the transaction. The 1934 Communications Act gave the Commission authority to determine if the transfer of certificates, licenses, and authorizations involved in the merger was in the public interest.[6] Under this broad public interest standard, the burden of proof is on the applicants, not the Commission. Nonetheless, the Commission used the analytical framework of the 1992 DOJ and FTC *Horizontal Merger Guidelines* for its review of competitive effects (FCC 1997, p. 37). The Commission was concerned with the effects of the merger on competition, even though many of the services involved were regulated. Market competition remained important both because moving to a deregulated market required the development of competition and because, in any event, regulation could not completely or costlessly constrain market power (FCC 1997, p. 45). Interested parties (e.g., the long-distance carriers) filed briefs with the FCC, as they had with the DOJ and states. Many opposed the merger and raised arguments discussed later in this chapter.

The Commission concluded that the applicants had failed to carry their burden of demonstrating that the transaction was in the public interest without any modifications. The FCC approved the merger, but only after Bell Atlantic and NYNEX made a series of commitments that the Commission believed would promote competitive entry and provide pro-competitive benefits sufficient to offset the otherwise negative effects of the merger. The Commission approved the merger on August 14, 1997. Later that day, Bell Atlantic and NYNEX consummated their merger.

POTENTIAL COMPETITION ISSUES

The merging firms were not current competitors in any market, but they might become competitors in the future if they did not merge. This was the competition issue that most concerned the authorities—at least as far as one can tell from the public record.[7]

---

[6]The FCC also has concurrent jurisdiction with the DOJ and FTC under sections 7 and 11 of the Clayton Act to determine if acquisitions of communications common carriers would have the effect "substantially to lessen competition, or to tend to create a monopoly," but in this case the FCC chose not to act under its Clayton Act authority (FCC 1997, pp. 29–33).

[7]Two other competitive concerns were raised. The first was that the merger would increase the incentives of the merged firm to engage in nonprice discrimination against long-distance carriers that would become its rivals once the merged firm was authorized to provide competing inter-LATA long-distance service. By providing poorer access services to long-distance companies, Bell Atlantic could harm the quality of service the long-distance carriers offered to customers both inside and outside Bell Atlantic territory. The harm to service offered to NYNEX customers would not benefit the long-distance service of a separate Bell Atlantic, but would benefit the merged firm (and similarly the effect of NYNEX discrimination on competing long-distance service supplied to Bell Atlantic customers would benefit only the merged firm). While regulation attempts to control such nonprice discrimination, merger could increase the willingness of the merged firm to risk detection and penalties because it would realize greater gains from discrimination (Brenner 1996, pp. 46–61). The second concern was that the merger would reduce the number of independent companies that regulators could use to "benchmark" the conduct of other carriers, and thereby potentially reduce the ability of regulators to design and enforce effective regulation (FCC 1997, pp. 146–156). For a more detailed discussion of each concern, see Brenner (1999).

The Potential Competition Doctrine

The courts have recognized two theories under which elimination by merger of a potential competitor may violate Section 7 of the Clayton Act (ABA Antitrust Section 1997, pp. 342–350).[8] First, competition could be reduced if, but for the merger, one of the merging firms would actually have entered a market supplied by the other, and that entry would have decreased concentration and increased competition. This is (somewhat confusingly) known as the "actual potential entrant" theory. Second, competition could be reduced if one of the merging firms were perceived as a particularly likely or effective potential entrant into a concentrated market supplied by the other, and this perceived possibility of entry disciplined suppliers in that market even without the entry occurring. This is known as the "perceived potential entrant" theory.

The perceived potential entrant theory played little role in the analysis of the Bell Atlantic-NYNEX merger. Entering and capturing a significant market share as a producer of most telecommunications services takes time and involves substantial sunk costs. Bell Atlantic or NYNEX could wait until entry occurred to respond with lower prices; the profitability of an entrant would depend then more on prices after entry than on pre-entry pricing. The perceived possibility that a firm might enter, without any actual entry, was unlikely to discipline pricing in markets supplied by Bell Atlantic or NYNEX.

The potential competition issue in this case centered on the question of whether the merger would harm competition by removing Bell Atlantic or NYNEX as a future, actual entrant into one or more markets served by the other. More specifically, attention focused on whether Bell Atlantic would have competed with NYNEX by supplying local telephone service in the New York metropolitan area, which was adjacent to Bell Atlantic territory in New Jersey, or in other parts of NYNEX territory.

Arguments of Bell Atlantic and NYNEX

The position of Bell Atlantic and NYNEX was straightforward. Bell Atlantic would not enter and compete with NYNEX if they did not merge; in legal terms, Bell Atlantic was not an actual potential competitor of NYNEX. Even if Bell Atlantic had entered, however, the merger would have had little effect on the structure of the market or on prices and service quality because many other firms were equally or better able to enter and compete effectively (NYT et al. 1996, esp. pp. 62–63). The merging parties presented the following evidence and arguments to support these positions.

First, Bell Atlantic had no plans to compete with NYNEX. Bell Atlantic's vice chairman filed an affidavit with the FCC in which he stated,

---

[8]Also see Kwoka (2001) for a discussion of the legal evolution of the potential competition doctrine.

"Bell Atlantic has not at any time had plans to enter NYNEX's local service markets" (FCC 1997, p. 239). NYNEX claimed that it had not perceived Bell Atlantic as a potential competitor in any New York local exchange or access market (NYT et al. 1996, p. 64). Therefore, the merging parties argued, Bell Atlantic could not be considered an actual potential competitor (or a perceived potential competitor).

Second, Bell Atlantic had no greater advantages as an entrant than did other companies, and thus was not particularly likely to enter markets served by NYNEX. Bell Atlantic claimed it had "no network facilities in New York from which to supply services, no existing customer base and no marketing presence or brand recognition of any significance" (NYT et al. 1996, p. 64). The merging parties claimed that many other firms had advantages greater than those of Bell Atlantic and were therefore more likely to enter than was Bell Atlantic. For example, interexchange carriers such as AT&T and MCI, competitive access providers such as MFS and Teleport, cable television companies such as Time Warner, and wireless providers such as Sprint Telecommunications Venture were more likely to enter because they could make use of their current network equipment, marketing and brand name recognition, or existing customer base (NYT et al. 1996, pp. 65–66).

Third, NYNEX already faced competition from many other suppliers. More than fifty competitive local exchange carriers were certified by the New York Public Service Commission to provide local service, with more applications for certification pending.[9] Competing firms already had deployed twenty-seven switches in New York City and been assigned eighty-two NXX codes, seventy-one of which also were in New York City; eighty-two NXX codes would provide telephone numbers for up to 820,000 customers.[10] The merging companies said NYNEX had lost customers to these competitors already, claiming that 50 percent of high-capacity dedicated lines in Manhattan for special access to interexchange carrier locations and between the local points of presence (or POPs) of interexchange carriers were supplied by CAPs. Nationwide, CAPS were said to have captured between 10 and 15 percent of the "national carrier access market."

Bell Atlantic and NYNEX went on to describe the activities of firms they saw as more likely entrants. Fiber deployment by MFS, a CAP, reached 638 buildings in New York City. Teleport, another CAP, had 3 switches and 600 New York area customers. Interexchange carriers were acting on plans to offer local dial tone service. AT&T had switches and other facilities under construction in Manhattan, and its recent purchase of McCaw Cellular gave it access to local networks. The merging firms quoted

---

[9]The evidence described here and in the next paragraph was presented in NYT et al. (1996, pp. 66–80).

[10]NXX refers to the first three digits of a seven-digit local telephone number. For traditional local telephone companies, the NXX identifies the exchange, or local switch, to which a customer's line is connected.

statements by AT&T's chairman that AT&T looked forward to opening up the local market and believed it could win one-third of that market over the next five to ten years. The two firms described MCI's plans to install fiber optic cable in Western Union conduits in various cities that would run through high-traffic corporate corridors accounting for a high proportion of long-distance traffic. An MCI subsidiary, MCImetro, had a switch and other facilities in the NYNEX region, and had installed an advanced SONEX fiber ring to carry traffic in New York City and parts of Westchester County. MCI had recently begun advertising local telephone service to businesses in large cities, including New York City.

Fourth, the 1996 Telecommunications Act promised to accelerate competition by lowering regulatory and technological barriers to entry into local exchange markets. The resale provisions in the Act made it possible for an interexchange carrier or cable television company to enter the local telephone market "with minimal investment and minimal risk" (NYT et al. 1996, p. 84). While full facilities-based entry required investment in sunk network costs, Bell Atlantic-NYNEX argued that the Act encouraged the development of facilities-based competition by requiring that incumbent carriers supply unbundled network elements or UNEs. In sum, they concluded, the 1996 Act "sharply reduced barriers to entry" (NYT et al. 1996, pp. 84–85).

Finally, Bell Atlantic and NYNEX claimed that the merger offered various efficiencies and other public interest benefits (although they denied that there would be any adverse effects of the merger for these efficiencies to offset). The increased size of the new firm would allow it to take advantage of economies of scope and scale. The merging parties told the New York Public Service Commission, "Without these economies of scale and scope (and concomitant efficiencies), New York Telephone would be far less able to compete in that it would not have an ability comparable to that of the large telecommunications companies to provide high quality service at competitive rates and to introduce new and innovative products and services" (NYT et al. 1996, p. 13). Other claimed efficiencies or benefits included: (1) saved research and development costs from the spreading of fixed R&D costs; (2) reduced unit costs from such sources as reduced corporate staff, and reduced costs for procurement, advertising, and information system development; (3) improved service quality from the application of each company's best practices; and (4) increased ability to enter and compete as a long-distance provider (NYT et al. 1996, pp. 43–59; FCC 1997, pp. 160–167).

Points of Contention

The Bell Atlantic-NYNEX arguments identified the major points for evaluating whether their merger would reduce competition by removing a potential entrant.

1. Did corporate plans, the firms' economic position, or both indicate that Bell Atlantic or NYNEX was a likely potential entrant into markets served by its merger partner?

2. Were the number and competitive strength of other firms that could and likely would enter in place of the merging firm sufficiently great that structural conditions in the relevant markets were unlikely to be affected if the merger eliminated one possible entrant?

3. Alternatively, was the merger's elimination of an entrant unlikely to affect competition because markets already were unconcentrated and competitive?

The Bell Atlantic-NYNEX arguments, and the points they identified, closely followed economic logic and tests that the courts have established for determining whether a merger violates the antitrust laws by eliminating a potential competitor.[11] There can be no competitive harm from loss of an actual potential competitor unless one of the merger partners would have competed with the other and a relevant antitrust market would function less competitively in the absence of entry by this competitor.

Not surprisingly, these issues became points of contention between the merging companies and those who argued that the merger did threaten competition. Answering such questions is always difficult because it requires peering into the future. Answers were particularly difficult to provide in this case because there was so little experience with, and thus evidence from, the operation of the market after the Telecommunications Act of 1996 had reduced regulatory barriers. The Act was passed only months before the merger was announced, and regulations implementing the new regime were still being written and disputed at the FCC and state commissions and in the courts. There was little or no market evidence on such critical questions as: How many firms would choose to compete with incumbent local exchange carriers, how successful would they be, and what types of firms were most likely to succeed? The controversy over these questions is discussed below after examining the issue of market definition.

Market Definition

In this case the various parties did not explicitly identify relevant antitrust markets—at least in the public record (FCC 1997, p. 49). Nonetheless, the

---

[11]The courts have established several prerequisites for showing that a merger violates the Clayton Act under the actual potential competition doctrine (ABA Antitrust Section 1997, pp. 342–350):

1. The market that one of the merging firms otherwise would have entered is concentrated.

2. Few other potential entrants are equally able to enter.

3. In the absence of the transaction, one of the merging firms in fact was likely to enter the market served by the other. More specifically, the firm had a means of entry other than the proposed merger, and that alternative means offered a substantial likelihood of promoting competition by deconcentrating the market or otherwise promoting competitive behavior.

parties disagreed about the critical issues, in part because, at least implicitly, they disagreed about market definition. Precise delineation of the antitrust markets in which telecommunications services are supplied is difficult, but important issues in this case turned on whether various groups of telecommunications services are supplied in the same or different product markets. Boundaries could exist between the relevant markets in which services are supplied because (a) the services are not good substitutes, (b) similar services are offered to different customer groups at different prices, or (c) one is a retail and the other a wholesale service.

At its most basic, the demand for a telecommunications service is the demand to transport information between point A and one or many points B, but not all means of conveying that information are close substitutes for all consumers. Those alternatives differ in cost and sometimes in other characteristics. Which alternatives are good substitutes often depends on the nature of a customer's demand (for example, the volume and frequency of use).

One prominent candidate for a boundary that separates product markets is the distinction between switched service and dedicated circuit services. A customer buying dedicated circuit service pays for a circuit or "pipe" of given capacity connecting two specific points, regardless of how much traffic is transported over the circuit while it is being leased. In contrast, a customer buying switched service can communicate with many different locations, and the amount paid often varies with the number and duration of calls. Dedicated circuits may be considerably less costly than switched service for business customers large enough to generate substantial traffic on particular routes over which they can spread the cost of a dedicated circuit, but much more costly than switched service for customers with less traffic or more dispersed traffic. Dedicated and switched services will be close in cost only for customers whose traffic falls in the right, intermediate range. Each type of service is used by enough customers for whom the other is not a good substitute that it is unlikely that most switched local and long-distance services are in the same market as most dedicated circuit services—even though it may be difficult to locate the precise market boundaries.

There also are market divisions based on the geographic dimension of service. (In some cases this may be seen as a matter of geographic market definition based on where the firms are "located" to provide service.) Few consumers would consider calling between, say, New York City and Albany to be a good substitute for calling between New York and Boston or between midtown and downtown Manhattan. Identifying separate, route-specific product markets usually serves little analytical purpose when the same set of carriers serves a group of routes with similar market shares.[12] At the time of the Bell Atlantic-NYNEX merger, however, at least three categories of

---

[12]Furthermore, the very nature of switched service is to provide calling to a collection of routes.

routes were supplied by different sets of carriers: local calling (which then was only rarely supplied by interexchange carriers), inter-LATA calling (supplied by interexchange carriers but not at that time by RBOCs), and intra-LATA calling (usually supplied by both interexchange carriers and local carriers).[13] Discussions of this merger did recognize these product market divisions, at least implicitly. Virtually all analysis of potential entry issues focused on product markets for local calling service in New York.

Product market divisions also may exist between services sold to different customer groups. An important issue in this case was whether local (switched) services supplied to residential customers and small businesses and those supplied to larger businesses were in different markets. They might be if it were possible to price discriminate among the services sold to different customer groups. Traditionally, the telephone companies charged different rates for local service to business and residential customers and, as the FCC has noted, residential and business customers may demand somewhat different bundles of service characteristics. In addition, some competing companies had installed lines and facilities in locations where they could serve business customers but where there were few residential customers.

Finally, market boundaries may be based on exactly what the firms actually produce. The 1996 Telecommunications Act requires local carriers— including Bell Atlantic and NYNEX—to allow their local service to be rebranded and resold by others. As a result, some carriers purchase service at wholesale rates from a carrier and act as a retailer by reselling it, rather than using facilities that they own or control to produce all the local service they sell to customers. In this situation, the analysis should distinguish between the merger's effects on competition in the production and supply of the underlying wholesale service and in the supply of retailing, much as one might want to distinguish the effects of a merger of petroleum companies on competition in petroleum refining and in gas station services. One way to do so is to identify separate markets for the production and the retailing of local telephone services.

General Prospects for Competition

Whether Bell Atlantic would compete with NYNEX absent the merger was significant only if NYNEX did not already face or would not soon face enough other competitors to ensure competitive conditions in all markets that Bell Atlantic was likely to enter. Bell Atlantic and NYNEX argued that NYNEX already faced competition from a large number of other firms, and that this competition would increase because the 1996 Act had substantially lowered entry barriers. Others disputed these conclusions and questioned the extent to which these present and anticipated competitors supplied the same markets that Bell Atlantic might enter.

---

[13]There also are differences in the firms that supply dedicated circuit services within metropolitan or regional areas and over national (or international) routes.

Bell Atlantic and NYNEX pointed to the growth of CAPs and their success in selling high-capacity circuits for special access, for traffic that long-distance carriers moved between their locations or POPs within a metropolitan area, and in a "national carrier access market." These, however, were all dedicated circuit services sold to business customers. The merging parties did not demonstrate that the product market should be defined so broadly as to place these dedicated services in the same product market as local switched services supplied to residences and small businesses.

Bell Atlantic and NYNEX cited as another index of competition the number of firms authorized (or seeking authorization) as competitive local exchange carriers (CLECs) by the New York Public Service Commission. The FCC gave little weight to this evidence. Authorization does not establish that a firm has the ability to become a substantial competitive presence and does not identify the market to be supplied. Many of these firms, according to the FCC, target large business customers with specialized service offerings (FCC 1997, p. 81). Some of these firms are CAPs expanding to supply local switched services to business customers, but the merging parties failed to show how the CAPs' success as suppliers of dedicated circuit service predicted substantial future market shares or significance in markets for local switched services, especially markets for supplying such services to residential and small business customers.

There was also a tension between the Bell Atlantic/NYNEX claims for the competitive significance of smaller firms in the near future and some of their efficiency claims for the merger. The merging companies claimed they would find it more difficult to offer competitive rates and innovative services as separate companies than as a merged firm, because as separate firms they would realize fewer economies of scale and scope. If, however, Bell Atlantic and NYNEX individually would be at a competitive disadvantage because of a limited ability to realize scale and scope economies, why wouldn't considerably smaller CAPs and newly certificated CLECs face scale and scope diseconomies that would make it difficult for them to put competitive pressure on a much larger NYNEX?

Bell Atlantic and NYNEX emphasized that resale and the availability of unbundled network elements (UNEs) under the 1996 Telecommunications Act sharply lowered barriers to entry, making it possible for many firms to enter and compete with NYNEX. They offered little analysis of the competitive significance of entrants that relied heavily on such inputs. On the one hand, an entering producer of local telephone service can reduce its sunk costs in the early stages of its entry by purchasing UNEs or service at wholesale. This could encourage the eventual development of competing sources of supply. On the other hand, an entrant's ability to constrain the exercise of market power by the incumbent remains limited so long as its ability to provide service continues to depend on purchasing wholesale services or UNEs from the incumbent local telephone company. By controlling the price that an entrant pays for these inputs, the incumbent can directly affect the entrant's costs and the price that the entrant can charge in downstream markets for telephone services sold to consumers, where it is in direct competition with the incumbent.[14]

Bell Atlantic and NYNEX did not identify how many announced sellers of local service in New York were planning only to resell NYNEX service. Nor did the merging parties distinguish between produced and resold service in the plans of firms that planned to market both. For example, they cited the optimistic prediction of AT&T's chairman that his company would sell one-third of local telephone service in the future, but did not discuss the likelihood that any such success, if at all possible, would involve a large component of resold service. Similarly, the merging parties presented no analysis of the extent to which other competing suppliers would have to rely on UNEs supplied by NYNEX in order to supply significant proportions of local service.

The DOJ/FTC *Horizontal Merger Guidelines* distinguish between uncommitted and committed entry. Uncommitted entry—which by definition does not require the entrant to commit substantial sunk costs—was unlikely to play a large role in local telephone markets, as the FCC observed (FCC 1997, p. 131). An entrant might reduce the sunk costs of installing its own network facilities by relying on resale and UNEs, but it would still face sunk costs for marketing and for nonrecurring charges for these same UNEs. Reliance on resale and UNEs also would limit competitive significance. Committed entry, the FCC argued, was not sufficiently easy to allay market power concerns: all but a small number of firms still faced substantial obstacles as entering suppliers of local service to residences and small businesses. Entry, and expansion of sales to large numbers of customers, would require very significant sunk costs, for both building network facilities and establishing brand reputations. Entry by firms other than those few with market advantages could not be relied upon as likely, timely, and sufficient (the tests set by the *Guidelines*) to prevent the exercise of market power in markets for local switched service (FCC 1997, pp. 132–134).[15]

The FCC and, apparently, the DOJ concluded that neither the level of competition at the time nor entry conditions ensured that all markets Bell Atlantic might enter would be fully competitive regardless of whether Bell Atlantic entered (FCC 1997; Joskow 2000). This was particularly true of a market for supplying switched local exchange service to residential and smaller business customers; many new CLECs, including CAPs transforming themselves into more general service local carriers, were concentrating

---

[14]The prices charged by the incumbent local telephone company for wholesale service and UNEs are subject to some statutory restrictions in the 1996 Telecommunications Act, and could be regulated. In that case, however, competitive performance in the downstream market would depend in part on regulatory constraints rather than on competitive forces.

[15]Joskow (2000, p. 187) indicates the primary concerns of the DOJ also focused on the merger's effects on entry into a market for supplying service to residential and small business customers in the New York City area.

on service to larger businesses. Thus, it remained important to examine whether, absent the merger, Bell Atlantic would have entered and competed with NYNEX, and how many others would be likely to do so. Two types of evidence were discussed: Did Bell Atlantic have plans to enter, and did it have economic advantages that would make it a likely successful entrant?

Evidence of Potential Competition:
Bell Atlantic's Plans to Enter NYNEX Markets

In focusing on company plans, the merging partners were following court precedent. The courts often have looked to company plans to provide evidence on whether one merger partner would have entered to compete with the other absent a merger.

Bell Atlantic's assertions that it had no company plans to compete with NYNEX relied on a careful definition of what constitutes "company plans": plans approved by governing levels of corporate management and supported by financial commitments. Bell Atlantic acknowledged that its staff had studied the possibility of entering New York markets, but it said that these studies had never matured into company-approved plans and, therefore, Bell Atlantic could not be considered an actual potential entrant (FCC 1997, pp. 240–241).

Bell Atlantic could hardly have denied that it had studied entering New York markets. In 1993 Bell Atlantic and TeleCommunications, Inc. (TCI) announced plans to merge and said that the merged firm would build on TCI's cable TV facilities to provide telephone service. An affidavit of a Bell Atlantic official stated:

> Outside Bell Atlantic's service area, BA/TCI will provide telephone service in direct competition against the incumbent providers of such services. Within approximately two and a half years of closing, I expect to be operating full service networks in competition with incumbent telcos in approximately 30 cities outside Bell Atlantic's current region. If the merger is completed on schedule, we expect BA/TCI to be providing competing local telephone services in geographic areas totaling more than 40 million people outside Bell Atlantic's current service area by the end of the 1990s. (Oliver 1994, pp. 8–9)[16]

At the time, NYNEX staff apparently thought that Bell Atlantic's entry plans probably included New York.[17]

---

[16]The affidavit was filed in connection with a request for waivers from the MFJ that would have been required to complete this merger.

[17]A NYNEX staff review at that time noted that TCI had substantial cable operations in the New York area and stated that Bell Atlantic might well enter the New York City market at some point. See the Affidavit of Jeffrey A. Bowden, submitted to the FCC, July 2, 1996, p. 4.

Bell Atlantic and TCI abandoned their merger, and Bell Atlantic later said it had decided not to pursue any of the entry strategies it had studied. Bell Atlantic's internal strategic plans and studies constituted important evidence, but they are not part of the public record. After they had been provided to the DOJ and the FCC, the FCC described some of their contents:

> Bell Atlantic's internal documents establish that Bell Atlantic was, until merger discussions were well underway, engaged in planning out-of-region entry into local exchange, exchange access, and long distance services in a number of locations in the NYNEX region, most notably LATA 132. The extent of planning reflected in the documents persuades us that Bell Atlantic would likely have entered LATA 132. The documents also show Bell Atlantic would have been most likely to target mass market, not business customers.[18]

The FCC rejected Bell Atlantic's claim that these documents represented only the activities of middle management and were not evidence that Bell Atlantic was an actual potential entrant because senior management had not formally approved and committed resources for entry. Formal approval of entry by the Bell Atlantic board of directors would have been conclusive evidence of intent to enter, said the FCC, but the planning revealed by the Bell Atlantic documents, under the continued supervision of senior management, was evidence supporting a finding that Bell Atlantic likely would have entered NYNEX markets but for the merger (FCC 1997, p. 75).

Evidence of Potential Competition: Sunk Assets

Economic analysis suggests another source of evidence for use in determining which firms are most likely to enter. To enter and supply service in competition with NYNEX, a firm had to have various inputs, some of which would be long-lived assets. The number of long-lived assets valuable for entry that various firms had already acquired provides information regarding the likelihood that each wanted to enter and whether each would succeed. A firm will enter a market only if it expects entry to increase its profits; the additional revenue it expects to earn by entering must equal or exceed the incremental costs it expects to incur. All else equal, a firm that has already sunk the costs of acquiring assets valuable for supplying the entered market will have lower incremental costs than a firm without those inputs, and thus is more likely to expect entry to be profitable.

According to a recent article, the economics staff of the DOJ evaluated the issue of potential competition by determining which firms had acquired

---

[18]FCC 1997, p. 73. LATA 132 covers essentially the same territory as NYNEX's New York Metropolitan Calling Area.

sufficient sunk assets to make their entry as a competitor of NYNEX fairly likely. Doing so allowed the Department's economists to avoid the "psychoanalysis" of trying to infer Bell Atlantic's intentions by examining who said what when and who did and did not approve which plans to enter (Joskow 2000, pp. 189–190).

Bell Atlantic and NYNEX claimed that other firms had greater advantages as entering suppliers of local telephone service than did Bell Atlantic, a claim others disputed. In economic terms, this was a dispute about whether Bell Atlantic had fewer assets that reduced the incremental costs of entry than did other firms. If many other firms possessed assets that left them as well positioned as Bell Atlantic to become viable, successful entrants, the loss of Bell Atlantic as an entrant would be less likely to result in increased market concentration and reduced competition, as the merger would not deter entry by those other firms.

Bell Atlantic and NYNEX emphasized that Bell Atlantic had no network facilities in NYNEX markets. When others countered that Bell Atlantic had switches in nearby New Jersey, Bell Atlantic argued that capacity constraints and the economics of using distant switches meant that these assets would not be valuable for entry in New York City.

Others pointed out that Bell Atlantic had in-place operational support systems developed for local service. These systems provide functions such as monitoring and measuring of usage, billing, service order and provisioning, network management, and customer service. They are complicated systems, costly to develop and crucial for providing high-quality local service (Mosca 1996, pp. 2–4). As an entering local service supplier, Bell Atlantic could have avoided not only the substantial cost of developing operational support software and procedures for local service, but also the inevitable glitches in service that occur as such systems are being debugged. Bell Atlantic also had corporate experience and know-how as a local service provider. It employed seasoned personnel with expertise in engineering and planning, as well as in operating local networks and in marketing local services. Bell Atlantic had been in business long enough to understand customer demands for service and support, to design and market services responsive to those demands, and to implement management structures facilitating the efficient delivery of such services. Bell Atlantic's experience and expertise also could have helped it to negotiate favorable interconnection agreements with NYNEX as the incumbent local carrier, and to present information to regulators describing how NYNEX should fulfill its obligations as an incumbent local carrier (FCC 1997, p. 127).

The merging companies argued that Bell Atlantic possessed no customer base in New York and no marketing presence or brand recognition of any consequence that would aid entry into NYNEX's markets. Such assets would be valuable if they lowered the cost of marketing and customer acquisition for an entrant. The FCC, however, pointed out that Bell Atlantic regularly advertised to its northern New Jersey customers via New York metropolitan area broadcast and print media that also reached customers in New York. The FCC also reported that marketing information in Bell Atlantic and NYNEX documents showed that Bell Atlantic enjoyed greater brand recognition or acceptance as a potential local service provider among customers in New York markets than did the smaller interexchange carriers, cable television providers, or CAPs. The FCC concluded that Bell Atlantic's brand recognition and reputation gave it an advantage in supplying local service to residential and small business customers in New York that, among possible entrants, was matched only by the three largest interexchange carriers: AT&T, MCI, and Sprint (FCC 1997, pp. 78–79, 82, 84, 86, 88).

There also was a dispute over the value for entry of assets possessed by other potential entrants. The merging firms pointed to the network facilities that cable TV firms, CAPs, and interexchange carriers had in NYNEX territory. Much existing cable TV infrastructure, however, was poorly suited to the provision of telephony. Cable firms were known to be investing in new plant facilities better able to support telephony, but the FCC pointed out that questions about the technological and financial constraints faced by these firms cast doubt on how soon they could become effective, competing suppliers of telephone service (FCC 1997, p. 86). CAPs had installed facilities in New York City and some other metropolitan areas, but typically had chosen locations within those areas best suited for providing service to concentrations of business customers. Interexchange carriers had designed and installed their network infrastructure to provide long-distance service, which limited their adaptability to local service; for example, new and different switches had to be used for local service. Similarly, the bulk of the infrastructure that the wireless carriers had installed was designed to provide mobile service; as such, it was less suited to providing service fully equal in quality to wireline local exchange service. Furthermore, rates for mobile service, and apparently the costs of supply, at least at that time, remained well above the rates charged for traditional local telephone service (FCC 1997, p. 90).

The merging firms stressed that interexchange carriers, cable firms, and CAPS—unlike Bell Atlantic—all had customers in NYNEX territory. The largest interexchange carriers did have customers and established brand names, albeit little reputation for local telephone service. Cable firms had customers, but their reputation was of doubtful value (Joskow 2000, p. 190). CAPS had business customers, but were largely unknown to most residential and even many small business customers.

Finally, the arguments of the merging parties did not address the possibility that Bell Atlantic need not enter de novo to deconcentrate markets. Bell Atlantic also might enter by combining with another firm that possessed an asset valuable for supplying local telephone service in New York that Bell Atlantic lacked. Bell Atlantic entry by this route might be deconcentrating if the other firm by itself would not have entered or could not by itself have commanded a market share and competitive significance as great as it could by merging with Bell Atlantic.[19] Arguably, the assets or advantages of Bell Atlantic and some other types of firms were complementary. Bell Atlantic possessed experience, reputation, and operational support systems for local switched telephony, but no network facilities in NYNEX areas; cable television firms and CAPs possessed network facilities but lacked local switched telephony experience, reputation, and operational support systems.[20]

In sum, Bell Atlantic probably was not uniquely well positioned to enter New York local service markets; but, from the perspective of what was known in 1997, a good case could be made that it was one of a limited number of potential entrants with comparable advantages for supplying local telephone service to residential and small business consumers. The FCC identified four firms as the most likely future, new suppliers to markets for local telephone service to residences and small businesses in the New York metropolitan area: Bell Atlantic, AT&T, MCI, and Sprint. According to Joskow (2000, p. 190), the DOJ also concluded that "at least" these four firms had "a subset of the requisite assets: brand name, infrastructure already in the market, access to customers, local exchange experience, etc." necessary for them to be considered likely future participants in the market for residential and small business customers.

How Many Potential Entrants Are Enough?

Were four significant potential entrants sufficient to ensure that elimination of one by merger did not pose a threat to competition? Bell Atlantic and NYNEX pointed out that the 1984 *Horizontal Merger Guidelines* say that the DOJ is unlikely to challenge a merger—all else equal—if three or more other firms possess advantages comparable in importance to those of the merging firm.[21] On a mechanical application of this standard to the FCC findings, the Bell Atlantic-NYNEX merger would not be challenged: the FCC identified exactly three other entrants with comparable advantages.

In a relatively stable but concentrated market, the 1984 *Guidelines* standard of three other firms with comparable advantages that are not current suppliers could promise sufficient entry that the merger would not reduce competition in the future. For example, suppose that entry by no more than one firm is likely to be profitable and viable. With three firms left to

---

[19]Of course, if the other firm would have entered on its own, a merger also might have a contrary effect by reducing the number of entrants.

[20]Bell Atlantic itself had claimed this complementarity of assets when it earlier argued that its contemplated merger with TCI would promote local telephone competition because its operational support and billing systems and technical experience would strengthen the cable company's competitive position as a supplier of local service. See Oliver (1994), pp. 9–10.

[21]NYT et al. (1996, p. 63). While the 1984 *Guidelines* otherwise largely have been superseded by later revisions, the revisions have not addressed the treatment of potential competition issues.

take the place of the merging firm as the single viable entrant, entry and future concentration might be approximately the same with or without the merger. Alternatively, analysis might indicate that entry could be profitable for all four well-placed entrants, but that entry by even two or three firms would deconcentrate the market sufficiently for it to perform competitively. In that case also, a merger that left three remaining potential entrants might not reduce competition in the future.[22]

It was doubtful that local telephone service markets resembled either of these situations, and the merging firms did not explain why the *Guidelines* standard should be sufficient in the particular, and rather unusual, circumstances of these markets. NYNEX had a monopoly or near-monopoly in supplying local switched telephone service to residences and small businesses in its local exchanges. It was far from obvious that entry by four firms would not result in a market that was less concentrated and more competitive than if three firms entered. Nor was it clear that only a subset of the four firms could become viable entrants, without or without the merger.[23]

More generally, to evaluate the effect of eliminating Bell Atlantic as a possible competitor of NYNEX in the future, it would be preferable to have more information than a count of entrants with and without the merger. It would be helpful to be able to predict how much market share Bell Atlantic could capture if it entered and, if merger prevented it from entering, how much of that share would instead be captured by NYNEX and by its competitors. In other words, one would like to project shares and calculate concentration in two scenarios: with and without entry by Bell Atlantic. With projected postmerger shares under each scenario, simulation models could be used to predict postmerger prices with and without the merger's effect on entry.

Apparently, both the FCC and the DOJ used such an analytical framework rather than simply counting entrants. The FCC used confidential information to assign hypothetical future market shares for both entering and incumbent carriers. The FCC did not report these hypothetical shares publicly, but the FCC did say that they showed that the proposed merger would increase the HHI by more than 200 points to a postmerger level above 3400 (FCC 1997, p. 142). The DOJ accounted for potential entrants in much the same way as it would account for uncommitted entrants using the *Horizontal Merger Guidelines:* it identified firms likely to enter absent the merger, and projected shares for those entrants as well as for firms already supplying the market (Joskow 2000). The practical difficulty of applying this framework, of course, was predicting future market shares with any degree of confidence—either with or without the merger.

---

[22]Kwoka (2001) recommends that the general standard be five, rather than three, other equally well-positioned entrants.

[23]The second alternative seems inconsistent with the tenor of Bell Atlantic-NYNEX arguments that the 1996 Telecommunications Act has resulted in low entry barriers.

THE DECISION

The DOJ cleared the merger with only a short statement that it had found the combination did not violate the antitrust laws. Joskow's later article indicates that the DOJ did view Bell Atlantic as one of relatively few potential entrants into a market for providing local exchange service to residential and small business customers in New York but, after analyzing the competitive effects of eliminating this potential entry, chose not to file a case (Joskow 2000). State commissions in NYNEX and Bell Atlantic territories also approved the merger. Some, notably the New York Public Service Commission, did impose conditions, but these addressed issues of service quality and state regulatory control more than they did competitive issues.[24]

The most complete public evaluation of the merger's competitive effects was that of the FCC. The FCC found that the applicants had not carried their burden of showing that the merger satisfied the public interest standard of the Communications Act (FCC 1997, pp. 8–12). The FCC found that the merger eliminated Bell Atlantic as a likely, significant competitor in markets to supply local exchange and exchange access service to residential and smaller business customers in the New York metropolitan area. But for the merger, the FCC concluded, Bell Atlantic had planned to enter. The FCC further concluded that eliminating Bell Atlantic by merger increased the risk that NYNEX would find it profitable to exercise unilateral market power. Bell Atlantic not only would have been a significant competitor in general, but also would have likely been the "second choice," or closest substitute, to NYNEX, for many consumers in the relevant markets (FCC 1997, pp. 101–108). The FCC concluded that elimination of Bell Atlantic as one of only five likely significant market participants—four likely entrants plus NYNEX—also substantially increased the risk of coordinated interaction in these markets (FCC 1997, pp. 121–124). The FCC maintained that the applicants had failed to show that such harm to competition would be mitigated either by easy entry conditions or by efficiencies generated by the merger. Therefore, the merger as proposed was not in the public interest.

Nonetheless, the Commission did approve the merger. The FCC found that the transaction was in the public interest when supplemented by commitments that Bell Atlantic and NYNEX made regarding how they would implement provisions of the 1996 Telecommunications Act (FCC 1997, pp. 13–14). Among these commitments were the following: (1) to develop operations support systems and interfaces that would make it easier for other firms to order UNEs and services to be resold; (2) to provide detailed performance monitoring reports to competing carriers that could help detect

---

[24]See "New York PSC Conditionally Approves Merger of Bell Atlantic, NYNEX" in *Telecommunications Reports,* March 24, 1997, p. 5.

poor performance or discrimination in the supply of UNEs or resold services; and (3) to set rates for interconnection and UNEs based on forward-looking economic cost. Many of these commitments addressed disputed issues between the merging firms and the competing companies with which they were negotiating interconnection agreements.

The FCC argued that these commitments would help other firms to enter or expand and thereby become more significant competitors. In this way, the commitments mitigated the competitive harm of eliminating Bell Atlantic as a likely competitor.

AFTER THE DECISION

The Hart-Scott-Rodino and FCC reviews of this merger had to rely on what was known at the time—and the view of the future was particularly hazy and uncertain in this case. We now have the luxury of several years of post-merger history.

The Bell Atlantic-NYNEX merger was neither the first nor the last merger of large local telephone companies. SBC Communications and Pacific Telesis, two of the RBOCs formed when AT&T divested local companies, merged a few months before Bell Atlantic and NYNEX completed their merger. SBC Communications went on to merge in October 1999 with Ameritech Corporation, another of the seven original RBOCs. In June 2000 Bell Atlantic merged with GTE Corporation, the largest of the telephone companies that had not been part of the Bell System (after which the merged entity began doing business under the name of Verizon). The DOJ and the FCC approved both later mergers. Potential competition, but with a novel twist, was an issue in each case, although other issues were more important than in the Bell Atlantic-NYNEX merger.[25]

As with Bell Atlantic-NYNEX, the FCC concluded that the SBC-Ameritech and Bell Atlantic-GTE mergers did harm the public interest because, absent the merger, the merger partners were among a small number of potential entrants most likely to compete to supply service to residential

---

[25]Another major issue also involved local competition. Opponents argued that the mergers would increase the incentives of SBC and Bell Atlantic to hinder efforts by local competitors to get access to UNEs and other inputs that they needed from SBC or Bell Atlantic, especially for novel services. A competitor expecting difficulties and reduced profits in one region would see reduced returns on investments that were necessary to offer the service anywhere rather than specific to the offering in that region. Consequently, the competitor would be less likely to invest to offer the service anywhere. Before the merger, SBC, for example, would not care that behavior limiting the success of an entrant in Dallas could make competitive entry less likely in an Ameritech market such as Chicago. After the merger, reduced competition in Chicago would benefit SBC, thereby increasing the payoff to behavior in Dallas that hindered entry in Chicago (and vice versa) and increasing the likelihood and magnitude of such behavior. (See FCC 1999, pp. 186–247; FCC 2000a, pp. 173–208) The FCC also was concerned, as with the Bell Atlantic-NYNEX merger, about the loss of benchmarking information for regulation (FCC 1999, pp. 101–185; FCC 2000a, pp. 127–172).

and small business customers in the other's regions. The FCC pointed to Ameritech plans to compete with SBC in St. Louis by building on the cellular service that SBC already provided in the city and on local service in its home region of Illinois and East St. Louis across the Mississippi River—plans abandoned only when merger discussions began (FCC 1999, pp. 78–81, 94–97). The FCC also concluded that, despite the absence of specific entry plans, Ameritech was a significant potential future participant in other markets in SBC territory, as was SBC in Ameritech territory.[26] In its order approving the Bell Atlantic-GTE merger, the FCC concluded that GTE was one of the companies most likely to provide significant future competition for local service to residential and small business customers in Bell Atlantic service areas adjacent to GTE service areas.[27]

The novel twist was that, far from disavowing any interest in out-of-region entry, these merging firms touted postmerger entry as a public interest benefit. Both pairs of firms claimed that their merger would enable them to pursue a strategy of entering to compete with incumbent local exchange carriers elsewhere—to provide service first to larger businesses, and later to residential and small business customers. SBC went so far as to claim that its primary reason for merging with Ameritech was to make possible a "National-Local Strategy" of out-of-region entry. SBC identified thirty-three markets that the merged firm would enter and provided a timetable for doing so (FCC 1999, pp. 259–266). Bell Atlantic and GTE said their merger would allow them to offer a bundle of services—including local service—to large business customers in twenty-one out-of-region cities within eighteen months of the merger (FCC 2000a, p. 219). The FCC, however, rejected the merging parties' claims that they would not have the capability or incentive to pursue these strategies without the merger. Since the benefits could be realized without the merger, they could not be weighed against harm due to the merger (FCC 1999, pp. 270–300, and 2000a, pp. 220–225).[28]

Again, neither potential competition concerns nor other issues induced the DOJ or FCC to try to block these mergers. The DOJ did require Ameritech to divest its cellular assets in St. Louis to another firm capable of providing conventional local service. The FCC, however, thought that this divestiture was insufficient to eliminate harm because the acquiring firm (which turned out to be GTE) had neither Ameritech's advantages of adja-

---

[26]The FCC pointed out that an SBC witness testifying earlier in California hearings for approval of its merger with PacTel had explained that SBC would not enter local service markets in California because SBC lacked the advantages in California that had caused SBC to consider entering to compete with Ameritech in Chicago. SBC argued that subsequent experience had caused it to abandon any thoughts of entering in the Chicago area (FCC 1999, pp. 82–83).

[27]The FCC concluded that Bell Atlantic had the capability to enter markets where GTE was the incumbent but lacked the incentive to do so since GTE service areas tended to be relatively rural and therefore less likely to offer the prospect of profitable entry (FCC 2000a, pp. 100, 106–119).

[28]The FCC also noted the strategies concentrated first on serving large business customers, for whom there were many more potential suppliers (FCC 1999, pp. 307–110, and 2000a, p. 223).

cency and brand name recognition nor the same intent to use these assets to provide local service (FCC 1999, pp. 96–97).

The FCC concluded that additional conditions on the merger were needed to mitigate the harm from the loss of potential competition. First, the FCC imposed conditions on both new mergers that had the same intent as the conditions imposed on the Bell Atlantic-NYNEX merger—to lower entry barriers. In addition, the FCC required the merged firms to carry out their strategies for out-of-region entry or face monetary penalties. SBC had to enter each of thirty markets within thirty months of closing the merger or face fines of up to $40 million for each market, or a total $1.2 billion across all markets (FCC 1999, pp. 398–399, 420–422). Bell Atlantic was required to invest $500 million on entry—of which half had to be spent on facilities-based service—or serve at least 250,000 customer lines within three years, or face fines of up to $750 million (FCC 2000a, pp. 319–323).

As of early 2002, SBC reported it had introduced service in twenty-two new markets and planned to enter at least eight more by April 2002, the end of the condition's thirty-month schedule, but also reported that in March 2001 it had scaled back its service offerings in these new markets in response to economic and regulatory conditions (SBC Communications 2001, p. 17). In late 2001 the FCC verified that Verizon had spent nearly $300 million toward its overall entry commitment and $113 million on facilities-based service by acquiring a competitive carrier (FCC 2001b). Neither SBC nor Verizon has been fined for failing to meet deadlines on their entry conditions. Both have been fined for not meeting other conditions, including those intended to lower barriers to entry. SBC has been fined a total of $56.2 million and Verizon about $6 million (Reuters 2002).

While competing local carriers have been entering and providing service in the years since the Bell Atlantic-NYNEX merger, the more optimistic predictions for local service competition have not been realized. AT&T, MCI WorldCom, and Sprint have been active as local entrants, especially where, as in New York, the incumbent RBOC has received authority to offer inter-LATA long distance, and the long-distance companies have wanted to offer a competing package of local and long-distance service. Many of the newer competing carriers, however, have had limited success and have faced financial difficulties, including even bankruptcy. Furthermore, much of the competing service that is available to residential and smaller business customers relies on the facilities of the incumbent carriers.

Table 3-1 summarizes data on local competition reported to the FCC. Nationwide, competing local exchange carriers, or CLECS, served only 9 percent of lines to end user customers as of the end of June 2001 and 5.5 percent of lines to residential and small business customers. Competitors have been more successful in New York, where the FCC identified twenty-three different CLECs that together served 23 percent of lines—a higher share of lines than in any other state. CLECs' 23 percent share of lines in New York was up from 8.6 percent at the end of December 1999, when Ver-

TABLE 3-1

Percentage of Reported End-User Lines Provided by Competitive Local Exchange Carriers

	Nationwide		New York State	
	Residential and Small Businesses	All Customers	Residential and Small Businesses	All Customers
December 1999	2.4%	4.3%	N/A	8.6%
June 2000	3.2%	6.0%	14.6%	15.8%
December 2000	4.5%	7.7%	19.2%	20.2%
June 2001	5.5%	9.0%	22.5%	22.7%

Sources: FCC (2000b, 2000c, 2001a, 2002)

izon was authorized to provide inter-LATA long-distance service to New York customers.

The FCC data also show, however, that much CLEC service is not provided over their own facilities. Nationwide, CLECs reported owning one-third of the lines they provide and acquiring the remaining two-thirds from another carrier, almost always the established incumbent carrier. CLECs could use an incumbent's lines with their own switches, but 74 percent of the lines that incumbent local carriers provide to CLECs are provided together with incumbent carrier switching. This means that about one-half of all CLEC service is simply the resale of service provided over incumbent local carrier facilities.[29] Finally, the FCC reports that as of June 2001 only about 11 percent of CLEC service, about 1.9 million lines nationwide, reaches customers over coaxial cable—as it would if cable television facilities were used to provide service (FCC 2002, Table 5). Cable systems have not become important providers of competing local telephone service.

CONCLUSIONS

There has been relatively little government enforcement activity under the potential competition doctrines recently, perhaps in part because of the difficult evidentiary burdens such activity would involve (ABA 1997, p. 350; Kwoka 2001). To demonstrate that a merger violates the antitrust laws under the actual potential competition doctrine requires showing (among other things) that one of the merging firms would have entered but for the

---

[29]Calculated as the 66.6 percent of lines CLECs report acquiring from other carriers multiplied by the 25.6 percent of lines that incumbent carriers report providing without switching, plus the 33.4 percent of lines CLECs report they own (FCC 2002, Tables 3 and 4).

merger and that the market in the future would be more concentrated and less competitive for the loss of this entry.

In this case, there was relatively strong evidence that, but for the merger, Bell Atlantic would have entered and competed with NYNEX in at least some relevant markets. Such evidence included the facts of Bell Atlantic's experience as a local carrier, location as a geographically adjacent carrier, and past public statements about an interest in entering local service markets outside its home territory. According to the FCC, internal Bell Atlantic documents provided strong evidence that the company had planned to compete with NYNEX.

The more difficult part of any case brought to block the merger would have been showing that the loss of Bell Atlantic as an entrant would have made markets substantially more concentrated and less competitive. This would have required projecting future market conditions in an industry in which past conditions have provided much less evidence on future conditions than is usually be the case. The 1996 Telecommunications Act made entry by competing suppliers of local services easier, but how much easier? What types of firms would prove to have the advantages necessary to make them successful entrants, and how much market share could they capture how quickly? How many firms would enter, and which services would they supply to which customers? These all were relevant questions for determining the effect on future market competition of eliminating Bell Atlantic as an entrant. When the merger was being reviewed in 1996 and early 1997, there was scant market experience under the new rules to answer such questions or provide a basis for evidence that could be presented to a court. From this perspective, it is not surprising that authorities examined the merger closely and expressed concern but in the end did not challenge it.

Years later it is still difficult to answer fully all of the relevant questions. Entrants have not been so successful, even in New York, that additional entry might not have made those markets more competitive. Six years after the passage of the Telecommunications Act of 1996 and four and one-half years after the Bell Atlantic-NYNEX merger, many CLECs have entered, but they have not captured a very large share of the market, especially over their own facilities. By any standard, local exchange markets even in New York remain highly concentrated. The evidence is less clear, however, on the extent to which entry of an independent Bell Atlantic would have had a substantial incremental effect on competition in local markets in New York, especially for residential and small business customers. Bell Atlantic, now Verizon, has promised to enter out-of-region markets, as has SBC. But to date incumbent local exchange companies seem not to have had a major impact as out-of-region entrants—at least in supplying residential and small business customers.

Would it have been different in New York if the Bell Atlantic-NYNEX merger had been blocked? The answer to this not-so-rhetorical question will never be known.

REFERENCES

ABA Antitrust Section. *Antitrust Law Developments,* 4th edn., 1997.

Brenner, Steven R. "Direct Testimony." Submitted to New York Public Service Commission in Case Nos. 96-C-0599 and 96-C-0603, November 25, 1996.

Brenner, Steven R. "Potential Competition in Local Telephone Service: Bell Atlantic-NYNEX (1997)." In *The Antitrust Revolution,* 3d edn. edited by J. E. Kwoka, Jr., and L. J. White, 116–142 New York: Oxford University Press, 1999.

Brock, Gerald. *The Telecommunications Industry: The Dynamics of Market Structure.* Cambridge, Mass.: Harvard University Press, 1981.

Federal Communications Commission. *Memorandum Opinion and Order.* File No. NSD-L-96-10, In the Application of NYNEX Corporation and Bell Atlantic Corporation For Consent to Transfer Control of NYNEX Corporation and Its Subsidiaries, August 14, 1997.

Federal Communications Commission. *Memorandum Opinion and Order.* CC Docket No. 98–141, In the Applications of Ameritech Corporation and SBC Communications Inc. For Consent to Transfer Control of Corporations Holding Commission Licenses and Lines, October 8, 1999.

Federal Communications Commission. *Memorandum Opinion and Order.* CC Docket No. 98–184, In the Application of GTE Corporation and Bell Atlantic Corporation For Consent to Transfer Control of Domestic and International Sections 214 and 310 Authorizations and Application to Transfer Control of a Submarine Cable Landing Station, June 16, 2000a.

Federal Communications Commission, Industry Analysis Division, Common Carrier Bureau. *Local Telephone Competition at the New Millennium,* August 2000b.

Federal Communications Commission, Industry Analysis Division, Common Carrier Bureau. *Local Telephone Competition: Status as of June 30, 2000,* December 2000c.

Federal Communications Commission, Industry Analysis Division, Common Carrier Bureau. *Local Telephone Competition: Status as of December 21, 2000,* May 2001a.

Federal Communications Commission. Letter from Carol E. Mattey, Deputy Chief, Common Carrier Bureau, to Jeffrey Ward, Verizon Communications, November 19, 2001b.

Federal Communications Commission, Industry Analysis Division, Common Carrier Bureau. *Local Telephone Competition: Status as of June 30, 2001,* February 2002.

Joskow, Andrew S. "Potential Competition: The Bell Atlantic/NYNEX Merger." *Review of Industrial Organization* 17 (March 2000): 185–191.

Kwoka, John E. "Non-Incumbent Competition: Mergers Involving Constraining and Prospective Competitors." *Case Western Reserve Law Review* 52 (Fall 2001): 173–209.

Mosca, W. K., Jr. "Affidavit." Attached to Petition of AT&T Corporation to Deny or, in the Alternative, to Defer Pending Further Investigation and Briefing, FCC Report No. 960205, September 23, 1996.

New York Telephone et al. "Initial Panel Testimony of New York Telephone, NYNEX Corporation, and Bell Atlantic Corporation." Submitted to New York Public Service Commission in Case Nos. 96-C-0599 and 96-C-0603, November 25, 1996.

Noll, Roger G., and Bruce M. Owen. "The Anticompetitive Uses of Regulation: *United States* v. *AT&T* (1982)." In *The Antitrust Revolution,* 2nd edn., edited by John E. Kwoka, Jr., and Lawrence J. White, 328–375. New York: Harper Collins College, 1994.

Oliver, B. D. "Affidavit." Submitted to the U.S. District Court for D.C., *U.S.* v. *Western Electric Company, Inc. and AT&T.* January 1994.

Reuters, "SBC, Verizon Pay Again for Access Faults," January 30, 2002 http://dailynews.yahoo.com/h/nm/20020130/tc/telecoms_fcc_penalties_dc_1.html.

SBC Communications Inc., *Annual Report 2001.*

Temin, Peter, with Louis Galambos. *The Fall of the Bell System.* Cambridge: Cambridge University Press, 1987.

CASE 4

The Long-Distance Industry: One Merger Too Many? MCI WorldCom and Sprint (2000)

Michael D. Pelcovits

INTRODUCTION

On October 4, 1999, MCI WorldCom and Sprint announced an agreement to merge. At the time of the agreement, the two companies were the second and third largest traditional long-distance companies in the United States, and the first and second (or third)[1] largest providers of Internet backbone service. Large portions of the two companies' business activities overlapped, which raised concern about competitive impacts, especially because the long-distance industry had consolidated significantly in the years prior to the merger announcement. MCI WorldCom itself was created by the merger of WorldCom and MCI one year earlier. This prior merger was hotly contested, and received government approval only after MCI agreed to divest its Internet business. In fact, Chairman William Kennard of the FCC remarked that with the approval of the WorldCom-MCI merger the industry was "poised just a merger away from undue concentration" (FCC 1998b).

The proposed merger was subject to intense scrutiny by a host of government agencies. After almost nine months of discovery, filings, meetings, and hearings, the applicants dissolved the agreement in the face of opposition from the U.S. Department of Justice (DOJ) and the Commission of the

Michael D. Pelcovits was Chief Economist of MCI WorldCom during this case. The author wishes to thank Tony Epstein for helpful comments. The views expressed in this chapter do not represent official views of MCI WorldCom.

[1]The parties to this case disputed Sprint's rank among Internet backbone providers.

European Communities (EC). The proposed MCI WorldCom-Sprint merger thus became the only merger between major telecommunications carriers that was derailed by the government.

This case is important in several respects. First, the merger defined the limits of the government's tolerance for consolidation in the telecommunications industry, which had experienced significant consolidation following the 1996 Telecommunications Act. The merger presented the government with the difficult task of predicting the structure of different segments of the telecommunications market at a time of major change in law and regulation, and it thus provides a fascinating look at the interactions of antitrust and regulatory policy. Second, the parties in the case presented a new tool—i.e., merger simulation models—which has become increasingly important in the analysis of mergers of differentiated consumer products. Third, economic analysis of the impact of the merger on the Internet market involved some interesting and controversial topics in the growing field of network economics.

Industry and Regulatory Background

On January 1, 1984, the Bell System, which consisted of local telephone, long-distance telephone, and manufacturing and research divisions, was broken up as a result of the DOJ's antitrust suit. Following the divestiture, seven separate regional Bell operating companies (RBOCs) provided local telephone service, and AT&T provided long-distance service and manufactured telephone equipment. The divestiture consent decree prohibited the RBOCs from offering long-distance service, information services, or manufacturing telephone equipment. Long-distance was defined as calling between 193 geographic areas, termed Local Access and Transport Areas (LATAs), created by and defined in the divestiture decree. At that time, it was not anticipated that local telephone markets would become competitive, so the underlying goal of the decree was to isolate the monopoly local service companies from downstream markets. This separation would eliminate the incentive that the local companies would otherwise have to engage in anticompetitive conduct that could distort or disrupt competition in these vertically related markets.

Competition in the long-distance market flourished in the years following divestiture. As shown in Figure 4-1, AT&T, whose market share was 90 percent in 1984, declined to a 43 percent share by 1998. During the same period, MCI WorldCom and Sprint increased their shares from 4.5 percent to 25.6 percent, and 2.7 percent to 10.5 percent, respectively.[2]

The orderly "deal" of the divestiture did not last long. Almost immediately, the RBOCs sought permission to enter long-distance markets, and several companies began to compete in niches of the local telephone mar-

---

[2]MCI WorldCom's share represents only MCI prior to the merger with WorldCom in 1998.

FIGURE 4-1   AT&T, MCI, and Sprint Shares of Total Toll Revenue in the United States, 1984–1998

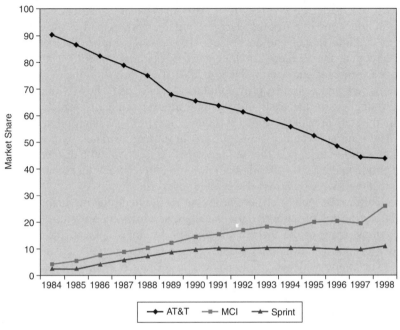

Source: FTC (1999c, Table 1.5).

ket, although they made insubstantial progress. Lobbying by RBOCs and would-be competitors in local markets eventually led to a new legislated deal with the passage of the Telecommunications Act of 1996. The Act ordered the RBOCs (and other local telephone monopolies) to unbundle the components of their networks and permit rivals to interconnect with their networks to facilitate entry into local markets. The Act also created a procedure by which the RBOCs could reenter long-distance markets on a state-by-state basis. At the time of the MCI WorldCom-Sprint proposed merger, however, the Act had not affected market structure in most of the country. Competition for local service, outside of core business areas, was nascent, and the only state where an RBOC had been authorized to provide long-distance service was New York.

Merger Review Process

Mergers of large U.S. telecommunications carriers are reviewed by many government agencies. First, the DOJ examines the merger under the Clayton Act, following the principles contained in the *Horizontal Merger Guidelines*. The DOJ follows the Hart-Scott-Rodino process, which requires merging companies to give prior notice to the DOJ, which can then collect information and documents from the applicants and other firms in the industry, so as to decide whether to file a lawsuit in Federal District Court seeking an injunction to block the merger. Until the merging parties provide the requested information and documents, they cannot complete the merger.

Second, the Federal Communications Commission (FCC) must approve the merger pursuant to Sections 214(a) and 310(d) of the Communications Act where carriers provide interstate services.[3] The FCC makes its determination on the basis of a "public interest standard," which differs from the standards of the antitrust statutes. The FCC has interpreted its role as determining "whether the applicants have demonstrated, by a preponderance of the evidence, that the proposed transaction, on balance, serves the public interest, considering both its competitive effects and other public interest benefits and harms" (FCC 1998b, par. 10).

Third, state public utility commissions in which the merging parties hold certificates of authority for intrastate services—permission to operate—must approve the merger. Finally, the EC must approve the merger under its antitrust laws, to the extent that the parties operate there as well.

The public evidence discussed below is primarily from the case filed at the FCC. The merging parties filed an application there in November 1999. Parties opposing the merger filed in February 2000, after which both the applicants and opponents filed additional comments. There was no FCC decision in this case, because the application was withdrawn after the DOJ decided to challenge the merger.

There is also evidence from filings before some of the state commissions. Several of the state commissions held hearings, which allowed for cross-examination of the experts who testified for the applicants and for their opponents; these hearings fill in some of the details on the economic evidence.[4]

Unlike many of the cases studied in this book, there is no final court decision resolving this case. As mentioned earlier, the DOJ filed a complaint to enjoin the merger in June 2000. At that point, the parties decided to dissolve the merger agreement rather than contest the case before a district court. After the parties withdrew their application to merge, however, the EC issued a decision declaring the merger to be incompatible with European law.[5]

This case study will proceed by presenting the economic arguments made by the applicants, following with evidence presented by private parties opposing the merger, and then summarizing the position taken by the

---

[3]The FCC also shares concurrent antitrust jurisdiction with the DOJ under the Clayton Act.

[4]For other details of the economic case, the author also relied on nonpublic presentations made by the Applicants before the DOJ and the EC.

[5]This decision is currently being appealed by WorldCom before the European Court of Justice, because of the company's concerns with the precedent set by the decision.

DOJ and the EC. Because of the complexity of the case, we will study the issues on a market-by-market basis.

MARKET DEFINITION

The proposed merger affected concentration and competition in many telecommunications markets. As is typically the case, the applicants claimed that markets should be defined broadly, in order to dilute the level of concentration found in markets where their business activities overlapped. The applicants claimed that telecommunications markets were evolving at a pace that was causing traditional market boundaries to crumble.

The major lines of business of the merging parties are shown in Table 4-1. The long-distance market is divided into two separate and distinct segments. The "Mass Market" consists of residential and small business customers who purchase voice long-distance service, which is sold primarily through direct marketing channels (e.g., telemarketing). Mass market customers buy services "off the shelf" without individualized prices or other terms. The "Large Business Market" consists of large corporate customers. These companies purchase a wide range of voice and data services, with most business conducted by bidding for large multiyear contracts tailored to the individual needs of each customer. The Internet backbone consists of high-capacity long-haul data networks that connect smaller networks and customers.

TABLE 4-1
Lines of Business and Market Presence

Market	MCI	Sprint	Other Firms
Long-Distance— Mass Market	Number 2	Number 3	ATT—Number 1 600 smaller firms
Long-Distance— Large Business	Number 2	Number 3	ATT—Number 1 New entrants: Qwest, Broad- wing, Frontier
Internet Backbone	Number 1	Number 2	Several other large firms; hundreds of small firms
Local Service	New entrant; concentrated in metro areas	Traditional carrier in a few smaller markets	Dominated by the RBOCs and GTE
Wireless	MMDS*	MMDS, PCS*	RBOCs, ATT

* MMDS stands for "multichannel multipoint delivery service"; PCS stands for "personal communications service" (a form of cellular telephone service).

The areas of concern to the government were the two major segments of the long-distance market and the Internet backbone. The applicants had to prove that the merger would not lead to too much concentration in either segment of the long-distance market. With respect to the Internet market, the applicants were prepared to divest Sprint's Internet assets rather than fight over the competition issues. Nonetheless, they still had to defend the issue of whether the divestiture of the Sprint assets would be sufficient to preserve effective competition for Internet backbone service.

Applicants' Case

The applicants argued that the traditional dividing line between local and long-distance markets was disappearing in favor of a new "all distance" market. The factors eroding the traditional market definitions were the expected entry of the RBOCs into long-distance, technological advances reducing the sensitivity of telecommunications costs to distance, and consumers' preferences for bundles of local and long-distance service. The most visible example of the evolution to an "all distance" market was the bundling of local and long-distance minutes by many wireless carriers. If the "all distance" market definition proposed by the applicants were adopted, MCI WorldCom and Sprint would fall in the ranks to number six and seven among all domestic carriers.[6]

According to the applicants, in the absence of their proposed merger the RBOCs would come to dominate this new market as they continued to gain long-distance authority because they controlled the "last mile" connection to the customer. The existence of large barriers to entry to compete for this last mile connection to the customer required the resources of the combined firm, which would be a more formidable competitor to vertically integrated RBOCs than the companies would be individually. This would give the firm the "scale and expertise to support a nationwide CLEC [competitive local exchange carrier] entry strategy" (Application, p. 15). One key part of the local entry strategy of MCI WorldCom and Sprint was to use newly acquired "multichannel multipoint distribution service" (MMDS) spectrum to serve as a "third wire" into the home.[7] MCI WorldCom and Sprint each controlled spectrum in large but non-overlapping geographic sections of the country. The applicants' case made a strong appeal to the public interest standard used by the FCC. They hoped that the FCC would focus on the difficult task of opening local markets and would allow the merger to proceed in order to serve this goal, even if competition in long-distance markets arguably was diminished until the RBOCs were permitted to enter the market.

---

[6]Sprint Corporation, Transferor, and MCI WorldCom Inc., Transferee, *Application for Consent to Transfer Control,* Federal Communications Commission, CC Docket No. 99-333, November 17, 1999, p. 4 (hereafter "Application").

[7]Telephone and cable TV are considered the first two wires into the home.

Opponents' Case

Opponents of the merger responded that the all distance market was an imagined future and that the merger ought to be evaluated under current market conditions (SBC Communications 2000, p. i.). The DOJ apparently agreed with this characterization, as its complaint made no mention of an all distance market and indeed carved up the industry affected by the merger into ten separate markets (DOJ 2000).

One market was the Internet backbone; the other nine markets related to long-distance service. Of these, two related to the mass market for long-distance. The DOJ divided this market into a domestic and an international market. International private line services, primarily used by large business customers and other long-distance companies, constituted another market. The other five markets related to services for large business customers and included the market for private line services (dedicated circuits used in any manner by the customer), the market for advanced voice services, and three separate markets for three kinds of data services: X.25 (an older protocol used by data networks), "frame relay" (the dominant type of data network at the time), and ATM ("asynchronous transfer mode," extremely high speed data networks).

THE LONG-DISTANCE MARKET

Long-Distance Competition—Network Coverage and Capacity

Domestic long-distance service is provided primarily over fiber optic lines that link together hundreds of carrier locations, known as points of presence (POPs), across the country. (Local telephone companies provide the connections between customers and the nearest POP of the long-distance company selected by the customer.) To build a long-distance network, a company must: obtain rights-of-way across the entire route of the network; dig trenches and lay fiber optic cable; place electronics at different points in the network to create and repeat light pulses and convert electronic (i.e., digital) signals into light pulses; install switches to route traffic; and set up computers and software to manage the network. A nationwide network extends between 15,000 and 30,000 route miles and costs several billion dollars to complete. Therefore, a fundamental issue to be resolved was whether there would be sufficient competition among different owners of long-distance networks following the merger.

The applicants claimed that the merger would not lead to undue concentration in long-distance because many carriers had recently built large fiber optic networks to compete with those of AT&T, MCI WorldCom, and Sprint. (The size of the fiber routes of long distance carriers is shown in Table 4-2.) Furthermore, they argued that the call-carrying capacity of fiber

TABLE 4-2
Fiber System Route Miles of Interexchange Carriers

	1991	1992	1993	1994	1995	1996	1997	1998
AT&T	32,500	33,500	35,000	36,022	37,419	38,704	38,704	39,576
MCI WorldCom	27,793	28,133	30,897	32,564	32,176	35,156	44,853	47,529
Sprint	22,725	22,799	22,996	22,996	22,996	23,432	23,574	23,574
Other carriers	3,909	3,919	4,263	4,548	4,437	8,913	18,468	49,100

Source: Kraushaar (1999)

optic lines could be expanded efficiently to meet demand. The reason for this is that once the fiber optic cables are placed in the ground, the electronics can be scaled to meet demand. Also, because of technological innovation in electronics and photonics, there is no constraint on the capacity of any fiber network to meet any conceivable increase in demand. From the standpoint of antitrust economics, this addressed a very significant factor, namely whether high sunk costs were required of new entrants and those expanding service to compete with the "Big 3" carriers.

The opponents did not dispute that the entrants were building large networks or that networks could be scaled to handle substantial increases in traffic. They did argue, however, that the entrants' networks did not have the geographic reach of those of the "Big 3." Consequently, the entrants had to depend on the "Big 3" to fill in the gaps in their networks in order to offer ubiquitous national coverage to their customers. The opponents concluded that the merger, by reducing the number of ubiquitous carriers from three to two, "raises the costs of providing service to new networks and adversely affects their ability to compete with the major carriers in providing long distance services" (Hausman 2000, p. 21). The difference in the reach of the competing long-distance networks, as claimed by the opponents, is illustrated in Table 4-3.

The applicants presented competing evidence and theories on the issue of geographic reach of the new carriers. First, they claimed that there would be only twelve LATAs (representing only 1.5 percent of the population) in which the number of facilities-based long-distance carriers would go from three to two as a result of the merger. Second, they said that an entrant did not need to fill in its network by buying from only one other carrier, but rather could assemble a network by piecing together portions from two or more carriers competing against the "Big 3." Therefore, the "Big 3" (or "Big 2," postmerger) did not have a network advantage that would give them market power.

The DOJ did not agree with the applicants that a network combining owned and leased portions was as good as a ubiquitous network under sin-

TABLE 4-3
Areas Served by Long-Distance Networks, 2000

Company	Points of Presence	LATAs Served (%)	Population Served (%)
AT&T	705	100	100
MCI WorldCom	740	99	100
Sprint	398	97	99
Qwest	136	55	81
Williams	110	49	78
Frontier	92	44	72
BroadWing	77	34	63
Cable and Wireless	35	16	48
Level 3	26	13	44

Source: Hausman (2000, p. 22).

gle ownership because of the complexity of providing high-quality, dependable service to sophisticated customers. In its Complaint, referencing the impact of the merger on competition for data services, the DOJ stated:

> Because each of these networks depends upon the ability of the provider to connect sites at diverse locations throughout the United States and, some cases, around the world, the provider must posses a vast network of optical fiber, POPs, nodes, switches, routes and other associated facilities. Because WorldCom and Sprint are two of only three such providers in the United States, the effect of the merger will be to eliminate one of the very few carriers that possesses the full range of facilities required to compete in these markets. (DOJ 2000, par. 135)

Residential Long-Distance Markets

At the time of the merger's announcement, most Americans were well acquainted with the intense rivalry among long-distance companies. Television advertising and incessant telemarketing constantly reminded customers that they could switch easily and at no cost among long-distance carriers, and many customers took advantage of this opportunity. Since divestiture, MCI WorldCom and Sprint had taken substantial market share from AT&T (see Figure 4-1), and many other carriers had entered the market and were serving residential subscribers across the country.

The opponents did not dispute these facts. Rather, the debate raged over the importance of the MCI WorldCom and Sprint brands in the marketplace. In a consumer products industry, where entry and expansion of new firms is relatively easy, a merger among the more established firms will harm consumers only if consumers do not regard the new entrants' products as good substitutes for those of the merging parties. The economists work-ing for the two sides in this case presented conflicting evidence on this issue. The applicants' economists argued that the new entrants in the long-distance markets were perceived as good substitutes for the "Big 3" carri-ers. By contrast, the opponents' economists argued that the brand name products of the "Big 3" were in a separate niche of the market from the new entrants. The parties argued their points in two ways: First, following a tra-ditional approach to antitrust, the parties presented evidence on the charac-teristics of the products offered by the carriers, the pricing strategies of the carriers, and consumers' tendencies to switch among carriers. Second, the parties offered models that estimated the potential impact of the merger on prices in the long-distance market.

Merger Simulation Models

Modeling of the effects of mergers is a relatively recent phenomenon, but it has become very popular, particularly for mergers of consumer products.[8] The models most in use are termed "unilateral effects models," which means that they assume that firms do not implicitly coordinate their actions, but rather act independently. By ignoring the possibility of coordinated be-havior, which could raise prices more than would be indicated by a unilat-eral effects model, these models provide a conservative estimate (one that is favorable to the applicants) of the potential impact of the merger on prices. This represents a significant shift in orientation by DOJ, which until recently focused on the potential effects of mergers through implicitly co-ordinated behavior (Shapiro 1995).

The merger models are based on the two major oligopoly models, Cournot and Bertrand, which have been used by economists for many decades. The Cournot model assumes that the firms adjust output, until each firm maximizes its profits given the output of the other firms. The Bertrand model assumes that firms adjust prices, until each firm maximizes its profits given the prices of the other firms. The Cournot scenario is most appropriate in industries characterized by homogeneous products where "capacity primarily distinguishes firms and shapes the nature of their com-petition" (*Merger Guidelines,* Section 2.22). The Bertrand model is more suitable for industries with differentiated products, including many con-sumer products, such as food, film, cars, and long-distance service.

In an industry producing differentiated products, the potential for harming consumers stems from the elimination of competition between two existing brands that are seen as close substitutes by many consumers. This does not necessarily mean that one brand will be eliminated, but rather that a single firm will now make pricing decisions for the two brands. Prior

---

[8]Among the many publications outlining this approach is Werden and Froeb (1994).

to the merger, a firm such as MCI WorldCom would only raise prices if it does not lose too much business to its rivals. After the merger, MCI World-Com would not consider the loss of business to the Sprint brand a cost of raising the price of the MCI brand products. According to this theory, the merger enables a firm such as MCI WorldCom to "internalize the financial consequences of its actions, and thus lessens competition" (Ordover and Willig 1993). The goal of the merger models is to estimate the strength of this effect. As in any concentrated industry, the models will always show some price increase when the number of competitors declines. The question is (1) whether this effect is significant and (2) whether it would be offset by efficiencies created by the merger.

Merger models have taken on particular importance in differentiated product industries because in these industries less formal (i.e., structural) analysis does not provide a very good basis for estimating the anticompetitive prospects of a merger. Structural analysis focuses on estimating market shares of the firms in the industry, which also requires setting the boundaries that define the market. The problem with this exercise is that many differentiated products are sold along a continuum, so there are no clear market boundaries or measures of market shares. Economists can debate endlessly about whether, for example, Gatorade, is in the same market as carbonated soft drinks. Moreover, the economic impact of a merger is hard to determine from structural analysis because "there probably is no simple relationship between the merging firms' shares and effects on price and welfare. . . . The key to a proper competitive analysis of a differentiated products merger is a careful consideration of the competition between the merging firms, and market shares do not necessarily indicate much about that" (Werden and Froeb 1996).

The mathematical formulation of merger simulation models involves two steps: a front-end selection and estimation of the demand system, which attempts to capture consumer preferences; and a "back-end simulation that maps the demand estimates, along with prices and shares, into a post merger price increase" (Froeb 1996). The greatest controversy surrounds the estimation of demand elasticities and the estimation or assumptions used to calculate cross-price elasticities.

A logit demand system is one of the most commonly used frameworks for merger simulation. Logit models state the demand for a product as the probability that a customer will choose the product rather than an alternative. The models usually specify the alternatives as the competing products in the same industry, as well as a single outside good that reflects the choice of "none of the above." A version of these models—the "antitrust logit model" (ALM)—was first developed by Werden and Froeb (1996) and assumes that each product is initially sold by a single firm, each firm has constant marginal cost, and fixed costs are very low. The implications of this model are that the prices of all the products in the industry increase as a result of the merger, but the magnitudes of increase are very different for different products. Nevertheless, welfare gains can arise in a merger because production will shift from smaller (less efficient) firms to larger (more efficient) firms. Also, the unilateral competitive effects from the merger can be mitigated by synergies that lower the costs of the merged firm.

Estimation of the competitive effects of a merger using the ALM requires information on only a handful of variables: prices and quantities for each firm, aggregate industry demand elasticity, and a single parameter controlling cross-elasticities of demand within an industry. The simulation is highly sensitive to this parameter, because it defines how close the competing products are to each other in the minds of consumers. The assumptions and structure of the model create a mathematical relationship between the cross-elasticity parameter and the marginal costs of the firms, however, so an alternative to estimating cross-elasticities directly is to rely on evidence of marginal costs. After selecting these inputs, the model is run and simulates the competitive interactions of the firms. It can then determine pre- and postmerger equilibria, and provide estimates of the effect of the merger on prices, quantities, profits, and consumer welfare.

There are many variations on this merger simulation model. It is possible to model more complex demand systems and also allow for single firms to produce multiple products. The first complexity introduced is often to allow for differences in the degree of substitutability among the products. This contrasts with the simple logit model, which assumes the same cross-elasticities with respect to a given product. For example, a nested logit model retains much of the character of the simple logit model, but allows different products to be grouped together if they are especially close substitutes. Other demand systems allow for even greater flexibility in the nature of demand relationships, but require more data to estimate parameters. The choice of demand system is very important for merger simulation because it influences the prediction of the changes in prices outside the neighborhood of the premerger equilibrium (Crooke et al. 1999).

One of the main reasons for the popularity of merger simulation models is the availability of abundant data on transactions from point-of-scale scanner data. The scanners at supermarkets and other retail locations provide data on revenues and units sold by UPC code. These data, which reveal customers' responses to changes in prices over many different time periods, provide econometricians with the ability to estimate own-price and cross-price elasticities. The richness of the data—each variety of a product is identified by a separate code (e.g., a two-liter bottle of Diet Coke), and data are often available on a weekly basis—creates its own set of problems (Hosken et. al., 2002). The econometrician must make a set of decisions on how to aggregate data (by product type, by geographic area, and by time period) to obtain meaningful results. These decisions introduce an element of controversy into the process, because they may have a significant impact on the outcome of the merger simulation model. Therefore, although merger simulation models give the impression of providing scientific precision to economic analysis of mergers, they do not eliminate the "art" of economics or the intensity of the conflict between battling experts in a merger case.

Applicants' Case

The applicants' position was that most customers perceived carriers other than the "Big 3" (which they termed the "emerging carriers") as very close, if not perfect, substitutes for the "Big 3" and especially for MCI WorldCom and Sprint. Since there were no barriers to expansion or new entry by the emerging carriers, the combination of MCI WorldCom and Sprint could not harm consumers. If the postmerger company were to raise prices, consumers would flock to the emerging carriers. In support of their case, the applicants provided evidence on market share and entry strategies of successful emerging carriers, as well as data on the willingness of customers to switch among carriers and classes of carriers.

As shown in Table 4-4, the emerging carriers' share in the residential market increased substantially during the years prior to the merger application.[9] The applicants further argued that new entrants had shown an ability to gain market share rapidly over relatively short periods of time. They cited the example of Excel Telecommunications, which increased its customer base from 223,000 to 3,800,000 in just eighteen months (Besen and Brenner 2000). Also, Talk.com had sold more than 1.5 million long-distance lines by January 1999, after first launching service in 1997. Talk.com's rapid ascent, which it described as "the fastest market share shift in the long distance industry's history," was a result of its partnership with AOL, which sold Talk.com to its customers.[10] The success of Talk.com and other long-distance services marketed by companies with established brands in other markets was further proof that value of the "Big 3" brands was very limited and not a source of actual or potential market power.

The parties also pointed to another major marketing phenomenon: low-price "dial around" service. Beginning in the mid-1990s, long-distance carriers began to promote service that did not require the customer to presubscribe to a new carrier, but instead allowed the customer to choose a vendor on a call-by-call basis by dialing extra digits. These services gained substantial market share very quickly. MCI WorldCom offered the most successful dial around products, 10-10-321 and 10-10-220, which accounted for 3 percent of the market. According to the applicants, the success of the dial around business, and especially MCI WorldCom's decision to sell these products *on an unbranded basis,* demonstrated the inability of

---

[9]Market shares measured in minutes and access lines show similar trends. Data on market shares in the residential market were not available to the parties for the year immediately prior to the merger, 1998. However, the data available on the emerging carriers' share of total toll revenue (residential and business combined) did show an increase (FCC 1999a, Table 11.3).

[10]Talk.com news release, January 5, 1999.

TABLE 4-4
Shares of U.S. Residential Toll Revenues, 1995–1997

	1995	1996	1997	Change in Share Points 1995–1997
AT&T	68.5%	63.3%	60.9%	−7.6
MCI	14.6	16.0	15.4	+0.8
Sprint	5.6	6.6	5.6	0.0
Others	11.3	14.1	18.1	+6.8

Source: FCC (1999a, tables 4.1–4.3).

the "Big 3" to set noncompetitive prices, either before or after a merger of two of them. Finally, the applicants pointed to the expected entry of the RBOCs into the long-distance market as another factor that would dilute the value of the MCI WorldCom and Sprint brands and the potential market power of the merged firm.

The applicants presented evidence of the use of "unbranded" carriers and of customer switching behavior in the two-year period prior to the merger application. The evidence was gathered from a survey conducted by the Paragren Company, which collected information on long-distance calling by 2000 to 5000 households every month from January 1998 through October 1999. Because Paragren sampled many of the same households for multiple months, one could observe how often households change the carrier they use and analyze the patterns of those changes.

The applicants provided the following conclusions based on the Paragren data:

1. *Customers are not loyal.* About one-half of MCI WorldCom's and Sprint's customers switched to another carrier over a twelve to eighteen month period. This means that carriers must actively win customers or they will lose share rapidly.

2. *Customers are willing to use emerging carriers.* Forty percent of customers used an emerging carrier sometime over the course of a year. This indicates that brand is not so important to many customers.

3. *Customers do not switch back and forth between MCI WorldCom and Sprint in unusually high volume.* Customers shifted from MCI World-Com to Sprint in numbers somewhat below what would be predicted by their shares, and from Sprint to MCI WorldCom just as frequently as would be predicted by their shares (Besen and Brenner 2000). These data indicate that MCI WorldCom and Sprint are not especially close substitutes for each other. This point was of particular importance for the unilateral effects modeling presented by the applicants, as it provided the rationale for using a model that treated all long-distance firms as equally good substitutes for each other.

Unilateral Effects Model Evidence

The applicants presented a unilateral effects model to the DOJ, which showed that the merger would lower the average long-distance price paid by residential consumers by an amount in the range of 0.2 percent to 0.8 percent (Hall 2000). The applicants presented a logit model, which as described earlier in this chapter, requires evidence on prices, quantities, market demand elasticity, and firm price elasticity.

Two approaches can be used to estimate the price elasticity of demand facing a single firm. First, elasticity can be calculated directly using econometric estimation based on historical information on price and quantity changes. Second, elasticity can be derived from a well-established theoretical relationship between profit margins and demand elasticity. Economic theory posits that at equilibrium a firm's profit margin will equal the reciprocal of its perceived demand elasticity.

The applicants calibrated the model using estimates of the firms' profit margins to determine demand elasticity. The estimates of profit margins were made based on an analysis of MCI WorldCom's internal costs, network utilization, and economic evidence regarding the cost of using capital goods. The applicants presented two versions of cost estimates based on whether advertising was treated as a fixed cost or a marginal cost—itself a very controversial issue. Estimates of marginal cost, calculated profit margins, and implied demand elasticities for MCI WorldCom are shown in Table 4-5. These elasticity estimates, and relatively similar estimates for Sprint (-4.7 or -6.5) and AT&T (-2.8 or -3.2), imply that the "Big 3" long-distance carriers did not have significant market power.[11] Even without any cost savings from the merger, the simulation model would predict an average price increase of less than 1 percent resulting from the merger.

The applicants estimated merger-specific cost savings primarily from reductions in Sprint's operating costs to the lower levels experienced by MCI WorldCom. The major categories of cost saving were: sales and administrative; costs of transporting traffic from local central offices to the long-distance network; and operator services. Also in one version of the model, reductions in Sprint's advertising costs were treated as a cost savings resulting from the merger. The total cost savings were projected to range between 13.5 percent and 18.5 percent of Sprint's costs. The final results of the model are shown in Table 4-6, which reports the predicted average change in prices for the merged firm, AT&T, the emerging carriers, and a weighted average for all long-distance carriers.[12]

The applicants staked their case on the claim that consumers regarded the emerging carriers as effective substitutes for the branded services of

---

[11]Even higher demand elasticities were reported in a econometric study published by Ward (1999).

[12]A version of the model was also run with the RBOCs in the long-distance market. The results for the weighted average long-distance price was -0.3 (with advertising not marginal) and -0.8 (with advertising marginal).

TABLE 4-5
MCI WorldCom Parameters

	Advertising not Marginal	Advertising Marginal
Marginal cost	69.2% of revenue	70.7% of revenue
Profit margin	30.8%	29.3%
Own-price elasticity	−3.3	−3.4

Source: Hall (2000).

TABLE 4-6
Results of Applicant's Unilateral Effects Model: Percentage Price Changes

	Advertising not Marginal	Advertising Marginal
Merged firm	−0.5	−2.2
AT&T	−0.1	−0.4
Emerging carriers	0.0	−0.1
Weighted average all carriers	−0.2	−0.8

AT&T, MCI WorldCom, and Sprint. The evidence on customer switching behavior and price-cost margins, used to back up this claim, was contested by very aggressive private party opponents to the merger.

Opponents' Case

The thrust of the opponents' case was that many consumers did not regard the emerging carriers as effective substitutes for the "Big 3." A merger of two of the three large carriers would thus lead to a significant diminution in competition and much higher prices paid by consumers. The opponents presented evidence on: the pricing and marketing behavior of the "Big 3"; the price-cost relationship of their services; econometric analysis of demand; and a merger simulation model that estimated expected price increases resulting from the merger.

The first step taken in a traditional antitrust analysis is the computation of HHI levels, pre- and postmerger. According to the opponents, the MCI WorldCom-Sprint merger "failed" the *Merger Guidelines'* HHI thresholds, thus creating a presumption of unlawfulness.[13] They estimated a premerger HHI of 2662 and a postmerger HHI of 3199, yielding a 537 point increase

---

[13] According to the *Merger Guidelines,* when a postmerger HHI exceeds 1800, it is presumed that a merger that increases the HHI by more than 50 points will be likely to create or enhance market power or facilitate its exercise.

in the HHI, well in excess of the *Merger Guidelines'* threshold of an increase in 50 points for an industry at this level of concentration.[14]

The opponents argued that the "generic" or emerging carriers could not constrain the prices of the "Big 3" branded products. They compared generic long-distance services to generic products in other consumer industries, such as soda, ice cream, and color film, where the availability of arguably generic products is not sufficient to constrain the price of the branded products. One argument used to support this point was that if consumers saw the generic products as effective substitutes, then "the branded products could not earn sufficient gross margins to fund the advertising that differentiates the brands" (Hausman 2000, p. 10). Thus, the importance of brands could be demonstrated by high margins, high advertising expenditures, or actual purchasing decisions made in response to price changes. In this case, the opponents presented the following evidence:

- Prices of brand name products were significantly higher for most customers than identical products available from generic carriers. Specifically, 45 to 75 percent of AT&T callers (depending upon their current calling plan) could save money buying from generic carriers. One-half of MCI WorldCom customers and one-third of Sprint customers could also save money buying from generic carriers.
- The "Big 3" advertise heavily to promote and differentiate their brands. In 1998, AT&T spent $1.4 billion, MCI WorldCom spent $948 million, and Sprint spent $671 million (Carlton and Sider 2000, p. 21).
- Market structure is very stable, with the identity and rank of the top three carriers not having changed for fifteen years or more.
- Long-distance companies had engaged in parallel pricing for many years.
- Customers face complex price schedules for long-distance, and thus place a high value on brand name.
- Long-distance rates net of access charges charged by AT&T to residential customers have increased over time.
- Long-distance rates to low volume customers (who use AT&T in greater proportions) are substantially above cost.

This evidence implied that the "Big 3" (or a post-merger Big 2) operated with substantial freedom from the competitive pressure of the generic carriers. Even if the carriers did not engage in coordinated pricing, this would mean that prices would be much higher after the merger. But the opponents claimed that the "Big 3" had coordinated pricing in the past, and

---

[14]This calculation was based on a market consisting only of inter-LATA toll. An alternative version was also presented, which included intra-LATA toll in the same market. It estimated that the merger would increase the HHI by 433 points (Hausman 2000).

that the merger would make coordination even easier and more effective at maintaining above-cost prices.

The opponents took the argument one step further, arguing that MCI WorldCom and Sprint were each other's closest competitors. While they both competed vigorously against AT&T, competition was especially intense over a specific group of customers: those with higher than average long-distance bills who had demonstrated a willingness to switch away from AT&T in the past. Several things demonstrated the intense competition between MCI WorldCom and Sprint. First, one of the two carriers usually responded to a pricing innovation by the other carrier by offering a similar product or service. (They argued that Sprint was usually the first to move in this game.) Second, MCI WorldCom and Sprint customers switched carriers more often than did AT&T's customers, implying that MCI WorldCom and Sprint each continuously needed to attract relatively larger number of customers than did AT&T. Third, contrary to the applicants' assertions, the opponents argued that MCI WorldCom and Sprint customers switched more frequently to the other carrier than would be predicted by market share alone.[15]

The opponents presented two models that estimated the impact of the merger on long-distance prices. The first model was a standard Cournot model of competition and was calibrated using price-cost margins for two long-distance products—standard message telephone service (MTS) and "discounted" MTS. This model also estimated the consumer welfare loss that would result from the merger. One version of this Cournot model assumed that the long-distance carriers did not cooperate in setting prices, which is the same assumption as the models discussed above. A second version of the model calculated the effects of the merger under the assumption that the long-distance carriers cooperated in pricing decisions.[16] The rationale given for this version of the model was that the "Big 3" had engaged in cooperative, oligopolistic pricing in the past.

As shown in Table 4-7, under the assumptions of this model, the merger would lead to a substantial increase in long-distance prices (between 7.5 percent and 21.6 percent) and a reduction of consumer welfare ranging from $1.8 to $3.9 billion a year, depending on whether carriers were assumed to collude on prices.

The opponents also presented a second merger simulation model, which was a Bertrand unilateral effects model, similar to the applicants' model described above. Unlike that presented by the applicants, however, this model did not treat all long-distance carriers as equally attractive substitutes. Rather, it estimated the relevant cross-price elasticities directly,

---

[15]Carlton and Sider (2000, p. 21). The main reason for the difference between the results of the applicants and opponents is that the two parties use different criteria for categorizing a customer's choice of a carrier as "primary."

[16]The economist sponsoring this model did not claim that long-distance carriers actively colluded, but rather engaged in tacit collusion.

TABLE 4-7
Results of Opponents' Cournot Merger Model

	Premerger	Postmerger Collusive Pricing	Unilateral Effects
P/C Margin (MTS)	0.763	0.805	0.780
P/C Margin (Discounted Service)	0.632	0.667	0.657
Price per Minute (MTS)	0.199	0.242	0.214
(change)		(increase by 21.6%)	(increase by 7.5%)
Price per Minute (Discounted Service)	0.128	0.141	0.137
Minutes of Use (billions)	163	148	155
Single Year Consumer Loss	—	$3.9 billion	$1.8 billion

Source: MacAvoy (2000, pp. 36–37).

TABLE 4-8
Opponents' Estimates of Own-Price and Cross-Price Elasticities

		Price Change by: Other Carriers	AT&T	MCI WorldCom	Sprint
Quantity Effect on:	Other Carriers	−1.33	0.47	0.12	0.04
	AT&T	0.16	−1.12	0.09	0.03
	MCI WorldCom	0.23	0.50	−1.33	0.06
	Sprint	0.30	0.61	0.22	−1.81
	Price-cost margin	75%	89%	75%	55%

Source: Hausman (2000, p. 13).

which showed MCI WorldCom and Sprint to be close substitutes for each other. Table 4-8 shows the elasticity estimates used in this merger simulation model. Entries in the table where the carrier is the same on the row and column correspond to own-price elasticities. For example, the own-price elasticity for AT&T is −1.12. Entries where the row and column are different correspond to cross-price elasticities. For example, the cross-price elasticity of a change in MCI WorldCom's price on Sprint's output is 0.22, meaning that if MCI WorldCom raises price by 10 percent, Sprint will sell 2.2 percent more long-distance.

The elasticity estimates and implied price-cost margins are dramatically different than the estimates presented by the applicants. Referring back to Table 4-5, the applicants estimated MCI WorldCom's own-price elasticity to be −3.3, compared to the −1.33 estimate of the opponents.

The corresponding price-cost margin estimates generated by the model are 30 percent by the applicants and 75 percent by the opponents. The analytical work of the parties corresponded to their qualitative assessments of the degree of competition in the long-distance market.

The opponent's merger simulation model was calibrated using the elasticity estimates shown in Table 4-8. The model assumed that the merger would not provide any efficiencies that would decrease marginal cost. The result of the model was a prediction that the merger would lead to an increase in price of 5.4 percent by MCI WorldCom, and 8.9 percent by Sprint.

The Department of Justice's Position

The Complaint filed by the DOJ objecting to this merger echoed many of the concerns and conclusions presented by the opponents. The DOJ argued that the "Big 3" had a unique position in the long-distance market:

> The Big 3 each have substantial competitive advantages in serving the mass market because of their respective brand equity and recognition, as well as the scale and scope of their respective operations, including near ubiquitous facilities-based networks, broad customer bases, storehouses of technological expertise and service experience, and corps of highly skilled, experienced personnel. (DOJ 2000, par. 163)

The DOJ rejected the interpretation of the evidence on consumer switching behavior presented by the applicants, and stated that a disproportionate number of customers leaving one of the two merger applicants switched to the other, thus proving the closeness of the two firms in the eyes of consumers. The DOJ also argued that the merger would facilitate coordinated or collusive pricing by the merged entity and AT&T. With regard to the emerging carriers, the DOJ cited the same evidence as the opponents, arguing that "despite the fact that for many years a large number of long distance carriers have been competing and, in many ways, have offered materially lower prices than the Big 3, none has ever successfully attracted a substantial share of the nationwide mass markets" (DOJ 2000, p. 29). According to the DOJ's reasoning, this meant that the postmerger "Big 2" would be able to raise prices without losing sufficient sales to the competitive fringe to make the price increase unprofitable.

Large Customer Markets

Economic analysis played a very limited role in the analysis of the large customer market. Thus, we will limit our discussion to a very brief summary of the parties' positions. Interestingly, this part of the case was possibly the most critical to DOJ's decision to oppose the merger.

There are many segments in this market, but the greatest competitive concerns were for the sophisticated services provided to national and multinational corporations. These services include: managed data networks used to connect multiple business locations, enhanced toll-free voice services with call-management features, and sophisticated billing and accounting systems.

Prior to the mid-1990s, the only major suppliers in this market were the large long-distance carriers: the "Big 3." As the geographic reach and sophistication of the new entrants' networks increased, some of them began to bid for and win the business of the large business customers. The applicants argued that the new entrants' success and rapidly increasing sophistication was sufficient to control any exercise of market power postmerger. In particular, they argued that the new entrants had deployed sophisticated data networks that were fully capable of providing the complete set of services demanded by the large customers. Further, they claimed that large, sophisticated customers did not need more than two or three competitors bidding for contracts in order to drive prices down to competitive levels.

The opponents and the DOJ viewed the market differently. They did not believe that new entrants could deliver the services that customers wanted and did not regard potential competition as a sufficient substitute for actual competition in a market dominated by only two large long-distance carriers, regardless of the sophistication of the customers. Substantial barriers to entry existed, in their view, due to the requirement that a competitor "obtain the ubiquitous facilities-based networks, technological expertise, account management and sales staff, and advanced operational support systems. . . . These carriers must also hire the numerous highly skilled personnel needed to provide the level of customer support that most large business customers require . . ." (DOJ 2000, par. 163).

Large business customers also convinced the DOJ that they would not shift large amounts of business to a new entrant until the entrant had gained a reputation for reliability. According to the DOJ this led to a "Catch-22," which created a long lag in the time that it took for new entrants to begin effectively competing with the "Big 3":

> CNS [customer network services] customers demand that their carriers have a reputation for reliability. Smaller carriers cannot get experience and references without winning CNS contracts, but their lack of experience and references prevents many large business customers from purchasing CNS from these carriers. The only way a potential entrant can surmount this hurdle is to establish a track record of reliability on secondary contracts for large business and, over time, develop a reputation sufficient for a large business to award it a CNS contract. This is a difficult process that usually requires several years of effort. (DOJ 2000, par. 164)

Resolution of this issue in a court, had the case gone that far, would have hinged on evidence (e.g., testimony and documents) from large customers. This evidence would be much more powerful than the applicants' or opponents' submissions or economic analysis, because customers are perceived as a disinterested party not inclined to bias their position toward the merging parties or their competitors.

THE INTERNET BACKBONE

MCI WorldCom and Sprint were the first and second largest Internet backbone providers, with respective market shares of 37 percent and 16 percent (DOJ 2000). Antitrust authorities in the United States and Europe previously had exhibited great concern over increased concentration in the Internet at the time of the proposed merger between MCI and WorldCom in 1997 and, as a condition of approving that merger, required MCI to divest itself of its Internet business. To secure approval of this merger, MCI WorldCom and Sprint proposed divesting Sprint's Internet business. This offer was rejected. The EC ruled that the state of competition was precarious in the Internet backbone market and that Sprint's divested Internet backbone would be a much-weakened competitor to the dominant MCI WorldCom.[17]

The State of Competition in the Internet Market

The Internet is an interconnected "network of networks" that carries packets of data between two or more computers through thousands of interconnected networks. The Internet is described as a mesh, because it connects tens of millions of independent computers, communications entities, and information systems, without any rigid controls limiting the paths that users can set up to communicate with each other (Pelcovits and Cerf 2002). Firms play a variety of roles in the Internet, including providing content, providing dial-up and dedicated (always-on) access to consumers and businesses, and connecting smaller networks to each other. According to the antitrust authorities, a separate antitrust market exists for the function of interconnecting the smaller networks. This function is performed by "backbone" networks, which operate high-capacity long-haul transmission facilities and are interconnected with each other (DOJ 2000, p. 10).

The antitrust authorities further divided the market into tiers based on the mechanism used by the carriers to compensate each other for interconnection and delivery of traffic. The "Tier 1" carriers, including about ten firms, typically maintained peering relationships with each other whereby they agree to exchange and terminate traffic destined to their own customers on a payment-free basis. Smaller carriers were assigned to a lower tier because of their reliance on services purchased from larger carriers to reach the entire Internet. Many of these small carriers maintain peering relationships with other small carriers located in the same geographic region.

---

[17]The applicants never submitted a formal divestiture plan to the Department of Justice, hence the DOJ did not discuss the competitive consequences of a divestiture in its Complaint.

The authorities believed that the Tier 1 carriers had the ability to control access to the Internet, and therefore saw increased concentration in this market segment as a threat to competition. A major reason for this heightened level of concern was the role played by network externalities.

The Internet, like any telecommunications network, exhibits externalities. Network externalities are present when the value of a service to consumers rises as more consumers use it (Katz and Shapiro 1985). Network externalities have a profound effect in some industries, driving markets to a winner-take-all outcome, where one standard or technology dominates all others. Two classic examples of this outcome are the successes of the VHS standard for videotapes and the QWERTY standard for keyboards. In other cases, such as the Internet, which is aptly called a "network of networks," the power of network externalities has been harnessed to allow many firms to participate by using common standards to facilitate interconnection. The issue that has concerned antitrust authorities is whether the seamless interconnection of the many providers of Internet transport (the "backbones") would be disrupted if one of the providers were to gain a large market share.

The antitrust authorities in the United States and Europe presented the following fact pattern and scenario to describe how a larger and stronger MCI WorldCom could come to dominate the Internet (DOJ 2000, par. 28):

(a)   The Internet is a hierarchical network, with the top "Tier 1" providers maintaining unique interconnection arrangements with each other. Lower-ranked providers, the second Tier, are dependent upon the Tier 1 providers for universal connectivity.

(b)   The Tier 1 industry, which according to the DOJ constitutes a relevant antitrust market, is highly concentrated. MCI WorldCom is the largest provider, by far. Further consolidation would change MCI WorldCom's incentive to cooperate with other firms on interconnection. The presence of network externalities would mean that MCI WorldCom would become much more valuable to the smaller networks, than the smaller network would be to the larger network. This would provide the larger network with the capability to leverage its size and disadvantage its rivals.

(c)   MCI WorldCom would attempt to degrade the quality of interconnection provided to its rivals to induce customers to switch and buy service from itself. This strategy would have a life of its own and lead to tipping or "snowballing" as MCI WorldCom got stronger and its rivals even weaker. The ultimate result could be total monopolization of the Internet backbone by MCI WorldCom.

The applicants disputed these arguments on empirical and theoretical grounds. They disagreed with the market definition, claiming that the Internet was not hierarchical, but a complex web of networks and customers who could easily divert traffic away from any single backbone provider. For example, Internet service providers (e.g., AOL and MSN) could find other ways to connect to large websites (e.g., Amazon), or use new storage technologies to "cache" content on their own networks and reduce their usage of the backbone. The applicant's position was that a network could not leverage externalities in circumstances such as these, where it did not have bottleneck control over access to its customers.

The economic analysis underlying the theory of a dominant Internet backbone was developed in the case by Cremer, Rey, and Tirole (1999). They created two Cournot models of the Internet backbone: one model with three firms, the other with four firms in the market. The firms differed only in the size of their embedded customer base.[18] Competition for new customers depended on the prices charged and on the size of the network or networks that could be reached. Prior to the merger of two of the firms, all of the networks gained from perfect interconnection. In the three-firm model, the combination of two firms into a single firm with greater than 50 percent market share could make it profitable for this firm to deny interconnection to the smaller firm. In the four-firm model, the combination of two firms into a single firm with 50 percent market share could make it profitable for the merged firm to deny interconnection to *one* of its competitors. After the demise of this competitor, the merged firm would have a market share in excess of 50 percent, and it would then be in a position to deny interconnection to its only remaining rival.

The antitrust authorities rejected the applicant's arguments at the time of the MCI-WorldCom merger and again at the time of this proposed merger. The hypothesized doomsday scenario of a dominant firm with a market share in the range of 50 percent had a powerful influence on the EC and the DOJ and set the stage for a rejection of the applicants' offer to divest the Sprint Internet backbone.

The applicants understood at the outset that a merger of their Internet backbone businesses would not receive government approval. At the time of the WorldCom-MCI merger, antitrust agencies exhibited great concern over concentration in the Internet, and required the divestiture of one of the two companies' Internet business. The critical question in the context of the proposed MCI WorldCom-Sprint merger was whether a voluntary divestiture of Sprint's Internet business would be sufficient to satisfy the antitrust authorities' concerns about competition in the Internet backbone.

Although divestiture of an overlapping asset would seem to resolve competition concerns, there are several reasons why it might not, depending on the circumstances. The key issue is whether the divested entity will remain an effective competitor in the market, or whether the loss of relations with the old integrated firm, or the divestiture process itself, will

---

[18]This model was first presented to the EC at the time of the WorldCom-MCI merger. A revised model was presented in this case, and a final paper was published.

weaken competition in the market (Federal Trade Commission 1999). In this case, the DOJ never rendered an opinion on the proposed divestiture. The EC, however, rejected the proposal in very strong terms:

> Given the high growth of the Internet and the importance attached by con-
> sumers to the quality of service, any proposed business for divestiture
> should be in a position to compete fully and effectively from the date of
> transfer of ownership. Any difficulty met by the divested entity could re-
> sult in a limitation to its growth and lead quickly to a relative lowering of
> its market share. The combination of the uncertainties . . . make it
> highly unlikely that the divested entity would exercise in the short to
> medium term any competitive constrain [*sic*] on the parties. (EC Decision
> 2000)

The economics of the Internet remains a very controversial issue, which is deeply enmeshed in regulatory and legal proceedings. We can expect to see a growing economic literature on this topic so long as the stakes remain so high.

CONCLUSION

Events subsequent to the collapse of the proposed merger support several of the key contentions of the applicants. Residential and small business long-distance service has become a very low-margin commodity, which has led to the rapid erosion of the profits and stock prices of the long-distance providers. MCI WorldCom and AT&T have both struggled to enter local markets in an attempt to retain their long-distance customer bases. Sprint has withdrawn several efforts to enter local markets as a new competitor and focused its efforts on increasing its share of the wireless market. The RBOCs are steadily gaining authority to offer long-distance service on a bundled basis with their local service, and they have been very successful in the states they have entered.

The other side of the coin is the large business market, where severe financial problems of the emerging carriers have undoubtedly hobbled their efforts to offer sophisticated services to large business customers in competition with the "Big 3." A merger of MCI WorldCom and Sprint certainly would not have helped the situation of the emerging carriers and may on balance have reduced competition for these customers' business.

The longer-term effect of the collapse of this merger will depend on how telecommunications markets develop as the RBOCs are allowed to enter long-distance markets across the country. Most observers are predicting that there will be additional consolidation as some of the long-distance companies are acquired by the RBOCs. Competition for many services will then depend on whether the RBOCs compete head-to-head from their home regions or whether they will instead maintain a détente and preserve monopoly power in their own markets. Under this second scenario, the loss of a powerful, independent large long-distance company may turn out to be very costly to consumers.

REFERENCES

Besen, Stanley, and Steven Brenner. *Declaration of Stanley Besen and Steven Brenner.* Attached to Reply Comments of Sprint and MCI WorldCom, FCC Docket CC No. 99-333, March 20, 2000.

Carlton, Dennis W., and Hal S. Sider. *Declaration of Dennis W. Carlton and Hal S. Sider.* Attached to Opposition of SBC Communications, Inc., Federal Communications Commission, CC Docket 99-33, February 18, 2000.

The Commission of the European Communities. *Commission Decision of 28 June 2000, declaring a concentration incompatible with the common market and the EEA Agreement,* Case No COMP/M. 1741 (2000).

Cremer, Jacques, Patrick Rey, and Jean Tirole. "Connectivity in the Commercial Internet." *Journal of Industrial Economics* 48 (December 2000): 433–472.

Crooke, Philip, Luke Froeb, Steven Tschantz, and Gregory Werden, "The Effects of Assumed Demand Form on Simulated Post-Merger Equilibria." *Review of Industrial Organization* 15 (November 1999): 205–217.

Federal Communications Commission. *Memorandum Opinion and Order,* Application of WorldCom Inc. and MCI Communications Corporation for Transfer of Control of MCI Communications Corporation to WorldCom, Inc., Federal Communications Commission, September 14, 1998a.

Federal Communications Commission. *Press Statement of FCC Chairman William E. Kennard on Merger of WorldCom and MCI.* September 14, 1998b.

Federal Communications Commission, Common Carrier Bureau, Industry Analysis Division. *Long Distance Market Shares, Fourth Quarter 1998* (March 1999a).

Federal Communications Commission, Common Carrier Bureau, Industry Analysis Division. *Trends in Telephone Service,* Industry Analysis Division, September 1999b.

Federal Communications Commission. *Statistics of Communications Common Carriers.* October 1999c.

Froeb, Luke, 1996. "Merger Simulation: the Guidelines, Cases and Economics." *http:// www.antitrust.org/mergers/economics/simulation.html.*

Hall, Robert E. *Presentation on behalf of the merging parties by Robert E. Hall to the U.S. Department of Justice.* April 26, 2000.

Hausman, Jerry A. *Declaration of Professor Jerry A. Hausman.* Attached to Opposition of SBC Communications, Inc., FCC, CC Docket 99-33, February 18, 2000.

Hosken, Daniel, Daniel O'Brien, David Scheffman, and Michael Vita. "Demand System Estimation and its Application to Horizontal Merger Analysis." Federal Trade Commission, *http://www.ftc.gov/be/workpapers/wp246.pdf,* April, 2002.

Katz, Michael, and Carl Shapiro. "Network Externalities, Competition, and Compatibility." *American Economic Review* 75 (June 1985): 424–440.

Kraushaar, Jonathan M. *Fiber Deployment Update: End of Year 1998.* Industry Analysis Division, Common Carrier Bureau, FCC, September 1999.

MacAvoy, Paul W. *Declaration of Paul W. MacAvoy on Behalf of SBC Communications Inc.,* Supplemental Submission of SBC Communications Inc., FCC, CC Docket No. 99-333, May 12, 2000.

Ordover, Janusz A., and Robert D. Willig. "Economics and the 1992 Merger Guidelines: A Brief Survey." *Review of Industrial Organization* 8 (1993): 139–150.

SBC Communications. *Opposition of SBC Communications Inc.,* FCC, CC Docket No. 99-333, February 18, 2000.

Shapiro, Carl. "Mergers With Differentiated Products." Address by Carl Shapiro, Deputy Assistant Attorney General, U.S. Department of Justice, November 9, 1995. (*http://www.antitrust.org/law/US/shapSpeech.html*).

U.S. Department of Justice and Federal Trade Commission. "Horizontal Merger Guidelines." April 2, 1992.

U.S. Department of Justice. *Complaint, U.S.* v. *WorldCom, Inc. and Sprint Corporation,* filed in the United States District Court for the District of Columbia, June 26, 2000.

Ward, Michael. "Product Substitutability and Competition in Long-Distance Telecommunications." *Economic Inquiry* 37 (October 1999): 657–677.

Werden, Gregory, and Luke Froeb. "The Effects of Mergers in Differentiated Products Industries: Structural Merger Policy and the Logit Model." *Journal of Law, Economics, & Organization* 10 (1994): 407–426.

Werden, Gregory J., and Luke M. Froeb. "Simulation as an Alternative to Structural Merger Policy in Differentiated Products Industries." In *The Economics of the Antitrust Process,* edited by Malcolm Coates and Andrew Kleit. New York: Kluwer Academic Publishers, 1996.

CASE 5

The BP Amoco-ARCO Merger: Alaskan Crude Oil (2000)

Jeremy Bulow and
Carl Shapiro

INTRODUCTION

In March 1999 British Petroleum Amoco (BP) announced its intention to acquire the Atlantic Richfield Company (ARCO) for $25.6 billion in stock. As one of the largest oil mergers ever, the BP/ARCO deal was sure to attract intense public attention as well as antitrust scrutiny. Attention was further heightened because the deal was part of a more general consolidation in the unloved oil industry. In particular, the BP-ARCO deal came close on the heels of the massive 1997 Shell-Texaco joint venture, BP's December 1998 acquisition of Amoco, and the then-pending Exxon-Mobil merger.

At the heart of the BP-ARCO deal was the combination of the firms' Alaska North Slope (ANS) crude oil reserves and related operations. The huge Prudhoe Bay oil field was the only one in the United States to have two operators. By 1999, with production having fallen by more than one-half since its 1988 peak, it had become far more efficient to have just one operator. Furthermore, the three primary owners of ANS—BP, ARCO, and Exxon—had disparate shares of oil and gas production. Exxon, for example, owned a larger share of the gas than the oil. This conflict made it more difficult for the partners to agree on an efficient development strategy.

Bulow served as the Director of the Bureau of Economics at the Federal Trade Commission at the time that the Commission reviewed the BP-ARCO merger. Shapiro served as a consultant and expert witness on behalf of BP and ARCO in the antitrust review and litigation of their merger. The opinions expressed here are an amalgam of the sometimes distinct views held by the two authors, and should not be attributed to the Federal Trade Commission, individual commissioners, or to BP or ARCO. We thank Simon Board, John Hayes, Paul Klemperer, and the editors for helpful comments on an earlier draft.

Overall, BP estimated it could save $100–200 million per year from reorganizing Prudhoe.[1] But the consolidation raised antitrust concerns. Exxon and some smaller investors were minority shareholders in the fields but did not operate in Alaska. Thus, the combined BP-ARCO would own 74 percent of ANS production and would operate every oil field in the state.

BP entered the antitrust review process with considerable optimism. From its perspective, the deal was quite "clean" on antitrust grounds. Downstream, BP had no West Coast refining and marketing assets, so the merger would not affect concentration there. Upstream, the overlap was in the production of crude oil, arguably a world market where the combined share of BP and ARCO was quite small. But BP also recognized that there were various upstream overlaps related to the exploration, production, and transportation of ANS.

The Federal Trade Commission (FTC), along with the states of California, Oregon, and Washington, was keenly interested in how the merger would affect the buyers of ANS, namely West Coast refineries, as well as final consumers, such as motorists. While the commission typically evaluates deals based on the effect on consumer welfare alone, as opposed to the sum of consumer and producer welfare, it presumed that an increase in prices charged to refineries would be largely passed along to final consumers. The state of Alaska had considerable interest in the deal, because of its strong financial interest in oil production (due to royalties, which dominate the state budget) and employment issues.

The FTC staff and the state of Alaska originally divided responsibility for the case so that the state would focus on the upstream (oil exploration and development, pipelines, and marine transportation) and the FTC mainly on the downstream (sales of ANS to West Coast refineries, impact on refined product prices). The theory behind this division of duties was that the state had more expertise in Alaska-specific issues, and that the interests of both the state and the Commission were to promote competition in exploration and development upstream. Downstream there was a divergence of interests, with the Commission preferring lower oil prices for consumers and the state preferring higher prices, which form the basis of its considerable royalties.[2]

While BP and ARCO dominated the North Slope, ARCO was also a major player downstream in California refining and marketing—businesses BP was not in. In fact, ARCO used all its own North Slope production and bought additional crude for its own refineries, raising questions regarding the treatment of captive capacity and the role of integrated firms in merger

---

[1]BP estimated the overall savings from its acquisition of ARCO at more than $1 billion per year, mostly from consolidating managerial and administrative operations.

[2]As we shall see, only after Alaska settled with BP by negotiating the Alaska Charter did the Commission begin to focus seriously on upstream issues.

analysis.[3] From a legal perspective, should the deal be viewed as "horizontal," since BP and ARCO were both major *producers* of ANS, or "vertical," since ARCO was a *net buyer* of ANS on the West Coast while BP was a major supplier to ARCO competitors such as Chevron and Tosco?[4]

The analysis of the BP-ARCO merger can be divided into two major parts: upstream issues in Alaska, and downstream issues on the West Coast.[5] We organize our analysis along precisely these lines, starting with the upstream issues. As we shall see, however, an upstream divestiture of assets negotiated between BP and the state of Alaska would prove to have a major impact on the downstream analysis.

THE UPSTREAM CASE:
EXPLORATION AND BIDDING FOR OIL TRACT LEASES

The state of Alaska and the federal government regularly auction off the rights to explore and drill for oil on new tracts of land on Alaska's North Slope (both on-shore and off-shore).[6] Under the terms of these auctions, bidders offer a price per acre, subject to a minimum. Winning bidders on a given tract of land obtain exclusive drilling and extraction rights to that tract, but must then pay rent on that tract as well as royalties on any oil that is extracted from it.

As any other sellers would, the state and federal governments benefit from competition in these auctions. The basic upstream antitrust issue was whether the merger of BP and ARCO would substantially reduce competition in these auctions, thus leading to a loss of revenue for the state and federal governments and perhaps to a slower rate of development of North Slope oil tracts.

There were good reasons for Alaska to fear that the merger would reduce its revenues from auctions of oil exploration and production rights. BP and ARCO had historically been the largest bidders in auctions of oil leases

---

[3]The issue of captive capacity was a common one for the FTC. Generally, it preferred to ignore captive capacity, as when it calculated the market share of Intel in microprocessors by ignoring IBM's production for its own use.

[4]Plus, some of ARCO's major competitors (Exxon) were integrated upstream while others (Chevron) had few or no assets in Alaska.

[5]There were also potential antitrust issues involving the Trans-Alaska Pipeline System (TAPS) and marine transportation of crude oil from Valdez, Alaska, to the U.S. West Coast. We do not explore those issues in this case.

[6]The Alaska Department of Natural Resources (ADNR) administers state leases. The Bureau of Land Management (BLM) administers lease sales for federal on-shore properties, and the Mineral Management Service (MMS) administers leases for offshore Outer Continental Shelf federal properties.

in the State of Alaska.[7] In the decade prior to the merger, ARCO accounted for 38.4 percent of all successful bids and BP for 20.2 percent.[8] Other major bidders were Chevron, Phillips, Anadarko, and Petrofina. The FTC estimated that BP and ARCO had been the top *two* bidders on about 15 percent of all the leases that the state had sold. A loss of revenue equal to the difference between the highest and second highest bids in those auctions would have cost the state and federal governments about $100 million in real terms over the bidding history of the North Slope. Recently, the two firms appeared to be in serious competition with one another in auctions on the western part of the North Slope, in the Alpine and the National Petroleum Reserve-Alaska (NPRA) fields.

As usual in any merger involving a bidding market, one must look at the key assets necessary to be an effective bidder, as well as the actual shares of the merging firms in winning, or placing, bids. Here, the key assets include (1) control over processing facilities and feeder pipelines valuable for oil production in new areas; (2) knowledge of the North Slope and experience in operating oil fields there; and (3) three-dimensional (3D) seismic data of the North Slope. In areas (1) and (2), BP and ARCO had advantages over other bidders and could be expected to have lower costs than their competitors for actually conducting North Slope operations. Anyone else who won an oil lease probably would need to negotiate with BP and/or ARCO to provide important services, such as processing facilities, pipelines, or operator services.

Due to their possession of 3D seismic data, BP and ARCO also had some informational advantage over other bidders. The magnitude and durability of this advantage was an issue in the merger review. The data were collected and initially processed by an independent firm, Western Geophysical, raising the possibility that other firms could also contract to obtain such data in the future (as well as obtain existing data as part of a divestiture package).

Information is critical in these auctions; put simply, auctions for oil leases are an information-intensive business. There are good reasons to believe that a bidder with superior information in an area will win the lion's share of the tracts in that area and make almost all of the money.[9] Unin-

---

[7]Some very interesting issues (beyond the scope of this case) arise in these auctions because joint bidding is common. Even the calculation of market shares is not straightforward in the presence of joint bidding.

[8]These bidding data are publicly available. See ADNR 1999.

[9]To illustrate, suppose that an oil field has a true value that is equally likely to be any amount between 0 and 100. One informed bidder knows the exact value, while others are literally clueless, other than knowing the distribution. Each firm submits a sealed bid, with the highest bid winning. Then the (Bayesian Nash) equilibrium is that the informed bidder will bid half the true value and the uninformed bidders will randomize in such a way that the highest bid among them will be equally likely to be any amount between 0 and 50. In this equilibrium, the informed bidder bids $v/2$ where v is the true value, and each uninformed bidder makes zero in expectation regardless of how much it bids: contingent on winning it knows that the true value must be between 0 and twice its

formed bidders do hold down the profits of the informed bidders—if the uninformed bidders did not participate, then a single informed bidder could win all the licenses for next to nothing—but the seller's revenue is considerably lower than when there is competition between *two* informed bidders.

The state of Alaska and the federal government had a strong interest in ensuring that they would receive full value for their property by having competition between equally well-informed bidders. If the two best-informed bidders were to merge, it might be necessary for the state and the federal government to protect themselves in other ways, such as by raising the minimum price or royalty rate at which they would lease fields. But increased minimum prices might cause some leases that otherwise would have been purchased to go unsold. This is hardly a phantom concern: Leases had been awarded on only about 40 percent of the acreage available in state auctions prior to the proposed merger.

During November 1999 Alaska negotiated an agreement with BP that was intended to preserve upstream competition in the bidding for leases and more generally to preserve competition on the North Slope. This agreement known as the "Alaska Charter", was unveiled on December 2, 1999. Under the terms of the Alaska Charter, BP would sell 175 thousand barrels per day (MBD) of ARCO's production to two other production companies[10] along with seismic data and other upstream assets that would make these companies stronger bidders on the North Slope.[11]

BP felt that the Alaska Charter fully addressed the upstream issues raised by Alaska and the FTC. It also believed that the state was the natural party with which to negotiate upstream issues since the FTC seemed focused on the downstream issues, and anyway the state had much greater expertise than the FTC in Alaskan production. Once the Alaska Charter was negotiated, Alaska and BP became allies, at least to the extent of arguing that the Alaska Charter dealt adequately with upstream competition issues. Nonetheless, the FTC later challenged the BP-ARCO merger in court primarily because of upstream issues.

It is doubtful that the FTC knew better than the state about competition within Alaska, but the FTC might have had a better sense of its own bargaining position. For example, the state may have been concerned that if it went to court the government would lose the case and the merger would go through as announced. The FTC probably recognized that BP would regard going to court as very costly. Furthermore, once the state had negotiated the

---

bid, while if the high uninformed bid is equally likely to be any amount between 0 and 50 the informed bidder will maximize expected profits by bidding v/2. See, for example, Klemperer (1999) for a primer on basic auction theory.

[10]BP was willing to sell all 175 MBD to one buyer if that was the FTC's preference.

[11]The Alaska Charter also required BP to divest the necessary pipeline and tanker capacity to bring this crude oil to the West Coast. We discuss the impact of the Alaska Charter on downstream markets below. The Alaska Charter is available at http://www.bp.com/alaska/ARCO/charter.htm.

Alaska Charter, its terms would have been binding on BP even if the FTC lost a bid to block the merger. In that sense, the Charter reduced the riskiness to the merger's biggest skeptics of going to federal court to block the merger.

One concern at the FTC was that while ARCO Alaska (the unit within ARCO conducting ARCO's Alaskan operations) was a going business, the smaller companies created or enhanced under the terms of the Alaska Charter might not be viable competitors. These concerns were partially based upon a study of divestitures conducted by the FTC's Bureau of Competition (FTC 1999). This study measured the success of a divestiture by whether the divested assets were later "operated viably" in the same industry they had operated in prior to the divestiture. Of twenty-two divestitures of whole businesses, nineteen were deemed successful by this measure. Of the fifteen divestitures of something other than whole businesses, only six were successful.[12] In addition, information economics implied that the commission should put a thumb on the scale in favor of divesting complete businesses rather than a set of assets cobbled together from two or more separate enterprises.[13] This "clean sweep" policy of selling whole businesses intact made three commissioners lean heavily in the direction of requiring a complete divestiture of ARCO Alaska, or at least something close to it.

The Alaska Charter was negotiated well before the FTC challenged the BP-ARCO deal in court. Therefore, it was natural and sensible to evaluate the impact of the proposed merger *given the Alaska Charter.* Though designed to deal with the *upstream* issues in the case, the Alaska Charter in fact eliminated the rationale for the commission's *downstream* case, which is precisely where the FTC's pre-Charter efforts had been concentrated. This realization gradually led to a change in the FTC's approach to the case, and affected the subsequent litigation in federal court.

WEST COAST CRUDE OIL SURPLUS, DEFICIT, AND ARBITRAGE CONDITIONS

The remainder of this case study focuses on the downstream impact of the merger. The basic downstream antitrust issue in the BP-ARCO merger was whether the acquisition of ARCO would allow BP to elevate the price of ANS crude oil to West Coast refineries. Ultimately, higher ANS crude oil prices might lead to higher prices of refined products, especially gasoline, on the West Coast. Certainly this concern was salient to politicians in Cali-

---

[12]There were scientific concerns about the study within the Commission; also, a proper study of the success of the Commission's divestiture policy should evaluate whether consumers were ultimately helped or hurt by the Commission's orders. The Bureau of Competition report ignored this important factor.

[13]A good example of the "sell a whole business" concept was the FTC's decision to ask Exxon Mobil to sell the Exxon jet oil business, which operated on a stand-alone basis, instead of the Mobil business, which did not.

fornia, Oregon, and Washington. To address these issues, we begin with some background information on the supply and demand of crude oil on the West Coast.

Quantities, Imports and Exports

In the mid-1970s, West Coast refineries relied largely on California crude oil and imported crude oils. Roughly 45 percent of the crude oil used in PADD V[14] was from California, 45 percent from imports, and 10 percent from Cook Inlet in Alaska. The West Coast was "in deficit"; that is, it was a large net importer of crude. Total use of crude oil was roughly 2.5 million barrels per day, or 2500 MBD.

These conditions were changed dramatically by Alaskan North Slope production of crude oil. ANS production started in 1977, peaked around 1990 at about 2000 MBD, and has now declined to about 1000 MBD, as shown in Figure 5-1.

When ANS production was high, the West Coast was "in surplus" as a net exporter of crude. But by 1999 the West Coast was again deeply in deficit, importing more than 600 MBD of crude oil, as shown in Figure 5-2. By 1999, some 42 percent of crude oil used on the West Coast was from Alaska, 33 percent from California, and 25 percent from imports; see Figure 5-3. Of the Alaskan oil, three-fifths was sold on the merchant market (this includes all of BP's ANS), and the rest was transferred internally (primarily ARCO and Exxon ANS crude oil used in their own West Coast refineries).

Crude Oil Prices

As a general principle, the price of ANS crude oil closely tracks other crude oil prices over time. Figure 5-4 shows the price of ANS and a number of other crude oils between 1989 and 1999. In this sense, crude oil prices on the West Coast are governed by conditions in the world crude oil market. The spike in prices in 1991, for example, reflects the Gulf War. The correlations among these different crude oil price series are very high, typically in the 0.97 to 0.99 range. However, price differentials between different grades of crude oil do vary somewhat over time. We will be examining these differentials closely. In particular, we look closely at the time series of the difference between the price of ANS crude oil and the price of the benchmark West Texas Intermediate crude oil (WTI).[15]

The price differentials between ANS and WTI crude oils can largely be explained by import and export arbitrage conditions. In the late 1980s and

---

[14]Much of the data in this industry actually covers Petroleum Area Defense District (PADD) V, which encompasses not only California, Oregon, and Washington, but also Alaska, Hawaii, and Arizona.

[15]ANS is more "sour" and thus cheaper than WTI, so the ANS-WTI price differentials are negative numbers.

FIGURE 5-1 Alaska North Slope Crude Oil Production, 1977–2005

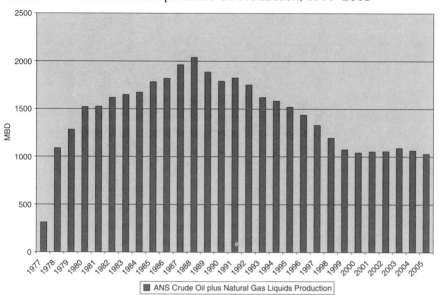

Source: State of Alaska Department of Natural Resources. Note: 2000–2005 data are projected.

early 1990s, the West Coast was in surplus, and foreign exports of ANS crude oil were prohibited. Therefore, some ANS crude oil had to be transported beyond the West Coast to the Virgin Islands and the Gulf of Mexico, where it would compete with WTI and other crudes. Competitive market arbitrage implied that the West Coast price should be the price in the alternative markets, *minus* the incremental transit costs. In the late 1990s, with the region in *deficit,* transit was going the other way. A competitive West Coast price for ANS crude oil should have reflected the price of crude in other markets, *plus* any incremental cost of shipping that crude to the West Coast. The price of ANS crude oil rose relative to WTI crude oil by about $1.50 from 1993 to 1995, as the market moved from surplus to balance and later into deficit (see Figure 5-2).

Ironically, the move from surplus to deficit both raised prices and reduced the chance that the merger would elevate ANS crude prices. Once the West Coast was in deficit, BP, ARCO, and Exxon were able to sell their oil at the cost of imports plus transit costs from a competitive world market. Increasing the shortage by exporting out of the region would not raise prices very much, as the supply of imports was highly elastic, and therefore would only be a viable strategy if transport costs were very low. By contrast, in the early 1990s it was theoretically possible that an increase in exports could have raised prices significantly by moving total supply from surplus to shortage, potentially making exports profitable for a large supplier, even one with high transit costs.

FIGURE 5-2 PADD V Imports and Exports, 1989–1999

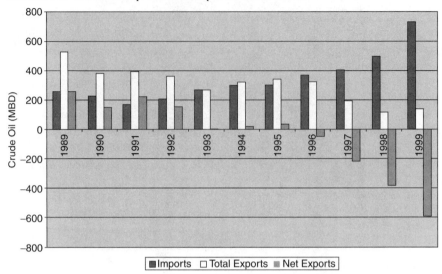

Source: Department of Energy (Energy Information Administration) and company data.

FIGURE 5-3 Usage of Crude Oil in PADD V, 1999

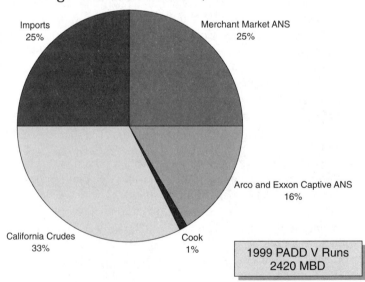

Source: Company data.

FIGURE 5-4 Monthly Prices (per barrel) for Select Market Crudes

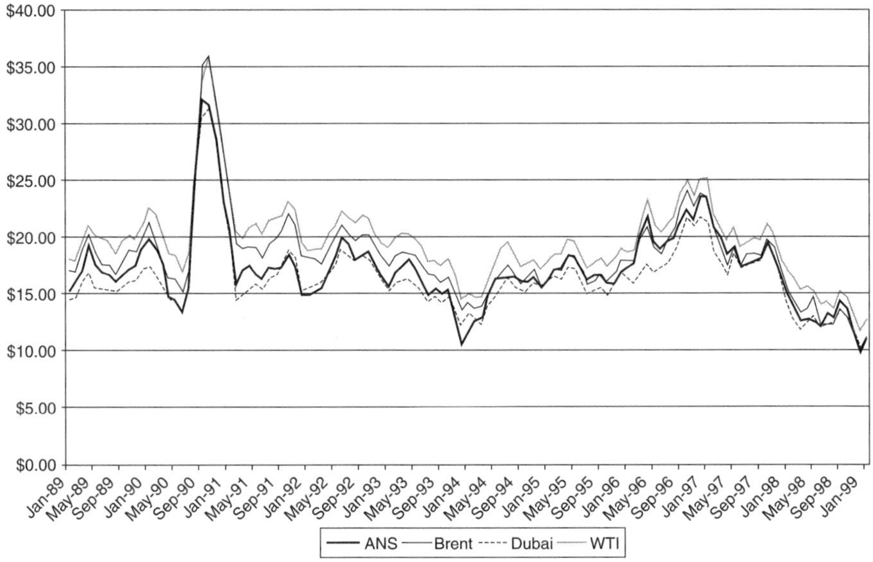

Source: Reuters (ANS), Nymex (WTI), Platts (Brent and Oman).

Demand for ANS since 1995

Since 1995, as shown in Figure 5-2, PADD V has increasingly relied upon imports to meet its crude oil needs. Data from this period provide strong evidence that West Coast refineries were capable of replacing ANS crude oil with foreign crude oils without incurring substantial incremental costs as a result of this substitution. In other words, the intermediate to long-term elasticity of demand for ANS crude oil on the West Coast is very high. Imported crude oils are very close substitutes for ANS crude oils.

The experience of California refineries is illustrative. From 1995 to 2001, ANS crude sold in California declined by 342 MBD, from 725 MBD to 383 MBD; balancing this, imports rose by 370 MBD, from 156 MBD to 526 MBD.[16] Despite this tremendous decline in ANS crude oil availability, the price of ANS crude did not rise at all relative to the price of WTI. In 1995, ANS crude sold for an average of $5.91 per barrel less than WTI; in 2001, the differential was actually higher, at $6.44.[17]

Declining ANS crude oil production is a wonderful natural experiment that reveals a great deal about the demand for ANS crude oil on the West

---

[16]Source: http://www.energy.ca.gov/fuels/oil/_crude_oil_receipts.html.

[17]These data are taken from the Energy Information Administration website. See http://www.eia.doe.gov/pub/oil_gas/petroleum/data_publications/petroleum_marketing_monthly/current/pdf/pmmtab22.pdf. In real terms the ANS discount declined slightly.

Coast. A huge, exogenous supply shock (gradually over a period of years) is perfect for statistically "identifying" the demand curve. Since large declines in ANS crude oil production were accommodated without any increase in price (since the West Coast went into deficit in 1995), we know that the shift from ANS crude oil to imported crude oils was quite inexpensive for West Coast refineries as a group. In other words, the intermediate-run elasticity of demand for ANS crude oil specifically is extremely high.[18] We say "intermediate-run" here because the decline in ANS crude oil production was widely anticipated, so refineries could and did plan to shift away from ANS crude oil. California refineries were required to renovate substantially to meet new environmental standards (specifically, to produce the so-called CARB gasoline required by the California Air Resources Board), and it was reasonable for refiners to increase their flexibility in the crude oils that they could process as part of their renovations.

This flexibility can be seen at the refinery level, as well as in the aggregate. Major refineries on the West Coast were owned by Chevron, ARCO, Equilon (a joint venture of Shell and Texaco), Tosco, and others. While some refineries made little change in their crude oil slate during the 1990s, others, most notably Chevron, made dramatic shifts toward greater use of imports.

Implications for the BP-ARCO Merger

The primary mechanism for raising West Coast prices after the merger would have been for BP to increase exports to the Far East. But experience from 1995 to 1999 showed that reduced ANS crude oil shipments would not, over the intermediate and long term, lead to higher crude prices. Even over the short run, it appeared that exports could only be profitable if shipping costs were extremely low.

For precisely these reasons, both of the authors concluded that the proposed merger would not elevate ANS crude oil prices on the West Coast in any significant way; this conclusion was even stronger after the negotiation of the Alaska Charter, which further reduced BP's incentive or ability to export ANS crude oil to the Far East. But these conclusions needed to be tested against, and reconciled with, evidence on BP's premerger ANS crude oil trading and export strategies, to which we now turn.

BP'S ANS EXPORT AND PRICING STRATEGY

We now examine how this high-level, long-term view of the market based on import and export arbitrage conditions contrasts with the short-term

---

[18]See "Market Definition in Crude Oil: Estimating the Effects of the BP/ARCO Merger," by John Hayes, Carl Shapiro, and Robert Town, for an econometric analysis of the demand for ANS crude oil.

strategies adopted by BP for exporting ANS crude oil and for pricing ANS crude oil to West Coast refineries.

BP's export, trading, and pricing strategies for ANS crude oil provide an excellent example of how basic economic principles can be used in business. BP's short-term trading activities, conducted in the context of a competitive world market for crude oil, illustrate nicely one of the basic tools of price theory, namely the distinction between price and marginal revenue. While there was some dispute over whether BP had any meaningful market power, even in the short run, there was little doubt that BP's export, trading, and pricing strategies applied standard microeconomic principles that are taught to students and are used by many businesses to maximize profits. There was never any suggestion that BP's basic export and pricing strategies were exclusionary or somehow "unfair." Rather, the question was whether they indicated that BP possessed market power, and, if so, whether that market power would be enhanced by its acquisition of ARCO.

Naturally, refineries may enjoy far less flexibility in their choices of crude oils over the short term (a few weeks or months) than over the intermediate or long term, when refineries can be modified to handle alternative crude oils. A close look at BP's sale of ANS to West Coast refineries therefore gives us an opportunity to explore the following classic puzzle: can a supplier exercise persistent *short-term* market power even if *long-term* demand is highly elastic?

When one looks more closely at the sale of ANS crude oil on the West Coast, the simple long-term picture driven by arbitrage conditions, while reflective of overall competitive conditions, becomes considerably more complex. To begin with, the *average* reported price of ANS crude oil (as used above) masks some variation in prices across different refinery customers. In fact, there was strong evidence that BP was able to exert some modest market power in the short run, even though in the medium to long term BP was very much subject to the powerful arbitrage constraints described above. The primary evidence regarding BP's short-term market power was BP's own pricing strategy and behavior; evidence on price discrimination was also present, but was murkier. We discuss these types of evidence in turn.

As we turn to look more closely at BP's trading strategies, it is well to bear in mind that here, as in other commodity markets, conditions change week to week and traders are always attempting to assess the strength or weakness of the market. In the West Coast crude oil business, demand can suddenly shift down if a refinery experiences an outage or if a pipeline carrying refined products has a fire; supply can be disrupted due to problems on the North Slope, on the Trans-Alaska Pipeline Systems (TAPS), at Valdez (the terminus of TAPS where ANS is loaded onto tankers), or with the oil tankers that bring oil from Valdez to the West Coast. Market conditions also shift if, for example, a refinery arranges for an extra cargo to be delivered from the Mideast and thus requires less Alaska crude oil in two or three months time. In short, even in highly competitive commodity markets, short-term supply and demand imbalances often occur, in some cases conferring short-term market power on certain market participants.

BP's Optimizer Model

BP's approach to selling ANS on the West Coast was highly scientific. BP used a tool called the Optimizer Model to inform its crude oil trading activities on the West Coast. Basically, the Optimizer Model was BP's attempt to estimate the short-run demand curve for ANS crude oil on the West Coast and to account for how spot prices would affect BP's revenues on its term contracts. By looking carefully at each refinery customer, BP attempted to estimate the price at which that customer would substitute imported crude oil for ANS. For example, the Optimizer Model might indicate that (given the price of other crude oils) a particular refinery would buy an extra 15 MBD of ANS crude oil if it could be acquired at $3.00 less than the price of WTI. This estimate of demand might depend on the availability of other crude oils as well as the prices at which different outputs (gasoline, jet fuel, diesel fuel) could be sold by that refinery, since the output mix would be affected by the input mix. BP used the Optimizer Model in two main ways, which we discuss in turn.

Exports to the Far East

First, BP sought to price discriminate between the West Coast and the Far East. BP sold a significant volume of its ANS crude oil to West Coast refineries according to term contracts that specified a price linked to the U.S. West Coast (USWC) spot price for ANS crude oil. Shipments to the Far East had the effect of "tightening" the West Coast market, thereby increasing USWC spot prices and yielding BP higher revenues on its West Coast term contracts. By some estimates, BP at times found it profitable to sell in the Far East for a netback (price less transportation cost) that was up to forty cents per barrel lower than it could get in California.[19] In economic terms, if BP sold the last cargo to Korea the price and marginal revenue from the shipment would be the same, but if BP instead sent this cargo to the West Coast the slight easing it would cause in West Coast contract prices (multiplied by the far larger volume sold under the term contracts than sold on the spot market) would mean that BP's marginal revenue would be forty to fifty cents below the price it would receive.

---

[19]The formula relating marginal revenue (MR) to price (P), when all competitors' quantities are held fixed, is $MR = P(1 + s/Z)$, where s is the firm's market share and Z is the demand elasticity. In this case if the price of crude oil was $15.00 a barrel and the elasticity of demand was -15, then if BP had a 40 percent market share there would be a $0.40 differential on the West Coast between marginal revenue and price.

Furthermore, it was often feasible for BP to get a Far East netback that was within forty to fifty cents of the West Coast netback. While the cost of shipping from Alaska to Korea on a *charter* was several dollars per barrel more than shipping to California, BP owned some excess shipping capacity in the late 1990s, since the decline in ANS crude oil production had left BP with more Jones Act[20] tankers in Alaska than it had capacity to use, at least until tanker retirements caught up with the production decline. All ships transporting Alaskan oil were and are Jones Act vessels. The decline in North Slope production created a short-run excess supply of Jones Act shipping capacity, which could not be practically used elsewhere. So effectively the marginal cost of shipping to the Far East instead of the United States, given that the crew and tanker were already paid for, was only the extra fuel cost. BP's excess shipping capacity made the short-term economics of exporting much more attractive than they would be if long-run costs had to be considered: It would never be profitable to build Jones Act tankers for the purpose of exporting from Alaska to Asia. The FTC's economic analysis thus implied that BP would stop exporting as soon as tanker retirements caught up with the decline in Alaskan oil production. In fact exports virtually ceased in April 2000.

BP's ability to influence the price of ANS through exports, at least in the short term, was highly significant to the FTC, which viewed the optimizer model as proof that BP had at least some market power. BP's contracts tying ANS crude oil prices to USWC prices instead of a world benchmark such as WTI represented some of the best economic evidence that the ANS crude oil prices moved somewhat separately from WTI prices. If the ANS crude oil price were rigidly tied to the WTI price, why would the vast majority of BP's contracts be based on a separate West Coast ANS crude oil price? After all, the USWC market had to be less liquid and more easily subject to manipulation. One explanation would be that refiners might have preferred USWC pricing if they thought that the prices that they would receive for their output would be more closely tied to the USWC price. But this would imply that differences between the USWC and world prices not only were likely to occur but to be passed through to consumers, an additional concern to the FTC.

However, if the Optimizer Model presented the clearest evidence that BP operated as though it had at least some market power, it also indicated that BP did not think it had very much at all. Even if BP exported to its physical limit (which it did not), the model predicted that West Coast prices of ANS crude oil would be only slightly higher than if there were no exports at all. The FTC's expert witness, Preston McAfee (2001), estimated that BP's exports raised the price of ANS by about a half a cent per gallon at the refinery level.

---

[20]The Jones Act (also known as the Merchant Marine Act of 1920) and related statutes require that vessels used to transport cargo and passengers between U.S. ports be owned by U.S. citizens, built in U.S. shipyards, and manned by U.S. citizen crews.

Negotiations with Refineries on the West Coast

BP negotiated terms and conditions separately with each refinery customer. These terms were then reflected in the Optimizer Model. In a purely competitive market everyone would be buying at the same margin of price over cost. BP claimed that some of the price differences across refineries were due to cost differences in supplying different refineries (it is cheaper to supply a refinery with superior port facilities, or a refinery that fits better with the supplier's marine logistics). But some of the price differences were simply the result of bilateral bargaining. While some within the FTC gave some credence to the cost explanations, others viewed price differentials among West Coast refineries as further evidence that BP had market power.

The Impact of BP's ANS Exports on Prices

While it was clear what BP was doing, because BP's thinking was so systematic, BP's actions probably had very little impact on the average price of ANS crude oil on the West Coast, and even less of an effect on gasoline prices. Certainly, if one takes the longer-term view described earlier, dramatically declining ANS shipments to the West Coast had no lasting impact on ANS crude oil prices, so BP's much smaller exports could not have had any lasting effect on crude oil prices, much less gasoline prices. Even if one focuses on the BP's short-term trading and exporting strategies, however, the magnitude of their impact was quite small, as we now demonstrate.

Crude Oil Prices

Exports of ANS crude oil to the Far East averaged about 80 MBD during the mid- to late-1990s.[21] Even assuming that all these exports were BP's (close) and that none of the exports would have been made in a competitive market (this is not correct; for example, West Coast refinery shutdowns would sometimes push California netbacks below Far East netbacks), then the impact on ANS prices would have been small—recall McAfee's estimate of a half penny a gallon. From a larger perspective, ANS production had declined by hundreds of MBDs during the mid- to late-1990s with no increase in the price of ANS relative to other crude oil prices, casting serious doubt on the proposition that 80 MBD of ANS exports would elevate ANS prices on the West Coast, given the elastic supply of imported crude oil.[22]

---

[21]The actual averages of exports from PADD V for 1995–1999 were 94, 94, 78, 54, and 74 MBD, returning to 92 MBD during the first four months of 2000. Source: Petroleum Supply Annual, various issues. It is fair to assume that the vast majority of these exports were ANS, and the vast majority of the ANS exports were sold by BP.

[22]The November 2002 earthquake in Alaska caused an unanticipated reduction in ANS supplies of about 3 million barrels (3 days' supply) but apparently did not affect West Coast prices. See Barrionuevo (2002).

Gasoline Prices

How would a penny per gallon elevation of the price of ANS crude oil affect average *gasoline* prices on the West Coast?[23] Here is an illustrative calculation.[24]

Economic theory says that if the downstream market is competitive then a parallel upward shift in the market marginal cost or supply curve should be passed through in proportion to the relative elasticities of supply and demand. The passthrough rate for increases in marginal costs is $S/(D + S)$, where D is the absolute value of the elasticity of demand and S is the elasticity of supply. It is fair to say that both supply and demand for gasoline are highly inelastic on the West Coast, so any estimate of the specific pass-through rate would involve the division of one small number by the sum of two small numbers, and therefore be of questionable reliability.[25]

A related issue was how much an increase in the cost of ANS crude oil would affect the marginal cost of production of refined products. This depends upon the elasticity of substitution between ANS and other crude oils, especially imported crude oils. As a first approximation, one could say that if ANS comprised 40 percent of the crude oil used on the West Coast, then a 1 percent increase in ANS crude oil prices might lead to a 0.40 percent increase in marginal costs.[26] So, even if 100 percent of any marginal cost increase were passed through to consumers, as would happen if the supply curve were flat, then the overall pass-through rate of ANS crude oil prices to gasoline prices would be 40 percent. If only ANS crude oil merchant market sales are counted, the relevant figure would be only 25 percent (see Figure 5-3).

Given the agreement by all of the FTC investigators in the Exxon-Mobil merger that the supply curve of refiners was quite inelastic, which would imply a lower pass-through rate, 45 percent seemed to be a reasonable working upper bound on the actual pass-through rate of ANS prices to gasoline prices. If this logic is followed, a penny a gallon of ANS crude oil would translate to an average of no more than 0.45 cents per gallon of gasoline, and probably quite a bit less.

---

[23]One barrel contains forty-two gallons. As a rule of thumb, one barrel of crude oil produces one barrel of gasoline. The production process involves some loss of volume, but this is made up by the addition of other inputs, which adds to volume. So, forty-two cents per barrel of crude oil translates roughly into a penny a gallon.

[24]The passthrough rate of crude oil prices to gasoline prices was the subject of considerable attention in the BP-ARCO merger. Space limitations do not permit us to develop this vertical part of the analysis further in the current case.

[25]The General Accounting Office (1999) estimated that the prices of ANS and certain comparable California crudes increased by $0.98 to $1.30 per barrel during the mid-1990s, but also estimated that the effect at the consumer level was "insignificant." Given the small change in the relative price of ANS over the 1990s while production declined by 1000 MBD, this estimate of the effect of 80 MBD of exports on crude prices seems implausibly high. However, a zero pass-through rate of refinery-level cost increases to consumers seems implausibly low.

[26]This would be precisely right with Cobb-Douglas production functions.

Furthermore, any price discrimination between refineries would be unlikely to affect retail prices. With perfect price discrimination an ANS crude oil monopolist would sell its oil to the same firms, in exactly the same quantities, as would occur in a market with price-taking, competitive ANS crude oil suppliers. While refineries would pay more in the price discrimination case for the same quantity of ANS crude oil, there would be no efficiency loss, implying that the quantity of all outputs produced at the retail level, and therefore all retail prices, would be exactly as in the competitive case. Compared to the simple monopoly (no price discrimination) case, where a monopolist could only raise its price by cutting output or, more likely, exporting, consumers would be *better* off with perfect refinery price discrimination because the monopolist would no longer need to export to get a high price and therefore would supply more to the domestic refiners.

One could envision that a modest increase in ANS crude oil prices resulting from exports might have some long-run impact on entry and exit from refining; however, due to the nature of the industry, that was very unlikely. First, no new refinery has been built in the United States in several decades, so de novo entry was highly unlikely in the best of circumstances. Second, while firms did invest in upgrading refineries to expand output by 1 or 2 percent per year, it is unclear whether BP's strategy served to dampen or increase such investment. A byproduct of many refinery upgrades was to reduce the refiner's dependence on any specific crude oil such as ANS. If BP behaved opportunistically, then a refiner might be *more* motivated to upgrade. (Recall the very high long-run elasticity of demand for ANS.) Third, in at least one case it appeared that BP's price discrimination helped keep a marginal refiner in business. The impact of this action was probably to *enhance* downstream competition, to the benefit of consumers.

Implications for the FTC's Merger Review

To summarize, there were legitimate reasons to believe that BP's strategy of exporting some ANS crude oil to the Far East had a slight upward effect at certain times on West Coast ANS crude oil prices, perhaps as much as a penny a gallon. At most this could have translated into 0.4 cents per gallon of gasoline. BP disputed these price effects, pointed out the inconsistencies between such alleged price effects and the longer-term evidence on ANS crude oil production and prices, and argued that ANS prices were at competitive levels. But BP's Optimizer Model, BP's trading strategies, and BP's exports to the Far East were central to the FTC's view of the proposed merger. Because of these exports, and the Optimizer Model, FTC lawyers took the position that BP already enjoyed some market power prior to its acquisition of ARCO. Still, such a finding would not be sufficient to challenge the acquisition, which would require the FTC to show that BP's merger with ARCO would strengthen or sustain BP's market power.

WHAT ABOUT ARCO?

As just explained, some in the FTC placed great weight on the observation that BP exerted some market power in the short term. They considered BP's exports to the Far East as proof that BP had monopoly power over ANS crude oil, and sought to use the merger review, and associated settlement, to prevent such exports in the future.

However, the conventional question in merger analysis (as called for under the Clayton Act) is whether the proposed merger will *reduce* competition, not whether one of the merging parties enjoyed some premerger market power. In particular, in following its own *Horizontal Merger Guidelines,* the FTC would ask whether the proposed merger would *raise* the price of ANS crude oil sold on the West Coast. Even without any consent decree, BP's incentive to export would be increased only marginally by the merger, and then only for the short time until its excess shipping capacity was retired. And once BP and Alaska agreed that BP would sell a significant fraction of ARCO's reserves as part of an upstream settlement it appeared that the merger would actually *reduce* BP's incentive to export, thereby slightly *lowering* West Coast prices, as we show below. Therefore, once the Alaska Charter was negotiated, it was not possible economically to justify blocking the merger based on the downstream case.

WHAT HAPPENED

We now turn to the resolution of the case.

Alaska Charter

The Alaska Charter was designed as an *upstream* remedy. However, what the Alaska Charter fixed most persuasively was any *downstream* problem based on BP's trading and export strategies. Prior to the Alaska Charter, ARCO's production of ANS was equal to roughly 90 percent of its consumption. The Charter required the sale of half of the ARCO production. This meant that ARCO's ANS crude oil production would only be 45 percent as great as its consumption. After the divestiture, ARCO's interest would be in *lower* ANS crude oil prices: For every barrel of ANS crude oil that ARCO consumed it would produce 0.45 barrels of ANS crude oil, so a $1 per barrel price increase would cost it fifty-five cents per barrel consumed. But the FTC's estimate of the pass-through rate implied that ARCO would be able to raise retail prices by at most forty-five cents for every dollar increase in ANS crude oil prices. So after its divestiture, ARCO would lose at least a dime on the dollar from an ANS crude oil price increase.

Now consider the merger. BP clearly gained from any increase in ANS crude oil prices; but if ARCO lost, then the net gain to BP from any price increase would be lower postmerger than premerger. The merger would *reduce* incentives for exports and therefore lead to *lower* West Coast ANS crude oil prices, so long as the merger would not cause any decline in upstream production. In other words, the BP-ARCO merger, along with the Alaska Charter, would be *better* than the status quo for West Coast consumers.

Some in the FTC had a second concern about the Charter that was at best controversial. As part of an earlier deal to pass legislation permitting ANS crude oil exports, BP had committed to California Senator Feinstein that it would use costly, inefficient Jones Act vessels on any shipments of oil from Alaska to the Far East. A new buyer might not be so constrained and therefore would have lower shipping costs to the Far East. Those lower costs might lead to more exports in a competitive market and therefore higher U.S. prices. The argument really boiled down to claiming that the antitrust authorities, in their role as protectors of U.S. consumers, should examine closely transactions that would involve the sale of assets to competitive firms with highly efficient export technologies, on the grounds that such acquirers would increase exports and therefore raise domestic prices.[27] While this might be politically attractive as trade policy, it is not, in our view, sound competition policy.

BP's Offers

In response to the FTC economists' concerns, BP agreed to alter its supply contracts so that they would be indexed to crude oil prices other than ANS spot prices. This meant that BP would no longer have any incentive to export based on West Coast marginal revenue being less than price. The contracts committed BP's ANS crude oil for years to come (after accounting for usage at the ARCO refineries and the Alaska Charter), so that BP would be net "short" of ANS crude oil. In fact, BP would in the position of benefiting from relative *declines* in the price of ANS crude oil! While these contracts were favorable to refiners, who benefited from knowing that the FTC was forcing BP to renegotiate, they did create a litigation dilemma for the FTC: It meant that the buyers of ANS crude oil were virtually unanimous in wanting the deal to go through so their contracts would become effective.

The FTC has a general tendency to be wary of contractual remedies, relative to divestitures. The two reasons in favor of accepting contracts in this case were that the identified downstream problem appeared to be contractual in nature, and that the problems appeared to be short term. That is, the initial incentive to export came from the indexing of the contract prices to the USWC price instead of the WTI price. In any event, within two or three years BP would no longer have the shipping capacity needed to ex-

[27]Perhaps a more charitable view would be to say that the majority viewed the Jones Act as a tax that benefited American maritime workers and it wanted firms to make decisions that were independent of this tax.

port. Furthermore, with a five- to ten-year contract, refineries would have plenty of time to eliminate any dependence they might have had on ANS crude oil. The only coherent reason for the FTC to reject BP's offer would thus have to be based on a concern that the real problem was not with the downstream markets at all but with the upstream ones.

Settlement

After the FTC turned down the Alaska Charter and the supply contracts as inadequate, BP made a series of "improved" offers. Ultimately BP was willing to sell as much production as ARCO owned, but it had a preference for selling part of BP's old acreage and part of ARCO's rather than all of ARCO's, to maintain some of the merger efficiencies, especially the consolidation of Prudhoe under one operatorship.

There was a heated debate within the Commission about the final BP proposals. Many of the staff argued that even though it appeared likely that BP would ultimately agree to sell all of ARCO Alaska, the deal on the table was better than that for consumers and for economic efficiency. Others, citing the Divestiture Study, claimed that the BP proposal to sell parts of both its and ARCO's holdings was a classic case of "mix and match," that is, a motley collection of assets that would be less likely to be a viable business than the current ARCO Alaska. But in this case selling the assets inefficiently did not make economic sense for BP, given the demand elasticity for ANS. That is, the reduction in revenues from selling an inefficient package would overwhelm any price increase BP might enjoy because of reduced output caused by an inefficient asset package. Furthermore, BP's proposals all made logical sense in terms of being designed to maximize the efficiencies that the company had claimed from the very beginning of the investigation.

On February 2, 2000, the Commission voted three to two to sue BP and ARCO and block the merger. Two months later, BP's CEO John Browne, not eager to go to court against the government of a country where he had major operations, decided to accede to the FTC's divestiture demands. The final deal announced on April 13, 2000, was that BP would sell the entire business of ARCO Alaska to Phillips Petroleum. Because ARCO Alaska was organized as a separate company, all of whose stock was owned by ARCO, in some ways this made for an easier divestiture than a sale of assets.

One additional issue arose—whether the consent order should include a ban on exports, by either BP or Phillips. There were three good reasons for opposing such a ban. First, there are times when exports are efficient, as when some West Coast refining capacity is out of operation. It is difficult to write a rule that only prohibits "inefficient" exports. Second, such a remedy would be "regulatory" rather than "structural" as the Commission generally preferred. Indeed, with the other aspects of the settlement and with BP's declining shipping capacity it was highly unlikely there would be any exports even in the absence of such a provision. Also, an export ban did not appear to correct any competition problem associated with the merger, especially given the divestiture of ARCO Alaska to Phillips. Third, Congress had explicitly allowed exports in 1995, reversing a long-time ban. It did not seem to be the FTC's place to overrule Congress. Three commissioners agreed with this logic, and the export ban was defeated three to two.

Postscript

After the merger was finalized, BP, Phillips, and Exxon worked out a way to gain the efficiencies initially visualized by BP. Prudhoe Bay is now operated by BP, which owns 26 percent compared to 36 percent each for Exxon and Phillips.[28] Oil and gas ownership rights were traded among the three companies to better align their incentives and make efficient investment decisions more likely.

An interesting organizational angle relates to the fact that BP and ARCO were unable, over many years, to find a way to renegotiate their working arrangements at Prudhoe Bay, despite the very substantial efficiencies associated with having one rather than two operators of the field. Perhaps their inability to eliminate the awkward dual-operatorship regime was due to fierce pride regarding North Slope know-how. BP, seeing itself as the best oil company in the world, naturally thought it should be the operator; Sir John Browne even got his start on the North Slope. Alaska was the crown jewel of ARCO's exploration and production operations and the place where ARCO trained many of its best people. ARCO may well have thought that because Alaska was so much more important to it than to BP that ARCO was the more appropriate operator; in any event, it would have been demoralizing for the ARCO employees to give up the ARCO operatorship in Prudhoe. After the sale, Phillips had no such corporate history, and quickly cut a deal with BP.

According to the *Merger Guidelines,* for the efficiencies from a merger to be considered as an offset to anticompetitive effects, they must be merger-specific. Did the switch to one operator at Prudhoe Bay qualify as merger-specific? The efficiencies could not have been achieved without a merger, but they were in fact achieved with a merger *cum* divestiture.

There have been no exports of crude oil from Alaska to the Far East since the deal closed.

CONCLUSIONS

BP-ARCO is one of several examples of major oil mergers that occurred in the last years of the Clinton administration. It is fair to say that in each of these cases the companies agreed to divestitures that went well beyond

---

[28]BP also operates the Prudhoe "satellite" fields, which have essentially the same ownership structure as the main field.

what many believed were necessary to protect competition. While in many industries the changes in antitrust policy associated with the shift from the Clinton administration to the Bush administration may prove to be marginal, the oil industry is one area where a new majority at the FTC may lead to a significant shift in antitrust enforcement.

REFERENCES

Alaska Department of Natural Resources. "FTC Briefing Presentation Acquisition of ARCO by BP-Amoco" available at http://204.126.119.8/oil/products/slideshows/ftc%5Fbriefing%5Fapr1999/index.htm, April 1999.

ARCO, British Petroleum, and the State of Alaska. "Charter for Development of the Alaskan North Slope." (Alaska Charter). http://www.bp.com/alaska/ARCO/charter.htm. November 1999.

Barrionuevo, Alexi, "Diversification Checks Prices of Fuel in Pipeline Shutdown." *Wall Street Journal,* November 7, 2002.

California Energy Commission. "Oil Supply Sources to California Refineries." http://www.energy.ca.gov/fuels/oil/_crude_oil receipts.html. February 2002.

Energy Information Administration. "Petroleum Marketing Monthly." See http://www.eia.doe.gov/pub/oil_gas/petroleum/data_publications/petroleum_marketing_monthly/current/pdf/pmmtab22.pdf. May 2002.

Energy Information Administration. "Petroleum Supply Annual." Various issues.

Federal Trade Commission, Bureau of Competition. "A Study of the Commission's Divestiture Process." See http://www.ftc.gov/os/1999/9908/divestiture.pdf. August 1999.

General Accounting Office. "Alaskan North Slope Oil: Limited Effects of Lifting Export Ban on Oil and Shipping Industries and Consumers." GAO/RCED-99-191. Available at http://www.gao.gov/archive/1999/rc99191.pdf. July 1999.

Hayes, John, Carl Shapiro, and Robert Town. "Market Definition in Crude Oil: Estimating the Effects of the BP/ARCO Merger." Mimeo. 2002.

Klemperer, Paul. "Auction Theory: A Guide to the Literature." *Journal of Economic Surveys* 13 (July 1999): 227–286.

McAfee, R. Preston, "West Coast Gasoline Prices." Prepared statement before the Committee on Commerce, Science, and Transportation, Subcommittee on Consumer Affairs, Foreign Commerce, and Tourism, United States Senate, April 25, 2001.

Efficiencies and High Concentration: Heinz Proposes to Acquire Beech-Nut (2001)

Jonathan B. Baker

INTRODUCTION

Mergers may benefit the economy by allowing firms to reduce costs or develop better products. Yet the Supreme Court has in the past questioned whether cost savings or other efficiencies from merger should ever count in favor of a transaction that increases market concentration substantially. In 1967, the Court announced that "[p]ossible economies cannot be used as a defense to illegality" in merger review.[1] The Court had previously explained that for courts to assess whether social or economic benefits can justify an otherwise anticompetitive merger goes beyond the ordinary judicial competence and is inconsistent with congressional intent.[2]

The government's *Merger Guidelines* of the same era, issued in 1968, were only slightly more sympathetic: They recognized that efficiencies might justify an otherwise anticompetitive merger, but limited the defense to "extraordinary cases."

The case against considering efficiencies in the analysis of mergers among rivals (horizontal mergers) has, perhaps surprisingly, been made forcefully by both Richard Posner and Robert Bork—influential antitrust

The author testified as an economic expert on behalf of the merging firms. He is indebted to Michael Black, Steven Brenner, Christopher Cavanagh, Edward Henneberry, Richard Higgins, John Hilke, David Glasner, Richard Ludwick, Steven Salop, Marc Schildkraut, and John Woodbury.

[1]*Federal Trade Commission* v. *Procter & Gamble Co.,* 386 U.S. 568, 579 (1967).

[2]*U.S.* v. *Philadelphia National Bank,* 374 U.S. 321, 371 (1963). Section 7 of the Clayton Act, the principal statute under which mergers are reviewed, does not explicitly mention efficiencies.

commentators who have enthusiastically encouraged the courts to consider efficiencies in antitrust analysis generally (Posner 2001, pp. 133–143; Bork 1978, pp. 123–129).[3] Posner and Bork contend that an efficiency defense would make merger analysis intractable in litigation, for several reasons. The cost savings likely to result from merger are easy to claim but may be hard to prove or disprove, particularly given that most of the relevant information is in the hands of the merging firms, who are interested parties.[4] It may also be difficult to determine how soon the same efficiencies might have been realized through less restrictive means short of merger, such as internal growth or managerial changes. In addition, courts may be unable practically to weigh the efficiency benefits of a transaction against the likely harm to competition from loss of a seller.[5] Accordingly, Posner and Bork conclude, the best institutional means of accommodating the concerns about the competitive harms from mergers among rivals in concentrated markets with the concerns about deterring efficient transactions is to address the possibility on average rather than case-by-case: by allowing mergers to proceed unless market concentration is substantial, and ignoring the efficiency justifications in specific cases otherwise.

Notwithstanding these concerns, the trend in antitrust law has been toward considering the efficiencies from merger in individual cases. Although the Supreme Court decisions from the 1960s that seemingly forbid an efficiency defense remain formally controlling, they are widely understood today as reflecting the perspective of an earlier era during which merger law was thought to vindicate noneconomic concerns, such as halting trends toward market concentration in their incipiency and protecting small business (along with the economic concern of preventing the exercise of market power). As such concerns have come to take a back seat to economic concerns across much of antitrust, judicial hostility to efficiencies has steadily decreased. Since 1979, the Supreme Court has recognized an efficiency defense in a related area of the law, the analysis of agreements among rivals (horizontal agreements) under the Sherman Act.[6] Here, as elsewhere in antitrust, the Supreme Court has backed off from bright line rules in favor of flexible standards that permit judges to consider the full range of factors relevant to the analysis of likely competitive effects, and thus hold out the promise of reducing errors in deciding specific cases.

---

[3]Other influential commentators, including Philip Areeda, Donald Turner, and Oliver Williamson, have been more sympathetic to allowing an efficiency defense to challenged mergers (Kolasky and Dick 2002; Williamson 1968).

[4]Moreover, mergers may reduce profits on average (Ravenscraft and Scherer 1987), consistent with anecdotes suggesting that many claimed and even legitimately anticipated efficiencies never materialize.

[5]Indeed, commentators do not agree how this weighing should occur in principle—particularly to what extent production cost savings not directly benefiting consumers of the products in the relevant market should count—as that issue implicates an ongoing debate over the purposes of antitrust law.

[6]*Broadcast Music, Inc.* v. *Columbia Broadcasting System, Inc.,* 441 U.S. 1 (1979).

Taking their cue from this judicial trend, and perhaps also in recognition of the finance literature that emphasizes the importance of the "market for corporate control" (acquisitions) as a means of weeding out bad management and moving assets to their highest-valued uses, the federal antitrust enforcement agencies have been willing to consider seriously the efficiencies from merger in deciding whether to challenge proposed acquisitions for at least two decades. Similarly, the lower courts today do not interpret the 1960s Supreme Court decisions as foreclosing all consideration of efficiencies in the analysis of mergers.

While the modern trend in the lower courts is to recognize efficiencies as a defense, and the government's *Merger Guidelines* were revised in 1997 to articulate a detailed approach to such a defense, the courts and antitrust enforcement agencies have nevertheless been skeptical about accepting an efficiency defense when market concentration is high. The *Merger Guidelines* state: "Efficiencies almost never justify a merger to monopoly or near-monopoly,"[7] and efficiencies have never been the primary reason for the failure of a government challenge to a horizontal merger in court (Berry 1996, pp. 526–528; Conrath and Widnell 1999, pp. 688–690).[8] Heinz's proposed acquisition of Beech-Nut—a merger of two of the three leading U.S. producers of baby food—might have been the first court decision to uphold a challenged horizontal merger primarily on grounds of efficiencies, but a favorable district court decision was overruled by an appellate court panel unwilling to accept the efficiencies that had been credited by the district court judge in a market where postmerger concentration was very high.

Both sides in the litigation over the merger of Heinz and Beech-Nut accepted that the case turned on whether baby food consumers would benefit or be harmed by the proposed acquisition.[9] As will be seen, Heinz and Beech-Nut claimed that the merger would produce variable cost savings that would lead to greater competition and lower prices within the relevant market, while the FTC contended that the merger would instead reduce

---

[7]This statement can be understood as premised in the economics of decision theory (Beckner and Salop 1999). Striking the right balance between adopting readily administrable decision rules and ensuring a full economic analysis is often difficult. Agencies and courts may thus be led to rely upon rebuttable presumptions based on easily observable information. From this perspective, the issue raised in *Heinz* is whether it is appropriate for courts and enforcers to depend on the shortcut of basing decisions primarily on market concentration when concentration is high, or whether a more complete competitive effects analysis would be practical and potentially lead to a different answer.

[8]Efficiencies have, however, at times persuaded the antitrust enforcement agencies not to challenge a proposed merger among rivals.

[9]Thus, the case could be decided without reaching two contested questions about the welfare standard in antitrust law. First, when the merging firms participate in multiple markets, should courts permit a merger likely to raise price to consumers in one market on the ground that consumers in some other market would benefit even more through substantially lower prices? Second, should courts permit a merger likely to raise price on the ground that the production cost savings exceeds the allocative efficiency loss? This situation is most likely to arise when the merger would produce large fixed cost savings, unlikely to benefit consumers in the relevant market, while the output reduction within the relevant market resulting from the merger would be small.

competition and prices would likely rise. Accordingly, the merger of Heinz and Beech-Nut provides an opportunity to consider whether efficiencies are an intractable subject for litigation and whether antitrust law properly accounts for the possibility that mergers among rivals could benefit society.

THE BABY FOOD INDUSTRY

In 2000, around the time of the proposed merger, three firms accounted for the sale of virtually all jarred baby food in the United States. Gerber, the leading firm, with more than 65 percent of U.S. sales, is a subsidiary of Swiss pharmaceutical conglomerate Novartis. Heinz, a food product company best known for its ketchup, had a share in excess of 17 percent. Heinz is also a leading seller of baby food in Europe. Beech-Nut, the major holding of Milnot, an investment firm, accounted for more than 15 percent of U.S. sales. Beech-Nut had previously been owned by seven different companies, including, most recently, two large food products concerns. Milnot acquired Beech-Nut in 1998 from Ralston Purina, which had purchased the company less than ten years before from Nestlé. (Another firm, Earth's Best, an organic brand, had a small and decreasing share, and was largely ignored during the merger litigation.)

Gerber and Beech-Nut are "premium" brands, with a strong reputation attractive to buyers. Heinz, in contrast, is a "value" brand, playing a role in the market similar to that of private label products in other markets. The Heinz brand name assures customers that the product is safe and healthy, but the brand appeals mainly to value-conscious shoppers who purchase it primarily because of its low retail price. At retail, Heinz sells at a discount averaging about 15 percent to the price of the Gerber and Beech-Nut products. Beech-Nut baby food generally sells for a price similar to that of Gerber's products, or at a small discount.

Supermarkets do not carry all three major baby food brands. Shelf space and restocking costs are high for product lines characterized by many varieties sold in small jars, and evidently exceed the benefits of providing buyers with additional product variety once the supermarket has added a second brand. The great majority of supermarkets carry two of the three major brands; virtually none carry three, and a small fraction carry only one brand. There are no private label baby food products, presumably for a similar reason.

Gerber, the leading firm, is sold in virtually every supermarket. In contrast, Heinz and Beech-Nut compete to be the second brand on supermarket shelves. That competition is roughly even from a national perspective: Heinz is carried in grocery stores accounting for about 40 percent of supermarket sales, while Beech-Nut is found in stores with about 45 percent of grocery sales. But each second brand has areas of geographic strength: metropolitan areas where each is the second brand in most supermarkets and where the other brand has little presence. For example, Heinz is the primary second brand in many cities in the Midwest, and Beech-Nut is the primary second brand in many metropolitan areas in the Northeast and Far West. Both brands have more than 10 percent of local sales in only about one-fifth of the major cities, largely concentrated in the Southeast. It is not surprising that Beech-Nut and Heinz exhibit strength in different regions: Scale economies in metropolitan area distribution and promotion make it costly, for example, for Heinz to serve a small number of retail outlets in a heavily Beech-Nut area. Indeed, the firms do not generally consider themselves to be significant players in a city where they have less than 10 percent of local sales.

This pattern of distribution imposes transactions costs on shoppers who wish to substitute between baby food products sold by Beech-Nut and Heinz. The two firms' products are virtually never on the same grocery shelves. Moreover, a customer of Beech-Nut in a core Beech-Nut area will typically have difficulty locating Heinz baby food products within the same city, and vice versa.

The metropolitan areas in which both Heinz and Beech-Nut have a nontrivial presence have probably been increasing as a result of supermarket consolidation. Many chains prefer to carry the same brands in all their stores, in order to obtain scale economies in inventory management, to enhance their negotiating leverage in dealing with suppliers, and to guarantee a consistent product line to those shoppers who patronize multiple stores in the chain. (But not always: A supermarket chain may also wish to vary some products across stores in order to cater to neighborhood tastes, as with some ethnic foods.) On the rare occasions when a chain carrying Heinz as its second baby food brand merges with a chain carrying Beech-Nut, the merged firm may hold an "all-or-nothing" shelf space competition between the two, ending with one brand taking over the other's position on the merged supermarket's shelves. Shelf space competition also occurs in other settings, as when Heinz or Beech-Nut approaches nonconsolidating supermarkets with offers to displace its rival for the position on the shelf not held by Gerber.

Beech-Nut and Heinz compete for the second slot on the supermarket shelf and influence the retail price set by the grocery store through merchandising payments from the manufacturer to the grocer (trade spending). Most contracts between supermarkets and baby food manufacturers are not fully specified in writing, so many of their aspects are worked out informally. The agreements typically involve a mix of fixed (lump sum) payments and payments that vary with the amount sold, roughly half fixed and half variable on average. The fixed payments are payments for shelf space for either new or existing products. The variable payments function more like discounts from the wholesale list price and give the retailer an incentive to lower the retail price: With a lower retail price, the grocer can sell more, and thereby increase the payment from the baby food producer. Gerber, by contrast, does not pay for or even compete for a place on the supermarket baby food shelf because its high market share and strong brand reputation automatically place it in a strong negotiating position with retailers.

THE PROPOSED MERGER

In February 2000, Heinz agreed to acquire the parent firm that owned Beech-Nut. The merging firms justified the transaction as a way to lower costs and improve products, much to the benefit of the companies and consumers. Heinz intended, after a year's transition, to sell only under the Beech-Nut label, produce baby food exclusively in Heinz's production facility, and share the cost savings from consolidating production with consumers by charging the low Heinz value price for the premium Beech-Nut product. The proposed merger would give Heinz distribution for its baby food in grocery stores accounting for the great majority of food sales.

Heinz planned to close Beech-Nut's old, high-cost labor-intensive production facility in Canajoharie, New York. That plant's production lines are laid out vertically over several floors. Its production processes are relatively unautomated: They require frequent intervention by workers who must measure and add ingredients, move ingredients over large distances around the plant on carts, and set and monitor temperatures by hand. Production would be shifted to Heinz's modern, highly automated Pittsburgh plant, which was reconstructed during the early 1990s as a facility for making baby food and other food products, such as private label soup. At Canajoharie, 320 workers produced 10 million cases of baby food each year, while 150 workers produced 12 million cases at Pittsburgh. Beech-Nut could not expand output cheaply at Canajoharie. In contrast, Heinz's Pittsburgh plant was operating at only 40 percent of its dedicated baby food capacity, and could add Beech-Nut's production volume and still have 20 percent of the plant's baby food capacity available for future growth. The merger would also allow the consolidated baby food production to take advantage of Heinz's six regional distribution centers, which handle all Heinz's food products, permitting the merged operations to share in the resulting scale and scope economies of distribution. The merging firms estimated that these efficiencies would permit Heinz to produce and distribute the Beech-Nut brand at a variable cost savings of about 15 percent.

THE FTC's CHALLENGE

In July 2000, the Federal Trade Commission (FTC) decided to challenge Heinz's proposed acquisition of Beech-Nut. That decision was controversial within the FTC. Both the legal and economic staffs that had investigated the merger recommended that the Commission decline to challenge it, and two of five commissioners voted against the challenge. The FTC's complaint seeking a preliminary injunction was tried in Federal District Court in late August and early September 2000.

The FTC emphasized that the baby food industry was highly concentrated, both nationally and in most metropolitan areas, and that the merger would increase concentration substantially. The FTC defined a jarred baby food product market and both a national geographic market and more localized city-specific geographic markets. Nationwide, the Herfindahl-Hirschman Index (HHI) of market concentration would rise as a result of the proposed transaction by 510 points to 5285, and in many cities the level and increase in concentration would be even greater. These are large numbers by the standards of the *Horizontal Merger Guidelines* or past merger cases. The number of significant sellers would fall from three to two. The Commission also observed, and the merging parties did not disagree, that entry would not be expected to defeat any exercise of postmerger Heinz–Beech-Nut's market power. For the FTC, the transaction was in a highly suspect category: a merger leading to duopoly in a market protected by significant entry barriers.

To explain how competition would be harmed by this increase in market concentration, the FTC focused on the loss of wholesale competition between Beech-Nut and Heinz for shelf space. The FTC saw shelf space competition between the two as pervasive.[10] It argued that the repeated efforts that each firm made to take retail accounts from the other amounted to a constant threat to each other at all grocery chains. The loss of this wholesale competition for the second baby food slot on the grocery shelf would harm competition in several ways, according to the Commission.

First, the loss of wholesale competition as a result of the merger would remove a key impediment to tacit collusion among the baby food producers in their sales to consumers. Coordination between Heinz and Gerber is prevented today by the threat that Beech-Nut would respond to higher grocery prices for baby food by undercutting Heinz's wholesale price to grocery stores and taking away Heinz's shelf space. Similarly, Beech-Nut refrains from colluding tacitly with Gerber, even in core Beech-Nut cities where Heinz has limited presence, by the threat presented by shelf space competition from Heinz. Moreover, with a trend toward consolidation among supermarket chains, Heinz and Beech-Nut were increasingly obtaining significant space on retailer shelves in cities where that presence had previously been limited; this trend could only increase the competitive discipline conferred by shelf space competition between the two.

Second, the reduction in shelf space competition would give the merged

---

[10]One FTC commissioner, in explaining his vote to sue, also argued that the merger would have been harmful even if competition between Heinz and Beech-Nut were instead limited, as the merging firms contended (Leary 2002, pp. 32–33). If the merging firms were not competing aggressively premerger, he suggested, that conduct would likely have reflected tacit coordination, which should not be rewarded by allowing the firms to merge and cease competing altogether. But the FTC did not allege premerger tacit coordination in court.

firm a unilateral incentive to raise price without need for coordination with Gerber. With less shelf space competition would come less trade spending and thus less financial incentive for grocery stores to keep retail prices of baby food low. In addition, according to the Commission, Heinz's plan to drop the Heinz brand in favor of the Beech-Nut label also would harm buyers by reducing consumer choice. In place of two alternatives to Gerber—a higher-priced Beech-Nut brand with strong reputation, and a Heinz brand that competed more on price than quality—consumers would have only one. Moreover, the merger would remove from the market a firm, Beech-Nut, that the FTC saw as innovative in the past, particularly in spurring the development and marketing of additive-free products.

Finally, the FTC regarded the shelf space competition at wholesale as worthy of protection under the antitrust laws for its own sake, independent of any effect it might have on retail prices or other dimensions of retailer conduct. Even if this competition did not benefit buyers directly, it would do so indirectly by benefitting grocery stores. Moreover, the FTC contended that harm to consumers should be presumed from the loss of wholesale competition in order to protect the government's ability to prosecute substantial increases in concentration upstream, including mergers to monopoly, even if the effect of the transaction on retail competition is hard to identify.[11]

With postmerger market concentration so high and entry unlikely, the FTC contended, the merger presented a clear and substantial danger to competition. Under such circumstances, efficiencies from merger could overcome the competitive concern only if the efficiencies were extraordinary indeed. But when the FTC reviewed the parties' efficiency claims, those claims were found wanting. In particular, the FTC challenged the efficiency claims of the parties as not cognizable under *Horizontal Merger Guidelines* standards: They were unproved and overstated; they could have been achieved through practical means short of merger (e.g., investment in brand reputation by Heinz, plant modernization by Beech-Nut, or the sale of Beech-Nut to some other buyer); and they would result from an anticompetitive reduction in consumer choice (the loss of the Heinz brand). Even if these efficiencies were cognizable, the FTC also contended, they were insufficient in magnitude to outweigh the likely harm to competition, in part because they would not be spread across the entire output in the market where competition is threatened.

THE MERGING FIRMS' DEFENSE

The merging firms saw Gerber as a dominant firm with the premerger ability to exercise market power, and Beech-Nut and Heinz as firms with lim-

---

[11]In other industries, for example, this situation might arise if the upstream product (intermediate good) accounted for a small cost share of the downstream (final) product.

ited competitive influence. Accordingly, the merger would do little to enhance Gerber's ability to exercise market power even absent efficiencies. Moreover, Beech-Nut and Heinz argued that their combination, by generating efficiencies, would promote competition with Gerber, leading prices to fall.

Challenging Gerber's Dominance

The parties' view of Gerber's role was based on evidence about market structure, firm conduct, and market performance. With respect to market structure, Gerber controlled more than 65 percent of baby food sales, and its only significant rivals, Beech-Nut and Heinz, had little incentive to challenge Gerber's dominance because they were each limited in their ability to expand. Beech-Nut could not increase output cheaply because it produced baby food in an old, high-cost plant. Its variable costs of manufacturing were 43 percent higher than those of Heinz (and likely also of Gerber), and its variable costs of production and distribution were 15 percent higher overall. Heinz could not expand cheaply because it sold a value brand that was limited in attractiveness to the many consumers who favored Gerber's and Beech-Nut's premium products.

Moreover, both firms were limited in their ability to expand, according to the merging parties, by the difficulty of obtaining distribution by grocery stores that did not already carry their brands. The second position on grocery shelves did at times change hands, but the shelf space rivalry between Heinz and Beech-Nut was circumscribed, and the incumbent firm held the upper hand. In an all-or-nothing competition to serve a grocery chain that previously sold Beech-Nut in some divisions and Heinz in others, the baby food manufacturer that already served most of the chain tended to win. Similarly, the firms' efforts to convince nonconsolidating supermarkets to displace their rival for the second position on the shelf had not led to much change in distribution patterns, as incumbents held an advantage in maintaining their existing shelf space.

The incumbency advantage had several sources. In order for Beech-Nut or Heinz to expand its distribution to stores it did not currently serve, it had to take shelf space away from the other contender for the second position on the supermarket baby food shelf. Doing so required it to outbid its rival for shelf space. In addition, the baby food producer had to compensate the grocery store for the costs of restocking stores and alienating the long-time customers of the rival brand. Moreover, the advertising and promotional costs of developing and maintaining a brand reputation are high. The payoff of such expenditures would be lower for Beech-Nut, for example, if it attempted to expand in a city in which it was carried on few grocery shelves, than it would be for Heinz, which had greater supermarket distribution in the same city. Under such circumstances, any promotional effort that reached the entire city would largely go to customers who patronized stores where Beech-Nut's product was not available.

The limited distribution of Beech-Nut and Heinz reduced the profitability of investments to develop significant innovation, forestalling these firms' efforts to expand by introducing major new products. Heinz did not provide marketing and promotional support to products that were not available to at least 70 to 80 percent of customers, in part to avoid wasting a substantial fraction of its national advertising budget. In addition, access to less than half the potential market (40 percent for Heinz; 45 percent for Beech-Nut) limited these firms' ability to spread the large fixed costs of new product development. Gerber's incentive to innovate was also muted, in its case by the prospect that new products would primarily cannibalize its own dominant existing sales. Consistent with this view, aggregate sales of baby food had not been rising; retailers commonly described the category as "sleepy"; and most recent new product introductions were more marketing sizzle than substance, or else (as in the case of high-priced organic baby food) attractive to only a small segment of buyers.

Because so many grocery shelves were unavailable to Heinz, the company concluded before the merger that it would be unprofitable to introduce two major baby food innovations it had contemplated. The Environmental Oasis program was a "field to fork" quality assurance program intended to convince consumers that Heinz baby food is more nutritious and safe than anything they can make themselves. This program was successful for Heinz's Italian affiliate, perhaps because of concerns about the food supply there in the wake of Chernobyl. Heinz also found that it would be unprofitable to introduce baby food produced using a new technology, aseptic production, that it had considered marketing as a high-priced, higher-quality product line for sale in addition to its regular brand. The aseptic production method would improve baby food taste by allowing Heinz to sterilize the product with less cooking time, and it would allow Heinz to introduce an attractive new product packaging (a microwavable and resealable pudding pack).

Firm conduct and market performance also suggest that Gerber was a dominant firm. Gerber was the pricing leader when wholesale prices changed; it arguably set the pricing umbrella for the industry. In addition, Gerber's prices had been rising faster than the prices of food in general during a period in which input costs were largely unchanged, which was again consistent with some ability to exercise market power.

Absent the merger, the parties contended, neither Heinz nor Beech-Nut had much incentive or ability to take on Gerber. Without this merger, the industry would continue to perform poorly, with prices in excess of competitive levels and limited new product introductions. In contrast, the acquisition would promote industry competition by removing all the impediments to expansion by Gerber's new (merged) rival. The merged firm could combine Heinz's low-cost automated production process with Beech-Nut's premium brand reputation, allowing the merged firm to produce a premium product at less cost and making it profitable for that company to reduce the premium product's price. Access to at least 85 percent of grocery shelves would make advertising and promotion cost effective in all major cities, and would make it profitable for the merged firm to introduce innovations such as Oasis and aseptic production.

The high market concentration resulting from the merger was beside the point. It was not generated by the dominant firm's entrenching its position by gobbling up a smaller rival; it flowed instead from the merger of two smaller firms that would create competition where competition had previously been limited.

Questioning the FTC's Theories

In addition to explaining why the merger would promote competition, the merging parties also questioned the competitive effects theories proffered by the FTC. In doing so, they challenged both the FTC's claim that competition between Heinz and Beech-Nut kept prices low premerger and the FTC's view that the efficiencies from merger would have little competitive significance.

Unilateral Competitive Effects

First, the merging parties contended that the merged firm would be unlikely to raise the retail price of baby food unilaterally. In part, the parties argued, it was hard to be concerned about the loss of head-to-head competition for consumers when there was little retail competition between Beech-Nut and Heinz even before the merger. After all, the two brands were never on the same grocery shelf, and in most cities only one of the brands was widely available. Moreover, the merging firms and a number of grocers indicated that both Beech-Nut and Heinz priced against Gerber, not against each other.

The lack of significant retail competition between Heinz and Beech-Nut was also demonstrated using systematic empirical evidence. The merging firms presented estimates of cross-price elasticities of demand in a sample limited to metropolitan areas in which both Heinz and Beech-Nut accounted for at least 10 percent of retail sales ("mixed" markets), and thus both had a nontrivial presence in (different) stores. The study estimated that a 5 percent decline in the Beech-Nut price would lower the quantity of Heinz sold by about 0.1 percent (cross-price elasticity of demand of about 0.02)—a buyer response that is trivial in practical economic significance and insignificant statistically. By comparison, a 5 percent decline in the Gerber price would lead to a 3.1 percent reduction in the quantity of Heinz sold (cross-elasticity slightly greater than 0.6). Similarly, a 5 percent decline in the Heinz price would lead to a 0.6 percent reduction in Beech-Nut's quantity sold (cross-elasticity of 0.12)—again small in practical terms, though significant statistically. A 5 percent Gerber price decline would again have generated a larger output reduction, here 4.0 percent (cross-elasticity of 0.8).

The FTC chose not to present alternative empirical demand elasticity estimates. Rather, it challenged the implications of these studies with grocer testimony that the two products competed at retail. In addition, the FTC raised a statistical concern about the merging parties' demand elasticity study. It pointed out that the demand analysis was based on shelf prices, not transaction prices, because it did not account for the effects of promotional coupons issued by Beech-Nut and Heinz. The merging firms responded that the absolute level of merging firm couponing was small during the sample period, and that the key cross-elasticity results were not biased from the omission of a variable accounting for this activity because almost all the coupons distributed by Heinz and Beech-Nut during the sample period were through direct mail, sent to new mothers in a steady, uniform way, uncorrelated with the retail price.[12]

The merging firms presented a second systematic empirical study that also showed that retail competition between Beech-Nut and Heinz was insubstantial. This study compared prices for 4 oz. jars in "core" Beech-Nut or Heinz metropolitan areas (defined as those where Beech-Nut or Heinz was the only firm aside from Gerber that accounted for more than 10 percent of baby food sales) with prices in "mixed" markets (where all three firms accounted for at least 10 percent of sales), and controlled for cross-city differences in the cost of grocery retailing. The empirical analysis found that baby food prices were little different in practical economic terms, and not different statistically, between markets where Beech-Nut and Heinz were both available and markets where only one of the two could be found alongside Gerber on grocery shelves. The FTC again chose not to present a competing analysis of the data. Instead, it responded primarily with testimony from some grocers that where both are present in the same areas, they depress each other's prices as well as those of Gerber.

The merging firms also questioned the FTC's claim that the loss of shelf space competition between Beech-Nut and Heinz would lead to higher retail prices for baby food. According to the firms, the *incremental* trade spending prompted by a bidding war for a retail account was mostly fixed, not variable. Grocery witnesses agreed with the prediction of economic theory: Increases in fixed trade spending would not be passed through to baby food buyers. The increased revenues could instead go to shareholders in the form of higher profits. Or, if those higher supermarket

---

[12]The omission of an explanatory (right-hand side) variable does not bias the estimated coefficients in a linear regression if the omitted variable is not correlated with the included variables (Greene 2000, pp. 334–337).

profits were competed away, the beneficiaries would be supermarket customers generally—the store might widen aisles or say open longer hours, for example—rather than baby food purchasers in particular.

The results of a third systematic empirical study presented by the merging firms were consistent with this economic analysis. The study analyzed the retail price effects of bidding competition for shelf space between Beech-Nut and Heinz. Grocery stores served by Heinz were divided into two groups, based on whether Heinz and Beech-Nut had competed for the shelf space at the time that the most recent agreement had been reached. The results showed no significant difference, either statistically or in practical economic terms, in retail prices for either firm with products on the shelf (Gerber or Heinz) related to whether there had been wholesale competition between Beech-Nut and Heinz in the past. In response, the FTC pointed to instances, drawn from grocer testimony or merging party documents, where the threat that a supermarket would switch its choice of second brand seemed to be associated with retail price competition.

Coordinated Competitive Effects

The merging firms questioned the FTC's view that the acquisition would make tacit collusion among the major baby food manufacturers more likely. They questioned the feasibility of coordination in general, given the time lag in the ability of the two firms to detect wholesale price cuts by each other. They also cited a recent decision by an appellate court rejecting an allegation that the baby food producers had expressly colluded.[13]

More importantly, the efficiencies that the parties saw flowing from the transaction played a central role in the merging firms' response to the government's coordination story. According to the firms, the efficiencies should not be understood as somehow justifying an otherwise anticompetitive merger; rather, they were the reason that the merger would promote competition affirmatively.

The cost savings from plant consolidation were, in the view of the merging firms' efficiency expert (later quoted with approval by the district court judge), "extraordinary." The variable costs of manufacturing the Beech-Nut line would fall by 43 percent, and the variable costs of all production and distribution activities would decline by 15 percent. The merging parties argued that these extraordinary variable cost savings would give the merged firm a powerful incentive to lower price. It would do better by lowering price and taking market share away from Gerber than by colluding tacitly with Gerber at a higher market price but lower market share.

Put differently, the merging firms argued that they would pass through all of the variable cost savings resulting from the acquisition to consumers. Heinz indicated that it would charge the low Heinz value price for the premium Beech-Nut product, thus lowering the price of Beech-Nut by about

---

[13]*In re Baby Food Antitrust Litigation,* 166 F.3d 112 (3d Cir 1999).

15 percent, the full amount of the variable cost savings in production. This prediction was credible, according to Heinz, because of the company's history of passing through similar cost savings achieved in the production or distribution of other food products in its portfolio, including cat food and ketchup. More importantly, an economic analysis showed that the likely pass-through rate in the absence of postmerger coordination was very high, at least 50 percent and quite possibly the 100 percent that the company claimed.

The pass-through rate is the proportion of variable cost savings that result in lower consumer prices. For example, if a firm lowered price by 5 percent when its variable costs fell by 10 percent, its cost pass-through rate would be 50 percent. Even a monopolist has an incentive to lower price if its variable costs decline: With a uniformly lower marginal cost curve and downward sloping demand, it necessarily equates marginal revenue with marginal cost at a higher level of output and lower price. For example, a monopolist with a linear demand will pass through 50 percent of any reduction in marginal cost.[14]

The shape of the firm's demand curve is an important determinant of the pass-through rate. The pass-through rate depends on the *curvature* of demand (the rate of change in the slope or elasticity). If a firm sells at a price in excess of marginal cost, as is common for producers of differentiated products, and the seller's demand grows substantially more elastic as it lowers price, then the firm has a powerful incentive to give buyers the benefit of a cost reduction by reducing price. Under such circumstances, the seller would likely benefit more by lowering price to expand output, thus capturing a positive price-cost margin on the many additional sales it makes, than it would by keeping price (and thus the price-cost margin) higher while limiting its output expansion. The more that the firm's demand curve is shaped in this way, the greater is the incentive for the seller to pass through cost reductions to buyers in the form of lower prices.

According to the merging firms, the demand curves facing both Heinz and Beech-Nut had a curvature that strongly favored a high pass-through rate. Heinz's marketing experience was that its sales became dramatically more responsive to price cuts as the gap between its retail price and that charged by Gerber increased. Econometric estimates of the demand for both the Heinz brand and the Beech-Nut brand, based on functional forms that did not constrain the curvature of demand, also showed that each firm's demand grew much more elastic when the firm's price declined slightly—so much so as to make plausible Heinz's claim that a cost reduction would be fully passed-through to consumers. Rivals' anticipated reactions to price changes can also affect the incentives to pass through cost reductions, but

---

[14]A firm's pass-through rate can be interpreted as the ratio of the slope of firm-specific (residual) demand to the slope of firm marginal revenue. The intuition is that when faced with a reduction in marginal cost, the firm will increase output so that marginal revenue declines by the same amount. (Bulow and Pfleiderer 1983).

simulation studies suggested that the competitive interaction among firms was a minor determinant of the pass-through rate for Heinz and Beech-Nut relative to the curvature of demand. Accordingly, this economic analysis demonstrated that the pass-through rate for cost savings from the merger of Beech-Nut and Heinz would likely be very high, at least 50 percent and quite possibly the 100 percent that the company claimed.

Heinz would want to compete aggressively postmerger by passing through all its baby food cost savings to consumers, according to the merging firms. The merger solved the problems that had previously limited both Heinz's and Beech-Nut's abilities to expand. It would give Heinz a premium brand, permit the Beech-Nut brand to be produced in a low-cost facility, and give the merged firm the national distribution required to make major innovation profitable. The transaction would thus effectively create a "maverick" firm with the ability and incentive to expand output (Baker 2002). Such a firm would not find it profitable to settle for its premerger market share, even if coordination with Gerber would facilitate an increase in the market price. Rather, with its new ability to expand inexpensively and to introduce new products, the merged firm would do better by taking market share away from Gerber. The resulting divergence in incentives between Gerber and Heinz would undermine the possibility of postmerger coordination. Not surprisingly, Gerber's internal documents predicted more intense competition following the merger; they did not predict a more cooperative environment.

If the merger led Heinz to compete aggressively and to pass through all the variable cost savings in production and distribution to consumers, then the quality-adjusted price of baby food would decline by 15 percent. Beech-Nut buyers would be able to purchase their premium brand for 15 percent less; Heinz buyers would be able to purchase a brand worth up to 15 percent more for the same low price they had previously paid;[15] and Gerber customers would get the option to switch to a premium brand at a 15 percent discount, possibly leading Gerber to reduce price as well. In this way, the merging firms argued, the efficiencies would benefit all buyers in the baby food market.

Loss of Wholesale Competition

Finally, the merging firms questioned the FTC's view that the transaction should be blocked because it would end head-to-head wholesale competition for shelf space between Beech-Nut and Heinz, without regard to

---

[15]The Heinz brand name would be withdrawn from the market, leading the FTC to voice a concern that consumers would be harmed from the reduction in product variety. The merging firms responded that the Heinz brand name primarily conveyed a low price to purchasers, not other characteristics valued by baby food buyers. In consequence, consumers would not be harmed by the removal of this brand so long as some other brand, here Beech-Nut, was sold at the low Heinz value price. Moreover, the merging parties noted, the merger would also increase product variety by facilitating the introduction of a new product line, based on Heinz's aseptic production process.

whether the FTC could demonstrate an adverse effect on retail prices. The loss of wholesale competition between the merging firms does not necessarily mean a loss of shelf space competition taken as a whole, because a reinvigorated Heinz would likely compete with Gerber for prime shelf space postmerger, inducing Gerber to pay grocers for shelf space for the first time. Moreover, any loss of wholesale competition is inextricably linked to the benefits that the merger creates for retail competition. The merging firms questioned whether a court should object to an increase in wholesale prices if that outcome were necessary in order to reduce the retail price of baby food.

THE COURTS DECIDE

The FTC, unconvinced by the merging parties' arguments, voted to seek a preliminary injunction to stop the merger on July 7, 2000. A five-day evidentiary hearing in federal district court took place during late August and early September. The district court decision was issued on October 19, 2000.

The district court sided with the merging firms.[16] The court agreed with the FTC that the high and increasing market concentration resulting from the transaction created a presumption that the merger would harm competition and that entry was not easy. But it found that the defendants had successfully rebutted the presumption arising out of market concentration by proving extraordinary efficiencies. "When the efficiencies of the merger are combined with the new platform for product innovation, . . . it appears more likely than not that Gerber's own predictions of more intense competition . . . will come true."[17]

The district court rejected the FTC's competitive effects theories. The merging firm would not be likely to raise the retail price unilaterally because retail competition between Heinz and Beech-Nut was limited and because the wholesale competition between the two did not benefit consumers. The court relied in part on the merging firms' econometric evidence in reaching this conclusion, and rejected the FTC's claim that the exclusion of coupons from the price data made the studies unreliable.[18] Nor would coordination be likely in the market postmerger. Rather, the district court found it "more probable than not" that the merger "will actually increase competition" in the baby food market.[19]

---

[16]*Federal Trade Commission* v. *H. J. Heinz Co.,* 116 F. Supp. 2d 190 (D.D.C. 2000), *rev'd* 246 F.3d 708 (D.C. Cir. 2001).

[17]*Heinz,* 116. F. Supp. 2d at 199.

[18]*Heinz,* 116 F. Supp. 2d. at 196 n.6.

[19]*Heinz,* 116. F. Supp. 2d. at 200.

The FTC appealed.[20] On April 27, 2001, a unanimous appellate panel reversed the district court.[21] The appeals court concluded that the efficiencies evidence accepted by the district court was insufficient, both as a defense and as a basis for showing that postmerger coordination would be unlikely. Without the efficiencies evidence, defendants could not prevail over the inference of harm to competition arising from the reduction in the number of sellers and the increase in market concentration.

The appeals court pointed out three main problems with the district court's factual findings on efficiencies. First, the district court should have considered the reduction in total variable cost, rather than merely the reduction in the variable costs of manufacturing. Second, the district court should have analyzed the magnitude of the cost reductions over the merged firms' combined output, rather than with respect to Beech-Nut alone. Third, the district court did not satisfactorily explain why the efficiencies could not be achieved through reasonable and practical alternative means, with less competitive risk than would arise from merger. The court of appeals suggested in particular that Heinz could have gotten to the same place by investing the money it was spending to acquire Beech-Nut on improving recipes and promoting a premium brand name.

The court of appeals also dismissed the district court's conclusion that postmerger collusion was unlikely on the ground that defendants had failed to show that the difficulties of solving the "cartel problems" of reaching a consensus and deterring cheating "are so much greater in the baby food industry than in other industries that they rebut the normal presumption" of anticompetitive effect that would apply in reviewing a "merger to duopoly."[22] In addition, the appellate court found that the district court had erred in concluding that Heinz and Beech-Nut did not really compete at retail and in concluding that the merger would promote innovation.

The court of appeals went to unusual lengths to reverse the district court opinion. An appeals court must accept the district court's findings of fact, unless the district court committed clear error. This highly deferential standard promotes the efficient use of judicial resources by limiting the scope of appeals.[23] But here, the appellate panel engaged in what one commentator has termed "an extraordinary amount of appellate factfinding" (Kolasky 2001, p. 82).

---

[20]Judge Bork, whose influential antitrust book argues against permitting an efficiency defense to mergers, filed an amicus brief to the appeals court in support of Heinz's acquisition of Beech-Nut. He contended that courts should allow a merger between two smaller firms that would create a stronger competitor against a firm that was dominant before a merger and would otherwise likely remain dominant. The brief did not address whether this position was tantamount to asking the court to accept an efficiency defense.

[21]*Federal Trade Commission* v. *H. J. Heinz Co.*, 246 F.3d 708 (D.C. Cir. 2001).

[22]*Heinz*, 246 F.3d at 380–81.

[23]Compare, for example, the appellate court's deference to the factual findings of the district court in *U.S.* v. *Microsoft Corp.*, 253 F.3d 34 (D.C. Cir. 2001), handed down by the same court of appeals a few months after the decision in *Heinz*.

In concluding that the district court did not look at total variable cost or at cost savings spread over the merging firms' entire output, the appeals court overlooked the evidence that Beech-Nut's total variable costs of production would decline 15 percent by shifting production of its brand to the Heinz facility, and the evidence that Beech-Nut customers would pay 15 percent less while Heinz customers would obtain a premium product at a value price. The appellate panel's theory that Heinz could have created a premium brand on its own had not been pressed by the FTC and overlooked the evidence that Heinz could not profitably make major new product investments absent national distribution, and had not done so. The appeals court's conclusion that no reasonable district court judge could have found that Heinz and Beech-Nut did not really compete at retail relied on the anecdotal testimony of some witnesses that was inconsistent with the anecdotal testimony of other witnesses, and gave no weight to the systematic empirical studies of retail competition introduced by defendants and relied upon by the district court. In contrast, when the appeals court rejected the district court's conclusion that the merger would promote innovation, its central complaint was that the evidence on which the district court relied was not statistically significant, and hence highly speculative.

The appellate court's thoroughgoing rejection of the district court's opinion appeared to be rooted in its skepticism about the efficiency defense, particularly when the merger would lead to a highly concentrated market. This concern was signaled in an order that the appeals court issued to prevent consummation of the merger while the appeal was pending, where the court noted: "[A]lthough there is much to be said for recognizing an efficiencies defense in principle, the high concentration levels present in this case complicate the determination of whether it should be permitted here."[24] The same theme was emphasized when the court of appeals issued its decision on the merits: "[T]he high market concentration levels present in this case require, in rebuttal, proof of extraordinary efficiencies, which the appellees [merging firms] failed to supply."[25] The court of appeals was so concerned about the competitive dangers flowing from high market concentration that it arguably created a new legal standard, raising the bar for the defense. In order for the district court to conclude that coordination would be unlikely in this highly concentrated market with entry barriers, the court of appeals held, the district court would have to find that the difficulties of colluding are not just high in some absolute sense; they must be "unique" to the baby food industry, and "so much greater . . . than in other industries that they rebut the normal presumption" that concentrated markets protected from entry are ripe for tacit collusion.[26] The appeals court's skepticism about

[24]*Federal Trade Commission* v. *H.J. Heinz Co.,* 2000 Trade Cas. (CCH) P73,090 (D.C. Cir. 2000). Only one member of the circuit court panel issuing this order was on the panel that ultimately decided the appeal.

[25]*Heinz,* 246 F.3d at 720.

[26]*Heinz,* 246 F.3d at 724–25.

an efficiencies defense when market concentration is very high stands in contrast to the way the courts treat entry: Ease of entry undermines proof of anticompetitive effect no matter how high the market concentration.[27]

In defense of its perspective on high concentration and efficiencies, the appeals court speculated that even if the defendants were correct in predicting that the postmerger Heinz would compete aggressively with Gerber in order to increase its market share, that incentive might at some time dissipate, and the two would eventually come to see their interest in tacitly colluding rather than competing.[28] Had it accepted the defendants' view of premerger industry conduct, however, the court might have seen the possibility of increased competition followed by tacit collusion as superior to the present situation, in which the dominant firm, Gerber, continues to exercise market power free from serious challenge.

LOOKING FORWARD

The appellate court decision ended Heinz's attempt to acquire Beech-Nut. This outcome did not arise as a matter of law: The legal result was merely that the district court was ordered to enter a preliminary injunction, leaving the parties free to pursue the case in a full administrative trial at the FTC. Instead, as is common in merger litigation, the delay that further proceedings would impose, combined with their uncertain outcome, undermined the business reasons for the transaction.

With respect to merger policy generally, the appeals court's decision leaves open the possibility that an efficiencies defense could succeed in other cases—or even could have prevailed in this very case if the litigation were to have continued through an administrative trial.[29] But the strong rejection of the "extraordinary" efficiency claims in *Heinz* calls into question the extent to which the courts will be willing to accept an efficiency defense when the market is highly concentrated.

REFERENCES

Baker, Jonathan B. "Mavericks, Mergers and Exclusion: Proving Coordinated Competitive Effects under the Antitrust Laws." *New York University Law Review* 77 (April 2002): 135–203.

---

[27]*U.S.* v. *Waste Management, Inc.,* 743 F.2d 976 (2d Cir. 1984); *U.S.* v. *Baker Hughes, Inc.,* 908 F.2d 981 (D.C. Cir. 1990). It may be appropriate for courts to be more skeptical of an efficiencies defense than an entry defense, however, to the extent the evidence relevant to efficiency analysis is more likely to be under the defendants' control and to the extent efficiency claims tend to be more speculative.

[28]See *Heinz,* 246 F.3d at 725.

[29]*Heinz,* 246 F.3d at 725.

Balto, David. "The Efficiency Defense in Merger Review: Progress or Stagnation?" *Antitrust* 16 (Fall 2001): 74–81.

Beckner, C. Frederick, and Steven C. Salop. "Decision Theory and Antitrust Rules." *Antitrust Law Journal* 67, no. 1 (1999): 41–76.

Berry, Mark N. "Efficiencies and Horizontal Mergers: In Search of a Defense." *San Diego Law Review* 33 (May–June 1996): 515–554.

Bulow, Jeremy I., and Paul Pfleiderer. "A Note on the Effect of Cost Changes on Price." *Journal of Political Economy* 91 (Feb. 1983): 182–185.

Calvani, Terry. "Rectangles & Triangles: A Response to Mr. Lande." *Antitrust Law Journal* 58, no. 2 (1989): 657–659.

Conrath, Craig W., and Nicholas A. Widnell. "Efficiency Claims in Merger Analysis: Hostility or Humility?" *George Mason Law Review* 7 (Spring 1999): 685–705.

Federal Trade Commission Staff. "Enhancing the Analysis of Efficiencies in Merger Evaluation." In *Anticipating the 21st Century: Competition Policy in the New High-Tech, Global Marketplace,* vol. 1, chapter 2. Washington, D.C.: Federal Trade Commission, May 1996.

Fisher, Alan A., and Robert A. Lande. "Efficiency Considerations in Merger Enforcement." *California Law Review* 71 (Dec. 1983): 1580–1696.

Greene, William H. *Econometric Analysis,* 4th edn. Upper Saddle River, N.J. Prentice-Hall, 2000.

Kolasky, William J. "Lessons from Baby Food: The Role of Efficiencies in Merger Review." *Antitrust* 16 (Fall 2001): 82–87.

Kolasky, William J., and Andrew R. Dick. "The Merger Guidelines and the Integration of Efficiencies into Antitrust Review of Horizontal Mergers." Unpublished manuscript, May 24, 2001.

Leary, Thomas B. "An Inside Look at the *Heinz* Case." *Antitrust* 16 (Spring 2002): 32–35.

Marcus, David. "Two and Three, Sponsored by the FTC." *Corporate Control Alert* (Sept. 2000): 11–17.

Muris, Timothy J. "The Government and Merger Efficiencies: Still Hostile after All These Years." *George Mason Law Review* 7 (Spring 1999): 729–752.

Ravenscraft, David J., and F. M. Scherer. *Mergers, Sell-Offs, and Economic Efficiency.* Washington, D.C.: Brookings Institution, 1987.

Williamson, Oliver E. "Economies as an Antitrust Defense: The Welfare Trade-Offs." *American Economic Review* 58 (March 1968): 18–36.

PART II

Horizontal Practices

The Economic
and Legal Context

Anticompetitive horizontal practices may occur in market settings ranging from fragmented industries to true monopolies. The nature of the practices, however, is likely to differ in each case. In an industry with many firms, the primary concern is with efforts at explicit collusion or implicit coordination in order to increase profitability above the competitive minimum. Where the number of firms is small—that is, in an oligopoly—the same possibility of explicit or implicit price cooperation or collusion exists, but anticompetitive conduct also may include some strategies by a firm to disadvantage or drive out its rivals or to deter possible entrants. Such strategies of predation and exclusion also may arise in the case of monopolies and dominant firms, whereas those firms engage in price coordination less frequently since they face few if any capable rivals.

The antitrust laws address this broad spectrum of anticompetitive conduct. Section 1 of the Sherman Act forbids any "contract, combination, . . . or conspiracy in restraint of trade . . ." , language intended to prevent collusion among firms. Section 2 of that act prohibits actions that would "monopolize, or attempt to monopolize" a market. This is directed at acts designed unfairly to achieve or maintain market dominance. Section 5 of the Federal Trade Commission Act encompasses all of this in its sweeping ban on "unfair methods of competition."

Issues of horizontal practice differ from the problems addressed in Part I of this book. There the focus is upon market concentration and especially increases in concentration as a result of mergers that affect the intensity of competition in the industry. The practices discussed in this section are not the result of any structural change in an industry. Rather, they represent behavior patterns that arise within a given industrial structure as firms seek to increase their profitability either through closer cooperation with horizontal competitors or through aggression against one or more of them. We address these two categories of concern—cooperation and aggression—in that order.

CARTELS, COLLUSION, AND COOPERATION

A simple demonstration in microeconomics shows how a mutual agreement on price can increase profits in the market and likely profits to all firms, possibly up to the equivalent of the monopoly level. From a social perspective, this outcome has the same effect as shown in the introduction to Part 1 for the case of monopoly or merger with market power: Deadweight loss is created, and surplus is transferred from consumers to producers. Mutual agreement may mean a range of things—cartels, collusion, and tacit cooperation. Cartels are formal, generally enforceable agreements among sellers. Collusion is the case of relatively formal but illegal agreements, while tacit cooperation involves informal coordination of behavior, which has uncertain legal implications.

Cartels are prohibited in most countries except in limited circumstances such as export promotion, some agricultural marketing agreements, and (according to some) certain sports league activities.[1] Cartels among countries, however, are not subject to such prohibitions and have sprung up in many primary product markets ranging from coffee to crude oil. The experience of these cartels demonstrates that success is by no means assured. The reasons for this bear examination, since the factors that prevent a cartel from succeeding must also stand in the way of an industry's efforts at collusion or tacit cooperation. Put differently, if an industry cannot come to an explicit agreement, it is even less likely to succeed using less powerful strategies such as collusive agreements or tacit cooperation.

Broadly speaking, cartels must be able to (1) reach an agreement and (2) enforce adherence to the agreement. Economic theory and empirical evidence indicate that the following considerations with respect to the market, sellers and buyers, and demand conditions make efforts more likely to succeed in the effort to raise price and profitability:[2]

- the fewer are the number of firms;
- the more similar are firm sizes;
- the more difficult is entry;
- the more similar are firms' costs;
- the greater is product homogeneity;
- the smaller and more frequent are orders;
- the more available is information about rivals' prices;
- the more stable is demand;

---

[1]See Case 11 by Franklin Fisher, Christopher Maxwell, and Evan Sue Shouten in this part.

[2]For a discussion of the rationale for these factors, see industrial organization texts such as Scherer and Ross (1990) or Carlton and Perloff (1999).

- the smaller and more numerous are buyers; and
- the lower are fixed costs.

The same factors play a role in firms' efforts to collude.[3] Collusion is, however, a considerably more complicated strategy than a cartel. The fact that collusion is illegal makes it more risky to pursue, as well as more difficult to implement, since the agreement is not legally enforceable. Despite that, the appeal of higher profits prompts firms to enter into collusive agreements with surprising frequency.[4]

The most common form of agreement among firms involves less formal, "tacit" modes of coordination. Much economic theory and empirical analysis have been devoted to examining the nature of firm interactions in general and the likelihood of spontaneous cooperation in particular. The relevant theory dates back at least to Augustin Cournot, who in 1838 demonstrated that above-competitive profitability can arise even in the absence of explicit agreements, so long as firms are sufficiently few and respond passively (and myopically) to each others' choices of quantities. Though Joseph Bertrand in 1883 demonstrated that in the case of price competition among firms selling identical products profitability would drop to competitive levels, even for a duopoly, more recent theoretical work has shown that even price rivalry among firms selling *differentiated* products will yield an equilibrium with above-competitive profitability.

While these theories generally predict above-competitive levels of price and profitability, they do not imply that monopoly levels are likely, since firms' individual incentives do not extend to that degree of cooperation. This proposition is readily shown with the aid of the famous game theoretic formulation known as the Prisoners' Dilemma. In the stylized example in Figure II-1, suppose there are two players A and B, each with price strategies we can label HI and LO. HI may usefully be thought of as the price consistent with cooperation or collusion, while LO maximizes each firm's *individual* profitability without regard to its rival or to joint profits. We assume that each firm makes its price choice independently but with knowledge that the resulting profit will also depend on its rival's price choice—the essence of oligopoly.

Player A rationally evaluates its two alternatives in light of what rival player B might do. If player B selects HI, then of A's two choices, its payoff is greater from LO (15) than from HI (10). On the other hand if player B selects LO, A is *still* better off choosing LO (4 versus 2). Remarkably, then,

---

[3]For evidence regarding the importance of many of these in actual conspiracies, see Hay and Kelly (1974).

[4]Case 10 by John Connor in this part represents a good example of a recent experience with a cartel in action. Both Case 8 by Robert Porter and Douglas Zona and Case 12 by Kenneth Elzinga and David Mills in this part illustrate the economic and legal challenges of determining whether a conspiracy exists in a market.

FIGURE II-1 A "Prisoners' Dilemma" Pricing Game

PLAYER B

regardless of what A expects B to do, A earns greater profit by choosing LO! LO becomes what is known as A's "dominant strategy"—better regardless of its rival's choice of strategies. The same result holds for player B,[5] so that the equilibrium of the game occurs at LO-LO despite the fact that each firm's profit (and total industry profit) falls well short of its maximum at HI-HI. This outcome illustrates the powerful effect of competition—the risk that one's rival will pursue its own interests—in conditioning the outcome of the process.

This compulsion toward strong competition is the result of the one-period ("static") nature of the game. Most business interactions are not one-period, however, so game theory has also investigated equilibria in multi-period games, either of finite or infinite length.[6] Treating a multi-period game as a sequence of one-period games with the structure shown in Figure II.1, it is straightforward to show that HI-HI may also be an equilibrium. To see this, consider player A's choices beginning at that point. Player A could, of course, choose the LO strategy that was unbeatable in the one-period game, but if it did (and Player B chose HI), its rival would surely retaliate by also choosing LO in the following period. That would produce first-period profit for A equal to 15, followed by a never-ending series of 4, as shown in the time profile of profits in Figure II-2. The alternative is that player A sticks with HI, so that if B does as well, A earns a payoff of 10 indefinitely. Comparing the two time profiles, it is clear that unless player A's discount rate is quite high—that is, unless it values first-period profits very much more than profits in later years—the longer period of modest profits

---

[5]This holds for player B since the game described here is symmetric: Player B confronts exactly the same payoffs from its choices as does player A.

[6]Infinite business games are not especially plausible either. Theory has shown, however, that finite games of *unknown* length are in fact much like those of infinite length. See, for example, Church and Ware (2000).

FIGURE II-2 Time Profile of Profits

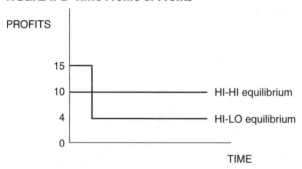

from cooperation may well yield it a higher present value of profits.[7] This result—that a cooperative equilibrium may result from purely tacit interactions—and the circumstances that may cause it are crucial ingredients in modern oligopoly theory.

In a number of cases such spontaneous cooperation may not succeed, but something short of a full-blown conspiracy may suffice. For example, in some markets there may be one distinctly unfavorable condition that prevents what otherwise would likely be successful cooperation. If that one condition can be remedied, higher profits may then result. Such devices are called "facilitating practices" and are illustrated by each of the following:

- "Most favored customer" clauses, which reduce each seller's incentive to cut prices to some customers by requiring equivalent rebates to other customers;

- Long-term customer contracts and exit fees from contracts, which may insulate existing sellers from new competitors and handicap existing firms in bidding away each other's customers;

- Advance pre-announcements of price changes or rapid ex post dissemination of such changes, which may assist oligopolists' efforts to come to an agreement on and to maintain prices.

Each of these mechanisms may facilitate anticompetitive outcomes in the market.[8] From a policy perspective these have the advantage of being easier to remedy than are the underlying conditions that give rise to, say, purely tacit coordination. The dilemma for policy in this area is that most of these so-called "facilitating practices" cannot simply be prohibited since they also have benign or pro-competitive explanations. Disentangling the two remains a major challenge for economics and policy.

---

[7]In the present case cooperation is an equilibrium for any discount rate less than 20 percent. Circumstances characterized by high discount rates include companies facing imminent financial crises that need cash upfront, and countries with pressing development needs. Each of these cases is associated with players' defecting from the agreement, as theory predicts.

[8]A good analytical discussion of these various practices can be found in Salop (1986). See Hay (1999) for an illustration of facilitating practices in the Ethyl case.

Three further considerations round out this brief review. First, collusion and coordination may occur not only with respect to price and quantity, but also with respect to capacity, product characteristics, advertising, research and development, and virtually any strategy variable. Most of the same broad considerations apply to these other dimensions of competition and cooperation, though details such as sunk costs, certainty, and time lags can play important roles (Scherer and Ross 1990). Second, perfect collusion or cooperation is not necessary for success. Sellers in an industry may be considerably better off simply by moderating the rivalry among themselves, even if full monopoly cooperation is not achieved. Third, higher price and profitability tends to spawn entry and erosion of market power. That outcome does not indicate "failure," since the alternative may be zero profits, nor does it imply that policy has no role. The latter depends upon the relative timing of policy action versus the market-induced decline in market power.

Antitrust

The longest-standing precedent in all of U.S. antitrust policy has been the per se prohibition on explicit price fixing. Beginning with the *Trans-Missouri Freight Association* case[9] and strongly affirmed in the *Trenton Potteries*[10] decision, the Supreme Court has ruled that price fixing is an automatic violation of the Sherman Act, invoking its ban on "contracts, combinations and conspiracies in restraint of trade." The Court explicitly rejected the defense that the resulting price might be "reasonable." This per se approach stems from a literal reading of Section 1 of the Act, but it is also an efficient rule for certain types of conduct.

Per se prohibition is an appropriate policy stance in any of three circumstances: where the action always has adverse consequences; where it always has either adverse or at best neutral consequences; or it *almost* always has adverse or neutral consequences and its positive outcomes are both infrequent and difficult to distinguish. Each of the first two cases represents fairly clear grounds for a per se rule since neither prohibits beneficial actions.[11] The third case is more problematic in that it concedes the possibility of occasional policy error—attacking beneficial actions. The justification is that these outcomes are relatively few and very costly to identify. A "perfect" rule in these circumstances would be very costly to administer (all possible cases would have to be fully examined), and the result might not be correct categorization in any event.

Given the earlier economic discussion, the court's per se approach to price fixing would seem entirely appropriate. To be sure, the courts have

---

[9]*U.S. v. Trans-Missouri Freight Association,* 166 U.S. 290 (1897).

[10]*U.S. v. Trenton Potteries Co. et al.,* 273 U.S. 392 (1927).

[11]The second may not be entirely free of controversy insofar as it occasionally attacks actions that are completely neutral in their market effects.

muddied the waters a bit by some minor inconsistencies in their treatment of price fixing, notably in the Depression-era *Appalachian Coals*[12] decision. Yet over its long history antitrust policy has been largely free of ambiguity: Conspiracy equals conviction.

More recently, the courts have been presented with substantial arguments as to the benefits of allowing direct competitors in certain circumstances to coordinate pricing and other matters. That circumstance has been said to arise when coordination is required in order for a product simply to be offered at all. That is, transactions costs or some other impediment would otherwise cause a market failure. Beginning with the *ASCAP/BMI*[13] cases, the Supreme Court has accepted this logical possibility and in those cases in fact allowed price coordination.

One consequence of this exception to the per se ban is that companies being investigated for price coordination may now argue that they fall within the exception. Such was the case in both the NCAA case[14] and in the MIT financial aid dispute that is discussed in Case 7 by Gustavo Bamberger and Dennis Carlton in this part.[15] In principle this might force the enforcement agencies and courts first to decide that issue before applying the per se rule in any matter, thus threatening to undermine the per se approach altogether.[16] In an effort to prevent this and to preserve the administrative ease of the per se rule, the agencies have developed a so-called "modified per se" approach toward such practices. This approach asks a series of questions designed summarily to filter out all those practices that lack any such justification, treating them under the standard per se rule and leaving only a very small fraction of cases for a more comprehensive analysis.[17]

No similarly tidy approach has been found for exchanges of information among firms that might set the stage for a tacit agreement. Since neutral and even beneficial effects are possible—for example, sharing information about future demand can help correct errors by individual firms—no per se prohibition seems appropriate. Yet many such exchanges clearly can aid in the process of coordinating price, output, and capacity decisions to the detriment of consumers. Here the courts have tried to fashion rules from the particulars of each case brought before them. In the *Container Corpo-*

---

[12]*Appalachian Coals, Inc. v. U.S.*, 288 U.S. 344 (1940).

[13]*American Society of Composers, Authors, and Publishers et al.* v. *Columbia Broadcasting System Inc.*, 441 U.S. 1 (1979); *Broadcast Music, Inc.* v. *CBS*, 441 U.S. 1 (1979).

[14]*National Collegiate Athletic Association* v. *Board of Regents of the University of Oklahoma and University of Georgia Athletic Association*, 468 U.S. 85 (1984); see Horowitz (1999).

[15]The MIT case was part of *U.S.* v. *Brown University et al.*, 805 F. Supp. 288 (E.D.Pa. 1992).

[16]Strictly speaking, one might say that there is no longer a per se rule if there is an exception to it.

[17]The first question asked is whether the practice is "inherently suspect"; that is, whether absent an efficiency justification, it is automatically anticompetitive. If not, then a rule of reason must be applied right away. Next is asked whether there is a plausible efficiency justification. If not, the practice is subject to per se prohibition. If there is, then a full inquiry is required. This approach was first adopted in the FTC case, *Massachusetts Board of Registration in Optometry*, 110 F.T.C. 549 (1988).

ration case, for example, the Supreme Court struck down exchanges of price information among direct competitors when they involved customer-specific information (which is the most helpful in detecting "cheating" on an understanding among sellers) and when industry characteristics suggested that an agreement was likely to have an adverse market effect.[18]

If the effects of a particular practice depend on the facts of each case, a so-called "rule-of-reason" must be used instead of per se. The rule-of-reason is appropriate when a practice may have either adverse or beneficial effects, both in significant proportion, and when these alternative outcomes can be readily distinguished in actual practice. While information exchanges fall into this category, a brief review of the courts' attempts to draw relevant distinctions illustrates the difficulties. For example, trade associations cannot take any action intended to force compliance by their members with published prices, but they are permitted to collect and disseminate considerable price information, some of it clearly helpful in efforts at coordination. Moreover, the courts have been somewhat more tolerant of exchanges of information about non-price matters, apparently in the belief that these pose a lesser risk of coordination or that coordination is less likely to affect the market adversely.

Further problems have accompanied the courts' recent efforts to judge so-called "facilitating practices"—those institutional arrangements and mechanisms that promote coordination among companies without explicit agreements. These cases have involved such practices as adherence to common pricing books that reduce the complexity of pricing heterogeneous products (as in the *GE-Westinghouse* case[19]), the use of most-favored-customer clauses as incentive-altering devices (as in the *Ethyl* case[20]), and reliance upon central data bases to disseminate, virtually instantaneously, information about competitors' prices (as in the Airline Tariff Publishing (ATP) dispute[21] that is discussed in Case 9 by Severin Borenstein in this part). The courts have been willing to consider some of these practices as undue intrusions on the market process, but their insistence on guidance regarding circumstances in which these represent anticompetitive behavior as opposed to normal business practice had been a common theme. They have often found such guidance lacking.

From the enforcement agencies' perspective, the advantage of the facilitating practices doctrine is that it allows antitrust action against instances of tacit collusion that are aided by such practices. The courts have been extremely reluctant to convict companies for purely tacit collusion,

---

[18]*U.S.* v. *Container Corp. of America, et al.,* 393 U.S. 333 (1969). Paradoxically, the Court acted in this case despite quite ambiguous evidence as to the likelihood of success.

[19]*U.S.* v. *General Electric Co. et al,* C.A. No. 28,228 (E.D.Pa.) (Dec. 1976).

[20]*In re Ethyl Corp. et al,* FTC Docket no. 9128, 1975; *E.I. DuPont de Nemours & Co.* v. *FTC,* 729 F.2d 128 (1994); see Hay (1999).

[21]*U.S.* v. *Airline Tariff Publishing et al.*

since that comes close to prohibiting conduct that seems virtually inevitable in an oligopoly setting (for example, responding to a rival's price change in a similar fashion). Moreover, prohibition is not straightforward since it is not altogether clear what action by companies should be proscribed. For these reasons purely tacit cooperation has been largely outside the reach of the antitrust laws and is likely to remain so unless in particular cases it is clear that some facilitating practice plays a crucial role and unless the courts are persuaded of the practicality of action against it.

MONOPOLIZATION: PREDATION AND EXCLUSION

Economic Theory

Oligopolists and dominant firms have a wider range of possible anticompetitive actions at their disposal than simply collusion and cooperation with their rivals. In particular, they may pursue strategies designed to improve their own profitability by aggressively attacking their rivals (actual and potential) and thereby weakening their constraining influence. For example, when a firm willfully excludes potential entrants from its market, drives one or more of its present rivals out, or disciplines its rivals for their conduct, the extent of (long-run) competition in the market may be lessened. Such statements of principles, however, obscure the great difficulty in determining precisely which practices, and under what circumstances, should constitute antitrust violations. Indeed, the answers to these questions have changed over time and are still undergoing change as economic understanding advances. Our discussion here will focus on two categories of conduct: predation and exclusion.

There is a longstanding and extensive body of antitrust law and economic analysis concerning predatory pricing. What might be termed "classic predation" involves a leading firm that increases output so as to lower market price and impose losses on its smaller rivals. Those rivals are eventually forced to exit, leaving the predator firm with unconstrained, or at least less constrained, market power. The new market equilibrium involves a yet higher market price and additional consumer harm. This scenario, together with other allegations of anticompetitive practices, has often been said to explain the rise of Standard Oil to dominance of petroleum markets in the late nineteenth century. There is no dispute that many of Standard's rivals exited the market and that it came to possess substantial market power, but a century after the fact, many continue to argue that Standard was simply a tough, efficient competitor, and that its displacement of its smaller, less capable rivals was inevitable.

This debate typifies the controversy that has always surrounded allegations of predatory conduct. Chicago School adherents, in particular, have argued that the circumstances under which predation can succeed are very limited, that rational firms will therefore rarely attempt it, and hence that predation is not a significant policy problem. They note that the dominant firm's larger size implies that it will incur losses proportionally greater than those of the target firms, the proportion being its share relative to that of its rivals. Thus, the would-be predator is likely to injure itself more than it damages its rival. Moreover, even if successful in driving rivals out, the dominant firm will benefit from this strategy only if it has the protection of entry barriers in the post-predation period. Without such barriers, any effort by the firm to raise price will simply induce entry, and it will never recoup the losses that it initially incurred. All of these considerations, it has been argued, make predation rarely rational (McGee 1958).

This conclusion received support from studies of the history of predating cases. Many instances of alleged predation have been found to arise from rivals confronted by hard competition by more efficient larger firms, with adverse consequences for their own market share and profitability but not necessarily adverse consequences for competition. Some analysts therefore concluded that instances of true predation are sufficiently rare that they can be safely ignored—indeed, are best ignored, since efforts to distinguish predation from legitimate and beneficial price reductions would likely endanger the latter. While this inference goes too far for most observers, there is widespread agreement that true predation is considerably less common than alleged.

Modern economic analysis has advanced this debate by demonstrating that predation may be quite rational, and hence entirely plausible, under certain circumstances. This new analysis is based on models of information asymmetry and/or strategic behavior and falls into three broad categories:[22] First, a dominant firm may predate in one market or against one competitor in order to deter competitors in other markets in which it may operate, or in the future against competitors in the same market. Even if "irrational" when considered in isolation, such conduct may create a reputation for aggressive response that discourages any other competitors from initiating action. The value of that reputation justifies the expenditure in the initially targeted market.

Another possible mechanism arises if the dominant firm has a "deeper pocket"—that is, greater financial resources with which to battle its rival, due to differential access to capital markets. Differential access arises when small firms have to pay a premium to borrow funds, either because lenders favor the prospects of the leading firm or perhaps because the leading firm deliberately disrupts the business prospects of smaller rivals.

Finally, some economic models have shown that a dominant firm may use pricing in an effort to convince ("signal") actual and potential rivals that it has lower costs. The most straightforward way to send that signal is to pick a price consistent with being a low-cost firm—that is, a low price. Ri-

---

[22]For an extended discussion, see Ordover and Saloner (1989).

vals will not know that this signal may be false, so they may decide that they would be better off tempering their actions or simply operating in some other market.

These new models of rational predation are central to any economic discussion of the topic, but none of them provides a simple and clear guideline for what constitutes predatory pricing. That is, practical policy is not easily based on such possibilities, although many have attempted to formulate decision rules to help guide policymakers (see, for example, Brodley et al. 2000). Most rules also allow for predation that varies from the classic model—for example, predation by a nondominant firm (Burnett 1999); or predatory price cuts targeted at particular rivals (Pittman 1984); or predation involving strategic use of product innovation (Ordover and Willig 1981), product proliferation (Schmalensee 1979), product replacement (Menge 1962), advertising (Hilke and Nelson 1983), and cost manipulation (Salop and Scheffman 1983). Which of these might be employed depends on the circumstances—in particular, the aggressor firm's perception of the most readily exploitable weaknesses of its rivals. All of these make clear how diverse predatory conduct may be, and how correspondingly difficult a task is the fashioning of a comprehensive rule.

Closely related to the strategy of attacking present rivals are actions by a dominant firm or monopoly to exclude firms contemplating entry into a profitable market. There are a wide variety of such exclusionary practices, including selective price discounting in niches or to customers most likely to be subject to entry, new product introduction and placement that makes entry less attractive, long-term contracts or tie-ins with present customers to deny demand opportunities, advertising directed at specific niches and potential entrants, denial of necessary inputs to rivals, and so forth.[23] For these to be effective, economic theory teaches that the actions or threatened response must be credible; that is, the leading firm must actually follow through because it is rational for it to do so. Otherwise, the firm's threats will not be taken seriously, and they will fail to deter entry. Credibility is enhanced by sunk costs, first move advantages, and other irreversible strategies.[24]

The first of these models, and the ones that have continued to receive the most attention, are those examining how capacity expansion may rationally be used to preempt entry opportunities. Early work by Spence (1977) and Dixit (1980) showed how the incumbent may select capacity and commit to a strategy that alters the best response of possible entrants. By leaving little opportunity for viable operation by an entrant, the result may be either no entry at all, or at worst entry on a smaller and less competitive scale. A host of such models have now been developed, examining various assumptions and parameters giving rise to credible entry deterrence

---

[23]Among relevant references, see Aghion and Bolton (1987) and Scherer (1979).

[24]For a good discussion of these, see Church and Ware (2000).

and extending the results to the large number of other strategy variables noted above.[25] The upshot of this research has been to place entry deterrence and related strategies on a sound theoretical footing and to provide some guidance as to the conditions that make them plausible.

Entry deterrence represents willful conduct aimed at preserving monopoly power. Another strategy is illustrated by "essential facilities," those for which access is necessary for effective operation in a market. Incumbents that deny prospective entrants such access can control the structure and conduct within the wider market dependent on that necessary input. Since essential facilities often (but not always) arise in the case of network industries, further discussion of the issues raised will be postponed until Part IV.

Quite a different category of conduct that raises possible concern involves exclusionary practices arising in related—often vertically related—markets. More will be said about these in Part III, but some issues deserve mention here as well. For example, a company whose product dominates one market may seek to link the purchase of that product to another where they have no such dominance but are interested in establishing a presence. Such "leveraging" of market power from one market to another may displace rivals in the second, "competitive" market and raise barriers to subsequent entry. Although some economists had argued that leveraging cannot extend monopoly power, more recent models (e.g., Rasmussen et al. 1992) have demonstrated how leveraging may indeed have that consequence. The conditions under which this is a rational, profit-maximizing strategy for the incumbent firm, however, remain imperfectly specified in practice.

In sum, there is clearly an enormous variety of practices that dominant firms may employ to handicap both small rivals and entrants. Many of these—increasing capacity, choosing to deny a competitor admission to some organization, operating in related markets, and so forth—may also have innocent purposes and raise no competitive concerns. It is an ongoing challenge for economics to determine the circumstances that distinguish pro- versus anticompetitive consequences.

Antitrust

Antitrust law has not been able to await resolution of these conceptual and practical difficulties before dealing with allegations of predatory and exclusionary behavior. Clearly, the difficulties of distinguishing predation from hard, but honest and pro-competitive, conduct by large firms can easily result in policy errors. Treating dominant firm actions too harshly is likely to stifle the very competition that antitrust policies were designed to foster. A policy that is too lenient, on the other hand, risks harm to competitors and

---

[25]For extended discussion, see Shapiro (1989) and Martin (1993).

consumers alike. At various times the enforcement agencies and courts may have made mistakes of both types.

Early cases against monopolies and dominant firms revealed the courts' inclination to interpret adverse effects on competitors as evidence of predation. In the previously mentioned *Standard Oil* case the dominant firm was alleged to have engaged in nasty practices toward rivals. Whether this was true or not, it was primarily on that basis that the Supreme Court found that Standard "monopolized" its market. But in cases where a firm's dominant position was achieved without victimized rivals, the opposite verdict was reached. Thus, market dominance by U.S. Steel that resulted in higher prices was found not to violate the antitrust laws since there was no evidence of "brutalities and tyrannies" against smaller rivals.[26] In fact—and not surprisingly—its higher prices drew favorable reviews from its competitors.

Judicial focus on and hostility toward the conduct of large firms may have reached its peak during the 1960s. Cases involving mergers, price discrimination, and monopolization routinely included allegations of predatory conduct by some leading firm in the market. In the *Utah Pie* case,[27] for example, large food manufacturing firms were convicted of predatory price discrimination against a local firm despite the fact that the latter remained the market leader and was profitable throughout. Such decisions raised questions as to whether price competition itself was being sacrificed to protect smaller firms.

In an effort to advance the debate concerning predatory conduct, two leading antitrust scholars (Areeda and Turner 1975) published an analysis seeking to establish enforceable rules for predation. In their analysis, Areeda and Turner did not claim that predation would never occur. Rather, they sought to limit judicial prohibitions on low prices to those cases that they believed were demonstrably anticompetitive by contemporary economic standards. Their survey of various possible price and cost patterns led them to conclude that anticompetitive effects were likely only if the leading firm priced below its own marginal cost, and they proposed using average variable cost as a surrogate for marginal cost.

This Areeda-Turner rule now has many critics, but the criticism in no way detracts from the importance of its contribution. For one thing, in the confusion that had pervaded judicial opinions with respect to predation, the concreteness of the Areeda-Turner rule had an immediate attraction, and many (but not all) courts seized upon it for their own use. Moreover, that original rule caused an explosive growth in research attempting to clarify the economics of predation and to develop an operational rule to identify it. Unfortunately, the latter goal has proven elusive, and the major advances in economic understanding of rational predation have made virtually no im-

---

[26]The language is taken from *Standard Oil.*

[27]*Utah Pie Co.* v. *Continental Baking Co.*, 386 U.S. 685 (1967).

pression upon the courts (Klevorick 1992). Instead, the Court has continued to insist on evidence regarding the relationship between cost and price, and more recently has added a virtual requirement that recoupment be shown possible.[28]

Analogous difficulties have arisen with policy toward exclusionary behavior by dominant firms. Distinguishing legitimate conduct—even hard competition—by a dominant firm from anticompetitive exclusion of potential competitors is as formidable a policy task as determining true predatory conduct. Examples of alleged exclusion include cases brought against such familiar dominant firms as Kodak, IBM, Kellogg/General Mills/General Foods, and DuPont. In *Berkey* v. *Kodak,*[29] the plaintiff alleged that Kodak sought to monopolize film and photo finishing by its introduction of a new camera/film system without pre-disclosure to rivals in film and processing.

A whole series of cases brought by peripheral equipment manufacturers[30] and later by the Justice Department against IBM alleged selective price discounting, strategic equipment modification, and other harmful practices designed to exclude potential entrants. In the breakfast cereal case[31] the Federal Trade Commission (FTC) developed a novel economic argument that the three major manufacturers shared a monopoly and collectively "packed product space" with new cereals so as to leave inadequate opportunity for new entrants. The FTC also pursued monopolization allegations against DuPont for using its cost advantage in the market for the paint whitener titanium dioxide to preclude expansion by rivals.[32]

With minor exceptions all of the defendant firms in these cases prevailed. The court ruled that Kodak had no obligation to pre-disclose product innovations for the benefit of rivals. IBM won most of the myriad private suits that it faced, and the Justice Department ultimately withdrew its suit. The FTC acquitted the three breakfast cereal manufacturers, in part balking at the proposition that "more products" could somehow be anticompetitive. In the DuPont case, the FTC concluded very explicitly that a dominant firm is under no obligation to avoid hard competition against smaller or newer rivals, regardless of the fate that might befall these rivals.

The view that a dominant firm should have much the same degree of discretion in its behavior as a competitive firm is not well-founded in economics. The same behavior may be benign when employed by a small firm but have quite different consequences in the hands of a dominant firm. Policy shifts in this direction relaxed restraints on the conduct of dominant firms, and the number of such cases—both government and private—dwin-

---

[28]See Elzinga (1999) on *Matsushita* and also Case 20 by Aaron Edlin and Joseph Farrell in Part IV.

[29]*Berkey Photo* v. *Eastman Kodak Co.,* 603 F.2d 263 (2d Cir. 1979).

[30]See Brock's (1989) discussion of several cases brought by peripheral equipment manufacturers against IBM.

[31]*In re Kellogg et al,* FTC Docket No. 8883 (1981).

[32]For an extended analysis of this case, see Dobson et al. (1994).

dled sharply during the 1980s. More recently, however, the enforcement agencies and courts have on occasion been persuaded of instances in which dominant firms' actions have crossed the line. This appears to be the case in both the *Kodak*[33] and *Microsoft*[34] proceedings discussed in Part IV of this volume. These and other cases may imply greater enforcement and judicial receptivity to claims of anticompetitive actions based on the focused application of economic theory and evidence.

REFERENCES

Aghion, Phillip, and Patrick Bolton. "Contracts as a Barrier to Entry." *American Economic Review* 77 (June 1987): 388–401.

Areeda, Philip, and Donald Turner. "Predatory Pricing and Related Practices under Section 2 of the Sherman Act." *Harvard Law Review* 88 (February 1975): 697–733.

Brock, Gerald W. "Dominant Firm Response to Competitive Challenge: Peripheral Manufacturers' Suits against IBM (1979–1983)." In *The Antitrust Revolution,* edited by John E. Kwoka, Jr. and Lawrence J. White, 160–182. New York: Harper-Collins, 1989.

Brodley, Joseph, Patrick Bolton, and Michael Riordon. "Predatory Pricing: Strategic Theory and Legal Policy." *The Georgetown Law Journal* 88 (August 2000): 2239–2330.

Burnett, William. "Predation by a Nondominant Firm: The Liggett Case." In *The Antitrust Revolution,* edited by John E. Kwoka, Jr. and Lawrence J. White, 239–263. New York: Oxford University Press, 1999.

Carlton, Dennis, and Jeffrey Perloff. *Modern Industrial Organization,* 3d edn. Reading, Mass.: Addison-Wesley, 1999.

Church, Jeffrey, and Roger Ware. *Industrial Organization: A Strategic Approach.* Boston: Irwin McGraw-Hill, 2000.

Dixit, Avinash. "The Role of Investment in Entry Deterrence." *Economic Journal* 90 (March 1980): 95–106.

Dobson, Douglas C., William G. Shepherd, and Robert D. Stoner. "Strategic Capacity Preemption: DuPont." In *The Antitrust Revolution: The Role of Economics,* edited by John E. Kwoka, Jr. and Lawrence J. White, 157–188. New York: Oxford University Press, 1994.

Elzinga, Kenneth. "Collusive Predation: *Zenith v. Matsushita.*" In *The Antitrust Revolution,* edited by John E. Kwoka, Jr., and Lawrence J. White, 220–238. New York: Oxford University Press, 1999.

Hay, George. "Facilitating Practices: The Ethyl Case," In *The Antitrust Revolution,* edited by John E. Kwoka, Jr., and Lawrence J. White, 182–201. New York: Oxford University Press, 1999.

---

[33]See Case 17 by Jeffrey MacKie-Mason and John Metzler in Part IV. This is a different case against Kodak than the one previously discussed.

[34]See Case 19 by Daniel Rubinfeld in Part IV.

Hay, George, and Daniel Kelly. "An Empirical Survey of Price-Fixing Conspiracies." *Journal of Law & Economics* 17 (April 1974): 13–38.

Hilke, John, and Philip Nelson. "Noisy Advertising and the Predation Rule in Antitrust." *American Economic Review* 74 (May 1984): 367–371.

Horowitz, Ira. "The Reasonableness of Horizontal Restraints: NCAA (1984)." In *The Antitrust Revolution,* edited by John E. Kwoka and Lawrence J. White, 202–219. New York: Oxford University Press, 1999.

Klevorick, Alvin. "The Current State of the Law and Economics of Predatory Pricing." *American Economic Review* 83 (May 1993): 162–167.

Martin, Stephen. *Advanced Industrial Economics.* Cambridge, Mass: Blackwell, 1993.

McGee, John. "Predatory Price Cutting: The Standard Oil (N.J.) Case." *Journal of Law & Economics* 1 (October 1958): 137–169.

Menge, John. "Style Change Costs as a Market Weapon." *Quarterly Journal of Economics* 76 (November 1962): 632–647.

Ordover, Janusz, and Garth Saloner. "Predation, Monopolization, and Antitrust." In *Handbook of Industrial Organization,* Vol. 1, edited by R. Schmalensee and R. Willig, 537–596. Amsterdam: North-Holland, 1989.

Ordover, Janusz, and Robert Willig. "An Economic Theory of Predation." *Yale Law Journal* 91 (November 1981): 8–53.

Pittman, Russell. "Predatory Investment: *U.S.* v. *IBM.*" *International Journal of Industrial Organization* 2 (December 1984): 341–365.

Rasmusen, Eric, Mark Ramserer, and John Wiley. "Naked Exclusion," *American Economic Review* 81 (December 1991): 1137–1145.

Salop, Steven. "Practices That (Credibly) Facilitate Oligopoly Coordination." In *New Developments in the Analysis of Market Structure,* edited by J. Stiglitz and F. G. Mathewson, 265–290. Cambridge, Mass.: MIT Press, 1986.

Salop, Steven, and David Scheffman. "Raising Rivals' Costs." *American Economic Review* 73 (May 1983): 267–271.

Scherer, F. M. "The Welfare Economics of Product Variety: An Application to the Ready-to-Eat Cereals Industry." *Journal of Industrial Economics* 28 (December 1979): 113–134.

Scherer, F. M., and David Ross. *Industrial Market Structure and Economic Performance.* 3d edn. Boston: Houghton Mifflin, 1990.

Schmalensee, Richard. "Entry Deterrence in the Ready-to-Eat Breakfast Cereal Industry." *Bell Journal of Economics* 9 (Autumn 1978): 305–327.

Shapiro, Carl. "Theories of Oligopoly Behavior." In *Handbook of Industrial Organization,* Vol. 1, edited by R. Schmalensee and R. Willig, 329–414. Amsterdam: North-Holland, 1989.

Spence, Michael. "Entry, Capacity Investment, and Oligopolistic Pricing." *Bell Journal of Economics* 8 (Autumn 1977): 534–544.

CASE 7

Antitrust and Higher Education: MIT Financial Aid (1993)

Gustavo E. Bamberger and
Dennis W. Carlton

INTRODUCTION

In 1991, the U.S. Department of Justice's Antitrust Division ("the Government") sued the Massachusetts Institute of Technology ("MIT") and the eight colleges and universities in the "Ivy League"—Brown University, Columbia University, Cornell University, Dartmouth College, Harvard College, Princeton University, the University of Pennsylvania, and Yale University. According to the Government, the nine schools violated Section 1 of the Sherman Act by engaging in a conspiracy to restrain price competition for students receiving financial aid. The Government claimed that the schools conspired on financial aid policies in an effort to reduce aid and thereby raise their revenues.

The schools responded that the Sherman Act did not apply to them because they are not-for-profit institutions. Furthermore, they justified their cooperative behavior by explaining that it enabled them to concentrate aid only on those in need and thereby helped the schools to achieve their socially desirable goals of "need-blind" admission coupled with financial aid to all needy admittees. Without collective action, the schools argued, there would be less financial aid available to needy students, with a resulting decrease in the number of lower-income students attending those schools.

Dennis Carlton testified as an expert witness on behalf of MIT. Gustavo Bamberger assisted in the development of the economic analysis underlying Carlton's testimony. This chapter is based in part on Carlton et al. (1995). We thank Greg Pelnar for his assistance and John Kwoka, William Lynk, and Larry White for helpful comments.

All of the Ivy League schools signed a consent decree agreeing to stop the challenged cooperative activity. MIT refused to sign and went to trial. In September of 1992, MIT was found to have violated the Sherman Act.[1] Government investigations against several schools outside of the Ivy League continued. Soon after the trial ended, Congress passed the Higher Education Act of 1992, allowing colleges and universities to engage in certain cooperative conduct aimed at concentrating aid only on needy students. In September of 1993, the court of appeals overturned the district court's verdict and ordered a new trial.[2] The Government subsequently dropped all investigations against other schools and reached a settlement with MIT that allows MIT to engage in most of the conduct that the Government had challenged.

This case raises several interesting and important issues about the treatment of not-for-profit institutions under the antitrust laws. Should the antitrust laws apply to not-for-profits, and if so, how? Specifically, how should the application of the antitrust laws to not-for-profit firms differ, if at all, from their application to for-profit firms?

This chapter describes the economics of not-for-profit schools and the schools' actions that were challenged by the Government, with the economic arguments and evidence relied on by each side. It then discusses the findings of the district court and the court of appeals. It also summarizes the settlement reached by MIT and the Government. It concludes with a discussion of the issues raised by this case and more recent developments in the application of the antitrust laws to not-for-profit institutions.

THE ECONOMICS OF NOT-FOR-PROFIT SCHOOLS

In the standard models of firm behavior used by economists, firms are assumed to have a simple objective—maximize profits. These profits are enjoyed by the owner or owners of the firm. A not-for-profit firm, however, typically is barred from paying out any profits it may earn (and there are no "owners" to whom profits could be paid). In the United States, not-for-profit firms typically are organized under IRS Regulation 501(c)3.[3] This regulation legally constrains the actions of a not-for-profit firm, specifically preventing the disbursement of any excess revenues over costs. Under the IRS code, private donations made to a not-for-profit institution can be deducted from the donor's taxable income and thus reduce the donor's tax. In this way, both the donor and the general tax-paying public support not-for-profit institutions.

---

[1] *U.S. v. Brown University, et al.*, 805 F. Supp. 288 (E.D. Pa. 1992).

[2] *U.S. v. Brown University, et al.*, 5 F.3d 658 (3rd Cir. 1993).

[3] MIT and the other Ivy League schools are 501c(3) corporations.

Although not-for-profit firms are relatively rare in the U.S. economy, several sectors of the economy are dominated by not-for-profits. Most higher education in the United States is provided by not-for-profit institutions. These institutions are either public, such as state universities, or private not-for-profit schools. In addition to most institutions of higher education, most religious and cultural institutions are not-for-profit. Similarly, most hospitals in the United States are organized as not-for-profits.[4]

Not-for-profit firms often are created to achieve (or attempt to achieve) a particular goal or goals that the firm's founders believe are socially desirable.[5] Some not-for-profit firms, such as educational institutions, solicit donations. Donors who would be reluctant to donate to a for-profit firm for fear that the owners would simply keep the donation do not face that concern in the case of not-for-profits because of the legal constraint on distributing funds.[6] Because for-profit firms may not have incentives to achieve certain goals that are considered socially desirable, not-for-profit firms can be viewed as a response to a "market failure."[7]

In the case of colleges and universities, the institution likely is interested in achieving various goals. For example, colleges and universities typically are thought to be interested in:[8]

- providing a quality education
- enhancing the general welfare of their students
- enhancing the general welfare of their faculty and administrators
- sponsoring high-quality and innovative research
- providing innovative teaching programs
- satisfying alumni and other potential donors' preferences.[9]

Because these institutions have various goals (not all of which are mutually consistent), it is difficult to specify precisely the "objective function" of the institution—that is, it is difficult to specify what exactly a particular school is attempting to maximize.

The not-for-profit nature of schools explains many school practices that would be unusual in a for-profit world. Schools maintain many prohibitions on transactions that would be inefficient in a profit-maximizing context. For example, schools such as MIT and the Ivys do not allow students

---

[4]See Hansmann (1980) and Lynk (1995).

[5]However, some not-for-profit firms may be formed to maximize the profits of other firms. For example, a not-for-profit trade organization likely takes actions intended to increase the profits of the firms it represents.

[6]Of course, donors are concerned that their donations will be well spent.

[7]See Hansmann (1980, p. 845).

[8]See, for example, Hopkins (1988).

[9]The MIT Alumni Association filed a brief in support of MIT in this case.

to buy admission (or at least there is no formal procedure for doing so) if they have poor grades. It seems likely that MIT and Harvard as well as many other schools could abandon need-blind admissions and profitably auction off their last five admission spots without a material decline in either their reputation or quality of the student body, but with a significant increase in revenue.[10] Since constraints on trading are generally undesirable, the behavior of schools can be reconciled with reasonable behavior only because of the complicated nature of each school's not-for-profit objective function.[11]

THE CHALLENGED CONDUCT

The history and development of the challenged conduct was not a disputed issue during the trial. Unlike most alleged price-fixing cases, both sides agreed on the basic facts.

In the 1950s, members of the Ivy League met to discuss the desirability of not bidding for "star" athletes. These meetings were called "Overlap meetings" (because they discussed students who were admitted to "overlapping" schools), and the schools participating in the meetings were called the "Overlap schools." Schools adopted the rule that no athlete could receive aid beyond that justified by financial need, and financial need was calculated according to a common formula. The meetings soon took up the issue of whether such a rule was sensible for nonathlete students. The schools reasoned that if they were forced to bid for star students who had no financial need, the schools would have less money to give out to other students who had such need. Before the 1950s, few schools had significant scholarship programs, and the Ivys were accessible primarily to the wealthy.[12] The purpose of the Overlap meetings, according to the participating schools, was to concentrate scarce financial aid only on needy students to enable such students to attend.

A student's aid package consists of two components. One is called "self help," which represents what a student contributes and is based on loans or jobs that the school may provide or help the student gets.[13] The other is grants (also known as scholarships), which are outright gifts to students. For most schools, grants and scholarships come primarily from either the Government (primarily through Pell grants) or the institution itself. A student pays for his or her education from grants, self help, and "family

---

[10]It is undoubtedly true that many schools do show preference to alumni and large donors and that this is a rough way of "selling" admission. MIT gives applicants of alumni and donors no preference.

[11]See Rothschild and White (1993) for a discussion of other school practices that are inconsistent with profit maximization.

[12]See Clotfelter (1991).

[13]There often may be a subsidy component to a loan that a student receives.

FIGURE 7-1 The Sources of Students' Tuition Payments.

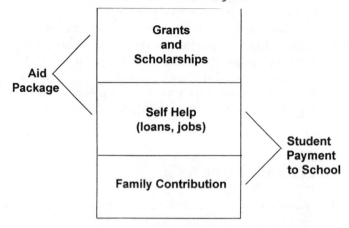

contribution." The sum of the first two categories is the student's aid package. The sum of the last two categories is what the student pays to the school (Figure 7-1). The Overlap schools reached agreement with each other on the family contribution for commonly admitted students seeking financial aid, so that regardless of which Overlap school a student was admitted to, the student's family contribution was identical. (Notice that even if gross tuition levels differed among schools, the Overlap schools equalized family contribution.) Some Overlap schools reached agreement on the division of the aid package between self help and grants, whereas others—including MIT—did not.

The number of schools participating in Overlap meetings grew over time. By the 1970s, there were regular meetings among the Ivys plus MIT and fourteen other prestigious schools.[14] The schools participating in Overlap meetings: (a) agreed to give aid based only on need; (b) agreed on a common methodology to define need; and (c) met to discuss individual cases of commonly admitted students.[15]

At the Overlap meetings, a listing of commonly admitted students was circulated among the schools together with each school's proposed family contributions for each student. In cases of significantly differing proposals

[14]The Ivys and MIT met together. The other fourteen schools also met together and some of these schools also met with certain members of the Ivy/MIT group. The other fourteen Overlap schools were Amherst College, Barnard College, Bowdoin College, Bryn Mawr University, Colby College, Middlebury College, Mount Holyoke College, Smith College, Trinity College, Tufts University, Vassar College, Wellesley College, Wesleyan University, and Williams College.

[15]A valid inquiry is whether the Overlap schools could have market power in view of their small share of total undergraduate enrollments in the United States (less than 1%). For example, the total undergraduate enrollment of all the Overlap schools was less than that of the total undergraduate enrollments of the Universities of Illinois, Michigan, and Wisconsin. If the Overlap schools lacked market power, it would be hard to explain why the Overlap process existed.

(ones that differed by more than several hundred dollars), the schools would discuss their justification for the family contributions and would agree to compromise on a common figure or (less often) agree to disagree. There were initial disagreements on about 10 to 20 percent of the commonly admitted students applying for financial aid.[16] The initial disagreements usually arose either because schools had different information (e.g., if an applicant had an older sibling at a school, one school could have more complete information than another about family finances) or because the schools had varying degrees of sophistication in analyzing complicated financial holdings (e.g., the treatment of a low reported income that took advantage of various tax shelters).

ECONOMIC ARGUMENTS AND EVIDENCE

The Government's Claims

According to the Government, there was little need for economic evidence in this case—the undisputed facts were enough to condemn MIT's conduct under Section 1 of the Sherman Act. The Government offered five arguments. First, the Government argued that the Sherman Act applied to MIT's financial aid policies because the collecting of fees from students and their families is a commercial activity governed by the antitrust laws. According to the Government, "financial aid is a discount from the list price that is offered to certain customers. Universities grant discounts in their own self-interest, just as do other businesses that compete in the market place."[17] The Government also argued that "[t]he selling and discounting of educational services involves a fundamentally commercial aspect of the higher education industry."[18]

Second, the Government argued that because MIT's financial aid policies constituted commercial activity, "MIT's status as a 'non-profit' corporation does not shield its anticompetitive conduct from the Sherman Act"[19] and that the "higher education industry" has no antitrust immunity.[20] In-

---

[16]See Dodge (1989).

[17]Memorandum of Law in Support of Government's Motion for Summary Judgment, Civil Action No. 91-CV-3274, United States District Court for the Eastern District of Pennsylvania, ("Government's Memorandum"), at 87.

[18]Government's Memorandum, at 86. The Government distinguished the "commercial nature" of MIT's financial aid policies from the issues involved in *Marjorie Webster Junior College, Inc.* v. *Middle States Association of Colleges and Secondary Schools, Inc.,* 432 F.2d 650, 654 (D.C. Cir.), *cert. denied,* 400 U.S. 965 (1970), which, according to the Government, stood for "the fairly unremarkable proposition that non-commercial activities, not related to pricing, are outside the scope of the Sherman Act" (at 92).

[19]Government's Memorandum, at 88.

[20]Government's Memorandum, at 92.

stead, the Government contended that an analysis of a challenged practice "must focus on the conduct in question, not on the nature of the industry involved or the organizational form of the actors."[21]

Third, given that the challenged conduct constituted commercial activity, the Government argued that the Overlap process was "garden variety price fixing."[22] The purpose of the price fix was to agree on the number and amount of discounts (grants) from list price (tuition) that the schools would offer. However, the Government did not allege a conspiracy to fix the list price, that is, the gross tuition level charged by the schools.[23]

Fourth, the Government further claimed that the inevitable consequence of the collective behavior of the Overlap schools was to increase the schools' net tuition revenues.[24] Indeed, the Government argued that even in the absence of evidence that average net tuition actually rose, the consequences of the school's actions were so inevitable that the conduct should be condemned as a per se violation of the antitrust laws.[25] The Government argued that "[t]he critical issue in applying the per se rule is whether the court has had experience with the type of restraint in question, not whether it has had experience in a particular industry."[26] According to the Government, although the terminology used by MIT and the Ivys differed from that used in most industries, it was easy to translate that terminology into "standard economic terms":

> "Tuition, Room and Board" and other compulsory charges is the list price of college attendance; "financial aid" and "merit scholarships" are selective discounts offered to some students. The "family contribution" is the net price for college attendance, that is, the list price minus the discount. By agreeing to fix family contributions . . . and to ban merit scholarships, MIT and the Ivy League institutions have engaged in a trade practice that the courts have experience with and have prohibited time and time again—price fixing.[27]

---

[21]Government's Memorandum, at 91.

[22]District Court Trial Transcript, at 725.

[23]The Government's theory implied that the schools increased revenues by colluding on the net tuition charged to needy students, but not to rich students. The Government did not explain why conduct allegedly intended to extract higher tuition payments ignored the students with the most money.

[24]The Government did not allege that the challenged conduct reduced the schools' output. For example, the Government did not claim that the Overlap process had reduced enrollments at the Overlap schools.

[25]Conduct that courts have found almost always harms competition is condemned as a per se violation without any analysis required of the effect in the specific case at hand. Conduct that might or might not harm competition is analyzed under a "rule of reason," where analysis of the effects of the conduct determine its legality. (In practice, however, the distinction between per se and rule-of-reason analyses often is not sharp.)

[26]Government's Memorandum, at 82.

[27]Government's Memorandum, at 84.

Finally, the Government argued that "social policy" justifications for the challenged conduct were irrelevant even under the rule of reason: "[N]o justification for price-fixing is allowed and no analysis of the specific factors involved in a particular industry is required."[28] According to the Government, the Supreme Court "has consistently rejected social or quality-based justifications for anticompetitive conduct" under the rule of reason.[29]

MIT's Position

Unlike most defendants in a price-fixing case, MIT did not dispute that it engaged in the challenged conduct—MIT readily admitted that it met with the other Overlap schools and discussed financial aid packages for individual students. However, MIT vigorously disputed the Government's characterization of its conduct as an attempt to raise net tuition revenues.

MIT had four responses to the Government. First, MIT argued that, as a threshold matter, the challenged conduct did not constitute "trade or commerce" and thus was not proscribed by the Sherman Act. MIT argued that it and the other Overlap schools "engaged in Overlap to advance educational access and socioeconomic diversity and to maximize the effective use of private charitable funds. In so doing, they neither sought nor obtained any financial or commercial benefit," and therefore MIT's conduct should not be subject to the antitrust laws.[30] Furthermore, MIT argued that because the actual cost of an MIT undergraduate education exceeded the total revenue received from every student (even those receiving no financial aid), all grants of financial aid constituted a form of charity, not a reduction from "list price." Thus, according to MIT, the conduct at issue "involved the coordinated distribution of private, charitable funds to qualified but needy students to help them defray the expenses of an education at MIT."[31]

MIT argued that the legislative history of the Sherman Act showed that it was not intended to apply to the charitable activities of not-for-profit educational institutions. For example, in 1890 Senator Sherman argued that there was no need to amend his proposed act to exempt temperance unions:

> I do not see any reason for putting in [an exclusion for] temperance societies any more than churches or schoolhouses or any other kind of moral or educational associations that may be organized. Such an association is not in any sense a combination or arrangement made to interfere with interstate commerce . . . I do not think it is worth while to adopt the

---

[28]Government's Memorandum, at 79.

[29]Government's Memorandum, at 79.

[30]Massachusetts Institute of Technology's Brief in Opposition to the Antitrust Division's Motion for Summary Judgment ("MIT's Brief"), at 44.

[31]MIT's Brief, at 40.

> amendment [relating to] temperance societies. You might as well include churches and Sunday schools.[32]

Second, MIT argued that if the court decided that the Sherman Act did apply to the challenged conduct, that conduct should not be condemned as a per se violation but instead should be analyzed under the rule of reason. MIT argued that the per se rule should be applied only to types of conduct where "a court can look back upon unambiguous judicial experience demonstrating that the challenged practice is a 'naked restraint of trade with no purpose except stifling of competition.' "[33]

MIT argued that the court did not have unambiguous judicial experience with the type of challenged conduct because the firms acting collectively were not-for-profit institutions, whereas most antitrust cases involve for-profit firms. According to MIT, the court should not condemn conduct practiced by not-for-profits simply because that same conduct when practiced by for-profit firms would harm competition. That is, even though the court's experience shows that when profit-maximizing firms meet to set price, they almost always intend to increase prices and profits (and thereby harm consumers), the same is not necessarily true when not-for-profit schools meet to set financial aid policy collectively.

In particular, MIT argued that the Government's claim that net tuition revenues inevitably would increase as a consequence of the collective action was wrong as a matter of economic theory. Even if the Government's argument generally were true for profit-maximizing firms, it was not true for not-for-profit firms. Because not-for-profit firms maximize a multiattribute objective function, it simply is not possible to predict inevitable consequences from cooperative price setting. As a matter of economic theory, the cooperative efforts of the Overlap schools could indeed be to conserve their financial aid so as to achieve their stated goal of enabling greater numbers of needy students to attend their schools.

Third, MIT argued that the challenged conduct was justified on "social welfare" grounds that the Government endorsed. In particular, MIT argued that the challenged conduct was needed to conserve aid for only the truly needy and claimed that the Overlap conduct helped the Overlap schools achieve their goals of need-blind admissions with a guarantee of full aid if admitted. Moreover, the schools believed that their policies were entirely consistent with the Federal Government's financial aid policy. With minor exceptions, federal money can be given *only* to needy students. A meritorious high-income student generally cannot receive any federal aid. Moreover, students receiving any federal aid usually cannot receive supplemental awards from a school beyond demonstrated financial need.

---

[32]MIT's Brief, at 40 (citations omitted).

[33]MIT's Brief, at 58, citing *White Motor Co. v. United States,* 372 U.S. 253, 263 (1963).

MIT pointed out that the Government seemed specifically to endorse collective behavior by MIT and the Ivys when used to make aid decisions for student-athletes. The consent decree signed by the Ivys provided that:

> Nothing in this Final Judgment shall prevent defendants that are members of a common athletic league from: (1) agreeing to grant financial aid to recruited athletes or students who participate in athletics on the sole basis of economic need with no differentiation in amount or in kind based on athletic ability or participation, provided that each school shall apply its own standard of economic need.[34]

MIT argued that if the Government believed that such agreements were reasonable for athletes, it made no sense to argue that similar agreements were per se illegal when applied to nonathletes.[35]

Finally, MIT argued that if the challenged conduct were evaluated under the rule of reason, the empirical evidence showed that the Overlap agreements produced no antitrust harm. MIT argued that the economic rationale for a per se rule against collective price setting is that price typically rises as a result of the collective action. Because this underlying rationale does not apply necessarily to not-for-profit schools, MIT claimed that the only way to determine whether the collective agreements on aid raised price is to study what happened as a result of the agreements. MIT's expert economist performed such a study and found no statistically significant basis for the claim that the collective action raised average net tuition per student at the Overlap schools.[36] Thus, MIT argued that the statistical evidence did not support the Government's hypothesis that the collective action inevitably must have increased the Overlap schools' net tuition revenues.[37]

MIT's expert investigated through a multiple regression analysis whether average net tuition per student was higher at schools that engaged in the challenged conduct. A multiple regression analysis is a well-accepted standard statistical procedure used to examine the factors influencing a variable of interest, such as average net tuition per student. Through a multiple regression analysis, it is possible to isolate the effect of a single variable in a complex factual environment containing multiple variables. In the regression analysis offered by MIT, other characteristics of a school that could affect average net tuition per student in addition to participation in the

---

[34]MIT's Brief, at 78 (quoting consent decree entered into by the Ivy League schools).

[35]Similarly, the Government has not opposed the NCAA's collective enforcement of limits on athletic aid packages.

[36]The Government's expert economist agreed that average net tuition per student was the appropriate variable to study.

[37]In the typical alleged price-fixing conspiracy, the conspiring firms are accused of raising price and restricting output. Because a school's "output" is multidimensional, measuring the effect of Overlap on output is difficult. The Government provided no evidence nor made any claim that the challenged behavior reduced the Overlap schools' output.

Overlap agreement were accounted for. For example, whether a school is a private or public institution or whether a school has a religious affiliation could influence average net tuition. By accounting for these other factors, an analyst can obtain estimates of the effect of Overlap membership on the average net tuition per student charged by a school.

The variables used to explain average net tuition per student at a particular school were:

1. Whether the school had a religious affiliation (this variable is labeled NONRELIG in the regression analysis)

2. Percentage of students scoring more than 700 on the SAT verbal or math test (SAT)

3. Real state per-capita disposable income in the state where the school is located (YDPC)

4. Percentage of applicants accepted (PCTACC)

5. Percentage of undergraduates not receiving need-based aid (PCT-NOAID)

6. Percentage of class completing a degree (COMPDEG)

7. Type of school, as determined by the Carnegie Foundation for the Advancement of Teaching (DOCTOR1, DOCTOR2, RSRCH1, RSRCH2)

8. Real endowment per full-time equivalent student (ENDOW)

9. Whether mandatory fee information was unavailable (FEEMISS)

10. Whether the school was MIT or in the Ivy League (IVY)

11. Whether the school was one of the non-Ivy League Overlap schools (NONIVY)

The analysis was based on annual data for each of these variables for the years 1984–1990 for approximately 160 private schools. Adding public schools to the analysis did not have a substantial impact on the results.[38]

MIT's expert analyzed yearly data as well as an average over the entire 1984–1990 period, and found that the results were unambiguous—there was no statistically significant evidence that membership in Overlap was associated with higher average net tuition per student. A typical result is presented in Table 7-1, which shows, for example, that

---

[38]Experiments with different models and estimation techniques found substantially similar results—the Overlap conduct did not result in statistically significant higher average net tuition per student at the Overlap schools, holding constant school characteristics.

TABLE 7-1
Weighted Average Net Tuition Regression Results,
1984–1990 (standard errors in parentheses)

Intercept	2299.47
	(2429.07)
IVY	−322.42
	(678.72)
NONIVY	130.37
	(463.81)
RSRCH1	1042.21
	(435.09)
RSRCH2	1062.57
	(514.05)
DOCTOR1	545.66
	(551.02)
DOCTOR2	−1143.27
	(493.21)
FEEMISS	−540.82
	(294.78)
PCTACC	−27.89
	(11.97)
PCTNOAID	43.58
	(9.44)
SAT	2.31
	(11.16)
YDPC	0.36
	(0.07)
COMPDEG	45.68
	(16.64)
NONRELIG	1343.18
	(250.19)
ENDOW	−5.95
	(3.77)
R^2	0.726
Number of Observations	162

1. All else equal, MIT and the Ivy League schools charged slightly *less* than non-Overlap schools (i.e., the estimated coefficient on IVY is negative but not significantly different from zero).

2. All else equal, schools that were not religiously affiliated charged, on average, roughly $1,350 more than schools that were religiously affiliated (i.e., the estimated coefficient on NONRELIG is about 1350).

3. Highly selective schools were more expensive, all else equal, than less selective schools. For example, a school that accepted 25 percent of its applicants charged roughly $1,400 more on average than a school that

accepted 75 percent of its applicants (i.e., the coefficient on PCTACC times 50 equals about 1400).

Thus, MIT argued that the evidence provided no statistically significant support for the Government's position that the Overlap agreements raised the average net tuition per student charged by the Overlap schools.[39]

THE RESULTS

The District Court

After a ten-day bench trial, the District Court for the Eastern District of Pennsylvania found that MIT had violated Section 1 of the Sherman Act. The court rejected MIT's contention that the challenged conduct did not constitute commercial activity: "[t]he court can conceive of few aspects of higher education that are more commercial than the price charged to students."[40]

Although the court accepted the Government's position that the Overlap conduct affected commerce and thus was susceptible to attack under the Sherman Act, the court refused to find the Overlap process per se illegal. The court observed that "[m]erely because a certain practice bears a label which falls within the categories of restraints declared to be per se unreasonable does not mean a court must reflexively condemn that practice to per se treatment."[41]

The court did not, however, undertake an in-depth rule-of-reason analysis of the Overlap conduct. Instead, the court ruled that the challenged conduct should be examined using an abbreviated rule-of-reason analysis. The court deemed that a full-scale rule-of-reason analysis was not needed because the Overlap conduct was "so inherently suspect" that "'no elaborate industry analysis'" was required to demonstrate its anticompetitive character.[42]

The court ruled that "[since] the Ivy Overlap Agreements are plainly anticompetitive, the Rule of Reason places upon MIT 'a heavy burden of establishing an affirmative defense which competitively justifies this apparent deviation from the operations of a free market.'"[43] The court held that

---

[39]At trial, the Government's economist presented regression studies that he claimed showed that the Overlap conduct did increase average net tuition per student at those schools. These results were based on a small subset of the data used in MIT's analysis. MIT argued that the Government's studies were flawed.

[40]*U.S.* v. *Brown University, et al.,* 805 F. Supp. 288 (E.D. Pa. 1992), at 298.

[41]*U.S.* v. *Brown University, et al.,* 805 F. Supp. 288 (E.D. Pa. 1992), at 299.

[42]*U.S.* v. *Brown University, et al.,* 805 F. Supp. 288 (E.D. Pa. 1992), at 303, quoting *FTC* v. *Indiana Fed'n of Dentists,* 476 U.S. 447, 459, 106 S.Ct. 2009, 2018 (1986).

[43]*U.S.* v. *Brown University, et al.,* 805 F. Supp. 288 (E.D. Pa. 1992), at 304, quoting *NCAA* v. *Board of Regents of the University of Oklahoma, et al.,* 468 U.S. 85, 113, 104 S.Ct. 2948, 2966 (1984).

evidence that the challenged conduct did not affect the prices charged by the Overlap schools did not provide an affirmative defense for the conduct. "Even accepting MIT's premise that Overlap was revenue neutral [i.e., did not affect average net tuition per student], to say that a restraint is revenue neutral, by itself, says nothing of its procompetitive virtue."[44]

The court rejected MIT's justification for Overlap and concluded:

> The court is not to decide whether social policy aims can ever justify an otherwise competitively unreasonable restraint. The issue before the court is narrow, straightforward and unvarnished. It is whether, under the Rule of Reason, the elimination of competition itself can be justified by non-economic designs. The Supreme Court has unambiguously and conclusively held that it may not.[45]

The Court of Appeals

Both the Government and MIT appealed certain portions of the district court's ruling. In September 1993, the court of appeals for the Third Circuit ruled (by a 2-to-1 majority) that the district court had erred in several respects and remanded the case to the district court for retrial.[46]

The court of appeals first examined whether the challenged conduct constituted trade or commerce. The court of appeals upheld the district court's finding and ruled that providing educational services in return for payment (whether discounted or not) is a commercial activity that subjects MIT to the antitrust laws. However, the court of appeals noted that "[a]lthough MIT's status as a nonprofit educational organization and its advancement of congressionally recognized and important social welfare goals does not remove its conduct from the realm of trade or commerce, these factors will influence whether this conduct violates the Sherman Act."[47] Thus, the court of appeals ruled that the social goals of MIT's policy were relevant in an antitrust analysis.

The court of appeals also addressed whether the district court erred by using a rule of reason, instead of a per se, approach in evaluating Overlap.[48] The court of appeals upheld the district court's ruling that Overlap was not per se illegal and held that Overlap's "alleged pure altruistic motive and alleged absence of a revenue maximizing purpose contribute to our uncer-

---

[44]U.S. v. *Brown University, et al.*, 805 F. Supp. 288 (E.D. Pa. 1992), at 304.

[45]U.S. v. *Brown University, et al.*, 805 F. Supp. 288 (E.D. Pa. 1992), at 305.

[46]In dissent, Judge Weis argued that the Sherman Act should not apply to the challenged conduct because MIT was a not-for-profit firm and argued that the district court should have granted judgment in favor of MIT.

[47]U.S. v. *Brown University, et al.*, 5 F.3d 658 (3rd Cir. 1993), at 668.

[48]MIT argued that the district court erred by not using a full-scale (as opposed to an abbreviated) rule-of-reason analysis; the Government argued that the district court erred by not finding Overlap to be per se illegal.

tainty with regard to Overlap's anti-competitiveness, and thus prompts us to give careful scrutiny to the nature of Overlap, and to refrain from declaring Overlap per se unreasonable."[49]

The court of appeals disagreed with the district court's ruling that the effect of Overlap on average net tuition per student was irrelevant. The court of appeals ruled that "the absence of any finding [by the district court] of adverse effects such as higher price or lower output is relevant, albeit not dispositive, when the district court considers whether MIT has met [its burden of establishing an affirmative justification for Overlap]."[50]

The court of appeals also ruled that the district court erred by not investigating more fully MIT's procompetitive and noneconomic justifications for the Overlap conduct. The court of appeals noted that MIT had proffered procompetitive economic justifications for Overlap. For example, the court of appeals explained that if Overlap increased consumer choice (by allowing needy but able students to attend MIT who otherwise would not have attended), then "rather than suppress competition, Overlap may in fact merely regulate competition in order to enhance it, while also deriving certain social benefits. If the rule of reason analysis leads to this conclusion, then indeed Overlap will be beyond the scope of the prohibitions of the Sherman Act."[51] The court of appeals ruled that "[t]he nature of higher education, and the asserted pro-competitive and pro-consumer features of the Overlap, convince us that a full rule of reason is in order here."[52]

Finally, the court of appeals held that "[e]ven if anticompetitive restraint is intended to achieve a legitimate objective, the restraint only survives a rule of reason analysis if it is reasonably necessary to achieve the legitimate objectives proffered by the defendant."[53] If, on remand, the district court found that MIT could persuasively justify Overlap, then the Government would have an opportunity to prove that a reasonable but less restrictive alternative existed that could meet Overlap's objectives.

The Settlement

The new trial called for by the court of appeals did not take place because the Government and MIT reached a settlement in December of 1993. Under the terms of the settlement, MIT and other schools are allowed to engage in Overlap-type behavior, including pooling of student information. Agreements not to give merit aid and to use common principles to determine aid are allowed, but discussions about individual students' financial aid are not.

---

[49]*U.S. v. Brown University, et al.,* 5 F.3d 658 (3rd Cir. 1993), at 672.

[50]*U.S. v. Brown University, et al.,* 5 F.3d 658 (3rd Cir. 1993), at 624.

[51]*U.S. v. Brown University, et al.,* 5 F.3d 658 (3rd Cir. 1993), at 677.

[52]*U.S. v. Brown University, et al.,* 5 F.3d 658 (3rd Cir. 1993), at 678.

[53]*U.S. v. Brown University, et al.,* 5 F.3d 658 (3rd Cir. 1993), at 678–679.

Audits to detect schools that deviate significantly from the agreed-upon common principles for awarding aid are allowed.

DISCUSSION

Economic Efficiency

To many economists, the economic content of the antitrust laws is simple: prevent inefficiency.[54] Did Overlap affect economic efficiency? If the Overlap process left the schools' revenues and class size unchanged and prevented the use of merit aid at those schools, then the Overlap process likely transferred income that otherwise would have gone to meritorious non-needy students toward other students. The Overlap conduct also probably resulted in a different allocation of students to schools than otherwise would have occurred—a larger number of needy students attended the Overlap schools.[55]

There is no necessary inefficiency generated by Overlap; instead, its major effect is better characterized as income redistribution.[56] The Government argued that there was a class of consumers harmed by the Overlap conduct—namely, meritorious high-income students. But if Overlap primarily redistributed income, then for every winner, there was an equal loser. There is no necessary efficiency loss from income transfers.

The general hostility that most economists (including us) have toward cooperative price setting in the profit-maximizing sector should not lead to an automatic condemnation of a practice that is focused primarily on equity

---

[54]Others have argued that efficiency should not be the sole goal of the antitrust laws. See, e.g., Lande (1989) and Pitofsky (1979).

[55]The schools claimed that Overlap allowed them to obtain a diverse group of students. As a general matter, it is unclear how to determine whether one mix of students is more efficient than an alternative mix because there is no unambiguous agreement on what "output" a school should be trying to achieve. As a theoretical matter, it is possible to justify the Overlap conduct on the basis of efficiency in matching. Suppose that students care about the quality of their classmates. Then given the quality attributes of each person, one can ask whether competition can achieve the optimal allocation of students to schools. This problem is similar to one posed by Koopmans and Beckmann (1957) and studied by Roth and Sotomayor (1990). (See also Telser, 1978.) These studies show that unconstrained competition cannot always achieve an optimal allocation. This finding can provide a possible theoretical justification for limitations on the use of prices and for cooperative assignment of students to schools. We are unaware of any empirical attempts to examine this potential justification. (See Hansmann and Klevorick, 1993.)

[56]If the Government were correct and the Overlap conduct had raised the schools' revenues, then the cooperative action would seem similar to a cartel. Even here, the not-for-profit schools could argue that they differ from a profit-maximizing cartel because any increased revenues that they receive are more likely to be spent on desirable causes. Except perhaps in unusual cases, the enforcement problem associated with determining whether the increased revenues were spent productively strike us as so great that it would not be desirable to allow such a defense even for not-for-profit institutions. Moreover, the danger of the cooperative agreement's causing inefficiency increases as average net tuition per student rises.

concerns and appears to have few if any efficiency consequences and that would never arise (at least, for the motives claimed by MIT) in the profit-maximizing sector.[57] No cartel of profit-maximizing firms would cooperate *solely* to redistribute income among its customers.

If one articulates goals for the antitrust laws other than economic efficiency, one can justify condemning many practices. For example, if one assumes that the antitrust laws guarantee unrestricted competition under all circumstances, then by assumption the Overlap conduct violates this goal. But that standard would condemn many practices generally viewed as pro-competitive. For example, policies that reduce information costs or that allow a manufacturer to use vertical restrictions on distributors to encourage the provision of services often are considered procompetitive. Yet in each case some individuals may be harmed. Consumers with low search costs or consumers with no need for service would benefit if the antitrust laws forbade such policies, even if, overall, consumers gain from these policies. Thus, any sensible antitrust policy must involve some balancing of harms and benefits to consumers.

Social Goals

Was the Overlap conduct necessary to meet MIT's and the other schools' social goals? In particular, does assisting needy students require collective action, or would it be possible for each school to meet the same goal by unilaterally implementing its own financial aid policy?

MIT presented expert testimony that without Overlap, competition for star students would break out in the future and financial aid to needy students would be reduced.[58] The adverse consequences of such an effect on the needy could be especially pronounced in light of recent trends in financing higher education.[59] Federal support for higher education declined substantially since its high point in the 1970s. For example, real federal aid (grants plus loans) per enrolled undergraduate student dropped by about 15 percent between 1975 and 1988 (see Table 7-2). Real federal grants per enrolled undergraduate student fell by about 60 percent over the same time period. Furthermore, the real cost of a college education increased by almost 40 percent during the same period. The combined effect of reductions in total aid and increases in tuition caused the real price paid per student to rise by at least 50 percent between 1975 and 1988.[60] To offset the decline in federal grants and aid, states and schools have expanded their grant and aid

---

[57]Even in the profit-maximizing sector, cooperation can sometimes be efficient, e.g., among firms in a network industry. See Carlton and Klamer (1983). Cooperation among competing (profit-seeking) teams in a sports league also may be efficient; see, e.g., Noll (1982).

[58]The demise of Overlap apparently led to some bidding for students by at least some former Overlap members. See, for example, Carlson and Shepherd (1992, p. 569).

[59]See McPherson and Schapiro (1991) for a detailed study of financing trends.

[60]See Clotfelter (1991) and *Statistical Abstract of the United States* (1991).

TABLE 7-2
Ratio of Aggregate Merit Aid to Need Aid by Carnegie Classification[a]

Carnegie Classification	Number of Schools	1984 Ratio Merit Aid to Need Aid	1989 Ratio Merit Aid to Need Aid
Research I	11	0.1467	0.1730
Research II	8	0.1880	0.1946
Doctoral I	4	0.1426	0.2139
Doctoral II	9	0.3032	0.3758
Liberal Arts I	40	0.0759	0.1313
Total	72	0.1339	0.1800

[a] Based on schools with available information.

Sources: Peterson's Annual Survey of Undergraduate Institutions and the Carnegie Foundation for the Advancement of Teaching.

awards. Data show that merit aid has generally become increasingly important as a fraction of institutional aid. As schools grant more aid, they grant it increasingly to meritorious non-needy students. In the early 1990s, several schools (including Brown University and Smith College, former participants in Overlap) announced that they would no longer maintain "need-blind" admissions policies.[61]

Since 1998, financial aid competition among at least some of the Ivies appears to have increased. In 1998, for example, Princeton announced that it would no longer consider the value of a student's family home when it determined financial need; the change in Princeton's policy effectively increased aid to applicants from relatively wealthy families. Princeton also eliminated loans for students from families earning less than $46,500. According to press accounts, other top schools, including Harvard, Stanford, and Yale, responded by increasing their aid offers.[62] In February 2001, Princeton announced that it would replace all student loans with grants, thereby reducing a student's payment to the school (see Figure 7-1).[63] According to Ronald Ehrenberg, director of Cornell's Higher Education Research Institute, Princeton's new policies have resulted in competitive responses from other Ivies, such as Harvard, Yale, and MIT (Seaman and Tesoriero 2000).

Two recent studies confirm our prediction that Overlap did not increase the Overlap schools' average net tuition. Because the Overlap meet-

[61]See Lubman (1994) and Stout (1992).

[62]See Clayton (2001). Netz (2000, p. 7) reports that "[b]eginning in January 1998, [financial aid] competition did heat up immensely, in both the methods used to determine a students financial need and the form in which such need would be met. However, this increase in competition did not occur until four years after the case was finally settled, and seems likely to have been triggered by something other than the lawsuit."

[63]In July 2001, the presidents of twenty-eight private colleges, including Stanford and Yale, adopted standards for calculating a family's "ability to pay" (e.g., is home equity considered?). Princeton and Harvard did not agree to adopt the standards. See Marcus (2001).

ings ended in 1991 and the Overlap process was not subsequently reinstituted, post-Overlap information not available at the time of our study is now available. This new information can be used to analyze the effect of Overlap by comparing the schools' Overlap and post-Overlap average net tuitions. Hoxby (2000, pp. 35–36) finds that the demise of Overlap did not reduce tuition revenues received by the Overlap schools. Netz (2000) also finds that the average net tuition received by the Overlap schools did not change significantly after Overlap meetings ended.[64] Neither of these studies included information from the period after the change in Princeton's aid policies, and the impact of the post-1998 changes is not clear. Some observers, however, argue that the new policies have increased the competition for top students, with the result that lower-income students will receive less financial aid. Ehrenberg, for example, argues that "low-income kids, those not at the top academically and students who do not have as much information on how to play the game" will be harmed by the new policies (Seaman and Tesoriero 2000).

Did Overlap achieve its goal of increasing access of the needy to Overlap schools? It is difficult to measure quantitatively whether Overlap did achieve its social goal, and little systematic evidence was presented at trial. Ideally, one would want evidence on the family income of entrants to examine whether Overlap affected the income distribution of its entrants by allowing a larger number of needy students to attend. Though such income data are not available in sufficient detail to perform a study, data are available on the percentage of the entering class that is black or Hispanic, a variable that likely is roughly related to income. Although these percentages are only rough proxies for income, they should provide some indication of Overlap's effect.

Studies performed by the authors found evidence that Overlap increased black enrollment by a statistically significant amount.[65] The magnitude indicates that for the typical school, Overlap increased black enrollment to about 5 percent during the period 1984–1990 from the about 3 percent that would otherwise be predicted. These results provide indirect evidence to support MIT's claim that Overlap did achieve its social goal. The evidence is weaker for Hispanics than for blacks that Overlap improved access.[66]

Hoxby (2000) confirms the finding that Overlap achieved its goal of increasing access of the needy to the Overlap schools. Based on a compar-

---

[64]Netz (2000, fn. 20 and table 5) reports that the estimated coefficient on an "Overlap dummy" in the post-Overlap period is "statistically significantly unchanged from the value before the meetings ended."

[65]See Carlton, Bamberger, and Epstein (1995).

[66]Although these results provide evidence that Overlap did increase access to these schools, it is not clear that the collective setting of financial aid awards by a group of schools is an optimal way for society to ensure access to higher education.

ison of outcomes in the last five Overlap years to the first five years after Overlap ended, Hoxby finds that the demise of Overlap resulted in fewer relatively needy, black, and Hispanic students at the Overlap schools.[67]

Recent Developments

The relevance of the difference between for-profit and not-for-profit firms in an antitrust analysis has emerged as a factor in other contexts. For example, in 1996, the Federal Trade Commission (FTC) filed suit to block a proposed merger between two not-for-profit hospitals in Grand Rapids, Michigan.[68] The district court denied the request.[69] First, the court found that the usual assumptions made in an analysis of a proposed merger of for-profit firms should not apply automatically to an analysis involving not-for-profit firms. Second, the court relied on empirical evidence that mergers of not-for-profit hospitals do not lead generally to price increases.[70] Finally, the court ruled that the fact that some consumer groups could be harmed by the proposed merger should not automatically lead it to block the merger if other groups of consumers could benefit significantly from the merger.

Not-for-Profits and Antitrust Law

If Overlap did provide the needy with increased access to the Overlap schools, then it would seem that such an effect could be relevant to MIT's defense under a rule of reason.[71] But is such a defense possible under the antitrust laws?

The antitrust laws and most economists generally are hostile to collective price setting. In numerous cases, the Supreme Court has not allowed profit-maximizing firms to justify their cooperative actions to set prices on the basis of reasonableness of the prices that have been set.[72] Only when the

---

[67]See Hoxby (2000, pp. 31–33).

[68]*FTC* v. *Butterworth Health Corporation and Blodgett Memorial Medical Center,* (W.D. Mi., Southern Division, 1996). The not-for-profit status of hospitals also was considered in (among other cases) an earlier hospital merger challenged by the U.S. Department of Justice. See *U.S.* v. *Carilion Health System,* 707 F. Supp. 840 (W.D. Va., 1989), discussed by Eisenstadt (1999).

[69]The FTC appealed the district court's ruling. The court of appeals for the Sixth Circuit affirmed the district court in July of 1997.

[70]The court relied on the writings and testimony of William Lynk. Lynk and Lexecon were retained by the defendants.

[71]A related question is whether MIT or the Government should have the burden of proving the effect of Overlap on access of the needy to schools. In *NCAA* v. *Board of Regents of University of Oklahoma, et al.,* 468 U.S. 85 (1985), the Court ruled that the NCAA bore "a heavy burden" to prove the procompetitive effects of its action because of the elevated price and reduced output of its actions. See the discussion by Horowitz (1999). Here the evidence does not support such overall adverse price and output effects, so it is unclear whether MIT should bear such a "heavy burden."

[72]See, e.g., *U.S.* v. *Trans Missouri Freight Assoc.,* 166 U.S. 290 (1897), *U.S.* v. *Addyston Pipe & Steel Co.,* 175 U.S. 211 (1899), *U.S.* v. *Trenton Potteries Co.,* 273 U.S. 392 (1927), and *U.S.* v. *Socony Vacuum Oil Co.,* 310 U.S. 150 (1940).

collective actions generate unusual efficiencies has the Court allowed collective price setting.[73] Although it is possible to label the greater access of the needy to Overlap schools as an unusual efficiency and thereby fit this case within existing antitrust precedent, we think it clearer to ask and answer the question of whether the antitrust laws leave room for a not-for-profit firm to use the achievement of social goals as a valid defense for collective behavior.

The most relevant precedent is *Professional Engineers,* where the Court struck down an agreement by a not-for-profit trade association that restricted price competition for the stated purpose of assuring quality.[74] The trade association, composed of profit-maximizing members, promulgated restrictions on bidding to raise price and increase safety. In that case, the Court's concern was clearly that, as a result of the agreement, price would be raised to all consumers. The Court suggested that any ethical rule with an overall anticompetitive effect is forbidden.[75]

We believe that there are two features of the MIT case that distinguish it from *Professional Engineers.* First, unlike *Professional Engineers,* there was no alleged output restriction and, as already described, no finding of a price effect. Second, the membership of the Overlap group, unlike the trade association, consisted of not-for-profit firms.

With no effect on total output or average price, the achievement of desirable social goals can, we believe, provide an economic defense of MIT's conduct without violating the logic of existing antitrust precedents.[76] We believe that this result is sensible because these 501(c)3 institutions receive that special status in return for the performance of valuable social goals presumably not achievable through competition of profit-maximizing firms.[77] Indeed, if the achievement of a social goal is not a justification under the rule of reason for competing not-for-profits to engage in collective action—and only the more traditional justification of improved efficiency is recog-

---

[73]*Broadcast Music Inc. et al.* v. *CBS et al.,* 441 U.S. 1 (1979). The Supreme Court does not characterize its decision in this way but instead says that the price action was "ancillary" to the production of a new product. Indeed, in other cases, the Supreme Court specifically states that it will not consider efficiency in a "price fixing" case. Such a view simply replaces the question of whether there are unusual efficiencies with the question of what is "price fixing" and what is "ancillary."

[74]*National Society of Professional Engineers* v. *U.S.,* 435 U.S. 679 (1978). The Supreme Court has recognized the distinction between for-profit and not-for-profit firms in applying the antitrust laws. See, e.g., *Goldfarb* v. *Virginia State Bar,* 421 U.S. 773, 788–9, n. 17 (1975). It is unclear how much of this distinction has been preserved after *Professional Engineers.* See Justice Blackmun's concurring opinion in *Professional Engineers.* The dissent by Justices White and Rehnquist in *NCAA* recognizes explicitly the need for schools to be able to defend their conduct by referring to non-economic goals.

[75]See the concurring opinion of Justice Blackmun in *Professional Engineers,* who does not endorse such a suggestion.

[76]If there were an output restriction or elevated average price, *Professional Engineers* would condemn the behavior.

[77]For profit-maximizing firms and perhaps for not-for-profits composed of profit-maximizing members, the achievement of social goals would not seem an appropriate defense for collective price setting because the achievement of social goals is not what those firms are intended to do.

nized—then no collective action of competing not-for-profits is likely possible under the antitrust laws, because economists' notions of improved efficiency usually will not apply to collective action of not-for-profits engaged in aspects of income redistribution or achievement of social goals.[78]

REFERENCES

Carlson, D., and G. Shepherd. "Cartel on Campus: The Economics and Law of Academic Institutions' Financial Aid Price Fixing." *Oregon Law Review* 71, no. 3, (Fall 1992): 563–629.

Carlton, D., G. Bamberger, and R. Epstein. "Antitrust and Higher Education: Was There a Conspiracy to Restrict Financial Aid?" *Rand Journal of Economics* 26 (Spring 1995): 131–147.

Carlton, D., and J. Klamer. "The Need for Coordination Among Firms with Special Reference to Network Industries." *The University of Chicago Law Review* 50 (Spring 1983): 446–465.

Clayton, M. "Princeton University's Shift from Loans to Grants Could Change How Schools—and Students—Negotiate Financial Aid." *Christian Science Monitor,* February 13, 2001, p. 11.

Clotfelter, C. "Financial Aid and Public Policy." In *Economic Challenges in Higher Education,* edited by C. Clotfelter, R. Ehrenberg, M. Getz, and J. Seigfried. Chicago: University of Chicago Press, 1991.

Dodge, S. "Overlap Group Makes Aid Process Fairer Targets of Inquiry Argue." *Chronicle of Higher Education,* October 11, 1989, p. A32.

Eisenstadt, D. "Hospital Competition and Costs: The Carilion Case." In *The Antitrust Revolution,* edited by John E. Kwoka and Lawrence J. White. New York: Oxford University Press, 1999.

Hansmann, H. "The Role of Nonprofit Enterprise." *Yale Law Journal* 89 (April 1980): 835–901.

Hansmann, H., and A. Klevorick. *Competition and Coordination in Markets for Higher Education.* New Haven, Conn.: Yale University Press, 1993.

Hopkins, D. "The Higher Education Production Function: Theoretical Foundations and Empirical Findings." In *The Economics of American Universities: Management, Operations and Fiscal Environment,* edited by Stephen Holnack and Eileen Collins. Albany State: University of New York Press, 1998.

Horowitz, I. "The Reasonableness of Horizontal Restraints: NCAA (1984)." In *The Antitrust Revolution,* edited by John E. Kwoka and Lawrence J. White. New York: Oxford University Press, 1999.

Hoxby, C. "Benevolent Colluders? The Effects of Antitrust Action on College Financial Aid and Tuition." NBER Working Paper Series, Working Paper 7754 (June 2000).

---

[78]For a different view, see Salop and White (1991); Morrison (1992); Carlson and Shepherd (1993); and Shepherd (1995).

Koopmans, T., and M. Beckmann. "Assignment Problems and the Location of Economic Activities." *Econometrica* 25 (January 1957): 53–76.

Lande, R. "Chicago's False Foundation: Wealth Transfer (Not Just Efficiency) Should Guide Antitrust." *Antitrust Law Journal* 58 (1989): 631–644.

Lubman, S. "The Tradition of Need-Blind Admissions Is Starting to Die." *Wall Street Journal,* January 5, 1994.

Lynk, W. "Nonprofit Hospital Mergers and the Exercise of Market Power." *Journal of Law and Economics* 38 (October 1995): 437–461.

Marcus, A. "The Market Maker; Princeton May Be One of the Oldest and Most Privileged of American Universities, but When It Comes to Financial Aid, It's out on the Cutting Edge." *Money,* October 2001, p. 122.

McPherson, M., and M. Schapiro. *Keeping College Affordable.* Washington, D.C.: The Brookings Institution, 1991.

Morrison, R. "Price Fixing Among Elite Colleges and Universities." *University of Chicago Law Review* 59 (Summer 1992): 807–835.

Netz, J. "The End of Collusion? Competition after Justice and the Ivy League Settle." Working Paper, Purdue University (Fall 2000).

Noll, R. "The U.S. Team Sports Industry: An Introduction." In *Government and the Sports Business,* edited by R. Noll. Washington, D.C.: Brookings Institution, 1982.

Pitofsky, R. "The Political Content of Antitrust." *University of Pennsylvania Law Review* 127, no. 4 (April 1979): 1051–1075.

Roth, A., and M. Sotomayer. *Two-Sided Matching: A Study in Game Theoretic Modeling and Analysis.* Cambridge: Cambridge University Press, 1990.

Rothschild, M., and L. White. "The University in the Marketplace: Some Insights and Some Puzzles." In *Studies of Supply and Demand in Higher Education,* edited by C. Clotfelter and M. Rothschild. Chicago: University of Chicago Press, 1993.

Salop, S., and L. White. "Antitrust Goes to College." *Journal of Economic Perspectives* 5 (Summer 1991): 193–199.

Seaman, B., and H. Tesorio. "How Much Do I Hear for This Student?" *Time,* April 16, 2001, p. 44.

Shepherd, G. "Overlap and Antitrust: Fixing Prices in a Smoke-Filled Classroom." *Antitrust Bulletin* 50 (Winter 1995): 859–884.

Statistical Abstract of the United States. Washington, D.C.: Government Printing Office, 1991.

Stout, H. "Education: Many Colleges Face More Cuts on Basic Services." *Wall Street Journal,* August 3, 1992.

Telser, L. *Economic Theory and the Core.* Chicago: University of Chicago Press, 1978.

CASE 8

Bidding, Bid Rigging, and School Milk Prices: *Ohio* v. *Trauth* (1994)

Robert H. Porter and
J. Douglas Zona

INTRODUCTION

Sometime between May and August every year, school district officials throughout the country independently solicit bids on annual supply contracts for milk and other products. In response to the solicitations, dairies that are in a position to supply school milk submit bids for procurement contracts. The majority of these procurements employ sealed bid auctions, in part because federal guidelines require the purchasing method to be as competitive as possible. Typically, the low bidder is selected to supply milk in half pints to the schools during the following school year. According to a study by the U.S. Department of Agriculture, 86 percent of dairy purchases for the 1996–1997 school year used a formalized bidding procedure. The value of the contracts totaled more than $700 million.

In 1993, representatives of two dairies from Cincinnati, Ohio (Meyer Dairy and Coors Dairy), confessed to rigging bids in school milk auctions in the 1980s. These individuals testified that they had rigged bids with each other and with Trauth Dairy. Their testimony was offered as part of a settlement of the criminal and civil cases against them. Together they paid several million dollars to settle the cases. The bid-rigging scheme described in their testimony was one of respecting incumbencies. If one of the cartel members had served a particular school district in the previous year, then

The authors consulted for the state of Ohio in the matters described in this chapter.

other conspirators were to submit high complementary bids that would not undercut the incumbent firm's bid, or else refrain from bidding. The testimony described frequent communication among these competitors as the specific details of the scheme were worked out through the bidding season.

Trauth Dairy, another Cincinnati dairy that was implicated by the whistle-blowers, maintained that there was no conspiracy. Instead, they claimed that the statements by their competitors were designed to ruin them and drive them from these markets, to the benefit of the whistle-blowers. They maintained their innocence through several trials, criminal and civil.

In 1994, the state of Ohio charged thirteen dairies, including Meyer, Coors, and Trauth, with collusion and bid rigging in school milk auctions for the years 1980 through 1990 inclusive.[1] Collusion in auctions is an agreement among a group of firms that is designed to limit competition between the participants. The analysis of collusion or communication among bidders is more difficult than the analysis of competitive bidding, in part because the nature and effects of conspiracy depend on the specifics of the situation.

Because the direct evidence of the extent of the conspiracy was disputed, economic evidence was gathered in addition to other kinds of evidence as the state set out to make its case. Three types of economic evidence were collected: (1) evidence on the incentives to collude in these markets; (2) evidence as to whether the behavior of the alleged conspirators was more consistent with competition or collusion; and (3) evidence on the extent of damages caused by the alleged bid rigging.[2]

The first category of economic evidence concerns the incentive to collude. As we describe below, the details of the procurement process, the nature of milk processing and delivery, and the characteristics of demand for school milk are such that collusive agreements among suppliers may be relatively easy to reach and maintain. Collusion appears to be a pervasive phenomenon in school milk auctions.[3] There have been investigations of price fixing in auctions for the provision of school milk in more than twenty states, beginning with a Florida bid-rigging case in 1988. More than 130 federal criminal cases have been filed, and many states have also filed charges. Guilty pleas have been entered in at least a dozen states, and fines have been levied in excess of $90 million. About ninety people have been sent to jail for average sentences of six months.

---

[1]*Ohio* v. *Louis Trauth Dairy,* 856 F. Supp. 1229, 1237 (S.D. Ohio 1994).

[2]Our analysis complements a recent empirical literature on the detection of bid rigging. Porter and Zona (1993) describe bid rigging in New York State highway paving jobs on Long Island in the early 1980s. Pesendorfer (2000) examines school milk bidding data from Florida and Texas. Hewitt, McClave, and Sibley (1996) and Lee (1996) also analyze the Texas data. Lanzillotti (1996) describes bidding for school milk contracts in Kentucky. The papers by Baldwin, Marshall, and Richard (1997) and Bajari (1998) compare collusive and noncooperative bidding for Forest Service timber contracts and Minnesota highway improvement jobs, respectively.

[3]See, for example, Henriques and Baquet (1993) and Lanzillotti (1996).

We then analyze the behavior of the defendants relative to a competitive benchmark. We conclude that the bidding behavior of the accused dairies was more consistent with collusion than with competition. For example, some of the defendants exhibit patterns of both local and distant bid submissions. That is, they submit bids relatively near their plants and they also submit bids well beyond their local territories. Further, the distant bids by the defendants tend to be relatively low. In contrast, bids by a group of firms that were not named as defendants are an increasing function of the distance from the school district to a firm's nearest plant. These features of bidding by the defendants are consistent with territorial allocation of districts close to the dairies' plants to restrict competition and relatively competitive bidding at more distant locations, which were perhaps outside the area of territorial allocation. If bidding for local districts had been competitive, local bids should have been lower than distant bids, because shipping costs were lower and because the Cincinnati area has several potential local suppliers. The relationship between bidding behavior and distance is notable, because processed milk is relatively expensive to ship (since its value is low relative to its weight) and competition is therefore localized.

Third, we also analyze the effect of the collusion on prices paid by the school districts in Ohio as a result of the collusion as identified. We estimate that collusion caused school districts to pay about 6.5 percent more for school milk in the affected area during the period analyzed, and much more than that in some locations.

CHARACTERISTICS OF OHIO SCHOOL MILK MARKETS

Market outcomes are determined by three factors: the nature of demand, the nature of the production process, and the nature of competitive interaction among suppliers. In the case of school milk, demand and cost characteristics are relatively easily described. The more difficult problem is determining the nature of competitive interaction given the demand and cost characteristics; that is the focus of a subsequent section.

There are more than six hundred school districts in Ohio. Most districts award annual contracts for the supply of school milk. For example, a district will indicate that it expects to purchase 50,000 half pints of whole white and 30,000 half pints of whole chocolate milk. (This corresponds to a student population of about 450.) A bid submission consists of a list of prices for the various products. In addition to specifying categories of milk, the district may require its supplier to provide coolers (for the refrigeration of milk), straws, or napkins. Escalator clauses with price indexed to the price of raw milk are also provided in some bid requests to reduce the risk to the dairy that is associated with submitting a bid on an annual contract, since the price of raw milk can fluctuate substantially over a year.

Demand for school milk is relatively insensitive to the price charged. School milk programs are subsidized, and milk demand may be inelastic in any event. An estimate of the responsiveness of school districts' demand for milk to price, using data on a cross-section of school districts in Ohio, indicates that price is not a statistically significant determinant of demand despite substantial variations in price. If school district purchasing is inelastic, a firm that controls the supply of milk for a particular district could profit from a substantially higher price in that district.

The competitive price will depend on the costs of potential suppliers. We now describe the most important components of these costs. Dairy processors receive raw milk from dairy farmers in the area. The price charged for raw milk is typically regulated through an elaborate federal marketing order (FMO) system based on location and type of milk. Although some milk producers are unregulated, the market would tend to produce a single price for both regulated and unregulated raw milk in the long run. The cost of the raw milk contained in a typical half pint purchased by a school district is about seven cents. (This figure varies seasonally and from year to year.) Raw milk is processed by standardizing the butter fat content (e.g., 2 percent or skim) and then pasteurizing, packaging, and delivering it. Typically, potential suppliers of school milk pay about the same amount for raw milk, and they use much the same technology to pasteurize, package, and deliver. Many firms use the same suppliers of packaging materials, typically paying about two cents per half pint for packaging. As described below, we would expect incremental costs to be similar across different suppliers or potential suppliers. Any differences in long-run incremental costs would likely arise from differences in distance from the plant to the district.

When bids are solicited by school districts, firms in a position to supply will submit a bid. Which firms are in a position to supply the district? A firm must have access to a supply of school milk. The potential suppliers of school milk fall into one of two categories: processors, which process and package raw milk in the half pint containers demanded by schools; and distributors, which often purchase milk wholesale from the processors and re-sell it to a school district.[4] For any firm interested in selling its own milk in school milk markets, the costs of a processing plant may represent a substantial entry barrier. For those processors for which we have data, the school milk business represents a small fraction of their total revenues, typically less than 10 percent. Although a processing plant is necessary to process

---

[4]There are many distributors active in Ohio school milk markets, but the relationship between processors and distributors can be classified into relatively few categories. First, some distributors are granted exclusive territories and offer bids using the affiliated processor's name or stationary. Second, some distributors purchase milk wholesale from one or more processors and sell it to schools using their own name. These distributors often switch processor affiliations from year to year, presumably to get better terms. Finally, but not as frequently, distributors can provide delivery to the processor for a fee. Since all three arrangements coexist in the market, any particular type of distributor/processor relationship is unlikely to convey a competitive advantage.

school milk, school milk is only one of many products. To our knowledge, no firm has ever built a processing plant solely to supply school milk.

Thus, the decision to build a plant hinges on considerations in other product markets, such as supplying wholesale to supermarkets or to other institutions such as restaurants. (It should also be noted that there was substantially more exit than entry of processing plants in Ohio during the 1980s.) The costs of the processing plant that are directly attributable to school milk are therefore quite small. We conclude that only those firms that have access to a milk processing plant, largely put into operation for other reasons, would have the ability to enter the school milk business selling their own product.[5]

If a firm has a plant that is relatively close to the school district in question, what costs would be incurred should the firm submit a bid and win the contract? For example, are there any important fixed costs associated with serving school districts? Because data on the fixed costs of supplying school milk are not available, we analyze the size distribution of firms in Ohio. For those companies participating in school milk markets, the scale of operations ranged from one firm supplying milk to about 1 percent of Ohio public school students annually to another that supplied about 7 percent of the students. Firms producing on vastly different scales coexist in these markets, even though marginal costs seem to be quite similar, indicating that the fixed costs associated with the school milk business for a dairy serving other customers are likely to be relatively small.

Given that a firm has a processing plant and is in the school milk business, there are incremental costs associated with starting service to a new school district, such as the costs associated with providing a cooler and adding the district to existing delivery routes. The delivery portion of total incremental cost may also be related to the number of deliveries per week for the new district and how well it fits with the firm's existing route structure.[6] There are three main options for delivery: some dairies have dedicated school milk routes; others add school deliveries to their regular retail commercial routes; and other dairies use local delivery subcontractors for these services. Frequently, a dairy will utilize more than one option. Of course, delivery costs vary with distance. A typical delivery cost is on the order of a penny per half pint for local deliveries.

The cost of coolers is small relative to the other costs of school milk. For example, a sixteen-case cooler can be purchased currently for $1100. Using an eight-year depreciation schedule, which probably underestimates a cooler's useful life, this figure implies a cost of about 0.2 cents per half pint for a cooler that chills approximately 70,000 half pints per year.

---

[5]As noted earlier, firms can and do enter the market for the distribution of other firms' processed milk. Thus, entry barriers into distribution would be lower.

[6]Absent collusion, bidders will not know exactly which school districts they will ultimately serve when they bid on individual contracts. That is, they will not know the outcome of future contract lettings.

In summary, the cost of ingredients for a half pint of milk is on the order of about seven cents, packaging costs are about two cents, and delivery costs to serve a nearby school district are about one cent. Total delivered incremental costs are on the order of ten cents per half pint during the period analyzed. We expect these incremental costs to be independent of the scale of operations and similar across firms (after accounting for proximity). Fixed and other one-time costs will affect a dairy's decision whether to enter or exit the school milk business, whereas the incremental costs of supplying an additional half pint of milk or servicing another district are relevant for its pricing decisions.

The market characteristics described so far suggest competition among firms producing a homogeneous product with similar and constant incremental costs. Firms are likely to have good information about the costs of their competitors, since most cost changes affect all firms similarly. There are unlikely to be substantial informational advantages in the market. School districts would be willing to pay high prices for school milk, if they had no other choice. Competition is likely to be localized, because of the regulation of raw milk prices and because of relatively high transportation costs.

FACTORS FACILITATING COLLUSION

There are many features of Ohio's school milk markets that may affect the dairies' competitive interaction. Specifically, there are a number of characteristics that facilitate collusion.[7]

1. Firms compete only on price. Under the terms of the contract, the winning bidder supplies the product with specified characteristics (e.g., butter fat content or flavoring). A cartel need only coordinate submission and bid decisions, and not other characteristics of the product, which simplifies cartel operations.

2. The school districts' policy of publicly announcing bids and the identity of the bidders allows cartel members to detect "cheating" from cartel agreements. Undercutting and cheating on collusive arrangements would not go unnoticed, so a collusive arrangement is therefore more likely to be stable.

3. Most school districts held their auctions annually but at different times during a year, and they acted on their own.[8] The disorganized letting of contracts (as opposed to all contracts being let on a particular day, for

---

[7]These characteristics are prevalent in other markets. See, for example, Porter and Zona (1993).

[8]Some school districts occasionally band together in cooperatives and solicit bids for the group. However, cooperative arrangements historically have not prevented districts from soliciting bids individually.

example) allows cartel members to adjust bidding behavior during the bidding season to allocate market shares, and it provides an opportunity for nearly immediate retaliation for "bad cartel citizenship."

4. The predictability of the demand for school milk from year to year allows threats of future retaliation in response to deviations to be credible.

5. The fact that the markets themselves are easily defined according to school district boundaries permits allocations by assignment of territories.

6. The set of firms potentially submitting bids in a particular market is small and quite stable.

7. These firms use similar production processes and therefore face similar cost structures. The similarity of potential suppliers makes it more likely that a group of firms could agree on joint behavior.

8. The same dairies encounter one another in more than one market, and so competition may not be fierce.[9] Contact between competitors in multiple markets (school districts as well as wholesale accounts) makes collusive schemes that allocate markets more feasible.

9. The practice of obtaining competitors' price lists through retail customers (e.g., grocery stores) was common, if not universal. Advance notification of list price increases can lead to supra-competitive prices: The practice allows communication of intentions of competitors (Holt and Scheffman, 1987).

10. Dairies are frequently customers of one another. This facilitates direct communication and allows a pretext for meetings between competitors. The practice allows communication of pricing information (even for products that are not purchased) through full price lists. Holt and Scheffman (1988) condemn this practice as potentially facilitating collusion.

11. The many dairy trade associations in Ohio also allow a pretext for meetings of competitors. Most meet on a regular basis to discuss issues of mutual interest. These associations obviously understand the legal dangers since the minutes of these meetings often indicate that they begin by reading a statement warning members not to discuss prices.

According to the testimony of the Meyer and Coors representatives, these factors were of more than theoretical importance. Even if one ignores their testimony, a cartel among firms operating in the area is plausible and

---

[9]Bernheim and Whinston (1990) show that multimarket contact in a repeated market setting "relaxes the incentive constraints that limit the extent of collusion."

would be to the benefit of each of the participants. Since competition is localized, prices will fall to competitive levels only in areas where there is a sufficient number of local competitors. Distant competitors are disadvantaged by transportation costs and can only discipline price increases to a certain extent. The competitive significance of each supplier is directly related to its relative distance from the school district. Any elevation of price that is achieved through collusion could, in some circumstances, be defeated by the entry of new firms from outside the market. In the case of school milk, entry will not take the form of a new firm's setting up a processing plant; instead, it will be in the form of bids from firms whose plants are farther away. In this way, the transportation cost for distant non-cartel entrants will constrain the ability of a cartel to raise prices, but if collusion is effective then prices could be elevated by a significant amount. If local firms could coordinate their bidding behavior, then some profits could be earned without stimulating entry from distant suppliers. The reaction of any school district is unlikely to limit the ability of a cartel to raise price. As noted above, demand for school milk is inelastic, and school districts would continue to purchase milk even at elevated prices, to the detriment of the school districts and to the benefit of cartel members.

A scheme of respecting incumbencies is one way for a cartel to coordinate bidding behavior. Such a scheme would be attractive if cartel firms were near each other, as some are in this case. This mechanism avoids the cartel problem of allocating school districts of varying profitability (due to a location or level of service required) among the cartel members. Another way of coordinating bidding behavior would be the assignment of geographic territories to individual firms. Territorial assignment would be a more practical collusive mechanism when firms are geographically separated and some firm has a clear advantage in serving a particular district.

A MODEL OF COMPETITIVE BEHAVIOR

In a competitive market, firms in the school milk business face two interrelated decisions. First, should the firm submit a bid in a particular district? Second, if a bid is submitted, what should the bid level be? We address these decisions in turn in the subsections below. Here we describe a model of competitive bidding.

Porter and Zona (1999) estimated an econometric model of bidding behavior using a data set provided by the state of Ohio that contains information on school milk procurement for as many as 509 of the approximately 600 school districts in the state from 1980 through 1990, inclusive, with approximately 60 different bidders participating at some point in the sample. We created a control group composed of nondefendant firms that bid on Ohio school milk contracts. The data set contains information on the identity of the districts, their location and enrollment, and the timing of

TABLE 8-1
Characteristics of Ohio School Milk Data Set

Year	Number of School Districts or Cooperatives	Total Enrollment in School Districts	Number of Plants Operated by Submitting Dairies	Number of Dairies Submitting Bids	Average Price Per Half Pint ($0.00)	Average FMO Price for Raw Milk
	(a)	(b)	(c)	(d)	(e)	(f)
1980	366	1,257,925	54	43	0.1282	0.0718
1981	398	1,379,619	50	44	0.1295	0.0769
1982	415	1,371,164	46	40	0.1295	0.0760
1983	436	1,415,281	48	40	0.1288	0.0764
1984	448	1,430,644	53	38	0.1313	0.0741
1985	463	1,460,697	48	35	0.1322	0.0708
1986	481	1,457,437	47	36	0.1304	0.0700
1987	494	1,566,591	46	33	0.1310	0.0701
1988	509	1,520,635	44	30	0.1338	0.0666
1989	491	1,564,869	43	26	0.1389	0.0708
1990	412	1,296,587	43	26	0.1575	0.0797

Notes: Dollars per hundred weight FMO (federal milk order) #33 Class 1 Fluid Milk; 186 half pints per hundred weight; prices quoted for July of each year.

contract lettings; information about who submitted bids, and the nature of winning and losing bids, such as prices and compliance with district speci-fications, that were submitted to each district. Table 8-1 provides some de-scriptive statistics for each year in our sample.

According to data obtained from the U.S. Department of Agriculture, a total of sixty-eight milk processing plants had sales in Ohio at some point during the sample period and potentially could have supplied school milk. Figure 8-1 displays the location and owners of the forty-six plants that sup-plied school milk in 1987. Superimposed on the plant location map in Fig-ure 8-1 is an index of dairy concentration.[10] The darker the area, the more concentrated is the ownership and control of local school milk processing facilities. Figure 8-1 shows that the markets in the northeast section of Ohio are the least concentrated, and if they are competitive they should have the lowest prices, all else equal. Columbus and the southernmost tip of Ohio have markets where the supply of school milk is concentrated in the hands of relatively few producers. Over the period 1980–1990, the number of plants serving Ohio school districts fell from fifty-four to forty-three, and the number of firms fell from forty-three to twenty-six.

Table 8-2 shows the distribution of bidder distances in the Ohio data. The table also shows the distribution of potential supplier distances in the

---

[10]We measure concentration using the Herfindahl index. For market shares we use the fraction of plants within seventy-five miles of the region that are owned by each firm.

FIGURE 8-1 1987 Regional Supply Concentration and Plant Locations

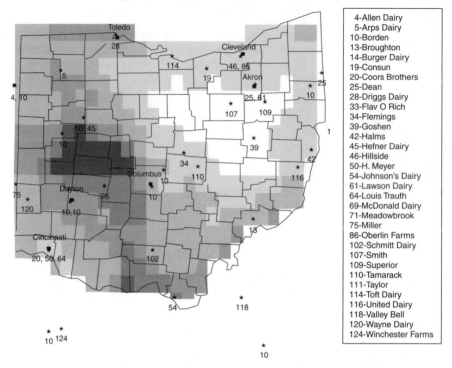

4-Allen Dairy
5-Arps Dairy
10-Borden
13-Broughton
14-Burger Dairy
19-Consun
20-Coors Brothers
25-Dean
28-Driggs Dairy
33-Flav O Rich
34-Flemings
39-Goshen
42-Halms
45-Hefner Dairy
46-Hillside
50-H. Meyer
54-Johnson's Dairy
61-Lawson Dairy
64-Louis Trauth
69-McDonald Dairy
71-Meadowbrook
75-Miller
86-Oberlin Farms
102-Schmitt Dairy
107-Smith
109-Superior
110-Tamarack
111-Taylor
114-Toft Dairy
116-United Dairy
118-Valley Bell
120-Wayne Dairy
124-Winchester Farms

Note: The concentration of an area is represented by its shading; white represents a completely unconcentrated area while black represents an area serviced by a single supplier.

data. Approximately 85 percent of the firms supplying school milk in a given year do so from plants located less than seventy-five miles from the school district. Firms considering entry in order to supply milk to distant school districts appear to be disadvantaged by distance, even if they have a plant in operation.

The distribution of processing plants in the state and the apparent disadvantage of shipping long distances cause districts to receive a relatively small number of bids on school milk. For the districts in the data set, 45 percent received only one bid, 34 percent two bids, and 18 percent three bids. Even though there are a large number of potential bidders for any particular auction, very few actually bid. The mean number of bids is 1.8. The small number of bids submitted indicates that dairies may not have important private information. If bidders knew their own costs as well as the costs of other potential suppliers, then it seems plausible that bidding by only one or two dairies would be observed. The low-cost supplier would submit a bid just below the cost of the next lowest cost supplier, and the latter would be indifferent between bidding at its own cost and not bidding. About 43 per-

TABLE 8-2
Probability of Bidding and Winning Conditional on Distance from Plant to School District

Distance in Miles	Number of Districts	Probability of Bidding	Proportion of All Bids	Probability of Winning	Proportion of Winning Bids
	(a)	(b)	(c)	(d)	(e)
0–10	2115	19.5%	20.1%	13.6%	22.9%
10–20	3197	14.0	21.7	8.9	22.5
20–30	3840	7.6	14.2	4.9	15.0
30–40	4526	5.5	12.1	3.4	12.1
40–50	5637	2.3	6.3	0.9	4.2
50–60	6440	1.9	5.9	1.0	5.0
60–70	5314	1.4	3.7	0.5	2.0
70–80	6732	1.4	4.7	0.8	4.4
80–90	5200	1.0	2.5	0.6	2.5
90–100	4885	1.2	2.8	0.7	2.8
100–150	26079	0.5	6.1	0.3	6.6

Notes: Columns (b) and (d) report, for each distance category, the percentage of districts in which firms submitted a bid or the winning bid, respectively. Columns (c) and (e) total 100 percent and report the fraction of all bids or winning bids, respectively in each distance category. Results are based on a total of 2053 submitted bids from control group firms out of 73,965 bid opportunities; 1260 of these were winning bids.

cent of all bids are submitted by the firms with the plants closest to the district, and 8 percent by the firms with the second-closest plant. Among winning bids, 49 percent are submitted by the firms with the closest plants, and 8 percent by those with the second-closest plant.

Bid Submission

In a competitive market a firm will submit a bid in a particular district whenever the probability of winning is relatively high and when the expected return covers both the costs of preparing the bid and the incremental costs of supplying the district. A model of bidding behavior should account for variables that reflect the potential bidder's absolute and relative advantage in serving a district. For example, variables that may be important in characterizing these advantages include whether or not the firm (1) has significant transportation costs to the particular district, as reflected by the distance from the district to the plant; (2) is a distributor or a processor of milk; (3) is the closest potential supplier (and so the most likely low-cost supplier for that district); (4) is the second closest, and hence likely the second least costly potential provider; (5) is bidding on a large or small school district, as larger districts may require more time and energy to prepare a bid; and (6) can efficiently provide the specified milk under the terms of the contract (whether or not coolers are required, or whether fixed price or indexed contracts are specified, for example).

From available bidding data, we estimated how these factors affect the decision whether to submit a bid by the control group of nondefendants. See Porter and Zona (1999) for more detail. The results from this estimation are then used as a benchmark for comparison with the behavior of the defendants.

The econometric results can be summarized as follows. Processors are more likely to submit bids than distributors, all else equal. This may reflect the fact that distributors tend to run a single school milk route, while processors tend to run several routes with school delivery. Firms, especially distributors, are more likely to submit a bid in one particular direction as opposed to all around their plant. This may reflect the effects of existing route structures. Firms are less likely to submit bids to school districts that are farther away from their plants than they are to closer districts. This probably reflects absolute cost differences. Districts that request coolers or straws receive fewer bids than districts that do not. The other specification items do not affect bidding behavior in a statistically significant way.

The likelihood of submitting a bid is a decreasing function of distance. Figure 8-2 displays the impact of distance on the probability of bidding for a hypothetical firm in the control group. To construct this figure we assume that the firm is the closest supplier to districts less than ten miles from its

FIGURE 8-2 Predicted Probability of Submitting a Bid by Distance

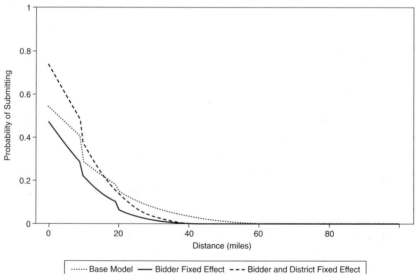

Note: Variables that are not related to distance are set to their mean value, except processor is set to one, closest is set to one at distances less than 10 miles, and closer is set to one at distances between 10 and 20 miles

plant and the second-closest potential supplier at distances between ten and twenty miles. The three curves correspond to three different specifications. There are two steps in the predicted probability of bidding where the firm loses its locational advantage and becomes neither the closest nor the second-closest potential supplier. The probability of bidding by this hypothetical firm is above 50 percent at zero distance, but nearly zero beyond seventy-five miles.

Bid Level Contingent on Submission

In competitive markets, a firm submitting a bid chooses its bid to maximize expected profit. A bid cannot be increased indefinitely; the higher the bid, the lower the likelihood of winning. To the extent that bids are costly to submit, it would not be profit maximizing to submit bids that have no probability of winning. A firm maximizing expected profit trades off higher profits against a lower probability of winning.[11]

Equivalently, bidders choose their markup over costs. The markup is affected by the probability of winning the auction, which depends on the likelihood of other firms submitting bids. The markup is chosen to maximize expected profit given the level of cost. There are two categories of variables that would tend to explain bidding behavior. First, there are variables that may contribute to cost, such as distance from the plant to the district; whether or not the bidder is a processor; whether or not coolers or other items are required or supplied; the number of required deliveries; and whether or not there is an escalator clause. Second, there are variables that reflect competitive characteristics of the market: the bidder's relative cost advantage and the number and costs of other suppliers. For example, if a bidder is the closest vendor, then that bidder can bid more than it would otherwise without decreasing the probability of winning. A second example is a variable that affects the probability that a firm submits a bid. Firms that are likely to submit bids on particular districts are those that have a high probability of winning and those expecting to earn relatively high profits in the event that they win the auction.

To analyze bid prices, we constructed a summary measure of each firm's bids for the various milk products, with 2 percent chocolate used as the base product. We measured the effects of the competitive factors described above on the bid levels of the control group of nondefendants. Figure 8-3 summarizes how control group bids vary with distance. We plot predicted bids for a hypothetical control group firm holding variables other than distance constant. The figure incorporates the effect of distance on the probability of submitting a bid and the resulting impact on the bid. Figure 8-3 presents the results for three different specifications of the control

---

[11]See Wilson (1993), McAfee and McMillan (1987), or Milgrom and Weber (1982).

FIGURE 8-3 Predicted Level of Submitted Bids by Distance: Control Group

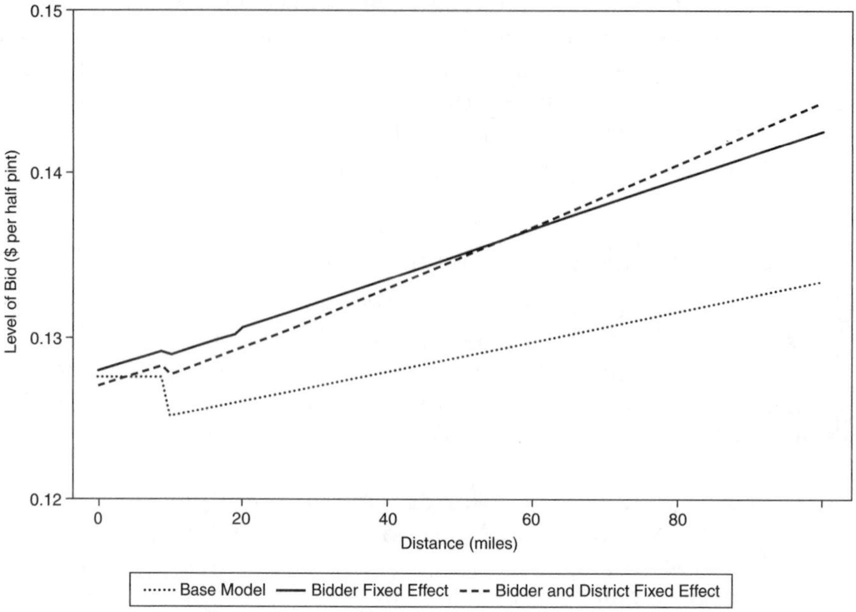

Note: Variables that are not related to distance are set to their mean value, except processor is set to one, closest is set to one at distances less than 10 miles, and closer is set to one at distances between 10 and 20 miles

group bidding model. A bid one hundred miles away would be between one and two cents higher than in a district adjacent to the plant, all else equal. Firms in the control group are unlikely to submit bids to districts at these distances from the plant, however. Firms closest to the district have some competitive advantage, but that advantage diminishes with distance.

Bidding by nondefendants is consistent with competitive bidding under standard models of spatial competition, where each firm may exercise local monopoly power. As described above, competition is localized, because of the regulation of raw milk prices and because of relatively high transportation costs.

BEHAVIOR OF DEFENDANTS

Comparison to Control Group Behavior

We now examine the bidding practices of the three dairies located in Cincinnati—Meyer, Coors, and Trauth—and compare them with the control group. We consider both the bid submission decision and the level of the bid contingent on submission.

Porter and Zona (1999) tested for differences between the estimated control group bid submission model and that estimated for each of the Cincinnati dairies. For each dairy, we reject the hypotheses that the defendants submitted bids according to the control group model at conventional significance levels under all the specifications considered. There are also significant differences in the statistical process generating the level of bids. That is, the bidding behavior of each of the Cincinnati dairies differs from the control group. Behavioral differences are not necessarily the result of anticompetitive behavior. We are interested in how the behavior of each of the defendants differs from the control group, given that they differ.

Comparison to a Collusive Strategy

We are faced with a standard problem in antitrust economics: distinguishing between competitive and collusive behavior.[12] Porter and Zona (1993) identified collusion in highway construction auctions by (1) focusing on bid levels rather than submission decisions, because conspirators apparently submitted complementary bids; (2) identifying differences in the determinants of cartel bids relative to that of other firms; and (3) observing that cartel bids seemed not to be cost based, except for the lowest cartel bid, in contrast to the bids submitted by other firms. Because these differences exist, we conclude that conspiracy with complementary bidding is more likely than not.

In a study of a nineteenth-century railway cartel, Porter (1983) proposed statistical tests to identify whether competition or collusion is more consistent with observed data based on pricing patterns over time. Some observed price fluctuations do not appear to be the result of demand shifts or changes in observable cost factors. Instead, the observed pattern of occasional price wars, following periods of unusually turbulent market shares, is unlikely to be observed under competition. Under a specific theory of conspiracy, such a pattern is possible. The existence of such a pattern informs an inference of collusion.

Our strategy for the problem at hand is similar. The nondefendant firms behave, on average, in a manner consistent with competition. We have concluded that the Cincinnati dairies behave in a statistically significantly different manner relative to the nondefendant firms. Is it likely that these differences are attributable to idiosyncratic effects of cost or competition? If not, are the differences attributable to independent factors, or are there suspicious patterns of correlation? We now address these two questions.

There are many alternative methods of colluding in auction markets.[13] For example, conspirators could refrain from bidding against each other by

---

[12]Baker and Bresnahan (1992) discuss related methods of detecting the exercise of market power.

[13]Hendricks and Porter (1989) describe several collusive mechanisms, and why the detection of collusion is necessarily case specific.

allocating exclusive territories. Alternatively, they could submit several bids at inflated levels, where the number of bids may be intended to create the appearance of competition. In either event, the members of the ring know that competition has been limited in the affected markets. Any of these firms know that if they submit a bid they do not have to worry about being undercut by another ring member. Observed bids will differ from competitive bidding because the conspirators have coordinated their actions. The expected winning bid will be higher because conspirators have coordinated their actions, whether or not a conspirator wins the auction.

Since distance is an important factor in the control group model, we focus on that dimension. Moderate increases in shipping distance are associated with large declines in the probability of submitting a bid (Figure 8-2). Similar increases in distance are associated with increases in submitted bids in the control group (about 10 percent at seventy miles in Figure 8-3). We examine the deviations of defendant firms' bidding behavior from the control group predictions in this context.

Consider first the differences between predicted and actual bid submission behavior for each of the three Cincinnati dairies, at various distances. There are some notable patterns. First, all three dairies bid more frequently than the control group model predicts for districts within 30 miles of their plant. Second, Meyer is unusually likely to bid in districts 100 to 110 miles away, and Trauth in districts 60 to 80 miles away.

We also compare actual bids[14] to the control group prediction. The bids of Meyer and Trauth decrease relative to the control group prediction significantly with distance. In particular, their bids are significantly lower in the distance ranges where they were unusually likely to bid—Meyer at 100 to 110 miles, and Trauth at 60 to 80 miles. As further evidence, consider bid level regressions, comparable to the control group regressions, for the three Cincinnati dairies. For both Meyer and Trauth, which submitted distant bids, bid levels are a significantly decreasing function of distance. In contrast, the distance bids are significantly higher for the control group.

To focus on whether firms behave in a parallel fashion, we tested for statistical independence in the probability of bidding for the defendant firms using a standard pairwise procedure. Under the null hypothesis of independent action based on public information and the specifications of our bid submission model, knowledge of whether one particular firm bids should not help predict whether another firm also bids. Under an alternative hypothesis of either complementary bidding or territorial allocation, the submission decisions are interrelated, and knowing how one cartel member behaves helps predict what the other does. In the case of complementary bidding, if one cartel member bids, then other ring members also bid. In this case the unexplained portion of the competitive bidding equation is posi-

---

[14]By actual bid, we are referring to the summary bid measure, rather than any element of the vector of bids that the firm may have submitted.

tively correlated across cartel firms. In the case of territorial allocation, if a particular cartel member bids, then other cartel members will tend not to bid. Then the unexplained portion of the competitive bidding equation is negatively correlated across cartel members. The test for independence, or zero correlation, that we used has power against both alternatives. The results indicate that the unexplained portion of the Coors submission decision was positively correlated with the unexplained portion of the Meyer decision, and similarly for Coors and Trauth, and for Meyer and Trauth. All three correlations are significant at any standard level.

We perform a similar analysis for the level of the submitted bids. Under the null hypothesis of independent action based on public information and the maintained specification of the bid level equations, knowledge of what one particular firm bid does not help predict what another firm will bid. Under an alternative hypothesis of complementary bidding, knowing that one cartel member bid above the predicted level helps predict whether other cartel firms will bid above that level. If one cartel member bids high, then other ring members are also likely to bid high. The pairwise correlation coefficients are positive and significant for all three pairs.

Our results support the testimony by representatives of Meyer and Coors. The behavior of Coors, Meyer, and Trauth is consistent with a complementary bidding scheme in the area close to their plants, since more bids than expected are submitted at distances of less than thirty miles. Further, these bids tend to be relatively high. The correlation results for these three firms are also consistent with a complementary bidding scheme. There are statistically significant correlations in bid submissions by these firms, suggesting that if one of these firms bids, then the others also tend to bid (to a greater extent than their proximity, size, and other factors would predict). In addition, when these firms bid on the same districts in the same years, their bids tend to move together to a greater extent than their proximity, size, and other factors would predict.

It is difficult to craft a competitive story where bid levels decrease with distance, as they do for these firms. The behavior of the Cincinnati dairies is suspicious, even without a comparison with the behavior of nondefendant firms. We believe that the collective behavior of these three firms is best characterized as collusive.

The Defendants' Response

Not surprisingly, the defendant dairies disagreed with our interpretation of the evidence. They criticized our econometric approach on several grounds. For example, they noted that the list of explanatory variables in our econometric model of bidding behavior was incomplete, in that they could point to a number of other factors that might also affect the decisions of whether to bid, and at what level. However, they did not provide a theoretical argument or any econometric evidence to indicate that the effect of omitting these variables would necessarily bias our tests in any particular direction. Instead, the force of their argument was that the model did not fit as well as one might like, and our conclusions therefore were suspect.

Second, they argued that the control group was not a cohesive group, because one could reject the hypothesis that they all bid according to exactly the same bidding model, and therefore a comparison of the defendants to the average behavior of the nondefendants is not an interesting exercise. However, Porter and Zona (1999) report that the bidding behavior of all but three of the fifteen nondefendant firms (those for which there are sufficient data to conduct the test) is not significantly different than the average behavior of the remainder. This contrasts with the defendants, all of whom have significantly different behavior.

Finally, the defendant dairies argued that econometric evidence alone cannot distinguish between an overt conspiracy and tacit collusion, whereby the dairies charged high local prices without ever communicating with each other.

EFFECT OF COLLUSION ON PRICES PAID

On the assumption that a conspiracy involving all the southwestern Ohio defendants was in force throughout the 1980s, what were the likely damages? Our methodology for estimating damages to the plaintiff school districts involves determining the percent markup in price attributable to collusion in various auctions.

Using regression techniques, Porter and Zona (1999) estimated the effect of variables that determine costs for the most efficient provider and other variables on the standardized price of the winning bid. The sample covers about four hundred districts, including those outside of the southwestern region. Annual dummy variables control for changes in the raw milk price, changes in uncertainties in the raw milk price over time, and changes in the costs of packaging year to year. We also control for district enrollment, the number of deliveries, and other characteristics of the school district. We include two location variables, to account for the effects of (1) the distance from the closest plant to the school district, as we expect price to be increasing with distance to the closest plant as shipping costs increase, and (2) the distance between the district and the second-closest plant. When the latter distance is large, all else equal, we expect the price paid by the school district to be higher since the closest firm can charge a higher price.

We also control for the effects of differing levels of competition in each of the markets. We measured competition in these markets using the number of equivalent firms defined by the inverse of the Herfindahl index.[15]

---

[15]The Herfindahl index is based on the fraction of school milk processing plants within seventy-five miles of the district controlled by each processor. If there are ten owners of ten processing plants within seventy-five miles, then the Herfindahl is 1/10, and the number of equivalent firms is ten. If

We expect higher prices in more concentrated markets where fewer firms compete with one another.

If there is collusion in these markets, prices are on average above the competitive level. Therefore, we include in each regression an index of collusion based on the number of conspirators in this case who are within seventy-five miles of the school district in question.[16] We also include an interaction between the collusion index and the number of equivalent firms, since the effect of a restriction of competition will depend on the initial level of competition. We interact these indices of collusion with the annual dummy variables so as to measure, to the extent they exist, differences in the degree of collusion from year to year.

In our regression we predicted the winning bid using 2 percent chocolate milk as the base product. In general, the coefficients are of the anticipated signs and statistically significant. The number of firms in the market, as measured by the variables described above, indicates the significant effect of concentration on the price paid by the school districts.

The predicted increase in price caused by collusion in these auctions is measured as the difference between the predicted value when indices of collusion are included and the predicted value that is obtained when all indices of collusion are set to zero. The difference is the predicted percentage change in price resulting from collusion. The estimated effect of collusion is small in 1983–1984 and after 1989, consistent with the market participants' testimony that the cartel agreement broke down in those years.

The average effect of collusion on price is an increase of about 6.5 percent. This is consistent with our estimate of the average effect of distance on school milk bids. If, for example, two nearby firms conspired to serve a district adjacent to their plants and faced competition only from firms located at least fifty miles from that school district, then prices could be about one half penny (or about 5 percent) higher than they would be otherwise. Districts that are farther from potential competitors face higher markups and districts closer to the plants of competitive firms pay lower markups.

SUMMARY AND AFTERMATH

Our analysis exploits specific features of school milk markets, and we would not necessarily advocate using similar methods to study other auction markets. For example, an unusual feature of Ohio school milk auctions is that few bids are submitted, even relative to school milk auctions in other

---

there are ten dissimilar firms, the Herfindahl index will exceed 1/10, and the number of equivalent firms will be less than ten.

[16]The index of collusion is the difference between the inverse of the Herfindahl index assuming competition and the inverse Herfindahl assuming collusion.

states. An important component of strategic decisions in this market is whether to submit a bid.

We also focus on the role of distance in bidding decisions. Processed milk is relatively expensive to ship, and competition is localized. We emphasize the fact that two of the three Cincinnati dairies tend to submit relatively low bids for distant school district contracts, and yet submit higher bids close to their plant. We document these patterns with a bidding model that ignores characteristics of potential rivals, except to the extent that we control for district specific fixed effects, in large part because we cannot be sure whether other firms were indeed rivals. In the case of the Cincinnati dairies, this omission should bias the results in their favor. Had they competed aggressively, bids for nearby districts should have been relatively low, as there were three local potential suppliers. Yet prices in Cincinnati were relatively high, especially in comparison with the dairies' distant bids. This price pattern is consistent with local monopoly power, but local monopoly power is consistent only with collusion.

The detection of collusion in auction or other markets is necessarily case specific, since the details of a collusive scheme depend on a number of factors. The study of auction markets can nevertheless inform the study of collusion in other markets. Data are often available on the bids of all participants in an auction, and the auction rules define the set of strategic considerations. Under these circumstances, a detailed study of strategic behavior is feasible, and it may be possible to isolate behavior that is inconsistent with competition.

This case study describes some features of a conspiracy among a group of neighboring suppliers, when the conspirators are protected locally from competition by the transportation costs borne by distant suppliers, and when the conspirators compete on a relatively equal footing with other firms outside their local market. In this case, lower prices at more distant locations are consistent with a local conspiracy and inconsistent with competitive behavior.

The case brought by the state of Ohio against the Cincinnati dairies was settled in 1996 before it could go to trial. Earlier, the federal government lost a criminal conspiracy case in 1995 that centered on the testimony of the Meyer and Coors representatives. In the federal trial, the defense described this testimony as unreliable, on the grounds that it contradicted previous statements of innocence before a grand jury. The federal case did not rely on statistical or economic evidence. The state preferred to settle rather than to go to trial with the same direct evidence, which would be subject to similar questioning. The economic evidence was intended to corroborate this testimony and to assess the amount of damages. It is very difficult to distinguish overt conspiracy from tacitly collusive behavior with economic evidence, which is typically not regarded as sufficient to establish liability.

In 1993, the Department of Justice adopted a "corporate leniency policy" under which the first person to confess participation in a collusive scheme is immune from prosecution, assuming that they were not the lead conspirator, and all other participants are subject to harsh penalties. This policy has induced a "race to the courthouse," and recent government cases have relied heavily on the testimony of participants in the conspiracy. Department of Justice officials believe that this policy is now their most effective weapon in combating cartels (e.g., Hammond 2001).

REFERENCES

Bajari, Patrick. "Econometrics of the First Price Auction with Asymmetric Bidders." Unpublished manuscript, 1998.

Baker, Jonathan B., and Timothy F. Bresnahan. "Empirical Methods of Identifying and Measuring Market Power." *Antitrust Law Journal* 37 (1992):3–16.

Baldwin, Laura, Robert Marshall, and Jean-Francois Richard. "Bidder Collusion at Forest Service Timber Auctions." *Journal of Political Economy* 105 (August 1997): 657–699.

Bernheim, B. Douglas, and Michael D. Whinston. "Multimarket Contact and Collusive Behavior." *RAND Journal of Economics* 21 (Spring 1990): 1–26.

Hammond, Scott. "Lessons Common to Detecting and Deterring Cartel Activity." In *Fighting Cartels—Why and How?* Goteborg: Swedish Competition Authority, 2001.

Hendricks, Kenneth, and Robert H. Porter, "Collusion in Auctions." *Annales d'Economie et de Statistique* 15–16 (July–Dec. 1989): 217–230.

Henriques, D., and D. Baquet. "Investigators Say Bid Rigging Is Common in Milk Industry." *New York Times,* May 23, 1993.

Hewitt, Cynthia, James McClave, and David Sibley. "Incumbency and Bidding Behavior in the Dallas–Ft. Worth School Milk Market." Unpublished manuscript, 1996.

Holt, Charles A., and David T. Scheffman. "Facilitating Practices: The Effects of Advance Notice and Best-Price Policies." *RAND Journal of Economics* 18 (Summer 1987): 187–197.

Holt, Charles A., and David T. Scheffman. "A Theory of Input Exchange Agreements." Mimeo, Federal Trade Commission, Bureau of Economics, 1988.

Lanzillotti, Robert F. "The Great School Milk Conspiracies of the 1980s." *Review of Industrial Organization* 11 (August 1996): 413–458.

Lee, In K. "Non-Cooperative Tacit Collusion, Complementary Bidding, and Incumbency Premium." *Review of Industrial Organization* 15 (September 1999): 115–134.

McAfee, R. Preston, and John McMillan. "Auctions and Bidding." *Journal of Economic Literature* 25 (June 1987): 699–738.

Milgrom, Paul R., and Robert J. Weber. "A Theory of Auctions and Competitive Bidding." *Econometrica* 50 (September 1982): 1089–1122.

Pesendorfer, Martin. "A Study of Collusion in First-Price Auctions." *Review of Economic Studies* 67 (July 2000): 381–411.

Porter, Robert H. "A Study of Cartel Stability: The Joint Executive Committee." *Bell Journal of Economics* 14 (Autumn 1983): 301–314.

Porter, Robert H., and J. Douglas Zona. "Detection of Bid Rigging in Procurement Auctions." *Journal of Political Economy* 101 (June 1993): 518–538.

Porter, Robert H., and J. Douglas Zona. "Ohio School Milk Markets: An Analysis of Bidding." *RAND Journal of Economics* 30 (Summer 1999): 263–288.

Wilson, Robert. "Strategic Analysis of Auctions." In *Handbook of Game Theory,* vol. 1, edited by Robert J. Aumann and Sergiu Hart, 227–279. Amsterdam: North-Holland, 1993.

Rapid Price Communication and Coordination: The Airline Tariff Publishing Case (1994)

Severin Borenstein

A firm announces a price increase and shortly thereafter its competitor announces its own increase to the same price level. Is that price fixing? Most antitrust economists and lawyers would say no. What if the announcements are made and changed rapidly? What if each firm makes many announcements before they settle down at identical prices? Finally, what if the prices being announced are to take effect at some future date so that no sales actually take place at these prices while the announcements are being made? This is a gray area of the antitrust laws. While an agreement among competitors to fix prices is per se illegal, computer technology that permits rapid announcements and responses has blurred the meaning of "agreement" and has made it difficult for antitrust authorities to distinguish public announcements from conversations among competitors.

These were some of the issues that were raised in the U.S. Department of Justice's investigation of the major U.S. airlines and the Airline Tariff Publishing Company (ATPCO), which is owned by the airlines and disseminates price change information to airline and travel agent computer systems. The investigation began in 1991, and the resulting case was settled with a consent decree in March 1994. The case never went to trial, and therefore it set no formal precedent. Still, the legal pleadings, negotiations, and the final consent decree indicate some of the difficult antitrust issues that are raised by rapid price announcements as well as the impact of new communication technologies on those issues.

Severin Borenstein consulted for the U.S. Department of Justice in this matter. For helpful comments and discussions, I am grateful to Dennis Carlton, Rob Gertner, Rich Gilbert, John Kwoka, Carl Shapiro, and Larry White.

THE AIRLINE INDUSTRY IN THE EARLY 1990s

From the time of airline deregulation in 1978 through the early 1990s, the airline industry was in a state of nearly constant upheaval. At the time of deregulation, the U.S. domestic jet air travel market included about twenty competitors ranging from small regional carriers to the largest national and international airlines. Immediately following deregulation, many startup airlines entered the domestic market. Concentration at both the national and the route level fell in the first five years following deregulation. Most of the startups were small regional airlines. Under the financial pressure of competition, few were ever able to turn a profit. By the mid-1980s, airlines were folding faster than new ones were entering, and many were disappearing through merger. A merger wave in the middle and late 1980s, along with more exits during that time, raised the Herfindahl-Hirschman Index for domestic air travel from 854 at the beginning of 1985 to 1074 at the beginning of 1990.

Two of the most important and unforeseen developments in the industry following deregulation were the airlines' moves to hub-and-spoke networks and their increased sophistication in pricing and marketing their products. The hub system created a natural area of dominance for a carrier. Since most cities do not have sufficient traffic to support hubs for two different carriers, a typical big-city airport is likely to be dominated by a single airline. From its hub, an airline would offer nonstop service to many or most of the country's other large cities and many small cities in the region of the hub. Such a network also lends itself naturally to offering change-of-plane service between airports for which the hub is a convenient intermediate stop. These routings could compete with nonstop service offered by a carrier that has a hub at one of the end-point airports. For instance, while Northwest was the only carrier to offer nonstop service between its Detroit hub and Los Angeles, it had less than 60 percent of the traffic in that market. The remaining traffic flowed over competing carriers' hubs: with Continental, changing planes in Denver; with American, changing planes in Chicago; with United, changing planes in Denver or Chicago; with Delta, changing planes in Salt Lake City.

The major carriers also became very sophisticated in marketing and pricing their products following deregulation. They developed customer loyalty plans that reinforced their dominance at their hubs. These included frequent flyer programs and travel agent commission override programs (TACOs). TACOs are effectively "frequent booker" programs for travel agents: Agents are rewarded for directing a high proportion of their bookings to the airline. Airlines also offered corporate discount programs that rewarded a corporation for concentrating its air travel with just one airline. The debate about the efficiency versus market power enhancement properties of these programs is still active, but there is general agreement that these programs led to greater airport concentration.[1]

Believing that hubs delivered significant competitive advantages, and forecasting continued growth in the industry, the remaining carriers in the late 1980s invested heavily in new equipment. The world's largest producer of jet aircraft, Boeing, reported record sales, and the delivery lag on some aircraft grew to many years. Carriers continued to establish new hubs in ever smaller cities, including Dayton, Raleigh-Durham, and Kansas City. By early 1990, however, it was apparent that the industry had overinvested in aircraft capacity. Demand was not expanding as rapidly as expected, and hubs at smaller airports were frequently turning out to result in more costs than benefits to the hub carrier. As the 1990–1991 recession hit and the Gulf War reduced even domestic air travel demand, newspapers reported that fleets of commercial aircraft were being grounded and stored in the Mohave desert. Many carriers went into financial distress and a number entered Chapter 11 bankruptcy proceedings: Eastern (1989), Continental (1989), Braniff (1989), Pan Am (1991), America West (1991), Midway (1991), and TWA (1992). As a whole, the industry reported record losses in 1990, 1991, and 1992.

AIRLINE PRICING

By the time the ATPCO investigation began in 1991, airlines had developed very sophisticated systems for setting fares, determining the number of seats available at each price, and disseminating this information to customers, travel agents, and other airlines. On a single route, such as Minneapolis-Atlanta, a carrier was likely to have more than a dozen different fares available at a time, and to have still more listed fares that were unavailable because no seats had been allocated to that fare category.

ATPCO is a central clearinghouse for distribution of fare change information. Each day airlines send to ATPCO information on new fares to be added, old fares to be removed, and existing fares to be changed. At least once a day, ATPCO produces a compilation of all industry fare change information and sends that computer file, which includes thousands of fare changes, to a list of recipients. The list includes, among others, all of the major airlines and all four of the computer reservation systems (CRSs) in the United States—Sabre, Apollo, Worldspan, and System One. Each CRS company operates a networks of computers that travel agents and airlines use to access flight, fare, and seat availability information on virtually any

---

[1]For a description of market power that might result from these loyalty plans and increasing hub concentration, see Borenstein (1992). For an alternative view, see Carlton and Bamberger (1996).

airline in the world. Thus, information sent to the CRS becomes available to consumers, travel agents, and all other airlines by the following morning.

To follow the ATPCO case, it is important to understand the information that is transmitted by ATPCO. Fare information that airlines submit to ATPCO includes a fare basis code (a "name" of the fare), the origin and destination airports, the price, first and last ticket dates, first and last travel dates, and any restrictions on the use of the fare (e.g., advance purchase; minimum stay; blackout dates; type of consumer who can buy it, such as clergy; or a specific routing or set of flights to which the fare applies). First and last ticket dates indicate when the carrier or a travel agent can sell tickets on the fare, while first and last travel dates indicate the range of dates on which travel can occur under the fare. By setting a future first ticket date on a new fare or setting a future last ticket date on an existing fare, a carrier could announce a fare increase, but delay its implementation until a specific future date. This ability to pre-announce price increases became a central focus of the investigation.

Ticket and travel dates, and all restrictions, are submitted as a "footnote" to the fare. Each footnote has a "footnote designator," which is a name for the footnote. Footnotes do not follow a numerical order, but are simply given footnote designators by the submitting airline. The use of fare basis codes and footnote designators as possible modes of communication also became a focus of the investigation.

"COMPETITIVE" PRICING IN IMMEDIATE-RESPONSE OLIGOPOLY MARKETS

While the ATPCO case involved a complex set of institutions and markets, one of the issues at its core was quite basic: When a small number of firms selling a homogeneous good can monitor one another's prices and respond to changes almost immediately, what is the likely outcome? In such a case, collusive pricing can result even without any sort of explicit communication among the firms. Acting unilaterally, each firm recognizes that price cuts will be matched immediately, so cutting price makes sense only if the firm would prefer an equilibrium in which all firms charged the new lower price. This greatly reduces the incentive to compete on price.

Gertner (1994) explored the outcome in such a market when firms have different costs and capacity constraints. His work, which is motivated by and refers frequently to the airline industry, concludes that if firms are not too different, the outcome in immediate-response markets will still be close to the collusive outcome and the price will be dictated by the firm that prefers the lowest price. This occurs because higher-cost firms have nothing to offer a low-cost firm in return for its agreeing to a price above its own profit-maximizing levels. Of course, if the firm that prefers the lowest price differs across markets, there may well be room for trades in which each firm agrees to a higher price than it would like in one market in return for increasing price closer to its preferred level in another market. Gertner also finds that if firms differ sufficiently in costs or other attributes, one firm may be able to sustain a lower price than others with none wanting to change its price given the prices charged by others. This result relies on the lower-cost firms' having a capacity constraint. In such a case, the higher-cost firms are better off allowing the low-cost firm to fill its capacity and then selling to the remaining demand than matching the price of the lower-cost firm and gaining a higher market share. Thus, even though the airlines differed in costs and other attributes, the ability to monitor one another's prices closely and respond very quickly could still result in prices well above the competitive level.

This line of economic research, however, has a mixed message for antitrust. On the one hand, low-cost monitoring and quick response raise concern that prices will end up at supracompetitive levels and will harm consumers. On the other hand, this may happen without any further facilitating circumstances—that is, without any actions that are clearly in violation of antitrust laws. It is not an antitrust violation for a firm unilaterally to charge high prices. Not only does such a circumstance present a dilemma for the prosecution of an antitrust case, it also makes it difficult to devise a remedy to the situation. Neither "charge lower prices" nor "stop responding to the actions of other firms" are realistic remedies under the antitrust laws (though the former is the basis for much of economic regulation).

THE JUSTICE DEPARTMENT'S CASE

On December 21, 1992, the U.S. Department of Justice filed antitrust charges against ATPCO and eight major airlines.[2] The complaint charged that the airlines, through ATPCO, had colluded to raise price and restrict competition in the airline industry. The Justice Department argued that the airlines had carried on detailed conversations and negotiations over prices through ATPCO. It pointed to numerous instances in which one carrier on a route had announced a fare increase to take effect a number of weeks in the future. Other carriers had then announced increases on the same route, though possibly to a different fare level. In many cases cited, the airlines had iterated back and forth until they reached a point where they were announcing the same fare increase to take effect on the same date. In cases where one airline did not announce that it would post the same fare increase as the others, the increase generally did not take place. In such situations it was common for carriers to "roll" their fare increases—that is, to move the

---

[2]The airlines were Alaska, American, Continental, Delta, Northwest, Trans World, United, and USAir.

effective date further into the future, in order to give the carrier that had not announced a matching fare increase more time to do so.

The DOJ garnered this information simply from the records of the ATPCO. It also had documents from each airline's daily internal fare change reports, which included phrases of the nature "we are waiting to see if [carrier name] is going to go along with our proposed increase," "we are abandoning the increase on [city1]-[city2] because [carrier name] has not matched," and "[carrier name] is now on board for the [date] increase to [fare level] on [city1]-[city2]." The DOJ argued that the announcement of fares that are to take effect at a later date allowed the airlines to negotiate over prices without ever offering those prices to the public. While none of the announcements was binding, such "cheap talk" can still aid collusive behavior.[3]

The DOJ's case also was based on patterns of multimarket coordination that it claimed to have identified. The complaint argued that the carriers were using fare basis codes and footnote designators to communicate to other airlines linkages between fares on different routes. A typical example of the allegation went something like this: Say that airline A1 has a hub at city C1 from which it serves a route to city C3 with nonstop flights, as illustrated in Figure 9-1. Airline A2 has a hub at C2, which is between C1 and C3. Airline A2 is offering a relatively low fare in the C1–C3 market with service that requires a plane change at C2. This low fare is siphoning customers from the nonstop service that A1 offers on the route. A1 would like A2 to raise its fare on the C1–C3 route.

If that were the whole story, however, A1 would not have much ability to bribe or coerce A2. However, A2 serves C2–C4 with nonstop service, and A1 offers change-of-plane service on that route over its hub at C1—exactly the reverse of the previous situation. A1 could strike a deal with A2 in which each carrier agrees not to undercut the other's nonstop service with its own fares that require a plane change at its own hub.

The DOJ argued that in such situations the ATPCO system of fare basis codes and footnote designators offered the sort of sophisticated communication necessary to spell out and agree upon such a deal. Here's one way the DOJ said it would work: A1 would institute a new fare on C2–C4 that undercut A2's fare on that route, and A1 would give this new fare the same or a similar fare basis code as A2 was using for the fare A1 was unhappy with on C1–C3, thus signaling to A2 the connection between the two fares. A1 would then put a short last-ticket date on this new fare, indicating that it would be available for only, say, two weeks. It would also put in a fare on the C2–C4 route that matched A2's current fare and would give that fare a first-ticket date that was the same as its last-ticket date for the cheaper fare. A1 would then wait to see if A2 got the message. If it did, A2 would put a last-ticket date on its fare on C1–C3 that was the same as the last-ticket date

---

[3]See Farrell and Rabin (1996) for a thorough discussion of the effects of cheap talk on collusion.

FIGURE 9-1 Carriers with Overlapping Networks.

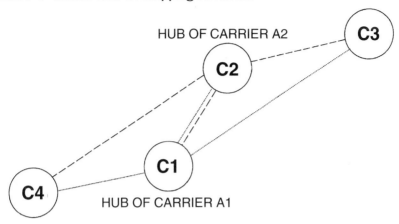

A1 had put on its cheap C2–C4 fare and would add a new fare that matched A1's fare on C1–C3 and had the same date for its first-ticket date. If that happened, then two weeks hence each carrier, without further action, would raise its fare on the other's nonstop route so that it was no longer undercutting the nonstop route with change-of-plane service.

If A2 did not get the message or respond in the way that A1 wished, A1 could roll forward its last-ticket date on its cheap C2–C4 route. By refiling the fare with a different last-ticket date, A1 could also make sure that this fare again showed up on A2's daily list of new fares, just in case A2 had overlooked it the previous time.

The DOJ argued that the combination of future first-ticket dates and fare basis codes or footnote designators that allowed an airline to highlight a link between two fares on different routes made it much easier than it would otherwise be for two airlines to "negotiate" over fares on different routes. With these facilitating devices, the Department asserted, the airlines could make clear the "trades" they were offering: raising price on one route in return for a rival raising price on another route.

THE AIRLINES' DEFENSE

While under Section 1 of the Sherman Act blatant price fixing has been found to be per se illegal, in reality there are many cases that do not fit that mold. Often, as in the ATPCO case, the action under scrutiny is not secret meetings of executives in smoke-filled rooms. In this case, no face-to-face meetings were alleged. Rather, the airlines were accused of making very frequent statements that amounted to a negotiation over price. The statements were also made in public insofar as travel agents and others with access to a CRS could follow the rounds of announced future price changes. The basis of the Supreme Court's view that blatant price fixing is per se illegal is that there is no credible argument that such behavior could benefit consumers or competition. The airlines asserted that there was a clear argument that the actions at issue could benefit consumers, so that any examination should be under a rule-of-reason standard.[4]

The airlines responded to the specific DOJ charges by pointing out that all firms price in response to the actions of their competitors. They argued that each carrier was acting in its own independent best interest when it raised price. It would be unrealistic to think that a carrier would set its fares without considering the response that they could anticipate from other airlines. Once it was recognized that it is legitimate for an airline to consider the likely response from it competitors, the airlines argued that the DOJ allegations were indistinguishable from competitive behavior. A carrier probably would not want to cut price if all its competitors would match. Likewise, an airline will not be able to make a price increase "stick" if other airlines keep their prices at a lower level.

One can draw a parallel with a market that is undeniably competitive, such as the wheat market. For the price of wheat to increase, some seller must be the first to raise its price. It will do so in the belief that the competitive equilibrium price is higher than the current level. If it is incorrect, then most other wheat sellers will not follow, and the first firm will lose all or most of its sales. It then will be forced to reduce its price again. It has done nothing anticompetitive, but rather has engaged in a normal part of the price discovery process in a competitive market. As recently as June 1993, the Supreme Court found in *Brooke Group Ltd. v. Brown & Williamson Tobacco Corp.* that such parallel pricing is likely to occur in competitive or oligopolistic markets without collusion.[5] In a slightly earlier case, the Supreme Court had stated that "conduct that is as consistent with permissible competition as with illegal conspiracy does not, without more, support an inference of conspiracy."[6]

The defendants argued not only that the observed parallel price movements were consistent with competition, but that pre-announcements of price increases were in the interest of consumers. Far from being devices for price fixing, the airlines asserted that such advanced warnings to consumers were a device for creating consumer benefits and maintaining goodwill. They submitted hundreds of affidavits from travel agents praising the airlines' policy of advanced notice on price rises and making dire predictions if such notices were eliminated. The travel agents said that con-

---

[4]Carlton et al. (1997) make this argument persuasively.

[5]See *Brooke Group Ltd. v. Brown & Williamson Tobacco Corp.*, 61 U.S.L.W. at 4703. Also see Burnett (1999).

[6]*Matsushita Electric Industrial Co. v. Zenith Radio Corp.*, 475 U.S. 574, 597 n. 21 (1986). Also see Elzinga (1999).

sumers became very angry when the price of a ticket increased between the time that the traveler reserved the seat and actually purchased the ticket. Many agencies reported having programs to notify their loyal customers of pending fare increases that were likely to affect them. It was clear that the travelling public was used to receiving plenty of warning of fare increases and that, *holding fare levels constant,* they would prefer to continue to get advanced notice of increases.

The airlines supported their argument that consumers value information of future price increases by introducing evidence about the bookings "surge" that had occurred prior to some price increase. They focused on a few incidents in 1991: heavily advertised fare wars that ended at a certain date, a date that had been widely publicized in advance. The airlines showed that bookings surged just before the end of these "sales" and then fell substantially in the days following the price increase. In one of these incidents, the surge had been so dramatic and the demand for bookings so great as to cause the Sabre CRS, the largest in the United States, nearly to crash on the night before the discounts expired.

The airlines also defended advanced notice of price increases by pointing out—in an argument reminiscent of the *Ethyl* case—that airlines engaged in such advanced warnings on monopoly routes as much as on competitive routes.[7] This demonstrated, the airlines argued, that the primary consideration in pre-announcing fare increases was maintaining goodwill with consumers, not signaling to competitors.

Further, the defendants argued, the price-fixing theory was refuted by the fact that airlines didn't pre-announce price decreases. They pointed out that there is no goodwill justification for delaying a price decrease in order to give advanced warning rather than putting it in place immediately. On the other hand, they contended, price cuts are very destabilizing to cartels, so a member of a price-fixing conspiracy would be as, or more, concerned with getting the approval of its fellow conspirators for a price decrease as for a price increase. Thus, if airlines were to use advanced notice of price changes to support a price-fixing conspiracy, they would be more inclined to preannounce decreases.

The airlines recognized that documents received by the DOJ in the discovery process had indicated a few occasions in which one carrier had retaliated against another's incursion into its area of dominance by cutting fares on routes dominated by the aggressor airline. They argued, however, that this was a natural part of the competitive process. If other carriers hit you where it hurts, you turn around and hit them back where it hurts them. This wasn't multimarket price fixing; it was aggressive, perhaps excessively macho, competition. If on a few occasions a pricing analyst got car-

---

[7]In the *Ethyl* case, one of the defendants demonstrated that the practices it had been accused of engaging in to facilitate collusion were the same practices that it had used decades earlier when it was the only producer of the gasoline additive. *E.I. DuPont de Nemours & Co.* v. *FTC*, 729 F.2d 128 (1984). Also see Hay (1999).

ried away with the conflict analogy, that was certainly not evidence of price fixing. Furthermore, if a carrier knows that another airline is likely to respond aggressively and to expand a fare war beyond a single market, it is only natural for it to be less inclined to initiate a fare cut even if it would otherwise like to. The point, the defendants argued, was still that all of this behavior was undertaken unilaterally by each airline, that no agreement was solicited or accepted.

All of the defendant airlines protested that they had never used fare basis codes or footnote designators to signal connections between fares or to communicate information to other airlines that might support price fixing. The few cases in which a fare basis code was found to contain the two-letter code of a rival airline were argued to be anomalies that did not constitute a pattern of collusive behavior. The airlines also explained that it was often easier to give certain fares the same footnote designators when they were likely to have the same restrictions for the foreseeable future or to give different footnote designators to fares with the same restrictions if it was believed likely that the restrictions on one would become different from the restrictions on the other.

Two other factors, the airlines asserted, made price fixing untenable in the airline industry. First, not all of an airline's prices were public. Airlines regularly cut special deals with large corporations. In return for a guaranteed amount of traffic from the corporation or share of the firm's business, an airline typically would offer some percentage rebate on all tickets. The size of that rebate was kept secret. Any carrier could cheat on a collusive agreement with these rebates and faced a low probability of detection. Second, airlines could not monitor how many seats a carrier was making available at each fare it published. An airline could effectively cut its prices by making a large number of seats available at its lower published fares. A competing airline could never be sure of the exact mix of passengers and fares that another carrier was serving.

Finally, the airlines argued that common sense didn't support the price-fixing story. The airlines were experiencing the largest annual losses in their history. Major airlines had recently entered Chapter 11, and two of the largest prederegulation carriers, Pan Am and Eastern, had been liquidated. New entry had nearly stopped since the middle of 1990, further indicating that the industry was not offering firms an attractive return on investment. If there was price fixing, it certainly wasn't making the airlines rich.

THE JUSTICE DEPARTMENT'S RESPONSE

While the DOJ continued to argue that the case could be prosecuted as a per se violation of Section 1 of the Sherman Act, both sides pursued arguments that would be relevant only under a rule-of-reason standard. The Department recognized that some consumers may have benefited from pre-announcement of fare increases. Rather, it argued that such benefits were likely to be very small in comparison to the opportunity that pre-announcement afforded airlines to coordinate price increases.

Furthermore, the DOJ argued that consumers also were often misled by last-ticket dates. A DOJ study found that about half of all last-ticket dates placed in the CRS systems turned out to be inaccurate. In some cases, they were rolled forward until all airlines on a route had announced the same increase, with only the last announcement being correct. In many cases, they were simply withdrawn if competing carriers did not go along. (On rare occasions, the increase was implemented sooner than the last-ticket date suggested.) Consumers who bought tickets sooner than they would have liked, due to pre-announced increases that never actually occurred, were made worse off by these announcements.

The airlines' "surge" data turned out to be less persuasive than appeared to be the case at first. The airlines had submitted surge data for only the largest and most highly publicized sales in the recent past. These were not the pre-announced increases that most concerned the DOJ, because the heavy advertising that accompanied these last-ticket dates made it very difficult for the carriers to "negotiate" through numerous changes in the dates and fares. The airlines did not supply surge data for more typical unadvertised increases or ones that came about after a number of different announced last-ticket dates and subsequent changes.

The Justice Department agreed that pre-announcement of price decreases would indeed be powerful evidence that they were being used for collusion, but argued that the absence of such announcements simply could be due to the airlines' awareness that such behavior would assure an antitrust investigation. The practice of pre-announcing price increases could still be a device intended to facilitate collusion. Similarly, while the use of pre-announcements on monopoly routes indicates that such announcements are not valueless to consumers, it does not indicate the predominant reason for use of pre-announcements on competitive routes.

The DOJ also suggested that the airlines had available a ready substitute for advance notices of fare increases, one that did not raise the antitrust issues that were the focus of this case: The airlines could guarantee a fare for some period of time after a traveler made a reservation. The guarantee could be for a few days, a week, or longer. Implementing such a system would not be trivial, however, since airline reservation systems were programmed only to ticket at the price effective at the time the ticket was purchased. A price-guarantee system would require that the computers maintain a record of the price in effect at the time the reservation was made. Opinions differed with regard to the cost of implementing such a program. Many of the airlines also argued that it would not substitute for pre-notification of price increases, as many customers would still be angry if they waited longer than the price guarantee period and found themselves facing an increased fare.

Finally, even if all last-ticket dates were accurate and if fare guarantees could not viably replace them, a simple "back-of-the-envelope" calculation indicated that the total savings to consumers from early warning of price increases was likely to be very small. Here's how such a calculation could be done: Assume that on a typical route, price increases were implemented once every sixty days (which is more often than actual) and that a typical fare increase is 5 percent. Assume that advance notice of the increase caused a full day of bookings that would have occurred after the increase to instead take place before. For an increase that is not advertised outside the CRSs, this is a very large surge effect. This would mean that one-sixtieth of consumers would receive a savings of 5 percent due to the advance notice of price increases, or an average savings of slightly less than 0.1 percent per traveler on the route. Of course, those consumers who missed the fare increase date due to the absence of pre-announcement would be unhappy about paying the increase, but for the entire group of travelers on the route, the average savings is likely to be extremely small. If the pre-announcements aided collusion to any noticeable extent, it is likely that consumers would benefit from their elimination.

Two points were made in response to the assertion that discounting to corporations made collusion implausible. First, even if sales to corporations remained competitive because of secret discounting, there was no reason to think that this disciplined prices to all other consumers. Corporate discount tickets accounted for less than 10 percent of volume on nearly all routes, so this still left a large proportion of the market subject to the collusive prices. Second, the corporate discounts were mostly discounts off list prices. In the short run, with these discount agreements in place, any increase in the list price would be reflected proportionally in the discounted prices as well. Of course, in the longer run, if the market for corporate discount passengers were competitive, list price increases would be largely offset by greater proportional corporate discounts.

The issue of seat availability is a complex one. Airlines expend a great deal of effort to try to figure out the proportion of seats their competitors sell at each published fare, but they are not entirely successful. At any point in time, however, they can see whether a competitor has any seats available at a given price—in airline parlance, whether a "bucket" is open or closed. Thus, if one carrier attempts to cheat on a collusive price by offering a greater number of seats at lower listed prices, competitors can observe that it is keeping a low-price bucket open and can keep their own corresponding bucket open as well. This is not a perfect substitute for knowing a competitor's total sales in each bucket, but it means that no airline can secretly undercut its rivals by having a low price available when others don't.

The Justice Department argued that profit levels were not relevant to the investigation. DOJ investigators pointed out a number of cases in which the colluding firms were in poor financial health. While collusion is likely to raise profits compared with the same market without collusion, there are many cases in which colluding firms lose money. In the ATPCO case, it was noted that the airlines had made massive investments in capacity just before the 1990–1991 recession hit, leaving them with aircraft that were depreciating without even providing services. Besides the costs of holding excess capacity, the existence of that capacity lowered each firm's marginal cost of serving a given route, thus putting downward pressure on prices. This is part of the normal economics of markets with large fixed capital investments. Though excess capacity depresses prices and causes firms to report losses, economists agree that this is the efficient economic response to such situations. Even if firms colluded in such a situation—and the desire to do so is likely to be great—they may not be able to raise prices to the point that they can cover the cost of all prior investment errors.

FASHIONING A REMEDY AND NEGOTIATING A SETTLEMENT

As the Justice Department continued the investigation in 1992, a question hung over the case: If the Department could prove its case and prevail at trial, what remedy should it seek? Parallel price movements of competing firms are not generally illegal. DOJ was reluctant to pursue a settlement that would place such restrictions on how or how often firms could change their prices. Through the discussions with the defendants and the memos written by each side, the case came to focus on two issues: the pre-announcement of price increases and the alleged use of fare basis codes and footnote designators to communicate linkages between prices on different routes. It became apparent to all involved in the case that rapid information transmission was inherent in the computer technology in use in the industry. The DOJ would not easily be able to prevent airlines from "proposing" fare increases and then withdrawing those fares relatively quickly if competitors didn't match.

Instead, the Department decided to pursue remedies that it hoped would make it more costly and less effective to use the system for collusive bargaining. First, the DOJ proposed the elimination of last-ticket dates except in situations in which the carrier was engaged in significant advertising through newspapers, television, radio, or other media intended to inform consumers of the last-ticket date. The idea was that such announcements are clearly aimed at consumers, and making changes to such information after it is advertised is costly and potentially harmful to the carrier's reputation. (Later in negotiations between the airlines and the DOJ, it was agreed that carriers could also post a last-ticket date if it was only to match the last-ticket date of another carrier, which had advertised that date.) Likewise, airlines would not be able to pre-announce prices that would go into effect in the future, that is, they could not use future first-ticket dates. Thus, an airline could advertise "Sale Ends November 30," but could not say what the price would be after November 30.

Some airlines argued that requiring a carrier to advertise a sale in print, television, or other media would raise the cost of running a sale and would thus discourage price cutting. There was, however, no requirement of advertising to run a sale, only to put a last-ticket date on the sale. An airline was free to cut its price for any period of time it liked without advertising. It could not, however, put a last-ticket date on the fare in its listing with ATPCO unless it also communicated in some direct fashion to consumers. It was also unclear what sort of a short-term sale an airline would want to run without advertising. The point of cutting price is to increase sales as much as possible to make up for the lower price a firm receives from those who would have bought even at the high price. A sale without advertising seems more likely to decrease revenue from those who would have bought at the high price while minimizing the increase in total sales.

The other major condition of the proposed remedy was on the use of fare basis codes and footnote designators. The Justice Department proposed that these codes could contain only the basic information they were said to contain: abbreviations that indicated fare class, minimum stay or advance purchase, and other restrictions. In the course of the case, examples had come to light in which one carrier had put the two-letter airline code of another in a fare that appeared intended to retaliate against that competitor. Similarly, the DOJ's proposed remedy restricted the use of footnote designators to make them more generic and less able to convey information about the connection between different fares. A carrier would be required to use the same footnote designator for *all* its fares that had footnotes with identical information: such as first and last travel dates. Carriers generally had many footnote designators that pointed to footnotes containing the same information. In addition, carriers would not be allowed to list footnote designators that pointed to "empty" footnotes, ones that had no further information about the fare. This practice had also been observed during the investigation in situations where it appeared to be used to identify connections between fares on different routes.

THE CASE FILING AND PARTIAL SETTLEMENT

On December 21, 1992, the DOJ filed the case accusing all eight of the airlines under investigation of price fixing through the ATPCO. As it often does, the DOJ had, prior to filing, engaged in lengthy informal discussions of the case and settlement talks with the defendants. Thus, along with filing the case, the Justice Department also announced a settlement with United Airlines and USAir. Under the settlement, the airlines did not admit guilt on any of the charges, but they agreed to abide by the DOJ's proposed remedies. In particular, United and USAir agreed to stop announcing most price increases in advance of the date on which they took effect. Instead, most price increases would have to take effect at the time they were announced.

Under the Tunney Act, a settlement of a government antitrust case such as this one must be approved by a federal court. The idea behind the Tunney Act was to ensure that the government didn't cut a backroom deal with specific defendants in return for favors. The court must review the settlement, hear arguments from all interested parties, and determine that the settlement is in the public interest.

At the Tunney Act hearing, which took place shortly after the settlement with United and USAir was reached, the other accused airlines argued strongly against the settlement. Their arguments were essentially the same as they had used in responding to the government's investigation: first- and last-ticket dates are for the purpose of informing consumers and give significant benefits to them; airlines act unilaterally but are of course influenced by the prices that other carriers charge; the evidence did not support the feasibility or practice of collusion in this market; and any signaling or attempt to coerce competitors to raise price was an anomaly.[8]

In responding to these filings, the DOJ examined the airlines' incentive for making such an argument. The Justice Department argued that if the airlines' pleading was accurate, they would have no incentive to oppose restrictions being placed on their competitors, United and USAir, in the use of first- and last ticket dates and other complex information transmission through ATPCO. The DOJ argued that accepting the nonsettling airlines' arguments would imply that they would gain a significant competitive advantage versus United and USAir. In fact, two of the nonsettling carriers stated that they would not accept the proposed settlement for themselves, because it would put them at a competitive disadvantage against other airlines that were not part of the case.[9] If this were true, the DOJ argued, one would expect the other airlines to be happy to see United and USAir subjected to these restrictions.

In contrast, DOJ submitted, if the techniques that United and USAir had agreed to cease using had been part of a system of price coordination, one would indeed expect the nonsettling airlines to fight it. If these facets of ATPCO filings had supported coordinated behavior, the inability of United

---

[8]Some of the airlines also argued that the proposed settlement could raise fare levels. If airlines found it more difficult to raise prices, they might be less inclined to experiment with lower fares, because it would be difficult to return to the pre-discount level. Of course, this same argument applies to nearly any impediment to collusion: if firms cannot collude as easily as previously, they might be less inclined to start a price war. The argument is not logically inconsistent, but there does not appear to be any evidence that impeding collusion reduces aggressive price competition.

[9]In a pleading shortly after the settlement with United and USAir, Delta stated that it had not discontinued the use of first- and last-ticket dates because if it did so, it "would be at a competitive disadvantage with respect to the remaining airlines that would be operating under no similar restriction." TWA made a similar argument. Joint Response of the Airline Tariff Publishing Company, Alaska Airlines, Inc., American Airlines, Inc., Continental Airlines, Inc., Delta Air Lines, Inc., Northwest Airlines, Inc., and Trans World Airlines, Inc., to the Court's order of May 24, 1993, requesting information, June 28, 1993. p. 10.

and USAir to use them would be nearly as harmful to the other airlines as if they had been forced to accept these restrictions on their own behavior. Thus, their arguments against the settlement with United and USAir may have undermined the procompetitive case the other defendants had made for the suspect behavior.

THE FINAL SETTLEMENT AND ITS EFFECTS

Despite the protests of the other defendant carriers, the settlement with United and USAir was accepted by the courts under the Tunney Act. Shortly after, the other six defendants entered further negotiations with DOJ. On March 17, 1994, a final settlement of the ATPCO case was announced. The other six airlines agreed to nearly the same restrictions as had United and USAir. The consent decree is to last for ten years, until 2004. Until that time, these airlines cannot use footnote designators and fare basis codes to convey anything but the most basic information; they cannot link different fares with special codes; and they cannot preannounce price increases except in the case of widely publicized sales.

While the settlement restricts behavior that the DOJ believed facilitated the communication of information that supported collusion, it does not restrict the fares that a carrier can offer or when the carrier can begin or end their availability. This was made clear in a memorandum filed with the settlement at the request of American Airlines. Two examples detailed in the memo make clear the freedom that airlines still have and the difficult antitrust issues that remain. The DOJ, as part of the settlement, accepted that neither of the following scenarios would constitute a violation of the consent decree:

> Scenario 1: At noon on Friday Airline A transmits 10% fare increases on certain city-pairs to ATPCO. The increased fares become available for sale through CRS at 5 p.m. that same day. On Saturday, Airline B transmits 5% increases to ATPCO on the same city-pairs. Airline A withdraws its 10% fare increases on Sunday when it learns that competing airlines have not offered matching fares for sale. Airline B withdraws its 5% increased fares. The following week, on Friday, Airline A raises its fares 5% on those city-pairs where Airline B had raised its fares 5% the previous week. On Saturday, Airline B matches Airline A's 5% fare increases, and both Airlines thereafter offer those fares for sale.

> Scenario 2: Airline A offers for sale a low fare (e.g., $101) for travel on a route that is important to Airline B. Airline B matches the $101 fare for travel on the same city-pair and also offers for sale a $101 fare for travel on a city-pair that is important to Airline A. Airline B withdraws both $101 fares after one day. Airline A then withdraws its initial $101 fare the next day.

The DOJ stated that these scenarios involved the offering of bona fide fares for sale that are available to consumers at the time they are published. Because they involved a change in the carrier's economic behavior in the marketplace, and were not intended solely to communicate a carrier's planned future fare changes, the DOJ agreed that they would not be forbidden under the consent decree.

Beyond clarifying the settlement, these scenarios also described the way that prices have been set in the industry since shortly after the December 1992 settlement with USAir and United. Since that time, the airlines have implemented most of their fare changes on weekends, when a very small share of tickets are actually sold because most travel agencies are closed. It is now common for an airline to post price increases on a Friday afternoon, which then become available in the CRSs on Saturday morning. If its competitors in the markets do not match the increase by Sunday afternoon, the airline withdraws the increase Sunday night, so that the original lower prices are in effect on Monday morning (Hirsch 1993). If its competitors match, the higher fares remain in effect.

The ATPCO case raised some of the most subtle and challenging issues in enforcement of Section 1 of the Sherman Act, the cornerstone of U.S. antitrust law. Unfortunately, because the case never went to trial, the ATPCO case set no legal precedent. Furthermore, because the remedy fashioned addressed only institutional aspects of the airline industry, today it provides little guidance as to where in the gray area of Section 1 legitimate communication ends and price fixing begins. It did, however, clarify the DOJ's willingness to pursue cases of coordinated pricing through rapid communication, as well as the types of arguments that are likely to arise in such cases.

The consent decree that concluded the case expires in 2004. While many things have changed in the airline industry since the case was settled, the fundamental issues of rapid communication and price coordination remain. When the DOJ reviews the case at the expiration of the consent decree, one question will be whether the settlement had the desired effect. This is a difficult question to answer since the counterfactual outcome—what would have happened if there had been no DOJ investigation or settlement—is not easy to discern. On a systemwide basis, it is extremely difficult to know if fares would have been higher or lower without the settlement, because many other factors changed during the years surrounding the case.

An alternative approach, however, may shed some light on the settlement's impact. There are certain routes for which many parties argued that the ability of airlines to communicate through ATP was particularly valuable in raising fares. If ATP communication was especially effective on these routes, one might then ask whether, following the settlement, prices on these routes fell *relative* to prices on other routes.

The routes on which ATP communication might be especially beneficial to airlines in coordinating prices are those on which nonstop flights from hub airports compete with change-of-plane itineraries available for the same route. The idea is that these are routes on which competing airlines are most likely to have different preferred prices; nonstop providers offer a higher quality product and are likely to see the passengers on the city-pair as the primary source of revenue for the flight, while carriers that serve the route only with a change of plane offer a lower quality product and face incremental costs that depend on the opportunity cost of the two or more flights on which passengers travel to get to the same destination. It was also suggested that ATP was used to coordinate implicit agreements not to undercut one another on such routes: "I won't cut fares on flights out of your hub if you won't cut fares on flights out of my hub."

To investigate this question, I examined 387 routes from hubs on which change-of-plane itineraries competed significantly with nonstop service, with each constituting at least 20 percent of the traffic for travel on the city-pair during 1990 (before the ATP case).[10] Comparing prices on these routes to the national average prices for routes of similar distance, it appears that prices on these routes *increased* relative to the national average following the settlement. In 1990, distance-adjusted prices on these routes were about equal to the national average. Prices increased on these routes relative to the national average over the ensuing six years, until they were 10 percent above the national average by 1996. Over the same period, routes from hubs that were predominantly nonstop (less than 20 percent change-of-plane passengers) held steady at about 20 percent above the national average, reflecting the premium for nonstop routes from hubs on which there is little competition.

This is only one simple analysis, and certainly not the final word, but it does cast doubt on the efficacy of the settlement. Sometime around 2004, the DOJ will have to reach its own conclusion on this issue. If it determines that the settlement did not affect prices, it will then have to decide whether the consent decree was ineffective in addressing a genuine antitrust problem or whether the problem of rapid communication wasn't so important after all.

REFERENCES

Borenstein, Severin. "The Evolution of U.S. Airline Competition." *Journal of Economic Perspectives* 7 (Spring 1992): 45–73.

Burnett, William B. "Predation by a Nondominant Firm: The Liggett Case (1993). In *The Antitrust Revolution: Economics, Competition, and Policy,* 3d edn., edited by

---

[10]These were all routes that met the share criteria and included Chicago O'Hare, Atlanta, Dallas/Ft. Worth, Denver, St. Louis, Detroit, Minneapolis, Pittsburgh, Houston Intercontinental, Charlotte, Salt Lake City, Memphis, Dayton, Cincinnati, or Raleigh/Durham.

John E. Kwoka, Jr., and Lawrence J. White, 239–263. New York: Oxford University Press, 1999.

Carlton, Dennis, and Chip Bamberger. "Airline Networks and Fares." Unpublished manuscript, 1996.

Carlton, Dennis W., Robert H. Gertner, and Andrew M. Rosenfield. "Communication Among Competitors: Game Theory and Antitrust." *George Mason Law Review* 5 (Spring 1997): 423–440.

Elzinger, Kenneth G. "Collucive Predation: *Matsushita* v. *Zenith* (1986)." In *The Antitrust Revolution: Economics, Competition, and Policy,* 3d edn., edited by John E. Kwoka, Jr., and Lawrence J. White, 220–238. New York: Oxford University Press, 1999.

Farrell, Joseph and Matthew Rabin. "Cheap Talk." *Journal of Economic Perspectives* 10 (Summer 1996): 103–118.

Gertner, Robert H. "Tacit Collusion with Immediate Response: The Role of Asymmetries." Unpublished manuscript, 1994.

Hay, George A. "Facilitating Practices: The Ethyl Case (1984)." In *The Antitrust Revolution: Economics, Competition, and Policy,* 3d edn., edited by John E. Kwoka, Jr., and Lawrence J. White, 182–201. New York: Oxford University Press, 1999.

Hirsch, James S. "Fliers Discover They Don't Fare Well on the Weekends." *Wall Street Journal,* July 30, 1993, B1.

CASE 10

Global Cartels Redux: The Amino Acid Lysine Antitrust Litigation (1996)

John M. Connor

INTRODUCTION

In the evening of June 27, 1995, more than seventy FBI agents simultaneously raided the world headquarters of Archer-Daniels-Midland Company
(ADM) in Decatur, Illinois, and interviewed a number of ADM officers in
their homes. Serving subpoenas authorized by a federal grand jury sitting in
Chicago, the agents collected documents related to ADM's lysine, citric
acid, and corn-sweeteners businesses. Within a day or two, investigators
had also raided the offices of four other companies that manufactured or imported lysine. These subpoenaed documents, together with hundreds of secret tape recordings of the conspirators' meetings and conversations, built a
strong case that five companies had been illegally colluding on lysine prices
around the world for three years.

The FBI raids were widely reported in the mass media and unleashed a
torrent of legal actions, some of which were still unresolved seven years
later.[1] The three major federal antitrust actions were the result of an under-
cover investigation by the U.S. Department of Justice (DOJ) that had begun

John M. Connor provided expert opinions for a law firm representing plaintiffs in the class action
encaptioned as *Amino Acid Lysine Antitrust Litigation,* MDL No. 1083 (Northern District of Illinois 1996). He also wrote opinions as a consultant for the Antitrust Division of the U.S. Department of Justice during the sentencing phase of its criminal trial *U.S. v. Michael D. Andreas et al.,*
in which three officers of the Archer-Daniels-Midland Co. were prosecuted for lysine price fixing.

[1]By the end of fiscal 1996 (June 30, 1996), ADM was a defendant in an antitrust suit or target of a
government investigation in seventy-nine cases, of which twenty-one related to lysine. In subsequent fiscal years, the number of active suits or investigations varied from twenty-two to forty-one
(ADM 2001). In 2002, ADM was appealing a lysine conspiracy fine levied by the European Commission and faced three indirect-purchaser suits in lysine.

in November 1992 with the cooperation of the ADM lysine division president. The first suit was a treble-damages class action settled in the summer of 1996. A few months later, the DOJ sought and obtained convictions for criminal price fixing by the five corporate lysine sellers. Although all the corporate members of the cartel pleaded guilty and paid historic fines, not all of the executives who managed the conspiracy were willing to plead guilty. Therefore, the DOJ prosecuted four lysine executives in a highly publicized jury trial held in Chicago in the summer of 1998; three of the four were found guilty and heavily sentenced.[2] The five corporate conspirators were later investigated and fined by the antitrust authorities of Canada, Mexico, Brazil, and the European Union.

Within a year of the FBI raids, more than forty civil antitrust suits were filed in federal district courts by direct buyers of lysine, each suit incorporating multiple plaintiffs. In early 1996, approximately four hundred plaintiffs were certified as a single federal class, and the case called *Amino Acid Lysine Antitrust Litigation* was assigned to a judge of the U.S. District Court of Northern Illinois. In April 1996, the three largest defendants offered the class $45 million to settle the damages allegedly caused by their price fixing. Final approval of the settlement occurred in July 1996.[3] Additional follow-up suits included about fifteen actions filed by farmers, consumers, and other indirect buyers of lysine in the courts of six states and two Canadian provinces. ADM was further distracted by derivative shareholder suits charging mismanagement by the company's managers and board of directors.

The three federal lysine cases were important for at least four reasons. First, it was the U.S. Government's first completely successful conviction of a global cartel in more than four decades.[4] Under the leadership of Attorney General Thurman Arnold, the DOJ had obtained convictions of scores of companies that had been members of international cartels that had operated between the two world wars. These suits had been initiated in the late 1940s and were completed by around 1950. Prior to the 1996 lysine convictions, the Government had attempted to prosecute only three international cartels. In all three cases, the DOJ failed to prevail at trial either because essential evidence located abroad could not be subpoenaed or because juries would not convict U.S. businessmen on the testimony of their foreign co-conspirators.[5]

---

[2]The transcript and exhibits of *U.S. v. Michael D. Andreas et al.* are a major source of primary information on the lysine cartel (Tr.); exhibits from this trial are labeled Tr. Ex. In late 1999, three top ADM officers were sentenced to long prison terms; Andreas got a thirty-six month sentence, the maximum allowed by the Sherman Act (Kanne et al. 1999). One defendant, a managing director of Ajinomoto of Japan, remains a fugitive.

[3]The two other defendants settled for almost $5 million about a year later.

[4]Although the Federal Trade Commission successfully prosecuted one international cartel (*Mylan Laboratories* 1998), nearly all naked cartel cases are handled by the DOJ because of the latter agency's unique authority to bring criminal cases.

[5]Prosecutions of the uranium cartel (1978) and industrial diamonds (1994) were hampered by the

Second, the conviction of the lysine cartel was the first public manifestation of a sea change in enforcement priorities by U.S. and overseas antitrust officials. Prior to 1995, less than 1 percent of the price-fixing indictments by the DOJ involved at least one non-U.S.-based corporation or non-U.S. resident. By contrast, beginning during 1998–2000 more than one-half of all criminal price-fixing indictments were brought against international conspirators (Connor 2001a, Figure 1.1). The investigation of the lysine cartel led directly to the discovery and successful prosecution of thirty multinational corporations that participated in global price fixing in the markets for lysine, citric acid, sodium gluconate, and ten bulk vitamins. Since 1996, more than a score of global cartels have been uncovered and prosecuted by the DOJ, the Competition Policy Directorate of the European Commission (DG-IV), and other antitrust agencies around the world. Cartel enforcement remains a high priority for the Antitrust Division of the DOJ, which is devoting 30 percent of its resources to criminal price-fixing prosecution.[6]

Third, the lysine cartel case demonstrated the government's intention to apply tough, "blue-collar" investigative techniques to what had been formerly been treated as a gentle, "white-collar" activity. In the three-year investigation that preceded the FBI's 1995 raid, the DOJ used all of the tools that it habitually employs in gathering evidence against drug cartels or other forms of organized crime, including seeking the cooperation of foreign police organizations. During guilty plea negotiations with targeted cartel conspirators, prosecutors have made deft use of a wide range of possible sanctions to instill cooperation, including threatening crippling fines, imposing significant prison sentences, and barring convicted felons from entering U.S. territory.

Finally, the lysine cases and those that followed soon thereafter showed that the sanctions for criminal price fixing had escalated enormously in the 1990s. Not only has Congress steadily raised the statutory fine for Sherman Act violations (up to $10 million for corporations), it also in 1994 made criminal antitrust violations felonies instead of misdemeanors. Combined with the U.S. Sentencing Guidelines first promulgated in 1987, corporate price fixers are now liable for criminal penalties as high as "double the harm" caused by a cartel. That is, corporations can be fined by the government up to twice the monopoly overcharge generated by a cartel, an amount that can easily exceed the $10 million statutory cap when market sales are large (Connor 2001a, pp. 84–88). ADM, the leader of the lysine cartel, was fined

---

absence of witnesses and documents outside U.S. jurisdiction. The DOJ lost at trial when prosecuting one member of the thermal fax paper cartel in 1995. Finally, although the DOJ was victorious in a U.S.-Canada cartel that fixed the prices of plastic dinnerware (1996), that cartel was only tangentially international in scope.

[6]In Fiscal 2002, the division planned to allocate 258 full-time equivalent positions (FTEs) to this activity (DOJ 2002). However, if one adds the resources of U.S. Attorney offices and the FBI, about 3000 FTEs are devoted to fighting cartels, at an annual cost of $440 million.

$100 million for its role in two criminal price-fixing schemes—a record amount that was twice eclipsed in the late 1990s by leaders of highly injurious global cartels.[7]

In fiscal years 1998–2001, the Antitrust Division collected more than $2 billion in fines for criminal price fixing, of which more than three-fourths was from members of international cartels (DOJ 2002). The EU's DG-IV, which operates on a somewhat delayed schedule, imposed record fines of 1.84 billion euros on hard-core cartels in 2001 alone; these fines are loosely based on the cartels' overcharges to customers in Europe. Both U.S. and EU authorities are empowered to base their fines on worldwide overcharges rather than their jurisdictional injuries, and the U.S. DOJ has done so at least twice.

U.S. Government fines are mere paper cuts compared to the financial wounds that may be inflicted by plaintiffs in civil actions. Direct buyers suing in federal courts, the principal focus of this chapter, are entitled to seek treble damages. In some cases, direct buyers abroad are permitted to seek treble damages in U.S. courts.[8] However, antitrust liability does not stop there. Nearly twenty states allow residents who are *indirect* purchasers to sue in state courts, most of which permit treble damages. In addition, state attorneys general increasingly have banded together to pursue antitrust claims in federal courts (*parens patriae* suits) to recover treble damages for their state governments and for corporate and individual indirect buyers residing in their states. For example, in October 2000 the attorneys general of more than forty states announced a settlement totaling $340 million to be paid by the six largest members of the vitamins cartels. Not counting the losses associated with derivative shareholder suits, legal fees, and reputational effects, corporations accused of criminal price fixing now face maximum antitrust liabilities that range from *eight to twelve times* the cartel's U.S. overcharges.[9] The fines and prison terms meted out to cartel managers have also risen.[10]

The major role played by economic analysis in horizontal price-fixing cases is the calculation of the *overcharge* on buyers in markets affected by a cartel. The overcharge is the value of purchases of a cartelized product actually made, minus what the sales would have been for the same volume of product absent the cartel. Accurate estimates of conspiracy-induced overcharges are important not only because of recovery of civil damages, but

---

[7]ADM was the second firm to be fined above the $10 million statutory cap, but the first to be widely reported by the business press and popular media. In 1999 Hoffmann-La Roche paid $500 million for its participation in six global cartels for bulk vitamins.

[8]A decision of the U.S. Court of Appeals for the Second Circuit gives standing to buyers of art in London auctions (Katzman et al. 2002).

[9]The lower estimate assumes that the DOJ bases its double-the-harm fine on U.S. affected sales only; the higher estimate uses global sales, which are typically three times domestic.

[10]One German CEO, the ringleader of the graphite-electrode cartel, paid a U.S. fine of $10 million to stay out of prison. In 2002, the chairman of an art-auction house was fined $7.5 million for price fixing (Markon 2002).

also because overcharges are the basis for the calculation of government fines. In criminal price-fixing cases that are prosecuted under the per se standard of proof, the U.S. Sentencing Guidelines in force require federal prosecutors to impose fines on corporations and individuals that are based on overcharge calculations. For corporations, unless prosecutors have evidence that the overcharge on sales was 10 percent or less, the fine for criminal price fixing is double the cartel's overcharge.[11] For individuals, base fines are either figured at 1 percent to 5 percent of the overcharge, or, under an alternative statute, fines up to $25 million are assessed from a sliding scale that also depends on the size of the overcharge. In summary, both corporate and personal penalties for price fixing are in principle closely related to cartel overcharges.

The primary purpose of this case study is to illustrate the computation of overcharges in a forensic setting with data drawn from the lysine cartel of 1992–1995. Most of the issues regarding calculation arose during preparations for the private federal class action *In re Amino Acid Lysine Antitrust Litigation* in the summer of 1996. However, as additional time and economic data became available, more refined estimates of the lysine cartel overcharge became possible for the sentencing phase of the criminal case, *U.S.* v. *Michael D. Andreas et al.* All told, four of the five recognized forensic methods of overcharge calculations can be illustrated with the lysine case. This study also illustrates the deterrence effects of the current levels of financial sanctions for criminal price fixing.

ECONOMICS AND LAW OF CARTELS

A cartel is an association of two or more legally independent entities that explicitly agree to coordinate their prices or output for the purpose of increasing their collective profits. Some cartels are organized by state agencies or government-owned corporations; other cartels have been formed by multilateral treaties to attempt to smooth commodity price cycles. This case study is concerned only with private business cartels that operate unprotected by the cloak of national sovereignty.

Economics views cartels as a special type of oligopoly, an extralegal joint venture of businesses that are normally rivals in the same industry. The mission of a cartel is to increase the joint profits of its members to a level as close as possible to that of a monopolist; the strategy of a cartel is to implement one or more of the "restrictive business practices" popularly known as price fixing. Cartels almost always agree to raise their list prices, to lower total production, or both; they may also reinforce this basic decision by fixing market shares for each member, allocating specific customers, impos-

---

[11]If the 20-percent-of-sales criterion is used, the base fine is raised by a complex list of factors that yields a numerical culpability multiplier. The DOJ brings 90 percent of its price-fixing indictments as criminal matters.

ing uniform selling conditions, sharing sales information, monitoring price agreements, pooling and redistributing profits, adopting a method for punishing deviants, and hiding or destroying evidence of their activities. The time and management resources required to negotiate the formation of a cartel and to carry out its agreements can be substantial.

Economic models of cartels emphasize the necessity of high concentration and of product homogeneity in an industry (Stigler 1964; Dick 1998; Connor 2001a). Without small numbers of member-sellers and reasonably standardized products, the transactions costs of forming and maintaining a group consensus would become too high relative to the anticipated increase in profits. Moreover, because there is always a profit incentive for cartel members to cheat on the cartel's agreement (i.e., to sell more or at a lower price than that agreed upon), only small numbers and homogeneity will keep the information costs of detecting cheating within acceptable bounds. Other conditions believed to facilitate the formation or successful operation of cartels include large numbers of buyers, a small amount of noncartel production capacity, equality of production costs across firms, and relatively stable or predictable demand conditions. High barriers to entry into the industry will facilitate the formation and longevity of cartel agreements.

Section 1 of the 1890 Sherman Act deems cartels per se illegal. An explicit agreement to fix prices is a "conspiracy in restraint of trade," irrespective of the agreement's actual impact on market prices or output. The competition laws of other industrialized nations state that the the illegality of a cartel should be determined using the rule of reason. In practice, however, non-U.S. competition-law agencies routinely prosecute all naked cartels that they discover. In the EU rare exceptions are made for cartels with significant benefits for consumers from technological innovation. Many countries, including the United States, permit registered export cartels to operate.

Strict enforcement of laws against overt price fixing is a public policy widely supported by economists and legal scholars of all stripes. They may differ as to the causes giving rise to collusive behavior and as to the likelihood of long-term success, but they are united in their evaluation of the negative economic effects of cartels. Effective cartels cause unrecoverable losses in production and consumption, transfer income from customers to the stakeholders of cartel members, and often engage in wasteful rent-seeking expenditures (Posner 2001, ch. 1).

INDUSTRY BACKGROUND

Lysine is an essential amino acid, a building block for proteins that speed the development of muscle tissue in humans and animals. Food derived from animal and marine sources normally provides humans with sufficient lysine to ensure healthy muscle development. Certain vegetables, soybeans in particular, are also good sources of amino acids; expensive pharmaceutical-grade or "natural" lysine is chemically extracted from vegetable matter.

In 1956, scientists in Japan discovered that amino acids can be produced as a by-product of bacterial fermentation (Connor 1999). By 1960, two Japanese companies, Ajinomoto and Kyowa Hakko, were selling commercial quantities of lysine utilizing these new biotechnologies. From the beginning, lysine was produced by fermentation at a far lower cost than chemically extracted lysine; continuing improvements in production technologies have brought the cost of so-called synthetic lysine down to less than one-fifth that of pharmaceutical lysine. The lower prices of lysine in turn made it cost-effective to incorporate manufactured lysine into animal feeds. Today, well over 90 percent of the world's lysine supply is made by biotechnology and is used as a supplement in animal feeds, principally for swine, poultry, and aquaculture.

Evolution of the Industry

Worldwide demand for lysine by animal-feed manufacturers soared from nothing in 1960 to almost 70 million pounds in 1980, at prices of around $1 to $2 per pound. In the 1980s, global consumption of lysine grew by 16 percent per year; in the 1990s, volume growth was still a heady 12 percent annually (Connor 2001a, ch. 7). In the early 1990s, approximately two-thirds of the demand for lysine originated in North America and Western Europe, areas with the highest levels of meat consumption and with consumers most willing to pay for lean meats.

The Japanese duopoly initially satisfied global demand by exporting from its two domestic plants. Ajinomoto made the first move abroad by building a large plant in France in 1974. Kyowa Hakko opened its first overseas lysine plant in Mexico in 1980 and its second in Missouri in 1984. Ajinomoto, which had about twice the capacity of Kyowa Hakko, responded by opening its own U.S. lysine plant in Iowa in 1986. After they were up and running, the Japanese firms implemented significant capital expansions to their plants outside Japan every two or three years.

Lysine was a Japanese duopoly until 1980, when the South Korean conglomerate Sewon opened a new plant in its home country. Sewon never expanded through direct investment abroad, instead relentlessly expanding its sole plant and exporting most of its output to Asia and Europe. Sewon reached its goal of achieving a 20 percent world market share by the late 1990s, but at the cost of massive borrowing.

Because feed-grade lysine is a homogenous product, the lysine oligopoly was able to collude successfully at least three times prior to 1992 (Connor 2001a, pp. 167–169). They fixed prices in Japan in the 1970s (Tr., pp. 908–909) and 1980s (Tr., pp. 1670–1894) and in Europe in the 1980s (Tr., pp. 2197–2522). From 1986 to 1990, Ajinomoto and Kyowa Hakko fixed prices and divided the U.S. lysine market 55 percent-45 percent (Tr., pp. 1670–1894). The U.S. price of lysine at times reached just over $3 per pound in the late 1980s. In brief, when the lysine biotech industry consisted of two or three Asian producers, collusive behavior was more often the norm than was uncooperative or classic competitive behavior.

Entry in the 1990s

Patents on high-yielding microbes and technological secrecy largely prevented new firms from enjoying the high growth and large profits being made in the lysine industry. Leading French and German biotechnology firms attempted to form lysine joint ventures in the 1970s and 1980s, but their efforts were thwarted (Connor 2001a, pp. 169–170). With two exceptions, only very small scale entry occurred in the 1990s (Connor 2001a, pp. 176–178).

   In early 1991, two newcomers turned the lysine industry into a five-firm oligopoly. ADM, according to a plan finalized in late 1989, opened the world's largest lysine manufacturing plant at its headquarters in Decatur, Illinois, in February 1991. Within eighteen months, ADM's plant had expanded global production capacity by 25 percent above year-end 1990 levels; by 1993, ADM's single plant accounted for one-third of global capacity (780 million pounds). ADM's strategic objective was to acquire a global market share equal to that of the industry leader, Ajinomoto. Ruthless price cutting by ADM and the sudden appearance of large excess capacity caused lysine prices to plunge 45 percent in the first eighteen months of the Decatur plant's operation. Global oversupply was exacerbated by the simultaneous opening of a smaller plant in Indonesia controlled by the South Korean food firm Cheil Sugar Co. ADM's aggressive entry into the lysine industry was the precipitating event in the formation of a new lysine cartel in 1992.

Cartel Behavior, 1992–1995

Ajinomoto, Kyowa Hakko, and Sewon began meeting as early as April 1990 to try to forge a plan to cope with ADM's entry, but they were fatalistic about ADM's impending success.[12] After ADM began production, the Asian manufacturers repeatedly signaled their willingness to raise lysine prices, but ADM appeared to be steadfast in its drive to share global dominance. By mid-1992, ADM had captured an impressive 80 percent of U.S. sales and was exporting more than one-half its production. Ajinomoto and Kyowa Hakko experienced large operating losses in late 1991 and early

---

[12]Details may be found in Connor (2001a, ch. 8) and Appendix A of Connor (2000). Many of these facts were corroborated by testimony or exhibits from the 1998 criminal trial (Tr.). For popular accounts of the cartel, see Eichenwald (2000) and Lieber (2000). The final legal decision is Kanne et al. (2000).

1992. In June 1992, the U.S. transaction price (manufacturers' delivered price) reached $0.68 per pound, which was $0.10 per pound below ADM's long-run marginal cost (see discussion of costs below).

By early 1992, the Asian incumbents were considering asking ADM to join them in a more cooperative arrangement. It must have seemed something of a godsend when in April 1992 the president of ADM's lysine division showed up in Tokyo with another more senior ADM officer to propose the formation of a lysine "trade association."[13] Under the cover of establishing such a trade group, Ajinomoto, Kyowa Hakko, and ADM officers met in Mexico City in June 1992. This was the first of twenty-five multi-party price-fixing meetings among the five corporations that joined the cartel; dozens of supplementary bilateral meetings by regional sales managers and hundreds of telephone calls cemented agreements on prices in as many as thirteen countries or regions. The price agreements covered only dry feed-grade lysine.[14] In early 1993, a brief price war broke out among the conspirators, mainly because of ADM's insistence that the participants had to agree to global market shares. After a top-level meeting in October 1993 resolved the issue, the cartel displayed a high level of harmony and consensus. Cheating was restrained in part by largely accurate monthly reporting of each company's lysine sales volume to all the members of the cartel.

The lysine cartel ended with the FBI raid on cartel offices in June 1995, almost exactly three years after the first price-fixing meeting had occurred. During that time, the average U.S. transaction price of lysine rose from $0.68 per pound when the cartel began operating to a plateau of $0.98 (October–December 1992), fell again to $0.65 (May 1993), and rose quickly again to above $1.00 for most of the remainder of the conspiracy period (Figure 10-1). Prices in the EU closely tracked those in the United States, albeit at a level $0.10 to $0.25 higher.[15] Target prices were also higher than the U.S. target price in Latin America, Japan, Oceania, and most parts of Asia (Connor 2001a, p. 238). However, in the rest of this study, only U.S. prices will be analyzed.

The Costs of Collusion

As mentioned above, there is considerable sentiment among some economists that the costs of forming and maintaining a collusive contract are so

---

[13]A year or two later, the International Amino Acids Manufacturers' Association was formed and recognized as a "working party" of the Agriculture Directorate of the European Commission.

[14]In the U.S. market ADM sold a somewhat diluted aqueous version delivered in tanker trucks to nearby customers. On an active-ingredient basis, liquid lysine was less expensive but highly correlated in price movements to the powder form. Liquid lysine accounted for well under 5 percent of the U.S. market.

[15]The correlation in prices is even higher when one compares the U.S. price in dollars to the EU price in Deutschmarks. That is, the US$/DM exchange rate, which is rather unpredictable, introduced more variability into the European price because the conspirators used the dollar to fix prices quarterly.

FIGURE 10-1 Lysine Transaction Prices, U.S. and EU Markets, 1991–1996

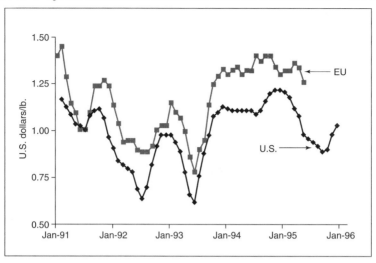

Note: U.S. prices from sales by the four largest manufacturers (see Appendix A of Connor (2000) for details). EU prices from a European Commission notice published on the *RAPID* web site in 2001, in euros, translated into U.S. dollars at the prevailing monthly interbank exchange rate.

high that the incidence of cartels is low and their lives fleeting.[16] The history of the lysine cartel and related global cartels prosecuted in the late 1990s does not support this sanguine view.

Internal memoranda and extensive trial testimony by cartel participants confirm that the conspirators anticipated that the rewards from price fixing would far outweigh the costs of operating the cartel (Connor 2001a, ch. 8). At a key meeting in late 1992, a top ADM official expressed the expectation that their recently concluded agreement would generate $200 million in joint profits in a global market for lysine that varied from $500 to $700 million in annual sales. His prediction, from ADM's perspective, was accurate; ADM would earn just about $200 million in profits from the cartel over three years with its one-third share of sales in the worldwide lysine market. Direct management costs of operating the cartel were modest. During the four years of

---

[16]An accessible treatment of the inherent instability of cartel agreements may be found in Posner (2001, pp. 60–69). Among the obstacles to agreement are an own-price elasticity of demand that is too high at the competitive price, uneven costs of production among potential cartel members, product heterogeneity, a steeply rising marginal cost curve, a large fringe of suppliers that will not join the cartel, lower costs of production by the fringe producers, and the difficulty of apportioning reductions in output among the cartelists. After the cartel is formed each member has an incentive to cheat by either cutting price or offering an improved product; cheating is difficult to detect; and virtually the only way to punish deviants is through expensive, self-destructive trigger mechanisms such as price wars. Many newer textbooks in industrial economics (e.g., Martin 2002) practically ignore cartels.

preliminary negotiations and actual cartel operation, each of the four (later five) companies sent two men to meetings held on average once every three months. Late in the conspiracy, regional sales managers became involved, but the total number of conspirators never exceeded forty (Connor 2000, app. A). Counting the monthly production reports and other communications submitted by each firm, it appears that each corporate member of the cartel managed the conspiracy with an input of fifteen to twenty-five mandays per year. Total labor costs for all corporate conspirators could not have exceeded $1 million for the entire duration of the conspiracy.

It is certainly true that the cartel members squabbled frequently and that the two smallest members, both South Korean companies, were strongly inclined to cheat on the price and market-share agreements. Infighting led to one sharp price war for a few months in 1993, the second year of the conspiracy. However, a number of techniques adopted by the cartel and the impressive diplomatic skills of the cartel's dual leaders, ADM and Ajinomoto, kept the effects of cheating to tolerable levels.

Among the most important practices that cemented cartel harmony was the tonnage quotas agreed upon in late 1993. Combined with accurate monthly sales reports and politic concessions of additional quotas to the two Korean firms, the market-share agreements would be honored with impressive precision throughout 1994 and into 1995. The formation of an amino acid trade association under European Commission sponsorship provided excellent cover for the group's illegal meetings in Europe and elsewhere. A compensation system was adopted to punish members that exceeded their quotas, but it was never necessary to implement the scheme. ADM, with its new efficient plant and ample excess capacity, frequently reminded the cartel of its willingness to flood the market with lysine; its threats were credible because it had twice driven the world price of lysine to below its own average total cost of production, inflicting operating losses upon the others. Moreover, ADM had taken the rare step of inviting its rivals in the lysine market to an intimate tour of its capacious production facilities. Finally, it should be recalled that the three largest Asian companies in the 1992–1995 cartel had a great deal of experience—nearly two decades worth—in organizing price-fixing schemes. ADM too, it is now known, was a serial price fixer.[17]

MEASURING THE OVERCHARGE

The monopoly overcharge is the difference between what a buyer has paid for a cartelized product and what a buyer would have paid absent the cartel. Under U.S. antitrust law, a successful plaintiff is entitled to treble the dollar

[17]ADM conspired to fix prices in the markets for sodium gluconate and citric acid; highly possible cases include corn sweeteners, monosodium gluconate, methionine, other nucleotides, carbon dioxide gas, and wine alcohol.

overcharge per unit, which is then multiplied by the number of units purchased.[18] Information on actual transaction prices and quantities sold is usually readily available from the parties in such cases, but the unobserved "but-for" price must be inferred using economic reasoning.[19] Enter the economists.

Methods of Calculation

There are five generally recognized methods of calculating an overcharge (Page 1996; Hovenkamp 1998). Proving an antitrust injury requires a preponderance of the evidence, but the amount of damages is decided according to a lower standard, that of reasonableness. Each of these five methods of computation probably meets the legal standard of reasonableness.

The *yardstick* approach involves the identification of a market similar to the one in which prices were fixed but in which prices were unaffected by the conspiracy. A yardstick market should have cost structures and demand characteristics highly comparable to the cartelized market, yet lie outside the orbit of the cartel's influence. Typically, the yardstick method is applied to cases of geographically localized price fixing. Because the lysine cartel was global in scope, the yardstick method could not be applied.

There were four feasible methods of estimating the lysine cartel's overcharge in the U.S. market. Two of them, the before-and-after method and the oligopoly-model method, were employed by economists acting as experts for the two sides in the civil treble-damages suit. Opinions and rebuttals were exchanged during May and July of 1996 prior to a fairness hearing for the federal class of plaintiffs and after the defendants provided monthly prices for 1991–1995. Two other methods of analysis, one using costs of production and the other a time-series econometric market model, were carried out in 1999 with the benefit of data from exhibits filed in the Chicago criminal trial.

The Before-and-After Method

This method has been used to calculate antitrust damages in U.S. civil cases since at least the 1920s (Hovenkamp 1998, p. 661), and it was one of the methods used in the treble-damages lysine case. "Before-and-after" is something of a misnomer because the "before" period is really any nonconspiracy period—whether before, after, or during an intermediate pause

---

[18]Equivalently, one may compute the *percentage* increase in price for each time period during the conspiracy, and then multiply these percentages by the *value* purchased in each period.

[19]Single damages under the law in most court circuits are precisely equivalent to the income transfer due to the exercise of market power. Single damages are slightly higher than the stream of monopoly profits accruing to the cartel members, because operating the cartel requires the expenditure of some management resources. In some circuits, the dead-weight loss may be permitted as an additional source of damages (Page 1996). Some legal theorists argue that a buyer's lost profits is a conceptually superior measure of damages (Hovenkamp 1998, p. 658).

in price fixing. It is important that the "before" period be one that is quite comparable to the conspiracy period with respect to demand and supply conditions. Shifts in buyer preferences, appearance or the disappearance of substitutes, and changes in the cost of production of the cartelized product during the affected period all can cause overstatement or understatement of the overcharge.

A precartel price is often presumed in legal settings to be the competitive price. "Cartel members . . . enjoy no presumption that they already had market power before the illegal act was committed" (Hovenkamp 1998, p. 660). However, even if a precartel period was arguably one of oligopolistic pricing conduct, the precartel price is still a reasonable benchmark so long as the determinants of pricing conduct did not change when the cartel was formed. That is, the before-and-after method is free of assumptions about the nature of the industry's noncartel competitive behavior. Prices during the postcartel period or during an intracartel price war might also serve as reasonable benchmarks. However, postcartel benchmarks may be affected by learning during the conspiracy; that is, when a cartel is formed in a competitive industry, its members may learn how to price tacitly after the cartel breaks up. If true, the overcharge would be understated. If prices fall to short-run marginal cost levels during a price war, the overcharge may be overstated.

In April 1996 ADM, Ajinomoto, and Kyowa Hakko offered the federal class of lysine direct purchasers (about 400 companies) $45 million to settle the suit. This offer came at a time when the DOJ's criminal investigation appeared stalled. Indeed, a rather unusual feature of this civil suit is that the settlement offer was made *four months before* the Government obtained the first of its guilty pleas. Normally, treble-damages suits are follow-on actions that are settled out of court or go to trial well after guilty pleas are made in a government case, pleas that are by law prima facie evidence in following civil actions. Moreover, civil plaintiffs can benefit from facts admitted in the pleas (e.g., conspiracy dates) or even the more extensive information gathered from a closed grand jury investigation. In this case, plaintiffs were provided with two slim bits of information: average U.S. monthly selling prices of lysine for the years 1990–1995, and annual sales of the four largest sellers (Cheil Sugar did not participate). From public sources the only other potentially useful data were list prices of lysine, international trade in lysine (value and volume), and U.S. prices for corn and soybeans. Corn prices drove most of the variability in the cost of manufacturing dextrose, the principal feedstock and largest input for making lysine.[20]

The decision the judge faced in July 1996 was whether the $45 million proposed settlement was fair and reasonable (Connor 2001a, pp. 451–454).

---

[20]Dextrose was the foundation for fermentation in Ajinomoto's and ADM's U.S. plants; Kyowa Hakko's Missouri plant used sucrose. Dextrose accounted for 38 percent of variable costs of manufacturing lysine in ADM's plant and 32 percent of total manufacturing costs (Connor 2001a, p. 257).

The proposed settlement had been hammered out behind the scenes in about three months by the lead class counsel and the law firms representing the lysine makers. In the interests of expediency, the judge had awarded the role of lead class counsel on the basis of a fixed-fee auction that provided the class counsel with "little incentive to maximize the recovery for the class" (Coffee 1998, p. B6).[21] Many of the larger lysine plaintiffs were dismayed at the small size of the award and what they perceived to be unassertive legal representation. They had to weigh two options: (1) stay in the class and take a riskless three cents on the dollar, or (2) opt out of the class and face the uncertainty of either a higher settlement or no settlement at all. Naturally, it was in the interests of the potential opt-outs to persuade the judge to reject the proposed settlement.

The main issues with respect to calculating the overcharge were the length of the affected period and the but-for price. It is conventional to use the conspiracy period for the affected sales period, but recall that the defendants had not yet agreed to plead guilty. Consequently, the opt-out plaintiffs had to depend on press reports that the conspirators had first met in June 1992 and had continued colluding until the FBI raid in June 1995. Because there appeared to be lags between the time the cartel set a list price and the time the transaction price fully responded, August 1992-December 1995 was chosen as the affected sales period.[22]

The hypothetical nonconspiracy benchmark price was the most contentious judgment that had to be made. Given the paucity of price observations (only seventy-one months), three periods seemed to be the leading candidates: (1) average prices prior to August 1992; (2) a nadir in prices in mid-1993 caused by a disciplinary price war; and (3) prices after June 1995. Ideally, but-for prices should be long-run equilibrium prices, averaged over fairly long periods, perhaps one to three years. However, prices from the February 1991–July 1992 period were affected by an earlier lysine cartel as well as ADM's massive entry. Not only was market structure shifting, but also costs were changing because of ADM's learning-by-doing. ADM's new plant suffered a number of contamination incidents during its first year, but very few thereafter. That is, most of the early precartel period appeared to be in disequilibrium.

Like the summer of 1992, the summer of 1993 also seemed to be a return to a regime that exhibited highly competitive pricing conduct; journalistic sources, later confirmed by memoranda of the cartel's meetings around

---

[21]The fee was capped at $3.5 million for any settlements above $25 million. The firm hired no economists to analyze the overcharge issue. The legal fees, at 7 percent of the settlement, were very low by historical standards.

[22]Lags were created by 30- to 45-day price protection clauses in most sales contracts, by delivery chains (particularly overseas deliveries), and information lags. In fact, the observed lags were mostly between two to four months except for minimal spot sales. The lags appeared to be asymmetric: longer when prices were declining and shorter when responding to upward changes in list prices by the sellers.

this time, reveal that bickering among cartel members resulted in a return to aggressive pricing behavior (Connor 2001a, pp. 224–229). When they became available, ADM's production records showed a surge in output in early 1993 that probably triggered the crash in lysine prices (Tr. Ex. 60–67). In consideration of these factors, the opt-out plaintiffs chose May–June 1992 and April–July 1993 as the but-for periods. Perhaps accidentally, prices averaged $0.70 per pound in both periods.

However, the third candidate period did not appear to be useful for competitive benchmarking. First, only six data points were available for the postcartel period, and the effects of cartel behavior might well lag for several months after the cartel was exposed. Second, the shadow price of lysine[23] had forced the cartel to drop its prices in early 1995, but then, just after the FBI raid, it climbed precipitously for the rest of 1995. One might hazard that the former cartel members had learned how to collude tacitly by following movements in the shadow price, because other demand and supply factors did not seem to explain the late-1995 rise in prices.

ADM's main line of defense was to criticize the simple before-and-after analysis (White 1996, 2001). The major flaws in the plaintiffs' method were alleged to be: (1) the benchmark price would have been generated by non-cooperative oligopolistic behavior rather than purely competitive conduct; (2) the price increases observed after the summers of 1992 and 1993 could have been seasonal rather than conspiratorial; and (3) the affected period chosen by the plaintiffs' expert was too long. As a matter of legal strategy, it is worth noting that because the lysine defendants had not yet admitted guilt, their experts would not be expected to present alternative overcharge estimates to the judge. Thus, demonstrating weaknesses in the plaintiffs' case was virtually the only option available to obtain a fairness ruling favorable to the defendants.

All three of these criticisms are logical possibilities. All of the economists working on the case agreed that the U.S. (and indeed global) lysine industry was a classic oligopoly. Sales concentration was high (Herfindahl index above 3000), buyer concentration was low, the product is perfectly homogenous, and several barriers to entry were present. "In sum, the lysine industry had virtually all the characteristics of an industry in which *implicit* oligopolistic coordination of some kind would likely have arisen in the absence of the *explicit* conspiracy" (White 2001, p. 28). If true, the but-for equilibrium price would, according to most oligopoly theories, be above the competitive price, and the overcharge significantly lower.

However, a few features of lysine industry may have prevented the sellers from forming an oligopolistic consensus. Chief among them is the

---

[23]The shadow price of lysine was governed by a technical rule-of-thumb followed by the animal-feed industry. Three pounds of lysine and ninety-seven pounds of corn were nutritionally equivalent to hundred pounds of soybean meal. Thus, when the price of the complementary corn rose and the price of the substitute, soymeal, fell far enough, feed manufacturers could stop buying manufactured lysine (Connor 2001a, pp. 210–211).

fact that two of the five sellers (ADM and Cheil) were brand-new to the industry; in other words, the major players did not have a sufficiently long history of strategic interaction to form *conjectures* likely to yield a stable implicit agreement. Prior to its entry into the lysine industry, ADM had no overlapping markets with any of the three incumbents (Connor 2000, app. E). Moreover, we now know that the principal form of oligopolistic conduct among the incumbents prior to the 1992–1995 cartel was explicit price fixing. Finally, internal contemporaneous documents show that ADM fully intended to put at least one of the incumbents out of business in order to achieve its announced goal of market-share parity with Ajinomoto (Connor 2001a, ch. 8). Predatory conduct by ADM, most likely to be effective in the U.S. market, could have driven the but-for price down to and even below the long run competitive price in 1992 and 1993. Had the Asian manufacturers not agreed to join an ADM-dominated cartel, ADM might well have continued predatory pricing beyond June 1992.

Seasonality of demand for lysine was well recognized by the managers of the cartel (Connor 2001a, pp. 211–212). It arises from swine feeding practices of producers in the temperate zones. With less than six full years of price data for lysine and no price series for comparable feed ingredients, it is difficult to be precise about the strength of seasonal effects.[24] The average difference between prices at the seasonal peak and prices at the seasonal trough (about 14 percent) could account for a difference in the calculated overcharge to be 10 percent less than an estimate that ignores seasonality (Connor 2001a, p. 269).

In most forensic settings, the affected period and conspiracy period are treated as identical. Both sides acknowledged that changes in transaction prices lagged changes in posted prices, the latter being the conspirators' direct price-fixing tool. In a retrospective evaluation of the cartel, a defendant's expert contends that a seventeen-to-nineteen-month period is the appropriate affected period (White 2001). He bases his position on the "unusual and suspicious" pattern of "uncharacteristic stability" in transaction prices from September or October 1993 to February or March 1995 (see Figure 10-1). The plaintiff's expert, on the other hand, continues to insist that information revealed by the Chicago trial provides additional support for a forty-two-month affected period (Connor 2001b). Without the luxury of additional time for more formal analyses it is not possible to determine the affected period definitively.[25]

---

[24]Seasonal effects are symmetric. The autumn run-up in lysine prices was followed by a spring decline, except in 1994 when the cartel was at its most effective. Because most lysine was consumed by farms in the Northern Hemisphere, peak demand in December–March was only slightly negated by the winters in the Southern Hemisphere.

[25]White's after-the-fact speculations do offer an insight into why the defendants offered a settlement consistent with a $15 million overcharge. Taking the nineteen-month affected period and the average prices for one year prior to September 1993 ($1.10 per pound) results in almost exactly a $15 million overcharge (Connor 2001b, p. 269). Again recall that the defendants' legal strategy

The Cournot Method

The defendants provided a second rebuttal to the plaintiffs' before-and-after analysis. They asserted that, had the cartel not operated, a noncooperative form of collusion would have been more probable than perfect competition (Warren-Boulton 1996). Further, the defendants specified the homogeneous Cournot model as the most appropriate one, because of its long-standing acceptance and widespread analytical use in economics. Over certain ranges of market conditions, that model predicted equilibrium prices that fell within the range of actual market prices observed during the cartel period. That is, the Cournot model implied that the cartel had been ineffective at raising prices by *explicit* collusion above prices generated by *implicit* (and legal) pricing coordination. Thus, the overcharge was zero.

Predictions from specific oligopoly models require structural parameters. In particular, the Cournot formula for calculating the profit-maximizing price needs three pieces of market information: the Herfindahl index of concentration, the own-price elasticity of demand, and the marginal cost of production. About the first item there was no disagreement; the Herfindahl index for three domestic manufacturers and two importers during the conspiracy was about 3500.[26] The other parameters were borrowed from the plaintiffs' own opinion, namely that document's assertion that $0.70 was the marginal cost (or close to it) and that the elasticity was around −0.5 to −1.0 during the cartel period.[27]

One problem with the Cournot model is that the formula can, under some assumptions, predict impossible prices. In layman's terms, the model can "blow up." For example, if the demand for lysine is highly inelastic (less than −0.35), then Cournot oligopolists would be predicted to set negative prices, no matter what the cost of production. Negative prices are rarely observed in natural markets, because prices generally must be set above the variable costs of production, and these costs are always nonnegative. Another problem with the Cournot model is that it is only one of many plausible oligopoly models; its popularity with economists rests more with its mathematical tractability than its consistency with the organization of natural markets. Given the lysine parameters just discussed, other equally plausible models such as price leadership by ADM produce equally untenable

---

may have discouraged them from presenting even minimal overcharge calculations because that would have been tantamount to an admission of guilt.

[26]Implicitly this assumes that a global cartel was viewing the U.S. market as geographically distinct from others. Internal records of the cartel's pricing decisions and its efforts to prevent geographic arbitrage tend to support this view. Global Herfindahl concentration was about 2500 in 1994 (Connor 2001a, tbl. 8.A.3).

[27]Connor (1996) opined that feeds were manufactured under fixed proportions, which implied poultry, swine, or meat elasticities of −0.10 to −0.50. These are retail-level elasticities calculated from precartel, more competitive periods; at the higher cartel-period prices, the elasticity will be higher in absolute value. This discussion took place in the context of his analysis of the deadweight loss from cartel pricing.

market price predictions. Moreover, the model that many economists would agree is the second most popular, the homogeneous Bertrand model, predicts *competitive* prices when there are two or more sellers. Finally, although possibly allowable as evidence in antitrust cases, the degree of econometric literacy required to comprehend formal oligopoly models greatly restricts their use in forensic settings.

The Cost-Based Approach

The cost-based approach and econometric modeling (discussed below) were not available to the economic experts doing battle in the 1996 federal civil proceeding, but they do shed light on the accuracy of the before-and-after method. The disparity between the two sides was an order of magnitude. Plaintiffs considering opting out of the federal class had a $150 million overcharge calculation before them, whereas the defendants' settlement offer of $45 million implicitly supposed a $15 million overcharge by the lysine cartel. Even were the plaintiffs to concede that seasonality was partially responsible for rising prices at the beginnings of the two phases of the conspiracy, their overcharge calculation would still have been about $140 million.

During the 1998 criminal trial of three ADM executives for lysine price fixing, prosecutors introduced the confidential production and sales records of ADM's lysine department as exhibits (Tr. Exhibits 60–67). These internal records provided ADM managers with monthly plant output and several costs (labor, energy, dextrose, other chemicals, overhead expenses, transportation, storage, and sales-office expenses) during the five years between 1991–1995. Figure 10-2 plots these costs of manufacturing and distribution against monthly physical plant output using regression analysis.

The plot appears to show considerable "scale economies" for levels of output up to 10 or 11 million pounds. In fact, the diagram really captures strong learning-by-doing effects, because all of the observations below 11 million pounds are drawn from the precartel period (February 1991–June 1992). Abundant testimony and the manufacturing records themselves support the fact that nearly all of the high-cost months were ones with "yield failures" due to contamination of fermentors.[28] As ADM learned how to sanitize its plant's fermentation reactors, contamination episodes ceased, and the costs of spoiled-product disposals disappeared. To a minor extent, unit costs also declined with increasing levels of output because fixed costs were being spread over larger units of production.

The most important feature of the average-total-cost curve shown in Figure 10-2 is the portion above 10 or 11 million pounds per month. During the conspiracy, plant output always exceeded 10 million pounds. Statis-

---

[28]In every case when costs jumped above about $0.80 per pound, the lysine/dextrose yield ratio dropped below 30 percent. Such episodes became rare after June 1992 or when production was above ten or eleven million pounds.

FIGURE 10-2 ADM's Lysine Manufacturing Costs, 1991–1995.

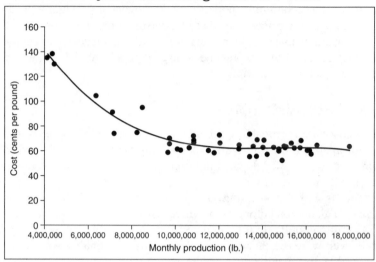

Source: Tr. Ex. 60–67.

tically, this portion is completely flat. It is true that manufacturing costs were affected by short-run changes in the price of dextrose, which in turn was closely related to the market price of corn. Nevertheless, total manufacturing costs hewed quite closely to the average of $0.63 per pound whenever production exceeded 10 million pounds. As plant output edged closer to its maximum of 18 million pounds, unit fixed costs dropped a bit. However, the decline in fixed costs was nearly perfectly balanced by higher selling costs incurred as ADM shipped higher shares of its U.S. production to overseas destinations. Thus, after June 1992 (the beginning of the likely cartel period), average total accounting costs of manufacturing and sales varied only within the $0.73 to $0.78 per pound range and were statistically unrelated to the quantity produced. Adding a fairly generous return on investment of 6 percent of sales brings the average total *economic* costs to $0.77 to $0.83 per pound of lysine.[29]

In competitively structured industries, profit-maximizing firms accept prices that are equal to their long-run marginal costs. Because ADM's total costs were effectively constant during the cartel period, it follows that the but-for competitive price would have been just about $0.80 during the affected period. This observation is reinforced by the fact that ADM's costs of production were equal to or lower than those of all four of its rivals in the lysine industry (Connor 2001a, p. 217). At a but-for price of $0.80, the ly-

---

[29]This is generous because it is ADM's own rate of return during fiscal 1990–1995 when its profits were bloated by several commodity cartels (Connor 2000, app. A). It is also well above the average return earned by publicly traded companies in similar industries.

sine overcharge for August 1992–July 1995 becomes $78 million, or 17.0 percent of U.S. sales of dry lysine (Connor 2001a, p. 444).

Econometric Modeling

With sufficient time and access to detailed price and cost information, statistical modeling is often the preferred analytical approach of forensic economists in estimating antitrust damages (see, e.g., Slottje 1999). With a rigorous model that is shown to fit the market's actual performance over time, the legal goal of isolating the effects of a defendant's illegal conduct from all other market forces appears to be achievable. Econometrics seems ideally suited to identifying "the only casual factor accounting for the difference between plaintiff's actual experience in the damage period and its but-for period . . ." (Page 1996, p. 36). Law journals and handbooks for lawyers in the antitrust field frequently include material on regression analysis for damages calculations (e.g., Fisher 1980; Page 1996; Hovenkamp 1999).

Morse and Hyde (2000) developed and tested an econometric model of the lysine industry using 1990–1995 monthly information. The main idea behind this model is to incorporate a sufficiently detailed list of market demand and supply factors so that most competitive market forces are accounted for; then variables are added to the model to capture the influence of a suspected conspiracy period. Morse and Hyde then test for and measure computed price differences that were (arguably) due to the conspiracy rather than to competitive market forces. For mathematical reasons, it is usually impossible to capture all of the factors that might affect market prices. As a result, modeling involves a degree of judgment about which factors have the highest priority for inclusion in the model; these decisions are informed by economic theory, knowledge about the industry, and data constraints. Initial testing of a model sometimes reveals statistical estimation problems that require the researcher to alter the regression equations.

Morse and Hyde (2000) managed to incorporate a fairly complete list of determinants of lysine demand: the number of hogs needed by U.S. slaughterhouses, red meat and poultry export demand, the price of a complement and a substitute (the shadow price discussed above), and the seasonality of lysine demand. On the supply side, an equation related ADM's U.S. production to the cost of three principal inputs: dextrose, other variable costs of manufacture, and capital. Both of these equations fitted the five years of data quite well, and the signs were the ones predicted by economic reasoning. Finally, an innovative feature of the model is an equation that permits the researcher to measure the degree of competitiveness ("conjectural variations") between ADM and its four rivals. Unlike the cost-based method, this modeling approach makes no assumptions regarding the intensity of competition before, during, or after the conspiracy.

In brief, tests of the econometric model show that during the year and one-half prior to the cartel's formation, ADM behaved in a highly (if not perfectly) competitive fashion relative to its rivals. While falling short of pure monopoly, ADM's conduct was calculated to have become distinctly more monopolistic after July 1992. Using the parameters that measure the degrees of market power, Morse and Hyde find that the lysine cartel's overcharge was $71 million.

CONCLUSION

One of the hallmarks of a rigorous scientific discipline is the ability to measure parameters of interest with precision. From this perspective, the highly variable estimates of the lysine cartel's U.S. overcharges could be interpreted as reflecting badly on empirical economics. After all, the overcharge estimates presented in this paper did vary by as much as ten-to-one as of the summer of 1996 when the first suit was being resolved. Plaintiffs in the class action had only a few weeks to decide whether to remain in the class and take a guaranteed immediate share of the $45 million settlement offer or to opt out of the class and take a chance on either a larger settlement many months in the future or possibly no compensation at all.

A more sanguine view of the damages these estimates present is that of a progressive movement toward greater precision, a movement made possible by additional information and the time to apply more complex analytical methods. If this latter view has more validity, then it implies that lysine buyers in the federal class were seriously disadvantaged when faced with the decision to accept or reject the proffered settlement.

In July 1996, the trial judge approved the $45 million offer as fair and reasonable. His decision seems to have been made for reasons unrelated to the economic evidence presented. Rather, he seemed most persuaded by the testimony of class counsel that this was a hard-fought deal that was unlikely to be improved. About thirty-three of four hundred direct buyers in the class indicated their disagreement by opting out of the settlement. Most of the opt-outs were larger firms with the legal resources to continue hard negotiations with the defendants. Although settlement terms are confidential, reports in the press suggested that the opt-out firms, with the benefit of guilty pleas that the lysine cartel members made in their criminal case, got at least double the amount per dollar of purchases than did the smaller buyers in the class (Connor 2001a, pp. 452–453). This trend—opt-outs becoming a larger share of the buyers and obtaining better settlements—continued in subsequent cartel settlements throughout the late 1990s (Connor 2001a, pp. 458–472).

With the benefit of hindsight and a great deal more information, it appears now that the first $150 million estimate by the plaintiffs was too high. Considering seasonality would have reduced the overcharge amount by about 10 percent or so. More importantly, the two periods selected to determine the but-for price were most likely unrepresentative predatory-type episodes that could not have been sustained for the entire three years of the cartel's operation. That is, ADM was punishing its future and actual cartel partners by unilaterally forcing prices down to the point where ADM was barely covering its variable costs.[30] Thus, the $0.70 but-for price was not enough to cover fixed costs and a normal return on investment. That is, in retrospect, a but-for price of $0.80 was closer to a long-run competitive price, suggesting that the true U.S. overcharge was around $80 million.

The federal lysine class and the opt-outs from the class eventually collected approximately $70 million from the cartel members; indirect purchasers of lysine obtained an estimated $15 million in state courts where such buyers have standing to sue (Connor 2001a, tbl. 16.A.1). Thus, U.S. lysine buyers as a group recovered slightly more than single damages; net of legal fees, buyers recovered less than single damages (Connor 2001a, tbl. 18.1). The lysine buyers' settlements were comparable to the settlements in two similar cartel cases that followed on the heels of the lysine case (Connor 2001a, p. 474). Direct buyers of citric acid and vitamins recovered 90 percent and 135 percent, respectively, of U.S. overcharges. These results reinforce Lande's (1993) conclusion that civil price-fixing awards are typically less than actual damages, never mind treble damages.

The *ex ante* perception of antitrust liability is a critical determinant of deterrence. If would-be price fixers expect that their monopoly profits will exceed the financial costs of antitrust fines and civil settlements, it is rational for them to form a cartel. In the Introduction above, it was noted that the potential antitrust liability in the United States is currently in the range of eight to twelve times the U.S. overcharges, and overcharges are only slightly larger than the monopoly profits from collusion.

One might argue that the best conjectures that a company could have made of their antitrust liability during 1988–1992, the period during which the recent crop of global cartels were established, would have been much lower than their actual penalties because of the changing legal landscape during the latter part of the 1990s. However, this is at best only a partial explanation for the spate of global cartels that were unmasked and punished after the lysine actions in 1996. In evaluating the deterrence capabilities of current antitrust sanctions, one must also consider three additional factors: the probability of an operating cartel's being detected and prosecuted, actual rather than maximum antitrust penalties, and the geographic location of the monopoly profits generated by a cartel.

Limited evidence from the United States and Europe suggests that the probability an established illegal cartel will be caught is somewhere between 10 percent and 20 percent (Connor 2001a, p. 79). Outside of North America and Western Europe the chances are negligible. Evidence from the three best-documented cartel cases of the late 1990s shows that U.S. crimi-

---

[30]Note that the lowest prices observed were $0.64 in July 1992 and $0.62 in June 1993. A cost-of-production analysis showed that ADM's average variable costs were $0.63, a result that is perfectly consistent with economic theory. That is, as a rule the lowest rational price a firm will accept or charge in the short run is generally the one that equals its variable economic costs of production.

nal and civil penalties approached but never exceeded double the U.S. overcharges. In the EU, these same cartels were made to pay fines about equal to single damages; the prospect of costly civil suits in Europe is dim. In Asia, cartel fines are small or nonexistent. A striking feature of most global cartels discovered since 1996 is that their sales and profits were distributed almost equally across North America, Western Europe, and the rest of the world. Taking into account each of these three general features of modern cartels and contemporary anticartel enforcement practices, it logically follows that global cartel deterrence requires actual monetary sanctions to exceed *five to ten times* worldwide overcharges, where the exact multiplier depends inversely on the probability of discovery. Treble damages will not deter global cartels.

The rationale of deterrence can be illustrated with financial information about ADM, the most heavily fined of the lysine conspirators. ADM's monopoly profits from fixing the U.S. price of lysine for three years were about $80 million. ADM paid a $70 million fine to the federal government, about $49 million to direct buyers of lysine, and $15 million to indirect buyers in state court cases (Connor 2001a, tbl. 19.4). Not counting legal fees and other intangible costs, ADM's *ex post* costs of collusion somewhat exceeded its U.S. revenues from collusion. On the other hand, ADM garnered approximately $100 million from its non-U.S. sales of cartelized lysine. The EU's $45-million lysine fine, Canada's $8-million judgment, and a few other minor actions abroad left ADM with a positive return of $25 to $35 million on its non-U.S. price fixing. Crime did not pay for ADM in the United States, but it did pay abroad. For its four co-conspirators, the lysine cartel was very likely a profitable venture.

REFERENCES

ADM. *Annual SEC Form 10-K Report for the Year Ending June 30, 2001 and Previous Years.*

Coffee, John C., Jr. "Securities Class Auctions." *The National Law Journal* (September 14, 1998): B6–10.

Connor, John M. *The Cost to U.S. Animal-Feeds Manufacturers of an Alleged Price-Fixing Conspiracy by Lysine Manufacturers,* affidavit presented in the case *In re Amino Acid Lysine Antitrust Litigation,* 1996.

Connor, John M. *Lysine Production, Trade, and the Effects of International Price Fixing,* 3d edn., Staff Paper 99-13. West Lafayette, IN: Department of Agricultural Economics, Purdue University (October 1999).

Connor, John M. *Archer Daniels Midland: Price-Fixer to the World,* 4th edn., Staff Paper 00-11. West Lafayette, IN: Department of Agricultural Economics, Purdue University (December 2000) (also http://agecon.lib.umn.edu/cgi-bin/pdf_viewpl ?paperid=2871&ftype=.pdf).

Connor, John M. *Global Price Fixing: Our Customers Are the Enemy.* Boston: Kluwer, 2001a.

Connor, John M. "'Our Customers Are Our Enemies': The Lysine Cartel of 1992–1995." *Review of Industrial Organization* 18 (February 2001b): 5–21.

Dick, Andrew R. "Cartels." *The New Palgrave Dictionary of Law and Economics,* edited by John Eatwell. London: Macmillan, 1998.

DOJ. *Fiscal Year 2001 Performance Report.* Washington, D.C.: U.S. Department of Justice, 2002.

EC. "Commission Decision of 7 June 2000 (Case COMP/36.545/F3—Amino Acids)." *Official Journal of the European Communities* (7 June 2001): L152/24–72.

EC. *Competition Policy Newsletter.* Brussels: Competition-Policy Directorate of the European Commission (February 2002): 29–43.

Eichenwald, Kurt. *The Informant: A True Story.* New York: Broadway Books, 2000.

Fisher, Franklin M. "Multiple Regression in Legal Proceedings." *Columbia Law Review* 80 (1980): 702.

Hovenkamp, Herbert. *Federal Antitrust Policy: The Law of Competition and Its Practice,* 2d edn. St. Paul: West Group, 1999.

Kanne, Michael S., et al. *Opinion, U.S. Court of Appeals for the Seventh Circuit in U.S. v. Michael D. Andreas and Terrance Wilson* (2000 U.S. App. LEXIS 14572). Chicago, June 26, 2000.

Katzman, C. J., et al. *Decision of the U.S. Court of Appeals for the Second Circuit in Kruman v. Christie's International PLC.* New York, March 25, 2002.

Lande, Robert H. "Are Antitrust 'Treble' Damages Really Single Damages?" *Ohio State Law Journal* 54 (Winter 1993): 115–174.

Lieber, James B. *Rats in the Grain: The Dirty Tricks of "Supermarket to the World."* New York: Four Walls Eight Windows, 2000.

Markon, Jerry. "Ex-Sotheby's Chairman Is Sentenced to a Year in Prison, Fined $7.5 Million." *Wall Street Journal Online,* April 23, 2002.

Martin, Stephen. *Advanced Industrial Economics,* 2d edn. Malden, Mass.: Blackwell Publishers, 2002.

Morse, B. Adair, and Jeffrey Hyde. *Estimation of Cartel Overcharges: The Case of Archer Daniels Midland and the Market for Lysine,* Staff Paper 08-00. West Lafayette, IN: Department of Agricultural Economics, Purdue University, October 2000.

Page, William H., ed. *Proving Antitrust Damages: Legal and Economic Issues.* Chicago: Section of Antitrust Law, American Bar Association, 1996.

Posner, Richard A. *Antitrust Law,* 2d edn. Chicago: University of Chicago Press, 2001.

Slottje, Daniel J., ed., *The Role of the Academic Economist in Litigation Support.* Amsterdam: Elsevier, 1999.

Stigler, George J. "A Theory of Oligopoly." *Journal of Political Economy* 72 (February 1964): 44–61.

Tr. Transcript of *U.S. v. Michael D. Andreas et al.,* U.S. District Court, Northern District of Illinois, Eastern Division, No. 96 CR 762, July to September 1998.

Warren-Boulton, Frederick R. *An Evaluation of "The Cost to U.S. Animal Feeds Manufacturers of an Alleged Price-Fixing Conspiracy by Lysine Manufacturers, 1992–1995."* Master File 95-C-7679, U.S. District Court for Northern Illinois, Eastern Division, 1996.

White, Lawrence J. *Declaration of Lawrence J. White, In re Amino Acid Lysine Antitrust Litigation.* Master File 95-C-7679, U.S. District Court for Northern Illinois, Eastern Division, 1996.

White, Lawrence J. "Lysine and Price Fixing: How Long? How Severe?" *Review of Industrial Organization* 18 (February 2001): 23–31.

Sports League Issues: The Relocation of the Los Angeles Rams to St. Louis (1998)

Franklin M. Fisher,
Christopher Maxwell, and
Evan Sue Schouten

INTRODUCTION

Sports leagues raise unique antitrust issues. Although most leagues consist of a collection of separately owned teams, each team is dependent on the others. No team could play even a single game without the cooperation of another team, and the production of a season of sports games, culminating in a championship, requires the joint efforts of all of the teams in the league. As a result, the question arises whether such a league is a single entity or a group of cooperating competitors. Are the league's rules pro-competitive, or do they constitute collusive restraint of trade?

Such issues have often challenged the courts. Their resolution is made no easier by the fact that they often arise in a proceeding brought by one of a league's member teams against the league or against the other members. In such cases, the plaintiff team often asserts that the league's rules are anticompetitive restraints on the freedom of its members. Evidently, there are situations in which the interests of a league as a whole and those of one or more individual members fail to coincide.

Nowhere has this phenomenon been more evident than in cases involving the relocation of team franchises. In the National Football League (NFL, or "the League"), the most famous cases are those stemming from

---

Portions of this chapter were taken from Fisher et al. (2000).

the move of the Oakland Raiders to Los Angeles and then back again.[1] Partly in response to the 1984 and 1986 cases, the NFL developed a process for making relocation decisions, a process that sometimes involves a relocation fee paid to the League. That process was challenged in 1997 in a case involving the move of the Los Angeles Rams to St. Louis.[2] This case study lays out the economic issues underlying relocation issues in the context of the St. Louis case.

CHRONOLOGY OF EVENTS

In 1988, the NFL Cardinals left St. Louis for Phoenix. This move occurred after the Cardinals' unsuccessful attempt to convince St. Louis to build a new stadium. St Louis's disappointed fans did not believe that Phoenix should be permitted to acquire "their" team.[3]

In response to the departure of the Cardinals, St. Louis passed a referendum granting the city permission to float bonds for the purpose of financing a new convention center. Construction began on the St. Louis Convention and Visitors Center (CVC) in 1993. The CVC facility included a stadium suitable for football. It was hoped that the existence of the new facility would ensure that St. Louis would be selected as one of the two anticipated NFL expansion sites. In late fall 1993, Charlotte and Jacksonville were chosen as NFL expansion sites. Lacking an NFL team, St. Louis contacted the Los Angeles Rams with the hope that it could convince the team to abandon Los Angeles and relocate to St. Louis.

On January 17, 1995, the Rams and St. Louis signed an agreement whereby the Rams agreed to relocate to St. Louis on terms very favorable to the Rams. Approximately two weeks later and in compliance with the NFL's relocation policy, the Rams notified the NFL of its intent to relocate. At a March 15, 1995, special meeting, the League voted to reject the Rams' initial relocation proposal. The Rams' second proposal, which was approved on April 12, 1995, included several modifications, among these a relocation fee.

---

[1]*Los Angeles Memorial Coliseum* v. *NFL,* 726 F.2d 1381 (9th Cir., 1984); *Los Angeles Memorial Coliseum Comm'n* v. *NFL,* 791 F.2d 1356 (9th Cir., 1986). These decisions are commonly known as Raiders I and Raiders II. See also *Oakland Raiders* v. *National Football League,* Los Angeles Super. Ct., No. BC 206388 (May 26, 2001).

[2]*St Louis Convention & Visitors Commission* v. *National Football League, et al.,* 46 F. Supp. 2d 1058 (Eastern District of Missouri, 1997), *aff'd,* 154 F.3d 851 (8th Cir. 1998). Franklin Fisher, supported by Charles River Associates, provided extensive expert testimony for the NFL. This paper is based on that testimony.

[3]Indeed, as early as 1985, in response to the Raiders move from Oakland to Los Angeles, Senator Thomas Eagleton (later a trial witness for the St. Louis CVC) sponsored a bill (S. 259, 99th Cong., 1985), the intent of which was "to protect the public interest in stable relationships among communities, professional sports teams and leagues." See http://thomas.loc.gov/cgibin/bdquery/D?d099:4:./temp/~bd9Jvq:l/bss/d099query.htmll.

The Rams moved to St. Louis and began playing the 1995–1996 season in the St. Louis CVC; their record was a disappointing seven wins and nine losses.[4] Subsequently, despite having succeeded in luring the Rams to St. Louis, the St. Louis CVC filed a $130 million lawsuit against the NFL.[5] Had the CVC won its claim, damages would have been trebled. Allegations included a Sherman Act Section 1 conspiracy claim, a Section 2 monopolization claim, and a tortious interference claim. With respect to the conspiracy claim, CVC alleged that the NFL Guidelines and Relocation Policies were illegal. According to the CVC, these guidelines and policies constituted a collusive action among twenty-nine separate firms (all of the NFL teams in the League at the time that the Rams relocated, other than the Rams).[6]

In its monopoly claim, the CVC alleged that the NFL was a monopsonist in a "market for professional football stadiums" and that the NFL had used its power to extract illegal profits from the St. Louis CVC.[7] In its tortious interference claim, the CVC alleged that the NFL used wrongful action to deny it a business advantage in dealing with the League's thirty teams.[8]

These claims placed several economic issues before the court. One issue was whether, for the purposes of determining the legality of the NFL's relocation rules and regulations, the NFL should be viewed as a single entity, a joint venture, or as thirty separate competing firms. With respect to this particular issue, although the plaintiff and the defendants jointly stipulated that the NFL was a joint venture (and thus should be judged by a rule of reason standard), the plaintiff still attempted to argue that the teams should be thought of as thirty separate, competing firms.[9] It alleged that these teams had joined together in an illegal cartel and that through this cartel they had established relocation rules and regulations. According to the plaintiff, these rules and regulations constituted an output restriction that the court should find illegal, per se. In fact, as the trial judge stated, the *Raiders I* court had previously addressed this question and found that the relocation rules and regulations were not illegal per se.[10] Rather, the *Raiders I* decision had found that relocations should be judged under a rule of reason standard.[11]

A second economic issue was whether or not the NFL had monopoly power in any relevant marketplace. The plaintiff's liability expert defined

---

[4]Four years later, the St. Louis Rams went on to win the 1999–2000 Super Bowl.

[5]*St. Louis Convention & Visitors Commission* v. *National Football League,* 46 F. Supp. 2d 1058 (1997).

[6]*St. Louis Convention & Visitors Commission* v. *National Football League,* 154 F.3d 851, 855–57 (1998).

[7]Ibid. at 856.

[8]Ibid.

[9]The NFL also preserved its position that the League was a single entity.

[10]*Los Angeles Memorial Coliseum* v. *NFL,* 726 F.2d 1381 (9th Cir., 1984).

[11]Similarly, Judge Easterbrook stated that the [National Basketball Association] "is sufficiently integrated that its superstation rules may not be condemned without analysis under the full Rule of

two relevant product markets: a "market for professional football"[12] and a "market for professional football stadiums in the US." The defendants asserted that neither alleged market constituted a relevant market for antitrust purposes, since both alleged markets excluded other products that constrained the exercise of any alleged monopoly power.

The final issue before the court was whether the NFL in any way restricted the NFL teams with which the city of St. Louis might speak. This was a factual question, and the court found no evidence that the NFL did this, although the plaintiff alleged that such a restriction was an inevitable effect of the League's relocation rules.[13] Near the close of the case, the judge dismissed the case and directed a verdict in favor of the NFL.[14] That judgment was affirmed by the Eighth Circuit in the fall of 1998.[15]

THE PRODUCT AND EFFICIENT ORGANIZATION OF A SPORTS LEAGUE

Many economists have noted the unique nature of the products produced and sold by leagues such as the NFL, Major League Baseball (MLB), and the National Basketball Association (NBA). Unlike most products sold in the marketplace, there is nothing to sell unless teams and their owners, through the formation of a league, cooperate to establish and enforce the rules of the game, determine the number of teams in the league, and ensure that the product sold in the marketplace has a particular look and feel that is commonly associated with the product.

It is not only economists who recognize the single entity characteristics of professional sports leagues. In the words of noted sports commentator Bob Costas (2000, pp. 42–43):

> [P]roperly understood, [a League] is less like 30 different restaurants and much more like 30 *franchises within a single restaurant chain.* They're

---

Reason." Judge Easterbrook further noted that for plaintiffs to prevail, they must establish "that the NBA possesses power in a relevant market, and that its exercise of this power has injured consumers." See *Chicago Professional Sports Ltd. Partnership* v. *National Basketball Ass'n,* 95 F.3d 593 (7th Cir., 1996). In the CVC case, had the parties not stipulated that the NFL was a joint venture, the court might have been asked to determine whether, for these purposes, the NFL should be viewed as a single entity. Were the NFL determined to be a single entity, for these purposes, a Section 1 claim would make no sense, as a single firm cannot conspire with itself.

[12]Plaintiff's Complaint alleged only one monopoly market, a market for NFL quality stadiums. As such, it is unclear why plaintiff's expert alleged that both the output market and input market were at issue. Professor Fisher addressed both in order to respond to the allegations of the CVC's expert witness.

[13]*St. Louis Convention & Visitors Commission* v. *National Football League,* 154 F.3d 851, 851–855 (1998).

[14]*St. Louis Convention & Visitors Commission* v. *National Football League,* 46 F. Supp. 2d 1058 (1997).

[15]*St. Louis Convention & Visitors Commission* v. *National Football League,* 154 F.3d, 851 (1998).

competitive, they all want profits and the prestige of a five-star rating, but they're not trying to put each other out of business. None can survive without the others. Leagues are, in the words of Notre Dame economist Richard Sheehan, a "joint effort," with all franchises needing to cooperate in some measure to generate revenues.

An important ingredient in the success of the league's product is genuine competition on the field of play and the perception by fans that there is such competition. One team alone cannot produce that. If a single team were to scrimmage against itself, fans would perceive it to be an exhibition rather than a true contest. A scrimmage would lack an essential component: genuine competition on the playing field. Even a small number of teams cannot produce the product that is produced by a sports league. That product is a series of games in the context of a league season. The elements of standings, playoffs, and championships are a very large part of what creates fan interest. The importance of statistics to fans is evidenced by the extent to which the news media reports these statistics.

It follows that at least a substantial portion of the economic value of a single NFL franchise is due to its membership in the League and what it derives from its joint participation in the production of the League's product. Even though star players are major assets, their star quality and popularity derive not only from their native abilities but also from their appearance in league games. Still, a basic question at issue in nearly every sports-related lawsuit is precisely what is and is not included in the "substantial portion" of economic value that each franchise derives from membership in the League.

To create and maintain interest in a league's product requires that fans perceive that the seasonal contest is a real one—a contest, so far as possible, among entities that truly compete on the sports field. Teams must be sufficiently independent to ensure that there is no limitation on their incentives to prevail on the field. This is required for the same reason that a league's product cannot be produced by a single team.

League sports thus demand a form of organization in which some local initiative and autonomy is both present and visible. Moreover, there are other, subsidiary benefits from such a form. For example, local knowledge and local contacts are likely to prove desirable in dealing with local authorities and local media. If such subsidiary reasons are all that is involved, a league might organize as a single entity with local profit centers. But the requirement of independent incentives to prevail on the field makes that form of organization generally unappealing, and most leagues have not adopted it. To preserve interest in the league's product, the teams must be seen to act independently in competing for players and coaches and in competing on the field of play. The interests of the team owners in winning must be genuine and made manifest by their actions.

As a result, successful leagues are typically organized with separate owners of teams and with certain decisions made at the local level. But not all decisions can be made at that level. Here is where the problem of externalities comes in.

DEALING WITH EXTERNALITIES

When a league organizes as a set of formally independent teams, it necessarily faces an incentive problem. The requirement that teams be seen to operate independently must be balanced against the possibility that the incentives to such independent action will lead to results privately profitable for one or more teams but detrimental to the league, and its customers, as a whole. This is an externality problem.

An "externality" occurs when one party's actions result in costs or benefits to others that are *not* reflected in the private profit-and-loss calculus of that party. In the case of professional sports leagues, externalities arise when a particular team fails to take into account the full costs and benefits of its actions to the league as a whole. Were leagues organized as centrally controlled operations, such problems would not exist; in effect, the externalities would be internalized.

Many, if not all, of the regulations that leagues impose on their members can appear restrictive. On the other hand, they can also be regarded as addressing externalities. For example, the player draft, restrictions on player trades, the salary cap, and salary minimum rules can all be seen as ways of dealing with the externalities that would otherwise occur if teams were permitted to compete unencumbered for players. If individual teams had complete autonomy in the hiring of players, richer owners or owners in more profitable cities would have an incentive to buy up the best players. This would be in their own interest, but it could reduce competitive balance and not be in the interest of the league as a whole, whose interests, as we shall see, are aligned with those of consumers. Restrictions on player mobility in the context of a collective bargaining relationship (e.g., the draft and restrictions on player trades) benefit the league as well as the players by helping to assure fans that every team has a chance to be competitive relative to the other teams. A salary cap attempts to ensure that all teams can afford to field competitive teams. A salary minimum prevents teams from selling off their players and taking the cash. Naturally, a salary minimum is also useful in persuading the players to agree to the salary cap and to other restrictions on movements; it guarantees them a certain share of revenues.

In summary, economists would all agree that leagues should be permitted to establish and enforce those rules that benefit consumers by helping the league to produce a better product. The disagreement arises in that economists do not all agree on precisely which rules those are.

PLAINTIFF'S CASE

The plaintiff's case depended on the crucial allegation that the NFL was a cartel comprising many "would-be" competitors who, but for the existence of the NFL, would compete both in the sale of professional football and for the inputs used in producing professional football. The NFL's purpose, according to the plaintiff's expert, was to establish and enforce policies that restricted competition both in the output and input markets. He cited the following factors in support of his conclusions: Each team was independently owned; each team acted independently in its input purchase decisions; and each team had its own "bottom line."[16]

The plaintiff alleged only that the NFL's relocation policies enabled the NFL to become a monopsonist with respect to a particular input used in the production of football: stadiums. The plaintiff's expert, however, did not limit his opinion to this issue alone. Rather, his testimony identified many League activities in which he believed the NFL's behavior was anticompetitive as a seller of NFL football "product" rather than as a purchaser/leaser of a particular input. Thus, in addition to condemning the NFL's rules governing relocation, the plaintiff's expert also condemned the League's negotiations on behalf of its member teams with the national television networks,[17] the League's labor contract with the Players' Association, and the League's determination of the number of its member teams. This extension of the scope of the alleged NFL wrongdoing led to issues that had little or nothing to do with leasing stadiums.

A prime example was the question of the relevant output market in which the NFL competed. In defining that market, the plaintiff's expert sought to determine whether the closest substitutes for NFL football were actually sufficiently close enough substitutes to limit any market power that the NFL might have. His analysis focused on other professional sports and concluded that they were not particularly good substitutes for NFL football.

The plaintiff's expert's conclusion that the products produced by other professional sports were not good substitutes was based on two separate studies that he undertook. In the first, he considered the collection of professional sports teams playing in different communities. If different sports teams produced products that were good substitutes for one another, he asserted, communities should be indifferent as to which particular sports their teams played. For example, among the communities with four professional

---

[16]In reality, each team faces many regulations regarding the use of inputs (for example, every team must comply with the conditions of the college draft and is limited in the number of players it may carry on its roster). Moreover, every team's "bottom line" is significantly affected by League-wide revenue sharing.

[17]Specifically permitted by Congress as a result of its passage of the Sports Broadcasting Act.

sports teams, we should observe different combinations of sports played by the communities' teams. One might even expect to see some communities where all four of their teams played the same sport (e.g., all four playing football). That sports teams do not distribute themselves more randomly must, he asserted, imply that the products produced by other professional sports leagues are not good substitutes for the product produced by professional football.[18]

The plaintiff's expert also prepared an econometric study that indicated that NFL ticket prices were not affected by the presence of other sports teams in a community. That analysis sought to explain NFL ticket prices on a team-by-team basis by analyzing the effect of the following variables on ticket prices: population, per capita disposable income, excess seating capacity, dummy variable for the year, the presence or absence of a second NFL team, whether the team had recently relocated, team performance statistics, and the presence of other sports teams. The plaintiff's expert found that, with the exception of the presence of other sports teams, all other variables had a statistically significant effect on a team's ticket prices. On this basis, he concluded that the products produced by other sports teams must not be good substitutes for NFL football.[19]

With respect to the question of the relevant market in which stadiums competed, the plaintiff's expert concluded that the market was extremely narrow. Those seeking investment funds for the building and/or maintaining of NFL stadiums either did not compete for funds with other large-scale community projects or such a question was of little relevance to the inquiry regarding the relevant marketplace. Rather, the relevant input market at issue was the market for professional quality football stadium leases. This conclusion led the plaintiff's expert to identify several of the relocation policies that he considered to be anticompetitive. Included among the policies deemed harmful to consumers were the guidelines governing when a team could relocate, the requirement that at least three-fourths of the NFL teams approve each proposed move, the right of the commissioner to interpret and establish policy, the ability of the League to review and approve stadium leases, and the provision that a relocation fee might be charged to the moving team. The plaintiff's expert asserted that all of these practices restricted competition among NFL teams for stadiums. He concluded that the result was too little investment in NFL stadiums, too few relocations occurring among NFL teams, and too much uncertainty regarding whether a proposed move would take place.

---

[18]By extension, this argument would suggest that if McDonald's and Burger King are good substitutes, we should observe some cities with only McDonald's restaurants and no Burger King restaurants.

[19]However, the regression results also indicated that for those communities with two NFL teams present, one team's ticket prices did not affect the other team's ticket prices, suggesting that NFL football was not a good substitute for itself.

DEFENDANTS' CASE

We now turn to the defendants' case. There were two key economic issues that arose in this case. The first was whether the NFL should be viewed as a single entity, a joint venture, or as thirty separate, competing firms. Although the plaintiff's expert concluded that the NFL teams were thirty separate firms, the defendants' expert concluded that, at a minimum, the NFL was a joint venture that produced a product that could be produced only as a joint product.

The second economic issue was whether or not the NFL had monopoly power in any relevant market. The defendants' expert concluded that neither the alleged "market for professional football" nor the alleged "market for professional football stadiums in the US" constituted a relevant market for antitrust purposes. Both proposed market definitions excluded products that constrained the behavior of the NFL.

THE NATURE OF THE NFL PRODUCT

In thinking about the first economic issue—whether the NFL should be viewed for these purposes as a single entity (or, at a minimum, a joint venture) or as thirty, separate, competing entities—it is crucial to consider the nature of the product sold in the marketplace.

The NFL produces a product: "NFL football." That product consists of a series of professional football games played by the thirty-two NFL teams over the course of an NFL season.[20] The season culminates with the Super Bowl, where the champions of the American and National Football Conferences play each other to determine the ultimate champion. The season ends with the NFL's Pro Bowl, which features the best players in the League.

As discussed above, the League's product must be produced by the League as a whole. The NFL as a whole works to ensure that the quality of NFL football generates fan interest. Relative competitive balance is a critical component to the NFL's (or any league's) popularity. Fans' interest is increased if their team is a potential champion—that is, if their team has a reasonable opportunity to win each game and also to compete for the championship. Team standings, winning streaks, rivalries, playoffs, championships, and the like are also very important parts of what makes NFL football a successful entertainment product.

The NFL has established revenue sharing as one of the many methods of achieving its goal of reasonable competitive balance among the member teams. An important example of revenue sharing is the equal sharing among all NFL teams of the revenues earned from the national television contract.

---

[20]When the St. Louis CVC sued the NFL, there were thirty NFL teams in the League. Since that time, the League has expanded to thirty-two.

These and other shared revenues help to ensure that each NFL team has the resources to field a competitive team.

In summary, NFL football can only be produced by the League as a whole. It follows that, if the League produces the product at issue, the League should be viewed as a single entity or, at a minimum, a joint venture. Moreover, regardless of whether or not the NFL has monopoly power as a single entity or as a joint venture, the NFL has a legitimate interest in the quality (measured by consumer appeal) of its own product.

PRINCIPLES OF MARKET DEFINITION

Turning to the second economic issue—whether or not the NFL has monopoly power in any relevant marketplace—we consider separately the market that includes the NFL product and the market that includes the leasing of stadiums. We begin, however, by reviewing the basic principles of market definition.

The question "What is *the* market?" is not well defined in economic analysis outside antitrust. As used in antitrust analysis, its answer consists of considering the products and producers that constrain any attempt by a seller to exercise alleged monopoly power, which is defined as the power to charge supranormal prices by restricting output or output quality.

One type of constraint that limits or eliminates monopoly power is demand substitutability—the alternatives available to buyers. These alternatives operate in the following manner. Suppose the company or group of companies being examined attempted to raise prices above competitive levels and thereby earn excess profits. They could not profitably raise prices if buyers could readily substitute the products of other companies.

A second type of constraint that can serve to limit or eliminate monopoly power is supply substitutability—the ability of suppliers who do not currently make demand-substitutable products to enter quickly and make such products in the event of an attempt by the alleged monopolist to charge supranormal prices. Obviously, supply substitutability differs from ease of entry in degree rather than in kind.

When defining a market and considering monopoly power, one must be careful in analyzing product differentiation and differences in quality. Markets can include products that differ in aspects other than price. In such markets, even though the products are not exactly the same, they still compete against each other for consumers' time and dollars. Prices in differentiated-product markets say nothing about monopoly unless differences in quality levels and differences in costs have been accounted for.

The point here is that the ability to charge a high price can be the reward for producing a high-quality product that is attractive to consumers. This ability is not monopoly power. Monopoly power in an output market involves the ability to charge high prices (relative to others) *without* offering superior products. It involves the power to charge high prices by restricting output, not by offering what, in terms of enhanced quality, is a larger output than would be the case if a lower quality product were offered.[21]

THE RELEVANT OUTPUT MARKET

NFL football is a product that is sold in two ways.[22] It is sold to fans attending games in person (this includes the "gate" and other stadium revenues), and it is sold for exhibition on television. The latter sale is a very important one: in 1994, average media revenues were nearly twice the size of gate and stadium revenues.[23] In both types of sale, the NFL competes with many other entertainment products that have differing characteristics and quality levels. The market is a differentiated-product market.

NFL football fans, who are one type of consumer of NFL output, have many ways to spend their leisure time; they do not have to watch an NFL football game. For instance, a television viewer may elect to watch professional basketball, hockey, baseball, or NCAA football or basketball, or attend a concert, see a movie, etc. Attendees at games also have a variety of choices as to how to spend their time. Indeed, when NFL fans were asked what they did in their spare time, they indicated that they participate in a vast array of leisure activities.[24] The NFL competes with these other forms of entertainment for fans' time and attention.

Regarding the revenues that the NFL derives from the sale of its product to television networks, the relevant output market is the national market for entertainment products. As we shall show, the League has no monopoly power in this differentiated-product market, and must compete aggressively to be successful. The League's control of its product is critical for that product's success in the highly competitive output market in which it competes.

That competition is especially strong in regard to television licensing. The vast majority of television programming is advertiser-supported. This means that advertisers, not viewers, are the buyers of television programming. Advertisers purchase time during NFL telecasts in an effort to reach customers who might be interested in buying their product. The value of NFL programming reflects its demographics, reach, and cachet value for advertisers. These same advertisers recognize that there are many other programs available on which they can attempt to attract potential customers.

---

[21]For a more detailed discussion of market definition, including a discussion of the "cellophane fallacy," see Fisher (2002).

[22]It is also sold by radio and through the Internet.

[23]"Suite Deals," *Financial World,* May 9, 1995, at 50.

[24]Interviews were conducted by ESPN Chilton.

While the NFL is good at attracting audiences with a significant number of male viewers (particularly, ages eighteen to forty-nine), many other television programs (including other sports programs, news, and prime-time programming) reach audiences with similar demographics. Moreover, these other programs deliver their audiences at similar prices (where prices are typically measured by CPMs, or the costs per thousand pairs of eyeballs). It is important to keep in mind that that the relevant comparison is not between the prices of advertisements on the NFL and on another program. Differences in these prices reflect, at a minimum, differences in audience sizes. It is more useful to compare CPMs. An analysis of CPMs indicated that the NFL prices were in line with those of other programs with similar demographics.

The existence of other programs where NFL advertisers can and do reach similar audiences at similar prices constrains the NFL from being able to raise its price above the competitive level. Were the NFL to attempt to charge supracompetitive prices, its advertisers would stop purchasing NFL spots and would instead purchase advertising spots on these other programs.[25]

In the absence of monopoly power, there is no anticompetitive reason for the NFL to restrict its output. The NFL wants and needs to appeal to fans—fans who have many other entertainment alternatives.

As we explain below, the NFL's relocation procedure assists this competition. We note, however, that even if such competition were more restricted, the League would still have a legitimate interest in sustaining the quality of its own product. We now consider the League's interests and actions in doing just that.

THE NFL HAS A PRO-COMPETITIVE INTEREST IN THE LOCATION OF ITS TEAMS

As we discuss in this section, the NFL has a pro-competitive interest in where its teams are located.[26] The financial success of the League is dependent on developing and retaining fan interest. This, in turn, is dependent on maintaining geographic diversity and franchise stability.

Geographic diversity reflects the national nature of the product, with live games being played *throughout* the country. Because the success of the League depends on fan interest, the League generally attempts to ensure that large population bases have access to live NFL football. Moreover, as

---

[25]For a more extensive analysis of this point, see Fisher et al. (2000).

[26]A separate, but related issue is whether the NFL has a pro-competitive interest in the number of teams in the League. While we do not address this topic directly (as it was not part of the Complaint), many of the same issues arise. We have argued elsewhere that the NFL also has a pro-competitive interest in the number of teams in the League.

avid fans are found throughout the country, the League attempts to ensure that teams are likewise spread out throughout the country.[27] If all of the teams were to move to the Northeast, for example, fans outside that region would eventually lose interest.

Geographic diversity is also important in competing with other television programming for the patronage of the television networks such as ABC, CBS, FOX, NBC, ESPN, and TNT. The NFL sells national television rights to telecast all NFL regular season and postseason games. These rights are a vital source of revenue for the League and its member teams. If NFL franchises were concentrated only in particular regions of the country, national networks would be far less interested in telecasting NFL games.

Further, the importance of television revenues means that the maintenance of geographic diversity is related to the maintenance of competitive balance. The maintenance of geographic diversity requires that the League adopt ways of sharing revenue, and this is done most importantly with revenue from television. If no action were taken by the League, the more profitable franchises would be able to spend more money on players and coaches than could the less profitable ones. This would lead to a decline in competitive balance and to fan interest.

The NFL's interest in the location of its teams, however, extends beyond geographic diversity. In generating and maintaining fan interest, the NFL also is necessarily committed to franchise stability and the fan loyalty that franchise stability encourages and rewards. The League has been subjected to tremendous nationwide criticism from its fans whenever a team has relocated (including, as we discussed above, criticism from St. Louis).

Franchise stability protects the identification of a particular team with a particular city and its fans. For example, the city of Pittsburgh is identified with the development of the steel industry. It is doubtful that the "Steelers" would have the same degree of identification with any other city. Changing team names is not sufficient to address this issue because once a team changes its name (e.g., Browns/Ravens), it takes on a new identity. As a result, the value created by the years of investment by the individual team, the city, and the League as a whole is significantly diminished.[28]

Franchise stability also protects rivalries, which are important to fan interest and fan loyalty. Rivalries such as Pittsburgh versus Cleveland, or the Cowboys versus the Redskins, do not develop overnight; they are the result of many years of intense competition, fan dedication, and substantial marketing investment by both the teams and the League. Relocations can destroy rivalries, undermining fan interest and causing harm to the League as a whole. Note that while a relocating team that is one half of a rivalry will

---

[27]According to a study conducted on behalf of the NFL, both NFL fans, in general, and avid NFL fans, in particular, can be found in nearly the same distribution throughout the United States as the population as a whole.

[28]In contrast to the NFL, during the short life of the USFL, which failed, there were a very large number of team relocations.

take account of the effect of rivalry destruction on itself when deciding whether to move, it will not take account of the similar effect on its rival team.

Franchise stability also protects existing investments, and encourages future investments by cities, states, and local businesses that support an NFL franchise. While local governments and business typically negotiate long-term contracts to help minimize their exposure to the risk of franchise relocation, they have been unable to eliminate all of this risk. The willingness of cities, states, and local businesses to invest in NFL football is influenced by the stability of NFL franchises. Hence, rules that promote franchise stability assist the League by providing local governments and businesses with additional security when they invest in stadiums or other League-assisting activities.

EXTERNALITIES AND FREE RIDING IN TEAM RELOCATION

The matter of team location is one in which the interests of the League and the interests of particular members will often not coincide. Indeed, this is an area in which externalities are likely to come into play.

To see this, observe that a team considering relocating from City A to City B will be interested in the relative extent of fan interest in the two cities, the related question of the relative support it can expect from public authorities and private businesses, and, of course, in the relative terms on which it can acquire or lease stadium facilities. But, while these matters will also be of interest to the League, there are other League interests that will not be fully reflected in the individual team's considerations. These are the interests of geographical diversity and franchise stability examined above.

When a team considers moving from A to B, it will not take into account the full effect that such a move has on the geographic diversity of the League. In the most immediate sense, the move may create scheduling difficulties for the League and, more importantly, leave a major television market without a franchise (as happened in Los Angeles when the Raiders and Rams both departed in the middle 1990s). In the longer run, a policy of permitting teams to relocate freely can have adverse impacts on the geographic distribution of teams, which in turn can affect fan interest and national television revenue. While each moving team may consider the effects of its move on its own share of such revenue, it is unlikely to take into account the effects on the shares of the other members of the League.

The same sort of phenomenon is even more marked in the case of franchise stability. We have already remarked that a team that makes up half of a traditional rivalry will consider only the effects of the loss of such a rivalry on itself in deciding to move; it will not consider the effects on the rival left behind. More generally, a policy of free team movement will lead to a situation in which fan interest drops and fans and local authorities and businesses feel insecure. A specific team that moves will not care about this effect on the League in general, but only about the effect on itself.

Beyond such considerations of negative externalities, there are also positive externalities involved in team movements, embodied in "free-riding." Free-riding occurs when one party takes actions that benefit another without being able to charge for such benefits. Since the incentives for action will not take account of such effects, the result will be inefficient. In effect, unless one gets paid, who will care to sow where another will reap?

In the context of a sports league such as the NFL, free-riding occurs when a team benefits disproportionately from the actions of the League and its member teams, without compensating the League and the other teams for those actions. Free-riding leads to inefficient outcomes because the League and its member teams will not have the appropriate incentives to invest in the promotion and development of the product if a particular team alone is allowed to capture disproportionate benefits from those efforts. Untreated, free-riding leads to economically undesirable or inefficient outcomes.

Team relocation often involves free-riding, as was illustrated by the St. Louis case. The value of the Rams in St. Louis was created by the promotion and development efforts of the entire League, not by the Rams alone. Indeed, the demand in St. Louis was for NFL football, not for the Rams' franchise specifically. St. Louis did not build an NFL-quality stadium to attract the Rams; rather, it began construction of its convention center (which included just such a stadium) with the hope that it would be awarded an NFL expansion team. Unless the League and its other member teams were appropriately compensated for the efforts to develop that demand, which was reflected in the extraordinary deal that the Rams were offered to move, the Rams would have enjoyed a free ride, and an inefficient outcome would have resulted. The incentives of the League and its teams to improve the product would be reduced if one of the teams could simply take advantage of such efforts by moving to a city where fan interest was great.

To sum up, in the absence of League relocation rules and regulations, an NFL team owner will have an incentive to move the franchise whenever the citizens of one city will pay more for that franchise than the citizens in the incumbent city. The League is interested in that calculation, also, but the interests of the League involve the consideration of other costs and benefits that the moving team will not take into account. Because those considerations involve the creation and maintenance of fan interest in the League's product, taking account of them is pro- rather than anticompetitive. It is the League's interest in its product and not the moving team's interests that coincide with those of its fans and consumers in general. A policy of permitting a team to relocate whenever it is in its private interest to do so will thus neither be efficient for the League as a whole nor pro-competitive, since the

League's interests stem from those of the fans and the maintenance of their interest.

Note in this regard that, with respect to relocations to cities that have no team (such as St. Louis before the arrival of the Rams), the interests of consumers and the League are necessarily aligned, provided the benefits of the relocation are appropriately shared to avoid free-riding. In particular, the League can have no anticompetitive output-restricting interest in preventing such a move. Games in St. Louis cannot materially affect ticket prices in other NFL cities. The number of nationally telecast games does not depend on the location of the teams. If a move makes the NFL more attractive to consumers taken as a whole, then it will be in the League's interest to permit it—again provided that a reasonable portion of the gain from the move can be appropriately shared.

A rule-of-reason analysis of a league's relocation rules should therefore be an analysis of whether those rules are reasonably designed to prevent the externality and free-riding effects described above. To such an analysis in the case of the NFL, we now turn.

ANALYZING THE NFL'S RELOCATION RULES AND PROCEDURES

The principal features of the NFL's relocation procedures are as follows. A team that wishes to relocate from A to B must make an application to that effect. Among other things, the application must cover issues of expected profitability in both cities, as well as fan support and the attitude of municipal authorities. The team must also cover the question of the adequacy of the actual and proposed stadiums and the terms of the leases. The team is not limited to the matters listed by the League, but may discuss any other issues that it deems relevant to its case.

The team's application is submitted to the commissioner, who then issues a report to the League's board. As with other major decisions, a vote to permit relocation outside a team's home territory requires a supermajority of three-quarters of all teams to pass. The League can, and often does, require the team to pay a relocation fee as a condition of the League's approval.

In the case of the Rams application, the commissioner's initial report raised a number of concerns regarding the various ways that the League, as a whole, might be affected by the proposed relocation. These issues included the potential impact on television viewers of the departure of an NFL franchise from the country's second-largest television city (and the loss of one of only two West Coast NFC franchises),[29] the possible disrup-

---

[29]As we mentioned above, the NFL is composed of two conferences, the National Football Conference (NFC) and the American Football Conference (AFC). Teams from within each conference

tion to the competitive balance among teams, and the League's right to earn the profits associated with its past efforts to develop that product—the free-riding issue. When it came time for the vote, the Rams' initial relocation proposal was rejected. A modified proposal, including, among other things, an indemnity provision and a relocation fee of $29 million, was approved.

In contrast to the plaintiff's assertions, the ability to charge such a fee, together with the supermajority rule, is in fact a crucial feature of solving the externality and free-riding problems.

As we have seen, the relocation of an NFL team can have negative effects on the League as a whole or on particular member teams. In addition, taking up a profitable opportunity can have a free-riding effect in which the relocating team preempts for itself an opportunity created by collective action. However, if the move were profitable for the League as a whole—and this can only happen if it were pro-competitive and hence in the interests of consumers generally—then the move should be permitted. In such a case, there must exist a way to share the benefits brought about by the move so that no League members lose and some gain. That sharing is accomplished largely or completely by means of the relocation fee, which thus serves both to offset the harms done by the move and to ensure that free-riding is no longer free but is appropriately priced.

The supermajority rule plays an important role here. When a team relocates, the effects on the other teams are not uniform. In the case of a dissolution of a traditional rivalry, for example, there will be an important special negative effect on the traditional rival who is left behind. Less dramatically, there can be scheduling problems that affect teams in one region more than in others. On the other hand, a team moving to a new location with a larger stadium or the ability to charge higher ticket prices may partly benefit those teams who play at the new location often and thus share in the gate.

The NFL's agreements with the players as to salaries require that a minimum percentage of certain League revenues flow to the players. When a team moves and total revenues rise, all teams will be obligated to raise salaries by the same percentage, even though the increase in revenues is not evenly spread among them. The relocation fee is a way of compensating teams for this as well as other disparities.

If relocations were approved by a simple majority, however, then some moves might be approved that would not be in the interests of the League as a whole. To see this, observe that because moves have different effects on different teams, there might be a simple majority of teams only relatively slightly injured by the move. Such teams would feel the move to be in their interests at a relatively low relocation fee (and a formula for sharing that

---

play against one another during the regular season. The two conference champions play against each other at the end of the season in the Super Bowl.

fee), even though some other teams might be very seriously negatively affected. Then a simple majority vote would approve the move even though, taking everything together, the teams collectively lost by it.

On the other hand, requiring unanimity would surely not work, as it would prevent moves that are in the interests of the League as a whole from taking place. If for no other reason, this could happen because of hold-up behavior, where a particular team or teams attempt to gain too large a piece of the relocation-generated pie by threatening to withhold their votes.

While there is no way to know that requiring a three-quarters supermajority is the efficient answer to such problems, it is likely that the correct requirement lies between a simple majority and a consensus.

The NFL's relocation rules and procedures therefore act to control the externality and free-riding problems and permit those moves that are in the pro-competitive interests of the League.

In the case of the move of the Rams, the League's system worked well. The operation of the relocation rules and regulations (including a provision for a relocation fee) led to a move that benefited the Rams, the League as a whole, the CVC, and consumers. The fact that the Rams gained was reflected by their willingness to compensate the league for the impact of the move. The fact that the League gained was reflected by its affirmative vote. The fact that the CVC gained was reflected by its willingness to pay for the Rams, even though it would have preferred to pay less.

It is important to note that the outcome that was in the consumers' best interest was achieved in this matter: The Rams moved to St. Louis and compensated the League for free-riding and harming other teams. The relocation rules did not prevent this from happening. Indeed, it is precisely because the rules worked that a mutually beneficial outcome was achieved. This happened because, as we have seen, the League's interests in such matters are to attract consumers in its competition in the output market. The move and the operation of the relocation rules and regulations were pro-competitive in that regard.

COMPETITION FOR INPUTS—IS THERE A "MARKET" FOR NFL FOOTBALL STADIUMS?

The plaintiff claimed that the NFL's relocation rules and procedures suppressed competition for the leasing (or purchasing) of stadiums. In particular, the St. Louis CVC claimed to be damaged because of the unfavorable terms it obtained in its negotiations with the Rams. The plaintiff claimed that the League created and exercised monopsony power (monopoly power as a buyer) in an input market—the supposed "market for stadiums meeting NFL requirements."

To analyze this claim requires consideration of the appropriate market definition involved. We have seen that market definition in the case of the alleged exercise of monopoly power by a *seller* requires considering what constrains that power—consideration of the alternatives to which buyers can turn and that other sellers can quickly provide. In the case of the alleged exercise of *monopsony* power by a *buyer,* market definition requires considering what constrains that power—consideration of the alternatives to which *sellers* can turn and that other *buyers* can quickly provide.

To begin such an analysis in the present case, one must ask what it is that the owners of football stadiums are actually selling. As we discuss below, it is too narrow an answer to this question to look only at the situation after a stadium has been built and negotiations with a particular team are under way. In thinking about this question, it is useful to distinguish private builders of stadiums and public authorities.

Private builders of stadiums are not in a narrowly defined business of providing only stadiums to NFL teams. Rather they are in the business of large-scale real estate development. Similarly, public authorities that are building or assisting with football stadiums are not in a narrowly defined business of attracting NFL teams. Rather, they are in the business of making their cities attractive to individuals and businesses, and NFL football is only one way of accomplishing this end.

Hence, the relevant input market here includes both large-scale private investments in real estate development and public investments designed to make cities attractive. While this includes *existing* and *potential* facilities suitable for a number of activities of which the exhibition of football is one, it also includes other large development projects in which public and/or private developers may invest (for example, the Arch, representing St. Louis as the Gateway to the West, and other local public goods such as museums, parks, hospitals, or public schools).

In examining competition in this input market, it is useful to divide the analysis according to whether the facility (the product of the investment) has already been constructed. This simplifies the analysis but in no way implies that there are separate markets for existing and potential facilities.

Potential Facilities

Since both private investment funds and public funds have many alternative uses, the NFL can have no monopsony power over facilities suitable for exhibiting professional football that have not yet been constructed. Stadium investors, both public and private, have many other attractive investment opportunities. Evidence is found in the controversy generated by stadium funding proposals. A typical discussion considers the relative merits of funding a stadium versus funding public works projects such as schools, fire and police protection, libraries, and garbage collection. For private investors, stadiums do not offer investors any economic investment return not easily obtained elsewhere.

Of course, potential facilities have an advantage over existing facilities when it comes to negotiating lease agreements. In particular, long-term contracting prior to a facility's construction protects all sides, given a stadium's large up-front costs and relatively small operating costs.

Existing Facilities

The analysis of existing facilities is more complex because some of these facilities are occupied by teams and some are not. The NFL's relocation rules may provide the owners of occupied stadiums with bargaining leverage over their home teams, since the rules hamper the ability of the teams to move. The plaintiff argued, however, that the rules provide moving teams (in particular, the Rams) with bargaining leverage over empty new facilities and that this amounts to deliberately attained monopsony power. The plaintiff argued further that the fact that the NFL requires stadiums to meet a number of specialized requirements narrows the market to NFL-standard stadiums.

Such an argument is confused. If we were considering the alleged monopoly power of a stadium *seller,* then the fact that the NFL has special requirements might be relevant, for it would limit the alternatives available to the buyer. But we are here considering the alleged monopsony power of the NFL as a *buyer.* The fact that it has special requirements does not limit the alternatives available to sellers.

This can be seen from the following analogy. Suppose that a maker of address labels were, without prior agreement, to print address labels with a specific name and address on them. Those address labels would meet special requirements, but would be essentially useless to anyone but the addressee. Having printed the labels, the maker could not then reasonably claim that the addressee had monopsony power because he or she required labels with a specific name and address.

So it was with the St. Louis CVC. Any negotiating leverage possessed by the Rams was created when the St. Louis parties committed the funds to construct and began building the Trans World Dome facility. By deciding to build the facility prior to signing long-term leases with potential occupants, the CVC placed itself in a far weaker negotiating position than would have been the case had the CVC first negotiated long-term leases. This had nothing to do with actions taken by the Rams or the NFL or with the League's alleged monopsony power.

Further, with respect to the effects of the NFL's relocation rules and procedures, those rules and procedures do not prevent stadium operators from talking with more than one potentially relocating NFL team (nor do they prevent an NFL team from talking with more than one stadium operator). There is simply no League prohibition against simultaneous bidding by teams for stadiums. Indeed, prior to the move by the Browns, a number of NFL teams discussed with Baltimore the possibility of relocating to that city.

The CVC also could have solicited bids from other franchises, but it apparently chose not to do so. Whether that choice was a matter of the negotiations between the CVC and the Rams or a decision by the CVC not to risk losing the Rams to another city, the choice was not imposed by the NFL's relocation rules and regulations.[30]

Existing facilities face what is commonly known as a *bilateral monopoly* situation when negotiating leases with a single NFL team. This is a bargaining situation in which both sides have the ability to influence the terms of the agreements.[31] In the course of negotiations under such circumstances, the two sides must determine how to divide the various revenues and costs associated with operating the facility and exhibiting NFL games there. In such a situation, both parties have an interest in achieving the economically desirable (efficient) outcome. Where they differ is the division of the surplus from doing so.

No output reduction and no economic inefficiencies resulted from the negotiated agreement between the St. Louis Rams and the St. Louis CVC. While the St. Louis CVC would doubtless have preferred a more favorable outcome, its failure to obtain one was of its own doing. There was no evidence that any other NFL team ever considered moving to St. Louis and none that such consideration was prevented by the NFL's relocation rules and procedures.

Even had this not been the case, it would have been wrong to conclude that NFL rules and procedures are anticompetitive. The rules and procedures are pro-competitive in that they assist with the production of a consumer-desired product on the output market. The accompanying effects on the input market may shift power in certain bargaining situations, but the shifts go both ways. In any case, even though from the viewpoint of a nail the entire enterprise of building a house is a conspiracy to hit it with a hammer, public policy must take a wider view.

THE OUTCOME AND SUBSEQUENT DEVELOPMENTS

In November 1997, near the conclusion of the trial, the judge dismissed the case and directed a verdict in favor of the NFL.[32] Approximately one year later, the Eighth Circuit affirmed the judge's decision. The CVC was prob-

---

[30]Evidence presented at trial showed that the St. Louis CVC believed the representative of the Rams when he told them that if they simultaneously negotiated with other teams, the club would terminate its negotiations with St. Louis. The St. Louis CVC never tested this claim by calling another team after starting negotiations with the Rams.

[31]Alternative uses of the stadium/convention center increased the bargaining position of the CVC with respect to its negotiations with the Rams. Alternative uses, such as conventions, also provide significant benefits to the community as a whole, including increased hotel and restaurant business. In fact, some have suggested that the benefits to St. Louis from alternative facility uses exceed the benefits from NFL football games.

[32]The *St. Louis Post-Dispatch* reported that an informal vote among the jurors at Denny's indicated that they would have voted in favor of the CVC.

ably not thinking about these courtroom defeats when the St. Louis Rams went on to win the Super Bowl two years later, only four years after the team's arrival in St. Louis.

The judge's decision was one of a growing number of significant, recent antitrust decisions favoring sports leagues. In 1996, the Seventh Circuit reversed a district court decision holding that the NBA was not a single enterprise. In that case, the Chicago Bulls challenged an agreement among the NBA teams that only the League, and not any individual team, could license the right to telecast NBA games in the national market. In reversing and remanding the case back to the district court for a retrial, the Seventh Circuit stated that it saw no reason why the NBA *"cannot* be treated as a single firm. . . . It produces a single product; cooperation is essential (a league with one team would be like one hand clapping); and a league need not deprive the market of independent sources of decision making."[33]

In yet another sports-related antitrust case, a group of professional soccer players sued Major League Soccer (MLS) and its member team shareholders. The plaintiffs claimed that either MLS was guilty of conspiracy or it had illegally exercised monopoly power. With respect to the conspiracy claim, the plaintiffs argued that the court should pierce the "veil" of a business organized as a single entity in order to determine whether participants within the corporation conducted activities that would have violated the Sherman Act had those participants been independent actors. The court dismissed this claim. It concluded that MLS was a single corporation incapable of conspiring with itself and its constituent members.[34]

With respect to the monopoly claim, the jury found that the plaintiffs had failed to prove that the relevant geographic market was limited to the United States or that the relevant product market was limited to Division I professional soccer players. Having failed to establish the relevant market, the plaintiffs could not establish that the relevant market was concentrated. The appellate court affirmed the decision.

In a recent case remarkably similar to that of the Rams, the Raiders claimed that the NFL had violated the Sherman Act, alleging that the NFL had illegally abused its monopoly power in the "market for stadiums offering their facilities to major league professional football teams in the United States" and in the "market for major league professional football including the geographic area around the San Francisco–Oakland Bay Area."[35] Prior to trial, the district court dismissed all antitrust claims and dismissed without prejudice the state law claims.[36]

---

[33]*Chicago Professional Sports Ltd. Partnership* v. *National Basketball Ass'n,* 95 F.3d 593 (7th Cir. 1996) at 598–99; emphasis in original.

[34]*Fraser* v. *Major League Soccer, L.L.C.,* 97 F. Supp. 2d 130 (D. Mass. 2000).

[35]Counterclaim and Third-Party Complaint, *National Football League* v. *Los Angeles Raiders* at 8.

[36]The Raiders refiled these claims in the L.A. County Superior Court. The case went to trial, and in April 2001 a jury found in favor of the NFL on numerous related claims (although some claims

Regarding market definition questions, the 1999 district court decision on behalf of the NCAA is yet another example of a recent antitrust decision recognizing that a sports league, or a product that it sells, does not constitute a relevant market. In that case, Adidas challenged the NCAA's rule limiting the amount of advertising that could appear on a student athlete's uniform and equipment as an unreasonable restraint of trade and an attempt to monopolize the "market for the sale of NCAA promotional rights."[37] In granting the NCAA's motion to dismiss Adidas antitrust claims, the district court rejected Adidas's market definition, stating that "Adidas has failed to explain or even address why other similar forms of advertising . . . are not reasonably interchangeable with NCAA promotion rights or sponsorship agreements."

Despite these significant victories for sports leagues, plaintiffs continue to bring antitrust lawsuits against the leagues. For example, Salvino, Inc., filed suit against both NBA Properties (NBAP) and Major League Baseball Properties (MLBP) alleging that NBAP and MLBP's separate decisions not to grant Salvino a license to use various marks on Salvino teddy bears is anticompetitive.[38] Many issues that arise in these cases are by now familiar. For example, in its case against NBAP, Salvino alleged that despite the fact that NBAP is structured as a single entity, the corporation is actually an illegal cartel. Moreover, according to the plaintiff, the relevant market at issue included *only* "professional basketball merchandise." NBAP contended that Salvino is incorrect with respect to both allegations and asserted that it has the pro-competitive right to determine how its marks are used. The questions at issue appear to be similar to those that have been addressed by earlier courts. But, as yet, no court has ruled on these specific issues.

Finally, we note that the recent decision by Major League Baseball to reduce the number of teams in its leagues prompted several significant responses, many of which are antitrust-related. However, these responses have been quieted for the next four years, as one of the provisions in the recently signed collective bargaining agreement between Major League Baseball owners and the players association is that there will be an elimination of contraction talks during the life of the four-year contract. But if discussions of contraction reemerge, many of the same issues as those discussed in this chapter are likely to prove relevant to Major League Baseball's ultimate decision to reduce the number of MLB teams in the league.

---

were not tried). In September 2002 a Superior Court judge, citing juror misconduct, ordered a new trial.

[37]*Adidas Am., Inc.* v. *National Collegiate Athletic Ass'n,* 64 F. Supp. 2d 1097, 1101 (D. Kan. 1999).

[38]*NBA Properties* v. *Salvino, Inc.,* and *Salvino, Inc.* v. *Major League Baseball Enterprises and Major League Baseball Properties, Inc.*

REFERENCES

Adidas Am., Inc. v. *National Collegiate Athletic Ass'n,* 64 F. Supp. 2d 1097, 1101 (D. Kan. 1999).

Chicago Professional Sports Ltd. Partnership v. *National Basketball Ass'n,* 95 F.3d 593 (7th Cir. 1996).

Costas, Bob. *Fair Ball: A Fan's Case for Baseball.* New York: Broadway Books, 2000.

Fisher, Franklin M., Christopher Maxwell, and Evan Sue Schouten. "The Economics of Sports Leagues and the Relocation of Teams: The Case of the St. Louis Rams." *Marquette Sports Law Journal* 10 (Spring 2000): 193–218.

Fisher, Franklin M. "Market Definition: A User's Guide." In *Workshop on Market Definition: Compilation of Papers.* The 4th Nordic Competition Policy Conference, Helsinki, Finland, Finnish Competition Authority.

Fraser v. *Major League Soccer, L.L.C.,* 97 F. Supp. 2d 130 (D. Mass. 2000).

Lhotka, William C. "Judge Throws Out St. Louis' Lawsuit against NFL," *St. Louis Post-Dispatch,* November 10, 1997.

Los Angeles Memorial Coliseum Comm'n v. *NFL,* 791 F.2d 1356 (9th Cir., 1986).

Los Angeles Memorial Coliseum v. *NFL,* 726 F.2d 1381 (9th Cir., 1984).

National Football League, *NFL Constitution and Bylaws,* § 4.3 (1984).

NBA Properties v. *Salvino, Inc.,* 99 CIV 11799 (LTS) (S.D.N.Y.).

Oakland Raiders v. *National Football League* Los Angeles, No. BC 206388. (Ca. Super Ct. May 26, 2001).

S. 259, 99th Cong. (1985).

St Louis Convention & Visitors Commission v. *National Football League, et al.,* 46 F. Supp 2d 1058 (Eastern District of Missouri, 1997), *aff'd,* 154 F.3d 851 (8th Cir., 1998).

"Suite Deals," *Financial World,* May 9, 1995.

The Brand Name Prescription Drugs Antitrust Litigation (1999)

Kenneth G. Elzinga and
David E. Mills

INTRODUCTION

Distribution issues are at the core of many antitrust disputes. The issues often concern price differences that manufacturers charge different buyers in alternate channels of distribution and how these prices are determined. Such were the questions raised in the largest antitrust case ever brought in the pharmaceutical industry: the Brand Name Prescription Drugs Antitrust Litigation (hereafter BNPDAL).[1]

BNPDAL began in the early 1990s when a group of retail pharmacies charged that every major pharmaceutical manufacturer selling prescription drugs in the United States: (1) price discriminated against retail drug stores in violation of the Robinson-Patman Act; and (2) conspired with each other and with the nation's largest drug wholesalers to refuse discounts to retail drug stores in violation of Section 1 of the Sherman Act. As summarized by economics consultants for several supermarket and drug store plaintiffs in the litigation, the contested pricing scheme purportedly arose from "a series of agreements and understandings among drug manufacturers developed in response to the emergence of managed health care in the 1970s and 1980s. While drug manufacturers began discounting extensively on sales to favored buyers, they allegedly agreed not to discount to retail pharmacies" (Weinstein and Culbertson, p. 258).

The authors, both of the Department of Economics at the University of Virginia, are consultants to SmithKline Beecham, one of the defendants in BNPDAL.

[1]MDL 997, U.S. District Court, N. District of Ill., Eastern Division.

The defendant manufacturers claimed that the discounts were decided upon unilaterally and were motivated by "meeting competition" considerations. The pharmaceutical companies also claimed that the disputed discounts were extended to buyers, such as hospitals and managed care organizations, because of their ability to "move market share" of their products, something retail pharmacies could not do. The defendant wholesalers claimed that they were merely the conduit for the manufacturers' discounts offered to certain buyers.

The litigation began with more than a hundred cases brought by (or on behalf of) some 40,000 retail pharmacies (i.e., independent drug stores, chain drug stores, and pharmacies in mass merchandising and food store chains). The cases were consolidated in federal court in Illinois, and a group of plaintiffs was certified (referred to as "the Class"). The Class consisted of retail pharmacies that purchased "prescription brand name drugs directly from any of the defendants." Members of the Class ranged in size from corner drug stores to Wal-Mart. Hospitals, clinics, nursing homes, and mail-order pharmacies were *not* plaintiffs in this litigation. Some plaintiffs exercised their right to opt out of the class and pursue their own individual claims (referred to as "Individual Plaintiffs").[2]

BNPDAL became one of the largest antitrust cases in American history. More than 1400 individuals were deposed in the course of this litigation, and more than 45 million documents were produced by the defendants. Many of the premier law firms in the United States and some of the most famous litigators represented the defendants. David Boies, one of the nation's most prominent lawyers, became involved in 2001 as lead counsel for one group of plaintiffs that opted out of the Class. Over twenty-five economists were involved in writing expert reports for the defendants. Before the trial, eleven of the seventeen original manufacturer defendants reached settlements with the class plaintiffs in which, collectively, they paid cash settlements of $700 million.[3]

Because the allegedly unlawful price discrimination in this case supposedly was sustained by collusion, the class action focused on the Sherman Act conspiracy elements of the plaintiffs' charges. For juridical reasons, the trial court scheduled separate trials for the Sherman Act (conspiracy) claims of the individual plaintiffs and for the Robinson-Patman (price discrimination) claims. The class action conspiracy case, thus far, is the only one to have been tried. The judge divided the conspiracy case from the price discrimination case on the grounds that the Sherman Act required proof of "un-

---

[2]The Individual Plaintiffs include some large drug chains such as Rite-Aid and Revco. Their litigation is still pending.

[3]The defendants who settled were American Cyanamid, American Home Products, Bristol-Myers Squibb, Glaxo Wellcome, Eli Lilly, Merck, Pfizer, Schering-Plough, SmithKline Beecham, Warner-Lambert, and Zeneca. Companies who elected to go to trial included G.D. Searle, Johnson & Johnson, and Ciba-Geigy.

lawful concerted action" by all the defendants, while the price discrimination claims might be shown "regardless of the existence of a conspiracy."[4]

The Sherman Act case brought by the Class went to trial in the fall of 1998, and for eight weeks the plaintiffs presented their evidence, at which point the defendants asked the judge to grant a directed verdict against the plaintiffs. In January 1999 he did so, thereby dismissing the plaintiffs' allegations of an industry-wide cartel.[5] The Class appealed to the Seventh Circuit Court of Appeals. In July 1999, the appellate court affirmed the lower court's judgment as to the Sherman Act case. Trial on the Individual Plaintiffs' claims remains to be scheduled.

THE MARKET FOR PRESCRIPTION DRUGS

To understand the economics of this case, it is necessary to understand some of the peculiar characteristics of the market for prescription drugs.[6] Most consumer goods are selected by consumers and purchased with consumers' financial resources. But prescription drugs are an exception for two reasons. First, "consumer sovereignty" does not apply to the consumption of prescription drugs because patients may buy only those drugs prescribed by a physician. The demands that pharmaceutical manufacturers face for specific drugs are not simply a function of patients' characteristics. Patients' preferences literally are "doctored" by prescribing physicians acting as agents for patients.

Prescription drugs also are an exception to the principle of consumer sovereignty because they often are not paid for directly by the persons who consume them. Increasingly, they are paid on behalf of patients by third-party payers such as employer health benefit plans and insurance companies. Third-party payment creates a "moral hazard" to the extent that the payer has no influence in the prescription generation process.[7] Under this arrangement, physicians and patients naturally focus on the therapeutic effects of prescription drugs and not on their costs. The cost is the payer's problem.

---

[4]*In re Brand Name Prescription Drugs Antitrust Litigation,* 1999 WL 33889 (N.D. Ill.), p. 10. The procedural history of BNPDAL is itself complex. The Sherman Act claims of the Independent Plaintiffs have not been tried nor have the Robinson-Patman claims of any plaintiffs been tried (as of April 2002).

[5]Directing a verdict essentially means that there is no reason for defendants to present their case because "no reasonable jury could reach a verdict" favoring the plaintiffs anyway.

[6]There are recent industry studies that provide a more comprehensive view of the pharmaceutical industry (Berndt 2002; Comanor and Schweitzer 1995; Deutsch 1998; Scherer 2000; Schweitzer 1997; and Spilker 1994).

[7]A moral hazard arises in situations where a fully insured person has the ability to change her behavior after purchasing insurance without the insurance company's being able to detect that she has done so.

Managed Care

Although they exist for good and necessary reasons, physician prescription writing and third-party payment have indirect effects that inflate the cost of providing prescription drug benefits to consumers. In time, as the magnitude of the indirect effects grew large, hospitals began to exert more influence over their doctors' generation of prescriptions, and managed care organizations were spawned to contain payers' prescription drug costs. Managed care organizations include staff-model health maintenance organizations (HMOs), independent practice association (IPA-model) HMOs, and pharmacy benefit managers (PBMs). Staff-model HMOs employ physicians to provide prepaid medical care exclusively to the patients whose health care benefits they manage. IPA-model HMOs provide prepaid medical care through networks of independent physicians. PBMs specialize in administering the prescription drug benefits of health insurance plans. Some PBMs (e.g., Medco) also dispense drugs by mail.

Hospitals and managed care organizations gained influence over drugs by (1) garnering control of the pharmacy benefits of large, closed patient groups, and (2) stimulating price competition among the pharmaceutical manufacturers for the business of these patients. The number of patients that are under some form of managed care in the United States has grown dramatically.[8]

The ability of hospitals and managed care organizations to reduce the cost of pharmacy benefits has been enhanced by growth in the number of generic prescription drugs and by growth in the number of brand name (patented) prescription drugs within various therapeutic categories (e.g., ACE inhibitors that treat high blood pressure or Histamine Antagonists that block gastric acid secretion). To the extent that there is competition among hospitals, among managed care organizations, and among third-party payers, the cost savings secured by managed care intervention in the prescription drug market will be passed on to employers and consumers.[9]

While the plaintiffs charge that competition is injured because pharmaceutical manufacturers deny retail pharmacies the same discounts offered to hospitals and managed care entities, the defendant manufacturers interpret the discounts in question as payments for *intervention* by hospitals and managed care organizations in the prescription generation process. In blunt terms, manufacturers reason that drug discounts are extended for exerting influence over physician prescribing behavior. Retail pharmacies, they argue, play a *dispensing* role rather than an intervention role in the

---

[8]In 1980, only 5 percent of all prescription drugs were under the influence of managed care organizations (Boston Consulting Group 1993, pp. 17–18 and Fig. 2–3). Today, the "four biggest PBMs provide prescription-drug benefits for about 200 million Americans" (Martinez 2001).

[9]Cost containment in the managed care segment of the health care industry is not limited to prescription drugs. Managed care organizations also exact discounts from physicians, hospitals, clinics, and retail pharmacies.

market. Retail pharmacies cannot influence physicians' prescribing behavior easily, and pharmacists in most situations are legally or ethically constrained from doing so. That is, if a physician prescribes a particular drug, the pharmacist may not substitute another drug without first contacting the physician and getting approval. Busy pharmacists cannot contact multiple physicians hoping to persuade them to approve hundreds of switches each week. Busy physicians will not entertain multiple calls from pharmacists suggesting changes in their written prescriptions.[10] In some circumstances, a pharmacist may not have to check with the prescribing physician if there is a generic substitute available for the particular drug that was prescribed. But, for most of the drugs at issue in BNPDAL, there are no generic equivalents available.

In short, the defendants reasoned, retail pharmacies do not exert the necessary influence with physicians to "move market share." From the perspective of an economist, manufacturers' discounts to hospitals and managed care organizations that move market share is a form of third-degree price discrimination, in response to differences in observed demand elasticities for individual companies' drugs.

The Chargeback System and Rebates

The contested discounts in BNPDAL are distributed differently to hospitals and managed care organizations depending on whether they actually dispense prescription drugs. Discounts to hospitals, staff-model HMOs, and PBMs that dispense drugs are implemented by means of a *chargeback* system that evolved from manufacturers' interactions with the drug wholesaler industry. The manufacturer charges wholesalers the wholesale price for a particular brand name prescription drug. But if a wholesaler then sells the drug to a hospital with whom the manufacturer has negotiated a discount, the wholesaler charges the hospital a price that encompasses the discount and "charges back" the discount to the manufacturer.

Discounts to managed care organizations work differently in most cases because these organizations, unlike hospitals, usually do not physically acquire and dispense pharmaceuticals. Prescription drugs that come under the aegis of managed care are distributed via the same drug wholesalers and retail pharmacies as other prescription drugs. But manufacturers' discounts to managed care organizations are implemented via *rebates* paid directly to these entities for the drugs prescribed by physicians and dispensed to patients who are under their care.

---

[10]This kind of activity is controversial. Senator Charles Schumer recently asked the Federal Trade Commission to investigate drug manufacturers' making payments to drug chains to promote certain prescription drugs to their consumers through phone calls and letters. See "FTC Is Asked to Study Promotion of More Expensive Drug Brands," *Wall Street Journal,* May 6, 2002.

Formularies

A formulary is the list of prescription drugs that physicians who practice in a hospital, or who treat patients whose health benefits are controlled by a managed care organization, may prescribe. One form of intervention by hospitals and managed care organizations is putting a particular brand name prescription drug on its formulary.[11] For example, a hospital might instruct its physicians to prescribe a particular antidepressant (e.g., Paxil) to the exclusion of other antidepressants (e.g., Prozac) in the same therapeutic class (i.e., Selective Serotonin Reuptake Inhibitors, or SSRIs, for treatment of depression). The physicians and pharmacists who determine the formulary may believe that the selected antidepressant is superior, or they may believe that it is comparable to others but its manufacturer has offered it to the hospital (or to patients covered by the managed care organization) at a lower price than rival products in the same therapeutic class.

Formulary access is not necessarily limited to a single drug within a therapeutic class. Therefore, another form of intervention is granting preferential, although not exclusive, formulary status for a manufacturer's brand name prescription drug to managed care organizations or hospitals.

THE TRIAL

The class plaintiffs and the six defendant manufacturers who did not reach a pretrial settlement with the plaintiffs proceeded to trial in 1998 on the Sherman Act conspiracy charge. The focus of the trial was whether the defendants colluded in their refusal to extend the same price discounts to retail drug stores that hospitals and managed care organizations received. The role that the plaintiffs attributed to manufacturers and wholesalers in the alleged conspiracy changed as the litigation proceeded. Before the trial began, the plaintiffs claimed that it was the manufacturers who started the cartel, and then brought the wholesalers on board—as "tools or reluctant accomplices." But at trial, the plaintiffs alleged it was the other way around: Wholesalers started the cartel, out of fear of retail buying groups, and "importuned the [m]anufacturers to join in their illegal conduct."[12] The judge criticized the plaintiffs for switching theories in the middle of the litigation.

Plaintiffs' Evidence of a Conspiracy

At trial, the plaintiffs presented four witnesses and a flood of deposition testimony in support of their conspiracy claim. Much of this testimony was of-

---

[11]The practice of offering discounts on prescription drugs to hospitals pre-dates the emergence of managed care organizations.

[12]*In re Brand Name Prescription Drugs Antitrust Litigation,* 1999 WL 33889 (N.D. Ill.), p. 10.

fered to support the claim that retail drug stores, like hospitals and health maintenance organizations who received discounts, also have the ability to "move market share" by influencing physician prescription patterns. If the plaintiffs could persuade the court that retail pharmacies, like hospitals and managed care organizations, were effective agents of intervention, this would undermine the defendants' economic justification for refusing to offer discounts to retail pharmacies.

The plaintiffs presented four live witnesses who had experience in the retail pharmacy business. The cross-examination of these witnesses ended up supporting the *defendants'* position instead. As the judge wrote, "[I]t was out of the mouths of [the plaintiffs'] live witnesses that the basic *independent* rationale for why the Defendants priced the way they did was first established in the record."[13] For example, a retail pharmacist in the Seattle area admitted to having once contended that "drugstores have little influence on the drug prescribed and cannot switch to alternative products as prices increase." Another plaintiff witness who had operated retail pharmacies admitted that for him to be involved in regularly switching his customers from the drug called for on the prescription to another drug was not only impractical but also unethical.[14]

The factual evidence offered in support of the plaintiffs' conspiracy theory was exclusively circumstantial and centered on trade association meetings attended by the manufacturers and meetings of the National Wholesale Druggists' Association (NWDA) attended by the wholesalers and manufacturers. The plaintiffs claimed that these professional gatherings provided the defendants with an opportunity to meet and discuss ways to prevent the outbreak of discounting to retail pharmacies. For instance, in reference to a panel discussion at a 1985 NWDA marketing conference in Atlanta, the Class offered as proof of conspiracy the "fact that the agenda for the panel discussion referred to [retail pharmacy] buying groups as a 'threat,'" even though, as the trial judge observed, "the presence of retail buying group representatives at this discussion undermines" this interpretation of events.[15] In reference to a 1986 study commissioned by NWDA that forecasted certain future developments in the brand name prescription drug industry, the plaintiffs inferred an attempt by manufacturers and wholesalers to coordinate a refusal to offer discounts to retail pharmacies. The judge reviewing the evidence presented about professional gatherings wrote that "[t]he fundamental weakness with the Class Plaintiffs' approach, and fatal to it, is that the Plaintiffs rely on speculation and conjecture rather than fair or reasonable inferences . . ."[16]

---

[13]*In re Brand Name Prescription Drugs Antitrust Litigation,* 1999 WL 33889 (N.D. Ill.), p. 6 (emphasis added).

[14]*In re Brand Name Prescription Drugs Antitrust Litigation,* 1999 WL 33889 (N.D. Ill.), pp. 2–3.

[15]*In re Brand Name Prescription Drugs Antitrust Litigation,* 1999 WL 33889 (N.D. Ill.), p. 8.

[16]*In re Brand Name Prescription Drugs Antitrust Litigation,* 1999 WL 33889 (N.D. Ill.), p. 9.

Plaintiffs' Economic Expert

Unable to present direct evidence for the alleged conspiracy, it was left to the plaintiffs' economic expert to resurrect the case. That expert testified that the manufacturers' discounts could not be explained by the ability of hospitals and health maintenance organizations to "move market share" because retail drug stores also had the ability to move market share in brand name prescription drugs. Further, having concluded that the defendants' economic justification for discounts was invalid, he testified that the circumstantial evidence presented by the plaintiffs was enough to prove that manufacturers' refusal to grant discounts to retail pharmacies was the product of collusion.

The plaintiffs' expert relied heavily upon the existence of price discrimination in the market for brand name prescription drugs to analyze the question of whether a conspiracy was afoot. He reasoned that if the market for brand name prescription drugs was competitive, competition should drive prices to the same level for all sales. His argument went like this: If a drug such as Lipitor sells at a high price to one customer, and a low price to another customer, arbitrage should eliminate (or narrow) the price differential unless there is collusion somewhere in the distribution chain. Because wholesalers did not abandon the low price managed care business to exploit opportunities in the high price retail business, and because manufacturers did not "go after" the business of the high price retailers by offering discounts that would eliminate the differential, he inferred that a cartel existed to maintain this profitable price discrimination scheme.

Upon cross-examination, the plaintiffs' economic expert admitted that, even without a cartel, different demand elasticities in different distribution channels could account for the observed price discrimination. He conceded that he had not studied whether pharmaceutical manufacturers faced different demand elasticities for brand name prescription drugs in different distribution channels.

The expert was unable to show to the court's satisfaction that retail pharmacies had the power to "move market share" the way that hospitals, nursing homes, and mail order pharmacies could. Upon cross-examination he was unable to back up his claim that retail pharmacies had even attempted to gain discounts based on their ability to deliver groups of customers to particular manufacturers.

Defendants' Motion for a Directed Verdict against Plaintiffs

In their mid-trial motions for a directed verdict against the plaintiffs, the defendants maintained that the Class had failed to prove a conspiracy to refuse discounts to retail pharmacies and, further, that discounts actually arose out of unilateral, profit-seeking behavior by the defendant manufacturers. The defendants argued that their pricing decisions to give discounts to hospitals and managed care organizations that influence the prescribing decisions of physicians were made independently. Likewise, the companies' refusals to extend discounts on single-source prescription drugs (e.g., those sold under the protection of a patent) to retail drug stores that lack effective intervention services were made independently. This explanation for discounts is supported by the manufacturers' practice of giving discounts to retail pharmacies to fill prescriptions for multisource drugs (e.g., those whose patents had expired)[17] where the pharmacy does have some ability to "move market share."[18]

Notwithstanding their independence, manufacturers acknowledged that their decisions concerning discounts were not made in a vacuum. The companies' chargeback and rebate contracts began as defensive measures to recover from or prevent lost sales in the burgeoning managed care sector as large hospitals and managed care organizations became more aggressive intervention agents. In effect, each manufacturer's discounts to managed care organizations were that company's unilateral response to the fact that it sells prescription drugs to customers with different elasticities of demand. The differing elasticities were created by the intervention capability of managed care organizations. By introducing price competition at the pre-prescription stage, managed care organizations *elasticized* prescription drug demands in the managed care sector. A 5 percent price reduction in this sector would increase unit sales of a manufacturer's product by a greater percentage than in the cash-pay (pharmacy) sector because managed care organizations can move large groups of patients from one drug to another so long as they have similar therapeutic effects. In response to the argument put forward by the plaintiffs' economic expert that price differences for brand name prescription drugs would be arbitraged were it not for collusion by manufacturers, the defendants attributed the absence of arbitration to the separation created by managed care organizations.

The plaintiffs' failure to prove a conspiracy, combined with the defendants' economic justification for the contested discounts, persuaded the court to grant the defendants' motion for a directed verdict. "Based on the evidence presented at trial, and viewing the evidence in the light most favorable to the Class Plaintiffs," the judge ruled that "no reasonable jury could reach a verdict in favor of the Class Plaintiffs" and entered judgment in favor of the defendants.[19]

---

[17]For instance, SmithKline Beecham had contracts with some retail pharmacies that gave rebates on the sale of Amoxil, the company's once-patented brand of the multisource antibiotic amoxicillin.

[18]Ironically, managed care entities also drive down the fees that retail pharmacies charge for dispensing drugs to patients under the control of HMOs. The dispensing fee for a prescription filled by a neighborhood pharmacist for a managed care customer is about 31 percent less than for a cash customer purchasing the same drug.

[19]*In re Brand Name Prescription Drugs Antitrust Litigation,* 1999 WL 33889 (N.D. Ill.), p. 17.

The Court of Appeals

The plaintiffs appealed this ruling to the U.S. Court of Appeals for the Seventh Circuit. In July 1999 the court of appeals upheld the directed verdict on the collusion allegations, but with one exception. The circuit court expressed concern that there could have been an agreement among the defendant drug manufacturers (but not the defendant wholesalers) to increase their prices in line with the Consumer Price Index (CPI). If a group of manufacturers, at one point, agreed to increase their prices in lockstep with the CPI, this arrangement could eliminate the need to have meetings about the timing and magnitude of future price increases.[20] But limiting drug price increases to increases in the CPI was considered by drug manufacturers as a means of warding off more direct government price controls. The judge held that such discussions among defendants were not a violation of the antitrust laws; corporations, like private citizens, have a right to petition their government and seek to avoid adverse regulations; and they have a right to do so collectively. Subsequently, on February 9, 2000, the trial judge dismissed the "CPI conspiracy" element of the case.

PRICE DISCRIMINATION AND PRESCRIPTION DRUGS: THE ROBINSON-PATMAN ISSUE

In a conventional Robinson-Patman Act case, a group of buyers of some input or product are in head-to-head competition but some of them allegedly are disadvantaged because they pay a higher price for the input or product than their rivals pay. The plaintiffs in BNPDAL claimed that this was their situation. The defendants responded that conventional Robinson-Patman analysis does not apply in BNPDAL because the favored customers are not in head-to-head competition with retail pharmacies. Retail pharmacies in fact are not generally in competition with hospitals for access to a hospital's in-patient customer base; in like fashion, they generally do not compete with managed care entities in the provision of intervention services to steer prescriptions for large patient groups. As discussed earlier, the defendants reasoned that retail pharmacies are *dispensing* agents rather than *intervention* agents.

Functional Discounts

In some markets, simply buying in large volume results in a customer receiving a "quantity discount." The pricing practice at issue in this case, however, differs from a quantity or volume discount. Prescription drug dis-

---

[20]*In re Brand Name Prescription Drugs Antitrust Litigation,* 186 F.3d 781, 787 (CA 7, 1999). If tying prices to the CPI was a political strategy on the part of drug companies to ward off government price controls, a "CPI conspiracy" might have resulted in lower prices.

counts are paid for intervening on a large scale in the prescribing process, not for dispensing large quantities of prescription drugs.[21] For example, the American Association of Retired Persons (AARP) operates one of the nation's largest mail-order pharmacies. But during the relevant period, the AARP did not generally receive rebates or chargebacks from pharmaceutical manufacturers because it did not have a formulary, and it does not control prescribing patterns for its member-customers.

If volume discounts *were* granted to a large drug store chain, this would not increase total sales of any particular drug. This is because retailers, even large chains, do not actively manage their prescription customer base; they do not have formulary control, and they have not made the extensive investment in information technology that is necessary to intervene effectively on a large scale. With a discount, the favored retail pharmacy might expand its own sales of a particular drug (at the expense of sales of the same drug at other pharmacies); but without inducing additional prescriptions this would not increase the manufacturer's overall sales.

In BNPDAL, the manufacturers maintained that from an economic perspective, chargebacks and rebates are not "discounts" from wholesale prices given to dispensing firms, such as the plaintiffs, but payments to firms who intervene to affect prescribing patterns. The overarching goal for the manufacturer is that the payment would increase the probability that its drugs will be chosen over generic or name brand therapeutic substitutes. In antitrust parlance, the defendants claimed that these payments properly should be viewed as *functional discounts:* payments for a marketing function that pharmaceutical companies would find costly to perform themselves.[22]

In support of the functional discount interpretation, manufacturers pointed out that rebates and chargebacks were arrived at on a contract-by-contract basis, after weighing the expected cost of the discounts against the expected gain from the customer's proposed intervention services. On the basis of these calculations, a customer would be offered one discount for listing a manufacturer's brand name prescription drugs on a formulary, a larger discount for giving that drug preferred status on a formulary, and an even larger discount for an explicit market share achievement on behalf of that drug.

For example, one defendant's contract provided discounts on one of its drugs for formulary access and for market share performance at a nursing home. The contract provided "a 4% rebate on all [usage if the drug] is made

---

[21]"Price discounts depend more on the ability to substitute among alternative suppliers than on sheer buyer size" (Ellison and Snyder 2001).

[22]Functional discounts are not unique to the drug industry. For example, in the food industry, a manufacturer might offer a grocery chain a 3 percent functional discount to induce the grocer to build an end-of-the-aisle display of the manufacturer's product, to be in place for two weeks, at each store location in the chain. From an economic perspective, through the vehicle of the discount, the manufacturer is purchasing marketing services for its brand, trying to swing customers to it and away from competitors.

available, unrestricted, on the . . . formulary" and provided additional rebates based on the "internal market share" achieved by the drug. These additional rebates ranged from 3 percent, for an internal share of 25–30 percent, to a 10 percent rebate for an internal share of 70 percent or more.

The defendant manufacturers claimed that retail pharmacies are offered discounts for products where they are positioned to influence the interbrand choices of consumers. Multisource drugs, as mentioned previously, provide examples. Other examples are over-the-counter medicines and consumer medical products, where pharmaceutical companies recognize that retail pharmacies can "move market share" by influencing interbrand choices of consumers.

Meeting Competition

Under the Robinson-Patman Act, a seller is permitted to charge a lower price to one customer if the lower price is offered to meet the low price of a competitor. In Robinson-Patman Act terms, this is called the "meeting competition" defense to a charge of price discrimination. Individual defendants in BNPDAL argued that this defense should apply to them.

For example, a particular pharmaceutical company would argue that its discounts (whether in the form of rebates or chargebacks) to managed care and hospital customers began as a defensive reaction. The manufacturer might notice that its efforts to influence physicians associated with the managed care entities through office visits were not working; the manufacturer might then learn that its competitors were gaining preferential access on the formularies of these customers by offering price breaks. The firm losing out would offer a discount or rebate in return for the buyer's favor. As this firm "met" the price of its various competitors, the divergence between list prices that retail pharmacies paid and the discounted price that intervention specialists were offered began to increase. "Meeting competition" became the process by which functional discounts were tendered and grew.

"Meeting competition" is not just a legal concept under the Robinson-Patman Act. Analyzing the "meeting competition" process in the drug industry affords an opportunity to understand both the economic concept of "price" and how competitive market processes operate in many oligopolistic markets.

In economic analysis, the "price" a seller charges includes all the terms of trade associated with the transaction. This means that in order to assess whether a firm "meets" the price of a rival, one cannot simply compare nominal prices; it is not a matter of simple arithmetic observation. Two firms might offer a drug in the same therapeutic category at *different* nominal prices, and a customer might view the offers as *equally attractive.* This would be the case if there were an offsetting advantage to the higher price drug in its ease of use, the absence of side effects, its relative lack of drug interactions, its delivery time, or other attributes.

Competition being "met" through price differentials is not unique to the pharmaceutical industry. If the products offered by two rivals in a market are different in quality, then this difference may require that their market prices be *different* (the lower quality product selling for less) in order for one seller to "meet" the price of the other. If a customer is evaluating an offer from a new supplier, comparing it with the terms offered by its current supplier, the customer may recognize that it will incur *switching costs* if it changes suppliers. In such a case, a new supplier may not be able to "meet" the price of a rival unless it offers a price sufficiently below the incumbent supplier's to cover the buyer's costs of switching vendors. If a manufacturer bundles different products together, where the aggregate price of the bundled assembly is less than the sum of the list prices for the products in the bundle, another drug company that cannot replicate that bundle may have to offer a very attractive price on products that it does sell in order to "meet" the price of the bundle.

This means that the economic focus of "meeting competition" should be on a notion of price that embraces all aspects of the contract, and not just the nominal price of the drug alone. The implication of this for BNPDAL is that "meeting competition" may mean offering a price low enough to get on a formulary. If a pharmaceutical company does not offer a price attractive enough to get on formulary, it may never be a vigorous competitor for the patient base served by that formulary. Such a company obviously has not "met" the competition.[23]

Economic analysis explains what keeps a firm, in the drug industry or elsewhere, from charging a price substantially below "meeting competition." In economic theory, firms are profit maximizers. Consequently a seller will not want to exceed by very much the reduction that is required to meet the competition and gain the business. Such a firm would be sacrificing profit unnecessarily. Unless firms in the pharmaceutical industry were adopting a predatory pricing strategy, or behaving irrationally, they would have no unilateral incentive to offer prices more attractive than is necessary to get the business.[24]

Third Degree Price Discrimination, Prescription Drugs, and Consumer Welfare

Class plaintiffs reason that manufacturers' refusal to offer discounts on prescription drugs to retail pharmacies is the product of collusion. They claim

---

[23]How do pharmaceutical companies learn about the "prices" they may have to meet? Customers may share this information (though they have an obvious incentive to dissemble); sales representative may gather intelligence about rivals' prices; and a firm's market research may uncover what its competitors are charging.

[24]The evidence about competition in the pharmaceutical industry does not suggest predatory pricing on the part of the defendants (i.e., charging prices below cost so as to drive rivals from the marketplace); nor is there evidence that the defendants offered low prices to favored buyers because the defendants were irrational or that they were doing so for eleemosynary reasons.

that if drug manufacturers were compelled to extend to retail pharmacies discounts like those offered to hospitals and managed care organizations, prices would fall uniformly to their lowest levels for all the defendants' customers. Competition among retail pharmacies and other customers, they argue, would enforce uniform low retail prices. Defendants counter this reasoning by claiming that discounts were extended to any and all customers who demonstrated an ability to "move market share" for their brand name prescription drugs.

From an economic perspective, the manufacturers' pricing practices are best explained by the theory of third degree price discrimination (Scherer 1997). Third degree price discrimination occurs when a firm with market power separates its customers into classes distinguished by demand elasticities and charges different prices to the separate customer groups. These prices vary among groups according to the "inverse elasticity rule," which holds that customers with low price elasticities of demand are charged high prices and customers with high price elasticities of demand are charged low prices. If the firm can identify such customer classes, and if arbitrage between classes can be prevented, price discrimination is more profitable than charging a uniform price to all.

Viewed through the lens of third degree price discrimination, the contested discounts in BNPDAL are explained by differences in the observed price elasticity of demand for individual companies' drugs in different channels of distribution in the industry. Retail pharmacies' demands for specific brand name prescription drugs are less elastic than the demands of hospitals and managed care organizations. This is because retail pharmacies do not maintain formularies and do not intervene on a large scale with physicians to steer prescriptions to particular drugs.

Under the plaintiffs' theory of the discounts, a ruling that eliminated preferential pricing to favored buyers would cause all prices to fall to the levels paid by the most favored customers. However, under the defendants' theory, such a ruling would cause prices to seek a higher, uniform level that reflects underlying market power. As one Robinson-Patman scholar put it, "[i]f a seller by law must lower all his prices or none, he will hesitate long to lower any" (Rowe 1951, p. 959). Under the defendants' hypothesis, the prices retail pharmacies pay would not fall, if uniform pricing were imposed on the industry, but the prices hospitals and managed care organizations pay would rise.

The consequences of the discounts in BNPDAL for aggregate economic welfare obviously would be different under the theories offered by the plaintiffs and the defendants. The plaintiffs contend that uniform pricing would reduce prices and increase aggregate economic welfare. The defendants contend that uniform pricing would raise prices and decrease aggregate economic welfare. Of course, whether aggregate economic welfare increases or decreases when a price discriminating firm is forced to charge uniform prices is not transparent. In some circumstances, economic welfare may increase. But in other circumstances, it may decrease. Scherer (1997, p. 253) examines this issue in BNPDAL and concludes "that the dead-weight losses attributable to discrimination are likely at most to be small."

One reason why third degree price discrimination in the brand name prescription drug industry may increase aggregate economic welfare vis-à-vis mandatory uniform pricing is found in the *Ramsey pricing* principle. This principle, which has familiar implications for pricing in regulated industries and for tax policy, holds that in markets where scale economies are so great that marginal cost pricing is neither feasible or desirable, welfare-maximizing prices are not uniform. Instead, welfare-maximizing prices in different segments of the market vary according to the inverse elasticity rule. Danzon (1997) has taken this line of reasoning one step further, arguing that Ramsey pricing, rather than uniform pricing, is the proper benchmark for socially optimal pricing in the pharmaceutical industry because of scale economies lodged in low marginal production costs and high, fixed, research and development costs. Danzon shows that competition among drugs that are therapeutic substitutes drives prices in the direction of Ramsey-optimal prices. That is, the price differentials that arise in the competition among the manufacturers of differentiated but substitutable drugs maximize overall welfare. These prices are better for consumers than uniform prices.

The generally ambiguous effect of third degree price discrimination on aggregate economic welfare in a given market stems from the consequence that the uniform price that would emerge in the absence of price discrimination is lower than the discriminatory price for some buyers and greater than the discriminatory price for others. Whether the welfare gains from lower prices to some buyers exceed or fall short of the welfare losses from higher prices to others varies from case to case. Elsewhere, we have given another reason why price discrimination in the market for prescription drugs would increase aggregate economic welfare vis-à-vis mandatory uniform pricing in the industry (Elzinga and Mills 1997). We argue that in the case of price discrimination in the drug market, the gains exceed the losses because there likely are no losses. That is, price discrimination of the kind that arose in the market for prescription drugs lowered the price to some patients and increased the price to none.

Unlike standard textbook examples of third degree price discrimination, the price discrimination in this litigation was not provoked by a monopolist separating its customers into existing groups with different given demand elasticities. Rather, it was provoked by managed care entities garnering control of the prescription drug benefits of large groups of patients and bargaining for the best deal with the manufacturers of drugs that are therapeutic substitutes. As a result of this intervention, the demands for prescription drugs in the managed care segment of the market were *elasticized,* resulting in discounts from the manufacturers. Since the demands for prescription drugs outside the managed care segment were not affected by this activity, the discounts elicited by managed care did not cause the price of prescription drugs to increase for any patient. Prices fell in one segment of the market but did not rise in another segment. In such a situation, the effect of discriminatory prices on aggregate economic welfare would be positive.

Economists who submitted expert reports for the defendants echoed one theme repeatedly: Using the antitrust laws to enforce uniform pricing would be unfortunate public policy. If uniform prices were required, they contended, this would raise the cost to a manufacturer of offering a discount, since the discount would have to be applied to all buyers. Thus, if uniform prices were required, manufacturers would be discouraged from giving any discounts.[25]

Status of the Remaining Cases

Several of the Independent Plaintiffs' cases have been transferred to the U.S. District Court for the Eastern District of New York for trial on the Sherman Act claims. But all of the Robinson-Patman claims remain before the original court. With the failure of the Class to prove that drug manufacturers colluded to deny discounts on brand name prescription drugs to retail pharmacies, the best remaining hope for plaintiffs in BNPDAL is a favorable judgment on the Robinson-Patman claim. As of this writing, some of the defendants have reached settlements with plaintiffs on the price discrimination charge, and the judge has not yet scheduled a trial to resolve the dispute among the remaining litigants.

REFLECTIONS ON BNPDAL

To appreciate the social backdrop of this case, it is helpful to recall the political philosophy of *populism* in which small business units, be they farmers, independent retailers, or manufacturers, are accorded social precedence over large organizations. BNPDAL appears to pit the independent pharmacist against the giant drug manufacturer.[26] At the same time, BNPDAL pits the efficiency philosophy of antitrust enforcement against the populist philosophy. The Robinson-Patman Act in particular reflects the populist philosophy. The act was New Deal Depression-era legislation passed in part to protect the existence of small, independent businesses against the superior buying power of new and larger competitive organizations. If antitrust were

---

[25]Mandating uniform pricing is akin to offering all buyers what in international trade is called a "most favored nation" status. Most antitrust economists are opposed to "most favored customer" clauses because they can reduce price competition and therefore harm consumers (see Berndt [1994] and Baker [1996]).

[26]This appearance is deceiving in that many of the plaintiffs, such as Rite-Aid, Wal-Mart, and CVS, are large corporations in their own right.

decided on the basis of populist sympathies, the "little guy" would always win.

The last quarter-century of antitrust has subordinated those populist sympathies to economic principles that stress consumer welfare and economic efficiency more than protecting small firms. Directing antitrust's focus to efficient resource allocation rather than the protection of any particular form of business organization is the most important contribution economic analysis brings to antitrust policy.[27]

The Sherman Act claim of the Class failed at trial for the lack of proof that manufacturers conspired to deny retail pharmacies discounts. The trial judge and the Seventh Circuit Court of Appeals found that the chargebacks and rebates that manufacturers extended to hospitals and managed care organizations, but not to retail drug stores, were arrived at independently and were a competitive response by the manufacturers to changes in the health care sector caused by the growth in managed care. While the Robinson-Patman claim has not yet been tried, the plaintiffs cannot win the price discrimination dispute unless they can discredit the defendants' economic justification for discounts in the managed care sector of the prescription drug market, namely that discounts are paid for intervention in the prescription generation process and occur as part of the process of meeting competition.

The paradox of this part of the case is that the retail pharmacists' problem is not manufacturers' refusal to discount prescription drugs per se, but their own reluctance or inability to introduce practices that effectively "move market share" of brand name prescription drugs. The response of pharmaceutical manufacturers to the emergence of intervention by managed care entities strongly suggests that if retail pharmacies develop mechanisms for intervention, as distinguished from dispensing prescription drugs, payments for intervention services would be forthcoming.

Evidence of responsiveness to intervention on the part of the manufacturers is provided by recent developments involving the states in their capacities as health care insurers. The Maine legislature passed a law in 2000 that sought to leverage the state's drug-purchasing power over Medicaid patients to negotiate discounts that would apply to residents who lack private health insurance with prescription drug benefits. The U.S. First Circuit Court of Appeals upheld this law in a decision in 2001 (Connolly 2001).[28]

As reported in *The Wall Street Journal,* in May 2001 "Florida lawmakers approved an innovative effort to slow Medicaid spending increases by creating a list of preferred drugs. To get on the list, manufacturers had to offer the state a 10% supplemental rebate on top of a federal rebate, which

---

[27]"The view that the guiding principle of the antitrust laws should be efficiency, rather than the taking of resources from one group and granting them to another, has gained increasing acceptance among legal and academic scholars" (Carlton and Perloff 2000, p. 604). "The only legitimate goal of American antitrust law is the maximization of consumer welfare" (Bork 1978, p. 51).

[28]*Pharmaceutical Research and Manufacturers of America* v. *Maine Department of Human Services,* 249 F.3d 66 (2001).

averages 15.1%. If a drug isn't on the list, doctors must get verbal authorization from a phone bank of pharmacists and pharmacy technicians before the prescription can be filled" (Gold 2002, p. A3). The "added inconvenience" of getting authorization is intended to shift prescriptions toward the preferred drugs.[29] Subsequently, the state of Michigan introduced a similar program.

Other states have implemented programs to reduce the cost of prescription drug benefits for state employees and retirees. West Virginia led the way in this effort. The state found in 2001 that the number of patients covered by its health plans was insufficient to win significant rebates from the pharmaceuticals industry, so it approved a plan to form a multistate drug-purchasing pool. Since then, officials from Maryland, Mississippi, Missouri, North Carolina, South Carolina, and Washington have formed a drug-purchasing pool to control the cost of their employees and retirees' prescription drug benefits. *The Wall Street Journal* reports that the "states plan to develop a common preferred-drug list for their employee health plans. By using lower co-payments to persuade many plan members to take certain drugs, the states hope to negotiate rebates from makers in return for having their products included" (Gold 2001, p. B6). Subsequently, eight northeastern states met to discuss a similar plan.

CONCLUSION

The cost of health care is one of the nation's most talked-about social problems. Prescription drugs are only about 8 percent of this cost. Physician services and hospital care involve even larger resource costs. But the nation's aggregate bill for prescription drugs is not small. In 2001, pharmaceutical expenditures in the United States exceeded $130 billion.[30]

Price competition for pharmaceutical sales became more intense in the 1970s and 1980s because of managed health care organizations that, along with hospitals and nursing homes, began to direct groups of patients to particular firms to secure lower prices. Hospitals and nursing homes also found that they could gain more attractive prices through the strategic use of their formularies and prescribing patterns for patients under their care. The resulting price competition was positive for consumers of (and payers for) prescription drugs in the managed care sector.

Retail pharmacies, which merely dispense the product but do not prescribe or control its use, were unable to leverage this competition to their

---

[29]*Pharmaceutical Research and Manufacturers of America* v. *Rhonda M. Medows,* 184 F. Supp. 2d 1186, 2001. The Pharmaceutical Research and Manufacturers of America, a trade group representing the manufacturers of brand name prescription drugs, brought a lawsuit in federal district court in Tallahassee that challenged the law. In January 2002, a federal judge let the law stand.

[30]Source: PhRMA Industry Primer at www.phrma.org/publications/publications/primer01 and www.phrma.org/publications/publications/profile02/appendtables.pdf.

advantage. The result is the antitrust lawsuit described in this article. If the plaintiffs were to prevail in BNPDAL, pharmaceutical companies might be required to offer the same contract terms to all buyers. This could make pharmaceutical manufacturers reluctant to extend discounts to any of their customers, and could discourage further experimentation in pricing and marketing strategies by the defendants. At a time when these pricing strategies serve to hem in the costs of health care, an outcome that discourages discounting is not likely to benefit consumers.

REFERENCES

Armstrong, David, and Ann Zimmerman. "FTC Is Asked to Study Promotion of More-Expensive Drug Brands." *The Wall Street Journal,* May 6, 2002, B1.

Baker, Jonathan B. "Vertical Restraints with Horizontal Consequences: Competitive Effects of 'Most-Favored-Customer' Clauses." *Antitrust Law Journal* 64 (Spring 1996): 517–534.

Berndt, Ernst R. "Uniform Pharmaceutical Pricing: An Economic Analysis." Washington, D.C.: American Enterprise Institute, 1994.

Berndt, Ernst R. "Pharmaceuticals in U.S. Health Care: Determinants of Quantity and Price." *Journal of Economic Perspectives* 16 (Fall 2002): 45–66.

Bork, Robert H. *The Antitrust Paradox.* New York: Basic Books, 1978.

Carlton, Dennis W, and Jeffrey Perloff. *Modern Economic Organization.* Reading MA.: Scott, Foresman and Co., 2000.

Comanor, William, S., and Stuart O. Schweitzer. "Pharmaceuticals." In *The Structure of American Industry,* 9th edn., edited by Walter Adams and James Brock, ch. 7. Englewood Cliffs, NJ.: Prentice-Hall, 1995.

Connolly, Ceci. "Court Backs Maine Drug Price Curbs." *The Washington Post,* May 18, 2001, A2.

Danzon, Patricia M. "Price Discrimination for Pharmaceuticals: Welfare Effects in the US and the EU." *International Journal of the Economics of Business* 4 (November 1997): 301–321.

Deutsch, Larry L. "Pharmaceuticals: The Critical Role of Innovation." In *Industry Studies,* 2d edn., edited by Larry L. Deutch, ch 4. New York: M. E. Sharpe, 1998.

Ellison, Sara F., and Christopher M. Snyder. "Countervailing Power in Wholesale Pharmaceuticals." *Social Science Research Network Paper Collection* (July 2001).

Elzinga, Kenneth G., and David E. Mills. "The Distribution and Pricing of Prescription Drugs." *International Journal of the Economics of Business* 4 (November 1997): 287–300.

Gold, Russell. "Judge Allows Drug Rebates in Florida Law." *The Wall Street Journal,* January 3, 2002, A3.

Gold, Russell. "Six States Plan to Pool Purchases to Limit Prescription-Drug Costs." *The Wall Street Journal,* October 17, 2001, B6.

In re Brand Name Prescription Drugs Antitrust Litigation, 1999 WL 33889 (N.D. Ill.).

In re Brand Name Prescription Drugs Antitrust Litigation, 186 F.3d 781 (CA 7, 1999).

In re Brand Name Prescription Drugs Antitrust Litigation, 2001 WL 59035 (N.D. Ill.).

Martinez, B. "Merck-Medco Policy on Switching to Costlier Drugs Is Scrutinized." *The Wall Street Journal,* August 30, 2001, B2.

Pharmaceutical Research and Manufacturers of America v. *Maine Department of Human Services,* 249 F.3d 66 (2001).

Pharmaceutical Research and Manufacturers of America v. *Rhonda M. Medows,* 184 F. Supp. 2d 1186 (2001).

Rowe, F. M. "Price Discrimination, Competition, and Confusion: Another Look at Robinson-Patman." *Yale Law Journal* 60 (June 1951): 929–975.

Scherer, F. M. "How US Antitrust Can Go Astray: The Brand Name Prescription Drug Litigation." *International Journal of the Economics of Business* 4 (November 1997): 239–256.

Scherer, F. M. "The Pharmaceutical Industry." In *Handbook of Health Economics,* Vol. 1b, edited by A. J. Culyer and J. P. Newhouse, 1297–1336. Amsterdam: North Holland, 2000.

Schweitzer, Stuart O. *Pharmaceutical Economics and Policy.* New York: Oxford University Press, 1997.

Spilker, Bert. *Multinational Pharmaceutical Companies.* New York: Raven Press, 1994.

Weinstein, R., and J. Culbertson. "How U.S. Antitrust Can Be on Target: The Brand-Name Prescription Drug Litigation." *International Journal of the Economics of Business* 4 (November 1997): 257–264.

PART III

Vertical and Related Market Issues

The Economic
and Legal Context

Vertical and complementary market relationships between firms continue to be areas of change for both microeconomics and antitrust policy. The issues involve firms that either are in a customer-supplier with each other (vertical) or that sell complements; as will be argued below, the latter type of relationship is often analytically similar to the former, and we will treat them similarly.

There is a history prior to the 1970s, for both law and economics, of muddy thinking and muddled analysis in this area (White 1989). At least part of the problem seems to have been difficulties in conceptualizing the relationships and in recognizing their fluidity; even terminology (e.g., "vertical restraints," "foreclosure," "refusal to deal") may have played a role as well.

We will first address the economics of these relationships, and then address the law.

ECONOMICS

Some Fundamentals

A *vertical relationship* describes the business relationship between a supplier and a customer. Thus, a wheat farmer and a flour miller, the flour miller and a bread baking factory, the baking factory and a supermarket, etc., are each in a vertical relationship with the other. Often these relationships are described as "upstream" (the supplier) and "downstream" (the customer) relationships. Another way of describing them is that each party in principle is always facing a "make or buy" decision with respect to the goods or services of the other.[1]

This last point highlights the possibility of *vertical integration:* Verti-

---

[1] Overviews can be found in Katz (1989), Perry (1989), White (1989), and Comanor and Rey (1995, 1997). Recent articles include Choi and Stefanidis (2001), Chen (2001), and Carlton and Waldman (2002).

cally related activities that are (or could be or formerly were) located in separate (customer-supplier) businesses could be combined and integrated "under one roof" in a single enterprise. Thus, the farmer might decide to mill his wheat himself and then sell the flour to the baker, or the miller might decide to grow his own wheat; equivalently, the baker might decide to open its own retail outlet, or the supermarket might start baking its own bread.

In turn, these illustrations highlight the fluidity of vertical arrangements. In principle, almost any vertical relationship *between* firms could be vertically integrated into a *single* entity, and almost any vertically integrated entity could be broken into two separate, vertically related firms. There is thus no "natural" extent of vertical integration for a firm; which of its inputs it "makes" or "buys" is always a situationally specific issue, driven by factors that we will discuss below.

Further, even the question of who is the "upstream" party and who is the "downstream" party is situationally specific. For example, manufacturers typically sell their goods to distributors or retailers, who in turn sell to the public, but sometimes manufacturers "buy" distributional services (e.g., through the payment of fees and commissions) while retaining title to the goods until they are sold to the public. Who is "upstream" and who is "downstream"?

At the opposite pole from vertical integration is the spot market. Here buyers and sellers each appear on an ad hoc basis, determined by their respective needs to participate in the market and engaging in one-at-a-time transactions.

In between the two extremes is a wide range of vertical arrangements between buyers and sellers that are agreed to by both parties and that limit the behavior of one or both; these are often embodied in legally enforceable contracts and are frequently termed *vertical restraints*. By thereby giving one party some control over the other party's actions, these arrangements are, in essence, a form of partial vertical integration. These arrangements include:

- long-term contracts;
- franchising;
- licensing;
- tying;
- bundling;
- exclusive dealing;
- requirements contracts;
- full-line forcing;
- refusals to deal;
- territorial restraints; and
- resale price maintenance.

Just as the extent of vertical integration is situationally specific, so is the presence or absence of vertical restraints.

Finally, firms are often in a relationship that appears to be neither horizontal (i.e., competitors) nor vertical (customer-supplier). For example, both the flour miller and the yeast manufacturer sell inputs to the bread baker. The relationship between the flour miller and the yeast manufacturer is neither horizontal nor vertical; they are selling complements. However, we could instead envisage an alternative structural relationship, whereby the flour miller sells his flour to the yeast manufacturer, who then sells a flour-yeast mix to the baker; for many analytical purposes (e.g., evaluating mergers), the two alternative arrangements yield similar outcomes. Accordingly, much of the discussion in this part applies equally strongly to vertical arrangements and to relationships between sellers of complementary goods.

Why Vertical Integration?

As the previous section indicated, vertical relationships embrace a broad spectrum of possibilities, from the vertical integration of activities within one firm to spot market transactions between firms, with various intermediate possibilities. Let us begin by considering the contrast between vertical integration and spot market transactions. Though there would seem to be advantages to the latter arrangement, reliance on the spot market may entail considerable informational and transactions costs (Coase 1937). Presumably, profit-seeking firms will search for the arrangements that offer them the most profitable opportunities. Whether this will involve "making" (i.e., vertically integrating) or instead "buying" will thus be driven in an immediate sense by perceived profit opportunities. But, in a larger structural sense, whether activities are integrated or in separate enterprises will be related to a host of potential factors, including:

- the technologies of the production processes;
- business strategies;
- managerial capabilities;
- customer preferences;
- legal requirements or restrictions;
- tax considerations;
- product-related informational issues;
- the presence (or absence) of market power; and
- the pursuit or protection of market power.

Vertical integration is often a means of taking advantage of technological complementarities, reducing transactions costs, gaining greater control over production processes (e.g., so as to preclude opportunistic behavior by suppliers), overcoming informational deficiencies, and/or internalizing externalities. The problem of "successive monopolies" or "double marginalization" is a good example of this last phenomenon (Tirole 1988, ch. 4). If an upstream monopolist sells to a downstream firm that is also a monopolist, the former firm will include its profit margin in its price; the latter firm thus buys that input at a price that is in excess of marginal cost, which in turn will cause the downstream firm to set a price that is excessively high, and both firms' sales volumes and profit levels suffer. The fundamental problem is that of an externality (each firm ignores the effects of the other's market power), and vertical integration between the two firms internalizes that externality and allows the combined firm to sell at a lower price that also yields higher profits.[2]

But vertical integration may also be a means by which a firm creates or enhances market power, by raising entry barriers and/or raising rivals' costs. A dominant upstream firm may be able to disadvantage its upstream rivals by integrating downstream (e.g., through merger) and reducing its upstream rivals' access to distribution; or, equivalently, a dominant downstream firm may integrate upstream and thereby disadvantage its downstream rivals by reducing their access to suppliers.[3] Also, vertical integration downstream may be a means by which a firm can more effectively practice price discrimination and thereby raise its profits.[4]

If vertical integration is to have anticompetitive effects, however, market power must actually or potentially be present. Conversely, if market power is absent, there is a strong presumption that the vertical structure is benign or beneficial. Such a determination, however, requires a delineation of a market. Unfortunately, the *Merger Guidelines'* paradigm of market delineation for merger assessment (discussed in Part I) does not apply to efforts to delineate markets in instances where market power is alleged to be already present;[5] and no satisfactory substitute has yet been devised (White 2000).

---

[2]The double-marginalization problem also provides a good example of the parallel between vertically related firms and complementary sellers. If two complementary sellers are monopolists and each ignores the other's monopoly power, then the downstream price will be too high, both sellers' profits will suffer, and a merger between the two would internalize the externality. This point is raised in the discussion of the GE-Honeywell proposed merger in Case 16 by Barry Nalebuff in this part.

[3]Note that these scenarios imply that an input (including distribution) is essential and good substitutes are not easily available.

[4]The social welfare consequences of price discrimination, however, are ambiguous; see, for example, Schmalensee (1981) and Kwoka (1984).

[5]Since a profit-maximizing monopolist maintains its price at a level where (by assumption) a higher level would be unprofitable, a price *increase* test (such as the SSNIP) for determining whether a market can be monopolized should always find that even the true monopolist cannot profitably raise its price from the current level (as is true also for a competitive firm). Thus, this test would mistakenly find that even the true monopolist appears to be just another competitor.

Why Vertical Restraints?

As was argued above, vertical restraints can be conceptualized as agreements that allow one or both parties to restrict the actions of the other and that thus can be considered partial vertical integration. The same forces—technology, managerial capabilities, etc.—that influence the presence or absence of vertical integration tend also to influence the presence or absence of these arrangements.[6] Often a manufacturer will have strong ideas about the way in which its product should be distributed and promoted at the retail level, but does not have the managerial capabilities to undertake the retailing itself. Vertical restraints are a means by which these ideas can be implemented without the necessity of the less-efficient full vertical integration. However, though they often promote efficiency, vertical restraints may also be a means for attaining or enhancing market power.

The pluses and the minuses for various vertical restraints include the following:

- Resale price maintenance (RPM) involves the specification of the retail price by an upstream entity (e.g., the manufacturer).[7] RPM that sets a minimum price can be a means by which a manufacturer can induce the provision of point-of-sale services, especially information, by its retailers, each of whom might otherwise be tempted to free-ride on the services of others;[8] but RPM may also be a cover for a horizontal conspiracy among retailers or among manufacturers (Telser 1960).

- Territorial restrictions involve a manufacturer's restricting the territories in which its retailers can locate or the locations of customers to whom they can sell.[9] The restrictions can allow a manufacturer to avoid duplicate sales efforts and free-riding (e.g., on the advertising of others) among its geographically dispersed retailers; but the restrictions may also permit the manufacturer more effectively to practice price discrimination or to enforce a retailer-inspired conspiracy to allocate markets and restrict competition (White 1981).

- Long-term contracts between a manufacturer and a distributor provide both parties with greater levels of certainty, which can be valuable for planning and investment (and help avoid "hold-up" or other opportunistic

---

[6]Often the efficiency rationale for these practices can be best comprehended by imagining how the relevant behavior would appear if the two firms that are parties to the vertical restraint were vertically integrated.

[7]In the examples below we will use "manufacturer" to represent generally an upstream entity (supplier) and "retailer" to represent the downstream entity (customer).

[8]RPM that sets a ceiling on prices may be a way to restrict the market power that is created for a retailer when a manufacturer also grants an exclusive territory to the retailer. See the discussion of the *State Oil* litigation in Case 13 by Gustavo Bamberger in this part.

[9]Similar restrictions may apply to the category of customer to whom the distributor can sell, with similar rationales.

behaviors by one side or the other) (Williamson 1983); but such contracts may also restrict the access of rival manufacturers to distribution services, thus raising their costs of distribution, or raise barriers to entry (if distribution services are an important bottleneck for that line of products).

- Exclusive dealing involves the manufacturer's insisting that the retailer sell only that manufacturer's line of goods.[10] The manufacturer may thereby achieve the focused effort of the retailer and prevent free-riding by other manufacturers; but the practice may also raise rivals' costs or barriers to entry, similar to the effects of long-term contracts.

- Refusals-to-deal involve the manufacturer's choosing to distribute its product through some retailers and not others. The practice permits the manufacturer to enforce other types of restraints (by refusing to sell to a retailer that does not abide by the restraint) and to avoid selling through retailers who the manufacturer believes do not enhance the goodwill of the product. But refusals-to-deal may similarly help the manufacturer effect anticompetitive outcomes from other restraints or may simply make some retailers' existences more difficult (which may adversely affect other manufacturers).

- Tying and bundling can be a means of ensuring quality and improved overall performance of a product or service; but these practices can also be used to price discriminate, to raise prices for the combined package,[11] or to raise rivals' costs and barriers to entry.[12]

- Franchising and other licensing arrangements can allow the originators of an idea to extend its use and maintain quality control over its use, without their engaging in the direct production (in which they may have little relevant expertise) themselves; but these arrangements may also be used to effect ties or other vertical restraints.

Further, as was true for vertical integration, the presence or absence of actual or potential market power is crucial for judgments about these practices; and the issue of market definition is just as important and just as unresolved.

ANTITRUST LAW

A broad range of the antitrust laws' provisions have been used to attack vertical and complementary market arrangements:

---

[10]Equivalently, a retailer may insist that manufacturers sell only to it and not to other retailers. This version is raised in the Toys "R" Us dispute that is discussed in Case 15 by F. M. Scherer in this part.

[11]See the discussion of the Kodak case in Case 17 by Jeffrey MacKie-Mason and John Metzler in Part IV.

[12]See the discussion of the Microsoft case in Case 19 by Daniel Rubinfeld in Part IV.

- The Sherman Act's Section 1 prohibition on any "contract, combination . . . or conspiracy in restraint of trade . . ." has been used to challenge vertical restraints.
- The Sherman Act's Section 2 condemnation of "monopolization" has been used to challenge vertical restraints and vertical integration itself.
- The Clayton Act's Section 3 specifically forbids contracts imposing a restraint whereby the customer "shall not use or deal in the goods, supplies, or other commodities of the lessor or seller" where the effect "may be substantially to lessen competition or tend to create a monopoly."
- The Clayton Act's Section 7 (which was discussed in Part I) has been used to challenge vertical mergers.

For the discussion that follows it is useful to classify the antitrust treatment of vertical arrangements into four areas: vertical integration; restraints involving prices; territorial restraints; and other non-price restraints.

Vertical Integration

Section 2 of the Sherman Act has been used, albeit sparingly, to attack vertical integration that appeared to promote or enhance market power. The 1911 *Standard Oil*[13] decision resulted in vertical dissolution (e.g., oil pipelines' being separated from refineries) as well as horizontal dismemberment (refineries in different geographic regions were separated into independent companies). The 1948 *Paramount*[14] case resulted in the separation of movie exhibition (theaters) from distribution and production. The Justice Department's *AT&T*[15] case and 1982 consent decree, which separated long-distance and equipment from local telephone service, was grounded on the DOJ's theory that AT&T's vertical integration encompassing local service, long-distance service, and equipment manufacturing, when buttressed by imperfect local and national economic regulation, created competitive distortions (Noll and Owen 1994).

Section 7 of the Clayton Act has been used to prevent vertical integration through merger. Even before Section 7 was strengthened in 1950, the DOJ was able successfully to challenge General Motors' substantial stock ownership position in its major supplier of paints and finishes, Du Pont.[16] In the heyday of merger prohibition victories of the 1960s, vertical mergers (as well as horizontal mergers) were regularly challenged and stopped.[17]

---

[13]*U.S. v. Standard Oil of New Jersey et al.*, 221 U.S. 1 (1911).

[14]*U.S. v. Paramount Pictures et al.*, 334 U.S. 131 (1948).

[15]*U.S. v. AT&T*, 524 F. Supp. 1336 (1981), 552 F. Supp. 131 (1982).

[16]*U.S. v. E.I. Du Pont de Nemours and Co. et al.*, 353 U.S. 586 (1957).

[17]See, for example, *Brown Shoe Co. v. U.S.*, 370 U.S. 294 (1962); *Reynolds Metals Co. v. F.T.C.*, 309 F.2d 223 (1962); and *Ford Motor Co. v. U.S.*, 405 U.S. 362 (1972).

Fewer vertical mergers received scrutiny in the 1980s and 1990s, as the enforcement agencies came to understand the more favorable economic assessment of these mergers' effects. Nevertheless, some mergers did require modifications before they were approved, because of the agencies' concerns about the creation of horizontal market power, through the strategies of raising rivals' costs and/or raising barriers to entry (White 1985; Nelson and Stoner 1999; Besen et al. 1999). And in 2001 the Department of Justice (DOJ) showed its continuing attention to vertical issues by challenging the acquisition by Premdor Inc. (a manufacturer of finished residential molded doors) of the Masonite Corp. (a manufacturer of "doorskins," the essential molded input for these doors) and requiring the divestiture of some facilities before approving the acquisition (Katz 2002).

Resale Price Maintenance (RPM)

In the 1911 *Dr. Miles Medical Co.*[18] case the Supreme Court declared that RPM was a per se violation of Section 1 of the Sherman Act, thus placing RPM in the same condemned position as horizontal price fixing. The Court has repeatedly upheld that position in subsequent cases, although in the 1980s it raised the evidentiary standards for finding a defendant guilty of RPM.[19]

An important new development in the 1997 *State Oil*[20] case involved maximum RPM. In 1968 the Supreme Court had declared that maximum RPM was a per se violation of Section 1, in the *Dr. Miles Medical* tradition.[21] But, as discussed in Case 13 by Gustavo Bamberger in this part, the Court decided in *State Oil* that maximum RPM should be judged under a rule of reason.[22]

Territorial Restraints

The Supreme Court first addressed territorial (and customer classification) restraints in 1963 and declared that it felt that not enough was known about them to condemn them as per se violations of Section 1 of the Sherman Act.[23] Four years later, however, the Court reversed itself and declared such

---

[18]*Dr. Miles Medical Co.* v. *John D. Park and Sons Co.,* 220 U.S. 373 (1911).

[19]If some neighboring retailers complain to a manufacturer that retailer X is shirking on service and is cutting prices, and the manufacturer subsequently terminates that retailer, does that constitute evidence of a RPM scheme? In *Monsanto Co.* v. *Spray-Rite Service Corp.,* 465 U.S. 752 (1984), and *Business Electronics Corp.* v. *Sharp Electronics Corp.,* 485 U.S. 717 (1988), the Supreme Court declared that more than just this fact pattern would be necessary for conviction.

[20]*State Oil* v. *Khan,* 188 S. Ct. 145 (1997).

[21]See *Albrecht* v. *Harold,* 390 U.S. 145 (1968).

[22]It is noteworthy that the DOJ and the Federal Trade Commission (FTC) entered a joint amicus brief in the *State Oil* case, urging this outcome.

[23]See *White Motor Co.* v. *U.S.,* 372 U.S. 253 (1963).

practices as per se offenses.[24] In 1977, however, the court reversed itself again and declared in *GTE-Sylvania*[25] that these practices should be judged under the rule of reason.[26] The Court's position on this issue has remained unchanged since then.

Other Non-Price Restraints

Until the mid-1970s the Supreme Court and the enforcement agencies were generally hostile toward tying, exclusive dealing, and other non-price vertical restraints. In 1949, for example, the Court declared that "tying agreements serve hardly any purpose beyond the suppression of competition,"[27] and in 1958 it declared tying to be a per se offense.[28] Long-term contracts, requirements contracts, and other restraints were routinely found to be illegal by the courts, largely based on their "restrictive" nature.

Since the 1970s, however, the approaches of the courts and the enforcement agencies have become more sophisticated. The Supreme Court has added successive exceptions and evidentiary burdens to plaintiffs' efforts to win a tying case (but the Court still maintains that tying is a per se offense),[29] and the other non-price restraints are judged under the rule of reason. The Supreme Court clearly stepped back from this trend in its *Kodak*[30] decision. But as the discussion in Case 17 by Jeffrey MacKie-Mason and John Metzler in Part IV indicates, the decision involved Kodak's motion for summary judgment,[31] and not the explicit merits of tying, and the Court considered sophisticated economic arguments from both sides before reaching its decision.

The enforcement agencies have moved away from a formalistic focus on "restrictions" and "foreclosure" and instead have focused their attention on those practices that seem likely to raise rivals' costs or raise barriers to entry. For example:

- The DOJ's first investigation and consent decree with Microsoft in 1995 (Gilbert 1999) focused on Microsoft's practices that raised barriers to

---

[24]See *U.S.* v. *Arnold, Schwinn and Co. et al.,* 388 U.S. 365 (1967).

[25]*Continental T.V.* v. *GTE Sylvania,* 433 U.S. 36 (1977).

[26]A discussion of this case, and the cases that led up to it, can be found in Preston (1994).

[27]*Standard Oil Co. of California* v. *U.S.,* 337 U.S. 293, 305–306 (1949).

[28]See *Northern Pacific Railway Co.* v. *U.S.,* 365 U.S. 1 (1958).

[29]In its unanimous dismissal of a tying case in 1984, the Court barely failed (by a 5-4 vote) to eliminate tying's per se treatment and adopt a rule of reason approach. See *Jefferson Parish Hospital District No. 2* v. *Edwin G. Hyde,* 466 U.S. 2 (1984).

[30]*Eastman Kodak Co.* v. *Image Technical Service, Inc., et al.,* 504 U.S. 451 (1992).

[31]In essence, Kodak was arguing that even if all of the facts alleged by the plaintiffs were true, the plaintiffs as a matter of law could not win their case. The Supreme Court decided that Kodak had not sufficiently supported that claim.

entry in PC operating systems; the DOJ's subsequent challenge to Microsoft, which is discussed in Case 19 by Daniel Rubinfeld in Part IV, focused on Microsoft's efforts to protect its market power in PC operating systems by raising rivals' costs.

- The FTC's dispute with Intel, discussed in Case 14 by Carl Shapiro in this part, featured the FTC's concerns that Intel's refusals to share intellectual property could raise barriers to entry.

- The FTC's prosecution of Toys "R" Us, discussed in Case 15 by F. M. Scherer in this part, highlighted the agency's concern that Toys "R" Us's actions (insisting on preferential treatment by toy manufacturers) raised rivals' costs.

- The DOJ's suit against Visa and MasterCard in 1998 involved the agency's concerns that the two card associations' prohibitions on their member banks' issuing any other credit cards except Visa and MasterCard raised rivals' costs and barriers to entry.[32]

- In 1999 the DOJ sued Dentsply International, Inc., a manufacturer of artificial teeth, claiming that its policy of refusing to sell its teeth to dealers that carried other manufacturers' teeth raised rivals' costs (Katz 2002). Dentsply's motion for summary judgment was denied in 2001,[33] and a trial on the merits was held in the spring of 2002.

In sum, vertical relationships are unlikely any time soon to be a settled area of economics or of antitrust law.[34] As we argued above, vertical arrangements between firms are always situationally specific. And if changes in technology or consumer preferences or other environmental conditions lead a firm to decide to change its vertical arrangements, there may well be customers or suppliers or rivals who are disadvantaged by the change and feel aggrieved. Lawsuits may well follow, and there will almost always be credible efficiency arguments that can be offered to counterbalance any anticompetitive claims. Creative economic theorizing about the pluses and minuses of vertical arrangements will surely continue. And a set of economically sound principles for delineating markets in such cases, so as to make sensible judgments about the presence or absence of market power, are absent.

Vertical arrangements will remain a rich stew indeed.

---

[32]The DOJ also sued to restrict the practice of banks that were major issuers of one card brand having a representative on the board of governors of the other card brand's association. In 2001 the DOJ won its claim as to the restrictive card issuances but lost on the governance issue. See *U.S.* v. *Visa U.S.A., et al.,* 163 F. Supp. 2d 322 (2001).

[33]See *U.S.* v. *Dentsply International, Inc.,* Memorandum Opinion, March 30, 2001.

[34]As MacKie-Mason and Metzler point out, the *Kodak* case alone has been followed by seven circuit court opinions on similar issues, with deeply divided results.

REFERENCES

Besen, Stanley M., E. Jane Murdoch, Daniel P. O'Brien, Steven C. Salop, and John Woodbury. "Vertical and Horizontal Ownership in Cable TV: Time Warner-Turner (1996)." In *The Antitrust Revolution: Economics, Competition, and Policy,* 3d edn., edited by John E. Kwoka, Jr. and Lawrence J. White, 452–475. New York: Oxford University Press, 1999.

Carlton, Dennis W., and Michael Waldman. "The Strategic Use of Tying to Preserve and Create Market Power in Evolving Industries." *RAND Journal of Economics* 33 (Summer 2002): 194–220.

Chen, Yongmin. "On Vertical Mergers and Their Competitive Effects." *RAND Journal of Economics* 32 (Winter 2001): 667–685.

Choi, Jay Pil, and Christopher Stefanidis. "Tying, Investment, and the Dynamic Leverage Theory." *RAND Journal of Economics* 32 (Spring 2001): 52–71.

Coase, Ronald H. "The Nature of the Firm." *Economica* 4 (November 1937): 386–405.

Comanor, William S., and Patrick Rey. "Competition Policy toward Vertical Foreclosure in a Global Economy." *International Business Lawyer* 23 (November 1995): 465–468.

Comanor, William S., and Patrick Rey. "Competition Policy towards Vertical Restraints in Europe and the United States." *Empirica* 24 (No. 1–2 1997): 27–52.

Katz, Michael L. "Vertical Contractual Relations." In *Handbook of Industrial Organization,* edited by Richard Schmalensee and Robert Willig, 655–721. Amsterdam: North-Holland, 1989.

Katz, Michael L. "Recent Antitrust Enforcement Actions by the U.S. Department of Justice: A Selective Survey of Economic Issues." *Review of Industrial Organization* 21 (December 2002): 373–397.

Kwoka, John E., Jr., "Output and Allocative Efficiency under Second Degree Price Discrimination." *Economic Inquiry* 22 (April 1984): 282–286.

Nelson, Philip B., and Robert D. Stoner. "Defense Industry Rationalization: Lockheed Martin (1995)." In *The Antitrust Revolution: Economics, Competition, and Policy,* 3d edn., edited by John E. Kwoka, Jr. and Lawrence J. White, 430–451. New York: Oxford University Press, 1999.

Noll, Roger G., and Bruce M. Owen. "The Anticompetitive Uses of Regulation: *United States* v. *AT&T* (1982)." In *The Antitrust Revolution: The Role of Economics,* 2d edn., edited by John E. Kwoka, Jr. and Lawrence J. White, 328–375. New York: HarperCollins, 1994.

Perry, Martin K. "Vertical Integration: Determinants and Effects." In *Handbook of Industrial Organization,* edited by Richard Schmalensee and Robert Willig, 183–255. Amsterdam: North-Holland, 1989.

Preston, Lee E. "Territorial Restraints: *GTE Sylvania* (1977)." In *The Antitrust Revolution: The Role of Economics,* 2nd edn., edited by John E. Kwoka, Jr. and Lawrence J. White, 311–327. New York: HarperCollins, 1994.

Schmalensee, Richard. "Output and Welfare Implications of Monopolistic Third-Degree Price Discrimination." *American Economic Review* 71 (March 1981): 242–247.

Telser, Lester G. "Why Should Manufacturers Want Fair Trade?" *Journal of Law & Economics* 3 (October 1960): 86–105.

Tirole, Jean, *The Theory of Industrial Organization.* Cambridge, Mass.: MIT Press, 1988.

White, Lawrence J. "Vertical Restraints in Antitrust Law: A Coherent Model." *Antitrust Bulletin* 26 (Summer 1981): 327–345.

White, Lawrence J. "Antitrust and Video Markets: The Merger of Showtime and The Movie Channel as a Case Study." In *Video Media Competition: Regulation, Economics, and Technology,* edited by Eli M. Noam, 338–363. New York: Columbia University Press, 1985.

White, Lawrence J. "The Revolution in Antitrust Analysis of Vertical Relationships: How Did We Get from There to Here?" In *Economics and Antitrust Policy,* edited by Robert J. Larner and James W. Meehan, 103–121. New York: Quorum, 1989.

White, Lawrence J. "Present at the Beginning of a New Era for Antitrust: Reflections on 1982–1983." *Review of Industrial Organization* 16 (March 2000): 131–149.

Williamson, Oliver E. "Credible Commitments: Using Hostages to Support Exchange." *American Economic Review* 73 (September 1983): 519–540.

CASE 13

Revisiting Maximum Resale Price Maintenance: *State Oil* v. *Khan* (1997)

Gustavo E. Bamberger

INTRODUCTION

State Oil, a distributor of gasoline, entered into a three-year gasoline supply agreement with Barkat Khan in January 1992. By the terms of the supply agreement, Khan was required to purchase all of his gasoline from State Oil. The supply agreement also effectively established the *maximum* retail price that Khan could charge for gasoline. After Khan's business failed, he sued State Oil, claiming that the supply contract constituted an illegal maximum vertical price-fixing agreement.

The dispute between Khan and State Oil eventually reached the Seventh Circuit Court of Appeals and the Supreme Court. The court of appeals ruled that State Oil's contract with Khan was illegal under the appropriate Supreme Court precedent from 1968, *Albrecht* v. *Herald Co.,* 390 U.S. 145. But the court of appeals strongly criticized the 1968 decision, and encouraged the Supreme Court to overturn it. The Supreme Court took the opportunity presented to it by the State Oil–Khan dispute to reexamine *Albrecht,* and agreed with the court of appeals that the earlier case had been decided incorrectly. As a result, *Albrecht* was overturned, and contracts between a distributor and a retailer that specify a maximum retail price are no longer always illegal.

Antitrust claims in the United States are decided under one of two standards, typically referred to as "per se" or "rule-of-reason." Although in practice the distinction between per se and rule-of-reason offenses often is

Bamberger submitted an expert report on behalf of Khan. The author thanks John Kwoka and Lawrence White for their helpful comments.

not sharp, a per se offense refers to conduct that courts have found is almost always anticompetitive—the classic example is horizontal price fixing by members of a cartel.[1] In the case of a per se violation, no defense is allowed for the practice, and a court does not need to investigate the competitive effects of the challenged practice.

In contrast, the rule of reason is used to investigate conduct that may or may not be anticompetitive. As the Seventh Circuit Court of Appeals has explained: "Challenged practices that do not fall within any of the per se categories are subject to the broader-ranging inquiry into effect and motives that goes by the name of the 'rule of reason' and that requires the plaintiff to prove that the defendant's conduct actually (or with a high likelihood) reduced competition."[2]

The treatment of "vertical" restrictions under U.S. antitrust law—for example, restrictions imposed by a manufacturer or distributor on its dealers—has long been unsettled and controversial. The antitrust treatment of exclusive territories (a form of non-price vertical restriction), for example, has varied over time. In *White Motor Company* v. *U.S.,* 372 U.S. 253 (1963), the Supreme Court ruled that territorial restrictions imposed by White Motor on its distributors should be evaluated under the rule of reason. But four years later, in *U.S.* v. *Arnold, Schwinn & Company,* 388 U.S. 365 (1967), the Supreme Court ruled that exclusive territories were per se illegal—according to the Court, the use of such restrictions was "so obviously destructive of competition that their mere existence is enough." In *Continental TV* v. *GTE Sylvania Inc.,* 433 U.S. 36 (1977), the Supreme Court overruled its prior *Schwinn* decision and reinstituted the rule of reason for exclusive territory cases.

Antitrust rulings in vertical price restriction cases have an even longer history. The Supreme Court first addressed the issue in *Dr. Miles Medical Co.* v. *John D. Park & Sons Company,* 220 U.S. 373 (1911). *Dr. Miles* involved the practice of "resale price maintenance," in which a manufacturer typically specifies the *minimum* price that a distributor or retailer can charge for the manufacturer's product. In *Dr. Miles,* the Supreme Court found that such vertical contracts were per se illegal. Congressional legislation in 1937 and 1951, however, allowed states to pass "fair trade" laws, under which resale price maintenance was allowed. These laws were repealed in 1975, and resale price maintenance has been per se illegal since then.[3]

---

[1]Even horizontal price-fixing agreements may escape per se treatment. In *U.S.* v. *Brown University, et al.,* for example, the Court of Appeals for the Third Circuit ruled that a horizontal pricing agreement between nonprofit institutions should be evaluated under the rule of reason; see the discussion in Case 7 by Gustavo Bamberger and Dennis Carlton in Part II.

[2]*Khan* v. *State Oil,* 93 F.3d 1358 (7th Cir. 1996), at 1361.

[3]See Carlton and Perloff (2000, at 637–639) for a brief discussion of antitrust rulings in exclusive territory and resale price maintenance cases.

The Supreme Court also addressed the use of *maximum* prices in vertical agreements. *Albrecht* v. *Herald Co.,* 390 U.S. 145 (1968) examined contracts between the publisher of the *St. Louis Globe-Democrat* and newspaper distributors. The *Globe-Democrat* provided its distributors with exclusive territories for the home delivery of newspapers, and specified the maximum retail price that a distributor could charge. The Supreme Court ruled that the contract constituted a vertical price-fixing agreement and was thus a per se violation of Section 1 of the Sherman Act.

The Court's *Albrecht* decision was widely criticized for years. In the 1970s, for example, Robert Bork (1993, p. 281), in his criticism of several of the Supreme Court's rulings in vertical price restriction cases, complained that "the Supreme Court has even gone so far as to declare per se illegal a manufacturer's attempt to fix *maximum* resale prices. . . . There could, of course, be no anticonsumer effect from such price fixing." Similarly, Richard Posner (1976, p. 157)—who would later play a key role in *State Oil* v. *Khan*—commented that "[i]t is difficult to understand what proper antitrust question is raised by [the defendant's conduct in *Albrecht*]." Notwithstanding these criticisms, *Albrecht* remained the law of the land until the Supreme Court's *State Oil Co.* v. *Khan* decision.

In the following sections, I first summarize the factual background of the dispute between State Oil and Khan. I then review the history of the case; I also discuss the antitrust treatment of vertical maximum price restrictions in the light of *State Oil* v. *Khan.* Finally, I revisit *State Oil* v. *Khan* in the context of a rule-of-reason analysis.

BACKGROUND

In January 1992, State Oil entered into a three-year lease with Barkat Khan for the operation of a gasoline station/convenience store in Addison, Illinois, a western suburb of Chicago located in DuPage County; at the same time, Khan agreed to be exclusively supplied with gasoline by State Oil. By the terms of the supply agreement, the wholesale price paid by Khan to State Oil was determined in relation to a recommended retail price established by State Oil:

> The Landlord [State Oil] shall charge the Tenant [Khan] for each transport of gasoline at the recommended retail pump price less margin and sales tax. The Tenant's margin will be $0.0325 (three and $\frac{1}{4}$ cents) per gallon. In the event the Tenant elects to sell at retail at a price in excess of the recommended retail pump price established by the Landlord, the Tenant shall pay the Landlord a sum equal to the difference between the retail pump price at which the gasoline in question has been sold, and the recommended retail pump price established by the Landlord multiplied by the number of gallons sold. In the event the Tenant elects to sell at a retail

pump price below the recommended retail pump price established by the
Landlord, the Tenant shall not be entitled to a reduction in price to cover
the difference.[4]

Thus, if Khan sold gasoline at a price higher than the recommended retail
price, his margin would nonetheless equal 3.25 cents per gallon; if Khan set
a price below the recommended retail price, his margin would be less than
3.25 cents per gallon. As a result, Khan could earn at most 3.25 cents per
gallon on his gasoline sales.

In addition to the margin he earned from the sale of gasoline, Khan
also earned a margin on convenience store sales. In 1992, Khan's gross
margin from convenience store sales accounted for about 65 percent of the
total gross margin he received from operating the gasoline station/conve-
nience store.[5]

Pursuant to his lease with State Oil, Khan had to make a monthly payment to State Oil. By the end of 1992, Khan was not able to meet his lease
obligations. At the end of January 1993, State Oil terminated Khan's lease
and petitioned a state court to appoint a receiver to operate the former Khan
location. A receiver was appointed and ran the station until September
1993.

The receiver was an experienced operator of gasoline stations who did
not consider himself bound by the terms of Khan's supply contract with
State Oil. By the beginning of May 1993, he had decided to set retail prices
so that he received a lower margin on sales of regular gasoline but a higher
margin on sales of premium gasoline.[6] He believed that by doing so, he
would increase traffic through the gasoline station and convenience store
and receive a higher average margin per gallon of gasoline sold. That is, he
expected the demand for regular gasoline to be more elastic than the demand for premium gasoline.[7] As a result, he expected to increase total gasoline and convenience store sales.

Information on the receiver's retail price and margin per gallon by type
of gasoline was not maintained. However, information was retained on gallon sales by type of gasoline, and average margin per gallon. This evidence
suggested that the receiver's new pricing policy was successful. First, as expected, sales of regular gasoline as a percentage of total gasoline sales increased substantially. For example, during the five-month period May to
September 1992—when Khan operated the station—regular gasoline sales

---

[4]Quoted in "Memorandum in Support of Plaintiffs' Motion for Summary Judgment on Count II,"
Barkat U. Khan and Khan & Associates, Inc. v. *State Oil Company,* in the United States District
Court for the Northern District of Illinois, Eastern Division, Case No. 94 C 00035.

[5]Based on Khan's U.S. Corporate Income Tax Return for 1992.

[6]Khan and the receiver each sold three types of gasoline—regular, premium and "mid-grade." Relatively little mid-grade gasoline was sold; the receiver set the same margin on mid-grade and premium. For the purpose of my discussion, I combine mid-grade and premium (into premium).

[7]My description of the receiver's actions are based on a discussion with the receiver.

accounted for about 55 percent of total gallons sold; one year later, during the five-month period May to September 1993—after the receiver stopped pricing so as to earn 3.25 cents per gallon of gasoline sold—regular gasoline sales were about 68 percent of the total. Second, total gasoline sales were 20.8 percent higher in May–September 1993 than in May–September 1992.[8]

The available evidence indicated that the 20.8 percent increase in gasoline sales was attributable, in part, to the receiver's revised pricing. According to the receiver, there were no substantial changes in competitive conditions between 1992 and 1993—e.g., no gasoline stations were closed during 1993 in the immediate vicinity of the former Khan location. However, total demand in the area for gasoline apparently was higher in 1993 than in 1992. The Illinois Department of Revenue reports monthly gasoline sales by county, and that information showed that gasoline sales in DuPage County were 11.6 percent higher in May through September 1993 than in the comparable five-month period in 1992. Thus, the receiver's sales increased by a substantially higher percentage than sales in the county in which the station was located.[9]

Finally, the overall margin earned by the receiver on all sales of gasoline for the May through September 1993 period was 3.82 cents per gallon, or 17.5 percent higher than the maximum that Khan could have received under the terms of his supply contract with State Oil. This increase in the overall average margin shows that the receiver's increase in margin (i.e., more than 3.25 cents per gallon) for sales of premium gasoline must have been substantially higher than the receiver's reduction in margin for regular gasoline sales.

HISTORY OF THE CASE

District Court

Khan brought suit against State Oil in Federal District Court, claiming that the supply contract between Khan and State Oil violated Section 1 of the Sherman Antitrust Act.[10] Khan did not argue that the supply contract was illegal because it resulted in an anticompetitive harm, such as higher prices to consumers. Instead, Khan argued that the contract was a "clear-cut case

---

[8]The statistics in the text are derived from financial records provided by Khan and the receiver and were reported in a damage analysis filed on behalf of Khan.

[9]The former Khan location accounted for only a small percentage of total sales in DuPage County. Information for smaller areas (e.g., Addison, Illinois, the town in which the gasoline station was located) was not available.

[10]The litigation at the District Court and Court of Appeals levels was *Khan* v. *State Oil.* Because State Oil appealed the Court of Appeals verdict to the Supreme Court, the Supreme Court case is known as *State Oil* v. *Khan.* I refer to all of the litigation as *State Oil* v. *Khan.*

of vertical price fixing" and thus per se illegal.[11] In particular, Khan argued that the "recommended" retail price was effectively a maximum price because Khan would have no economic incentive to charge more than that price.

State Oil denied Khan's claim. First, it denied that the supply contract constituted vertical price fixing because under its terms Khan was free to charge any price he chose for gasoline. Second, it argued that even if the supply contract constituted vertical price fixing, it should be evaluated under the rule of reason, not under the per se standard. Furthermore, because Khan had failed to present any evidence that the contract was anticompetitive—as would be required in a rule-of-reason analysis—Khan's complaint should be dismissed.

The district court agreed with State Oil that the legality of the supply agreement should be evaluated under the rule of reason. Because Khan failed to provide any evidence that the supply contract had an adverse effect on competition, the district court granted State Oil's motion for summary judgment on Khan's price-fixing claim.

Court of Appeals

Khan appealed the district court's decision to the Seventh Circuit Court of Appeals. In a decision written by Chief Judge Richard Posner—who had criticized *Albrecht* twenty years earlier—the court of appeals overruled the district court. The court of appeals agreed with Khan that the supply agreement between State Oil and Khan constituted a vertical price-fixing agreement, and that vertical price-fixing agreements were per se illegal. The court of appeals based its conclusion that vertical maximum price-fixing was per se illegal on *Albrecht*. But the court of appeals also argued that *Albrecht* was mistaken and should be overturned.

The court of appeals began by investigating State Oil's claim that the supply agreement did not set a maximum retail price because Khan was allowed to charge a higher price so long as he turned over any proceeds that reflected a greater than 3.25 cent per gallon margin to State Oil. The court of appeals was not convinced by the State Oil claim:

> State Oil . . . denies that the provision in the contract pertaining to Khan's charging a price above the suggested retail price is a form of price fixing. It points out that Khan was free to charge as high a price as he wishes. This is true in the sense that it would not have been a breach of contract for Khan to raise his price. But the contract made it worthless for him to do so. . . . Generally when a seller raises his price, his volume falls; and if his profit on each unit sold is frozen, the effect of his raising

---

[11]"Memorandum in Support of Plaintiffs' Motion for Summary Judgment on Count II," at 3.

price will be that he loses revenue: he will sell fewer units, at the same profit per unit.[12]

The court of appeals concluded that "State Oil engaged in price fixing."

The court of appeals then turned to whether maximum price fixing is illegal per se. The court of appeals noted that a distributor (e.g., State Oil) may want to impose a maximum retail price on a dealer (e.g., Khan) for pro-competitive reasons. For example, if State Oil granted Khan an exclusive territory—so as to encourage more efficient marketing—and Khan thereby gained some measure of market power, a maximum retail price could prevent Khan from exploiting that market power.[13] State Oil would not share in any of the proceeds generated by an exercise of market power by Khan—indeed, such an exercise of market power would harm State Oil by reducing the amount of gasoline it sold to Khan. Thus, State Oil would have an incentive to constrain the exercise of market power by Khan through the use of a maximum retail price. In this case, State Oil's incentives would be aligned with those of consumers.

But the court argued that despite the potential pro-competitive explanations for setting a maximum retail price

> the Supreme Court has thus far refused to reexamine the cases in which it has held that resale price fixing is illegal per se regardless of the competitive position of the price fixer or whether the price fixed is a floor or a ceiling. The key precedent so far as the present case is concerned is *Albrecht v. Herald Company* . . . , a damages suit like this where the Court held over a vigorous dissent that the action of a newspaper publisher in fixing a ceiling at which its distributors could resell the newspaper to the public was illegal per se.[14]

Although State Oil argued that *Albrecht* was no longer the view of the Supreme Court, the court of appeals rejected State Oil's position. Instead, the court of appeals concluded that the district court had erred and that Khan's "antitrust claim should not have been dismissed."[15]

But the court of appeals made clear that it believed that *Albrecht* was bad antitrust law:

> [D]espite all its infirmities, its increasingly wobbly, moth-eaten foundations. . . . *Albrecht* has not been expressly overruled. . . . And the Supreme Court has told the lower federal courts, in increasingly emphatic, even strident, terms, not to anticipate an overruling of a decision by the Court; we are to leave the overruling to the Court itself. . . . *Albrecht*

---

[12]*Khan* v. *State Oil,* 93 F.3d 1358 (7th Cir. 1996), at 1360.

[13]Khan did not claim that he had been granted an exclusive territory by State Oil.

[14]*Khan* v. *State Oil,* 93 F.3d 1358 (7th Cir. 1996), at 1362.

[15]*Khan* v. *State Oil,* 93 F.3d 1358 (7th Cir. 1996), at 1365.

was unsound when decided, and is inconsistent with later decisions by the Supreme Court. It should be overruled. Someday, we expect, it will be.[16]

Supreme Court

Not surprisingly—given the court of appeals' unambiguous encouragement—State Oil appealed the Seventh Circuit's decision to the Supreme Court. In its decision, the Supreme Court accepted the court of appeals' analysis, and took up its invitation to reconsider *Albrecht.* In a unanimous decision, the Supreme Court overruled *Albrecht.*

The Court's analysis began by reviewing relevant Supreme Court precedents: "A review of this Court's decisions leading up to and beyond *Albrecht* is relevant to our assessment of the continuing validity of the *per se* rule established in *Albrecht.*"[17] The Court began with its *Dr. Miles* decision, in which it

> recognized the illegality of agreements under which manufacturers or suppliers set the minimum resale prices to be charged by their distributors. . . .
>
> In subsequent cases, the Court's attention turned to arrangements through which suppliers imposed restrictions on dealers with respect to matters other than resale price. In *White Motor Co. v. United States* [citation omitted], the Court considered the validity of a manufacturer's assignment of exclusive territories to its distributors and dealers. The Court determined that too little was known about the competitive impact of such vertical limitations to warrant treating them as *per se* unlawful. Four years later, in *United States v. Arnold, Schwinn & Co.* [citation omitted], the Court reconsidered the status of exclusive dealer territories and held that . . . a supplier's imposition of territorial restrictions on the distributor was "so obviously destructive of competition" as to constitute a *per se* violation of the Sherman Act.[18]

The *Albrecht* decision came in the year after *Schwinn,* and the Court noted that the *Albrecht* Court's ruling was influenced by prior decisions in *Schwinn* and related cases.

Nine years after *Albrecht,* the Court overruled *Schwinn* in *GTE Sylvania.* The Court explained that the *GTE Sylvania* decision was, in part, based on the widespread criticism of *Schwinn.* The Court also noted that the *GTE Sylvania* was informed by "scholarly works supporting the economic utility of vertical nonprice restraints."[19]

---

[16]*Khan* v. *State Oil,* 93 F.3d 1358 (7th Cir. 1996), at 1363.

[17]*State Oil* v. *Khan,* 188 S. Ct. 275 (1997), at 279.

[18]*State Oil* v. *Khan,* 188 S. Ct. 275 (1997), at 279.

[19]*State Oil* v. *Khan,* 188 S. Ct. 275 (1997), at 280.

The Court recognized that *Albrecht* had been met with the same types of criticism as *Schwinn,* and again relied on such criticisms to overturn a precedent: "Thus, our reconsideration of *Albrecht*'s continuing validity is informed by several of our decisions, as well as a considerable body of scholarship discussing the effects of vertical restraints. . . . So informed, we find it difficult to maintain that vertically-imposed maximum prices could harm consumers or competition to the extent necessary to justify their *per se* invalidation."[20]

Thus, in *Schwinn,* the Supreme Court deemed a vertical restriction—the use of exclusive territories—per se illegal, but then overruled its precedent, based in large part on criticism of its prior decision by economists and antitrust scholars. Similarly, the Court characterized maximum retail price constraints as per se illegal in *Albrecht,* but used *State Oil* v. *Khan* to overrule its precedent, again based in large part on economics-based criticisms of the earlier decision.

In contrast, the per se illegality of minimum retail price constraints remains in place, although that standard also has been widely criticized—indeed, the same types of arguments that were directed at *Schwinn* and *Albrecht* have been used to criticize the Supreme Court's position in minimum price constraint cases. The *Khan* Court made clear, however, that it continues to distinguish between minimum and maximum vertical price restrictions, and that minimum vertical price restrictions remain illegal per se.[21]

VERTICAL MAXIMUM PRICE RESTRICTIONS AFTER *STATE OIL* v. *KHAN*

Although the Supreme Court abandoned the per se standard for vertical maximum price restrictions, it did not, however, go as far as clearing such restrictions of all antitrust scrutiny. In particular, it refused to adopt a standard of per se legality:

> In overruling *Albrecht,* we of course do not hold that all vertical maximum price fixing is *per se* lawful. Instead, vertical maximum price fixing, like the majority of commercial arrangements subject to the antitrust laws, should be evaluated under the rule of reason. In our view, rule-of-reason analysis will effectively identify those situations in which vertical maximum price fixing amounts to anticompetitive conduct.[22]

---

[20]*State Oil* v. *Khan,* 188 S. Ct. 275 (1997), at 282.

[21]See *State Oil* v. *Khan,* 188 S. Ct. 275 (1997), at 283.

[22]*State Oil* v. *Khan,* 188 S. Ct. 275 (1997), at 285.

Some commentators have criticized the Court's decision to apply the rule of reason to maximum vertical price restrictions. Blair and Lopatka (1998, p. 179), for example—whose prior writings on vertical restrictions were cited by the *Khan* Court—argue that

> [a]lthough Khan contributed significantly to sound antitrust policy, the decision is flawed. It replaced the rule of per se illegality, not with a rule of per se legality, but with the rule of reason. In the context of maximum vertical price fixing, a test of reasonableness makes little sense. The practice has no discernable anticompetitive consequences in any setting. Further, the content of the test is a mystery, and therefore its application is unpredictable.

In what circumstances could vertical maximum price fixing be found to be anticompetitive under the rule of reason? In its *Khan* decision, the Court referred to the justifications given for the per se treatment of maximum vertical price restrictions in the *Albrecht* decision, and argued that the conduct described in *Albrecht* "can be appropriately recognized and punished under the rule of reason."[23] Thus, the Court suggested that the anticompetitive explanations given for vertical maximum price restrictions in *Albrecht* could be the basis for a rule-of-reason finding of illegality. However, none of the Supreme Court's three *Albrecht* explanations seems likely to support a rule-of-reason-based finding of anticompetitive effect.

The first explanation of anticompetitive effect provided by *Albrecht* is that "[m]aximum prices may be fixed too low for the dealer to furnish services essential to the value which goods have for the consumer or to furnish services and conveniences which consumers desire and for which they are willing to pay."[24] But this argument implies that the manufacturer or distributor would take actions that were not in its self-interest. Indeed, the *Khan* Court recognized the flaw in this theory: "such conduct, by driving away customers, would seem likely to harm manufacturers as well as dealers and consumers, making it unlikely that a supplier would set such a price as a matter of business judgment."[25]

The second argument advanced by *Albrecht* is that "[m]aximum price fixing may channel distribution through a few large or specifically advantaged dealers who otherwise would be subject to significant nonprice competition."[26] This argument is similar to the first, and likely to be insufficient to support a finding of anticompetitive effect for the same reason—a manufacturer would not be expected to take actions that limit its dealer network, unless it were efficient to do so. Again, the *Khan* Court recognized the flaw

---

[23]*State Oil* v. *Khan,* 188 S. Ct. 275 (1997), at 283.

[24]*Albrecht* v. *Herald Co.,* 390 U.S. 145, at 152–3.

[25]*State Oil* v. *Khan,* 188 S. Ct. 275 (1997), at 283.

[26]*Albrecht* v. *Herald Co.,* 390 U.S. 145, at 153.

in *Albrecht*'s explanation: "It is unclear, however, that a supplier would profit from limiting its market by excluding potential dealers. . . . Further, although vertical maximum price fixing might limit the viability of inefficient dealers, that consequence is not necessarily harmful to competition and consumers."[27]

The final *Albrecht* explanation relies on converting a maximum vertical price restriction into a minimum vertical restriction. In particular, *Albrecht* argued that "if the actual price charged under a maximum price scheme is nearly always the fixed maximum price, which is increasingly likely as the maximum price approaches the actual cost of the dealer, the scheme tends to acquire all the attributes of an arrangement fixing minimum prices."[28] This explanation also seems unlikely to support a finding of anticompetitive effect in a rule-of-reason evaluation of a maximum vertical price-fixing claim.

If maximum vertical restrictions are in place, a dealer is not prevented from cutting price below the maximum. *Albrecht* avoided this difference between maximum and minimum prices by referring to situations in which "the maximum price approaches the actual cost of the dealer." Although it is correct that a dealer would typically have no incentive to cut its price if the maximum price imposed on it equaled the dealer's costs, there is, in general, little or no reason to be concerned about minimum price restrictions if the minimum price is set at or near cost. Thus, in a situation in which a minimum price could be objectionable—i.e., a minimum price substantially above dealer cost—the dealer whose maximum price is restricted could cut price, and a maximum vertical price restriction is unlikely to be equivalent to a minimum vertical price restriction.[29]

Other explanations not discussed by the Court could, however, provide a basis for such a finding that a maximum vertical price restriction could be anticompetitive. One potential antitrust attack on maximum vertical price restrictions was discussed by the court of appeals. The court of appeals notes that "[t]he difference between what a supplier charges his dealer and what the dealer charges the ultimate customer is, functionally, compensation to the dealer for performing the resale service."[30] That is, the margin that a dealer earns can be thought of as the "price" that the dealer charges for performing the resale function. Thus, by setting a maximum retail price, a manufacturer could reduce the "price" it pays for resale service, perhaps below the otherwise market-clearing price. If the manufacturer is competing with other manufacturers for dealers, this is an unprofitable strategy. But if a manufacturer is a monopolist, such a policy could reduce output of

---

[27]*State Oil* v. *Khan*, 188 S. Ct. 275 (1997), at 283.

[28]*Albrecht* v. *Herald Co.*, 390 U.S. 145, at 153.

[29]As I have discussed, there is widespread criticism of the Supreme Court's position that minimum vertical price restrictions are per se illegal.

[30]*Khan* v. *State Oil*, 93 F.3d 1358 (7th Cir. 1996), at 1361.

the final good, leading to higher prices, lower distribution costs, and higher profits for the manufacturer. That is, a monopolist manufacturer could exercise monopsony power over its dealers.

Although this explanation is correct as a matter of economic theory, it seems unlikely to be of practical importance in many, if not most, industries. The exercise of monopsony power would be possible only if a monopolist manufacturer faced an upward-sloping supply curve for buying dealer services. If not, the manufacturer could not reduce the price of dealer services.[31] But the supply curve of dealer services—at least in the long run—is unlikely to be upward sloping. As Blair and Lopatka (1998, pp. 161–162) explain:

> A positively sloped supply curve implies that the resources necessary to provide the services in question are specialized to the needs of the buyers under consideration. Thus, if the buyer demanded less, the supplier would not be able to shift to an alternative buyer. The resources necessary to provide distribution services, however, tend not to be specialized to the needs of the buyers under consideration. Thus, if the buyer demanded less, the supplier would not easily be able to shift to an alternative buyer. The resources necessary to provide distribution services, however, tend not to be specialized. If a single purchaser of some kind of distribution services attempted to depress price, dealers would switch to other buyers desiring the same kind of services; if a group of firms in the same industry conspired to offer a depressed price for distribution services, dealers would switch to buyers in other industries.

A different potential attack on such restrictions is provided by a recent analysis of the *Khan* decision. In it, Blair et al. (2000, p. 221) conclude that "one can unequivocally endorse jettisoning the *Albrecht* rule of per se illegality, and that the Supreme Court's decision to retain a rule of reason was correct. Allowing the pendulum to swing to per se legality as many economists seem to advocate would have been a mistake." The Blair et al. (2000) attack on maximum vertical price restrictions is based on a generalization of the "successive monopoly" model of vertical price restrictions.

A standard (pro-competitive) explanation for the use of maximum vertical price restrictions is that they can be used to solve the "successive monopoly" problem. Suppose that a manufacturer has market power and that the demand for its product can be increased by the provision of dealer services. To encourage the provision of these services, the manufacturer may choose to award exclusive territories, so as to prevent one dealer from free-riding on the promotional efforts of another dealer. But by creating exclu-

---

[31]In general, the exercise of monopsony power requires an upward-sloping supply curve. Carlton and Perloff (2000, p. 107), for example, explain that "[l]ong-run monopsony power is impossible if the long-run supply curve is flat, because then price cannot be lowered below the competitive price."

sive territories, the manufacturer creates market power for its distributors. To prevent the exercise of market power by its dealers, the manufacturer uses maximum vertical price restrictions.

Blair et al. (2000) develop a model in which the dealer chooses the retail price and a level of service provision. They assume that the manufacturer cannot control the amount of service provided by dealers. By imposing vertical price restrictions, the manufacturer can prevent the exercise of market power by its dealers. But the dealers may respond to the reduction in retail price by reducing the provision of service—because each additional sale becomes less profitable if retail price is constrained, the dealer's incentive to provide service is reduced.

Because a reduction in dealer services will tend to reduce consumer demand, and the reduction in retail price will tend to increase consumer demand, Blair et al. (2000, p. 217) argue that the net effect of maximum vertical price restrictions is ambiguous: "Absent service at the distributor stage, maximum resale price restraints always lead to an increase in output. When we generalize the model to include service by the distributor, however, the effect on output is ambiguous." Blair et al. (2000) argue that because consumer welfare increases as output increases, a rule-of-reason approach to maximum vertical price constraints implies an "output test"—if output increases as a result of imposing a maximum retail price, the practice is pro-competitive; but if output declines, the imposition of maximum retail prices should be condemned under the rule of reason.[32]

STATE OIL v. KHAN REVISITED

In addition to overruling *Albrecht,* the Supreme Court remanded *State Oil* v. *Khan* to the court of appeals "for consideration of whether State Oil's maximum price-fixing violated the Sherman Act under the 'Rule of Reason,' as distinct from the per se rule."[33] But Khan elected not to provide a rule-of-reason analysis, and the court of appeals considered the argument waived. Instead, Khan argued that the price restrictions in the supply contract he signed with State Oil should be considered minimum price restrictions and thus per se illegal. The court of appeals concluded that Khan's argument was "plainly without merit" and thus remanded the suit to the district court with directions to dismiss the suit.

But what would a rule-of-reason investigation have shown if one had been conducted? It is clear that lifting the vertical price restrictions had an economic effect—the receiver's average margin and total sales increased.

---

[32] The Blair et al. (2000) model assumes that the upstream firm is a monopolist. It is unclear whether the authors would apply their output test in a situation where the firm that imposes the vertical restrictions competes with other upstream firms.

[33] *Khan* v. *State Oil,* 143 F.3d 362 (7th Cir. 1998), at 363.

What is less clear is why State Oil would impose a policy that reduced its total sales.[34] Klein (1999) provides one possible explanation. Klein explains that State Oil may receive a higher (wholesale) margin per gallon of premium gasoline than per gallon of regular gasoline. If that were the case, State Oil would be interested not only in the total amount of gasoline it sold to Khan, but in the mix of those sales between regular and premium gasoline. In particular, State Oil would want to sell a relatively high percentage of premium gasoline and would want to prevent Khan from charging a high price for premium. That is, "the dealer's shift in gasoline demand towards regular and away from premium hurts the gasoline supplier by producing a mix of premium and regular gasoline sales that is not jointly profit maximizing [i.e., does not maximize the joint profits of State Oil and Khan]" (Klein 1999, p. 56).

Evaluating the competitive effect of the vertical maximum price restrictions imposed on Khan is complicated by the fact that Khan was selling two products—regular and premium—that were affected differently by the imposition of the price restrictions. Ignoring the different demands for the two products leads to the apparently anomalous finding that lifting the vertical restrictions resulted in both an increase in price (i.e., the average dealer margin increased) and an increase in total output.

Were the State Oil maximum vertical price restrictions anticompetitive because they resulted in lower sales of regular gasoline (although higher sales of premium gasoline)? Other contractual practices not generally condemned by the antitrust laws can harm one group of consumers and benefit a second. To take a closely related example, consider the case of territorial restrictions adopted to encourage dealer services such as the provision of information. Territorial restrictions that result in additional information to consumers also can shift a dealer's sales mix. By increasing the amount of information available to potential consumers, the policy will presumably tend to increase the sales of products for which information is relatively more important (e.g., those that are more complicated) at the expense of products for which information is less important. If the territorial restrictions lead to higher retail prices for all products, then the restrictions could harm consumers who buy products for which information is not important and benefit consumers who buy information-intensive products. This type of shift in sales mix can be profitable for the manufacturer if its margin on information-intensive products is higher than for other products.

A rule-of-reason analysis generally will not condemn territorial restrictions of the type in my previous example (especially if the manufacturer imposing the restrictions is one of many competing in a market). Thus,

---

[34]Because convenience store sales were important to profitability, Khan could have reduced the margin on regular gasoline sales even if he were constrained to a 3.25 cents per gallon margin on premium sales. Presumably, he could have increased his total sales even more than the receiver. Whether this would have been a more profitable strategy than pricing so as to receive a 3.25 cent margin on every gallon sold is not clear from the available evidence. See Klein (1999, p. 55).

condemning the same type of result—that is, a vertical restriction that led to higher sales of one product but lower sales of a second—under the rule of reason because it was generated by a vertical price restriction instead of a vertical non-price restriction would create an inconsistency in the treatment of the two types of restrictions with no basis in economics.

CONCLUSION

The per se illegality of vertical restrictions has long been criticized by economists because economists have shown that these practices often benefit consumers. Largely as a result of such criticism, the per se illegality of exclusive territories—a vertical non-price restriction—was replaced by a rule-of-reason treatment of the practice in 1977. Almost twenty years later, the Supreme Court used *State Oil* v. *Khan* to further narrow the range of vertical practices that are per se illegal. The Supreme Court's decision to overrule a prior decision was again largely based on economic analysis of the prior ruling. It is unclear how these practices will be analyzed under the rule of reason, however, because the Supreme Court provided little guidance on how maximum vertical price restrictions could be shown to have an anticompetitive effect.

The *State Oil* decision also is important because of what it did not do: Despite the criticisms by economists that have long been made of the per se treatment of minimum vertical price restrictions, the Supreme Court used *State Oil* v. *Khan* to reaffirm explicitly its view that such restrictions remain per se illegal. Thus, the Supreme Court has not fully accepted the economic analysis of its earlier rulings on vertical restrictions.

REFERENCES

Blair, Roger, James Fesmire, and Richard Romano. "Applying the Rule of Reason to Maximum Resale Price Fixing: *Albrecht* Overruled." In *Industrial Organization: Advances in Applied Microeconomics,* vol. 9, edited by Michael R. Baye. New York: JAI Press, 2000.

Blair, Roger, and John Lopatka. "The *Albrecht* Rule after *Khan:* Death Becomes Her." *Notre Dame Law Review* 74 (October 1998): 123–179.

Bork, Robert. *The Antitrust Paradox: A Policy at War with Itself.* New York: Free Press, 1993.

Carlton, Dennis, and Jeffrey Perloff. *Modern Industrial Organization,* 3rd edn. Reading, Mass.: Addison Wesley Longman, 2000.

Klein, Benjamin. "Distribution Restrictions Operate by Creating Dealer Profits: Explaining the Use of Maximum Resale Price Maintenance in *State Oil v. Khan.*" In

Supreme Court Economic Review, vol. 7, edited by Ernest Gellhorn and Larry Ribstein. Chicago: University of Chicago Press, 1999.

Posner, Richard. *Antitrust Law: An Economic Perspective.* Chicago: University of Chicago Press, 1976.

CASE 14

Technology Cross-Licensing Practices: *FTC* v. *Intel* (1999)

Carl Shapiro

INTRODUCTION

When do hardball negotiating tactics constitute violations of the antitrust laws? Consider the following fact pattern, which reflects real-world events during the 1997–1998 time frame:

> Intel is the leading manufacturing of high-end microprocessors, the brains of personal computers and workstations. Intergraph Corporation makes computer workstations that use Intel's microprocessors. Intel gives Intergraph, a valued customer, access to Intel's trade secrets (which are very useful when building computers based on Intel's chips) and advance samples of new Intel microprocessors.

> Intergraph sues Intel, asserting that Intel's microprocessors infringe on Intergraph's patents. As negotiations fail, the relationship between Intel and Intergraph deteriorates. Intel withdraws the special benefits that Intergraph had been enjoying. Intergraph asserts that Intel has monopoly power over the supply of microprocessors, that Intel's withdrawal of these benefits will greatly damage Intergraph's business, and that Intel's conduct is anti-competitive. Intel claims that its commercial response to Intergraph's lawsuit does not harm competition in any relevant market and that the Courts should not intervene to favor Intergraph in their patent dispute.

Is Intel's conduct anticompetitive and thus illegal under the antitrust laws? That is the central question explored in this chapter.

The author served as an expert witness of behalf of Intel in the litigation brought by the FTC against Intel, which is the subject of this case study. The views expressed here are those of the author alone and should not be attributed in any way to the Intel Corporation.

After an investigation lasting several months, in June 1998 the Federal Trade Commission (FTC) brought an antitrust lawsuit against Intel Corporation based on Intel's conduct toward Intergraph, and similar conduct toward Digital Equipment Corporation and Compaq, all in the context of disputes where Intel was accused of patent infringement. The FTC charged that Intel's practices were an abuse of Intel's monopoly position in microprocessors.[1] The Chairman of the FTC described the FTC's case against Intel as "one of the most widely noted antitrust enforcement actions involving intellectual property" (Pitofsky 2001).

The case attracted enormous media attention, in part because it took place contemporaneously with the Justice Department's monopolization case against Microsoft. Commentators asked whether the FTC was heading in a whole new direction with antitrust, since Intel's conduct was directed primarily at its *customers* rather than at its competitors, the normal (direct) victims in monopolization cases (Weinstein 1998, 1999). The FTC and Intel settled their dispute in March 1999, literally on the eve of trial. The FTC's case against Intel, in conjunction with a related private lawsuit described below, helped to define the antitrust limits on what dominant firms can do to gain competitive advantage using their intellectual property.

The next section provides some background for the case by discussing the tension between intellectual property rights and antitrust law, a tension that is evident in the FTC's dispute with Intel, and by describing the role of patents in the semiconductor industry. Subsequent sections provide a succinct summary of the facts surrounding Intel's conduct in each of the three patent disputes identified by the FTC; explain the FTC's theory of how Intel's conduct was anticompetitive; present Intel's response; and describe the settlement reached between the FTC and Intel. The final section discusses legal and economic developments since the case was settled and remarks on the lasting implications of the Intel case.

THE ROLE OF PATENTS IN THE SEMICONDUCTOR INDUSTRY

The FTC's case against Intel is first and foremost a case about *intellectual property and antitrust:* where do intellectual property rights end and antitrust limits begin? Before we turn to the antitrust issues that are central to the Intel case, we must first understand the role of patents, both in general and in the semiconductor industry.

---

[1]The FTC's website contains a trove of information about the case; see www.ftc.gov/alj/D9288/index.htm.

The Tension between Intellectual Property Rights and Antitrust

Patents, copyrights, and trade secrets—the primary forms of intellectual property—play an increasingly central role in our economy. Many companies consider their intellectual property to comprise their corporate crown jewels. Pharmaceutical companies place great value on the patents that protect their blockbuster new drugs. Hollywood is tireless in defending its copyrighted movies and music from unauthorized use. Microsoft zealously guards the copyrighted source code for its Windows and Office software. IBM earns substantial revenues each year by licensing its patents and trade secrets. Intel attaches enormous value on the patents that it has obtained, and the trade secrets it controls, in the semiconductor field.

The central role played by intellectual property reflects the fact that economic growth is often driven by innovation, and corporate competitive advantage often results from research and development (R&D) activities that give rise to patents, trade secrets, or copyrights. Large companies such as Microsoft and Intel invest billions of dollars each year in R&D.

Strong or dominant companies increasingly rely on intellectual property rights to earn a return on their R&D investments and to protect their market positions. Under these conditions, the tension that has always existed between intellectual property law—which grants innovators certain rights to exclude others from practicing their inventions—and antitrust law—which seeks to limit monopoly power and to promote competition— has become more visible and more important to our economy. As noted by Shapiro and Varian (1999), the proper treatment of intellectual property rights under the antitrust laws has become a more pressing and more central policy topic as we move into the "Information Age." Gilbert and Tom (2001) document that innovation and intellectual property rights became more common elements of antitrust cases brought by the FTC and the U.S. Department of Justice (DOJ) during the 1990s.[2]

In recognition of the growing importance of intellectual property in our economy, and the need to articulate how intellectual property rights intersect with the antitrust laws, in April 1995 the DOJ and the FTC jointly issued their "Antitrust Guidelines for the Licensing of Intellectual Property."[3] These "IP Guidelines" seek to inform the business community as to how licensing arrangements will be evaluated by the two antitrust enforcement agencies.

While the IP Guidelines have been well received, guidelines by their nature involve general principles and hypothetical situations; they cannot substitute for actual cases. Intel believed that its licensing practices com-

---

[2]Gilbert and Tom (2001) also provide a thoughtful discussion of the Intel case itself. Gilbert and Shapiro (1997) also discuss the antitrust treatment of licensing practices.

[3]These Guidelines are available at http://www.usdoj.gov/atr/public/guidelines/ipguide.htm. See also Klein (1997).

plied with the FTC's own Guidelines; the FTC felt otherwise. The FTC's case against Intel, along with the related private case involving Intel and Intergraph, provide additional guidance, above and beyond that in the IP Guidelines, to companies seeking to use their intellectual property rights to gain commercial advantage.

The Patent Thicket

With this background, we can ask how patents are actually used in the semiconductor industry, the industry in which Intel competes. Hall and Ziedonis (2001) provide a detailed discussion of precisely this issue.[4] They summarize their results as follows:

> Recent survey evidence suggests that semiconductor firms do not rely heavily on patents to appropriate returns to R&D. Yet the propensity of semiconductor firms to patent has risen dramatically since the mid-1980s. We explore this apparent paradox by conducting interviews with industry representatives and analyzing the patenting behavior of 95 U.S. semiconductor firms during 1979–1995. The results suggest that the 1980s strengthening of U.S. patent rights spawned "patent portfolio races" among capital-intensive firms, but it also facilitated entry by specialized firms. (Hall and Ziedonis, p. 101)

The increased patenting activity has created a "patent thicket" in the semiconductor industry.[5] The extent of the problem can be seen by looking at some basic data on patenting. Figure 14-1 shows that the number of U.S. patents issued each year containing the word "microprocessor," "processor," or "CPU" in their abstracts more than doubled during the 1990s to 4714 in the year 1998. Table 14-1 gives a breakdown for a number of companies in the microprocessor industry. The cumulative effect: more than 25,000 microprocessor patents were issued from 1988 to 1998.

To some extent, this surge in patenting simply reflects the highly innovative nature of the semiconductor industry. For the purposes of the FTC's case against Intel, however, the key point is that the role of patents in the semiconductor industry in the 1990s bore little resemblance to the "classical" role of patents on which the FTC's theory was based. According to the classical (one might say romantic) view of patents, inventors responsible for major inventions rely on the patent system to prevent others from copying their discoveries. While this view fits the pharmaceutical industry reasonably well, patents play a radically different role in the semiconductor industry. To see why, one must first understand three important ways in which

---

[4]Grindley and Teece (1997) provide further information about patenting in the semiconductor industry. Their evidence further supports the conclusions presented here.

[5]See Shapiro (2002) for a more complete discussion of the patent thicket and its implications for business strategy and antitrust policy. Heller and Eisenberg (1998) describe the "tragedy of the anti-commons" that can result from a thicket of patents.

FIGURE 14-1 U.S. Microprocessor Patents, 1988–1998

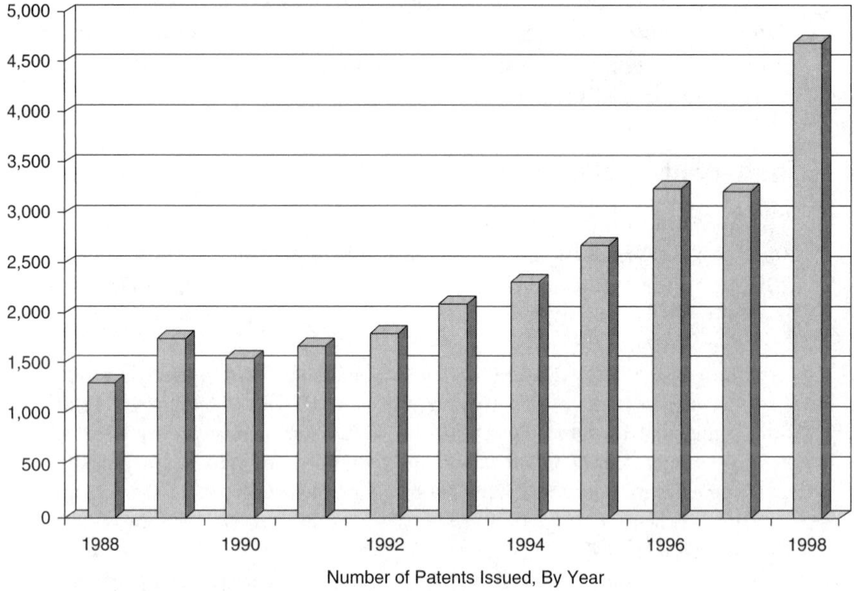

Number of Patents Issued, By Year

patents in our economy today differ from the classical role of patents just described.

First, many companies rely comparatively little on patents to appropriate the returns from their R&D activities (Levin et al. 1987; Cohen et. al. 2000). Instead, companies in many industries rely on trade secrets and time-to-market advantages to earn returns on their R&D expenditures.

Second, the propensity to patent (patents issued per dollar of R&D) has risen as more companies engage in *defensive patenting.* Defensive patenting refers to the practice of seeking patents in order to defend oneself from patent infringement actions brought by others. Under this strategy, the company does not plan to assert its patent proactively against others, but it can counterattack with its own patent infringement claims if sued for infringement (Kortum and Lerner 1998; Hall and Ziedonis 2001).

Third, there have been increasing concerns about the operation of the patent system itself (Merges 1999). The general thrust of the criticism is that the Patent and Trademark Office (PTO) has been too generous in granting patent rights. A common criticism is that the PTO lacks sufficient expertise to determine whether many patent applications in fact represent new and useful inventions as required under patent law.

Opportunism and "Hold-Up" by Patent Holders

Consider what all this means from the perspective of a successful company such as Intel. Each time Intel designs and produces a new microprocessor,

TABLE 14-1
U.S. Patents Containing the Words "Microprocessor", "Processor", or "CPU" in their Abstracts, Issued per Year to Selected Companies

	1988	1989	1990	1991	1992	1993	1994	1995	1996	1997	1998*	Total
AMD	8	13	14	8	7	12	13	14	30	51	98	268
DEC	6	17	18	23	35	38	46	31	40	22	28	304
Hewlett Packard	12	10	15	19	17	26	31	38	46	37	55	306
Hitachi	37	45	56	54	70	58	82	81	91	74	102	·750
IBM	60	68	73	67	99	149	149	162	221	228	307	1,583
IDT	0	0	0	0	1	0	2	1	4	3	3	14
Intel	4	9	4	10	14	23	45	69	114	112	146	550
Motorola	27	24	27	32	27	41	42	75	71	86	123	575
National/Cyrix	1	2	1	2	3	9	10	8	17	38	30	121
Rise Technology	0	0	0	0	0	0	0	0	0	0	0	0
Silicon Graphics	1	0	0	1	0	2	0	2	8	11	10	36
STMicroelectronics	0	1	1	2	2	1	2	2	9	6	13	39
Sun Microsystems	1	4	3	2	7	18	17	13	24	29	54	172
Texas Instruments	17	13	9	15	24	27	29	33	51	54	60	332
Total U.S. patents**	1,326	1,771	1,549	1,681	1,820	2,128	2,323	2,686	3,241	3,234	4,714	26,473

* Individual company counts for 1998 only include patents issued prior to October 31, 1998. Total U.S. patents reported for 1998 includes the entire year.

** Total U.S. patents refers to all patents issued by the U.S. Patent and Trademark Office, not just those received by the companies listed in this table.

Source: Data gathered from U.S. Patent and Trademark Office web site (http://www.uspto.gov). Year refers to patent issue date.

Intel faces some risk that it will be sued for patent infringement. A company suing Intel for patent infringement can be expected to ask the court for an injunction forcing Intel to stop shipping its microprocessors; both Intergraph and Digital sought such injunctions. Once Intel has invested billions of dollars in R&D and in a fabrication facility designed to make its latest chips, the losses Intel would suffer, were it forced to shut down production, would be staggering. In this very real sense, a type of "judo economics" is at work in the industry: The larger are a company's revenues, the more vulnerable is that company to a patent infringement lawsuit, other things equal.

If the classical view of patents applied, this would be a minor problem. Intel would merely refrain from copying patented technology, and it could avoid the risk of a devastating injunction against its flagship products. In the presence of the patent thicket, however, it is much harder for Intel to avoid this risk. A single microprocessor can potentially infringe on hundreds if not thousands of patents, many of which were not yet issued, and thus were invisible to Intel, when Intel was designing that microprocessor. Since many companies are working on similar aspects of semiconductor technology in parallel, and since patent applications are secret, it is common for one company to obtain a patent on a process or design element that was simultaneously developed and used by another company. The combination of simultaneous discovery, secrecy of patent applications, lags in the issuing of patents, a patent office that is generous to patent applicants, and the presumption of validity afforded to patents creates a potent mix.

F. M. Scherer stressed the danger of hold-up in his testimony at the FTC's Hearings on Global Innovation-Based Competition in 1995:

> Smaller firms, and even some rather large firms trying to develop a new product, are essentially finding themselves in a situation just like walking through a mine field: There are lots of unexploded patents out there, and you might just step on one and have your corporate leg blown off. . . . I find it a rather scary situation, to be honest. (see www.ftc.gov/opp/global/ GC112995.htm)

Clearly, some patent holders will be in a position to engage in opportunistic behavior relative to Intel. Intel is keenly aware of the dangers of hold-up and attempts to manage those risks, in part by entering into broad cross-licenses with others in the industry, such as IBM. Under these cross-licenses, each company can design and produce its products without fear of infringing on the other's patents. These licenses thus afford "design freedom," but not the freedom to copy. The rapid pace of technological advance in the industry in the presence of many such cross-licenses attests to their pro-competitive nature. As Hall and Ziedonis (2001) note, semiconductor companies seek patents in large part to be in a better position to negotiate these cross-licenses.

While cross-licenses between major players in the industry have proven effective, they are not as well suited to situations where the revenues at risk on the two sides are sharply different. When cross-licenses are negotiated, each side makes the case that its patent portfolio is strong and that the other side is earning substantial revenue (and profits) selling products that infringe these patents. When one side has few or no revenues at risk, that party gains an advantage in bargaining. For this reason, patent infringement actions brought by industry outsiders, or by firms with small market shares, can be the most difficult to resolve through cross-licensing. Texas Instruments is widely seen as having decided to exploit its patents to earn licensing revenues after its business took a turn for the worse (Grindley and Teece 1997). The extreme case of this tactic occurs when a firm that holds patents, but engages in no design or manufacturing activities, brings suit against a major industry player. For example, TechSearch sued Intel in 1998 asserting that Intel's Pentium chips infringed patents owned by TechSearch.[6]

INTEL'S CONDUCT DURING INTELLECTUAL PROPERTY DISPUTES

The facts surrounding the episodes giving rise to the FTC's case are relatively simple and for the most part undisputed.[7] For this reason, the FTC's case was largely about the proper legal and economic standard for conduct by a dominant firm, not a messy dispute over the facts, which makes the case especially attractive from the perspective of the antitrust economist.

Intergraph Corporation

The basic facts of the Intergraph dispute were described above. Some additional detail is useful, however, to understand better just how the dispute arose between Intergraph and Intel.

In 1987, Intergraph acquired the "Clipper" microprocessor technology from Fairchild Industries. Until 1993, Intergraph developed this technology for use in Intergraph's computer systems. Beginning in 1993, Intergraph gradually shifted from using the Clipper technology to building workstations and servers based on Intel's Pentium microprocessor architecture. By 1996, all of Intergraph's hardware sales were Intel-based systems.

In 1997, Intergraph informed a number of makers of computer systems (original equipment manufacturers, or OEMs) that they were allegedly in-

---

[6]TechSearch engages in no R&D, design, or manufacturing activities; rather, it buys patents and attempts to maximize their value. TechSearch acquired the patents it asserted against Intel from International Meta Systems (IMS), which had attempted (but failed) to develop a chip that was compatible with Intel microprocessors. In 1994, IMS filed a patent for a Reduced Instruction Set Computer (RISC) that could read Intel instructions; the patent was granted in 1996. Intel's spokesman has been quoted as saying about TechSearch: "This company exists solely for the purpose of purchasing patents and extorting funds from another company" (Takahashi 1999).

[7]The basic fact patterns below are taken largely from the FTC's complaint against Intel; see http://www.ftc.gov/os/1998/9806/intelfin.cmp.htm.

fringing certain Intergraph patents. These OEMs requested indemnification from Intel because the alleged infringement was based on these OEMs' use of Intel's microprocessors. Following these OEM requests, Intel sought to negotiate a cross-license with Intergraph. After the two companies were unable to reach agreement on the terms of a cross-license, Intel exercised its right under nondisclosure agreements (NDAs) with Intergraph to seek the return of intellectual property previously disclosed by Intel to Intergraph in the form of trade secrets and advance samples of unannounced products. Following indications that Intergraph was willing to negotiate with Intel, Intel withdrew this request for the return of its intellectual property and renewed its effort to obtain a cross-license with Intergraph. In November 1997, Intergraph filed a patent infringement suit against Intel in Federal District Court in Alabama.[8] In response to Intergraph's lawsuit, Intel demanded the return of its intellectual property from Intergraph. In April 1998, the court handling the private action between Intergraph and Intel issued a preliminary injunction requiring Intel to provide Intergraph with advance product information, advance samples, and production microprocessors on terms available to certain other large Intel customers.

According to the FTC's Complaint, "Intel cut off Intergraph's access to any of the Intel technical information necessary to continue developing in a timely and efficient manner new computer systems incorporating new Intel microprocessors" (FTC Complaint, p. 29). In particular, the FTC Complaint states that Intel: "cut off technical information that Intergraph needed in order to design systems based on Intel's newest chips"; "demanded return of microprocessor prototypes and refused to supply additional prototypes"; "failed to inform Intergraph of a bug Intel had previously discovered in an Intel chip that Intergraph was purchasing"; "acted to create uncertainty about Intergraph's future source of supply of Intel microprocessors"; and "otherwise engaged in conduct to create a perception in the computer industry that Intergraph was no longer capable of bringing to market in a timely manner new computer system products that incorporate Intel's latest microprocessor technology" (FTC Complaint, p. 29).

Compaq Computer Corporation

Compaq Computer Corporation ("Compaq") was the largest manufacturer of personal computers in the world during the mid-1990s. Compaq's 1997 revenues were $24.6 billion. The majority of Compaq's revenues during this time period were based on sales of Intel-based computers. Compaq was Intel's largest customer in 1997, purchasing more than $2 billion worth of Intel microprocessors. As stated in the FTC Complaint Counsels' Pretrial

---

[8]This private action, *Intergraph Corporation* v. *Intel Corporation,* 3 F. Supp. 2d 1255 (Northern District of Alabama), eventually led to an important ruling by the Court of Appeals for the Federal Circuit. The Intergraph case is discussed towards the end of this case study.

Brief (p. 36): "By manufacturing complementary components such as chipsets and motherboards, Compaq seeks to add value to its products—more features, greater reliability, and lower production costs." However, the FTC states that "Compaq's strategy of differentiating its computer systems came into conflict with Intel's strategy for expediting the adoption of new Intel microprocessors by the largest number of OEMs." More specifically:

> In 1994, Intel accelerated the expansion of its business from microprocessors into the systems area. Intel began to manufacture and sell chipsets and motherboards, and in some cases complete computer systems. It did so in order to provide OEMs with a vehicle for launching new generations of Intel microprocessors. By providing OEMs with a complete set of the building blocks needed to design Intel-based systems, Intel can speed the dissemination of each new generation of microprocessors. Intel's increased activity in the systems area heightened the risk that Intel would bump up against Compaq's portfolio of system-level patents. (Complaint Counsels' Pretrial Brief, p. 37)

As this quote reveals, the FTC recognized that Intel's strategy of selling chipsets and motherboards—*complements* to Intel's microprocessors—was designed to increase the sales of Intel's microprocessors, clearly a procompetitive goal.

In November 1994, Compaq sued Packard Bell (another PC maker) for using patented Compaq technology in Packard Bell computer systems. Since the allegedly infringing technology was part of Intel-supplied motherboards, Packard Bell requested indemnification from Intel. In May 1995, Intel formally intervened in the suit between Compaq and Packard Bell. Intel then stopped supplying Compaq with access to its trade secrets regarding Intel's Pentium II and Merced microprocessors, both of which were then in the design stage. Intel did not cut off the flow of all confidential information, and it did not demand the return of all Intel confidential information held by Compaq. Intel and Compaq executed a cross-license in January 1996, which ended the dispute between the two companies.

The FTC alleged that Intel's conduct "had a significant adverse effect on Compaq's ability to develop and bring to market in a timely manner computer systems based on Intel microprocessors, and would have posed an even more significant long-term threat to Compaq's business if Compaq had not agreed to license its technology to Intel" (FTC Complaint, p. 37). Intel asserted that Compaq was not in fact delayed in introducing the products to which the trade secrets withheld by Intel related.

Digital Equipment Corporation

Digital Equipment Corporation ("Digital") also designs and sells computer systems that incorporate Intel microprocessors. In 1997, Digital's sales of Intel-based systems accounted for roughly $2 billion of Digital's $14 billion of revenues. Digital purchased about $250 million worth of Intel microprocessors in 1997.

Unlike Intergraph and Compaq, Digital designed, developed, manufactured, marketed, and sold its own microprocessor products under the trade name "Alpha." Digital's Alpha microprocessors made relatively few sales, but they achieved a high level of performance during the mid- to late-1990s. As the FTC noted:

> Alpha has been able to garner only a small share of the microprocessor market, in significant part because software developers have generally not created Alpha versions of their Windows NT applications. In network industries parlance, Alpha has been unable to generate the "positive feedback" necessary to establish itself as a standard architecture. (Complaint Counsels' Pretrial Brief, p. 32)

Although not Intel's primary competitor, the Alpha microprocessor was one of the rivals of the new IA-64 microprocessors under development at Intel, including the "Merced" microprocessor, since introduced as Intel's high-end Itanium chip.

In May 1997, Digital sued Intel, alleging that Intel's Pentium processors infringed ten of Digital's patents. According to the FTC, "Intel responded to Digital's lawsuit by publicly denying Digital access to any of the Intel technical information needed to continue developing in a timely and efficient manner new computer systems incorporating new Intel microprocessors" (FTC Complaint, p. 19). As in the Intergraph case, Intel exercised its rights under its NDA with Digital, demanding that Digital return Intel's technical information and prototypes.

In November 1997, Intel and Digital settled their dispute. This settlement had three key components. First, the two companies entered into a cross-license, giving each company a license to the other's patents. Second, Intel purchased an underutilized chip fabrication facility from Digital at book value, arguably well above its market value. Third, Intel granted favorable pricing to Digital for future purchases of Intel microprocessors. Intel also assured Digital a continued supply of Alpha chips from the chip fabrication plant that Intel was acquiring.

The FTC investigated Digital's settlement with Intel separately, because the settlement involved the acquisition by Intel of a Digital fabrication facility. The FTC's basic concern with the *settlement itself* was that Digital would become dependent upon Intel for making Digital's Alpha chips, and thus that Digital would become a less effective or less independent competitor to Intel as a result of their settlement. The FTC resolved these concerns by entering into a consent order with Digital in April 1998 to ensure that Digital would retain sources for the design and production of Alpha chips that were independent of Intel.[9] Subsequent events have shown

---

[9]The consent order was announced on April 23, 1998; see www.ftc.gov/opa/1998/9804/digitala.

that Digital's Alpha microprocessor was not in fact an especially attractive product in the microprocessor market. Compaq later acquired Digital and phased out the Alpha microprocessor, which never attracted a large base of customers.

The FTC's approval of the Digital/Intel settlement did not, however, end Intel's entanglements with the FTC. To the contrary: partly as a result of its inquiry into the Digital/Intel settlement, the FTC's attention became focused on the tactics that Intel had used in its negotiations with Digital. The FTC's approval of the Digital/Intel *settlement* did not imply the FTC's approval of the *tactics* used by Intel in reaching that settlement. Instead, finding that Intel had employed similar tactics in prior disputes with Intergraph and Compaq, the FTC decided to bring an antitrust case against Intel for its conduct in these three episodes.

THE FTC's THEORY

Although some within the FTC felt that Intel's conduct was clearly "unfair," the FTC fashioned a complaint against Intel that contained the standard elements of a Sherman Act monopolization case: monopoly power in a relevant antitrust market combined with anticompetitive conduct to fortify that monopoly.[10]

Intel Had Monopoly Power

Since the FTC's case was based on the claim that Intel's conduct constituted monopolization, the FTC needed first to show that Intel had monopoly power in some well-defined relevant antitrust market. The FTC alleged that Intel had monopoly power in the market for general-purpose microprocessors.

The FTC supported this proposition by stating that "sales of Intel microprocessor products have accounted for approximately 80 percent of the total dollar sales of general-purpose microprocessors worldwide for each of the last five years" (FTC Complaint, p. 6). The FTC also described the entry barriers into the microprocessor market. The FTC listed sunk-cost investment and long development times, economies of scale, network effects, intellectual property rights, and reputational barriers as barriers to entry.

---

htm. For the FTC's complaint in the Digital/Intel matter, see www.ftc.gov/os/1998/9804/9810040. cmp.htm. The consent order itself can be found at www.ftc.gov/os/1998/9804/9810040.agr.htm. The FTC's analysis to aid public comment is available at www.ftc.gov/os/1998/9804/9810040. ana.htm.

[10]The most complete description of the FTC's case available to the public is Complaint Counsels' Pre-Trial Brief [Public Version], filed February 25, 1999; see http://www.ftc.gov/alj/D9288/ 990225ccpb.pdf. There the FTC states "Sherman Act standards are the logical starting point in the analysis of unfair conduct" (p. 4).

Intel's Conduct Harmed Competition

Next, the FTC claimed that Intel's conduct harmed competition in Intel's monopoly market, namely the market for general-purpose microprocessors. But how could Intel's conduct have an adverse impact on competition in the market for general-purpose microprocessors, where Intel's most direct competitor was Advanced Micro Devices (AMD), who was not a customer of Intel and not subject to the tactics at issue? The FTC Complaint (p. 39) stated:

> Because patent rights are an important means of promoting innovation, Intel's coercive tactics to force customers to license away such rights diminishes the incentives of any firm dependent on Intel to develop microprocessor-related technologies. Because most firms who own or are developing such technologies are vulnerable to retaliation from Intel, the natural and probable effect of Intel's conduct is to diminish the incentives of the industry to develop new and improved microprocessor and related technologies. Consequently, Intel's conduct entrenches its monopoly power in the current generation of general-purpose microprocessors and reduces competition to develop new microprocessor technology and future generations of microprocessor products.

This was the essence of the FTC's complaint: That the "natural and probable effect of Intel's conduct" would be to discourage "the industry" from developing "microprocessor-related technologies" and thereby entrench Intel's monopoly power. Notice that the FTC's theory was based on the proposition that "most firms who own or are developing such technologies are vulnerable to retaliation from Intel." This proposition will be tested below.

At the time that the FTC issued its complaint against Intel, its press release further articulated the FTC's theory of harm to competition:

> Innovation is critical to economic progress, and patents play a crucial role in encouraging that innovation. Intel's great contributions to this country's economic growth have been encouraged and protected by patents in the design and manufacturing processes for its semiconductor products. But if Intel can use its monopoly position in the market for microprocessors to prevent other firms from enforcing their own patents, other firms will have little incentive to invent new features to challenge Intel's dominance. As a monopolist, Intel can compete by producing better, cheaper and more attractive products. It cannot act to cement its monopoly power by preventing other firms from challenging its dominance. Intel has acted illegally. It has used its monopoly power to impede innovation and stifle competition.[11]

---

[11]FTC Press Release, June 8, 1998, "Intel Abuses its Monopoly Power in Violation of Federal Law: Agency Charges World's Largest Microprocessor Manufacturer Cut Off Customers and Competitors in Order to Stifle Competition and Impede Innovation." See http://www.ftc.gov/opa/1998/9806/intelc.htm.

In short, the FTC saw Intel's conduct as a form of expropriation of the patent rights of others through "coercion." If Digital could not protect its innovations from copying by Intel, the FTC argued, Digital would have less incentive to innovate in the future. Similarly, the FTC argued that OEMs such as Compaq and Intergraph might use their own "microprocessor-related" innovations to help sponsor competition by an Intel rival, but such sponsorship would be less attractive if other OEMs using Intel's chips could match these same innovations.

Intel's Conduct Had No Efficiency Basis

Under the antitrust laws, even a dominant firm that has acted in a manner that excludes competitors can defend itself by showing that its conduct served a legitimate business purpose. The FTC asserted that Intel's conduct, in each of the three disputes described above, "was not reasonably necessary to serve any legitimate, procompetitive purpose."[12]

In fact, the FTC went even further, inferring *anticompetitive* intent from Intel's actions. Specifically, the FTC took the view that Intel sacrificed short-term profits by disrupting its relationships with valuable customers, and doing so could only have been profitable because Intel stood to benefit over the longer run by protecting its monopoly.

INTEL'S RESPONSE TO THE FTC's THEORY

Intel had a radically different view than the FTC on all of these issues.[13]

Competition Faced by Intel

Intel argued that it lacked monopoly power over microprocessors. Intel emphasized two aspects of the microprocessor market. First, the price reductions and performance improvements for microprocessors have been simply extraordinary. Moore's Law, which states that microprocessor performance doubles roughly every eighteen months, has been operating for some twenty years. One is hard-pressed to find a market where consumers have experienced greater improvements in performance, and reductions in price, over such a sustained period of time. Intel, a great manufacturer, has continually pushed prices down and introduced dramatically faster and faster chips. Intel questioned whether this is the behavior of a monopolist.

---

[12]FTC Complaint, p. 30 (Intergraph), p. 36 (Compaq), p. 20 (Digital).

[13]The most complete description of Intel's position available to the public is Respondent Intel's Trial Brief [Public Version], filed February 25, 1999; see http://www.ftc.gov/alj/D9288/intelbrief.pdf.

Second, there have been regular price wars and market-share skirmishes between Intel and its most direct rival, Advanced Micro Devices (AMD). Here is one rendition from a *New York Times* article (Fisher 1999) reporting the price war that broke out between Intel and AMD just one month before the FTC was set to go to trial against Intel:

> Anyone who has watched the semiconductor industry for a while has seen this chain of events play out time and time again. Intel brings out a new generation of microprocessor; Advanced Micro rushes to offer a compatible product but manufacturing glitches keep volume low. Then, when Advanced Micro catches up and is ready to ship increased quantities, Intel cuts prices and prepares for the next generation of products.

In short, Intel argued that it was an aggressive and successful competitor in a market that was generating enormous benefits to consumers.

Although Intel disputed the FTC's assertion that Intel had monopoly power in the market for general-purpose microprocessors, the analysis below of Intel's conduct assumes that Intel indeed had such power.[14] In the context of the disputes described above, this assumption implies that Intergraph, Compaq, and Digital had limited ability to replace Intel's microprocessors with microprocessors from other suppliers. The analysis below further assumes, as alleged by the FTC, that Intel's refusal to provide trade secrets and advance product samples imposed substantial costs on Intergraph, Compaq, and Digital.[15]

Intel's "IP for IP" Policy

Intel also had an entirely different perspective than the FTC regarding the rationale behind its conduct and the competitive effects of the tactics it used when faced with patent infringement lawsuits by Intergraph, Compaq, and Digital. From Intel's perspective, the episodes with Intergraph, Compaq, and Digital were just three of many instances in which Intel had to deal with the exploding number of patents in the semiconductor industry and the ever-present danger of being held-up by patent holders acting opportunistically.

Keenly aware of the patent thicket, Intel had developed a policy of "IP for IP." Under this policy, Intel would use its intellectual property rights to negotiate cross-licenses and to defend itself if sued for infringement. The FTC's case was a direct attack on Intel's "IP for IP" policy. From Intel's perspective, the FTC wanted Intel to disarm unilaterally by continuing to

---

[14]The author's assignment in the litigation was to analyze the effects of Intel's conduct under the assumption that Intel had monopoly power, as alleged by the FTC.

[15]This proposition does not follow from the assumption that Intel had monopoly power, since Intel never refused to sell its microprocessors to these companies.

provide trade secrets and other valuable IP to companies that were asserting their IP against Intel.

Intel believed that its policy of "IP for IP" was a natural—and legal—way to use its valuable intellectual property to gain design freedom so that it could make the very best chips, to reduce its payments of royalties, and to limit its exposure to hold-up. While far from perfect as a defense—Intel was still at a strategic disadvantage by virtue of its enormous microprocessor revenues—this policy helped Intel be a more effective competitor without involving the offensive use of Intel's patents. In other words, Intel saw its policy of "IP for IP" as appropriate in the context of the wave of defensive patenting, and in the presence of the patent thicket in its industry. Intel's documents and the testimony of Intel's executives consistently supported this view that Intel's policy of "IP for IP" was a defensive strategy to deal with the patent thicket and was not designed to deter other industry members from engaging in innovation.

In contrast, the FTC's position was that Intel had no legitimate business justification for its actions. As noted above, the FTC took the position that Intel had previously benefited from offering technical assistance and confidential information to Intergraph, Compaq, and Digital, so Intel's decision to restrict or reduce the supply of confidential information and technical support to these companies was unjustified:

> From Intel's perspective, this aggressive strategy directed against its customers made sense because its objective was the preservation of its monopoly, and it was willing to reduce its short-run profits to do so (Complaint Counsels' Pretrial Brief, p.2).

> By terminating Intergraph's, Digital's, and Compaq's access to product information and samples, Intel gave up the benefits it obtained from the cooperative relationship it had previously enjoyed with each company. . . . *Aspen* teaches that the sacrifice of short term benefits is evidence of anticompetitive purpose and nature. (Complaint Counsels' Pretrial Brief, pp. 46–47)

The central economic issue here is not especially complex. Let us suppose that Intel's tactics had the purpose and effect of allowing Intel to negotiate more favorable terms for cross-licenses with Intergraph, Compaq, and Digital than Intel could have obtained had it continued to provide its trade secrets and advance product samples to those companies. In other words, suppose that Intel's tactics allowed Intel to lower its royalty costs and perhaps improve the quality of its chips by achieving greater design freedom. Are these "legitimate business justifications"?

The ability to achieve lower costs and improved product quality is the essence of "competition on the merits." Intel's efforts to reduce its royalty costs and to achieve greater design freedom by bargaining using its own intellectual property should at the very least count as a pro-competitive benefits, against which any anti-competitive effects should be balanced. In short, there is no economic basis for the FTC's position that Intel's attempt to lower its costs and to obtain design freedom should not count as a "legitimate business objective."

This conclusion is strengthened by knowledge of the perils facing Intel and other companies that are vulnerable to hold-up as a result of the patent thicket. Recall that both Intergraph and Digital sought injunctive relief to enjoin Intel from selling its flagship microprocessor products, while Compaq sought to enjoin Intel's sales of motherboards. As noted earlier, once Intel has sunk substantial costs in the design and production of its microprocessors, Intel may be subject to hold-up by patent holders whose actual contributions fall far short of the royalties they can extract from Intel. In fact, Intergraph fit the hold-up pattern quite well: Intergraph had already exited the microprocessor business and was trying to mine older patents. The Digital situation also fits the hold-up pattern: Digital's Alpha microprocessor had not been selling well, Digital appeared to be trying to make a graceful exit strategy, and Digital gained considerable financial benefits from its settlement with Intel, as described above.

The FTC's theory seemed especially strained in the cases of Compaq and Intergraph, which were simply not microprocessor rivals of Intel. The FTC did manage to construct a theory of how Intel's conduct towards Compaq and Intergraph could harm competition in the microprocessor market, but a far simpler explanation of Intel's conduct fit the facts very well: Intel was using its own IP as a bargaining chip in negotiations with others who were asserting their IP against Intel.

The FTC's "no business justification" position (a) did not seem to reflect accurately the role of patents in the semiconductor industry, especially the patent thicket; (b) gave little or no weight to the necessity and pro-competitive effects in this industry of cross-licenses that enable design freedom and reduce royalty payments, and (c) appeared to discount the very real danger of "hold-up" faced by Intel and other semiconductor manufacturers.

The Effect of Intel's Conduct on Microprocessor Competition

Intel also hotly disputed the FTC's claim that Intel's conduct had harmed competition in the microprocessor market.

The FTC asserted that "Intel's conduct preserved its monopoly by guaranteeing Intel's access to innovative technology" (Complaint Counsels' Pretrial Brief, p. 42). In other words, by insuring that it could offer the most advanced microprocessors, the FTC stated that Intel's monopoly position would be preserved. This notion—that it is anti-competitive for a monopolist to use its monopoly power to negotiate for better or cheaper inputs and thus to improve its product—is misguided. True, such cost reductions and product improvements will make it harder for others to topple the monopoly; but lower costs and higher quality are the essence of competition and should be encouraged. Exchanging one's own intellectual property to lower royalty costs and to help gain the necessary IP rights to make improvements is therefore also pro-competitive.

The FTC also asserted that "Deterring innovation was another means for Intel to preserve its monopoly." "The evidence will show that the ability of Intel to force licenses to the technology it desires will, over time, dull the incentive of other firms to innovate" (Complaint Counsels' Pretrial Brief, pp. 43–44). Here we have a coherent theory that can in principle be tested: Did Intel's conduct induce Intel's microprocessor rivals to reduce their innovative effects? The FTC's theory of harm to innovation failed to hold up to empirical testing.

The starting point for testing the FTC's theory is the identification of Intel's primary microprocessor rivals. As noted above, the most direct rival was AMD. Other companies with the capability to engage in microprocessor innovation included IBM, Sun, Hewlett-Packard, Digital, Samsung, Motorola, Silicon Graphics, Texas Instruments, Toshiba, and Hitachi.[16] We can sharpen the test of the FTC's theory by asking the following question: Did Intel's conduct induce these companies, who have the capability to engage in microprocessor innovation, to reduce their innovative efforts?

Observe that two conditions must hold for the FTC's theory even to get off the ground with respect to a specific microprocessor company: (1) the company in question must be a customer of Intel that receives Intel's trade secrets and advance product samples; and (2) the company must *not* have a cross-license with Intel, or else it would already have licensed its patents to Intel in return for a license to Intel's patents.[17] In fact, none of Intel's competitors identified by the FTC met these two conditions. AMD and Sun, for example, do not purchase microprocessors from Intel; and IBM, for example, has a cross-license with Intel (Intel's Trial Brief, pp. 28–29).

Despite this formidable obstacle, the FTC attempted to prove that Intel's conduct "chilled" innovation activity. But the evidence obtained during the discovery process simply did not support the "chill" theory. One after another, the major innovators in the microprocessor field, including IBM, Sun, Hewlett-Packard, and Digital, testified that their R&D efforts were *not* affected adversely by the Intel conduct at issue (Intel's Trial Brief, p. 5). The FTC acknowledged that it had no evidence linking Intel's conduct to R&D decision making at AMD, National Semiconductor (Cyrix), IBM, Sun, Hewlett-Packard, Samsung, Silicon Graphics, NEC Electronics, or several smaller companies, which together with Intel and Digital comprised all companies identified by the FTC as microprocessor innovators

---

[16]Recall that the analysis here assumes that Intel has monopoly power. Therefore, this list of rivals is best thought of as the list of firms that are best placed to engage in innovation that will erode Intel's monopoly power.

[17]It is theoretically possible that the future innovation incentives of a company that has signed a cross-license with Intel could be affected by Intel's conduct, since these cross-licensees have finite duration.

(Intel's Trial Brief, p. 13). The evidence was especially strong that Digital's innovation had not been adversely affected by Intel's conduct.[18]

The FTC was forced to take the position that the harm to innovation would take place gradually, and could simply not be detected yet, despite the fact that Intel had been following its policy of IP for IP for some time. As the FTC's economic expert stated, the consequences of Intel's actions would "unravel over a period of probably ten or so years, and it's just too early to assess those consequences" (Intel's Trial Brief, p. 29).

SETTLEMENT AND CONSENT ORDER

Following the FTC's procedures, the FTC action against Intel went before an administrative law judge (ALJ) at the FTC. Once the FTC's complaint was issued in June 1998, a docket was opened with the ALJ presiding. The actual hearing before the ALJ was scheduled to begin in March 1999. The FTC and Intel announced a settlement of their dispute on March 8, 1999.[19] Under the consent order negotiated by the FTC and Intel,[20] Intel agreed to continue to provide its trade secrets and advance product samples to customers that were suing Intel for patent infringement, with one significant exception: Intel would have such an obligation only if the customer agreed not to seek an injunction against Intel's manufacture and sale of its microprocessors. According to the FTC's Analysis to Aid Public Comment,[21] this exception

> strikes an appropriate balance, on a prospective basis, between the interests of Intel and its customers. If a customer chooses to seek an injunction against Intel's microprocessors, it cannot, under the provisions of this Order, be assured of continuing to receive advance technical information about the very same microprocessors that it is attempting to enjoin. If an

---

[18]Digital's Chairman, Robert Palmer, "testified that the company did not cancel, curtail, delay, defer, scale back, reduce, or otherwise limit any research and development related to microprocessors as a result of Intel's conduct" (Intel's Trial Brief, p. 12). Palmer also testified that Digital's settlement with Intel had left the Alpha microprocessor in a stronger position to compete than it had been prior to the dispute with Intel, and that Digital's ability and incentive to advance Alpha technology had increased as a result of the settlement with Intel (Intel's Trial Brief, p. 13). William Strecker, Digital Chief Technology Officer prior to Compaq's acquisition of Digital, testified that Intel's conduct had no effect on R&D related to the Alpha microprocessor. (Intel's Trial Brief, p. 13) Digital in fact signed a long-term cross-license with Intel. Even if Digital had received a higher lump-sum payment from Intel in the absence of Intel's tactics, this would have no effect on Digital's incentives to innovate during the long term of the cross license. Alternatively, if Digital had received running royalties, we would expect Intel's prices to be higher, harming consumers.

[19]For the FTC Press Release announcing the settlement, see http://www.ftc.gov/opa/1999/9903/intelcom.htm.

[20]The Consent Order can be found at http://www.ftc.gov/os/1999/9903/d09288intelagreement.htm.

[21]See http://www.ftc.gov/os/1999/9903/d09288intelanalysis.htm.

Intel customer nevertheless wishes to seek injunctive relief against Intel's manufacture, use, sale, offer to sell or importation, it remains free to do so, but without the protections in this Order. In all other circumstances, Intel is required to continue supplying technical information and product under the Proposed Order.

The beauty of this compromise is that it met the essential needs of both the FTC and of Intel. In particular, the FTC obtained some protections for customers suing Intel for patent infringement, under the theory that customers' ability to bring such lawsuits would serve to encourage their innovative efforts. From Intel's perspective, the settlement ended the FTC case against Intel and allowed Intel to bring its own intellectual property rights to bear in negotiations if the other party were seeking an injunction against Intel's microprocessors, the very type of hold-up that was of greatest concern to Intel. Both the FTC and Intel expressed satisfaction with the settlement, although Intel continued to assert that its conduct had not violated antitrust laws.

SUBSEQUENT DEVELOPMENTS

Although it had settled with the FTC, Intel's litigation with Intergraph continued. Recall that Intergraph had obtained a preliminary injunction from a federal district court requiring Intel to continue to provide it with trade secrets and advance samples. Intel had appealed this injunction to the Court of Appeals for the Federal Circuit (CAFC), the appeals court that specializes in intellectual property disputes.

In a major decision issued in November 1999, the CAFC ruled in Intel's favor.[22] The Court strongly supported Intel's view of its rights as a holder of intellectual property and of the limitations of Intergraph's antitrust case against Intel. In particular, the CAFC emphasized that Intergraph was not a competitor of Intel in the market in which Intel was alleged to have a monopoly, namely the microprocessor market. Citing substantial precedent, and relying on the fact that Intergraph and Intel were in a customer/supplier relationship instead of a competitive relationship, the CAFC could find no likelihood that Intel's conduct, even if it harmed Intergraph, violated the Sherman Act.[23] Here are three key quotes from the CAFC decision:

However, the Sherman Act does not convert all harsh commercial actions into antitrust violations. Unilateral conduct that may adversely affect another's business situation, but is not intended to monopolize that business,

---

[22]*Intel Corp.* v. *Intergraph Corp.,* 195 F. 3d 1346 (1999).

[23]On remand, the District Court dismissed Intergraph's antitrust case against Intel in March 2000.

does not violate the Sherman Act. . . . Intel's conduct with respect to Intergraph does not constitute the offense of monopolization or the threat thereof in any market relevant to competition with Intergraph. (*Intel* v. *Intergraph,* 494 F. 3d 1346, 1354-5, 1356)

Intergraph provided no support for its charge that Intel's action in withholding "strategic customer" benefits from Intergraph was for the purpose of enhancing Intel's competitive position. . . . No threat or actual monopolization is asserted to flow from the various rejected patent license proposals. Commercial negotiations to trade patent property rights for other consideration in order to settle a patent dispute is neither tying nor coercive reciprocity in violation of the Sherman Act. Although the district court calls Intel's actions "hardball," it is not the judicial role to readjust the risks in high-stakes commercial dealings. (*Intel* v. *Intergraph,* 494 F. 3d 1346, 1359)

Despite the district court's sensitive concern for Intergraph's well-being while it conducts its patent suit against Intel, there must be an adverse effect on competition in order to bring an antitrust remedy to bear. The remedy of compulsory disclosure of proprietary information and provision of pre-production chips and other commercial and intellectual property is a dramatic remedy for antitrust illegality, and requires violation of antitrust law or the likelihood that such violation would be established. In the proceedings whose record is before us, Intergraph has not shown a substantial likelihood of success in establishing that Intel violated the antitrust laws in its actions with respect to Intergraph, or that Intel agreed by contract to provide the benefits contained in the injunction. (*Intel* v. *Intergraph,* 494 F. 3d 1346, 1367)

Intel's perspective also has gained ground at the Federal Trade Commission. The current Chairman of the FTC, Timothy Muris, has in the past been quite explicit in his criticism of the approach taken by the previous Commission leadership to monopolizations cases, including the Intel case:[24]

FTC officials have pronounced their view regarding monopolization in court papers, speeches, and articles. The agency appears to believe that in monopolization cases government proof of anticompetitive effects is unnecessary. . . . In this article, I intend to demonstrate that the FTC's position on this issue is wrong: wrong on the law, wrong on policy, and wrong on the facts. [footnotes omitted] (Muris 2000, p. 694)

The Intel case thus leaves us with a question that is central to the antitrust law and economics of monopolization cases: What must the govern-

---

[24]Muris explicitly identifies concerns about hold-up as an area where the FTC is "wrong on the facts": "In rejecting suits by Intel's customers as a justification for Intel's refusal to supply information, the FTC appears to have ignored the implication of the relational contracts literature discussed [above]" (Muris 2000, p. 717).

ment show in terms of competitive effects before a monopolist's conduct is branded anti-competitive and thus illegal under the Sherman Act? The FTC's case against Intel may prove to have been the high-water mark for those who would set a low hurdle of proof of anticompetitive effects for the government in monopolization cases and for those who would take a narrow view of what constitutes a "business justification" for conduct alleged by the Federal antitrust agencies to be anticompetitive.

REFERENCES

Cohen, Wesley M., Richard R. Nelson, and John Walsh. "Protecting Their Intellectual Assets: Why U.S. Manufacturing Firms Patent (or Not)." NBER Working Paper No. 7552, February 2002, www.nber.org/papers/w7552.pdf.

Federal Trade Commission and U.S. Department of Justice. *Antitrust Guidelines for the Licensing of Intellectual Property.* www.usdoj.gov/atr/public/guidelines/ipguide. htm.

Fisher, Lawrence. "Price War between Advanced Micro and Intel Ravages Chip Stocks." *New York Times,* February 8, 1999.

Gilbert, Richard, and Carl Shapiro. "Antitrust Issues in the Licensing of Intellectual Property: The Nine No-No's Meet the Nineties." *Brookings Papers on Economics: Microeconomics* (1999): 283–336.

Gilbert, Richard, and Willard K. Tom. "Is Innovation King at the Agencies? The Intellectual Property Guidelines Five Years Later." *Antitrust Law Journal* 69, no. 1 (2001): 43–86.

Grindley, Peter, and David J. Teece. "Managing Intellectual Capital: Licensing and Cross-Licensing in Semiconductors and Electronics." *California Management Review* 39 (Winter 1997): 1–34.

Hall, Bronwyn, and Rosemarie Ham Ziedonis. "The Patent Paradox Revisited: An Empirical Study of Patenting in the U.S. Semiconductor Industry, 1979–1995." *Rand Journal of Economics* 32 (Spring 2001): 101–128.

Heller, M.A. and R. S. Eisenberg. "Can Patents Deter Innovation? The Anti-Commons in Biomedical Research." *Science* 280 (May 1, 1998): 698–701.

Klein, Joel I. "Cross-Licensing and Antitrust Law." (1997) available at http://www. usdoj.gov/atr/public/speeches/1123.htm.

Kortum, Samuel and Josh Lerner. "Stronger Protection or Technological Revolution: What Is behind the Recent Surge in Patenting?" *Carnegie-Rochester Conference Series on Public Policy* 48 (June 1998): 247–304.

Levin, Richard C, Alvin K. Klevorick, Richard R. Nelson, and Sidney G. Winter. "Appropriating the Returns from Industrial R&D." *Brookings Papers on Economic Activity* (1987): 783–820.

Merges, Robert P. "As Many as Six Impossible Patents before Breakfast: Property Rights for Business Concepts and Patent System Reform." *Berkeley Technology Law Journal* 14 (Spring 1999) 577–615.

Muris, Timothy J. "The FTC and the Law of Monopolization." *Antitrust Law Journal* 67, no. 3 (2000): 693–723.

Pitofsky, Robert. "Antitrust and Intellectual Property: Unresolved Issues at the Heart of the New Economy." Prepared Remarks at the Antitrust, Technology, and Intellectual Property Conference, Berkeley Center for Law and Technology, March 2, 2001. http://www.ftc.gov/speeches/pitofsky/ipf301.htm.

Shapiro, Carl. "Navigating the Patent Thicket: Cross Licenses, Patent Pools and Standard Setting." In *Innovation Policy and the Economy,* edited by Adam Jaffe, Joshua Lerner, and Scott Stern. Cambridge, Mass.: MIT Press, 2002.

Shapiro, Carl, and Hal R. Varian. *Information Rules: A Strategic Guide to the Network Economy.* Boston: Harvard Business School Press, 1999.

Takahashi, Dean. "Intel's Bold Steps to Thwart Foe in Patent Case." *Wall Street Journal,* April 16, 1999.

Weinstein, Michael. "Intel Case Gives Antitrust Law a New Twist." *New York Times,* June 9, 1998.

Weinstein, Michael. "Antitrust Case against Intel Stresses Customers, Not Rivals." *New York Times,* February 25, 1999.

Retailer-Instigated Restraints on Suppliers' Sales: Toys "R" Us (2000)

F. M. Scherer

INTRODUCTION

During the early 1990s Toys "R" Us[1] (hereafter, TRU), by a considerable stretch the largest retailer of toys in the United States, persuaded leading toy manufacturers to restrict the range of products they sold to warehouse clubs—a newly-emerging form of consumer goods retailing. The restrictions were challenged under the antitrust laws by the Federal Trade Commission (FTC) in May 1996.[2] The extensive litigation that followed clarified in important ways the kinds of "vertical restraints" a retailer could impose upon its suppliers and the role of efficiency defenses, and especially claims of free-riding on services provided by the retailer, in justifying such restraints.

INNOVATION IN RETAILING

The tensions that arose among TRU, warehouse clubs, and toy manufacturers during the 1990s were a natural sequitur from the several revolutions that occurred in retailing during the prior century and one-half (Chandler 1977, chs. 1 and 7; Adelman 1959; and Scherer 1999).

As the United States emerged from its great Civil War, most consumer goods were provided at retail by general stores or "mom and pop" stores.

---

[1]The company's logo prints the "R" backward, which is not easily accomplished in type-set publications. We use quotation marks to note that our usage is not strictly accurate.

[2]*In the matter of Toys "R" Us, Inc.*, docket no. 9278. The author was testifying expert economist on behalf of the Federal Trade Commission.

These outlets were challenged competitively at first in the larger cities by department stores and then by mail-order houses such as Sears, Roebuck. During the twentieth century new retailing approaches appeared successively in the form of the chain stores (such as A&P and Walgreen's), supermarkets, hypermarket chains (such as Kmart and Wal-Mart), and specialized "category killer" chains (such as Home Depot for hardware and garden supplies and Staples for office supplies). These innovations in retailing were often accompanied by reductions in the percentage margin between prices and wholesale merchandise acquisition costs (hereafter, percentage retail margin, or PRM), and hence reductions in the prices that consumers paid, to the competitive disadvantage of more traditional retailing forms.

The traditional retailers fought back in part by seeking governmental protection—e.g., in unsuccessful attempts during the 1880s and 1890s to secure state legislation curbing department stores' lower prices, through delays in the spread of free rural mail delivery aimed at inhibiting the growth of Sears, Roebuck, and in the passage of tougher anti–price discrimination laws (the Robinson-Patman Act) and laws enabling mandatory minimum resale price maintenance (so-called "fair trade" laws) during the 1930s. Gradually, these barriers proved ineffective or were repealed, and the retailing innovations took root and spread, with consumers as principal beneficiaries.

Toys "R" Us made important contributions to this innovative process. Founded by Charles Lazarus in 1948, with expansion to a Washington, D.C., branch first bearing the Toys "R" Us logo in 1954, it was one of the first category killer discount chains. It offered an unprecedentedly broad line of toys, encompassing some 16,000 different items (stock-keeping units, or SKUs) by the 1990s (reduced to roughly 11,000 in 1996), and priced its products to realize margins between selling price and acquisition cost well below the 40 to 50 percent values that were the norm in more traditional toy outlets. It reached the fifty-store threshold in 1974 and continued its expansion to operate 497 retail toy outlets in the United States during 1992, along with 126 stores in other nations, to which it had introduced the previously unfamiliar concept of systematically discounted toy prices.

The Rise of Warehouse Clubs

The warehouse clubs, among which the most important examples were Costco, the Price Club, Sam's (affiliated with Wal-Mart), Pace (affiliated with Kmart), and BJs, made further additions to retailing innovation history. At first, beginning in 1976, they sold merchandise mainly to small business customers. But in the late 1980s they began accepting individual retail customers who paid an annual membership fee of roughly $30, or approximately two percent of the average member's annual purchases. They purchased selected nationally branded food, appliance, electronic, automotive, and other consumer products in large quantities, transported them to austere warehouse-like buildings at low-rent locations, and moved them onto the selling floor still heaped upon the pallets with which they had been transported from the manufacturer to the store. Customers served themselves from the pallets and packed their purchases into oversize shopping carts after bringing them through a streamlined checkout counter. Despite selling a wide array of consumer products, the typical warehouse club outlet carried only some 3000 individual SKUs, with the product mix varying over the year to reflect both seasonal demands and the opportunistic purchases made by the clubs' buyers. Because the product mix varied so widely, shopping at the clubs was viewed by many consumer members as a kind of treasure hunt—one never knew what specials one might encounter.

Because of their extraordinarily low overhead, the large volumes in which members typically bought, and the annual admission fee, the clubs were able to offer their goods at uniformly low percentage retail margins— on the order of 9 to 12 percent. By 1992, there were 576 warehouse club stores in the United States. Their appeal was spreading rapidly, and marketing researchers projected in 1992 that the number of club outlets would double during the following decade.

The low PRMs taken by the clubs on the 100 to 250 toy items they stocked, depending upon availability and season, were perceived as a serious threat by the management of TRU. Although its principal draw to consumers was the huge array of products TRU stocked, it also emphasized its role as a low-price, if not *the* low-price, outlet, leading consumers to sample that array. To be sure, it faced price competition from other toy retailers—increasingly, from hypermarkets led by Wal-Mart, which was expanding rapidly from its Arkansas base during the 1980s and 1990s, and which carried as many as 3000 toy items at seasonal peaks, sold at PRMs averaging 22 percent but considerably lower for "hit" items.[3]

TRU responded to this competition by varying its prices inversely with the popularity of the item, and hence with the extent to which consumers might make price comparisons at alternative outlets. The best-selling hundred or so TRU toys were sold at substantially discounted PRMs; margins then ascended into the 32–38 percent range for products ranked 1000 to 10,000 in sales volume. Especially after competition from Wal-Mart intensified, TRU recognized that it could not always be the lowest-price outlet, but it tried to keep prices of the most popular items close to those of the toughest rivals. Customers were drawn to TRU through the advertising of a few hundred low-margin, popular items (along with disposable diapers and baby formula, priced at razor-thin margins, and shelved near the back of the stores); TRU's profits were then enhanced substantially as the typical customer made several impulse purchases of higher-margin products.

With their uniform low-margin policies, the clubs added a new quantitative dimension to this marketing equation. The prices they asked on pop-

---

[3]Compare Steiner (1973, 1985).

ular items were seen by TRU executives as a serious threat to TRU's reputation as a low-price vendor, and hence to TRU's ability to draw customers in for additional higher-margin purchases. To be sure, this adverse "image" effect could be minimized by reducing TRU's prices on the relatively few popular products stocked by the clubs. TRU's initial reaction to the clubs' rapid ascent in the early 1990s was to make selective downward price adjustments, with a maximum negative impact on its retail margins estimated at roughly $55 million per year. But it sought a better solution.

Following preliminary discussions with many of the leading toy manufacturers, TRU made the club problem the main theme of its meetings with toy manufacturers at the New York Toy Fair in February 1992—the annual meeting at which retailers join manufacturers to scrutinize the newest toy designs and book orders for the forthcoming pre-Christmas peak season. Through these meetings, TRU articulated to toy makers what its policy would be toward manufacturer sales to warehouse clubs:[4]

- Toy makers should sell to the clubs no new or advertised products unless the clubs purchased the manufacturer's entire product line.

- All special products, exclusives, and close-out clearance items offered to the clubs should be shown to TRU first to see whether TRU wished to preempt the clubs and stock them itself.

- Old and basic products should be sold in special combination packages, e.g., with a bridesmaid doll added to a basic Barbie Bride doll package.

- There was to be no discussion between TRU and the toy makers as to the prices at which these special, typically more complex and costly, products were sold to the clubs.

The penalty for violation was that TRU would not purchase offending products.

Subsequent fine-tuning discussions clarified the basic theme: that the manufacturers would not sell to the clubs products that were identical to those stocked by TRU, rendering it difficult for consumers to make straightforward comparisons between club and TRU prices. Since TRU tended to order all products expected to become best-sellers or receive television advertising support, this meant that the clubs would be able to obtain only by happenstance the most popular "hit" merchandise. (Predicting what new toys will catch consumers' fancy is an extremely uncertain game; even the most experienced retailer executives err.)

Most of the leading manufacturers accepted TRU's new policy with minor variations, and the supply of best-sellers to clubs atrophied. Despite the continuing growth of club merchandise sales more generally and an increase in the number of club outlets to 695 in 1995, warehouse clubs' toy sales peaked at 1.9 percent of total U.S. toy sales in 1992 and then declined

---

[4]Opinion of the Federal Trade Commission, 126 FTC 415, 539–540 (1998).

to 1.4 percent in 1995. By 1993, TRU no longer found it necessary to adjust "high profile" products' prices downward to deal with club competition.[5]

THE ANTITRUST CHALLENGE

The clubs responded to these changes in part by threatening legal action against TRU and the manufacturers, but they also informed the FTC of what had happened. Following an investigation, the FTC, pursuing more activist policies after twelve years of relative inactivity during the Reagan and Bush administrations, issued in May 1996 a formal complaint charging TRU with diverse antitrust violations.

Critics of U.S. antitrust policy often assert that in responding to information provided by aggrieved rivals (e.g., the clubs, as rivals of TRU), the federal antitrust agencies are protecting "competitors" rather than the processes of competition and hence consumer interests, as should properly be their mandate. There are two responses to this criticism. First, antitrust agency staff are acutely aware of the criticism and try hard to limit their cases to those that serve the broad public interest. Whether they succeeded in the TRU case is for the reader to judge. Second, agency staff have only limited insight into what is happening in the vast world of business enterprise. Consumers too, and especially consumers at retail, lack the information needed to defend themselves against abuses. Without information from aggrieved market participants and other affected parties, the antitrust enforcement agencies would overlook many genuine violations of the antitrust laws.[6]

The complaint against TRU was the subject of a bitterly contested trial before an FTC administrative law judge, who found in September 1997 that the antitrust laws had in fact been violated.[7] As is customary, the judge's decision was appealed by the losing party, in this instance TRU, to the FTC as a whole. In a meticulously reasoned decision that was plainly intended to make a definitive pronouncement on the extent to which retailers could initiate restraints limiting the purchasing opportunities of their rivals, the four Commission members (one of the five commissioner slots was vacant at the time) affirmed that TRU had violated the antitrust laws.[8]

The Vertical Restraints

TRU was charged with, and found responsible for, two rather different violations of the antitrust laws. For one, the agreements it elicited from indi-

---

[5]Opinion of the Commission, 126 FTC 415, 597 and note 15 of the commission's opinion.
[6]See Scherer (1990).
[7]*In the Matter of Toys "R" Us,* initial decision, September 25, 1997, 126 FTC 415, 418.
[8]Opinion of the Commission, 126 FTC 415 (1998).

vidual toy manufacturers not to sell popular items to the warehouse clubs fell under the rubric of *vertical restraints*—that is, where a firm (i.e., a retailer) located at one tier in the chain from production to consumption imposes restraints upon the distribution practices of firms (in this case, manufacturers) located at a different tier in the chain. But in addition, TRU was accused of orchestrating a set of horizontal agreements among manufacturers to deny popular products to—i.e., to boycott—the warehouse clubs.

Antitrust law makes a distinction between unilateral vertical restraints—e.g., TRU announces, "If you sell product X to the clubs, we will not stock it, end of discussion, full stop"—and restraints between vertically stacked parties in the distribution chain that comprise a meeting of minds and hence mutual agreement between the parties. The relevant case precedents show greater willingness to accept vertical restraints imposed unilaterally, as compared to those achieved by agreement, without a detailed investigation of the pros and cons.[9]

Although TRU claimed that in announcing to toy manufacturers its intent not to stock products they sold to the warehouse clubs it imposed only unilateral restraints, the facts clearly established that what occurred was much closer to a bilateral meeting of minds. TRU executives met repeatedly with each major toy manufacturer to present their list of demands. There was give-and-take in the discussions to modify the policies and adapt them to special circumstances. TRU sought, and from at least ten leading manufacturers received, assurances that the manufacturers would conform to the negotiated restrictions on supply to clubs. TRU executives inspected in advance the special products toy makers proposed to sell to the clubs and in some instances requested, and obtained, modifications that differentiated them more clearly from products stocked by TRU. There was continuing feedback as TRU monitored the availability of manufacturers' products on the shelves of warehouse clubs and reported apparent policy violations to the manufacturers, threatened and in some cases removed offending products from TRU shelves (actions that standing alone would be unilateral), and through subsequent negotiations achieved policy convergence.

Considering this record, the Commission found that a series of anticompetitive vertical agreements were reached that prima facie violated Sherman Act Section 1, but whose legality depended upon the analysis of additional considerations, to be addressed here shortly.

The Horizontal Boycott

Three of the four FTC commissioners, with one dissenting, concluded that TRU also acted as the "hub" in a horizontal "hub and spoke" agreement among toy manufacturers to deny top-line and advertised products to the

---

[9]The precedents are discussed at length in the Opinion of the Commission, 126 FTC 415, 569–615.

warehouse clubs. Such horizontal agreements are treated harshly under the antitrust laws as illegal per se, with consideration of extenuating circumstances only when the agreements yield plausible efficiency gains that cannot be achieved through alternative policies restricting competition less—conditions that are difficult to satisfy.

What gave rise to a horizontal agreement problem was the fact that most leading toy manufacturers viewed the clubs as an attractive and rapidly growing outlet for their products, sales to which would among other things lessen their growing dependence upon TRU as their largest and most powerful customer. To placate TRU and prevent it from taking product placement actions detrimental to their interests, the toy makers were willing to go along with TRU's proposed restraints—but only if they could be assured that they were not, in so doing, sacrificing sales to rival manufacturers.

Toys are highly differentiated products; as a rule, one toy maker does not consider itself to be competing head-to-head with all other toy makers, but rather with only a handful of firms that offer products (especially advertised products) similar in function and design to its own products. The manufacturers expressed concerns to TRU that if they complied with the proposed TRU policies, specifically named rivals might not, causing them to sacrifice significant sales in the clubs. As a top TRU executive testified, "They would always tell us, 'I'm only there because my competitor is there.' And we would say, 'Well, he keeps saying he's only there because you're there.'"[10] To deal with the problem, he testified, "We communicated to our vendors that we were communicating with all our key suppliers. . . . We made a point to tell each of the vendors that we spoke to that we would be talking to other key suppliers."[11]

TRU executives repeatedly informed toy manufacturers that a "level playing field" was being maintained and that their rivals had agreed to pursue the TRU-suggested policies. They received manufacturer complaints about rival noncompliance and communicated back to the originators reassurances that perceived deviations had been eliminated. And this, three of the four FTC commissioners concluded, was a classic "hub and spoke" horizontal agreement.[12] The dissenting commissioner questioned the strength of the factual evidence supporting a horizontal agreement inference and argued that "TRU's very indispensability gave each toy manufacturer every incentive—every *unilateral* incentive—to knuckle under to TRU's demands regarding the clubs," rendering horizontal agreements among the manufacturers unnecessary.[13]

---

[10]Testimony of Roger Goddu, quoted in Opinion of the Commission, 126 FTC 415, 554.

[11]Ibid. at p. 55, from CX 1658 p. 278.

[12]Among the precedents cited was *Interstate Circuit Inc.* v. *U.S.,* 306 U.S. 208 (1939).

[13]Opinion of Commissioner Orson Swindle dissenting in part and concurring in part, 126 FTC 415, 620 (emphasis in original).

A limitation of both the horizontal and vertical agreement allegations is that the agreements were not pervasive among toy manufacturers. The vertical agreements were found to have been implemented only by ten named producers, the horizontal agreements by seven—to be sure, those who originated most of the nationally advertised toy products.[14] Electronic game maker Nintendo in particular rejected TRU's overtures, in part because it sold its products through electronic specialty stores and was therefore less dependent upon TRU. Nintendo's noncompliance in turn posed problems for rival Sega, which adhered only intermittently to TRU's proposed policy. And at times Little Tikes, a manufacturer of large blow-molded toys, opted out because compliance might jeopardize more voluminous sales to warehouse clubs by its parent, the Rubbermaid Corporation. But there are strong antitrust law precedents holding that substantial but less than complete compliance with restrictive agreements does not reverse the illegality of such agreements if the impact on consumers is substantial.

The Role of Market Power

An appreciable fraction of the testimony by economists in the TRU case addressed the question of whether TRU possessed "market power" in the sense defined by prior antitrust precedents. As events ensued, this emphasis was misdirected, since proof of market power is normally unnecessary to infer illegality when horizontal agreements are shown. But for the vertical aspects of the case, the existence of market power would strengthen an inference of illegality, since an actor at one stage in the vertical chain of distribution was more likely to implement restraints with a meaningful impact on consumers if the initiator at another stage had a powerful position, and significant anticompetitive effects would ensue if the restraints applied to substantial shares of the affected markets.

The concept of "market power," said by a reviewing appellate court to imply a degree of market dominance less than "monopoly" in the sense normally used by economists,[15] is not well defined. There are at least three ways of showing that it exists or does not exist—structure-oriented measurement of market shares in relevant markets, statistical analyses of the relationship between prices and market shares, and analysis of the effects of restrictive actions on market outcomes. All three avenues were pursued in the Toys "R" Us case.

Although there are hundreds of toy manufacturers and thousands of firms retailing toys in the United States, both markets exhibit what at face value would be called intermediate concentration levels. At the manufacturing stage, the top four U.S. suppliers during the early 1990s originated

---

[14]Opinion of the Commission, 126 FTC 415, 575.

[15]*Toys "R" Us, Inc.* v. *Federal Trade Commission*, 221 F. 3d 928 (2000).

from 34 to 45 percent of total toy supplies (many imported from southeast Asia), varying with whether only traditional or also video game toys are counted and to some extent with the data source used. However, the focus of TRU's clubs policy was on nationally advertised toys, and for those, roughly two-thirds of the national television advertising was done by only eight toy makers, three of them divisions of Mattel, the source inter alia of Barbie dolls. By accepted antitrust standards, toy manufacturing was sufficiently highly concentrated that an inference of "market power" could be supported.

At the retailing level, Toys "R" Us accounted for approximately 20 percent of all retail toy sales in the United States. However, all parties acknowledged that the relevant retail markets for toys were localized. TRU maintained stores principally in the larger metropolitan areas. Its marketing research revealed that in population areas within a thirty-minute drive from a TRU store, its average share of the total toy market was approximately 32 percent—again, a structural position sufficient to imply the existence of "market power" under the received vertical restraints precedents.

TRU maintained rich internal data on the competitive structure of the localized retail markets surrounding its U.S. sales outlets. Tapping these data and information on individual store percentage retail margins, economists representing TRU computed regression equations relating store PRMs to the number of significant rivals (mainly, hypermarkets such as Wal-Mart and Target as well as, briefly during the early 1990s, warehouse clubs) within a local market. They showed that TRU realized somewhat lower PRMs in markets with one or two major rivals than in markets where no major retailing rival existed, and that the presence of additional rivals beyond two made no significant difference. The PRM differences with and without major competition were said to be sufficiently small as to be de minimus. However, TRU adjusted prices to deal with local market conditions for only about 250 items, typically those that were nationally advertised and/or "hot," out of the nearly 16,000 items it stocked at the time. For the majority of SKUs, prices were uniform nationally. A witness for the FTC testified that, given the modest share of total TRU sales associated with the items whose prices were geared to local competitive conditions, the implied price differences on those competition-sensitive items could be as much as 6 to 7 percent—a not negligible magnitude.

Economists representing TRU argued, using regression and qualitative evidence, that TRU's ability to raise prices in any given retail market was severely constrained by the presence of vigorous low-price competitors such as Wal-Mart, Kmart, and Target, and therefore that TRU lacked the "market power" required to find its vertical restraints inconsistent with antitrust law. It is undoubtedly true that TRU's ability to raise prices was constrained by strong competitors. However, the argument skirted a fundamental point. The purpose of TRU's warehouse clubs policy was directed not toward raising prices in local retail markets whose structure reflected the encroachment of hypermarkets, but toward curbing additional and rising competition from warehouse clubs that could otherwise force *reductions* in retail prices. To the extent that TRU's warehouse club policies were successful in suppressing the clubs' competitive threat, downward price changes were avoided—a clear manifestation of market power. As the FTC concluded, rejecting the constrained price increase argument, "there is little question that the boycott of the warehouse clubs that TRU organized *could* and *did* lower output by avoiding a decrease in toy prices by TRU and TRU's non-club competitors."[16]

The "Free-Riding" Efficiency Defense

The U.S. courts have accepted as a defense to some vertical restraints the argument that such restraints help solve problems that would otherwise render the distribution of goods or services less efficient. The basic theoretical premise was formulated by Telser (1960). Telser observed that retailers often provide presale services that help consumers make well-informed product choices and, by enhancing the demand for the products, are valuable to manufacturers. Although other presale services might fall within the scope of Telser's argument, the standard example is a retailer that maintains display models in its show room, explains to consumers (or allows them to experiment and learn) how the product functions, and hence enlightens their choices. Providing these services usually entails costs for the retailer. However, consumers might visit the high-service retailer's show room, utilize the presale services, and then travel down the street to a low-service outlet and buy the product at discounted prices. In this case, the discount retailer is said to "free-ride" on services provided by the high-service retailer, and if such free-riding occurs with sufficient frequency, the high-service retailer will lose its incentive to provide desirable services and the market will implode to a low-service equilibrium. Restricting the availability of products to low-service retailers and/or preventing them from quoting steeply discounted prices restores the incentive for retailers to provide the desired presale services.

How important such free-riding market failures are in the real world, their implications for consumer welfare, and whether there exist alternative, less restrictive ways of solving the free-riding problem, are questions on which unusually intense disagreement exists among professional economists, with those advocating vertical restraints identified more or less closely with the so-called Chicago School of thought.[17]

There was little dispute over the fact that TRU provided valuable presale services. With its large selection of products, it acted as a kind of

---

[16]Opinion of the Commission, 126 FTC 415, 597 (emphasis in original).

[17]For sharply differing textbook views on the problem, compare Carlton and Perloff (2000 ch. 12); and Scherer and Ross (1990, ch. 15).

"showroom" for toy industry manufacturers, ensuring that most of their products, and not just the best-sellers, were available to consumers. It tended to order products for the Christmas rush a few weeks earlier than did other toy retailers and to take delivery of the products slightly earlier, helping the manufacturers economize by spreading their production over a longer time period. It claimed also that its early stocking decisions signaled to other retailers what products were likely to be in strong demand, but this was contradicted by evidence showing that other retailers, and especially the warehouse clubs, made purchasing decisions on the basis of their own independent market assessments, taking into account manufacturers' announced advertising plans. Perhaps most importantly, several times a year TRU placed in leading metropolitan area newspapers catalogue inserts with full-color illustrations of several hundred products featured on its shelves, informing consumers of what was available and at what prices.

There were, however, several logical and factual problems with the TRU free-riding argument. For one, TRU's large product selection was unlikely to have provided presale information on which consumers then freerode to make purchases at warehouse clubs. TRU merely put its products on its shelves, without providing the kind of demonstrative services emphasized in the original free-rider theories. The average price of items advertised in TRU's newspaper insert catalogues in the spring of 1997 was $45.41, the median price $29.99. With such low ticket prices, few consumers inspect the product in a TRU show room and then make a special trip to buy the item at a lower-price (e.g., warehouse) outlet. The FTC found no evidence that consumers "sought demonstration or explanation of a toy at TRU and then purchased the product at a club."[18] In addition, TRU derived direct competitive advantage in consumers' eyes from having the largest selection of toys, and thus its large stock conferred consumer image benefits upon itself and was not something on which rivals plausibly free-rode.

Second, the costs that TRU incurred to take early delivery of seasonal products and to inform consumers about available toys and their prices through its widely distributed catalogues and newspaper inserts turned out not to be very high. It was compensated for its early stocking practices by the deferral of invoice payment requirements—e.g., from June, when delivery was taken, to December, when sales were at peak levels. When products taken into inventory turned out to be "duds" in consumers' eyes, manufacturers compensated TRU for the ensuing closeout discounts by granting substantial retroactive wholesale price discounts. Indeed, manufacturers testified that no other retailer received deferred payment terms and closeout discounts as favorable as those accorded TRU. They also paid TRU advertising allowances to compensate for the cost of distributing catalogues to consumers. The case evidence revealed that more than 90 percent of TRU's

---

[18]Opinion of the Commission, 126 FTC 415, 603–604.

advertising outlays during the mid-1990s were reimbursed by manufacturers.[19] If TRU bore little of the cost of providing presale advertising and early product stocking, it was implausible to infer that free-riding by others on those services could lead it to eliminate them, as the standard theory of free-riding assumes.

TRU's principal economic witness attempted to demonstrate through a series of regression analyses that other retailers nevertheless experienced sales increases as a result of TRU's catalog advertising, and hence free-rode on that advertising. What ensued was a war of alternative regression equation specifications. The first TRU analysis revealed that for items featured in TRU's April 2, 1995, catalogue, TRU achieved substantial sales gains relative to non-advertised items. But in addition, other toy retailers experienced smaller but still appreciable sales gains on those items relative to non-advertised items. The FTC's economic expert questioned whether there might have been something special about the items selected for the April 1995 catalog that induced high subsequent sales growth independent of the advertising effect—an example of what econometricians call "omitted variables" bias. Re-estimating the original TRU regression equation with variables added to measure the pre-April growth momentum achieved by advertised as compared to non-advertised products, the FTC analysis showed that catalog inclusion indeed augmented TRU's sales, but had a *negative* impact on rival retailers' sales of the advertised products. Another round of competing regression equation specifications yielded similar inference reversals, prompting the administrative law judge to call a halt to the war and view the statistical inferences as not proven.

Finally, in rejecting TRU's free-rider defense, the FTC observed that before February 1992, when the warehouse club policy was announced at a Toy Fair, "no toy company document . . . even hints that 'free-riding' by one toy retailer on the efforts of another could be a problem in the industry."[20] Rather, TRU's concern was the damage that low warehouse club prices could do to its reputation as a low-price merchandiser and the necessity of reducing popular toys' prices to warehouse club levels to avert that adverse reputation effect. The first recorded mention of free-riding in the voluminous case record occurred later in 1992, when the clubs threatened to sue TRU and its suppliers for discriminatory sales policies. The record is silent as to whether the notion originated spontaneously or whether it was suggested by outside consultants hired to evaluate the legal threats. Whatever the origin, the Commission concluded that TRU's concerns about free-riding as a justification for its restrictive policies were a "pretext" and not a valid basis for the policies' implementation.[21]

---

[19]National television advertising was sponsored almost exclusively by the manufacturers, not TRU. Toy advertising outlays on television in 1995 amounted to roughly five times TRU's outlays for (mostly) local catalog advertising.

[20]Opinion of the Commission, 126 FTC 415, 567. See also pp. 579–580 of the opinion.

[21]Opinion of the Commission, 126 FTC 415, 607.

THE OUTCOME

Rejecting the free-rider defense and concluding that TRU had orchestrated both a horizontal boycott and restrictive vertical agreements, the FTC ruled that TRU had violated the antitrust laws. It ordered TRU to cease entering into vertical agreements with its toy suppliers that limited the supply of toys to discounters, to cease facilitating horizontal agreements among its suppliers concerning the sale of toys to other retailers, and to refrain from requesting information from manufacturers about their sales to toy discounters.

Throughout the proceedings, counsel for TRU openly expressed doubts that they could obtain a fair trial at the FTC combining as it does in a carefully compartmentalized way the functions of prosecutor and judge. TRU therefore sought, as many losing parties do, reversal from an independent federal appellate court. Operating in all parts of the United States, it could as the appealing party choose the jurisdiction in which to file its appeal. It selected the Seventh Circuit Court of Appeals, situated in Chicago, with three members of the University of Chicago law faculty as sitting judges. It presumably believed that its chances were best in the environment where the theory of free-riding had originated. If so, then it was mistaken.

A panel of three appellate judges headed by a University of Chicago law faculty member unanimously ratified the FTC's decision.[22] It found that the horizontal boycott and vertical agreements had violated Section 1 of the Sherman Act and that TRU's pleadings "fundamentally misunderstood the theory of free riding," since in the absence of TRU threats, most leading manufacturers wanted to sell to the clubs without restrictions and since, with manufacturers paying for most of TRU's presale services, there was little opportunity for meaningful free-riding.

THE AFTERMATH

The Federal Trade Commission's October 1998 decision finding TRU in violation of the antitrust laws precipitated a flurry of additional class action antitrust suits against TRU and leading toy manufacturers, some by private parties seeking compensation for damages sustained and one by the attorneys general of forty-four U.S. states plus Puerto Rico and the District of Columbia. "To avoid the cost and uncertainty of protracted litigation," TRU along with three toy manufacturers negotiated in 1998 and 1999 settlements valued at a total of $56 million, some paid in cash and most in the form of toys to be distributed to needy children.[23]

---

[22]*Toys "R" Us, Inc.* v. *Federal Trade Commission,* 221 F.3d 928 (2000).

[23]Annual Report, Toys "R" Us, 2000, "Other Matters" (www.shareholder.com/toy/toysrus00. t2000ar36); Canedy (1998); and Gargiulo (1999).

In addition to the rejection of its policies toward warehouse clubs, whose overall sales growth slowed during the late 1990s, TRU experienced increasing competition from hypermarkets, and especially from a Wal-Mart that was continuing its "march to the sea" and overtaking TRU as the nation's leading toy seller. Faulty purchasing decisions—inevitable in as fashion-sensitive a business as toy retailing—also contributed to net losses in its fiscal year ending January 30, 1999.[24]

The next two years brought a restoration of profitability, although not to the level of returns on stockholders' equity it had enjoyed during the early 1990s. TRU placed increasing emphasis on stocking toys for which it received exclusive selling rights from manufacturers and encouraged its sales staff to devote more of their time (estimated at 30 percent in 2002) to helping shoppers.[25] It continued to expand, operating 710 toy stores in the United States on February 3, 2001 (reduced by twenty-seven in 2002), and 491 toy stores outside the United States.

Pinpointing what role the FTC's intervention had in the change of TRU's fortunes could be the subject of a challenging research project.

REFERENCES

Adelman, Morris A. *A&P: A Study in Price-Cost Behavior and Public Policy.* Cambridge, Mass.: Harvard University Press, 1959.

Canedy, Dana. "Hasbro to End Suit with $6 Million Donation." *New York Times,* December 11, 1998, p. C-20.

Carlton, Dennis W. "Market Power and Vertical Restraints in Retailing: An Analysis of FTC v. Toys 'R' Us." In *The Role of the Academic Economist in Litigation Support,* edited by Daniel J. Slottje, 67–96. Amsterdam: Elsevier, 1999.

Carlton, Dennis W., and Jeffrey M. Perloff. *Modern Industrial Organization,* 3d edn. Reading, Mass.: Addison-Wesley Longman, 2000.

Chandler, Alfred D. *The Visible Hand: The Managerial Revolution in American Business.* Cambridge, Mass.: Harvard University Press, 1977.

Gargiulo, Linda. "Putting Children First in a Toy Settlement." *New York Times,* May 30, 1999, p. III-4.

Hays, Constance L. "Toys 'R' Us Plans to Lay Off 1,900 and Close 64 Stores." *New York Times,* December 29, 2001, p. C-1.

Scherer, F. M. "Sunlight and Sunset at the Federal Trade Commission." *Administrative Law Review* 42 (Fall 1990): 461–487.

Scherer, F. M. "Retail Distribution Channel Barriers to International Trade." *Antitrust Law Journal* 67, no. 1 (1999): 77–112.

---

[24]Toys "R" Us Annual Report, 2000, "Financial Highlights."

[25]See Hays (2001).

Scherer, F. M., and David Ross. *Industrial Market Structure and Economic Performance.* Boston: Houghton-Mifflin, 1990.

Steiner, Robert L. "Does Advertising Lower Consumer Prices?" *Journal of Marketing* 37 (October 1973): 19–26.

Steiner, Robert L. "The Nature of Vertical Restraints." *Antitrust Bulletin* 30 (Spring 1985): 346–359.

Telser, Lester G. "Why Should Manufacturers Want Fair Trade?" *Journal of Law & Economics* 3 (October 1960): 86–105.

CASE 16

Bundling: GE-Honeywell (2001)

Barry Nalebuff

INTRODUCTION

The economic theory of bundling has moved from the classroom and academic journals to the public policy arena. Its debut was dramatic. On July 3, 2001, the European Commission (EC) blocked the $42 billion merger between General Electric (GE) and Honeywell.[1] A primary reason for their objection to this combination was a concern over bundling.

This case study uses the context of the proposed GE-Honeywell merger to address the concerns raised by bundling.[2] We set out the theory as put forth by the EC and try to reconcile this theory with both the economic theory of bundling and the facts of the case. We discuss what is meant by bundling and explain when it is a potential problem and when it is not. Based on this understanding, we propose antitrust policy recommendations to deal with the novel issues raised by bundling.

BACKGROUND

On October 19, 2000, United Technologies Corporation (UTC) reported that it was in merger discussions with Honeywell. Three days later, a merger was announced—but the buyer was GE, not UTC.

---

[1]The merger was voted on by the twenty-member European Commission. Their vote confirmed the recommendation made by Competition Commissioner Mario Monti, who, in turn, was given a recommendation by the European Union Merger Task Force.

[2]The author was an economic expert for GE-Honeywell in their presentation to the European Union Merger Task Force. The application of bundling theory to the GE-Honeywell merger was done together with Patrick Rey, Carl Shapiro, Shihua Lu, and Greg Vistnes. The opinions expressed in this paper are solely those of the author.

This case generated a good deal of attention. General Electric is one of the most well-known and admired companies in the world. At $42 billion, this was a large merger even for GE. The proposed integration passed the scrutiny of the U.S. Department of Justice (DOJ). Because of the size of GE and Honeywell's European sales, the merger also had to be approved by the European Commission.[3] On July 3, 2001, that permission was denied.[4] The divergence of outcomes between the U.S. and European antitrust authorities added to the publicity of this case.

THE PLAYERS

GE's 2001 revenues exceeded $125 billion, and its businesses included everything from plastics and television (NBC) to financial services, power systems, medical imaging, and lighting. In the arena of aviation, GE produces aircraft engines on its own (GEAE) and through CFMI, a 50-50 joint venture with SNECMA (a French company). This joint venture accounted for a large majority of GE's engine sales, as CFMI is the exclusive provider of engines for Boeing's most popular plane, the 737. CFMI engines also power the Airbus A320 family and the A340-200/300. GE's own engines power the Boeing 777, 767, and 747 planes. They also power the Airbus A300, A310, A330, and the not-yet launched A380 super-jumbo aircraft.[5] In almost all of these cases, CFMI and GEAE compete with Pratt & Whitney (a division of UTC), Rolls Royce, or IAE (a PW/RR joint venture).

Honeywell started out in heating and environmental controls and over time developed a leadership position in aerospace.[6] Honeywell's position in avionics was enhanced through a series of mergers, most notably the purchase of Sperry Aerospace in 1986 and a merger with Allied Signal in 1999. Allied Signal was itself a leader in aerospace, the result of Allied Corporation's purchase of Bendix in 1983 and merger with the Signal Companies in 1985. Along with avionics, Honeywell's nonavionics aerospace products include auxiliary power units (which give power to the plane when on the

---

[3]"The Commission has authority to review all mergers, acquisitions and takeover bids and other deals that can be defined as a 'concentration', involving companies with a combined turnover worldwide in excess of €5,0 billion and European sales of at least €250 million" (Commission press release *IP/01/939*). See also Article 1 (2) (a) and (b) of the European Merger Control Regulation, Council Regulation 4064/89 EEC of 21 December 1989 on the Control of the Concentration between Undertakings, 1990 O.J. (L 257) 13, as amended by Council Regulation 1310/97 EC of June 30, 1997, 1998 O.J. (L 180) 1.

[4]While the parties have appealed the decision to the Court of First Instance of the European Communities, a judgment is not expected until sometime in 2003, too late to resurrect the prohibited transaction

[5]The GP7000 engine, designed to power the Airbus A380, is a joint venture between GE and Pratt & Whitney.

[6]Honeywell instruments helped guide Apollo astronauts Neil Armstrong and Buzz Aldrin's landing on the moon.

ground), starter motors, environmental control systems, aircraft lighting systems, engine accessories and controls, wheels, and braking equipment. In 2001, nearly one-half of Honeywell's $23 billion of revenue came from their aerospace division.

THE CASE AGAINST THE MERGER

To block a merger, the Merger Control Regulation requires the Commission to demonstrate that the proposed merger would lead to market dominance. According to European case law, dominance is defined as:

> a position of economic strength enjoyed by an undertaking which enables it to prevent effective competition being maintained on the relevant market by giving it the power to behave to an appreciable extent independently of its competitors, customers and ultimately of consumers.[7]

In this case, the claimed route to market dominance was unusual. It was not through the merger of competitors. Nor was it through a vertical integration of customer and supplier.[8] Given the depth and breadth of GE and Honeywell product offerings, there was a remarkable *lack* of overlap between the two companies. Instead, the focus of the merger review was on "conglomerate effects" or horizontal integration issues of bringing complements together.[9]

The Commission's case against the merger emphasized three linked points.

- First, the Commission claimed that GE had a dominant position in aircraft engines for large commercial aircraft and Honeywell had a leading position in avionics and nonavionics areas.

- Second, they claimed that the proposed merger would allow the new firm to bundle these complementary products. The bundling strategy would lead to price discounts that would give the firm an unbeatable advantage over its rivals.

---

[7]Case 27/76 *United Brands* v. *Commission* [1978] ECR 207 at 286.

[8]The very few areas of competitive overlap could have been resolved by divestitures. GE's role in speculative aircraft leasing and Honeywell's starter motor business did bring up some issues of vertical integration, which are not discussed here. See Pflanz and Caffarra (2002) for an excellent analysis of the unorthodox arguments made regarding the role of GE's leasing company, GECAS. A good summary of the commission's case regarding GECAS is presented in Giotakas et al. (2001).

[9]The Commission referred to this as a conglomerate effect. I prefer the term *horizontal integration of complementors* as it emphasizes the specific nature of the relationship—namely that their two products are used together by a common customer. Honeywell's customers are primarily the airframe manufacturers and airlines, not the engine maker. Thus, Honeywell is a complementor to GE as opposed to a supplier. (See Brandenburger and Nalebuff [1996] for a more formal definition of complementors.) Starter motors (and a few related components) are the exception to this rule.

- The third leg of the argument was that this advantage would lead to the exit of rivals and thus ultimately to strengthening the dominance of the merged GE.

As explained in the EU Final Decision (para. 355):

> Because of their lack of ability to match the bundle offer, these component suppliers will lose market shares to the benefit of the merged entity and experience an immediate damaging profit shrinkage. As a result, the merger is likely to lead to market foreclosure on the existing aircraft platforms and subsequently to the elimination of competition in these areas.

To an economist, the Commission's case was unorthodox. The concern was that under the merger prices would fall—not that prices would rise. The idea that bundle discounts could be an anticompetitive strategy was novel to this case.[10] A merger that created cost savings that resulted in lower prices would be permitted. But if the lower prices came from pricing efficiencies, this was viewed as anticompetitive. There was no discussion of whether the lower prices on the road to market dominance would or would not result in a net increase in the present discounted value of consumer surplus. Such considerations do not appear to be within the Commission's mandate.

Even to a lawyer, the Commission's case was unorthodox. The Commission did not demonstrate that the combination *would* lead to dominance, as required by its mandate. Rather, it emphasized the *theoretical* potential for future anticompetitive behavior.[11]

In this case study, we focus on the Commission's arguments concerning bundling. Not only is this aspect of the case novel, it also has wide-ranging implications for other mergers. We present the Commission's case for why bundling might create an antitrust issue, and then discuss whether the theory and evidence justified their conclusion.

It will help to define bundling at the outset. Many items are sold together in a package. That in itself does not mean that the items are bundled. The answer depends on how else and at what prices the items can be purchased. For example, if two items are *only* sold together and are not available separately, this is a case of pure bundling. This may be done via pricing or via technology.

---

[10]Range effects had been considered in a number of prior EU cases, including Coca-Cola/Amalgamated Beverages and Guinness/ Grand Metropolitan. These cases focused on distribution efficiencies rather than pricing strategies.

[11]Schmitz (2002) criticizes the decision on this basis: "Although it is probably true that the new company would indeed have the *potential* to bundle and it cannot be ruled out that at one point in time it might engage in this behavior, using this potential to conclude that the merger would strengthen a pre-existing dominant position within the meaning of Article 2 European Merger Control Regulation is questionable. . . . Describing the question of whether it is permissible to block a merger because of possible future bundling as theoretical, hardly fits the impact it has. . . . [T]he tool for this investigation is and must be Article 82 EC, not the European Merger Control Regulation."

Pure bundling becomes tying when one of the items, say item 1, is sold by itself, but item 2 is only available as part of a package with 1. Thus, the National Football League (NFL) has a season pass program to television viewers to watch every game of the season. This viewing option is only available on satellite TV and is not offered to cable viewers. Of course, satellite viewers can also buy a contract without the NFL season pass. Thus, we would say that the NFL season pass is tied to satellite TV.

The most general form of bundling is mixed bundling and this was the type of bundling emphasized by the Commission. In mixed bundling, two items are available both separately and as a 1–2 package. *What makes this bundling is that the package is sold at a discount relative to the individual items.* If the package is simply priced at the sum of its component prices, and these components are each available on an a la carte basis, then we do not call this bundling, as there is no strategic impact of the bundle pricing. Note that mixed bundling includes pure bundling and tying as special cases.

In this next section, we first present the argument as made by the Commission concerning mixed bundling and then question whether this theory of bundling was applicable to the case at hand.

THE ECONOMIC THEORY OF BUNDLING

The theory of bundling begins with Cournot (1838). Cournot considered the case of a monopoly seller of good 1 and a different monopoly seller of good 2 where the two goods are used together by the customer. Cournot used as an example the case of copper and zinc that are combined to make brass. Here one can think of the two goods as a jet engine and avionics.

Cournot's insight is that two monopolists, acting independently, will set an inefficiently high price. Were they to merge or coordinate their pricing, they would lower their prices and earn more money. The simple intuition is that the lower price of good 1 stimulates sales of good 2 (and vice versa) and this effect is not considered when goods 1 and 2 are sold independently.

It is not surprising that the merging firms make more money. What is unusual here is that prices *fall* so that consumers are also better off. The merger is a Pareto improvement. Thus the antitrust authorities should encourage such mergers.[12] We return to this issue when we discuss policy implications.

The Cournot example is the horizontal equivalent of "double marginalization." Each firm causes a negative externality on the complementary

---

[12]One of the ironies of this case is that if one took the view that GE and Honeywell each had a monopoly position then bundling would unambiguously improve welfare. The only possible source of harm would be on competitors. But if each firm (as a monopolist) does not face competitors, there is no harm done.

products by raising its price. When the two firms combine, they internalize this effect and lower prices. The simplicity of Cournot's argument has led to general confusion about when the theory is applicable.

In some ways this result is very general. It does not depend on the specific form of the demand function nor the cost function. It does not require that the goods be perfect complements. But there are several hidden assumptions on which the result relies. Two, in particular, are of concern to us.

First, the basic Cournot model does not consider the impact of the merger on any other firms in the market. This is by design. In Cournot, the producers of goods 1 and 2 are alone in the market. To apply this approach to the facts as interpreted by the Commission in the GE-Honeywell merger, we need to consider how the results change when the two merging firms are not alone in the market. Naturally, the results are more complicated.

There are now two reasons to cut price: market expansion and competition with rivals. Cournot looked at the price reduction as a way to increase the total market. Though the total demand for airplane engines can be expanded with a price reduction, the engine (along with avionics) is only a minority of the total airplane cost. The greater impact of a price cut is through the potential to gain market share from rivals.

Because there are rival firms, there will also be a response to a price cut. This response may offset the potential gain to the merging firms. Thus, we will want to consider the equilibrium impact on the nonmerging firms and on consumers to determine the overall social welfare implications.

A second reason why the Cournot framework may not apply to the GE-Honeywell merger is that the basic result depends on an unstated assumption: *that firms set a single price in the market to all customers.* This is a quite reasonable assumption for a typical consumer good, such as Microsoft Office. But it is not a reasonable assumption for the sale of large commercial products in which the two parties engage in extensive negotiation as part of the sale process. If firms can price discriminate or negotiate with each customer, then the advantage to bundling disappears.

Our focus here will be on the applicability of the Cournot model. There are other reasons to offer a bundle besides curing double marginalization. For example, even a monopolist seller of both good 1 and good 2 might be able to use bundled pricing as a way to improve its ability to engage in price discrimination.[13] This incentive to bundle is more important if there is demand for the goods individually (as is the true case with copper and zinc) than when all customers buy both goods (as is typically the case with jet engines and avionics).[14] We do not emphasize this aspect of bundling, as it did not play a role in the GE-Honeywell case.

---

[13]See, for example, Adams and Yellen (1976); McAfee, McMillan, and Whinston (1989); Bakos and Brynjolfsson (1999).

[14]There is still an advantage to bundling in a world where all customers buy a 1-2 package and the rival sellers of good 1 (and good 2) are imperfect substitutes. This advantage only exists so long as the firm cannot perfectly price discriminate.

COMPETING AGAINST BUNDLES

We first extend the original Cournot model to cover the case where the two sellers face competition in the market. The results from this approach were at the heart of the Commission's theoretical argument against the merger.

This approach is based on Nalebuff (2000). We consider the case with four firms in the market. There are two differentiated versions of the first good, produced by firms, A_1 and B_1 and two differentiated versions of the second good, produced by firms A_2 and B_2.

To model the product differentiation we assume that both A components are located at 0, while both B components are located at 1. (These locations "0" and "1" can be thought of as points in geographic space or in product characteristics space.) The two goods can be thought of as avionics and engines with the "A" firms being GE and Honeywell and the "B" firms being Pratt & Whitney and Rockwell Collins.

Because planes require both engines and avionics, the customer will purchase one unit of both components in the basket. Thus, each customer will buy one of (A_1, A_2), (A_1, B_2), (B_1, A_2), or (B_1, B_2).

Customers assemble the package that best suits their preferences. Each customer purchases the package with the smallest total cost, where total cost is composed of price plus a linear unit transportation cost. We assume that for each of the two goods, the customer's ideal location is uniformly distributed over [0, 1].[15] Location preferences for each good are independent.

There are three possible market structures. All four firms act independently; the two A firms bundle as do the two B firms, resulting in bundle-against-bundle competition; the two A firms combine, while the two B firms remain separate.[16]

Case 1: A_1, A_2, B_1, B_2 each separate

Case 2: A_1-A_2 combination versus B_1-B_2 combination

Case 3: A_1-A_2 combination versus B_1 and B_2 separate

Case 1: All Firms Act Independently

With a uniform distribution of customers and unit transportation costs, the equilibrium prices equal 1, and the market is evenly split between firms A and B.[17]

---

[15]Later we will explore cases where the sellers have more information as to the customer's preferences. This leads to a different distribution of customer locations.

[16]The case where the two B firms combine and the A firms remain separate leads to the same results.

[17]This result assumes "Bertrand" price competition between each of the pairs of competitors. We further assume that production has constant and equal marginal costs. With this assumption, profit margins are independent of costs, and so we employ zero marginal costs in the results below.

$$P_{A1} = P_{A2} = P_{B1} = P_{B2} = 1; \qquad \pi_{A1} = \pi_{A2} = \pi_{B1} = \pi_{B2} = 1/2,$$

where P_i is price and π_i is profit.

This case is the baseline from which we can evaluate the impact of co-ordinated pricing decisions. In this baseline case, consumers mix and match their preferred components and pay a price of 2 for their two-good customized bundle.

Case 2: Bundle versus Bundle

Here all the A firms coordinate their pricing and sell their product as a bundle against the B firms, who have also coordinated their pricing decisions.[18] Let bundle A sell for $P_A = P_{A1} + P_{A2}$, and bundle B sell for P_B, defined similarly. In this equilibrium

$$P_A = P_B = 1; \qquad \pi_A = \pi_B = 1/2.$$

Profits fall by 50 percent. This is because the aggregate bundle price has fallen by 50 percent. The price of the entire bundle is reduced to the prior price of each of the single components. In hindsight, the intuition is relatively straightforward. Cutting price brings the same number of incremental customers as when selling individual components. So the bundle price must equal the individual price in a symmetric equilibrium. Bundle against bundle is ferocious competition. Similar results hold for bundles with more than two goods as demonstrated in Nalebuff (2000).

Case 3: Bundle against Components

The pricing externality suggests that the bundler will have an advantage over the component sellers. But the results of case 2 suggest that this gain may be offset by an increase in competition induced by the A firms selling their products only as bundle. Which effect dominates?

$$P_A = 1.45; P_{Bi} = 0.86, P_B = 1.72; \qquad \pi_A = 0.91, \pi_{Bi} = 0.32$$

It turns out that the increased competition effect dominates so that bundling reduces Firm A's profits from 1 to 0.91. The bundler does roughly 50 percent better than the sum of the uncoordinated B firms. The market share moves from a 50-50 split to 63-37. But even with this gain in share, the bundler does about 10 percent worse than in the case where each component is sold in an uncoordinated fashion. The explanation is that the bundle takes away enough market share from the B firms so that the resulting

---

[18]For simplicity, we assume that consumers buy only one of the two bundles.

equilibrium prices are low enough to make the A firm worse off.[19] Thus, even though it leads to an advantage, there is no incentive to bundle.

These results, taken from Nalebuff (2000), consider the case of pure bundling—products A_1 and A_2 are only available as a bundle. To apply this model to GE-Honeywell, the results need to be extended to cover the case of mixed bundling.

Mixed Bundling

Rolls Royce presented to the Commission an extension of this model to include the case of mixed bundling.[20] While it is difficult to find a closed-form solution, the approximate equilibrium prices and profits can be found through simulation. The results are not identical to the pure bundling case, though they have the same flavor.

The A bundle is sold for a 19 percent discount below the pre-merger price of 2, and the component prices for A rise from 1 to 1.21. The B firms respond to this increased competition by lowering their component prices to 0.890.

$$P_A = 1.63, P_{Ai} = 1.21; P_{Bi} = 0.89, P_B = 1.78; \pi_A = 0.97, \pi_{Bi} = 0.40$$

Even with mixed bundling, the merging firm still sacrifices profits. Profits fall from 1.00 to 0.97 or 3 percent. Although its profits fall, firm A gains an advantage over its rivals. Firm A's market share is 55.4 percent and the rival's profits fall by 21 percent.

This model is obviously quite stylized. The results about whether or not the bundling is profitable can be reversed with relatively minor changes in parameter values or modeling assumptions. For example, bundling becomes more profitable the more items are added to the bundle (at least for the case of pure bundling).

While the biggest impact from lowering price comes from gaining market share, there is also the potential to expand the total market. As recognized by Choi (2001), even if this effect is small, it can be enough to make bundling profitable.

Thus, the commission reached the conclusion that economic incentives would lead a firm to engage in mixed bundling. That a firm that bundles obtains an advantage over its rivals is a relatively robust conclusion. But whether or not a multiproduct firm has an economic incentive to bundle is a much more delicate finding. And by the same token, so is the expected loss to the competition. Among other factors, it depends on the num-

---

[19]As the bundle grows in size, the gap in prices continues to grow and, consequently, so does the bundler's market share. Once the bundle has four or more items, equilibrium profits rise for the bundling firm. See Nalebuff (2000).

[20]The nonconfidential version is presented in Choi (2001).

ber of items in the bundle and the elasticity of total market demand. The results presented rely on a specific distribution of preferences, namely a uniform distribution. It is not clear if the results would be robust across different distributions of customer preferences.

The results also depend on the two goods in the bundle being of symmetric importance to the consumer. Clearly, the engine is more important than the avionics or even all of the potential Honeywell components combined.

An aircraft engine might have a $15 million price tag, while a piece of avionics could sell in the $100,000 range. Overall, the avionics components add up to less than 5 percent of the total aircraft cost. The basic model of bundling has the two products being symmetric in valuation. Nalebuff and Lu (2001) extend the earlier model to allow for asymmetry in importance. In the examples considered, there appears to be little incentive to bundle and minimal impact on competitors. In fact, with pure bundling and enough asymmetry, bundling actually *increases* the profits of all the players in the market.

The Rolls Royce model only examines the two-goods, two-vendor case. Realistically, the number of avionics and nonavionics goods purchased is in the several dozens, and the number of important vendors is at least a dozen. We need to understand not just whether mixed bundling is attractive or not, but also how much more attractive it is as the bundle size increases and what impact that increased bundle has on the market.

Thus, before we try to use these type of models to make predictions about the likely impact of a merger, the models need to be robust enough to capture some important elements of the real-world market.[21] If one takes the results of this model at face value, it is not clear why there should be any antitrust concern. Average prices fall in the market. Consumers are better off at the expense of firms.

One can make the argument that social welfare falls, but as Patrick Rey observed in his presentation to the European Union Merger Task Force this is truly an artifact of the model. As demand is inelastic, the only change in social welfare is due to a change in transportation costs. Since transportation costs are minimized in the initial symmetric equilibrium, *any* change would lead to a fall in social welfare. But this argument depends critically on the starting points being completely symmetric. If, for example, the merging firms have a superior position and a larger share, then the bundle discount can lead to increased efficiency.

---

[21]But even assuming for a moment that all of these issues did not exist, work by Patrick Rey shows that even on its own terms the Rolls Royce model was fatally flawed. In order to estimate the impact of the proposed merger, one needs to have coefficients on the model. The problem is that there is only one observation to use to estimate these parameters. Rolls Royce used the existing market shares. At best that would leave the model exactly identified. However, in this case the model was still underidentified. Thus, the impact of the merger would depend on the choice of some parameters for which there were no data to make an estimate.

The Commission's problem with bundling was not with the immediate loss to social welfare but rather with the long-run (and even short-run) impact on competition. Similar to the argument against predation, the Commission believed that rivals would exit and that GE-Honeywell would obtain and exploit a dominant position.

Dynamics

If one wants to consider the expected market dynamics, then there are other factors that should be taken into account. For example, is it realistic to imagine that the individual competitors would not respond in any way? One option for those firms is to invest in product improvements or cost reductions. Another option would be to offer a competing bundle.

For the B firms, offering a competing bundle would lead to a further reduction in profits, but it would also level the playing field (recall case 2). Firms may prefer to be in a symmetric position relative to a rival. They may prefer a lower but level playing field if they are worried that a bundler would use its profit advantage to position itself better in R&D or gain other advantages in a repeated game.

Even if the B firms did not want to offer a competing bundle, their customers could drive them to this outcome. Customers would stand to gain a great deal if they could create a bundle-against-bundle competition. Customers are anything but passive in this market and would use their power to influence the nature of competition.

The Rolls Royce model looked at the advantages of bundling when the competition was selling their products individually. *Whatever advantages may exist, they quickly disappear if the rival firms coordinate and offer a competing bundle.* Given the level playing field for rivals and the advantages to customers, a firm that introduces a product bundle cannot expect that rival firms will not offer competing bundles.

NEGOTIATING BUNDLES

The previous discussion suggests several potentially interesting questions for antitrust policy, but its relevance to the GE-Honeywell merger is doubtful. The reason is that the previous results on bundling all depend critically on the assumption that there is one price to all customers in the market. This is such a basic assumption to most economics models that it is usually not even stated. However, this assumption does not apply to the aerospace industry.

Customers don't pay list price for jet engines or avionics. Airplane customers are large and powerful. A vendor cannot ignore an airline that asks for a better price. Nor are vendors uninformed as to their customers' preferences. The vendors in this market spend a great deal of resources getting to know their customers. Vendors take into account previous purchases as well as technical performance differences between their products and those of competitors. Going into a competition a vendor has a good idea of where it stands; and by the end of the competition, it has a very good idea.

The result of this buyer power and vendor information is that prices are negotiated, not set by the seller. Examples of transaction prices confirm the fact that different buyers pay different prices. Every deal is negotiated, and the price is customized to the specifics of the situation.

In a world where firms negotiate prices with customers and do so with perfect information, the combination of two complementor firms is completely neutral. To see why, first take the case where a customer has a preference for the two firm A products. Imagine that the net advantages are equal to (0.2, 0.3). In this case, the A firms would be expected to win both competitions, whether the items are sold separately or if the firms merge and the products are sold in a bundle.

Before conceding defeat, the B firms would be willing to price down to marginal cost. In the case where the A goods are sold separately, Firm A_1 would be able to negotiate a profit up to 0.2 on good 1 and Firm A_2 could negotiate a profit of up to 0.3 on good 2. If the goods were sold as a bundle, then the merged firm A would be able to negotiate a profit of up to 0.5 on the bundle.

Nothing is different if firm B has an advantage in one (or both) of the goods. Take the case where the customer has a net preference for A products of $(-0.2, 0.3)$, so that the customer actually prefers B_1 to A_1. With individual pricing, firm A_1 would lose to B_1 and firm A_2 would beat B_2. If merged A firm tried to sell the two products as a bundle, it could do so, but only at a profit of 0.1. This would be worse than selling just the second good at a profit of 0.3.

These two examples are quite general. The point they illustrate is the following: When the customer type is known and prices are negotiated, bundling can never lead to higher profits. If the customers would have made all of their purchases from a single firm, bundling has no impact—on customers, prices, profits, or efficiency. If customers would prefer some products from A and others from B, then the combined firm will continue to offer the individual goods at their premerged prices. Forcing a bundle on the consumer can only lower firm A's profits. In effect, it would have to subsidize its disadvantage using profits it could have earned from products where it is strongest. This is no different from selling individual components at a loss—a strategy it can do but would choose not to, even without bundling.

One additional perspective can help with the intuition. Firms make profits only to the extent that their products are differentiated. Profits exist to the extent that the firm has an advantage with the customer. When a firm bundles two good products or two bad products together, the advantages (or disadvantages) sum up and there is no impact. But when a firm mixes good and bad products together, this mitigates the advantage and profits fall accordingly. With mixed bundling, there would be no bundle discount and thus no effect at all.

The perfect information negotiation model is designed to capture the basic nature of competition in this market. But, like all models, it presents a simplified description of the market. While vendors are well informed about the customer, their information is not always accurate. Firms can still negotiate prices even with good but imperfect information as to customer preferences.

The conclusion from this negotiation model is not a narrow result. The mathematics of the more realistic cases becomes more difficult, but simulation results suggest that bundling has little effect when vendors have good but not perfect information.

As one example, imagine that the firms don't know the customer's exact location (and thus preferences) but do know which firms the customer prefers.[22] Consider a customer who is known to prefer both A products.

In this case, bundling offers a small advantage. A firm that knows it has an advantage in all components can use a bundle to do a better job of price discrimination. Market efficiency increases. Competitors' profits fall, but their profits in this case were very low to start with.

In contrast, bundling is not profitable when the merging firm is at a disadvantage in all products. Here we also note that this is the case where rivals have the highest profits. Thus, bundling has the lowest impact when rivals make the most money.

Pure bundling or tying would be counterproductive in the two cases where the merging firm is better in one component and worse in the other. If the merging firm employs mixed bundling, then the majority of consumers do not take advantage of the bundle, and there is again a small impact of the mixed bundle.

Averaging across these four cases, the net impact of the mixed bundling strategy is reduced by 50 percent. This is in line with the improved information. Half of the uncertainty has been removed in the sense that each firm knows if it is ahead or behind, although not by how much.[23] Nalebuff and Lu (2001) show that with even better information, the impact of mixed bundling is even smaller.

The distribution used in generating the simulation results provides the results for a given type of customer with some uncertainty, but that leaves open the question of what is the proper distribution of customer types. The tightness of the distribution is a proxy for the quality of information in any particular negotiation.

---

[22]For more specifics on this approach, see Nalebuff and Lu (2001).

[23]Another way of putting this is that each firm knows which half of the line the customer is in and thus the range of uncertainty has been reduced by half.

The wide margin variations that we observe are indicative of high-quality information, but this is not something that has been empirically measured and calibrated to the model.

EMPIRICAL EVIDENCE OF DOMINANCE AND BUNDLING

Ultimately, the Commission's case against the proposed merger rested on a claim of market dominance. The starting point in this argument was that GE already had a dominant position in aircraft engines for large commercial aircraft. Recall that market dominance means that a firm can act independently of its rivals and its customers.

It almost follows from the definition that a firm without a commanding market share cannot have a dominant position in the market. The Commission presented its calculation that GE had a dominant position with a 52.5 percent market share of the installed base of engines on large commercial aircraft still in production:[24]

	GE	PW/IAE	RR/IAE
Narrow Body	51	22	27
Wide Body	54	31	15
Overall	**52.5**	**26.5**	**21**

Planes still in production leaves out planes still in service but no longer produced. While new engines are obviously no longer sold to planes no longer being built, this perspective misses the spare parts market. With spare parts an engine can be "sold" up to ten times over its working life. Pratt & Whitney, in particular, has a large annuity coming to it from selling spare parts to planes in service that are no longer being produced. Using the planes-in-service approach, GE's market share falls to 41 percent.

The calculation of market shares for PW (Pratt & Whitney) and RR (Rolls Royce) include the engines of IAE, a joint venture between Pratt & Whitney and Rolls Royce. IAE's market share is split evenly between PW and RR. In contrast, all of the market share of CFMI, the 50-50 joint venture between GE and SNECMA, is attributed to GE.[25] If CFMI is eliminated from consideration and we consider market share on planes in service, then GE's market share falls to 10 percent. If we attribute half of

---

[24]The data is of 12/31/2000. The table is reproduced from European Commission decision in Case No. COMP/M.2220—General Electric/Honeywell, paragraph 70.

[25]The Directorate-General Competition justified this calculation: "Although in legal terms GE and SNECMA jointly control CFMI, the only meaningful attribution of market shares for the purposes of analyzing the transaction could only be made to GE, to the extent that SNECMA is not an independent supplier of civil jet engines for large commercial aircraft. The analyses of the joint venture and of SNECMA's participation in other GE engine programmes indicated that SNECMA would act jointly with GE as a profit-maximising entity" (Giotakos et al. [2001]).

CFMI to GE and half to SNECMA, then GE's market share is still only 28 percent. Even if we use the planes in production and credit only half of CFMI to GE, then GE's market share is 36 percent.

In any of these calculations other than that of the Commission, GE's limited market share would practically preclude it from having a dominant market position. Which definition is correct?

There is no one correct definition of market share made in the abstract. The issue should be market share measured for what purpose. For example, if the purpose is to evaluate the firm's financial resources to continue investing in this business, then all of its revenue streams are relevant. Thus, PW can use earnings from its entire installed base (not just planes in production) to finance new investment. GE only gets one-half of the revenue from CFMI. Thus, for this purpose it would seem that the 28 percent number is most appropriate as it reflects GE's revenue share of today's market.

To understand future financial viability, one might also want to examine preorders on next generation planes, those that have been launched but are not yet in production (such as the A380, B777x). It is common for airplanes to be ordered in advance of production. As of 2001, Rolls Royce had a 40 percent share of the engines on these next generation planes, while GE and CFMI's combined share was second with 38 percent, and PW was third with a 21 percent share.

If market shares are used to provide evidence of market power, it would seem that most of CFMI's share should not be included in GE's share. This is because the great majority of CFMI's sales are not in a position to exercise any market power. Recall that CFMI is the exclusive provider of engines to the Boeing 737 plane.[26] Prior to entering this exclusive relationship, Boeing realized that its customers would be in an untenable bargaining position if CFMI were the sole provider. Thus, Boeing prenegotiated a deal with CFMI as part of the exclusivity contract.

For most engines, the airline purchases the engines separately from the plane. Having decided upon a 747, the airline can then put the engine order out to bid between GE, PW, and RR. But in the case of a 737 purchase, the customer negotiates with Boeing and the engine is included in the price. CFMI does not have the ability to control engine pricing on these orders. For that reason, a more appropriate measure of GE's market share used to measure market power would be its share of engines excluding its exclusive-contract sales.[27] This corrected share is on the order of 10 percent or 20 percent, depending on whether one looks at planes in service or just those in production.

If market shares are used to understand the potential for bundling,

---

[26]In addition to CFMI's exclusive sales contract for the Boeing 737, its CFM56 engines also power the Airbus A320 family and A340 long haul.

[27]There are some GE exclusive sales, such as for the two new "longer range" (LR) versions of the Boeing 777. Here, again, the engine is sold at prenegotiated terms. One would want to take out all of the exclusive engine sales in calculating a firm's ability to act strategically.

then, again, it would seem that CFMI's sales should not be attributed to GE. This follows for two reasons.

First, because the engine is offered to Boeing at a predetermined deal it is almost impossible to employ a bundled pricing strategy. If the customer has already bought the Boeing plane and CFMI engine, there is no gain in providing a retroactive engine discount for the purchase of Honeywell components. The company would do just as well to offer the discount directly on the Honeywell parts.

The only way even to offer a bundle discount would be to promise a *future* discount on Honeywell components if the 737 plane is purchased. This would only make sense if the discount would increase the 737 plane sales. (If the sales of 737s are unchanged, then there is no increase in demand for the CFMI engine, and hence the discount might as well be applied directly to the Honeywell components.)

There are practical problems with this approach. The cost of Honeywell components is small relative to the plane and engine. Thus, there is little ability for the tail to wag the dog. Second, the sale of avionics and other Honeywell components is done at a future time at a negotiated price. One party can't promise to give the other party a "better deal" in a future negotiation, as there is no baseline against which to measure what makes a better deal.[28]

Bundling would be further complicated by the fact that CFMI is a joint venture. Thus, the decision on offering a bundle price would have to be made by both GE and its partner SNECMA. By its charter, CFMI is always led by a SNECMA representative. The joint venture nature of the relationship complicates CFMI's ability to offer a bundle, as SNECMA has no incentive to help sell Honeywell avionics.

GE's ability to act strategically so as to gain market share is practically restricted to its own engine sales, and this is roughly 20 percent of the market for planes in production. A 20 percent market share does not put a firm in a position where it can act independently of its rivals and customers.

However one measures shares, there is no disagreement regarding the extensive use of bidding competitions, the emphasis on market intelligence, and the very dynamic nature of shifting market shares. But the same facts were viewed very differently on the two sides of the Atlantic. In the United States, the fact that GE had won several of the recent engine competitions was viewed as evidence of competition at work. In Europe, these recent wins were viewed as evidence of dominance.[29]

---

[28]To help make this clear, consider the following hypothetical bundling offer: If "New Air" purchases a 737 plane, GE will offer a $1 million rebate good toward the purchase of Honeywell avionics. When it comes time to negotiate the price of those avionics, Honeywell and the customer both factor in the $1 million discount when setting the price. Thus, if the negotiated price would have been $4 million, the new negotiated price would be $5 million, which achieves the $4 million post-rebate price.

[29]For a more detailed comparison of the U.S. and European approaches, see Patterson and Shapiro (2001) and DOJ (2001).

A contributing factor to GE's alleged dominance in engines was the company's unique financial strength. Excerpts from Giotakos (2001) demonstrate this perspective:

> GE Capital offers GE business enormous financial means almost instantaneously and enables GE to take more risk in product development than any of its competitors. . . . GE has also taken advantage of the importance of financial strength in the industry through the use of heavy discounts of the initial sale of the engine. . . . [T]hanks to its financial strength and incumbency advantages as an engine supplier, GE can afford to provide significant support to airframe manufacturers under the form of platform-programme development assistance that competitors have not been historically in a position to replicate. . . . Unlike any other engine manufacturer, GE can afford to pay for exclusivity and capture aftermarket, leasing and financial revenues.

Patterson and Shapiro (2001) show the dangers in the approach. They look at as these same activities as pro-competitive. Taking risks leads to innovation; discounting benefits customers. In the United States, entrenchment of a dominant firm is a discredited theory and is no longer grounds for challenging nonhorizontal mergers (DOJ 2001):

> Challenging a merger because it will create a more efficient firm through economies of scale and scope is at odds with the fundamental objectives of antitrust law. And there is no empirical support for the notion that size alone conveys any significant competitive advantage that is not efficiency-related.

Whether or not GE was starting from a dominant market position, the commission was concerned that this merger would allow GE to extend its dominant position to Honeywell products. The proposed route to this dominant position was through bundling. To what extent was this theoretical concern supported by evidence?

While the theory suggests that bundling is unlikely to be an important factor, there remains the empirical question: Do we see much evidence of bundling in aerospace? At first glance, the answer seems to be yes: Many bids are multi-item bids. Companies such as Honeywell and its competitors often make a bid to supply a long list of components. This led several observers and even industry participants to conclude that bundling was a feature of this industry.

However, the long list of items is also broken down into prices for each individual component. And the component prices add up to the "bundle" or package price. If there is no discount, then we don't consider this to be bundling.

Compare this situation to Microsoft Office. Microsoft's July 2001 list price for Office XP Professional was $547. One could also buy the components separately, but one wouldn't. Word, Excel, PowerPoint, Access each cost $339 separately, and Outlook was a bargain at $109. The total adds up to $1,465. The software package comes at a 60 percent discount compared to the individual items.

In the cases cited by the Commission, the claimed bundle discounts were much smaller—by an order of magnitude. The claimed bundle discounts were also much smaller than those predicted by the Rolls Royce model. Even more importantly, these discounts were evidence of negotiation and not of mixed bundling.

In cases where the Commission attempted to document examples of a mixed bundle discount the analysis failed to distinguish between a *discount* and a *discount conditional on buying a package.* As a result, the cases cited actually demonstrated the absence of mixed bundling.

Even if a discount were offered for buying a package, this does not mean that the discount would not be applied to individual items. In general, this would be a matter of speculation. However, in the cases cited by the Commission, the alleged mixed bundle *failed* to induce the customer to buy the entire package. Thus, it is possible to observe what prices were paid and whether or not the discount was in fact conditional on buying the entire package. In the cited cases, the customer was not penalized for breaking apart the bundle. Whatever discounts the customer was offered for purchasing the bundle were applied on a proportionate basis to the partial bundle that was ultimately purchased.

The evidence of bundling provided by the Commission undercut its own argument. If bundling was such an anticompetitive tool, then why did it fail to get customers to purchase products for which the firm was otherwise at a disadvantage? The fact that customers were able to get any discount offered without having to purchase the bundle confirms the industry perspective that it is a mistake to offer a bundle discount as this will simply end up coming back as a discount on whatever the customer ends up buying.

If bundling is to be a matter of concern, we should see contracts that are won, not lost. And these contracts should offer a substantial discount for buying the entire package over a la carte purchases.

THE (IM)PRACTICALITY OF BUNDLING ENGINES

The theory suggests that bundling will not lead to an advantage with negotiated prices. The evidence suggests that bundle discounts are not prevalent, if they even exist. But perhaps the combination of GE and Honeywell would create a new opportunity to offer an engine and avionics/nonavionics bundle. Even if this were desirable, there are institutional features of the airplane purchase process that make this type of bundling impractical.

We have already discussed the problems of bundling CFMI engines with Honeywell's avionics (and other nonavionic) equipment. These include the joint venture with SNECMA and the predetermined engine price for 737s. An additional factor that makes it impractical to bundle engines with other components is the timing of purchases. Typically, the engine choice is made well in advance of the choice of other components, such as avionics.

To see why this is a problem, consider how bundling would have to work. Once GE has won the engine competition, there is no incentive to give retroactive discounts on engines if the customer would also buy Honeywell avionics. This would be no different than giving a discount on the Honeywell avionics directly.

In order for there to be any possibility of bundling to work, it must be the case that at the time the engine selection is being made the customer is led to believe that by choosing the GE engine there will be a better price on Honeywell avionics. For example, the customer might be given a 10 percent discount for their later purchase of avionics if they have a GE engine. While this story is possible in some industries, it is not applicable to avionics. The reason is that all prices are negotiated so that a discount from list price has no bite. One person can't promise to give the other party a "better deal" in a future negotiation as there is no baseline against which to measure what makes a better deal. Here again, we see the importance of taking into account whether prices are fixed or negotiated.

The bundling of avionics components would seem to be much more practical than bundling engines and avionics. Indeed, this issue was considered only two years earlier when the commission approved the merger of Allied Signal and Honeywell. While there was some dispute as to whether bundling exists at all, even the Commission did not argue the Allied Signal-Honeywell merger had led to widespread bundling. From the Commission's perspective this was only because the merger was too recent and thus the impact of bundling had not yet been felt.

EVIDENCE THAT BUNDLING WOULD LEAD TO EXIT BY RIVALS

At the same time that the Commission was arguing that the Honeywell-Allied Signal bundling effects were slow to arise, the Commission took the stance that the GE-Honeywell merger would lead to nearly immediate exit or marginalization of rivals.[30]

Is exit (or marginalization) really likely in this business? Here the Commission seemed to rely on the dire warnings of some competitors. Of

---

[30]If the exit or marginalization were to occur more gradually, then one would want to take into account the benefits gained by customers during the period of lower prices. Such a calculation was never made.

course, these competitors are not disinterested parties. They would hope to block the merger or purchase various Honeywell "jewels" that the commission would require to be spun off.

Nor was there evidence provided that the rival firms were in any danger of exit. To the contrary, evidence was presented that showed the long-term viability of the rival firms. For example, the stock market's reaction did not anticipate the financial vulnerability of aerospace firms. From the time of the announced merger to the time of the EC hearing, almost all of the rival firms had a gain in stock price that exceeded the S&P 500 index. The firm that underperformed the index was GE.

One would not expect to see aerospace firms concede defeat quickly. Airframes are long-lived. The typical plane is on the market for twenty-five or more years. Thus, a contract gained today (or ten years ago) would provide a long stream of profits down the road. Hence, even if firms were precluded from new contracts, they are not going to disappear any time soon. In fact, the next plane for which the engine choice has not been made is the Boeing Sonic Cruiser, which is not set to debut until 2007 or later (if it is built at all).

In the aerospace industry there are several large players who have an interest in maintaining competition. Military purchases play this role. Both Rolls Royce and P&W have multibillion dollar annual revenues from military contracts, and there is a substantial amount of spillover between civilian and military work. While it could be argued that no single airline would be eager to provide the public good of maintaining competition, Airbus and Boeing (each of which has about a 50 percent market share and each of which works closely with airlines when making purchase decisions for the aircraft it designs) do have this incentive.

POLICY PRESCRIPTIONS

We have discussed at some length whether competition authorities should be worried about mixed bundling in the context of the GE-Honeywell merger. Putting relevancy to GE-Honeywell aside for a moment, in an environment in which the Cournot effect does exist, there remains the issue of what should be the antitrust policy toward a merger of two producers of complements, each with market power. Another way of saying this is that if we did indeed find a case where the Cournot effect was large, what should we do about it?

At first blush, the answer would seem to be nothing. Prices fall! Social welfare is higher. Consumers gain, and competitors lose. This is not the arena for antitrust authorities to get involved.[31]

---

[31]While the European law is concerned with market dominance, the economic rationale would be a concern about high prices. Here the problem is with low prices. The European law does not seem to take efficiencies into account that might lead to lower prices (Schmitz 2002).

The European Commission took a novel perspective. They were concerned that the long-run impact of the combination could be to put competitors out of business. Similar to a predatory pricing case, once the competitors were either hobbled or vanquished, the merging firm would have even more power to raise prices, and then social welfare would fall.

Unlike in the typical predatory pricing case, recoupment might or might not be an issue. Depending on the parameters and setup of the model, the combining firms might actually make money in the process of putting their rivals out of the market.

If we follow this line of reasoning, a several-part-test will follow. This test is an extension of one developed by Carl Shapiro and by the Department of Justice.[32]

1. Is there an incentive to bundle?

   a) Under what circumstances does the combined firm earn higher profits through a bundled pricing strategy?

   b) Did either firm have an opportunity to bundle prior to the combination? If so, is there evidence that bundling is a common practice in this industry?

      i) If we see bundling, then what is the marginal impact of increasing the potential scope of the bundle?

      ii) If we do not see bundling, then how do the opportunities created by this combination create a different incentive to bundle?

2. What is the immediate gain to consumers from lower prices?

   a) How much do we expect prices to fall due to bundling?

3. What will be the impact on competitors?

   a) How much will competitors' price fall?

   b) What will be the shift in share?

4. How long do we expect these lower prices to persist?

   a) How long do we expect the rivals will be able to hold out?

   b) Are rivals sufficiently close to exiting the market that this will tip the scales?

   c) Are there large customers with market power that have an incentive to keep multiple firms in the market?

5. If the rivals exit, what is the expected harm?

---

[32]The Shapiro test was presented to the Merger Task Force. The DOJ guidelines are described in a report submitted to the OECD roundtable on portfolio effects in conglomerate mergers, DOJ (2001).

a) Will other firms be able to enter the market?

b) Will large buyers be able to hold prices down?

c) Or, if prices rise, what is the expected damage?

In short, there are immediate benefits to the combination. How long can we expect these benefits to last? How likely is the potential harm, and how big is the potential harm? Or, even simpler, what is the present value of the net expected change in social welfare from allowing the combination?

Applying this approach to the GE-Honeywell case, the Commission stopped at step 1. Even if bundling were to threaten the long-term viability of competitors, no analysis was made of the trade-off. Properly discounted for time and the fact that the outcome is uncertain, was there any argument to be made that the net present discounted value would be negative? The Commission made a recommendation against a merger that by its own account would be expected to lower prices without demonstrating that the expected long-run harm would outweigh short-term gains.

REMEDIES

When the net impact of some conduct is negative, the next step is to look for remedies, either structural or behavioral, that would solve the problem. In the case of bundling a very simple behavioral remedy presents itself. The firm can commit itself not to bundle.

Since it was the potential to engage in this behavior that concerned the Commission, the fact that the merging parties would agree not to offer bundle discounts should signal that this was not an important element of their incentive to merge. And since it was the bundling behavior that had the potential to lead to dominance, without bundling there would be no dominance.

A no-bundle discount policy is straightforward. A firm can do that by having to provide an itemized breakdown of the package price and giving a price to each component in the package. The individual prices must add up to no more than the bundle price.

A bundle only works if it is offered at a discount to the components. A firm need not be regulated on what it can charge for each item. It can charge whatever it would like for components and for the bundle just so long as the combined price of the components is not more than the bundle.

The Commission rejected this approach based on its preference for structural over behavioral remedies. Yet this particular behavioral solution does not appear hard to monitor or enforce. If the component elements of a firm's bids are not itemized or add up to more than the package total, that would be an automatic violation.

CONCLUSIONS

In the Statement of Objections, the Commission presented a theory of bundling that was based on the premise that the merged firm would be able to bundle and would have a rational economic incentive to do so. The result of this bundling would be prices so low that competitors will be foreclosed.

When closer scrutiny was given to this argument, it turned out not to apply to the market for aircraft engines, avionics, and nonavionics products. The Commission subsequently abandoned its original approach:

> The various economic analyses have been subject to theoretical controversy, in particular, as far as the economic model of mixed bundling, prepared by one of the third parties, is concerned. However, the Commission does not consider the reliance on one or the other model necessary for the conclusion that packaged deals that the merged entity will be in a position to offer will foreclose competition from the engines and avionics/nonavionics markets.[33]

Instead, it based its decision on a new, dynamic, theory: Foreclosure of competitors would occur as a result of predation accomplished through the cross-subsidization of bundled sales.[34] As explained in the EU's Competition Policy Newsletter (Giotakos 2001):

> Thanks to GE's strong generation of cash flows resulting from the conglomerate's leading positions on several markets, following the merger, Honeywell would have been in a position to benefit from GE's financing surface and ability to cross-subsidise its different business segments, including the ability to engage in predatory behaviour.

There may be a simple explanation as to why reliance on the Rolls Royce model was so attractive to the Commission. If, in fact, a merged firm would make *more* money by reducing prices when selling complementary products, then there is no need to estimate the cost of predation (as there is none), and there is no need to estimate recoupment (as none is required). Moreover, the merger becomes the proximate cause of the price discounting, and so there is now a reason to think that this type of economically rational predation will occur postmerger even if it does not occur premerger.

Against this background, the Commission may have been disappointed to discover that the economic models upon which it had relied—the model advanced by Rolls Royce, and even the basic Cournot complements model—were unsuited to the task.[35]

---

[33]Paragraph 352 of the Decision.

[34]Predation was never seriously discussed in the Statement of Objections: There is only a *single* mention of predation in the SO, unrelated to the bundling theory, and this occurs in a footnote.

[35]The Cournot complements model has a crucial assumption, namely that each firm charges one price in the market to all of it customers. While this may be an acceptable assumption for a consumer good, it does not apply to the negotiated sales of aircraft engines and avionics. With perfect

Although the Commission abandoned the original model, it did not replace the flawed model with another model. Rather, the Commission switched to a dynamic theory of predation. But it never carried out any of the steps required to establish the facts necessary to support that theory.

In the end, the European Union Merger Task Force did back away from its economic theory of bundling. But it did not back down from its conclusion that bundling was a reason to block the merger. The decision in this case presents a challenge for the role of economic analysis in the design and implementation of antitrust policy.

REFERENCES

Adams, William J., and Janet L. Yellen. "Commodity Bundling and the Burden of Monopoly." *Quarterly Journal of Economics* 90 (August 1976): 475–498.

Bakos, Yannis, and Eric Brynjolfsson. "Bundling Information Goods: Pricing, Profits, and Efficiency." *Management Science* 45 (December 1999): 1613–1630.

Brandenburger, Adam, and Barry Nalebuff. *Co-opetition.* New York: Doubleday, 1996.

Choi, Jay P. "A Theory of Mixed Bundling Applied to the GE/Honeywell Merger." *Antitrust* 16 (Fall 2001): 32–33.

Cournot, Augustin. *Recherches sur les principes mathematiques de la theorie des richesses.* Paris: Hachette, 1838. English translation: *Research into the Mathematical Principles of the Theory of Wealth,* translated by N. Bacon. Mountain Center, Cal.: James and Gordon, 1995.

Department of Justice. "Range Effects: The United States Perspective," Antitrust Division Submission for OECD Roundtable on Portfolio Effects in Conglomerate Mergers, downloadable at www.usdoj.gov/atr/public/international/9550.pdf, 2001.

European Commission Decision in Case No. COMP/M.2220—General Electric/Honeywell, 2001. This decision can be downloaded at http://europa.eu.int/comm/competition/mergers/cases/index/by_nr_m_44.html#m_22

Giotakos, Dimitri, Laurent Petit, Gaelle Garnier, and Peter De Luyck. "General Electric/Honeywell—An Insight into the Commission's Investigation and Decision." *Competition Policy Newsletter* 3 (October 2001): 5–13.

McAfee, Preston R., John McMillan, and Michael D. Whinston. "Multiproduct Monopoly, Commodity Bundling, and Correlation of Values." *Quarterly Journal of Economics* 104 (May 1989): 371–384.

Nalebuff, Barry. "Competing against Bundles." In *Incentives, Organization, Public Economics,* edited by Peter Hammond and Gareth D. Myles, 323–336. London: Oxford University Press, 2000.

---

information, there would be no Cournot complements effect at all. Even with imperfect information, the Cournot effect is diminished to the extent that firms can differentiate between their customers. The evidence suggests that prices and profit margins vary substantially among customers. But the commission did not attempt to estimate the degree of uncertainty and distribution of preferences so as to employ the negotiation model presented to them.

Nalebuff, Barry, and Shihua Lu. "A Bundle of Trouble." Yale School of Management working paper, 2001.

Patterson, Donna, and Carl Shapiro. "Transatlantic Divergence in GE/Honeywell: Causes and Lessons." *Antitrust* 16 (Fall 2001): 18–26.

Pflanz, Matthias, and Cristina Caffarra. "The Economics of G.E./Honeywell." *European Competition Law Review* 23 (March 2002): 115–121.

Schmitz, Stefan. "How Dare They? European Merger Control and the European Commission's Blocking of the General Electric/Honeywell Merger." *University of Pennsylvania Journal of International Economic Law* 23 (Summer 2002): 325–383.

PART IV

Network Issues

The Economic
and Legal Context

The concepts of "network economics" and "network effects" are relatively new for microeconomics, and antitrust legal decisions have just recently begun explicitly to take them into account. But networks themselves—e.g., telephone, rail, pipelines, electricity, broadcasting, even highways—have been around for far longer. The economic issues that they raise—economies of scale, strategic uses of assets, refusals to deal, etc.—also have long histories, and they arise in many other contexts described in other parts of this book. Because of those other contexts, antitrust has had to confront network issues—often described in other terms—for a long time as well.[1]

We will first address the economics of networks and then the relevant antitrust law.

ECONOMICS

Some Basic Concepts

Technically, a network is a set of nodes connected by links. Because this definition does not convey much intuition some diagrams and examples will surely help.[2]

A Simple Network. Figure IV-1 portrays a simple "star" or "hub-and-spokes" network. The outer nodes (A,B,C, etc.) are all connected to each other through a central node S.[3] Examples of networks that look approximately like Figure IV-1 include:

---

[1]In addition to antitrust, many networks are subject to direct regulation of various kinds, often as a policy response to the kinds of features of networks that are discussed in the text below. See White (1999).

[2]Overviews can be found in Economides and White (1994), Katz and Shapiro (1994), Besen and Farrell (1994), Liebowitz and Margolis (1994), Economides (1996), and White (1999).

[3]A star is not the only possible configuration of a network. It could also be circular (e.g., some local computer networks; the highway "beltways" or "rings" around major cities) or all-points-connected (e.g., a local street grid in a city; "ham" radio connections). See White (1999).

FIGURE IV-1 A Simple Star Network

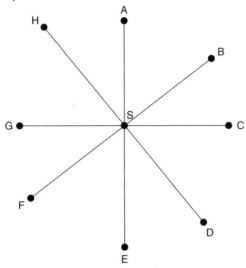

- a local telephone exchange, with the outer nodes as the users, the central node as the central switch that connects them, and the connecting links as the telephone lines (wires) that connect the users to the switch;[4] a local e-mail system could similarly be portrayed;
- a small airline ("hub-and-spokes") network, with the outer nodes as smaller (less central) airports, the central node as the "hub" through which passengers must travel (and usually change planes) if they want to fly from one peripheral city to another, and the connecting links (spokes) as the flights between the smaller airports and the hub; many local (metropolitan) commuter rail and bus systems have a similar structure;
- a local package or mail delivery system, with the outer nodes as pick-up and delivery customers, the central node as the sorting and routing facility, and the links as the collection and delivery routes;
- a local electricity system, with the outer nodes as electricity users, the central node as a generating station, and the links as the wires that carry electricity to users;
- a local radio, TV, or cable broadcasting system, with the outer nodes as listeners/viewers, the central node as the broadcasting facility, and the links as the over-the-air or over-the-cable broadcast transmissions.

Some important insights can be gained from even these simple examples. First, the central nodes really are central; all transactions must travel through or originate at that node. An immediate implication is that the cen-

---

[4]The telephone system is frequently described as a "switched network."

tral node can be characterized as a potential "bottleneck" for the system or an "essential facility": Without access to it, operation in the market is impossible.

Further, the capacity of that node is important for the system. If there is adequate capacity at the central node (or extra capacity can be added at relatively low cost), then extra users can be added to the network at relatively low cost. In essence, economies of scale for the central node and thus for the system are an important aspect of networks.[5]

These economies of scale are usually a component of economic models of networks, and they do seem to be present in many real-world networks. However, short-run capacity constraints can cause diseconomies of scale, which manifest themselves through congestion, delays, and static in these systems;[6] and whether additional capacity can be added at modest or substantially higher costs (including managerial and other "systems" costs) is an empirical question, and not a mandate of nature or the guaranteed result from an engineer's calculations.

Second, compatibility of the nodes and links is essential in order for transactions to occur. Compatibility is achieved through the nodes' and links' sharing (and adhering to) common specifications or standards. Compatibility standards may be of a physical nature:

- The telephone jacks must fit the wall receptacles;
- Rail gauge (track width) and wheel spacing, tunnel dimensions and freight car dimensions, etc., must fit with each other;
- Airport runways must be a suitable length for the airplanes that are expected to land and take off;
- Electrical plugs must fit the wall outlets; etc.

Compatibility standards may also be a technological phenomenon:

- The telephone equipment on a system must be capable of sending and receiving the same analog or digital information in order to be able to communicate;
- The voltage and cycle requirements of electrical appliances must be compatible with the electricity flow;
- Radio and television receivers have to be compatible with the broadcast signal; etc.

Third, there is an important distinction between the telephone, airline, and package networks and the electricity and broadcasting networks. The

---

[5]Scale and capacity issues may also be present for the links.

[6]Over-the-air broadcasting is the one exception among these examples, since congestion or delays are not relevant. The broadcast signal is a true public good: It is nonrival (one viewer/listener does not prevent another from viewing/listening) and nonexclusive (in the absence of scrambling, no one can be excluded from viewing/listening); see Pindyck and Rubinfeld (2001, ch. 18).

former networks are *two-way* networks: The outer nodes are all capable of both sending (initiating) and receiving transactions, and transactions can flow back and forth (two-way) between any two outer nodes (via the central node). By contrast, the latter networks are *one-way* or distributive networks: The outer nodes are capable only of receiving transactions from the central node, so the flow of transactions is solely (one-way) outward from the central node.

Fourth, so long as economies of scale are present, two-way networks enjoy positive *direct* "network externalities" (Rohlfs 1974, 2001): When an extra user (an additional external node) joins the network, the other users directly benefit.[7] Thus, if extra telephone users join a local exchange network, not only do they receive benefits from the calls that they make to and receive from others on the network, but the others benefit as well (by being able to receive and make more calls); the same effects occur for the airline and package systems.[8]

By contrast, the one-way networks do not generate direct network effects. There is no direct gain to one electricity user if another user joins the network (and no direct gain to one viewer/listener to another's tuning in). But there may be *indirect* network effects that operate through the economies of scale of the central node: More electricity users on the network permit the fixed costs of the central generating facility to be spread over the larger number of users and thus may permit lower rates to all users; more viewers/listeners may permit higher quality and a wider variety of programming to be broadcast.

Fifth, network members often have to make network-related investments: in equipment or location or in learning the technology of the system. Often these investments are "sunk"; that is, they are specific to that network and are not transferable to another (somewhat different) network. The differing compatibility standards—physical and/or technological—of networks can contribute to this sunk aspect of the investment.

A Slightly More Complex Network. In Figure IV-2 we expand the conceptual coverage of the diagrams by portraying two star networks that are connected by a "trunk" link. This expanded diagram could represent:

- two separate local telephone networks that are connected (through their two respective switches, S_A and S_B) by a long-distance trunk line; again, a more complex e-mail system could similarly be portrayed;
- two local or regional railroad freight collection and distribution systems, with S_A and S_B representing marshalling yards, connected by a long-dis-

---

[7]As Liebowitz and Margolis (1994) point out, whether the other users enjoy a net benefit will depend on whether the pricing of the network services takes these externalities into account, in which case the network owner will have internalized the externality.

[8]The assumption of adequate capacity—economies of scale—is crucial. If the extra user causes added congestion for the others, then the direct network effects could be negative.

FIGURE IV-2 Two Star Networks Connected by a Trunk Line

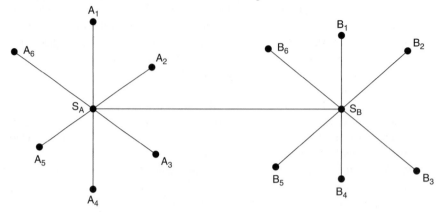

tance trunk line (or an airline route system with two hubs and a connecting route);

- an electrical system, with generating units A_i on the left (coordinated by S_A) and electricity users B_i on the right (with a voltage "step-down" facility S_B);
- a more complete cable TV model, with cable networks A_i on the left and subscribers B_i on the right, with S_A representing the cable system's "packaging" function, and with S_B representing the system's distribution "head end," from which the channels are electronically distributed to subscribers.

The characteristics of the simple star network carry over to the double star network: The central nodes, S_A and S_B, continue to have a bottleneck position vis-à-vis any outer node that is directly connected to it in its local system and also with respect to the outer node of any other local system that wishes to transact with an outer node in that central node's system; and economies of scale are an important feature, as are compatibility, standards, and the possibility of significant switching costs by users. Further, the first two examples involve two-way networks and direct network effects; the latter two involve one-way networks and indirect network effects.[9]

The double star allows us to expand the network concept to other systems that have network-like characteristics. For example, consider a system that consists of personal computer (PC) application software packages (the outer nodes A_i), a PC operating system (OS) (node S_A), a microprocessor (node S_B), and PCs (outer nodes B_i). Though this is not a physical network,

---

[9]Though both use the Internet, e-mail (including instant messaging) is clearly a two-way network, while the World Wide Web is primarily a one-way network.

it has the characteristics of a network: central nodes, economies of scale, and the importance of compatibility and standards (since all of the components must be able to function with each other). Further, the network effects are indirect (as is true for one-way networks): If an extra PC user joins the system, there is no direct benefit for other users.[10] But there are indirect benefits: As more users join the system, more software applications developers are willing to write software for this larger volume of users. So the incumbent users benefit from a greater variety of software available to them when more users join the system.[11] Also, users of a particular system may well find that their investments are system-specific, if the system's standards are different from those of other systems.

In sum, this PC-related system does indeed have the important characteristics of a network. Further, hardware-software combinations, such as video cassette recorders (VCRs) and VCR tapes, and compact disk (CD) players and CDs, and the combination of specialized machinery and its spare parts[12] have similar characteristics. The term *virtual network* is frequently used for such nonphysical systems.

Implications

There are a number of important implications of these network characteristics for market structure and behavior.

First, if the direct or indirect network effects are relatively strong, competition among networks—especially networks that are incompatible with each other—is likely to be unstable. Relative size itself will provide an important advantage to a larger network, which will cause it to attract an outsized fraction of new users (and of switchers), yielding greater size and greater advantage. A "bandwagon" or "tipping" effect operates.

The result (when network effects are strong) is likely to be a "winner-take-most" structure. Smaller networks will be able to survive only if they offer distinct features that are sufficiently worthwhile to their members to compensate for the smaller network size (and thus the smaller network effects) or if their users are locked into the network because of high switching costs.

Second, for such winner-take-most networks, there is likely to be fierce rivalry at the early stages of network development. Owners of rival networks will each hope to get an early advantage and start the bandwagon process. Such efforts are likely to include low introductory pricing (which others may claim is "predatory"); exaggerated claims for future product developments;

---

[10]An exception might be if users can talk to each other about their experiences with the system, useful tricks and shortcuts, etc.

[11]This greater variety is a scale-driven phenomenon.

[12]The Kodak litigation, which is described in Case 17 by Jeffrey MacKie Mason and John Metzler in this part, involved an equipment and parts combination that had these attributes.

lists of testimonials and endorsements by prominent customers; prominently announced alliances and joint ventures with some other network providers; and other efforts to create the impression of a bandwagon. In essence, the process of "competition for the market" may be crucial for the determination of the eventual structure of the market (and especially the identity of its dominant firm).

An immediate policy implication of this last point, but also a dilemma, is that antitrust enforcement may have to scrutinize carefully the early behavior and maneuverings of the network rivals, in order to prevent anti-competitive practices that could yield a subsequent structure that is then difficult to change (for the reasons discussed below). But it is during the early stages of a nascent network industry when information about the industry is the most hazy, the technological possibilities are the most vague, and the risks of harm from inappropriate interventions are the greatest.

Third, the central nodes of the network—as bottlenecks—are likely to possess market power vis-à-vis the other nodes in the network. The central node may be a physical facility, such as the central switch of a telephone network. Or the centrality of the network may be found in its compatibility standard. If the standard is proprietary, as is true for Microsoft's Windows operating system, the owner is likely to be able to exercise market power.[13] On the other hand, if the standard is in the public domain (as is true for railroad gauges and telephone jack design), a bottleneck problem is unlikely to arise.[14] Important determinants of the extent of the owner's market power will be the strength of the network effects and the size of users' switching or lock-in costs.

Fourth, entry by new networks (if they are not compatible with incumbent networks) is more difficult than in otherwise similar non-network industries, because the entrant suffers from the reverse network effects of small size and customer base. In essence, it is harder for an entrant to convince customers of other networks to sample its product or service, because the switchers lose any network-effects benefits from their old network as well as incurring any switching costs. Equivalently, the entry costs and risks for an entrant to attain a network size that approximates an incumbent may be quite large.[15]

Fifth, fundamental innovation involving incompatibilities with incumbent networks may be more difficult in network industries, because of the difficulties of attracting incumbent networks' customers to a new product. (Innovation that is compatible with a network standard and can easily be integrated with incumbent networks, however, should face fewer prob-

---

[13]See the discussion of Microsoft in Case 19 by Daniel Rubinfeld in this part.

[14]This may not prevent companies from attempting to create important differences for strategic purposes. AT&T, for example, sought to ensure that only its equipment would be used by arguing that equipment from other manufacturers would jeopardize the integrity of the telephone network. See Noll and Owen (1994).

[15]This appears to be the case for networks such as rail and local telephone service.

lems.)[16] Of course, cars did supplant horse-drawn carriages, CDs did replace vinyl records, and DVDs are replacing videotape formats. So fundamental innovation clearly can and does take place. Nevertheless, the process must be harder because of network effects and switching costs.

Sixth, decisions about compatibility or incompatibility among competing networks may have an important strategic component, as well as a technological component. If the owner of a network believes that its network is or will become the beneficiary of a bandwagon or tipping phenomenon, that firm is likely to be reluctant to interconnect—i.e., become compatible with—rival networks. This currently seems to be AOL's strategy with respect to its Instant Massaging e-mail system, as is discussed in Case 18 by Gerald Faulhaber in this part. This refusal to interconnect is the network technology equivalent of refusals to deal in the context of the vertical arrangements of Part III.

Further, if the setting of a compatibility standard is jointly determined by the members of an industry (say, through an industry association), there is the risk that political/strategic considerations may cause the choice of standard to become a vehicle for raising barriers to entry or raising rivals' costs, as incumbents choose a standard that they know will make entry more difficult or that might favor live-and-let-live incumbents over mavericks.

Finally, because of tipping and the subsequent inertia of a network market structure that has a dominant firm, the process that yields a market "winner" offers no assurance that the outcome represents the socially most efficient (say, greatest customer net satisfaction) network. Though the tipping could occur because the best network provider gets an early lead, chance events might cause another provider to get an early lead and then (because of bandwagon effects) dominate. Further, even if the best provider initially does dominate, subsequent technological change might argue for a new and improved network, which another firm could better provide. But the inertia of the network structure might foil the succession by the new provider.

In sum, networks embody special features that do raise extra concerns for antitrust policy. It is to antitrust that we now turn.

ANTITRUST

The above discussion illuminates the vast array of practices in network industries that might have anticompetitive purposes or consequences. Some of these practices are essentially the same as those that arise in the case of

---

[16]An exception would be if the incumbent network provider saw the existence of even a compatible innovative node or link as a threat to its core bottleneck position, as was the case in Microsoft's hostile reaction to Netscape's compatible browser.

non-network industries. In these instances the enforcement agencies and courts have dealt with them using the same underlying principles as would apply to non-network industries, but with attention to their network setting. Mergers between firms in network industries are analyzed using the *Merger Guidelines,* for example, but the analysis additionally reflects their cost and demand interdependencies.[17] Evaluation of alleged predatory conduct by firms in these industries recognizes the multimarket, multidimensional nature of network competition.[18]

In other cases, however, the competitive issues surrounding network industries are themselves distinctive or arise with unique properties. Here we focus on two of the most important categories of such issues: constrained access to the network, and mechanisms to induce network tipping. Each of these is assessed against the rule-of-reason prohibitions in Section 2 of the Sherman Act concerning monopolization and attempts to monopolize. We will provide a brief review of the manner in which the enforcement agencies and courts have brought this language to bear on them.

The issue of access was first confronted in the *Terminal Railroad* case of 1912.[19] One company controlled a key bridge as well as approaches and terminals serving that bridge at the St. Louis crossing of the Mississippi River. When that company was acquired by a group of the railroads using those facilities, the now jointly owned company could and did deny access to rival railroads that also sought to use them. The Supreme Court ultimately mandated access to the bridge, terminals, and approaches to those rivals. While this opinion is generally cited as the origins of the essential facility doctrine, it should be noted that this ruling was motivated more by the plight of horizontal competitors—the rival railroads that had to compete with the vertically integrated bridge/railroad company—than simply by the facility's being essential. As will be discussed below, in cases where a company owns a crucial facility without also competing with buyers of its services, the courts have adopted a different view.

Other cases involving "essential facilities"—sometimes couched in terms of denial of access, discriminatory access, and refusals to deal with unintegrated rivals—have involved the Associated Press's news reports,[20] electricity sold to municipal systems by Otter Tail Power,[21] the complicated

---

[17]See the discussions of the UP-SP merger in Case 1 by Lawrence White and John Kwoka, the Bell Atlantic-NYNEX merger in Case 3 by Steven Brenner, and the proposed MCI-Sprint merger in Case 4 by Michael Pelcovits (all in Part I). Also, Katz (2002) describes the DOJ's challenge to the proposed merger of United Airlines and US Airways in 2001 and its earlier challenge to Northwest Airlines' acquisition of a significant ownership share in Continental Airlines in terms of the network characteristics of these airline systems.

[18]See the discussion of the American Airlines predation dispute in Case 20 by Aaron Edlin and Joseph Farrell in this part and in Katz (2002).

[19]*U.S.* v. *Terminal Railroad Association of St. Louis,* 224 U.S. 383 (1912).

[20]*Associated Press* v. *U.S.,* 326 U.S. 1 (1945).

[21]*Otter Tail Power Co.* v. *U.S.,* 410 U.S. 366 (1973).

pricing and payment structure for ski lift tickets in Aspen,[22] terms of access to railroad trackage,[23] and computer reservation systems maintained by the major airlines (Guerin-Calvert 1994). In general, where the courts have viewed access to be a true bottleneck, as opposed simply to an impediment, they have been inclined to require access on some terms, though not necessarily equal terms. This inclination is diminished insofar as the crucial asset is the result of creative effort (e.g., as embodied in a patent), for which the courts have sought to ensure adequate returns, as opposed to the mere purchase of the asset (as in *Terminal Railroad*).

The case that most clearly and specifically articulated the essential facilities doctrine was the private monopolization case brought by MCI against AT&T.[24] The facts are well known: In order to provide long-distance telephone service, MCI needed to originate and terminate calls on local exchanges that were for the most part owned by AT&T, with whom MCI was competing in the long-distance market. Many of MCI's early years were spent battling in the courts and regulatory agencies for rights to interconnect with AT&T's local exchanges, and the courts ultimately found in MCI's favor. The opinion set out the following criteria for a finding of an antitrust violation under the essential facilities doctrine: (a) control of an essential facility by a monopolist, (b) a competitor's "inability practically or reasonably to duplicate it," (c) denial of use of the facility to a competitor, and (d) feasibility of providing the facility. The government's contemporaneous antitrust suit against AT&T was based on similar evidence of AT&T's strategy of anticompetitive denial of access to MCI (Noll and Owen 1994). This case was also resolved on terms that made clear the basic merits of this allegation.

Where outright denial of access or discriminatory terms of access are not employed, other stratagems are sometimes pursued. Foremost among these have been so-called "price squeezes," a practice designed nominally to permit rivals to acquire the critical input but in reality to do so only in a manner that undermines their ability to compete. In a classic price squeeze the integrated producer sets a price for sale of the crucial input to its final-product competitor(s) that, combined with the final product price, leaves too small a margin for viable operation of its rivals.

A prominent recent example in a network context is the *Town of Concord* v. *Boston Edison* case.[25] This case focused on actions by Boston Edison to secure wholesale price increases from state regulators, price increases that were then charged to the municipal electric companies in several towns, including Concord, Mass., supplied by Boston Edison. Combined with regulated retail prices, the higher wholesale prices left little or

---

[22]*Aspen Skiing Co.* v. *Aspen Highland Skiing Co.*, 472 U.S. 585 (1985).

[23]*Delaware & Hudson Railway Co.* v. *Consolidated Rail Corp.*, 902 F.2d 174.

[24]*MCI Communications Co.* v. *AT&T*, 708 F.2d 1081 (7th Cir. 1982).

[25]*Town of Concord* v. *Boston Edison*, 915 F.2d 17 (1st Cir. 1990).

no operating margin to the municipal utilities. The town's contention that they were being subjected to a price squeeze was rejected by the court. Its reasons—that electricity was a natural monopoly, that regulation was in place, that this result may reflect efficiencies—have been disputed elsewhere.[26]

As noted earlier, most essential facility and related cases involve the relationship of a vertically integrated company to its unintegrated rivals. Where such integration is *not* an issue, however, the courts have permitted greater discretion to the owner of a critical asset in determining who should have access to it. Many such cases arise as competitors seek membership in an organization that provides a distinctive aspect to a product or service in the market. Prominent cases have involved access and membership in credit card networks, ATMs, and real estate listing services. For example, when Dean Witter (which had launched the Discover Card) sought membership (through a bank it owned) in the Visa card network, the latter refused. Dean Witter sued, claiming a diminution of competition, a claim that the court rejected.[27] Rather, the court viewed the established network as a joint venture, entitled to its own membership and other business provisions without any obligation to make itself available to rivals. On the other hand, a substantial number of private suits have been brought against dominant ATM networks by rivals who have sought access to the systems. Many of these have been settled on terms that have allowed such access, indicating an apparent belief on the part of the dominant ATMs that full court proceedings would likely have gone against them.[28]

Apart from access issues, certain practices in network industries have also been a source of particular antitrust concern even though they arise in non-network industries as well. A key reason for this special concern is that networks are subject to "tipping," so that despite early competition there may ultimately be only one surviving network, or at least one very dominant network. Anticipating this, any single one of multiple competing networks at the outset may decide to engage in practices intended to undermine its rivals and thereby propel itself into the winner's circle. Similarly, when an incumbent dominant network is faced with the prospect of a new entrant, it may take actions designed to make such entry more difficult. Some of these practices may therefore have effects that are qualitatively or quantitatively different from non-network settings.

---

[26]For such discussion, see Kwoka (1992). It should be noted that price squeezes are by no means limited to network industries. These have been commonly alleged as alternative methods of eliminating competition in industries ranging from petroleum to aluminum. See, for example, *U.S.* v. *Aluminum Company of America,* 148 F.2d 416 (1945).

[27]*SCFC ILC* v. *VISA USA, Inc.,* 36 F.2d 958 (1994). See Evans and Schmalensee (1999) and Baker (1993).

[28]*BayBanks Inc.* v. *New England Network Inc.,* No. 86-3532-K (D. Mass. filed Dec. 9, 1986); *Household Bank F.S.B.* v. *Cirrus System, Inc.,* No. 87C2353 (N.D. Ill., filed Mar. 2, 1987); *Household F.S.B.* v. *Money Station, Inc.,* No. C-2-88-0274 (S.D. Ohio, filed Mar. 2, 1988). For a critique that argues that such easy access discourages the maintenance of rival networks, see Baker (1996).

Consider, for example, the practice of exclusive dealing, which may prevent encroachment on an incumbent's position in any market and thereby trigger a weighing of its beneficial and adverse competitive effects. In the context of a network industry, the ability to prevent or deter customer switching may keep new rival networks and technologies from gaining the customer base necessary for scale economies and long-term viability. Such "foreclosure" has been at the center of cases involving competition between Nintendo and Atari, and efforts by FTD to deter entry by rival florist networks.[29] These actions not only distort customer choice in the short run, but may also alter the long-run makeup of the industry.

Similarly, strategic use of standards and choices with respect to compatibility can alter the long-run structure of a network industry by inducing or preventing tipping of the market in favor of a particular technology or firm. Among the prominent antitrust cases that have confronted the question of the legitimate versus possibly anticompetitive use of compatibility in network industries have been the government's cases against IBM, AT&T, and Microsoft.[30] For example, the government alleged that IBM sought unnecessarily to manipulate the interface between its central processing units and certain peripheral equipment in order to thwart rivals from gaining a foothold in the latter. As previously mentioned, in the AT&T case the company sought to prevent attachment of non-AT&T equipment to the network, and Microsoft has been found to have employed a variety of strategies to reduce artificially the interoperability of its rivals' software. Among these are fee structures, product pre-announcements, and long-term contracts with buyers that the courts have found can be (and, in the case of Microsoft, were) intended to deter migration of users to alternatives to its dominant Windows operating system.

When confronted with such practices, the courts find themselves in the uncomfortable role of having to render judgments about the technical necessity versus strategic motives of individual company decisions, but it seems difficult to envision how else such matters can be resolved. Of course, antitrust has had a long history of having to deal with difficult questions. In that respect network concepts and analysis are but the latest challenge that the agencies and courts have had to confront. As more satisfactory answers to some questions are provided by economics, it seems highly likely that here, as elsewhere before in antitrust, those advances will find their way into enforcement and judicial decisions.

---

[29]For discussion of these and other cases, see Shapiro (1999).

[30]For issues of compatibility and standards in non-network contexts, see for example, *Radiant Burners, Inc.* v. *Peoples Gas Light & Coke Co.,* 364 U.S. 656 (1961) and *American Society of Mechanical Engineers, Inc.* v. *Hydrolevel Corp.,* 456 U.S. 556 (1982). A discussion of the disputes between IBM and peripheral equipment manufacturers can be found in Brock (1989). More general discussion can be found in Katz and Shapiro (1994).

REFERENCES

Baker, Donald I. "Compulsory Access to Network Joint Ventures under the Sherman Act: Rules or Roulette?" *Utah Law Review* no. 4 (1993): 999–1078.

Baker, Donald I., "Shared ATM Networks—The Antitrust Dimension," *Antitrust Bulletin* 42 (Summer 1996): 399–425.

Besen, Stanley M., and Joseph Farrell. "Choosing How to Compete: Strategies and Tactics in Standardization." *Journal of Economic Perspectives* 8 (Spring 1994): 117–131.

Brock, Gerald. "Dominant Firm Response to Competitive Challenge: Peripheral Equipment Manufacturers' Suits against IBM." In *The Antitrust Revolution,* 1st edn., edited by John E. Kwoka, Jr., and Lawrence J. White, 160–182. Glenview, Ill.: Scott, Foresman, 1989.

Economides, Nicholas. "The Economics of Networks." *International Journal of Industrial Organization* 14 (October 1996): 673–699.

Economides, Nicholas, and Lawrence J. White. "Networks and Compatibility: Implications for Antitrust." *European Economic Review* 38 (April 1994): 651–662.

Evans, David S., and Richard Schmalensee. "Joint Venture Membership: Visa and Discover Card (1993)." In *The Antitrust Revolution: Economics, Competition, and Policy,* 3d edn., edited by John E. Kwoka, Jr., and Lawrence J. White, 286–309. New York: Oxford University Press, 1999.

Guerin-Calvert, Margaret E. "Vertical Integration as a Threat to Competition: Airline Computer Reservation Systems." In *The Antitrust Revolution: The Role of Economics,* 2d edn., edited by John E. Kwoka, Jr., and Lawrence J. White, 432–468. New York: HarperCollins, 1994.

Katz, Michael L. "Recent Antitrust Enforcement Actions by the U.S. Department of Justice: A Selective Survey of Economic Issues." *Review of Industrial Organization* 21 (December 2002): 373–397.

Katz, Michael L., and Carl Shapiro. "Systems Competition and Network Effects." *Journal of Economic Perspectives* 8 (Spring 1994): 93–115.

Kwoka, John E., Jr., "Price Squeezes in Electric Power: The New Battle of *Concord.*" *Electricity Journal* 5 (June 1992): 30–37.

Liebowitz, S. J., and Stephen E. Margolis. "Network Externality: An Uncommon Tragedy." *Journal of Economics Perspectives* 8 (Spring 1994): 133–150.

Noll, Roger G., and Bruce M. Owen. "The Anticompetitive Uses of Regulation: *United States* v. *AT&T* (1982)." In *The Antitrust Revolution: The Role of Economics,* 2d edn., edited by John E. Kwoka, Jr., and Lawrence J. White, 328–375. New York: HarperCollins, 1994.

Pindyck, Robert S., and Daniel L. Rubinfeld. *Microeconomics,* 5th edn. Upper Saddle River, N.J.: Prentice-Hall, 2001.

Rohlfs, Jeffrey. "A Theory of Interdependent Demand for a Communications Service." *Bell Journal of Economics and Managerial Science* 5 (Spring 1974): 16–37.

Rohlfs, Jeffrey. *Bandwagon Effects in High Technology Industries.* Cambridge, Mass.: MIT Press, 2001.

Shapiro, Carl. "Exclusivity in Network Industries." *George Mason Law Review* 7 (Spring 1999): 673–684.

White, Lawrence J. "U.S. Public Policy Toward Network Industries." AEI-Brookings Joint Center for Regulatory Studies, 1999.

Links between Markets and Aftermarkets: Kodak (1997)

Jeffrey K. MacKie-Mason and
John Metzler

> The difficulty of obtaining parts, technical information and diagnostic software has effectively kept 3rd party service suppliers out of the advanced equipment service market[1]

> Both IBM and Xerox will sell spare parts, but we do not. This makes it more difficult for a third party to service our copiers.[2]

INTRODUCTION

In 1987 seventeen small companies filed an antitrust lawsuit against the Eastman Kodak Corporation ("Kodak"). These companies, several of them literally "mom and pop" operations, had been trying to compete with Kodak for contracts to provide maintenance service to end-use customers who owned expensive, durable Kodak photocopier or micrographics equipment. Eleven years later, there had been two district court opinions, two from the Ninth Circuit Court of Appeals, and one from the Supreme Court. Kodak appealed its guilty verdict to the Supreme Court one last time, but the Court refused to hear the appeal, and the case finally ended in 1998. Entire conferences have been devoted to the antitrust economics issues raised by *Kodak*, and numerous articles have been published in both legal and economics scholarly journals. Since the initial Supreme Court opinion in *Kodak*, there

---

MacKie-Mason was expert economist for the plaintiffs on liability issues, and testified at trial. Metzler assisted in the economic analysis.

[1]Trial Exhibit (hereafter, "Ex.") 99 at 6762, a Kodak report on micrographic service.

[2]Ex. 649 at 1315–1316, a Kodak internal document.

have been many closely related appeals court opinions, and they stand in sharply divided conflict on at least two issues. *Kodak* is one of the most significant antitrust cases of the last decade or two. It is also one of the most controversial, and the controversy is far from resolved.

In this case study we report on the history and status of *Kodak*. We focus on the economic issues. Although there is still sharp disagreement on the antitrust *policy* that should be followed in response to the economic issues, there is now a fairly broad agreement about the structure, assumptions, and results of the basic economic theories; remaining disagreements are largely about the facts specific to Kodak's situation. After summarizing the relevant factual and procedural background, we describe the theories. We then describe the economic analyses presented by the parties in court. We close by discussing several issues in the law and economics of antitrust that *Kodak* raises, but which have implications far beyond cases about durable equipment and maintenance.[3]

MARKET BACKGROUND

This case concerned Kodak's practices relating to parts for, and maintenance service on, micrographic equipment and high volume copiers. These machines are "durable" goods: goods that are purchased with the expectation of gaining utility from them for an extended period of time. ("Consumption" goods are purchased for the one-time utility that they provide.) Many durable goods, perhaps most, require ongoing maintenance for continued utility. For example, a copier with a burned-out light bulb generates little utility beyond that of an ordinary countertop.

Specialized terms have been developed to describe the markets in which these goods are sold. Consider a car, as an example: Because the utility derived from the car is what brings consumers into these markets, the market in which the car is sold is the "foremarket" or "primary" market. Demand for maintenance is composed entirely of consumers of the primary market good: Consumers don't demand brake service if they don't own a car. Therefore, we refer to the market for maintenance goods as the "aftermarket."[4]

---

[3]The first three subsections summarize a large number of facts. We believe it is fair to represent these as the undisputed facts, though of course almost no presentation of facts in a case is completely undisputed. In the interest of space, however, we do not provide specific citations to the trial evidence to support most of these background facts. When the trial evidence is summarized, we provide citations.

[4]Fore- and aftermarkets do not exist only for equipment and maintenance. For example, we could have a computer operating systems foremarket and application program aftermarkets.

Micrographics

Micrographics equipment is used for creating, filing, retrieving, viewing, and printing microforms. Microforms include microfiche, microfilm (for example, with back issues of *The New York Times*), and, for secret agents, microdots. These are variations on the same basic idea: Using optics and fine-grained film, it is possible to expose an image of printed matter onto film at a greatly reduced size, thereby reducing storage space. With another set of optics, the film image can be enlarged to the original size, then viewed or printed.[5]

Kodak invented this process in the late 1920s. Over the last seventy years, micrographics equipment has developed to encompass cameras, film processors, film duplicators, readers (enlarge microfilm for viewing or printing), COM (computer output to microfilm, devices that "print" to microfilm rather than paper), and CAR (computer automated retrieval, largely software/hardware combinations to automate handling large libraries of microfilm). Kodak remained a significant manufacturer and seller in most of these equipment categories.

Photocopiers

Kodak began manufacturing and selling high-volume photocopiers in the mid-1970s. These are large machines, weighing hundreds of pounds and generally selling for tens of thousands of dollars. High-volume photocopiers can handle from 60,000 to more than one million copies per month.

Maintenance

Both copiers and micrographic equipment require extensive, ongoing maintenance, consisting of service labor and parts. In this case, essentially all maintenance calls included a service component and many, perhaps most, required parts as well. Labor and parts are not required in fixed proportions. Among other things, they can vary due to the choice between part repair and replacement, and the use of preventative maintenance.

Kodak established a national network of service technicians to provide maintenance on its copiers, and another technician network for maintenance of its micrographics equipment. Kodak advertised the quality of its maintenance.

By the early 1980's, there were many, small independent service organizations (ISOs) providing maintenance on Kodak micrographic equipment. There were a few ISOs servicing Kodak photocopiers. These ISOs typically provided maintenance at prices 15 to 30 percent below Kodak. They provided service generally of the same quality as Kodak's. They at

---

[5]We use the present tense to discuss the technologies in this case, but we are referring to technologies current as of the issues in the case, covering approximately the years 1980–1995.

times provided customized maintenance options that Kodak would not provide.

The "Parts Policy"

In 1995 Image Technical Services (ITS) had won a large contract from the Computer Service Corporation (CSC) for micrographics maintenance. Kodak had been servicing CSC's equipment for about $200,000 per year with a four-hour guaranteed response time. ITS submitted a bid of $150,000 with the same four-hour response time guarantee. Kodak countered by lowering its bid $135,000. ITS came back with a bid of $100,000 and agreed to put a service technician on-site full time.

Shortly thereafter, Kodak instituted a policy of no longer selling parts for either copier or newly introduced micrographics equipment to ISOs.[6] This was clearly a change in practice for micrographics. Kodak had previously sold parts to anyone who ordered them and seemed to support the small ISOs. Kodak agreed that this was a change in policy, but claimed that the policy applied only prospectively: Kodak would only refuse to sell parts for equipment models introduced after the policy was announced.

It is not clear whether the change in *practice* on copier parts sales was also a change in policy. Kodak had previously sold copier parts to some ISOs and had referred the ISOs to Kodak's in-house technician help line for assistance. Kodak claimed such sales were unintentional.

Over time, Kodak increasingly policed its no-parts sales policy. It began tracking parts sales to ensure that equipment owners were not purchasing more than they would reasonably need for the equipment they owned. Kodak required prospective parts purchasers to provide proof of ownership of the equipment model for which they were ordering parts. It additionally required, for copier parts, certification that the customer had a Kodak-trained employee to effect the repairs. Kodak also required customers to agree to not resell parts.

PROCEDURAL HISTORY

The Initial Case and the Motion for Summary Judgment

In April 1987, ITS and several other ISOs filed suit against Kodak in the District Court, Northern District of California. The suit alleged that Kodak used its monopoly over parts to monopolize the service markets for its copiers and micrographics equipment; and that Kodak had conspired with its outside parts suppliers to preclude ISO access to parts, thereby monopolizing the service market; and that Kodak had tied its service labor to parts,

---

[6]The record is not clear on whether the policy was implemented in 1985 or 1986. It was not much enforced, if at all, prior to mid-1986.

thereby harming competition in the service market. These actions were alleged to violate Sections 1 and 2 of the Sherman Act.

Very early in the fact-finding process, Kodak moved for "summary judgment."[7] Kodak argued that there was no allegation that it had market power in the equipment markets. Kodak claimed that equipment customers had many alternatives available to them and made purchase decisions based on the total cost of ownership,[8] and thus any attempt by Kodak to extract higher profits from maintenance customers would result in equipment customers' taking their business elsewhere. Thus, because it could not have service market power, Kodak argued that as a matter of law it could not be found guilty of tying or monopolizing service markets. The judge agreed, and granted summary judgment.[9]

The ISOs appealed to the Ninth Circuit Court of Appeals, claiming that Kodak's arguments were purely theoretical. Various market imperfections could break the link between higher aftermarket prices and reduced foremarket sales, preventing foremarket competition from sufficiently disciplining aftermarket market power. The Ninth Circuit granted the appeal, overturned the summary judgment order and remanded the case for trial.[10]

Kodak appealed to the Supreme Court, which ruled in 1992. The Court agreed with the Ninth Circuit, and remanded the case for trial in district court.[11]

It is important to recognize the Supreme Court did *not* find that Kodak had illegally monopolized or tied. Nor did it find that parts or service were necessarily relevant markets. The Supreme Court found only that Kodak had not carried its burden of proof for summary judgment. Kodak had failed to convince the Court that economic theory proved that it was impossible for Kodak to be guilty. Rather, the Supreme Court concluded that the ISO's economic theories were plausible, and that Kodak's guilt or innocence hinged on the interpretation of the *facts* in the case: A trial would be required.

The Trial

On June 19, 1995, the jury trial of *ITS* v. *Kodak* began in district court. The trial involved sixty-three witnesses giving twenty-seven days of testimony. At the close of evidence, the plaintiffs dropped the tying claims. Therefore,

---

[7]"Summary judgment" is granted when the court is persuaded that, even if all disputed facts are resolved in favor of the non-moving party, the non-moving party cannot, as a matter of law, win the case. Essentially, it is a way to avoid wasting court resources.

[8]"Total cost of ownership" is the present discounted (expected) value of all costs associated with owning and using the machine, including future maintenance costs. This is also called "life cycle" analysis.

[9]1988 WL 156332 (N.D. Cal.).

[10]903 F.2d 612 (9th Cir. 1990).

[11]504 U.S. 451 (1992).

the only claims presented to the jury were that Kodak had monopolized the service markets for its high-volume copier and micrographics equipment. The alleged monopolizing acts were the restrictive parts policies, which leveraged Kodak's parts monopolies into service monopolies. The jury deliberated for thirteen days and returned a unanimous guilty verdict. Kodak was held liable for $24 million in damages, trebled to $72 million. On February 15, 1996, the district court issued a ten-year injunction requiring Kodak to sell parts to ISOs at nondiscriminatory prices.[12]

Kodak appealed to the Ninth Circuit Court of Appeals with three interesting economic points: Can Kodak be required to sell patented parts and copyrighted service software and manuals? Can "all Kodak parts" be a relevant market, despite the lack of substitutability between two different parts? Can a firm be convicted of monopolizing its *aftermarkets* without first being found to have obtained supracompetitive *systems* profits or prices?

On August 26, 1997, the Ninth Circuit ruled. The court rejected these three Kodak arguments and upheld the plaintiffs' verdict on all liability issues.[13]

ECONOMICS OF AFTERMARKET MARKET POWER

The central economic feature of *Kodak* was the dispute over theories of market power in aftermarkets. Kodak argued before the Supreme Court that primary market competition, as a matter of economic theory, precludes anticompetitive aftermarket actions. After the Supreme Court rejected this argument, Kodak argued at trial that the *presumption* should be that aftermarket power was unlikely and that Kodak's circumstances were consistent with this presumption. We refer to this as the "systems" theory. The plaintiffs argued that there are several theories showing commonplace circumstances under which a durable goods manufacturer could monopolize its aftermarkets. Therefore, they argued, there should be no presumption against aftermarket power. Further, the plaintiffs presented facts to demonstrate that Kodak both had and exercised market power. To present the arguments put forth on each side, we will use a very simple model of firm profits from a foremarket and an aftermarket.

Whereas a firm competing in a single good has only a single price lever, a firm participating in fore- and aftermarkets considers both prices

---

[12]*Image Technical Services, Inc., et al.* v. *Eastman Kodak Co.,* C 87–1686 (January 18, 1996) and *Image Technical Services, Inc., et al.* v. *Eastman Kodak Co.,* 1996-2 Trade Case. (CCH) ¶ 71,624 (N.D.Cal., Feb. 28, 1996).

[13]The court required a new trial to recalculate a portion of the damages because the plaintiffs' accounting expert and the fact witnesses did not sufficiently link some of the damages to the antitrust violation. *Image Technical Services, Inc., et al.* v. *Eastman Kodak Co.,* 125 F.3d 1195 (9th Cir. 1997).

(p^f, p^a) when maximizing profits.[14] The firm chooses these to maximize profits (π), which, on the assumption of constant costs (c^f, c^a), are:[15]

$$\pi = \pi^f + \pi^a$$
$$= (p^f - c^f)q^f(p^f,p^a) + (p^a - c^a)q^a(p^f,p^a).$$

We assume that the quantities demanded for each product depend on *both* prices, e.g., $q^f = q^f(p^f,p^a)$. That is, if the price of service rises, we generally expect the demand for primary market equipment to fall. This linkage between goods across markets is the essential feature of aftermarket economics. Most of the disputes can be summarized as arguments over how strong that link is under various factual circumstances.

We start by assuming that foremarkets and aftermarkets are perfectly competitive: $p^f = c^f$ and $p^a = c^a$. We are interested in whether a firm can increase its profits by acquiring market power in its aftermarket while its foremarket remains competitive. Thus, we are asking if a firm can profit overall by raising p^a above c^a. That is, the basic disagreement is whether, starting from competitive pricing, the sign of $\partial\pi^f/\partial p^a + \partial\pi^a/\partial p^a$ is positive or negative.

Economists on both sides agree that under most circumstances aftermarket profits can be increased, $\partial\pi^a/\partial p^a > 0$, but that there will be a simultaneous decline in foremarket profits, $\partial\pi^f/\partial p^a < 0$, because increasing p^a increases the overall cost of owning equipment and forward-looking buyers will reduce their equipment purchases. The debate, then, is about whether $\partial\pi^f/\partial p^a$ is sufficiently negative to offset monopoly aftermarket profits, and thus make aftermarket monopolization unprofitable overall.

Economists writing since the Supreme Court opinion, including at least one who testified for Kodak at trial, have largely agreed that there are circumstances under which aftermarket monopolization can be profitable overall; that is, $\partial\pi^a/\partial p^a > -\partial\pi^f/\partial p^a$.[16] We shall briefly describe some of the theories, in order to frame the facts and economic arguments presented at trial.

---

[14]Whether firms compete in prices ("Bertrand") or quantities ("Cournot") is not important here; we discuss "price" competition for convenience. However, focus on just price alone (or just quantity) *is* an important simplification. Consumers consider factors beyond just price when products are differentiated. Such differentiation is particularly true with "service" type goods: Two service programs might differ in technical quality, response time, flexibility of contract terms, provision of manufacturer-independent advice, and so forth. Kodak surveys showed that typical customers rated several factors as more important than price when choosing a service provider (see Ex. 264).

[15]Typically, aftermarket sales associated with a given foremarket sale will occur over a period of time. Therefore, what we refer to as aftermarket prices (for consumers) and profits (for firms) are actually discounted streams of future expenditure and profits, respectively.

[16]See, e.g., Borenstein, MacKie-Mason, and Netz (1995, 2000), Shapiro (1995), Carlton (2001), and Chen and Ross (1993). There is yet another issue, which is that under some circumstances even if it is profitable overall to monopolize an aftermarket, social welfare may be harmed only a little, or even improved, and thus legal antitrust intervention might be inappropriate. See footnote 26 below.

Preliminaries

Under what conditions might we expect foremarket competition to protect aftermarket consumers? That is, when might the total effect, $\partial\pi/\partial p^a$, be zero or negative, so that aftermarket monopolization is not attractive?

First, for the question to be interesting there must be at least some aftermarket power, which we define as $\partial\pi^a/\partial p^a > 0$. That is, the firm must have the ability to raise the aftermarket price above the competitive level and earn additional aftermarket profits, ignoring the effect on foremarket profits. This requirement implies two necessary conditions: There must be some protectable aspect to the aftermarkets, and some form of switching costs related to the primary market good.

Protectable aftermarkets mean that there are limited substitutes for, and limited entry into, the equipment manufacturer's aftermarket.[17] If aftermarket substitutes are widely available at competitive prices, say from independent parts manufacturers or service providers, increases in p^a will merely result in the firm's equipment customers making their aftermarket purchases from another supplier. That would imply $\partial\pi^a/\partial p^a \leq 0$.

Similarly, if equipment owners can switch at no cost from their existing equipment to a competitively priced alternative, a service price increase would induce consumers to sell their equipment and buy the alternative brand of equipment and service. It must be costly for current equipment owners to switch to another brand of equipment if the manufacturer is to have aftermarket power. There are two basic types of switching costs: inefficient used equipment markets, and complementary sunk investments that are specific to the given brand of primary good. An inefficient used equipment market means that the seller of a used primary market good cannot expect to recover the full economic value of the good when she sells it. This could be due to a lemons problem or to other causes.[18] We will refer to these as "financial" switching costs. Financial switching costs are coterminous with the economic life of the specific piece of equipment: Once a machine has zero economic value, there is no financial cost of switching to a new brand.

Switching costs from complementary investments arise when a firm needs to make investments in addition to the equipment and aftermarket good in order to utilize the equipment *and* these investments are of little value with any other brand of equipment. The classic example of complementary investment is custom applications software written for a specific operating system—switching to a new operating system requires rewriting

---

[17]This implies that the primary market is monopolistically competitive or a differentiated product oligopoly. It is difficult to conceive of protectable aftermarkets in combination with truly homogeneous primary market goods: If there are no differences among primary market goods, how can a given aftermarket good work only with one "brand" primary market goods?

[18]See Akerlof (1970). However, even a perfectly functioning used-equipment market might not eliminate financial lock-in resulting from installed base opportunism. See the text below.

the applications. Other switching costs include training and familiarization, converting data and archival file formats, custom configuration of peripherals, developing new relationships with expert, sales, and service personnel, and so forth. We refer to these as "technological" switching costs. Technological switching costs can extend beyond the economic life of an individual piece of equipment.[19]

The level of total switching costs puts an upper bound on the amount of surplus a firm can extract by exercising aftermarket power. Any attempt to extract the current owner's surplus in excess of the cost of switching results in the equipment owner's switching brands. However, there are situations where switching costs are large and this constraint might not be significant. When switching costs are significant, we say consumers experience *lock-in*.[20]

If aftermarkets are not protectable and switching costs are negligible, then we would generally expect no local aftermarket power, $\partial \pi^a / \partial p^a < 0$, and the systems theory would prevail.

Necessary Conditions for the Systems Theory

When a durables manufacturer has local aftermarket power ($\partial \pi^a / \partial p^a > 0$), systems theory proponents argue that linkage to a competitive foremarket will protect locked-in aftermarket consumers from monopoly exploitation. That is, $\partial \pi^f / \partial p^a$ is sufficiently large and negative so that a foremarket profit loss offsets the aftermarket profit gain. The argument is either that switching costs are low, so that current equipment owners can switch at low enough cost to constrain sufficiently the manufacturer's aftermarket power, or that new customers (and repeat customers upgrading or replacing their equipment) will see the high aftermarket prices and demand lower equipment prices to compensate, or will purchase elsewhere. What conditions are necessary to establish a sufficiently strong linkage between fore- and aftermarkets? Three have received the most attention: sufficient, low-cost information; effective simultaneity of fore- and aftermarket purchases; and competitive foremarkets for equipment. We explain each in turn.

Sufficient, Low-Cost Information

The systems theory assumes that consumers are aware of aftermarket prices, make reasonable assumptions about their own future demand for the

---

[19]This can lead to the confusing situation where future equipment purchases should properly be analyzed as aftermarket purchases: The choice of which primary market good to buy in the future is contingent on which is purchased today. Thus, technological switching costs increase competition in new product markets but reduce competition in mature markets. With new markets, firms compete vigorously to get a large base of locked-in customers; in mature markets, most customers are already significantly locked-in to a brand. See Klemperer (1987).

[20]For more on switching costs and lock-in, see Porter (1985), Williamson (1985), and Farrell (1985).

aftermarket goods corresponding to each primary market good, and use this information when making price comparisons. Thus, consumers are aware when a given primary market supplier charges supracompetitive prices in the aftermarket, and take their custom elsewhere.

Effective Simultaneity

Aftermarket goods and services are typically purchased later than fore-market equipment. Yet the systems theory requires that an increase in aftermarket prices be accompanied by an offsetting decrease in foremarket profits. This linkage requires what we call "effective simultaneity"; that is, the markets must operate as if the fore- and aftermarket purchasing decisions were being made simultaneously. Systems theory proponents suggest several ways in which effective simultaneity might be obtained. First, product lifetimes might be sufficiently short that current equipment owners will soon be purchasing new equipment, and will expect that, if charged high current aftermarket prices, they will be charged high prices in the future. (Note that this argument assumes low or nonpersistent *technological* switching costs, since these can lock in repeat purchasers beyond the life of their current equipment.) Second, the ratio of new potential buyers to existing owners may be sufficiently large that high current aftermarket prices will dissuade sufficient new buyers, because they expect to be charged high aftermarket prices. (This argument requires that the firm not be able to price discriminate openly between new and old buyers.) Both approaches require that a firm's pricing reputation is important because consumers consider the firm's past pricing.

Another approach to obtaining effective simultaneity is through warranties and long-term aftermarket contracts purchased at the time of equipment purchase. Similarly, the availability of rental or lease agreements that include the aftermarket good or service might restrain a firm's aftermarket power by reducing lock-in.[21] These arguments received little attention in *Kodak* (and similar cases) because aftermarket contracts extending for the full life of the equipment were never offered by Kodak.

Competitive Foremarkets

The third premise of the systems theory that durable manufacturers cannot have aftermarket power is that the equipment foremarket be competitive. The linkage argument requires that an attempt to charge high aftermarket prices will be foiled by strong competition in the foremarket.

Theories of Market Power in Aftermarkets

Kodak proposed to the Supreme Court in 1992 that as a matter of *law,* on the basis of the systems theory, it should be held that it was not *possible*

---

[21]However, these protect only against financial, not technological lock-in.

for Kodak to have aftermarket power, and thus the case should be dismissed without a full factual inquiry. Various economists—some involved in the case, some not—responded by showing that under plausible circumstances *any* of the necessary conditions of the systems theory might not hold and that the conclusion about lack of market power in the aftermarkets would then change. We shall now briefly describe the main theoretical challenges to the systems theory.

Installed Base Opportunism (IBO)

One theory disputes the assumption of *effective simultaneity.* For at least some customers, there is *not* simultaneity: those who already own equipment, and who are not about to replace it. Even if the other assumptions hold, the manufacturer could practice what is known as *installed base opportunism:* After customers are locked-in, surprise them by raising aftermarket prices above the competitive level.[22] Competition in the foremarket may force the firm to discount new equipment sales to offset the aftermarket price increase, thereby earning zero economic profits on new sales, but due to competition the firm was *already* earning zero profits on all customers. Now the firm gets excess profits equal to the total switching costs faced by its installed base. IBO will be especially attractive for mature and declining product lines, in which most revenues are from locked-in, rather than new, customers.

Costly Information

Consumers will rationally forgo complete life-cycle cost analysis if *sufficient low-cost information* is not available. Costly information also mitigates the effectiveness of reputation and thus undercuts the *effective simultaneity* assumption.[23] Since maintained durables often have lives of seven, fifteen, or even more years, and may have parts lists thousands of items long, obtaining sufficient information about future costs, and future user needs, can be quite difficult. In addition, both durables and their aftermarket goods and services may be highly differentiated. This means a complete analysis requires extensive information gathering about each of the various models and brands considered, as well as about many features other than price. Indeed, many aftermarket products—e.g., maintenance or software—have significant "experience" components: Potential buyers have great difficulty knowing their value *ex ante.*[24]

---

[22]Salop (1992) applied IBO theory to *Kodak.* The theory had been applied previously in other contexts. See, e.g., Williamson (1985).

[23]The plaintiffs presented this theory to the Supreme Court; Shapiro (1995) has discussed it.

[24]For some background on experience goods, see Carlton and Perloff (1994, pp. 601–602) and references and Tirole (1988, pp. 294–295) and references.

Imperfect Foremarket Competition

Another critique of the broad applicability of the systems theory relaxes the assumption of perfectly competitive equipment markets. Markets for expensive durable equipment are often quite concentrated; and even if they are not, there is often a substantial degree of product differentiation. Thus, we see the conditions for monopolistic competition, with each firm facing a downward-sloping residual demand curve.[25]

Klemperer (1987) has shown that in an oligopolistic market with switching costs the collusive output level can occur in a noncooperative equilibrium. When foremarkets are not competitive, it will be generally true that a manufacturer can increase its profits further by monopolizing the aftermarket (see, e.g., Borenstein, MacKie-Mason, and Netz 2000). Several authors have pointed out that one way in which aftermarkets can be used to increase foremarket profits is through price discrimination (for example, Chen and Ross 1993). Suppose that customers are heterogeneous in the utility they derive from the good and its aftermarket. This heterogeneity is not observable in the primary market. The heterogeneity is, however, related in some manner to the consumer's demand for the aftermarket good. This allows the equipment manufacturer to use aftermarket purchases as a metering device if he has an aftermarket monopoly, and thereby to extract additional profits.[26]

Imperfect Commitment

Borenstein, MacKie-Mason, and Netz (1995) present a model that is based on precisely the assumptions of the systems theory, and show that even then there will generally be supracompetitive aftermarket pricing, and harm to consumer (and overall) welfare. The main point is that when firms cannot sign complete contracts for aftermarket products that cover the full life of the durable good, and all contingencies, then *effective simultaneity* will generally be an *approximation,* and there will be at least some room to profit from the slippage.

The intuition is not hard: As soon as the firm has some locked-in customers, it can earn at least some monopoly profits by charging a supracompetitive aftermarket price. Due to foremarket competition it may lose some

---

[25]In high-volume copiers, Kodak and Xerox produced about 90 percent or more of all units sold during the relevant years. Not only was the market concentrated, but the products were also substantially differentiated.

[26]Chen and Ross (1993) have modeled the use of aftermarkets for price discrimination. They note that price discrimination itself has ambiguous welfare effects: The firm unambiguously increases its profits, but combined producer plus consumer welfare can either increase or decrease. Indeed, Hausman and MacKie-Mason (1988) have shown that price discrimination can even lead to a Pareto improvement if new markets are opened or economies of scale are significant. However, these concerns do not undermine the basic point: When a firm has foremarket power and can use the aftermarket to meter, it *will* earn higher profits due to aftermarket monopolization, contrary to the systems theory. It is still necessary to show antitrust *injury* from the profitable monopolization effort before winning a case.

foremarket profits and need to lower equipment prices, but the firm was only earning competitive (zero) profits before and the cost of a small foremarket price change at the margin is zero, or small compared to the aftermarket profit gain. That is, given switching costs and lock-in, a rational firm will always want to extract at least some of the aftermarket monopoly profit, even if foremarket competition prevents it from extracting all of the profit. The result does not require the surprise element of the IBO theory.

The consumer harm could be much larger if, for example, aftermarket monopolization reduces desirable product differentiation (such as variety in service terms or quality), or eliminates innovation that might have occurred in a competitive aftermarket (Borenstein, MacKie-Mason, and Netz 1995). Since this theory shows that the systems theory never holds completely, and that the magnitude of harm depends on the facts, it directly challenges the view that aftermarket monopolization should be strictly or even presumptively legal as a matter of law.[27]

THE ARGUMENTS PRESENTED IN THE SUPREME COURT AND IN TRIAL

Supreme Court (Summary Judgment 1992)

It bears repeating that *Kodak* first came to the Supreme Court as the result of Kodak's motion for summary judgment. This has two implications for the outcome: All questions about disputed facts were resolved for the non-moving party (the ISOs), and the moving party had to demonstrate that it could not be found guilty under any reasonable interpretation of the facts of the case. As the Supreme Court noted in its decision, the motion was heard early in the discovery phase of the case: The Court had a slim factual record upon which to base its decision.

Kodak argued that it faced substantial equipment competition in both copiers and micrographic equipment. Kodak claimed that it competed with Xerox, Canon, and others in copiers. It listed Canon, Anacomp, Bell & Howell, 3M, and others among its micrographics equipment competitors. Kodak argued that, given this equipment competition, any attempt by it to abuse its aftermarket customers would have a ruinous impact on its equipment sales: It could not *profitably* exploit whatever market power it had in its aftermarkets. Therefore, parts and service could not be distinct relevant markets for antitrust, and Kodak could not be guilty of tying or monopolization.

Under the case law, even if Kodak tied or monopolized, it might not be guilty if it had legitimate business justifications. Kodak asserted three pro-competitive business justifications: desire to provide quality maintenance,

---

[27]European Union law essentially presumes aftermarket monopolization is harmful—firms are required to sell parts. See Reed (1992)

desire to control its inventory costs, and desire to prevent the ISOs from "free-riding" on Kodak's investments in equipment, parts, and service.

The ISOs countered that customers were not perfectly informed and they faced high switching costs. Therefore, even if equipment markets were competitive, aftermarket customers might not be protected from abuse. The ISOs also argued that there was evidence that Kodak had engaged in IBO. Thus, they relied on two of the theories that undo the systems theory.

The Court rejected Kodak's argument in a detailed opinion. The Court noted that Kodak's theory required factual assumptions about the real world;[28] Kodak's theory was not compelling on purely theoretical grounds;[29] and Kodak's theory, rather than being supported by evidence in the record, was contradicted by the record.[30] Furthermore, the ISOs presented plausible explanations for why Kodak's theory didn't explain the evidence.[31]

Trial

The case at trial was somewhat different than the case argued before the Supreme Court. This difference stemmed in large part from the plaintiffs' discovery that Kodak had substantial market shares in what were very concentrated foremarkets.

Although this case involved copiers and various micrographics equipment, we will concentrate on the analysis of copiers. At the end, we shall briefly describe some differences in the micrographics part of the trial.

Plaintiffs' Arguments

The plaintiffs made three main arguments at trial: first, that Kodak had monopoly power over repair parts, and leveraged this power to maintain and extend a service monopoly; second, to rebut Kodak's main defense, that Kodak in fact had significant market power in the foremarkets; third, also in rebuttal to Kodak, that several factors sufficiently broke any linkage between fore- and aftermarkets.

Market Definition: The plaintiffs argued that there was a relevant market for the repair parts needed for Kodak copiers. The evidence indi-

---

[28]"Kodak's proposed rule [that "equipment competition precludes any finding of monopoly power in derivative aftermarkets" (504 U.S. 451 at 466, citing Kodak's Brief at 33)] rests on a factual assumption about the cross-elasticity of demand in the equipment and aftermarkets . . ." *Kodak,* 504 U.S. 451 at 469. That is, the Court recognized that the strength of the linkage depended on the factual circumstances of the case.

[29]"Thus, contrary to Kodak's assertion, there is no immutable physical law—no 'basic economic reality'—insisting that competition in the equipment market cannot coexist with market power in the aftermarkets." *Kodak,* 504 U.S. 451 at 471. Borenstein, MacKie-Mason, and Netz (1995) showed later that even Kodak's idealized conditions, stated in Justice Scalia's dissent, imply at least some market power in aftermarkets.

[30]*Kodak,* 504 U.S. 451 at 472.

[31]*Kodak,* 504 U.S. 451 at 473.

cated that many Kodak copier parts had no substitutes at all: They were unique to Kodak copiers. Furthermore, there were substantial costs involved in switching to another high-volume copier brand, indicating that customers would have an inelastic response to a significant increase in the price of Kodak copier parts. Last, there were barriers to entry into production of Kodak parts. Evidently a single firm controlling access to the parts could profitably raise prices substantially.

The "all parts" nature of the parts market definition was a departure from a strict interpretation of the DOJ/FTC Guidelines methodology. It resulted in clustering complements within the same relevant market. For example, fuser rollers and image loops were both in the relevant market. The plaintiffs argued that "all parts" were a relevant market based on the "commercial realities" of the case: If parts demanders could not get, for example, fuser rollers, they would have no demand for image loops. Kodak's parts manager testified that one would need "an assured supply of parts" to be in the service business.[32] Most customers would only deal with service providers who had an assured source of supply for all parts. Additionally, Kodak's policy applied to all parts, not just specific parts.

The switching costs that were relevant for parts were equally relevant for service labor, as were the theories undercutting the systems theory. Thus, a single firm controlling all service could profitably raise price substantially, and service was a relevant market.

Last, the plaintiffs argued that there was a relevant market for high-speed, high-volume (HV) photocopiers. Customer testimony, internal Kodak documents, and industry sources all strongly suggested that there was a distinct HV copier market and that it was a duopoly composed of Kodak and Xerox. This led the plaintiffs to define the HV copier market using copier speed, volume capability, and durability measures.[33]

Market Power: The plaintiffs contended that Kodak had market power in the parts market. Kodak had patents on various critical parts and refused to provide the specifications on others. There were entry barriers to parts production apart from the patents—in particular, significant minimum efficient scale.[34] Because a potential service competitor required access to all parts to compete, these restraints were sufficient to conclude that Kodak had monopoly power in the parts market.

---

[32]Tr. at 5585. Kodak used 9942 different parts in one year to service its installed base of copiers. It used 6430 different parts for servicing its micrographics equipment. Tr. at 5558–5559.

[33]The plaintiffs used two measures of copier speed (reproducing a single-sided, single-page document and a two-sided, multipage document), rated monthly copy volume, and weight (to reflect durability). Though some Japanese copiers with high single-page speeds were offered by the early 1990s, these units still fell far short of the Kodak and Xerox offerings in the other characteristics. See Tr. Ex. 724, 725, 726, 744, 752, 753.

[34]A copier parts manufacturer testified that, for most parts, he would need to be supplying parts for 2000 or more machines, roughly 5 percent of Kodak's installed base, to generate a sufficient return on design and tooling investments (ignoring technical and patent difficulties). Tr. at 818–820, 825–827.

Kodak also allegedly had market power in the service market. Kodak's market share was 98 percent.[35] There was evidence that Kodak restricted service contract options[36] and engaged in significant price discrimination across service customers, both of which are indicators of possible market power.[37]

The plaintiffs also argued that the equipment market did not discipline the exercise of market power in the aftermarkets. One significant piece of evidence was that Kodak did *not* engage in systems pricing. Where systems pricing requires that customers paying above-average service prices pay below average prices for their equipment and vice versa, there was essentially no statistically significant correlation between the prices customers paid for equipment and the prices they paid for maintenance. The data showed that customers paid widely different systems prices on a total-cost-of-ownership (TCO) basis.[38]

Plaintiffs gave several reasons for this unlinking:

- There were significant switching costs across copier brands.[39] In addition, shortly after introducing its parts policy Kodak increased switching costs within the Kodak service market by quadrupling the inspection and restoration fees that it charged for Kodak to begin servicing a copier bought from or previously serviced by someone other than Kodak.[40]

- Several equipment customers testified that they did not engage in TCO. A Kodak saleswoman indicated that her "TCO" proposals for customers included at most an initial few years of service while the equipment generally lasted much longer.[41] Kodak's expert testified that the inclusion of later renewal agreements was necessary for TCO calculations to be correct.[42]

- Kodak had market power in the equipment market. Kodak and Xerox were essentially the only suppliers in the high-volume copier equipment market.[43] There was also extreme price discrimination across equipment purchasers.[44]

---

[35]Ex. 730. This left the ISOs with 1/4 to 1/20 the share held by ISOs in some other high-tech industries. Kodak's expert said Kodak's share was 90 percent. Tr. at 4573:11–16.

[36]Ex. 215. For example, ITS offered CSC an on-site technician, but Kodak did not.

[37]Exs. 238, 239.

[38]See Ex. 743.

[39]Ex. 735. See also Plaintiff's Expert Report on Liability Issues for a more detailed analysis.

[40]Ex. 742. This action made it riskier to try ISO service: if you were not satisfied with the ISO, it would be very expensive to return to Kodak service.

[41]Tr. at 4511–4517.

[42]Tr. at 4587–4589.

[43]Ex. 748. The Herfindahl index for high-volume copiers was over 3100.

[44]Some customers paid 1.7 to 2.3 times as much for a given equipment configuration as other customers purchasing the same quantity.

The plaintiffs showed that when ISOs could obtain access to parts they could compete with Kodak for service contracts with lower prices and comparable quality. Kodak's own documents recorded that the parts policy helped Kodak exclude competition (see the quotes at the opening of this chapter). Therefore, the plaintiffs argued, Kodak's parts policy was used to maintain and extend its service monopoly.

IBO: Installed base opportunism was a prominent, though not the only, theory presented to the Supreme Court. It was not the central theory at trial for copiers, but the plaintiffs did present IBO evidence. Such evidence was more prominent for micrographics. Several customers testified that after a few years on Kodak maintenance, the price increased significantly. Additionally, a Kodak saleswoman testified that *renewal* maintenance agreement terms were more limited and less attractive than for agreements purchased at the time of equipment sales.[45] Thus, although there was not a specific date on which Kodak raised prices to *all* current owners of Kodak equipment, there was evidence that IBO was applied customer-by-customer. Further, earlier standard industry practice had been to permit independent service. Both IBM and Xerox had sold parts for their copiers. Kodak had sold parts for its micrographic equipment. Therefore, when Kodak implemented a policy to refuse parts sales, and thus stunted the development of ISOs as the market matured, customers were surprised to find that ISOs could not get parts and that prices were higher than they *would* have been, even if they did not rise in nominal terms.[46]

Kodak's Arguments

Kodak's expert testimony closely paralleled its Supreme Court case. This meant that it followed a significantly different framework than the plaintiffs' presentation. Kodak asserted the *presumption* that equipment competition precluded profitable abuse of aftermarket power and therefore "systems" were the relevant market.

Market Definition: Consequently, Kodak's market definition effort focused strictly on the copier equipment market. It claimed that the market was for copiers with a multicopy speed greater than 60 cpm. By ignoring throughput and durability, Kodak argued there was significant competition in the 1990s. Kodak also argued that the plaintiffs' price discrimination evidence did not indicate market power in a concentrated market, but rather hard customer bargaining in a vendor-competitive environment.[47]

Market Power in the Aftermarkets: Kodak's experts then addressed whether this competitive equipment market would adequately protect

---

[45]Tr. at 4511–4517.

[46]ISOs, when they could get parts, offered service at about 15–30 percent less than Kodak, and when Kodak competed head-to-head it cut prices drastically. See, e.g., Ex. 729.

[47]Tr. at 4634, 4669–4670.

Kodak's aftermarket customers.[48] They presented hypothetical examples to suggest that Kodak would lose profits from lost future systems sales if it overcharged aftermarket customers.[49] They asserted that it was reasonable to expect that Kodak would lose future sales if it exploited aftermarket power because a significant part of both its micrographic and copier sales were made to existing customers,[50] but they offered no direct evidence that repeat purchasers were responsive to aftermarket practices.

Kodak's copier expert suggested that switching costs were not significant. He did not analyze them in detail because he had concluded that it would not be profitable for Kodak to exploit lock-in even if it did exist.[51]

Kodak argued that information costs were also not significant. It presented evidence that several publications were available that gave guidance on how to conduct TCO as well as giving independent, if anecdotal, pricing information. Additionally, information cost effects are mitigated by the high proportion of repeat purchasers: Because such customers would be able to spread any costs of performing TCO over their several purchases, they would have lower information costs per equipment unit. Kodak's experts also noted that Kodak had spent considerable money developing an automated quote system that included pricing on initial service contracts. They argued that Kodak wouldn't have done this if either it was counting on customer ignorance or customers hadn't regularly asked for such TCO information.[52]

Kodak also pointed out that equipment manufacturers typically have large aftermarket shares. Kodak "invented" the Kodak aftermarket, inherently having a 100 percent share at the inception of the aftermarket. Thus, Kodak's "monopoly" share in the market was not the result of Kodak's parts policy, but was instead a natural effect of Kodak's having created the market.[53]

Business Justifications: Kodak claimed several pro-competitive business justifications for its parts policy. Kodak argued it had chosen to

---

[48]Kodak's economic expert on copiers believed that the systems *theory* was dispositive: He testified that merely knowing that Kodak had to compete with Xerox would have been sufficient for him to conclude that Kodak could not harm its aftermarket customers. Tr. 4515:23–4516:3.

[49]Ex. 3697 and Tr. at 4603–4608. However, the exhibit was based on the *assumption* that Kodak would lose all future systems sales to this customer. This is the exact assumption that the Supreme Court refused to accept as dispositive, demanding instead that the facts be examined. Kodak presented a similar exhibit in its micrographics presentation, using the same underlying *assumption*. Ex. 3768 and Tr. at 6010–6014, and 6323–6325.

[50]Seventy-five percent of Kodak's copier sales between 1986 and 1994 were to past or current owners of Kodak copiers. Ex. 3695. In micrographics, somewhere between 68 percent and 90 percent of purchases from 1990 to 1994 were to past or current owners of Kodak equipment. Ex. 3733 and Tr. at 5999–6000.

[51]This conclusion was based on Ex. 3697. See fn. 48 and related text.

[52]Tr. at 4592–4593.

[53]Kodak's expert presented evidence on other industries, including IBM copiers, in which ISOs had only a 5 percent market share. The IBM copier example is particularly apropos because IBM was required to sell parts for its equipment to anyone who asked. Tr. at 4578, Ex. 3693, 3692.

compete in the equipment market by adopting a strategy of providing high-quality maintenance. This and the avoidance of finger-pointing were reasons to prevent ISOs from servicing Kodak equipment.[54] Kodak claimed that it also needed to be the sole service provider so that it could control its parts inventory costs. Kodak argued that the ISOs were free-riding on its investment in developing maintenance methods, tools, and parts. Last, Kodak argued that its patents gave it the explicit right to refuse to sell patented parts.

Jury Findings

The jury returned a unanimous verdict against Kodak. Based on the written instructions from the judge to the jury (and on the written opinion of the Ninth Circuit, which reviewed the case), we can infer[55] that the jury concluded:

1. Equipment, parts, and service were distinct relevant markets.

2. Kodak had a parts market monopoly.

3. Kodak levered its parts monopoly to monopolize service.

ANTITRUST AND ECONOMICS AFTER *KODAK*

Kodak raises interesting issues about the role of economics in antitrust analysis that transcend the economics of aftermarkets. We shall briefly describe two here; space is too limited for a thorough treatment. First, should a plausible but relatively untested economic theory be sufficient, as a matter of law, to prevent a case from getting to a factual determination by a jury? Second, having gotten to the jury, where does the plaintiff's burden of proving the relevant market with *partial* equilibrium evidence in a *general* equilibrium world end?

Government intervention in markets, even when intended to correct market failures, is itself costly, and subject to error. The summary judgment procedure exists in part to balance the costs of intervention with the benefits of antitrust enforcement. A party can move for summary judgment on the basis that it will prevail as a matter of *law*, even if the facts are all interpreted in the other party's favor. Kodak made a somewhat novel motion for summary judgment: It claimed that on the basis of an *economic theory*, a showing that Kodak had market power would be impossible even if the

---

[54]Finger-pointing was described as the customer's inability to distinguish between poor service and poor equipment. Thus, Kodak claimed, it had the right to control service because poor service could harm Kodak's equipment reputation.

[55]Juries, unlike judges, do not issue written opinions to support their decisions, but the jury was instructed by the judge that it had to make specific findings on several questions before it could conclude that Kodak was guilty.

plaintiffs had the facts right. If the plaintiffs could not establish market power, Kodak would prevail. The question raised is whether courts should rely on a novel, untested economic theory to conclude that despite the facts, the plaintiffs would not be able to demonstrate market power.

When dealing with questions such as market power, courts necessarily rely on economic theories. However, it is our view that there should be a strong presumption against granting summary judgment on the basis of a theory that has not been well tested in previous cases, or for that matter in the economics literature. Kodak's theory had a superficial plausibility and was endorsed by Justice Scalia in his dissent to the majority Supreme Court position. However, as shown above, economic research since *Kodak* has established that the plaintiff's alternative theory is sound, and *additional* theories have been published and accepted under which market power in an aftermarket could exist.[56] When an opposing party offers a plausible alternative theory, judges are called on to evaluate the competing theories for correctness and appropriateness to the alleged factual setting, and since this is not their area of expertise, the risk of judicial error is high.

The second question, we think, is fundamental to the practice of antitrust economics: When it is impossible to do a complete, general equilibrium analysis of market interactions, how far does the burden of proof on the plaintiffs extend? Kodak argued in trial and in its appeal to the Ninth Circuit that since higher service profits might be offset by lower equipment profits under systems competition, the *plaintiffs* were obliged to show that *combined* profits were above competitive. Only then, Kodak argued, would the ability profitably to monopolize a service market be established; that is, only if Kodak *did* earn combined monopoly profits would plaintiffs have shown that it had market power. This is a difficult proof issue that we believe requires a policy judgment. Should it be the plaintiff's burden to prove that systems competition *did not* protect consumers from antitrust harm, or should it be the defendant's responsibility to prove that systems competition *did* protect consumer welfare?

In an ideal world, we would assess all interactions between a hypothetical monopolization and other markets. If, taking into account all interactions, it would not be possible for a defendant to harm overall social welfare, then we would not find it guilty of an antitrust violation. A complete, general equilibrium analysis will almost never be possible, yet clearly it is not consistent with antitrust policy to bar all plaintiffs from court because they are unable to perform such an extensive analysis. In general, all market definition analyses are partial equilibrium in nature.

Consider an example. Suppose Kodak asserted that by charging supracompetitive service prices, enough disgruntled customers would stop buy-

---

[56]Indeed, one of Kodak's expert economists at trial has published an article acknowledging the theoretical correctness of four of the alternative theories (Shapiro 1995).

ing Kodak film products that Kodak overall would not be able to earn supra-competitive profits. (Most micrographic equipment in this case requires film, and Kodak, of course, also sells other film.) Should plaintiffs also have the burden to prove that film profit losses do not outweigh service profit gains?[57] What if Kodak proposed an even more remote linkage? Where should the line be drawn?

The question raised about burden of proof and the proper bounds for practicing market definition apply generally. Plaintiffs practice and courts permit partial equilibrium analysis. However, this provides only general guidance. How far the plaintiff has to go is a policy question for Congress or the courts.

POSTSCRIPT I: DID THE SUPREME COURT LIMIT CLAIMS TO ONLY ONE ECONOMIC THEORY?

There have been at least seven circuit court opinions on aftermarket cases since the Supreme Court (1992) decision in *Kodak,* and the results are deeply divided on a fundamental issue. Three, we believe, clearly misread *Kodak.*[58]

These three opinions turned on the same question: Was the allegation of *installed base opportunism* the crucial issue in *Kodak?* The First, Sixth, and Seventh Circuits have now each held that a *surprise* change in policy is necessary for a finding of a separate aftermarket that can be monopolized when the foremarket is competitive.[59] Each has dismissed a plaintiff's claims, because there was no evidence or allegation of IBO.

The Supreme Court did not write that IBO was a single, special circumstance that permitted aftermarket power. The Court wrote:

---

[57]This is not so far-fetched. Kodak argued at trial that the line should be drawn not just around its equipment and complementary service, but around every product Kodak produced that a service customer might buy. Tr. at 6010–6014. Thus, Kodak argues for a presumption of "systems" wherever there are complementary products *and* that Kodak's "reputation" is sufficiently important to make a wide range of superficially unrelated product effective complements: Kodak couldn't overcharge micrographic service customers because they might, someday, be a prospective buyer for Kodak copiers.

[58]The three we believe are in error are: *Lee* v. *Life Ins. Co. of North America,* 23 F.3d 14 (1st Cir. 1994), cert. denied, 513 U.S. 964 (1994); *PSI* v. *Honeywell,* 104 F.3d 811 (6th Cir. 1997), cert. denied (1997); and *Digital Equipment Corp.* v. *Uniq Digital Techs., Inc.,* 73 F.3d 756 (7th Cir. 1996), 520 U.S. 1265. The other four are *Kodak* itself in its second visit to the Ninth Circuit; *United Farmers Agents* v. *Farmers Ins. Exchange,* 89 F.3d 233 (5th Cir. 1996); *Allen-Myland* v. *IBM,* 33 F.3d 194 (3rd Cir. 1994), and *Virtual Maintenance* v. *Prime Computer,* 11 F.3d 660 (6th Cir. 1993). Note that in two opinions, the Sixth Circuit is in conflict with itself.

[59]For example, the Sixth Circuit held "that an antitrust plaintiff cannot succeed on a Kodak-type theory when the defendant has not changed its policy after locking-in some of its customers." *PSI* v. *Honeywell,* 104 F. 3d at 820.

> The fact that the equipment market imposes a restraint on prices in the aftermarket by no means disproves the existence of power in those markets. . . . Thus, contrary to Kodak's assertion, *there is no immutable physical law*—no "basic economic reality"—insisting that competition in the equipment market cannot coexist with market power in the aftermarkets. (*Kodak,* 504 U.S. at 471 [emphasis added])

The Court emphasized that "marketplace realities" and market imperfections, such as high information costs and lock-in from switching costs, "could create *a less responsive connection* between service and parts prices and equipment sales" (*Kodak,* 504 U.S. at 473 [emphasis added]).

The *Kodak* Court made specifically the point that we described in the theoretical section above: The key factor in whether or not aftermarket power is possible is the strength of the link between the fore- and aftermarket responses to supracompetitive aftermarket pricing. The Court noted that *every* monopolist faces some constraints on its prices; the crucial question was the cross-elasticity between the aftermarket and the foremarket: How strong is the link?

This is the key factual issue for market definition in *all* antitrust cases. For example, slide rules can, to a degree, substitute for computers: is the linkage strong enough that consumers are protected from computer monopolization by slide rule competition? The Court agreed with the plaintiffs that the connection could be sufficiently weak due to IBO. The Court also stated that switching costs and high information costs could make the connection sufficiently weak. In short, the Court stated that *one theory* under which the systems view could fail is IBO; it did not state that this is the only theory. This point has been reinforced by the post-*Kodak* economic literature. Even one of Kodak's own expert economists has published an article in which four different theories are identified under which there is an opportunity to behave monopolistically in aftermarkets, with a reduction in consumer welfare (Shapiro 1995).

There is a consistent economic theme here: firms wish to maximize profits, and thus want to act like monopolists given the opportunity. However, only sometimes are monopoly profits possible. The crucial economic question is what market constraints there are on a firm's ability to charge supracompetitive prices or otherwise earn excess profits at the expense of consumers. When studying behavior in an aftermarket, one such market constraint may be the effect that aftermarket pricing has on foremarket profitability. This link should be analyzed in an aftermarket case. But there are any number of different circumstances under which the link is not sufficient to prevent monopoly harm. Simple, but incomplete economic theories should not provide antitrust immunity for entire classes of potentially harmful behavior. If plaintiffs in a case have a plausible alternative theory of aftermarket power, and allege facts consistent with the theory, the case should proceed to trial, as did *Kodak.*

POSTSCRIPT II: DO INTELLECTUAL PROPERTY RIGHTS GRANT IMMUNITY FROM ANTITRUST?

After the *Kodak* case was completed, another issue that arose late in the proceedings has become very controversial, and another conflict has emerged between appeals courts. The controversy concerns the extent to which patents should have protected Kodak from antitrust liability.

Kodak argued on appeal that the patents it had on some of its parts gave it the right to refuse to sell parts to ISOs. The Ninth Circuit ruled that protecting intellectual property is presumed to be a valid, pro-competitive business justification for refusing to sell or license. However, the court stated that this was a rebuttable presumption, and concluded that plaintiffs successfully rebutted the Kodak's patent defense by showing that only about 65 of 10,000 parts were covered by patents, and that the author of the Kodak parts policy testified that he didn't give any thought to protecting Kodak's intellectual property when crafting the policy.

The Federal Circuit, which is a special court created to hear appeals on cases in which patent issues are central to the case, has more recently ruled in the *Xerox* case that intellectual property owners have a much more general immunity from antitrust law: "'The antitrust laws do not negate the patentee's right to exclude others from patent property.'"[60] The *Xerox* case is remarkably similar to *Kodak* (it also involves a refusal to sell high-volume copier parts to ISOs), but the result was different: the court stated that firms could refuse to sell patented parts regardless of their motivation, in particular even if the motivation was to foreclose competition in a separate market such as service.

This conflict between two federal appeals courts is quite stark, and many authors have written about it in just the two years since the *Xerox* ruling (see, e.g., Katz and Safer [2002] and Boyle et al. [2002]). The issue highlights a long-standing area of controversy. Patent and other intellectual property laws establish property rights, which may create limited monopolies, in

---

[60]*In re Independent Service Organizations Antitrust Litigation (Xerox)*, 203 F.3d 1322 at 1325 (Fed. Cir. 2000), cert. denied, 531 U.S. 1143 (2001), quoting *Intergraph Corp.* v. *Intel Corp.*, 195 F.3d 1346 at 1362 (Fed. Cir. 1999). There is substantial uncertainty about what the *Xerox* decision even means. For example, in *U.S.* v. *Microsoft* (253 F.3d 34 at 63) the U.S. Court of Appeals for the District of Columbia cited *Xerox* when it wrote:

> Microsoft's primary copyright argument borders upon the frivolous. The company claims an absolute and unfettered right to use its intellectual property as it wishes: "[I]f intellectual property rights have been lawfully acquired," it says, then "their subsequent exercise cannot give rise to antitrust liability." Appellant's Opening Br. at 105. That is no more correct than the proposition that use of one's personal property, such as a baseball bat, cannot give rise to tort liability. As the Federal Circuit succinctly stated: "Intellectual property rights do not confer a privilege to violate the antitrust laws." *In re Indep. Serv. Orgs. Antitrust Litig.*, 203 F.3d 1322, 1325 (Fed.Cir.2000).

Yet, Microsoft's quoted argument above also claimed to rely on *Xerox* for support.

order to encourage invention and authorship, and endow the property owners with the right to engage in exclusionary conduct. The antitrust laws make some exclusionary conduct by a monopolist illegal. Both are seeking to enhance consumer welfare: Intellectual property law by leading to new ideas and inventions, antitrust law by limiting allocative inefficiency (high prices, reduced quality or variety) by firms with current market power. Thus, we have a situation in which both types of law are largely trying to accomplish the same thing (maximizing consumer welfare), but they come into conflict.

From an economic perspective, there should be some balancing: In some situations antitrust should restrict the way in which firms use their intellectual property, and in other situations intellectual property should be exempt from antitrust restrictions. The Supreme Court has repeatedly stated that intellectual property laws grant property rights, and those property rights are sometimes limited by antitrust (and other) laws. For example, in *Kodak* it wrote "[we have] held many times that power gained through some natural advantage such as a patent, copyright, or business acumen can give rise to liability if 'a seller exploits his dominant position in one market to expand his empire into the next.' "[61] However, at present the law is very unclear about when antitrust limits the ability of firms to refuse to sell patented goods, or to otherwise condition sale or licensing on anticompetitive conditions.

The Kodak case continues to be one of the most controversial antitrust cases of the modern era, although the controversy has expanded beyond whether aftermarkets can be profitably monopolized to also include conflicts between intellectual property and antitrust law. The particular conflict between *Kodak* and *Xerox* almost surely will need to be resolved by the Supreme Court in some future case. Today, some prominent observers believe that "recent cases, and particularly the Federal Circuit's opinion in *[Xerox]*, have upset that traditional balance [between intellectual property and antitrust] in a way that has disturbing implications for the future of antitrust in high-technology industries" (Pitofsky 2001). Other equally notable analysts believe that *Kodak* got it wrong, and *Xerox* got it right (Carlton 2001). Until the Supreme Court resolves the dispute, businesses and trial courts will not know what the law really is.

REFERENCES

Akerlof, G. "The Market for 'Lemons': Quality Uncertainty and the Market Mechanism." *Quarterly Journal of Economics* 84 (August 1970): 488–500.

Borenstein, S., J. MacKie-Mason, and J. Netz. "Antitrust Policy in Aftermarkets." *Antitrust Law Journal* 63 (1995): 455–482.

---

[61] 504 U.S. at 480 n.29 (quoting *Times-Picayune Publishing Co.* v. *U.S.,* 345 U.S. 594, 611 [1953]).

Borenstein, S., J. MacKie-Mason, and J. Netz. "Exercising Market Power in Proprietary Aftermarkets." *Journal of Economics and Management Strategy* 9 (Summer 2000): 157–188.

Boyle, P., P. Lister, and J. Everett, Jr. "Antitrust Law at the Federal Circuit: Red Light or Green Light at the IP-Antitrust Intersection?" *Antitrust Law Journal* 69 (2002): 739–800.

Carlton, D. "A General Analysis of Exclusionary Conduct and Refusal to Deal—Why Aspen and Kodak Are Misguided." *Antitrust Law Journal* 68 (2001): 659–84.

Carlton, D., and J. Perloff. *Modern Industrial Organization,* 2d edn. New York: Harper-Collins, 1994.

Chen, Z., and T. Ross. "Refusals to Deal, Price Discrimination, and Independent Service Organizations." *Journal of Economics and Management Science* 2 (Summer 1993): 593–614.

Farrell, J. GTE Laboratories Working Paper 85–15, 1985.

Hausman, J., and J. MacKie-Mason. "Price Discrimination and Patent Policy." *RAND Journal of Economics* 19 (1988): 253–265.

Katz, R., and A. Safer. "Should One Patent Court Be Making Antitrust Law for the Whole Country?" *Antitrust Law Journal* 69 (2002): 687–710.

Klemperer, P. "Markets with Consumer Switching Costs." *Quarterly Journal of Economics* 102 (May 1987): 375–394.

Pitofsky, R. "Challenges of the New Economy: Issues at the Intersection of Antitrust and Intellectual Property." *Antitrust Law Journal* 68 (2001): 913–924.

Porter, M. *Competitive Advantage.* New York: Macmillan, 1985.

Reed, C. "EC Antitrust Law and the Exploitation of Intellectual Property Rights in Software." *Jurimetrics Journal* 32 (Spring 1992): 431–446.

Salop, S. "Kodak as Post-Chicago Law and Economics." Unpublished manuscript 12/13/92, presented at ALI-ABA "New Directions in Antitrust Law," January 21–23, 1993.

Shapiro, C. "Aftermarkets and Consumer Welfare: Making Sense of Kodak." *Antitrust Law Journal* 63 (1995): 495–496.

Tirole, J. *The Theory of Industrial Organization.* Cambridge, Mass.: MIT Press, 1988.

Williamson, O. *The Economic Institutions of Capitalism.* New York: Free Press, 1985.

CASE 18

Access and Network Effects in the "New Economy": AOL-Time Warner (2000)

Gerald R. Faulhaber

INTRODUCTION

On January 10, 2000, Steve Case, CEO of America Online (AOL), and Gerald Levin, CEO of Time Warner, announced the acquisition of Time Warner by AOL. This merger was unique in many respects; it was at that time the largest merger ever proposed and consummated, valued at the time at $183 billion; it also was the first merger of "old" and "new" media, and by far the most significant Internet-related merger to date. The Federal Trade Commission (FTC) approved the merger with conditions on December 14, 2000. The Federal Communications Commission (FCC) approved the merger with conditions on January 19, 2001.

The principal economic issues at the FTC were: (1) Should the merged firm be required to offer its cable broadband Internet channels to Internet service providers (ISP) other than AOL? (2) Would AOL's acquisition of cable properties reduce its interest in deploying its ISP over digital subscriber lines (DSL), a competitive technology to cable for broadband Inter-

The author was Chief Economist at the Federal Communications Commission (FCC) from July 1, 2000, through June 29, 2001, during which time the FCC considered this merger and issued its order approving it with conditions. The author wishes to thank various colleagues at the FCC, seminar participants at the American Enterprise Institute, April 25, 2001; George Washington University Seminar, March 1, 2001; Antitrust Division of the Department of Justice, May 8, 2001; and at the Corporate Control and Industry Structure in Global Communications Conference, London Business School, May 15, 2001. I am particularly indebted to Professors Jeremy Bulow (Stanford GSB) and William Rogerson (Northwestern) for extensive conversations regarding the analysis of this merger at the FTC, where both of them were active participants in the process. The views expressed in this paper are those of the author only, and do not represent the views of the FCC or any other party.

net access, in territories where both AOL and DSL competed? The principal economic issue at the FCC was the ability of AOL to leverage its dominant position in text-based Instant Messaging (IM) into next generation IM services using the cable assets that it proposed to acquire.[1]

AUTHORITY FOR MERGER REVIEW

The merger plans were submitted to the FTC for antitrust review under Hart-Scott-Rodino.[2] In addition, the merger was also reviewed by the FCC, which is required by the Communications Act of 1934 to review all transfers of electromagnetic spectrum to ensure that such transfers are "in the public interest." This merger required that the CARS (cable television relay service) licenses[3] held by Time Warner be transferred to the new merged entity, AOL-Time Warner; therefore the merger was subject to FCC approval.[4]

The FCC's merger review authority is not without controversy. Merger parties frequently complain to legislators about undergoing two reviews, and legislators frequently complain that one antitrust agency is quite enough. Moreover, the FCC reviews mergers using a public interest standard and is therefore not limited to the Clayton Act's antitrust standard of "substantial lessening of competition." In fact, this public interest standard is not defined in the governing statute and is open to Commission interpretation (and court challenge). The Commission has been criticized for extending its writ to impose "voluntary" conditions on merging parties that perhaps are more properly considered under the Commission's formal rulemaking procedures. Nevertheless, the FCC's merger review authority has not been challenged in court nor has Congress sought to remove this authority; and it was not challenged in this merger.

---

[1]Additionally, both agencies had concerns that AOL's control of the Time Warner cable assets could lead it to favor its own entry, AOLTV, into the nascent Interactive TV market. This issue did not play a large role in the merger analysis of either agency. Documents of the agencies that detail their merger analysis, remedies, and orders are FTC (2000a), FTC (2000b), FTC (2000c), FTC (2000d), and FCC (2001).

[2]In the past, the FTC has reviewed mergers in the cable industry, such as Time Warner-Turner in 1996. However, the Department of Justice has handled mergers in telecommunications, such as the AT&T-TCI and AT&T-MediaOne mergers, also involving cable firms. In this case, the FTC assumed jurisdiction.

[3]Cable television firms transmit video signals to their individual metropolitan distribution points using microwave systems; the CARS licenses required to operate these microwave systems are granted by the FCC in its role as the nation's spectrum manager.

[4]This review authority is only granted for a spectrum license transfer; then-Commissioner Furchtgott-Roth pointed out that since Time Warner held the radio licenses in question, if Time Warner had acquired AOL, then no license transfer was required and the FCC would have no jurisdiction.

INDUSTRY BACKGROUND AND
THE MERGING PARTIES

Each company was a major player in its industry. AOL was founded in 1985 as a popular interactive services firm providing content and services to residential customers via dial-up modems. Originally, customers who subscribed to AOL were limited to AOL content and e-mail (as was typical of online service providers at the time). As the Internet grew in popularity, AOL also provided Internet access to the World Wide Web in addition to its proprietary content. Its simple intuitive interface and aggressive marketing led to extremely rapid growth in the late 1990s. At the time of the merger, AOL had 27 million subscribers (2 million in its Compuserve subsidiary), amounting to about 40 percent of total U.S. online subscribers. The second-largest online provider was EarthLink, with 4.7 million subscribers (Grice 2001), followed closely by Microsoft's MSN, with 4 million subscribers (Kapadia 2001).

Time Warner is both a content firm and a cable firm, created by the merger of Time Inc. and Warner Bros. in 1989. That merger brought together Warner's video and music content with Time's print and editorial content and cable assets. The 1996 merger of Time Warner and Turner Broadcasting added to both the content assets and the cable assets of the firm. At the time of the AOL merger, Time Warner's cable properties served more than 18 percent of U.S. cable households, ranking number two in the country after AT&T (which had purchased TCI and MediaOne).

It also owned (directly or through subsidiaries) leading cable television networks, such as HBO, Cinemax, CNN, TNT, TBS Superstation, Turner Classic Movies, the WB Network, and Cartoon Network. In addition, it owned several major music labels, the extensive video libraries of Warner Bros. and NewLine Cinema, and print media such as *Time, People,* and *Sports Illustrated.* Time Warner's cable assets were controlled by various subsidiaries, notably Time Warner Entertainment (TWE), in which AT&T owned a 25.5 percent nonvoting share as a result of its merger with MediaOne.

THE MAJOR ISSUES OF THE MERGER

Open Access

The merger attracted a great deal of interest from the press, from public interest and consumer advocate groups, and from competitors and firms that did business with either or both companies. In its comments on the previous mergers of AT&T-TCI and AT&T-MediaOne, AOL had taken a strong and very public position that cable firms should be required to provide "open access" to their broadband Internet facilities (the "IP pipe") to any ISP that so requested it. During 1999, the open access movement gained many adherents. After AOL and Time Warner announced their merger in January 2000, however, AOL changed its position, advocating voluntary open access and promising that it would provide such access on its Time Warner cable facilities when the merger was consummated. Open access was clearly the most salient issue when the merger was announced, due in part to AOL's *volte-face* on the issue after the merger announcement.

The ISP market in the United States experienced remarkable growth during the 1990s, from zero to about 7000 firms today, with over one-half of U.S. households connected to the Internet via an ISP. Until recently, almost all ISPs were reached by their customers via the voice telephone network and provided narrowband connections to the Internet. Customers initiated an Internet session by calling their ISP over the telephone system using a modem in or attached to their computer. In addition to connecting customers to the Internet via telephone, ISPs also provided e-mail services, disk space, web hosting, and portal services.

Broadband Internet connections, via either cable modems or digital subscriber line (DSL) over telephone lines, functioned quite differently. The connection had substantially higher bandwidth (> 200 Kbps, often 500 Kbps to 1 Mbps), and the connection from the customer to the Internet was continuous, dedicated, and "always on." No dialing was necessary. Even DSL service, which relied on telephone company access lines, used a high-bandwidth channel piggybacked on the standard voice access line and provided a dedicated "always on" connection. As a business matter, cable firms that provided broadband Internet service to customers provided connections via an ISP-like firm designated by the cable operator; the two most popular were Excite@Home, principally owned by TCI (later AT&T), and RoadRunner, principally owned by Time Warner. Each of these firms provided Internet connections and the IP pipe for cable firms other than their principal owners. For example, Excite@Home provided service for Comcast Cable. Customers had no choice of their ISP. There was concern that AOL coupled with Time Warner's share of RoadRunner would dominate the broadband ISP market postmerger.

On the DSL side, telephone companies that deployed DSL were required to provide the DSL channel on the access line to any firm that wished to offer DSL service, including the provision of co-location space at telephone company central offices and nondiscriminatory operations and installation support. This requirement was imposed by the FCC's interpretation and implementation of the 1996 Telecommunications Act's mandate to achieve competition in local exchange telephone service via resale of local access facilities. In effect, telephone companies offering DSL service had an open access condition imposed upon them. It was a particularly severe "common carrier–like" condition, in that all competitors had to be accommodated; the telephone company could not choose whom to accept. Not surprisingly, local telephone companies used the opportunity of this merger to lobby for the imposition of open access on this cable merger, or to be rid of it themselves.

Cable versus DSL

Prior to the merger announcement, AOL had been quite active in seeking arrangements with telephone companies deploying DSL to offer AOL Plus, a broadband version of AOL's flagship ISP service. This effort did not go particularly well; telephone companies were rolling out DSL service very slowly in 1998–1999, in spite of incentives provided by AOL. It is likely that this slow rollout was due to technical and operational problems, not to lack of enthusiasm for AOL (Faulhaber 2001). AOL's decision to buy itself a cable firm with broadband assets may well have been influenced by its somewhat negative experience with telephone company DSL deployment speed.

However, AOL's purchase of a cable firm with broadband assets could certainly dampen its enthusiasm for DSL, a competing technology. In fact, the power of AOL in the ISP market could have been used to direct customers in Time Warner cable franchise territories away from DSL and toward cable, thus lessening competition in the conduit market.

Instant Messaging

IM is a text-based means of near-real-time communication between customers who have signed up for the service. Customer A can send an "instant message" to customer B and receive an immediate reply, thus carrying on a text conversation.

This service has roots in the original Unix system, in which users on the same server could exchange messages in conversation mode. Instant messaging differs from e-mail in that it is a true dialogue, operating in synchronous rather than asynchronous mode.[5] AOL introduced the service as a feature for its customers in 1989. However, it became wildly popular when AOL added the "buddy list" feature in 1996. This feature displays a small window that lists all the customer's (self-designated) "buddies" with an indication of whether each buddy is on-line. This feature ensured that if the customer sent an IM to a particular buddy, the customer knew that the buddy would receive it immediately and could reply. With the advent of the buddy list, Instant Messaging became one of the most popular features of AOL.

---

[5]In synchronous mode, both communicating parties must be simultaneously present in order to respond to each other as they speak. In asynchronous mode, a communicating party leaves a message for the other party, who need not be there when the message is left. The other party responds to the message at some later date, leaving the response for the originating party who is not likely present at the time of response.

In 1997, AOL took the unusual step of offering AIM (AOL Instant Messenger) as a stand-alone free download on the Web for non-AOL subscribers.[6] AIM customers could IM both other AIM customers and AOL subscribers using IM, and vice versa; this is referred to as interoperation. In the same year, AOL bought ICQ, an IM provider based primarily outside the United States. However, AOL chose not to interoperate its AIM/IM services with ICQ.

In 1999, several firms established competitive IM services, including Microsoft, Yahoo!, Otigo, and Tribal Voice. However, these competitors quickly learned that few customers wanted to sign up for a service that couldn't IM with AOL's huge customer base, reported at the time to be more than 30 million subscribers. These competitors designed their IM client software to be compatible with AOL's IM protocols (which they earlier had published on the Web) to allow their IM client software to interoperate with AOL's AIM/IM. AOL chose to interpret these attempts to interoperate as "hacking" and took immediate steps to block such attempts. During the summer of 1999, various competitors' attempts were temporarily successful but quickly blocked by AOL. By year's end, AOL had demonstrated that it had both the will and the means to block all such competitor attempts to interoperate with its AIM/IM services.

AOL was criticized in the press for refusing to interoperate with other IM services. Indeed, many contrasted AOL's call for open access in the pending AT&T-MediaOne merger with their refusal to interoperate their AIM/IM services with competitors. AOL's response was that it had safety and security concerns on behalf of its customers and was unwilling to expose them to nuisance or even pornographic IMs from non-AOL sources. AOL did indicate that it would interoperate with competitors, but only when technical protocols were agreed to that ensured the safety and security of its IM customers.

ANALYSIS OF THE ISSUES

Open Access and DSL

On the face of it, a vertical merger between an ISP and a conduit has the beneficial effect of eliminating "double marginalization,"[7] and so should be

---

[6]All other features of AOL, such as chat rooms and proprietary content, are provided only to AOL subscribers. AIM represents the first and only (to this author's knowledge) departure from this policy.

[7]Double marginalization occurs when two vertically related firms independently set their prices; the upstream firm prices to maximize profit, the downstream firm takes that price as an input price and then determines its output price to maximize profit. The result is that the total price to the consumer is greater and the total profit of the two firms is less than if the two firms jointly maximized profit. Vertical integration solves this problem.

favored on grounds of efficiency. Though the merging parties did not use this argument, staff at both agencies understood this as a value to the merger. However, open access and the impact of the merger on DSL were viewed by the FTC as vertical foreclosure issues. In the case of DSL, the merger would make AOL less interested in DSL deployment in Time Warner franchise territory, thus reducing DSL's competitive position vis-à-vis Time Warner cable. This was of particular concern to the FTC staff, whose analysis stressed the importance of competition between the conduits (rather than among ISPs on the same conduit). If AOL withdrew its support for DSL, this could well lessen DSL's ability to compete with cable. The FCC staff, however, saw AOL's ISP strategy of ubiquity as trumping the potential profit impact of weakening DSL by not offering AOL over that conduit.

In the case of open access, a merged AOL-Time Warner could either deny access to Time Warner cable systems to any competing ISP, or it could charge a very high price for such access, a classic vertical price squeeze. In order to offer a customer broadband service, both the cable access and the ISP are complementary services. For the customer, the total price is what matters, not the price of each component. AOL could thus maintain an appearance of nondiscrimination by setting a high fee for access to its cable IP pipe and a low price for the AOL ISP service. This high fee would not permit other ISPs to compete with AOL and still earn a profit.

There are two rather different forms of open access. The first is the common carrier model (applied to the telephone companies' DSL service), in which the conduit provider must provide service to all competitors that demand it. The second is the "shopping mall" model, in which the conduit provider chooses several ISPs to carry on its system as a business decision. Both models were considered at the FTC and the FCC. At the FTC, the common carrier model was rejected as "too regulatory," but the second model became the core of the FTC's case and the eventual Consent Agreement.

The FCC staff had concerns about open access in this merger but recognized that the FTC would take vigorous action. As a result, open access played only a minor role in the FCC's findings. However, the FCC perceived that open access was an industry-wide issue, not simply an issue with this merger. The FCC had an advantage as a regulatory agency in that it had continuing authority over this industry beyond this merger (which the FTC did not), and in response to public demands for open access, it issued a Notice of Inquiry on High-Speed Internet Access on September 28, 2000.

During and after the merger, AOL professed to be in favor of open access and indicated that it would move toward sharing its IP pipe with a few selected ISPs after the merger.[8] This suggests that the shopping mall model

[8] Since the cable IP "pipe" is shared among customers (and therefore their ISPs), establishing rules and protocols for multiple ISPs to share is not technically trivial. It appears that these problems are

is perhaps the more accurate model, if AOL's protestations were to be believed. AOL accepted the general thrust of open access, but was suspicious of a regulatory-driven approach in which a government agency dictated the terms of open access. The ensuing negotiations between AOL and the FTC were less over the general thrust of open access than over the specifics of implementation. AOL also pledged to continue working with DSL providers to offer AOL broadband on DSL facilities, and offered little objection to the FTC's proposed remedy for DSL.

Surprisingly, there was no economic analysis of the threshold issue of whether or not open access was efficiency enhancing. Competition among upstream ISPs is not likely to produce lower prices to consumers, as the cable companies are (usually) monopolies in their markets and can extract all the rents from consumers. Further, since virtually all content is available over all ISPs, having multiple ISPs is unlikely to increase the content available to consumers. And lastly, it is possible that in a dedicated access context such as cable (as opposed to dial-up access) it is more efficient to integrate the ISP function with the IP pipe. Clearly, a careful economic analysis of open access is needed as a guide to policy.

Of course, pricing is critical in a vertical foreclosure case; what cannot be obtained by outright denial of access can be obtained by price strategies. The FTC considered an interesting pricing mechanism that promised to solve both vertical foreclosure problems of DSL and open access (the "Rogerson remedy"):[9] Time Warner could offer conduit services to AOL at whatever price it wished, and AOL could offer its ISP service at whatever (incremental) price[10] it wished. Customers would face the sum of the two prices. However, Time Warner was constrained to offer the same price for conduit services to any ISP on its system, and AOL was constrained to offer its ISP service on other broadband systems at the same (incremental) price as it offered over Time Warner systems. This remedy ensures that AOL does not unduly raise the conduit price and lower its ISP price on Time Warner (a vertical price squeeze) because it would then be required to charge the same low ISP price on other broadband systems at a loss. Conversely, it could not raise its price to DSL subscribers (thereby negotiating a hard bargain with telephone companies) without being forced to charge the same high price on Time Warner systems and suffer competitive losses. This elegant solution to the pricing problem placed only nondiscrimination con-

currently being solved, as various cable firms conduct multiple ISP trials. In contrast, DSL is not a shared technology.

[9]Devised by Professor William Rogerson of Northwestern University Department of Economics, who acted as a consultant to the FTC in the AOL-Time Warner case. Professor Barry Nalebuff of the Yale School of Organization and Management suggested a similar solution to the FCC at the FCC's *en banc* hearing of July 27, 2000. See http://www.fcc.gov/csb/aoltw/07-27-00_enbanc/yale.pdf.

[10]As a practical matter, the cable firm charges (say) $25/customer-month to the ISP, and the ISP charges the customer (say) $40/month, for an incremental ISP price of $15. In this example, the customer is "owned" by the ISP that bills the customer.

straints on AOL-Time Warner, otherwise letting them set prices where they wished and relying on the incentives inherent in the scheme for AOL to avoid anticompetitive pricing.

The elegance of this remedy rests on the presupposition that ISP access to a cable (or DSL) firm's IP pipe is a single, simple product with a single price. More likely, the conduit firm may offer a variety of prices for access, depending on the needs of its customers: (1) quantity discounts may be appropriate; (2) bundling of ancillary services such as web caching; and (3) whether the ISP chooses to perform its own customer account management or have the conduit firm do it. Of course, such price differentials among Time Warner service offerings have the potential to be anticompetitive. Policing a complex rate structure to ensure that such differentials are cost-justified becomes a highly regulatory exercise, and the remedy loses its elegance and could become a regulatory morass.

Instant Messaging

Several consumer groups as well as an Instant Messaging trade group (IM Unified) lobbied both of the commissions to adopt remedies requiring AOL to interoperate its popular IM service with other IM competitors, such as Yahoo! and Microsoft. Initially, IM was not considered a merger-specific problem; AOL had built up a compelling market lead in IM prior to the merger, and the merger did not appear to increase AOL's market power in IM at all. At both the FCC and the FTC, the IM issue was, at least initially, off the table.

IM did, however, present at least one troubling policy issue, since it was a communication service that in principle came under the FCC's regulatory jurisdiction. It was clearly a service subject to network effects, in which the value of the service to each customer depends upon how many (and who) other customers are available on the service, similar to the telephone system (more fully described in the Appendix). The first mover (which AOL was) could build up a large customer base (which AOL had) and refuse to interoperate with competitors (which AOL was doing), thus keeping the network effects proprietary.[11] Refusing to interoperate reduces the value of an IM system to each customer, as that customer can reach fewer people. However, it reduces the value of IM providers with smaller customer bases even more, giving these customers an incentive to switch to the larger provider.

In this simple model, the strategy of refusing to interoperate is profit-maximizing if the increase in customers gained from smaller IM providers more than offsets the loss of value to existing customers. If AOL were large enough to have this "critical mass" of customers, refusal to interoperate

---

[11]In the telephone system, proprietary network effects are avoided via regulation: All carriers are required to interconnect with each other.

could lead to near-monopoly and an almost insuperable barrier to entry for new entrants. In this view, though IM is not a merger problem, it may well be a regulatory problem, perhaps best left to the FCC. However, the FCC has a long history of forbearance of regulation from data communications services, including the Internet. Changing this policy in order to regulate IM was never seriously contemplated.

Others would argue that this is not a problem at all. Proponents of the "serial monopoly" hypothesis in dynamically competitive markets[12] would contend that the problem is self-correcting. Some new technologically advanced product will eventually overturn this dominance, resulting in a new temporary monopoly, followed by a new round of innovation.

Upon deeper analysis, the FCC staff learned that IM systems were enabled by databases of names, IM addresses, and presence information maintained on the IM provider's server(s), which was referred to as Names and Presence Directory (NPD). It was clear that the network effects of the IM service resides in the NPD, which is the list of all customers who have "signed up" for this communication service and are available for communications. In a proprietary IM system, the IM provider keeps its NPD proprietary, and only customers on that system can check the presence of and communicate with customers on that system. In an interoperating IM system, each IM provider shares the relevant information in its NPD with other providers, thus ensuring that customers of one system can check the presence of and communicate with customers of other systems.

However, today's text-based IM is simply one application of the underlying NPD. As IM providers roll out new IM services, the same NPD can be used to extend existing proprietary network effects into the new services. This raised the alarming possibility that as "next-generation" IM services were introduced, AOL could use its existing NPD to leverage its current network effects market power in text-based IM (the "earned monopoly") into "next-generation" IM services without diminution. If its current market power in text-based IM was particularly strong, then this power could be carried forward without loss into new markets, thus affording AOL "instant monopoly" in next-generation IM services.

Whether or not this concern required FCC action to forestall this leveraging of NPD market power into next-generation IM services depended on several things:

1. Did AOL have sufficient market power in text-based IM that was worth leveraging? The FCC analysis focused on whether or not AOL's customer base had surpassed the "critical mass"[13] that could lead to near-monopoly.

---

[12]See Evans and Schmalensee (2001) for a compelling statement of this case as applied to antitrust analysis.

[13]This is sometimes referred to as "tipping," or "the market has tipped."

2. Could this market power be leveraged into advanced next-generation IM services?

3. How confident was the FCC that such advanced IM services would emerge and that they would be NPD-based?

4. Without being able to identify or specify such services, how could a true next-generation IM service (as opposed to an incremental improvement) be characterized?

5. If the present text-based IM service was an "earned monopoly," why shouldn't that earned monopoly be extended into future generations of IM?

6. Were these advanced IM services related in any way to the merger?

7. What was an appropriate remedy?

In the event, a majority of commissioners was sufficiently convinced by the analysis that they approved a remedy, but the issue was controversial at both the staff level and the Commission level.[14] In brief, the major points of controversy were (1) and (6) above. The arguments for the other points can be briefly summarized first:

2. The technologists' analysis of the NPD concluded that existing network effects could easily be leveraged forward. All that was required was backward compatibility of IM client software.

3. Projecting monopoly problems with future as-yet-unrealized services certainly placed the analysis well outside standard antitrust work, perhaps necessarily given the fast-paced nature of change in this industry. The analysis thus focused on the NPD as the underlying asset that carried the network effects, and the ability of AOL to roll this asset forward to provide new services but maintain its existing monopoly.

4. The advent of broadband gave a conceptual benchmark for next-generation IM services: any service that required a broadband connection for its commercial viability was considered next-generation. As a practical matter, the benchmark service chosen (for the remedy) was two-way streaming video, which is only viable with a high-speed connection. The difference between text-based IM and streaming video IM appeared compelling enough so that the latter could safely be called "next-generation."

5. Through how many generations of products should network effects be leveraged to provide sufficient payback to an innovator? Intellectual

---

[14]Then-Commissioner and now-Chairman Michael Powell was particularly eloquent and forceful in his opposition to the IM remedy in his dissenting opinion, but he was by no means alone. For a more technical discussion of the IM analysis, see Faulhaber (2002).

property law suggests that there is a limit to this, after which excess returns are just that, and no longer considered quasi-rents. In this case, the FCC faces the same trade-off: If a remedy removes proprietary network effects for next-generation IM services, does that discourage future innovators from investing in the next "killer app"? On the other hand, does permitting AOL to use network effects into the indefinite future create a huge barrier to entry that would discourage current and future potential IM innovators? This is clearly a judgment call, as it is in intellectual property law. In this case, the FCC decided that a one-generation monopoly is enough.

7. The remedy was clear in this case: require AOL to interoperate with any other requesting advanced IM provider on a mutual basis prior to offering advanced IM services itself (defined as two-way streaming video). The proposed remedy clearly creates a disincentive for AOL to offer (otherwise worthwhile) advanced IM services that would cause them to lose the strategic advantage of non-interoperability. However, the remedy actually increases the incentives of competitors to introduce video streaming, thereby placing competitive pressure on AOL to introduce the feature itself. AOL must then choose either to interoperate or to lose the "feature war." Feature competition at the very least partially offsets the direct disincentive, and may actually hasten the arrival of both video streaming as well as interoperability.

We turn now to the more contentious IM issues: (1) Has the market tipped? and (6) Is advanced IM merger-specific? The economics of network effects and tipping are straightforward: If a critical mass of customers has been achieved by the largest provider (i.e., the market has tipped), then that provider's optimal strategy is to refuse interoperability with competitors for strategic advantage. If the critical mass has not been achieved, then that provider's optimal strategy is to interoperate with competitors.

Since AOL was clearly refusing to interoperate, the conclusion seemed clear. Of course, AOL could be refusing to interoperate for other reasons, and AOL proffered a number of reasons for not interoperating,[15] discussed in the next section. The FCC carefully considered each of these possible reasons and found no evidence to support them. As a result, the economic conclusion was that the current text-based IM market (and therefore the underlying NPD) had tipped, indicating that AOL had substantial power in the IM market available to be leveraged into next-generation services.

On the face of it, the concern (#6) with next-generation IM services made the issue merger-specific, since such services required broadband capability, which was exactly what AOL was acquiring in the merger: Time Warner's cable assets. Merging the NPD network effects with the Time

---

[15]AOL publicly committed to interoperation at the FCC's *en banc* hearing on the merger in August 2000, promising to interoperate "within the year," once it resolved certain security problems. As of this writing, AOL still does not interoperate with any competitors.

Warner IP pipe assets would enable the combined firm to offer and then dominate next-generation IM services that it might not be able to do absent the merger. However, AOL had the potential to leverage its NPD into next-generation IM services using *any* broadband facilities, including those of AT&T, Comcast, Cox, or other cable firms, provided it could contract with such firms to provide ISP services. It was not obvious that actual cable ownership changed AOL's strategic options regarding next-generation IM services. If that were the case, then this concern of leveraging network effects forward would not be merger-specific. There were, however, several reasons to believe that ownership of cable assets enhanced AOL's ability to leverage its existing NPD asset:

1. AOL apparently had been in negotiations with major cable companies for at least a year seeking to gain access to their broadband IP pipes for AOL Plus, their broadband offering. For whatever reason, none of these deals closed. Contracting, as a practical matter, was not apparently a good substitute for ownership.

2. The premise of this merger was that combining the AOL franchise with the conduit and content assets of Time Warner would enable the firm to bring new compelling features and services to customers "better, faster, cheaper." But if this superior performance was exercised to leverage an existing network-effects-barrier-to-entry into new services for almost one-fifth of U.S. cable households, then even the hope of new entrants with better technology, etc., overturning these network effects would fade away almost completely. If the merger delivered on its promise of "better, faster, cheaper," then the likelihood that the serial monopolist would soon be overturned was almost nil.

3. With control of cable assets covering one-fifth of U.S. households, AOL would have the potential selectively to degrade competitor IM services.[16] Such degradation would be difficult to prove in practice, but could well give AOL's advanced IM service a decided advantage over competitors.

These factors suggest that ownership of the cable assets would facilitate AOL's leveraging of the proprietary network effects in its NPD into next-generation IM services requiring broadband speeds. This economic analysis supported the merger-specificity of the problem.

AOL Objections

Although AOL claimed that it intended to interoperate "soon" and that in any event it had no interest in advanced IM services, it raised vigorous ob-

---

[16]Again, the FCC technical staff confirmed this possibility. Routers and servers designed for use by cable modem systems give operators "bit level" control of the content of the IP pipe, allowing them to discriminate among different services, such as IM. See Faulhaber (2002) for more detail.

jections to the proposed IM remedy (of requiring interoperability prior to offering advanced IM services), more so than any other part of the FCC's order. We review the objections here, with FCC responses.

1. *"Interoperation is technically difficult; even our competitors haven't accomplished it, and the IETF [Internet Engineering Task Force] hasn't achieved it either."*

The FCC's technologists did not find this assertion credible; their professional view was that interoperability of IM systems was only slightly more difficult than interoperability of e-mail, which is *technically* quite easy. Nor did AOL produce any evidence in support of this assertion.

The failure of AOL's competitors to interoperate was most likely due to the fact that the only provider really worth interoperating with was AOL since it had by far the largest customer base.

The IETF is not a formal standard-setting body; it adopts standards for which there is an effective consensus. In the case of IM standards, there was no effective consensus. The IETF's failure to settle on a standard was a consequence of consensus failure, not technical difficulty.

2. *"We are concerned that interoperation would put our customers at risk; we will interoperate when we can solve these safety and security problems."*

This was a legitimate concern; experience has shown that e-mail systems can bring junk mail, unwanted sexually oriented mail, and viruses, similar to the telephone system. AOL claimed to aim for a higher standard for IM, which could well be a welfare improvement for customers, perhaps worth the wait for interoperability. On the other hand, the argument could be merely a delaying tactic, pushing off interoperability until AOL had driven its competitors out of business.

AOL was unable or unwilling to support its "safety and security" argument. Support would have been easy to do, in any one of several ways:

- a clear and explicit statement of the criteria for a "safe and secure" IM system in order for AOL to be willing to interoperate with it;
- an "alpha" version of the software and protocols for implementing such a system; since AOL claimed to be working on such a system for a trial in August 2001, such a prototype should have been available in late 2000, but was never produced;
- a briefing by AOL engineers on how they were solving their "safe and secure interoperability" problems, and what their development timetable was; no engineers were produced to discuss this issue with FCC technologists.

AOL's unwillingness to provide supporting evidence (such as outlined above) for its safety and security argument tended to undermine what was likely its best case. In the event, the FCC reluctantly rejected this argument as without evidentiary support.

3. *"Customers can download various IM clients and keep them all on their computer desktop, using each when he/she wants. Interoperability is really unnecessary, as there is no cost to the customer of maintaining multiple IM clients. In fact, many of our customers do this."*

It is true that every IM download is free, so customers can indeed have multiple clients on their screen without paying a fee. However, very few customers keep multiple clients of any sort on their desktop, even when free. For example, most corporate customers can get any word processor or spreadsheet they wish without personal payment, but few maintain more than one for active use. Apparently, it is simply too troublesome for most customers to switch between applications. There is no reason to suspect that IM is any different. In fact, the use of multiple clients in IM is probably more difficult than with other applications, as it is a communications service. Being unable to communicate simultaneously with buddies on different systems appears to be a significant drawback. The fact is that many customers do use multiple IM clients, and some become quite adept at it. However, this is not an indication that the cost of doing it is low; rather, it is an indication that the *net benefits* are high, at least for customers that use multiple clients. It is likely that for this group, even a bad form of interoperability is better than none, and they are willing to put up with an awkward, manual form of interoperability.

4. *"Market share data from MediaMetrix[17] shows that Microsoft and Yahoo! had large customer base increases from July 2000 to September 2000, while AOL's customer base increase was more modest. If the market has tipped, Microsoft and Yahoo!'s customer bases would be shrinking, not growing. Therefore, the market has not tipped."*

This is the strongest economic argument that AOL made against tipping. If in fact the IM market were stable, then this objection would be compelling as a matter of theory. However, the market was not stable; it was (and is) growing quite rapidly. New customers are constantly entering the market, and their choice of provider is likely guided by marketing efforts of the providers, as they are likely to know little about the network effects of the business until they experience the service (and are unable to connect with friends on other services).

---

[17]There was some question about exactly what the MediaMetrix data measured. Apparently, MediaMetrix creates a sample of users whose computers are polled every 0.5 seconds to determine which (Windows) screen is active. AOL presented data on average use of various IM clients as well as the fraction of the sample that had used an IM client at least once in a month. However, different IM clients use different active screen strategies, so it is not clear whether this measure correlates with actual usage.

A model of network effects in a growing market is presented in Faulhaber (2002) in which under certain circumstances a growing market can indeed be tipped and yet competitors make investments in customer acquisition and grow their customer base as a result. The circumstances in which the theory leads to this prediction appear to comport with the circumstances present in the IM market at the time that MediaMetrix collected its data: July–August 2000. At that time, both Yahoo! and Microsoft were advertising their IM services quite heavily relative to AOL, yet all firms showed customer gains. Thus, competitor growth in customer base is not, as a matter of theory, dispositive of market tipping. Therefore, AOL's strongest economic argument against tipping, based on market data and a theory of tipping applicable in a mature market, did *not* contradict market tipping in a growing market.

AOL did raise serious objections to the IM tipping hypothesis. But it did not present serious evidence to support these objections (except in the case of the MediaMetrix data). Further, such support would not have been difficult to produce if the objections were valid. Absent such support, the FCC staff was unable to give credence to AOL's objections. Only in the case of the last objection did the FCC staff undertake significant analysis, even model building, to assess this quite serious objection.

THE REMEDIES

The processes by which mergers are resolved differ substantially between the two agencies. A merger review at the FTC (as at the Department of Justice) always anticipates the possibility of a complaint and trial should the agency have objections or insist on remedies. The agency's analysis and recommendations usually lead to negotiations between the agency and the parties, both seeking to obtain what they need and both seeking to avoid a trial. Should an agreement be reached, it is codified in a Consent Agreement.

At the FCC, no trial is anticipated. The legal context in which the review takes place is the CARS spectrum license transfer; this is accomplished by a Memorandum Opinion and Order (MO&O), which is adopted by the Commission. It is, of course, subject to judicial review, but not before an appeal to the Commission itself. The FCC has apparently never turned down a request for a license transfer as part of a merger, although it has been fairly free in imposing conditions on the merging parties.

Open Access and DSL

The FTC required AOL-Time Warner to negotiate an access deal in major markets before it would approve the merger. AOL chose EarthLink from a list of several "approved" ISPs. Additionally, when AOL offered broadband service over Time Warner systems (again, in major markets), it was required to enter into agreements with at least two other ISPs approved by the FTC within ninety days. If it failed to do so, the FTC's "monitor trustee" could select two ISPs and negotiate contracts for carriage. Somewhat weaker conditions were imposed for Time Warner systems in smaller markets.

Additionally, all AOL contracts with other cable systems or DSL systems would be available *(in toto)* to ISPs on Time Warner systems, and AOL-Time Warner was not permitted to discriminate in terms of services provided ISPs in favor of itself: The same service levels, the same usage and performance statistics, and the same points of connections were to be made available to all ISPs on AOL-Time Warner cable systems. AOL was also required both to price and to market its DSL offerings over telephone company facilities identically in both Time Warner cable areas and non-Time Warner cable areas. This latter condition ensured that AOL would not attempt to disadvantage DSL in territories where it competed with Time Warner cable by failing to deal or charging high prices.[18]

The FCC also adopted conditions related to non-affiliated ISPs on AOL-Time Warner cable systems, "narrowly tailored to augment that [FTC] decree by preventing AOL Time Warner from utilizing certain indirect means to disadvantage unaffiliated ISPs on its cable systems . . ." (FCC 01-12, January 22, 2001). These conditions impose nondiscrimination obligations on AOL-Time Warner with respect to choice of ISP, customer billing, first screen, and technical capabilities such as caching, quality of service, and other technical functions.

Instant Messaging

The FCC imposed the condition that AOL cannot offer advanced IM services until it satisfies one of the following three "grounds for relief":

1. AOL demonstrates that it has adopted a public standard of interoperability established by IETF or another official standard-setting body (interoperability by standard).

2. AOL enters into interoperability contracts with at least two IM providers, and stands ready to negotiate in good faith with other IM providers under the identical technical interoperability standards (interoperability by contract).

3. AOL demonstrates that it is no longer dominant in IM, either using market share data or other evidence.

Advanced IM services are defined to entail the transmission of one- or two-way streaming video over Time Warner facilities using AOL's NPD. In addition, this condition sunsets in five years.

---

[18]This provision has elements of the Rogerson remedy, discussed above.

This condition highlights the struggle of attempting to deal with future problems in a fast-moving industry. The FCC had no wish to insist that AOL adopt an industry standard when such a standard does not exist now and may never exist, not least because competitors may use the standard-setting process strategically. The FCC did not establish any technical standards of interoperability, preferring to leave that to independent technical standards boards or to the market. Additionally, the FCC wished to account for changing conditions; it could well be that a competitor could come to dominate the IM market as advanced IM services became available, and AOL would not then have market power. If this could be proved, then AOL would be relieved of the interoperability requirement (although as a business matter AOL would certainly wish to interoperate under these conditions).

Perhaps most important, if there really were no next generation IM services (or none that AOL wished to offer), then there was no interoperability requirement. The FCC gave tacit assent to the "earned monopoly" hypothesis, that AOL was entitled to the rents from its text-based IM innovation.

Monitor Trustee

As previously noted, antitrust agencies such as the FTC do not have continuing jurisdiction over the merged parties, while the FCC typically does. However, the conditions of the FTC Consent Agreement with the parties was sufficiently detailed in its compliance requirements that the FTC appointed a Monitor Trustee to act on its behalf to supervise AOL-Time Warner's conduct in implementing the agreement. The Monitor Trustee reports to the FTC but has considerable investigative power, including the ability to hire consultants and access to all records that he deems necessary to monitor compliance.

DENOUEMENT

One year after the merger, AOL-Time Warner was implementing a multi-ISP environment for its Time Warner cable systems. Technical difficulties had been overcome. Complaints from ISPs that had been unable to negotiate access were fairly steady, but multiple ISPs sharing a cable IP pipe appeared to be a reality.

The FCC's Notice of Inquiry into High Speed Internet Access attracted comment, as expected. The matter was under active consideration at the FCC, with a Notice of Proposed Rulemaking expected before midyear 2002. While there was no advance indication of the direction that the FCC intended to take on this matter, it would be quite surprising if the current market-oriented Commission would impose regulatory open access conditions (and thus raise costs) on the broadband access industry in which it had professed interest in encouraging investment.

Several months after the merger, both Microsoft and Yahoo! announced versions of their IM products that supported streaming video. However, without extensive broadband connections, this apparently had limited uptake. AOL continued to insist that it had no interest in such a product, while insisting that it was working hard on interoperation. Meanwhile, interoperation was still not a reality; one year after the merger, AOL was still aggressively blocking attempts of other firms to interoperate with AIM (Bowman 2002).

The FCC's IM condition drew some fire from consumer groups that had hoped the FCC would impose interoperability on the current version of IM. These groups viewed the condition as ineffectual. Generally, industry analysts did not see the condition as imposing any cost on AOL-Time Warner. The Internet community, ever alert to possible intrusions of government regulation into cyberspace, was relatively relaxed in their response to the condition.

It is clear that the short-term impact of the condition was virtually nil. On the other hand, the condition was designed to have an impact only in the future, and then only if there were a problem. In the absence of an obvious problem, the condition's short-term failure to cause costs to AOL-Time Warner should be considered a plus.

What of AOL-Time Warner itself? Subsequent events were not kind to the new media giant. At the time of the merger announcement, the combined stock market capitalization of the two firms was $290 billion (Loomis 2002); one year after the merger (and two years after the announcement) the merged firm's market capitalization was $135 billion, a loss of $155 billion in market capitalization. This loss in value was due in part to the significant downturn of Internet stocks, in part due to the advertising revenue downturn of the current recession, and in part due to the failure of AOL-Time Warner to live up to the impossible financial goals it giddily set for itself at the time of the merger.

LESSONS OF THE CASE

Without question, the two salient issues of this merger were open access (at the FTC) and advanced IM services (at the FCC). Both represented challenges to antitrust analysis that derive from the "new economy": Should we mandate access to new economy essential facilities, or do we let the market sort it out? Should we seek to negate a network effects barrier to new entry, or should we recognize such barriers as a necessary part of investment incentives in the new economy?

The FTC required open access, believing that more competition must be good and adopting what appears to be an aggressively regulatory remedy.

The remedy was a popular one; it was well received by consumer groups and the press. Whether customers are now better off than they otherwise would be remains unknown. The costs of this regulatory approach are not likely to be large; however, the precedent of having a Monitor Trustee provide ongoing supervision of an antitrust conduct remedy is somewhat disturbing. It is reminiscent of Judge Harold Greene's decade-long supervision of the AT&T breakup, essentially creating another layer of regulation on the telephone industry.

The FCC answer to the second question was in the affirmative to both parts. While there was economic analysis aplenty, the case raised troubling issues more generally for antitrust in the new economy.

Serial Monopoly and the New Economy

Some scholars working in the area of antitrust in dynamically competitive industries have argued that the competitive norm in such industries is temporary "winner take all" innovators, succeeded in rapid order by a new "winner take all" innovator, and so forth (Evans and Schmalensee 2001). The period of monopoly for each innovator is in fact a reward for innovation, and the temporary monopoly rents are merely the quasi-rents for a socially beneficial activity. Imposing "old economy" antitrust to break that monopoly in fact will lesson innovation as it lessens the legitimate rewards to that innovation. In this view, temporary monopolies generate the quasi-rents for innovation much as patent protection helps generate quasi-rents for a limited period of time.

The unstated assumption of the serial monopoly theorists is that somehow intellectual property protection is not available in these fast-moving markets. But even these scholars admit that anticompetitive behavior can still exist: for example, exclusive distribution contracts with today's monopolist can inhibit the rise of the next monopolist. The current serial monopolist, in this view, ought not to be permitted to use its temporary market power to forestall new innovators and thus turn itself into a permanent monopolist.

The FCC specifically recognized that AOL had earned whatever rents it could garner from its IM innovation, and that network-effects barriers to entry could well be part of this rent generation. It also recognized that a temporary monopoly should not be used to foreclose new innovators and thus create a permanent monopoly. Its judgment was that the merger would create just such conditions, and it sought to forestall such actions. Its remedy was designed to ensure that the next-in-line serial monopolist would not be foreclosed by the use of merger assets. In essence, it argued that network effects combined with merger assets that dramatically improve deployment capabilities is similar in effect to exclusive distribution contracts; it makes entry by the next serial monopolist almost impossible. Whether the factual case supports the remedy can be argued; but the theory of the case seems well within the confines of antitrust in the new economy. It also illustrates the difficulty of conducting the analysis and the case within those confines.

It also illustrates the dilemma of substituting antitrust enforcement (or nonenforcement) for intellectual property (IP) law. It may well be true that IP affords little protection to innovators in fast-moving markets, and perhaps antitrust enforcement needs to recognize the need for temporary quasi-rents to innovators. But the problem appears to be with the inability of IP law to afford protection in important fast-moving markets. This suggests that the appropriate policy conclusion is not to alter antitrust enforcement but rather to fix intellectual property law to provide such protection.

APPENDIX: NETWORK EFFECTS

Instant messaging fits the classic definition of a service imbued with network effects, in which the value to each customer depends upon the number of other customers (and who they are) who also use the service. The first example cited in the economics literature of a network effects business was telephone service, in which each customer only derives value from the system if they can use it to communicate with their friends, neighbors, and businesses they use (Rohlfs 1974): The more customers that subscribe to the telephone, the more each customer values subscribership. Other industries were found to exhibit this property, sometimes referred to as "demand-side scale economies"; for a review of the extensive literature on network effects, see Katz and Shapiro (1994). Particularly important early work is that of Katz and Shapiro (1985); an example of more recent research is Fudenberg and Tirole (2000).

Network effects can be beneficial. When all providers of a network service interconnect, then customers of even the smallest competitor get the benefits of connecting to everyone, which enhances competition. However, if a dominant provider chooses not to interconnect, then new entrants and smaller competitors can face a significant barrier to entry. If the provider is large enough, competitors may be driven from the market, and near-monopoly may result. A monopoly based on network effects may be particularly difficult to unseat, even with a superior service. Because of this result, network effects can raise important antitrust concerns. In an FTC Staff Report (1996), the staff found that "[i]n sum, demand-side economies associated with networks warrant a heightened degree of scrutiny in assessing denials of access . . ." Evans and Schmalensee (1996) also discuss the importance of network effects for antitrust enforcement.

However, it is not necessarily profit-maximizing for firms to refuse to interconnect (or, in this context, to interoperate). The theory suggests that in an industry with a number of firms of roughly equal size, the more profitable strategy is to interoperate.[19] Otherwise, a firm that refuses to interoperate may find its competitors agreeing to interoperate, thus establishing a critical mass and condemning the non-interoperator to lose share and eventually disappear as its customers move to the more attractive interoperating coalition.

There is some evidence that the Internet backbone market is a network effects business in which the larger players agree to interoperate ("peering"), as described in Kende (2000); see also Cremer, Rey, and Tirole (2000). But if a large provider dominates a network industry, that provider could refuse interoperability, driving its competitors' customers toward its own larger customer base and eventually (near-) monopolizing the industry. This phenomenon is colloquially referred to as the market "tips" in favor of the largest provider. "Tipping" occurs when a single provider reaches a critical mass of customers that are so attractive to others that competitors must inevitably shrink, in the absence of interoperation.

REFERENCES

Bowman, Lisa. "AOL Blocks Instant Massaging Start-up." *ClNet News,* January 30, 2002, at http://news.com.com/2100-1023-826625.html.

Cremer, Jacques, Patrick Rey, and Jean Tirole. "Connectivity in the Commercial Internet." *Journal of Industrial Economics* 48 (December 2000): 433–472.

Evans, David S., and Richard L. Schmalensee. "A Guide to the Antitrust Economics of Networks." *Antitrust* 10 (Spring 1996): 36–40.

Evans, David S., and Richard L. Schmalensee. "Some Economic Aspects of Antitrust Analysis in Dynamically Competitive Industries." NBER Working Paper No. W8268, May, 2001, at http://www.nber.org/books/innovation2/evans5-1-01.pdf.

Faulhaber, Gerald R. "Broadband Deployment: Is Policy in the Way?" presented at *Broadband Communications: Overcoming the Barriers,* AEI-Brookings Conference, October 4–5, 2001, at http://rider.wharton.upenn.edu/~faulhabe/Broadband%20Deployment%20Is%20Policy%20in%20the%20Way.pdf.

Faulhaber, Gerald R. "Network Effects and Merger Analysis: Instant Messaging and the AOL-Time Warner Case." *Telecommunications Policy,* forthcoming, 2002, at http://rider.wharton.upenn.edu/~faulhabe/NETWORK%20EFFECTS%20AND%20MERGER%20ANALYSIS.pdf.

Federal Communications Commission. "Memorandum Opinion and Order." CS Docket 00-30, FCC 01-12, January 22, 2001, at http://www.fcc.gov/Bureaus/Cable/Orders/2001/fcc01012.pdf.

Federal Trade Commission. "Competition Policy in the New, High-Tech Global Marketplace." Vol. I, FTC Staff Report, May, 1996, at http://www.ftc.gov/opp/global/report/gc_v1.pdf.

---

[19]In fact, interoperation in the case of roughly equal-sized firms is a dominant strategy; each firm is no worse off by offering mutual interoperation no matter what other firms do, and is strictly better off if at least one other firm offers mutual interoperation.

Federal Trade Commission. "Complaint." Docket No. C-3989, December 14, 2000a, at http://www.ftc.gov/os/2000/12/aolcomplaint.pdf.

Federal Trade Commission. "Analysis of Proposed Consent Order to Aid Public Comment." December 14, 2000b, at http://www.ftc.gov/os/2000/12/aolanalysis.pdf.

Federal Trade Commission. "Decision and Order." Docket No. C-3989, December 14, 2000c, at http://www.ftc.gov/os/2000/12/aoldando.pdf.

Federal Trade Commission. "Agreement Containing Consent Orders." December 14, 2000d, File No. 001 0105, at http://www.ftc.gov/os/2000/12/aolconsent.pdf.

Fudenberg, Drew, and Jean Tirole. "Pricing a Network Good to Deter Entry." *Journal of Industrial Economics* 48 (December 2000): 373–390.

Grice, Corey. "MSN's Down to EarthLink Strategy." *ZDNet,* February 13, 2001, at http://www.zdnet.com/zdnn/stories/news/0,4586,2684916,00.html.

Kapadia, Reshma. "Battle of the Behemoths: MSN Takes on AOL Time Warner." *Reuters,* February 5, 2001, at http://www.zdnet.com/zdnn/stories/news/0,4586,2682211,00.html.

Katz, Michael, and Carl Shapiro. "Network Externalities, Competition, and Compatibility." *American Economic Review* 75 (June 1985): 424–440.

Katz, Michael, and Carl Shapiro. "System Competition and Network Effects." *Journal of Economic Perspectives* 8 (Spring 1994): 93–115.

Kende, Michael. "The Digital Handshake: Connecting Internet Backbones." OPP Working Paper 23, September 2000, Federal Communications Commission, at http://www.fcc.gov/Bureaus/OPP/working_papers/oppwp32.pdf.

Loomis, Carol. "AOL Time Warner's New Math." *Fortune* 145 (February 4, 2002): 99–102.

Rohlfs, Jeffrey. "A Theory of Interdependent Demand for a Communications Service." *Bell Journal of Economics and Management Science* 5 (Spring 1974): 16–37.

Maintenance of Monopoly:
U.S. v. Microsoft (2001)

Daniel L. Rubinfeld

INTRODUCTION

In May 1998, the U.S. Department of Justice (DOJ), twenty individual states, and the District of Columbia filed suit against the Microsoft Corporation claiming that Microsoft had monopolized the market for personal computer (PC) operating systems and had used its monopoly to engage in a wide range of antitrust violations.[1] The case was tried in Federal District Court from October 19, 1998, through June 24, 1999. The court reached its findings regarding the facts of the case on November 5, 1999, and its legal conclusions on April 3, 2000. Microsoft's appeal to the Circuit Court of Appeals for the District of Columbia was decided on June 28, 2001, followed by extensive settlement discussions among the various parties—the Department of Justice, the states, and Microsoft. The appellate court affirmed the monopolization claim, reversed other findings by the district court, and remanded the case back to the district court to find an appropriate remedy. Following extensive settlement discussions among the various parties—DOJ, the states, and Microsoft—DOJ and Microsoft reached a settlement agreement. Nine states opted not to join the settlement, proposing a different remedy. A 32-day remedy trial was held, and, on November 1, 2002 the district court issued a remedy ruling. As this case study is going to press, it

Daniel Rubinfeld served as Deputy Assistant Attorney General for Economics at the U.S. DOJ from June 1997 through December 1998 and as a consultant to the Department of Justice in its case against Microsoft through most of 1999. He wishes to thank Franklin Fisher and the editors for helpful comments.

[1]*U.S. v. Microsoft,* Civil Action No. 98-1232. One state settled with Microsoft before the case went to trial.

appears very likely that the court's remedy will mark the end of the four-year case.

While its ultimate impact on antitrust jurisprudence remains unclear, there is no doubt that from the public's perspective *U.S.* v. *Microsoft* was the antitrust case of the 1990s, and arguably from a policy perspective one of the most significant antitrust cases of the twentieth century. The investigation, the trial, and its aftermath received wide press coverage throughout. A number of the major actors in the drama became household names, as much the result of the public relations battle among the parties as from the litigation itself.

At the heart of the *Microsoft* case was the Government's claim that Microsoft had engaged in a range of anticompetitive acts that were designed to maintain its operating system (OS) monopoly. The Government did not question the source of Microsoft's historical success. The Government did, however, claim that consumers were harmed by Microsoft's conduct, in part because consumers were paying higher prices for their operating system software, and in part because Microsoft's actions had reduced innovation in the software industry. In response, Microsoft argued that it was not a monopoly since it faced significant competitive threats in a highly dynamic industry. It further argued that its success should be seen as pro-competitive, since consumers had benefited as the result of the distribution of its high-quality, innovative software. If the court were to impose substantial antitrust remedies, Microsoft believed, competitive incentives would be reduced, which would lead to less, rather than more, innovation.

BACKGROUND

The Microsoft Corporation is a relatively young corporation, having begun its existence in the mid-1970s. Since that time, Microsoft has enjoyed exceptional and unparalleled growth, and in the process has made millionaires of thousands of its employees. Many attribute this success to Microsoft's skill and foresight, while others cite an element of luck; all would most likely agree, however, that Microsoft has shown an uncanny ability to adapt its business plans and to market innovative technology successfully. With success, however, has come antitrust scrutiny, with various governmental agencies and private plaintiffs questioning whether Microsoft has used a range of practices to restrain competition, to exclude competitors, and to expand its market power beyond the operating system market.

The first governmental investigation of Microsoft began with the Federal Trade Commission (FTC).[2] In 1990 the FTC undertook an investigation of Microsoft's software licensing practices with personal computer original equipment manufacturers (OEMs). After nearly three years of in-

---

[2]See, for example, Gilbert (1999).

vestigation, the five-member Commission failed to support the legal staff's desire to bring a suit against Microsoft (the vote was 2-2; one commissioner had not participated).

This victory for Microsoft was short-lived; the Department of Justice undertook its own investigation almost immediately. A year later, on July 15, 1994, DOJ filed a complaint, claiming that Microsoft's contracts with OEMs were exclusionary and anticompetitive and that their purpose was to allow Microsoft to maintain its monopoly in the market for personal computer (PC) operating systems (OSs). The case did not go to trial. Microsoft and the Government settled, with Microsoft signing a consent decree in which it agreed to restrict its licensing agreements along a number of dimensions. (The agreement was finally approved on June 16, 1995.)[3] An important aspect of the consent decree was the agreement that Microsoft could not condition or "tie" its operating system license to the license of other operating system products. However, the agreement did explicitly allow Microsoft to continue to develop "integrated" products.

The distinction between an anticompetitive tie and pro-competitive product integration was to become a central issue in the Microsoft litigation that followed. But there was an additional skirmish to be fought before the larger battle began. With the rapid development of the Internet came the need for software that would allow PC users to have easy Internet access. The first highly successful web browsing product came from Netscape. In a very short period of time Netscape's "Navigator" became the market leader, accounting for approximately 70 percent of browser usage in 1996.

While initially slow to realize the potential significance of the Internet, Microsoft was quick to redirect its efforts aggressively toward Internet browser software in 1996. A new antitrust issue arose when Microsoft required OEMs to license and to install Microsoft's browser, Internet Explorer (IE), into new PCs as a condition for obtaining a license to install the Windows 95 operating system. The Government sued, claiming that Microsoft's tie between IE and the OS violated the 1996 consent decree. Microsoft defended by claiming that IE and the OS were integrated products, and consequently its licensing arrangement should be seen as an exception to the 1995 consent decree. The Government was initially successful: On December 11, 1997, Judge Thomas Penfield Jackson ordered that Microsoft separate its Windows 95 OS and IE. However, on appeal the U.S. Court of Appeals for the District of Columbia sided with Microsoft, claiming that Microsoft had offered evidence that the combination of IE and the OS offered functionality that was not available without product "integration."[4] In a move that would later be seen as prescient, the appellate court made it clear that its decision was based solely on its reading of the consent decree and not on broader antitrust principles.

---

[3]*U.S. v. Microsoft Corporation,* 1995-2 Trade Cas. p. 71,096 (D.D.C. 1995).

[4]*U.S. v. Microsoft Corp.,* 147 F.3d 935 (D.C. Cir. 1998).

The battle began on May 18, 1998, when the U.S. Government, twenty of the states, and the District of Columbia brought suit against Microsoft. In its filing, the DOJ alleged that Microsoft had engaged in a range of practices involving operating system licenses with OEMs, contracts with Internet service providers (ISPs), and ties between the OS and its IE browser, all of which restrained trade in violation of Section 1 of the Sherman Act. The DOJ also alleged that Microsoft had attempted to monopolize the market for Internet browsers in violation of Section 2 of the Sherman Act. The heart of the Government's case was its allegation that Microsoft had engaged in a range of practices that aimed primarily, if not solely, to protect and maintain the Microsoft operating system monopoly.[5]

Some background will be useful at this point. In the years prior to the filing of the Government's case, it became apparent to Microsoft that the Netscape Navigator browser could serve as the foundation for a software "platform" that had the potential to compete with Microsoft's Windows 95 (and later Windows 98) operating system. Operating systems provide application programming interfaces (APIs) through which applications interact with the OS and through the OS with the computer hardware. Applications developers must write their programs to interact with a particular operating system's API. The time and expense of then "porting" the application to a different OS can be substantial. The term *platform* describes a set of APIs to which applications may be written.

Because of the huge volume of Windows operating system sales and the size of the network of OS users, a vast number of applications, including the highly successful Office suite, have been written for Windows. If a firm were successfully to offer a competing OS, it would, of necessity, need to offer a substantial number of applications, which would most likely include word processing and business productivity software. As Apple realized during the 1980s, failure to offer a range of applications that appeal to businesses is likely to hinder one's ability to grow market share.[6] Because much of the software development and marketing effort is sunk (i.e., cannot easily be of value elsewhere), the result is the presence of a significant "applications barrier to entry" to OS markets. The ability to reduce the significance of this barrier to entry is what made the Java programming language of particular interest to Microsoft and its competitors.

Netscape Navigator (and other browsers) relied on Java. Developed and marketed by Sun Microsystems, Java was a "cross-platform" language that offered to applications programmers the opportunity to write a program once, but to have that program run on all operating systems. Cross-platform Java effectively served as a form of "middleware," software that

---

[5]Unless otherwise stated, "Government" applies to the U.S. Department of Justice, the states, and the District of Columbia.

[6]In response to this concern, Apple licensed Windows 1.0 to Microsoft in exchange for a Macintosh version of the spreadsheet program Excel (and a one-year delay before the Windows version of Excel was offered).

sits on top of an OS, while at the same time serving as the foundation for other applications. According to the Government, Netscape threatened Microsoft because its browser had the potential to distribute cross-platform Java to independent software developers. If those developers chose to write to other OSs such as IBM's OS/2 or Linux (or if they wrote directly to browser APIs associated with Internet applications), the Windows monopoly would be at risk.

With respect to the maintenance-of-monopoly claim, the Government alleged that Microsoft had engaged in a range of practices whose purpose was to limit severely the commercial viability of the Netscape browser. These included an attempted market division with Netscape, and attempts to discourage Apple and Intel from participating in closely related, and potentially threatening, software markets. They also included a combination of exclusionary devices (including those mentioned previously) and other predatory acts aimed in part at Java and in part at the Netscape browser, an important means by which Java can be distributed to computer users. Exclusionary behavior is behavior that makes it more difficult for competitors to compete; predatory behavior arises when a firm forgoes short-run profits to drive a competitor from the market in the hope of recouping future profits in the same market or in some other market.

In its April 5, 2000, opinion, the district court found in favor of the Government with respect to its Section 2 claims, including both its core maintenance-of-monopoly arguments and a separate attempted-browser-monopolization claim. While determining that the browser-operating system tie and certain contractual practices violated Section 1 of the Sherman Act, the court found that the Government had not shown sufficient evidence that the exclusionary practices had foreclosed competition.

Judge Jackson then accepted the Government's proposed remedies, which included conduct remedies that would limit Microsoft's use of exclusive contracts and its control over the PC "desktop." He also supported the Government's proposal that Microsoft be divided into two smaller companies—an operating system company and an applications company. The latter would maintain control over the browser business, although the OS company would retain property rights with respect to the current version of the browser.

Judge Jackson agreed to stay his remedies until after the appeals court heard the case. In a highly unusual move consistent with the importance of the case, the entire eligible membership of the Appeals Court for the District of Columbia (rather than the usual three-judge panel) heard Microsoft's appeal of the case. The unanimous appellate decision was seen as a victory by the Government, but it did contain positive elements for both sides. From Microsoft's perspective, the opinion was successful because the appeals court (1) reversed Judge Jackson's decision that Microsoft had attempted to monopolize the browser market, and (2) remanded (sent back) the case to the lower court for a rehearing on the remedy issue. From the

Government's perspective, the decision was highly successful because (1) the court upheld both the maintenance of monopoly claim, and (2) along with it, the court condemned the wide range of exclusionary and predatory practices alleged by the government.

AN OVERVIEW OF THE ECONOMIC ISSUES

Two significant economic questions raised by *U.S. v. Microsoft* were:

1. Did the Microsoft Corporation possess monopoly power in the market for personal computer operating systems?

2. Did Microsoft maintain its monopoly power by a series of anticompetitive actions that unreasonably restrained trade?

In answer to the first question, the Government stated that Microsoft did possess monopoly power in the market for operating systems for Intel-compatible desktop personal computers. Microsoft responded that the relevant market for antitrust purposes is substantially broader than Intel-based PC OSs; it includes hand-held computer operated systems and servers. Moreover, Microsoft faces substantial competition from other computer OSs, threats from other non-OS platforms that can support applications, and threats from yet unknown innovations. Indeed, the very fact that Microsoft found it necessary to take action against Netscape and Java shows that those companies and their products are in the market. Consequently, Microsoft does not have monopoly power.

With respect to the second question, the Government argued that Microsoft foresaw the possibility that the dominant position of its Windows OS would be eroded by Internet browsers and by cross-platform Java. Microsoft engaged in a series of anticompetitive practices in order to protect the monopoly power of its Windows OS. Microsoft responded that it did perceive a competitive threat from Java and responded in a number of ways to combat that competitive threat. However, those responses were the reasonable and appropriate responses of a competitor and cannot be appropriately characterized as an attempt by Microsoft to maintain its OS monopoly.

The Government raised an additional question that focused specifically on the market for browsers. That question raised a third issue:

3. In order to thwart the competitive advantage of the Netscape Navigator browser, did Microsoft use many of the same acts to hamper severely Netscape's browsing software?

Because questions 2 and 3 raised similar concerns about the alleged anticompetitive acts by Microsoft, it is not surprising that the economic analysis associated with question 3 is closely related to the analysis of 2. While question 3 was supported by the district court, it was rejected by the circuit court of appeals, which argued that the Government had not proved that there was a separate and distinct browser market or that there were substantial barriers to entry in the browser market. To keep the discussion focused, this case study will analyze only claims 1 and 2.

As mentioned, the core of the Government's case lay in its second claim—that Microsoft had used illegal anticompetitive practices to maintain its OS monopoly. According to the Government, Microsoft's conduct, which preserved and increased barriers to entry into the PC operating system market (and which distorted competition in the market for Internet browsers) included:

1. Tying IE to the operating system (in effect requiring manufacturers to acquire Microsoft's Internet browser as a condition of acquiring Microsoft's Windows OS), thereby severely hampering Netscape's browser and blunting the threat that software developers, in writing for a browser platform, would create software for a non-Microsoft OS;

2. Excluding browser competitors from the most efficient channels of distribution (OEMs and ISPs), thereby requiring competitors to use more costly and less efficient channels;

3. Imposing agreements requiring OEMs not to remove Microsoft's browser or to substitute an alternative browser;

4. Imposing exclusionary agreements on ISPs, requiring them to boycott or disfavor Netscape and other browsers; these included agreements not to promote, distribute, use, or pay for Netscape's browser (or to do so only on less favored terms); and

5. Giving its browser away for free ("committing" itself to do so "forever") and paying others to take its browser.

The following section elaborates on the two central economic questions raised by the case, in the process describing first the positions maintained by each of the two sides and then by the courts.

DEBATING THE ECONOMIC ISSUES

Did Microsoft Have Monopoly Power?

The Government's Perspective

The Government alleged that Microsoft possessed monopoly power in the market for operating systems for Intel-compatible desktop PCs. To support that claim, the Government provided market share data that showed that Microsoft's share of PC operating systems was very high and had remained stable over time; indeed, its worldwide share of shipments of Intel-based operating systems had been approximately 90 percent or more during the 1990s. Furthermore, numerous OEMs—the most important direct customers for PC operating systems—believed that they did not have any alternative to the acquisition and installation of Microsoft's Windows operating system.

The Government chose to exclude Apple's OS from the relevant market, based on evidence that there was very little substitutability between Apple and Windows. However, Apple's exclusion did not play a significant role in the Government's analysis of the case, primarily because of its relatively small market share.

Of greater potential significance were non-desktop devices such as the Palm Pilot, which could arguably substitute at least in part for the PC. To the extent that they could, Microsoft's monopoly power in PC operating systems would become less important. From the government's perspective, it was not credible that a 5 or 10 percent increase in the price of Windows above a competitive level would make a large number of users choose Palm Pilots rather than PCs.[7] Moreover, even if non-desktop devices did at some point become serious substitutes for the PC, the Government argued that Microsoft's monopoly power would only become less important; it would not disappear.[8]

Note that in both the case of Apple and the case of hand-held devices, the crucial question (according to the Government) was not whether the hardware products involved competed with Intel-based PCs. That would matter if one were considering an alleged monopoly of PCs themselves. Rather, Microsoft's alleged monopoly was over *the market for operating systems* for PCs; hence, an appropriate test was whether a 5 or 10 percent increase in the price of *Windows* above a competitive level would induce customers to change OSs, or choose other hardware. This seems implausible, given that the price of Windows was only a small portion of the price of a PC at current prices, and would be even smaller had the price of Windows been reduced.

While high market shares are an important indicia of monopoly power, the Government's case had a broader foundation. In particular, there was direct deposition testimony from PC manufacturers—the most important direct customers for Windows—that a 5 or 10 percent price increase by Microsoft would not make them shift away from Windows. Further, Microsoft's internal documents made clear that the company did not take into account the prices of other operating systems in setting its own prices.

Both parties agreed that OSs are characterized by *network effects.* Users want an OS that will permit them to run all the applications programs they want to use. As a result, developers tend to write applications for the most popular OS; and applications software written for a specific OS typi-

---

[7]Although a hypothetical "small but significant non-transitory increase in price" is a central part of the DOJ-FTC *Merger Guidelines* paradigm for market definition, its use for monopoly determination is controversial. See, for example, White (2000).

[8]A similar argument applied to servers.

cally cannot run on a different OS without extensive and costly modifications or add-ons.

There are other network effects as well. For example, operating systems are complex; they exhibit network effects in part because firms are reluctant to reinvest in retraining workers, and in part because using multiple OSs vastly increases technical support costs. This gives firms an incentive to have the same OSs for all its own computers and the same OS that is widely used by other firms. Other network effects include the ease of exchanging files and the opportunity to learn from others.

As the result of economies of scale and network effects, the parties agreed that Microsoft's operating system success has led to many more applications (more than 70,000) being written for its operating system than for any other. This reinforced and increased Microsoft's market share, leading to still more applications being written for Windows than for other OSs, and so on. According to the Government, this positive feedback effect created an "applications barrier to entry" that made it difficult or impossible for rival OSs to gain more than a niche in the OS market. Indeed, the Government believed that Microsoft's share and power was not likely to be eroded by new entry as long as the applications barrier to entry remained strong.

The Government also considered Microsoft's argument that it faced significant competition from its own installed base of users. If so, Microsoft could not raise the price of new operating systems without fear that the installed base of users would choose not to upgrade their software. Indeed, Microsoft argued that it needed to continue to innovate for the same reason. While this installed-base argument relates to its pricing of upgrades, it does not apply to new computers, which are bought largely to take advantage of developments in hardware or software.

Microsoft's Response

Microsoft denied that it has monopoly power; indeed, Microsoft claimed that the Government's market definition was invalid. Stressing the network effects story, Microsoft argued that the appropriate focus should be on platforms, not on operating systems. Platform software offers standardized routines that allow software developers to avoid recreating code to perform standard operations. While the Windows OS was a platform (as were other OSs), Microsoft argued that other non-operating system software, "middleware," could also serve as a platform. For example, Lotus Notes is a popular form of middleware that is popular among network users because of its e-mail and other functionality. Another significant platform is the World Wide Web, which consists of servers that make information, including applications software, available to the public communications network.

Microsoft argued that it competed vigorously to maintain its position as provider of the leading software platform. Indeed, Microsoft maintained that had it not continually improved its software, it would have been displaced by competing platforms. Whether threatened by known or unknown, actual or potential competition, Microsoft argued that any market power that it enjoyed was temporary, and therefore not fairly characterized as monopoly power.

Microsoft also disputed the Government's view as to the significance of the applications barrier to entry. According to Microsoft, if this was a significant barrier, then neither Netscape nor Java could ever successfully attract the allegiance of independent software developers. But, according to Microsoft, that was inconsistent with the reality that Netscape and Java were serious threats, despite their initial lack of applications. (The Government responded, in turn, that it never claimed that the barrier was insurmountable; had it been, Microsoft would not have engaged in its anticompetitive behavior.)

In another defense against the claim that it had monopoly power, Microsoft relied on a standard static model for short-run monopoly pricing to argue that its Windows OS price was far below the price that a monopolist would charge. Assuming that there was monopoly power, Microsoft's economist calculated an elasticity of demand for Windows from information relating to the elasticity of demand for PCs, its OS market share, and the marginal cost of Windows (which was very low). Applying a "rule of thumb for pricing," Microsoft calculated that the short-run monopoly price for Windows was approximately $1800,[9] well in excess of the actual price (around $60). Hence, the Government was wrong to characterize Microsoft as having monopoly power.

The debate surrounding the short-run profit-maximizing price of Windows was an extremely active one during the trial, perhaps because it had implications for the private lawsuits that were to follow on the Government's case, and perhaps because it focused analytical attention on crucial short-run versus long-run and static versus dynamic distinctions. The Government objected strongly to Microsoft's claims, pointing out that since the marginal cost of Windows software is very low, the *short-run* profit-maximizing action for Microsoft is to price where the elasticity of demand that it faces is unity (when costs are zero, this maximizes revenue and profit). According to the Government, this is true whether or not Microsoft has monopoly power. According to the Government, the correct conclusion must be that something other than short-run profit maximization is happening, and in particular, Microsoft must be taking its OS monopoly profits in other ways (e.g., through higher priced applications). Moreover, according to the Government, Microsoft's pricing of its operating system (in particular its contractual prices to OEMs) is consistent with long-run profit maximization by a firm with monopoly power in a network market.

---

[9]See, for example, Pindyck and Rubinfeld (2001), pp. 333–334. According to the rule of thumb, the profit-maximizing price of a product is given by $P = MC/[1 + 1/E_d]$, where P is the price, MC is the marginal cost, and E_d is the elasticity of demand facing the firm.

The issue of how a profit-maximizing firm should price in a dynamic network market remains a complex one. In a network industry it is in any dominant firm's interest to account in its pricing strategy for a host of factors that could lead, other things equal, to a lower price than one would expect from a simplistic short-run theory. These include: (1) the value of keeping and growing one's installed base, the source of the significant network effects; (2) the possibility of creating increased demand for complementary applications, which in turn provides an additional revenue source; (3) the need to discourage software pirating; and (4) the imposition of binding restrictions on its OEM customers as part of its anticompetitive campaign to preserve long-run monopoly profits.

The Court's Perspective

While Judge Jackson's opinion did not focus on the pricing issue, his Findings of Fact (in November 1999) supported the Government's position on all significant market definition and monopoly power issues. The court understood that, when defining a market in a monopoly case, it is appropriate to emphasize the constraints on an alleged monopolist's power with respect to buyers of operating systems, not the constraints relating to producers of complementary products. Seen in this light, Navigator and Java were *complements* to the OS that could facilitate the writing of applications that were also complements. They were not substitutes and therefore should not have been defined as part of the same market.

The court also agreed that there was a significant "applications barrier to entry." While Apple had 12,000 applications and OS/2 had 2500, neither could compete with Microsoft, which had more than 70,000 applications, one of which was its dominant business suite, Microsoft Office.

The appellate court chose not to overturn Judge Jackson's findings of fact on these issues, in effect affirming the district court's finding that Microsoft had monopoly power in the operating systems market. The academic and policy debate about the nature of dynamic competition, the measurement of market power, and the appropriate framework in which to evaluate the pricing of firms with market power will, however, continue beyond the scope of the *Microsoft* case.

Did Microsoft Maintain Its Operating System Monopoly by Thwarting the Threat Posed by Netscape's Browser?

The Government's Case

The Government argued that Microsoft engaged in a range of acts whose primary purpose was to protect its operating system monopoly. The Government pointed out that in May 1995 Microsoft's CEO Bill Gates had warned his top executives that the browser could "commoditize" the OS. His fear was that if Netscape's browser was successful, programmers would be easily induced to write software for competing operating systems, to the detriment of Microsoft. The key to maintaining its monopoly was to thwart the success of the Netscape Navigator browser.

The Government emphasized that before Microsoft began giving away its browser for free, ISPs and retailers had distributed browsers separately from OSs; as a result, there was clear evidence that there had been demand for OSs without browsers and for OSs with a choice of browsers. This supported the Government's view that a free browser was not simply a competitive strategy to penetrate the browser market, and it also supported the Government's proposed remedy—that Microsoft allow OEMs to choose which browser to offer, or indeed, to offer no browser at all.

The Government argued that by bundling its browser with its OS and giving away its browser for "free," Microsoft prevented companies from successfully entering the browser market unless they successfully entered the OS market. The necessity of this "two-level" entry effectively increased the barriers to entry into the OS market, and thereby protected Microsoft's monopoly in operating systems. The Government believed that Microsoft recognized the threat from Netscape Navigator, because it was an Internet browser capable of supporting applications that were OS independent. By lessening reliance on the OS, the browser, while not performing all the traditional functions of an operating system, could have provided opportunities for competing OSs by reducing the applications barrier to entry. In sum, the Government placed great weight on the fact that Microsoft was concerned that browsers could ultimately develop into alternate platforms, thereby threatening its Windows OS.[10]

This threat was real, because the Navigator browser runs on many different operating systems, including Windows, the Apple Macintosh OS, and various versions of UNIX, including Linux. Netscape's browsers contain their own set of APIs to which applications developers can write their applications. As a result, applications can be developed that will run on browsers regardless of the underlying OS. Similarly, browsers could have reduced the power of the OS monopoly by facilitating the expansion of network computing, in which users with "thin clients" use a network to access applications residing on a server, rather than hosting the application on the PC itself.

According to the Government, Microsoft recognized that it could protect its dominant position in the PC operating systems market by gaining and keeping a large share of the business in Internet browsers and by preventing any other browser from gaining a share sufficient to threaten Microsoft's

---

[10]In April 1996, Bill Gates wrote that: "Netscape's strategy is to make Windows and the Apple Macintosh operating system all but irrelevant by building the browser into a full-featured operating system with information browsing. Over time Netscape will add memory management, file systems, security, scheduling, graphics and everything else in Windows that applications require. The company hopes that its browser will become a de facto platform for software development, ultimately replacing Windows as the mainstream set of software standards. In Netscape's plan, people will get rid of their existing PC and Mac applications in favor of new software that will evolve around the Netscape browser" (4/10/96 "The Internet PC," Plaintiff's Exhibit 336).

platform dominance or remain viable as a platform. Moreover, if Microsoft's Internet Explorer browser were the dominant browser and Microsoft decided to support only Windows-based technology, developers would have little incentive to create applications that were not Windows-based.

In furtherance of its argument concerning browser shares, the Government showed that Netscape's market share (70 percent in 1996) had declined significantly by 1997, to the benefit of Microsoft, and that this pattern was likely to continue into 1998 and 1999, as in fact it did. In the Government's eyes, the market for browser usage had "tipped" in favor of Microsoft. With hindsight, the tipping did occur; Microsoft's current browser usage share is more than 85 percent.[11]

In sum, the Government believed that a range of anticompetitive acts was taken by Microsoft to exclude competition in Internet browsers. These were acts that Microsoft would not have undertaken except to foreclose competition and to protect the applications barrier to entry. The specific actions included:

Market Allocation: The Government claimed that Microsoft engaged in a series of market allocation efforts (involving Netscape, Apple, and Intel) whose ultimate purpose was to minimize the competitive threat to its OS monopoly.

In June 1995, Microsoft had a business meeting with Netscape, the alleged purpose being to solicit this emerging competitor to engage in a market allocation scheme in which Microsoft would agree to let Netscape offer its browser without competition in the server market, while Microsoft would be given control of the PC browser market. If Netscape had agreed (it did not), Microsoft would have succeeded in eliminating its only serious browser competitor.

The Government believed that Microsoft also engaged in similar conduct with Intel. When Intel proposed offering certain platform-level software that conflicted with Microsoft's platform plans, Microsoft threatened, among other things, to withhold support for Intel's new generation of processors.[12] According to Intel's chairman, Intel ultimately "caved" and withdrew the effort, at least under its own brand, explaining, "Introducing a Windows-based software initiative that Microsoft doesn't support . . . well, life is too short for that."[13]

Finally, Microsoft had entered into an agreement with Apple that required Apple to make IE its default browser on all its Macintosh operating

---

[11]As of June 2000, the IE browser usage share was 86 percent (Clark 2000).

[12]Specifically, Microsoft attempted to convince Intel to agree not to engage in platform competition with Microsoft by developing its Native Signal Processing technology, which would have endowed microprocessors with enhanced video and audio capabilities. Because the NSP technology would have been available for non-Windows platforms, it could have presented a threat to Microsoft's monopoly power.

[13]July 8, 1996, Brent Schlender, "A Conversation with the Lords of Wintel," *Fortune:* Plaintiff's Trial Exhibit 559, p. 8.

systems. According to the Government, that agreement forced Apple to place all competing browsers in a folder, thereby removing other browsers from the desktop. Microsoft also limited Apple's ability to promote other browsers and tried to discourage Apple from developing its QuickTime streaming software, a platform threat to windows.

The Government viewed Microsoft's conduct with respect to Netscape, Intel, and Apple as consistent with its efforts to prevent browsers from becoming a threat to the applications barrier to entry. In each case (1) Microsoft was confronted with platform-level software to which applications programs could be written; (2) platform-level APIs threatened to erode the applications barrier to entry into PC operating systems by supporting applications programs that could be used with multiple operating systems; (3) Microsoft responded by attempting to get the supplier of the potential alternative platform-level software to agree to withdraw from offering it and to concentrate instead on products that did not offer platform potential; and (4) Microsoft was prepared to act to preclude the supplier of a potential platform-level software from succeeding in offering the platform, even if Microsoft's actions were not otherwise sensible from a business perspective.

Predatory Pricing: According to the Government, once Microsoft recognized the potential threat posed by Netscape's browser, Microsoft began devoting at least $100 million per year to develop IE and tens of millions of dollars a year on marketing and promotion. Despite the significant browser-related costs it was incurring, Microsoft distributed its browser at a negative price. The IE browser was not only given away free, but companies were also paid and given valuable concessions to accept, use, distribute, and promote IE. While a free browser might be a profitable "penetration pricing" strategy to grow its market, the Government cited Microsoft's internal documents to show that Microsoft undertook its browser development not to make money from browsers but to prevent Netscape's browser from facilitating competition with Microsoft's monopoly OS. Indeed, Microsoft had referred to IE as a "no-revenue product," at the same time that Microsoft emphasized the importance of the browser to Microsoft's competitive position.[14]

When it made its decision to supply IE without charge, Microsoft estimated that from 20 percent to 50 percent of Netscape's revenues came from licensing its browser (such revenues amounted to nearly $200 million per year). Microsoft's decision to price its own browser below cost was thus made when it knew that Netscape was charging for its browser and that Netscape depended on those revenues to continue to compete effectively. Indeed, Microsoft candidly described its pricing of its browser to Intel in an effort to convince Intel not to do business with Netscape, saying that Mi-

---

[14]Government Trial Exhibit 39.

crosoft was "going to be distributing the browser for free" and that "this strategy would cut off Netscape's air supply, keep them from gaining any revenue to reinvest in their business."[15]

A predatory pricing strategy is one in which the predator forgoes current profits in order to eliminate or cripple a competitor, with the expectation of recouping those forgone profits at some point in the future. In the Government's view, Microsoft's pricing strategy did not make sense as an ordinary business practice. It was giving away something (a "no-revenue product") that it had spent a lot of money to develop and distribute (forgone profits) and something for which the leading competitor was charging. It was only when Microsoft's gains from preserving and extending its monopoly (recoupment) were included that Microsoft's conduct appeared to be profitable. From the Government's perspective, the preservation of Microsoft's OS monopoly alone would permit recoupment. Indeed, the Government introduced contemporaneous Microsoft documents showing that the company's zero (or negative) price for its browser was not considered a way to earn competitive ancillary revenues.

Bundling and OEM Restrictions: Although IE was not "tied" or "bundled" with the retail version of Windows 95 when it was first released in the summer of 1995, Microsoft did bundle IE with Windows 95 in distributing Windows 95 to OEMs, and IE was bundled with all Windows 98 OSs that Microsoft distributed through retail or OEM channels.[16] (In Windows 98, the browser was "integrated," having been designed to share extensive code with the operating system.) According to the Government, Microsoft made the decision to bundle IE and Windows in one form or another even though there was demand for browsers separate from the demand for operating systems.

The Government also argued that Microsoft made its bundling decision not to achieve efficiencies, but to foreclose competition. The Government was not arguing that bundling per se was anticompetitive. Instead, because Microsoft did not give OEMs the option of taking Windows without the browser, it thus compelled those OEMs and users that wished otherwise to take IE nonetheless in order to get Windows. This foreclosure of competition arguably had an immediate harmful effect on consumers, whose choice of browsers was restricted. The harm was not simply to consumers who faced limited browser choice; other harms resulted from the unnecessarily cumbersome OS and from the limited options for those who preferred not to use a browser.

---

[15]Steven McGeady 8/10/98 Dep. Tr. 16–17.

[16]In the traditional terminology of economics, bundling relates to situations in which firms sell packages of two or more products for which there may or may not be separate consumer demand. Tying, a more general term (although often used interchangeably with bundling by economists) applies to cases in which there are separate demands for two products, but the consumer must purchase one product in order to obtain another. With this terminology, it is appropriate to describe the browser as having been bundled with and tied to the OS.

Microsoft also recognized that OEMs wanted the ability to develop their own desktops and to substitute Netscape's browser for IE. The Government suggested that Microsoft, fearing this threat in 1996, imposed screen and start-up restrictions to prevent OEMs from developing their own first screen or positioning competing browsers more favorably than IE. From the Government's perspective, had Microsoft simply viewed the browser as a complement to its OS, Microsoft would have had a clear incentive to support all browsers. A successful Netscape browser, for example, would increase the demand for the Windows OS. However, according to the Government, Microsoft saw the Netscape browser as a platform that would support substitute operating systems. Facing the threat of a potential substitute, Microsoft's OEM restrictions were rational, indeed profit-maximizing, but at the same time, they were also anticompetitive.

With respect to OEMs, Microsoft required the distribution of IE and restricted the distribution of other browsers. The agreements required OEMs that wanted to preinstall Windows 95 or Windows 98 on their machines to preinstall Microsoft's IE also. The agreements also limited the ability of OEMs to promote other browsers, or to substitute other browsers for IE. Indeed, until changes were prompted by an early 1998 stipulation between Microsoft and the Department of Justice, the agreements typically required that licensees not modify or delete any of the product software. This prevented OEMs from removing any part of IE from the OS, including the visible means of user access to the IE software, such as the IE icon on the Windows desktop or the IE entry in the "Start" menu.

Licensees were not contractually restricted from loading other browsers on the desktop. However, most OEMs preferred to load only one browser to avoid user confusion and the resulting consumer support costs and to avoid increased testing costs. In addition, some OEMs viewed the desktop and/or disk space as scarce real estate and were generally reluctant to preinstall more than one software title in each functional category.

Microsoft's restrictions on the startup screen were modified just before trial so that OEMs had somewhat more flexibility than when the restrictions were imposed. However, IE was still required to be installed on every PC, and the IE icon could not be removed. The result, according to the Government, was a significant exclusionary effect that ensured that IE was the *only* browser on most PCs shipped by OEMs. By January 1999, Navigator was on the desktop of only a very small percentage of PCs.

Exclusionary Agreements with Internet Service Providers: According to the Government, Microsoft required the promotion and distribution of IE and restricted the promotion and distribution of other browsers by striking deals with Internet service providers in order to protect Microsoft's business in operating systems. After OEMs, ISPs are the largest distributors of browsers.

While Microsoft's agreements with ISPs allowed them to distribute other browsers, Microsoft's contracts typically required that the ISPs not distribute other browsers to more than a relatively small fraction of their customers. Some ISPs had agreements that allowed them to distribute IE and Netscape without preferences; Microsoft's documents used the term "IE Parity" to identify these companies.

Microsoft also created a separate desktop folder for certain favored ISPs and entered into agreements with AOL, CompuServe, Prodigy, and AT&T to appear in it. The Government offered evidence that in doing so, Microsoft extracted promises from the ISPs not to deal with Netscape or to do so only on very unfavorable terms. Of particular importance was the agreement that Microsoft reached with AOL, which by early 1996 was being installed on a large number of PCs, to ship IE.

Typically, the ISP restrictive provisions involved percentage restrictions on shipping for larger ISPs and restrictions on promotional efforts for smaller ISPs. These limitations included: (1) requirements that 75 percent or more of the ISP software shipments include IE as the only browser, and that the ISP not ship a competing browser unless a customer specifically requested it; and (2) limitations that restricted the total shipments of non-Microsoft browsers by ISPs.

The Government stressed that, in its agreements, Microsoft offered ISPs valuable space on its desktop as well as direct payments in the form of rebates or bounties. In exchange, Microsoft placed requirements on ISPs that hindered their ability to promote or distribute Netscape Navigator. The Government viewed these provisions as anticompetitive. Their purpose and effect were to reduce the ability of competing browser manufacturers to distribute and promote their browsers through leading ISPs.

Microsoft's Response

Microsoft agreed that the Internet presented both an opportunity and a threat. The Internet expanded the market for platform software generally, and the demand for Windows in particular. However, the Internet was also a threat to Microsoft because it offered competitors an opportunity to gain control of the communications and language standards for the Internet, which would leave Microsoft at a severe competitive disadvantage.

Microsoft characterized its browser battle as part of a larger effort to maintain its position as the leading PC provider of the Microsoft Windows software "platform," the software code that can be accessed through APIs, and which therefore offers a wide variety of features and services to software developers. Microsoft argued that its responses to this threat were appropriate responses by a competitor. Microsoft did believe that Netscape's Navigator could become a competing software platform if it added sufficient APIs to become attractive to software developers. If successful as a platform, Navigator could influence Internet standards in ways that would be adverse to Microsoft. Microsoft argued that, as a result, it had every right to compete aggressively with its most serious platform competitor.

Microsoft further argued that its actions against Netscape were not predatory because they were directed toward improving its own browser and OS and were not conditioned on crippling or eliminating Netscape as a browser competitor. Microsoft claimed that it had decided as early as 1993 to incorporate Internet features into its Windows platform. It invested $100 million annually to develop new and improved versions of IE. Indeed, because of the success of those investments, the IE browser eventually equaled if not surpassed the Netscape browser in quality. However, because its Internet development did not proceed sufficiently quickly, Microsoft chose not to include the browser in Windows 95. Microsoft suggested that it had always planned to "integrate" its browser in its OS and that there were significant efficiencies associated with doing so. Its reward from investing in the browser was similar to the reward that it expected from other features that were integrated into the operating system; it came from the increased value of a Windows OS that would continue to remain the leading software platform.

With respect to the Government's market allocation claims, Microsoft responded that it had legitimate business reasons for meeting with Netscape, Apple, and Intel. In each case, there were pro-competitive reasons to have joint discussions. Indeed, as a general matter, discussions concerning software interfaces and complementary products with other software firms can be valuable to both parties and to consumers. Microsoft emphasized the complementary relationship between the Netscape browser and its OS, and similar arguments were made concerning Intel's software tools for video streaming, Apple's QuickTime software, and Microsoft's OS. Finally, in each case, Microsoft argued that no agreements were reached, that it did not intimidate its competitors into altering their behavior, and that its competitors continued to be successful. Thus, according to Microsoft, Apple continued to develop its QuickTime for Windows product, and Intel's software development was delayed, but not stopped entirely.

With respect to pricing, Microsoft responded that firms frequently give away software for free or at a very low price in order to compete in what could be a "winner-take-all" market battle. Moreover, Microsoft argued that offering a free browser with Windows 95 was the natural step toward a goal of integrating valued features into its OS, as it did with its Internet browsing functionality in Windows 98. Microsoft additionally argued that Netscape had alternative sources of revenue, since it could sell advertising on its web portal, Netcenter. Finally, Microsoft argued that the Government had offered no compelling evidence that Microsoft's policy of integrating features into its OS was not profit-maximizing apart from any predatory motives.

With respect to bundling and OEM restrictions, Microsoft believed that it was justified in restricting OEMs from altering the start-up process to preserve the quality and speed of the start-up process and to give each user a consistent, "seamless" experience. Microsoft also argued that it did not have substantial market power. Absent monopoly power (or, at least, significant market power), bundling is not a rational anticompetitive strategy. Rather, it is likely to be harmless and to serve a legitimate business purpose. Indeed, from Microsoft's perspective, the benefit gained by creating interdependencies between IE and Windows was greater than any anticompetitive effects of bundling that might be imagined.

Microsoft further claimed that there were efficiencies associated with bundling that would be lost were Microsoft forced to separate the browser functionality from that of the OS. Microsoft further argued that the Government's claim that every product design, particularly in the area of computer software, can make a plausible claim for some efficiency or benefit, missed the point. In Microsoft's view, browser functionality was an essential component of the operating system, and that separating the two products once they have been combined would be impossible.

Finally, Microsoft claimed that the absence of IE would undermine the quality of the OS, to the detriment of users. Microsoft distinguished Windows 98 from Windows 95 and thereby dismissed as irrelevant the Government's view that Microsoft had provided ways to remove IE in Windows 95—a function that would most likely not have been provided if it led to a decrease in the quality of the OS. They also argued that the Government's showing that it is possible within Windows 98 to remove the ability to browse the Web with IE and to replace IE with another browser with no appreciable decline in the quality of the Windows 98 OS was misleading, since the Government's expert removed only the visible means of accessing the browser and not the browser functionality itself.

With respect to its ISP agreements, Microsoft took the position that it was justified in competing aggressively for the distribution of its browser. Its success with AOL, for example, was due to its superior quality product and the desirable competitive terms that it offered. Microsoft stressed that its browser came in distinct "modules," which allowed AOL more easily to integrate the IE "technologies" into its own proprietary software. Finally, Microsoft argued that Netscape did not offer the same support as Microsoft, refusing, for example, to allow AOL to manage its popular web portal.

With regards to both OEM and ISP agreements, Microsoft argued "no harm, no foul." Microsoft offered evidence to support the view that Netscape had many channels through which it could distribute its browser. It could "carpet bomb" by mailing disks with CDs, or it could encourage individuals to download IE from the Web. Consequently, neither Netscape nor any other competitor was foreclosed from competing with Microsoft.

The Court's View

Judge Jackson strongly supported the Government's claims that Microsoft had used anticompetitive acts to maintain its OS monopoly. The court's condemnation of Microsoft's behavior with respect to maintenance of monopoly was widespread. In each of the four categories of activities listed above—market allocation; predatory pricing; bundling; and exclusionary agreements—the court sided with the Government.

Moreover, with respect to the bundling arguments, the court agreed that "tying" the browser to the OS was anticompetitive even apart from its contribution to Microsoft's maintenance of monopoly goal. Microsoft's only "victory" at the district court level was Judge Jackson's finding that the Government had not provided sufficient evidence that the OEM and ISP restrictions had foreclosed competition.[17]

The circuit court of appeals supported Judge Jackson with respect to the maintenance-of-monopoly arguments, thus strongly backing the core of the Government's case. Specifically, the court of appeals affirmed the district court's finding that the OEM and ISP restrictions described previously were anticompetitive. The appellate court also agreed with the core of the lower court's finding that the means by which Microsoft tied its browser to its OS was anticompetitive. Moreover, the appellate court made it clear that certain of Microsoft's marketing allocation efforts with respect to Apple and Intel were anticompetitive. The appellate court did, however, raise questions about the bundling-tying issue itself, remanding this issue back to the district court for further analysis of the benefits and the costs associated with Microsoft's bundling of IE and its OS.

Was Microsoft's Alleged Anticompetitive Behavior Harmful to Competition?

The Government's View

In the Government's view, Microsoft succeeded in effectively excluding Netscape almost completely from the personal computer OEM distribution channel. OEMs that license Windows were required to take (and not remove) IE. For most OEMs, including the largest, that meant including only IE with the PCs they shipped.

In evaluating the effectiveness of Microsoft's actions on browser competition, the Government argued that the relevant measure was Microsoft's share of browser *usage.* The evidence of Microsoft's foreclosure of Netscape and other browser competitors could be seen by comparing Microsoft's share of browsers distributed by ISPs that made IE their default browser with ISPs that did not make IE their default browser. At the end of 1997 Microsoft enjoyed a 94 percent weighted average share of browser shipments by ISPs who agreed to make IE their default browser, compared with a 14 percent weighted average share of browser shipments by ISPs

---

[17]Here, the judge arguably failed to note that the imposition of significant costs on competitors can harm consumers. Even if those rivals are not driven from the market, their ability to compete effectively can be reduced if their costs of browser distribution are raised significantly.

who did not make IE their default browser. Further, Microsoft's weighted average share of browser usage by subscribers to ISPs who made IE their default browser was over 60 percent. In contrast, Microsoft's weighted average share of browser usage by subscribers to ISPs who did not make IE their default was less than 20 percent.

Figure 19-1 shows Microsoft's monthly share of browser usage by three categories of ISPs, from January 1997 through August 1998. The top line shows Microsoft's share of usage among subscribers to AOL and CompuServe rising sharply. These companies (now merged) were chosen because they represented the largest ISPs (with a total of more than 11.5 million subscribers and about 65 percent of all subscribers to the services in the "Top 80" as of year-end 1997), and because AOL and CompuServe, as online service providers, were contractually restricted in their promotion and distribution of non-IE browsers to a greater extent than were most other ISPs.

FIGURE 19-1 Microsoft's Share of the Browser Market
Three-Month Moving Average of Usage by ISP Category

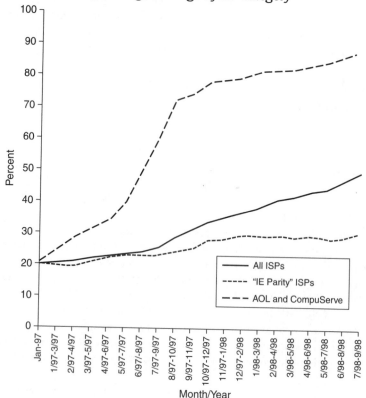

(*Source: AdKnowledge, Inc.*)

The middle line shows Microsoft's share for all ISPs. The bottom line shows Microsoft's share for the ISPs within the "Top 80," which Microsoft listed as having "IE Parity" (ISPs whose browser choice was not known to be contractually restricted), which had 10,000 or more subscribers, and for which data were available.

From the Government's point of view, the effects were striking. Microsoft's share of "IE Parity" browser usage—the category that is contractually neutral—rose in twenty months from 20 percent to just under 30 percent. This increase included the effects of technological improvement in IE as well as the effects of Microsoft's bundling and tying. By contrast, the "All ISPs" line showed an increase in Microsoft's share from 20 percent to 49 percent. Finally, for AOL and CompuServe, Microsoft's share rose from just over 20 percent to over 87 percent. (It is worth noting that the dramatic jump in that share occurred *before* the introduction of IE4—the improved version of IE—in October 1997.) Thus, contract restriction—not browser quality or ISP choice—was largely responsible for the overall decline in Netscape share.

The exclusion of Netscape and other competing browsers from the OEM channel has been even greater. Although several OEMs sought to replace IE with Netscape, none was permitted to do so. And the fact that IE was required to be included meant in most cases that *only* IE would be included.

Recall that because of its innovations and success in creating and distributing the world's first widely used browser, Netscape initially had a very large share of the browser market. Microsoft's browser share at the beginning of calendar year 1997 was approximately 20 percent and had been significantly lower earlier. Regardless of how share is measured, it is clear that Microsoft's browser share increased dramatically, and Netscape's browser share fell sharply, over the years 1997 and 1998. Indeed, as mentioned previously, Microsoft's browser share continued to increase through 1999 as well, reaching over 85 percent by mid-2000. The Government's claim that Microsoft's goal wasn't necessarily to drive Netscape completely out of business, but only to prevent Netscape from becoming the browser of choice for most consumers, was borne out by history.

Microsoft's Response

Microsoft responded at trial that its conduct was profitable without considering any gains from reduced competition because the wide distribution of its browser caused more people to buy PCs to browse the Internet, with the result that Microsoft was able to sell more copies of its Windows OS. In other words, browsers can be complements to operating systems to the extent that the sale of browsers can be used to increase demand for Windows. Moreover, Microsoft argued that it expected to benefit by improving the quality of its browser through innovative product development.

Microsoft argued further that, while it did compete aggressively to defend its market position, none of the actions to which the Government objected had harmed consumers, nor would they do so in the future. Moreover, Microsoft argued that it had not succeeded in eliminating the competitive threat posed by Netscape and Java. It argued further that AOL, which acquired Netscape during the trial, could choose to distribute the Netscape browser if it wished to do so. If AOL had decided to follow this avenue, the share of the browser market controlled by Microsoft would have diminished sharply.

Microsoft disputed the Government's measure of browser market share, offering numbers that suggesting that the market for browsers had not yet tipped in Microsoft's favor. Microsoft further argued that the allegedly restrictive distribution agreements with ISPs did not foreclose Netscape, because Netscape had many opportunities to distribute its browser—through PCs and ISPs, and through downloads. Microsoft further argued that Netscape could have marketed its browser more effectively, but had failed to do so.

The real source of Netscape's decline, according to Microsoft, was that Microsoft had won the battle of Internet browsing technologies on the merits—it simply had a better product. Rather than being anticompetitive, its actions to (1) invest $100 million annually in its browser; (2) invest heavily in the distribution of IE; (3) integrate its browser into Windows; and (4) reach a contract with AOL to have AOL use IE technologies for its own subscribers, were pro-competitive. From Microsoft's perspective the Government failed to distinguish these pro-competitive acts from a narrower set of acts that the Government viewed as anticompetitive.

The Court's Perspective

Judge Jackson's Findings of Fact supported the Government's view that Microsoft's anticompetitive acts caused immediate harm. According to the court:

> To the detriment of consumers, . . . Microsoft also engaged in a concerted series of actions designed to protect the applications barrier to entry, and hence its monopoly power, from a variety of middleware threats, including Netscape's Web browser and Sun's implementation of Java. Many of these actions have harmed consumers in ways that are immediate and easily discernible. They have also caused less direct, but nevertheless serious and far-reaching, consumer harm by distorting competition. (paragraph 409)

> By refusing to offer those OEMs who requested it a version of Windows without Web browsing software, and by preventing OEMs from removing IE—or even the most obvious means of invoking it—prior to shipment, Microsoft forced OEMs to ignore consumer demand for a browserless version of Windows. . . . Those Windows purchasers who did not want browsing

software . . . had to . . . content themselves with a PC system that ran slower and provided less available memory than if the newest version of Windows came without browsing software. By taking the actions listed above . . . Microsoft forced those consumers who otherwise would have elected Navigator as their browser to either pay a substantial price (in the forms of downloading, installation, confusion, degraded system performance, and diminished memory capacity) or content themselves with IE. None of these actions had pro-competitive justifications. (paragraph 410)

Many of the tactics that Microsoft has employed have also harmed consumers indirectly by unjustifiably distorting competition. The actions that Microsoft took against Navigator hobbled a form of innovation that had shown the potential to depress the applications barrier to entry sufficiently to enable other firms to compete effectively against Microsoft in the market for Intel-compatible PC operating systems. That competition would have conduced to consumer choice and nurtured innovation. . . . It is clear . . . that Microsoft has retarded, and perhaps altogether extinguished, the process by which . . . middleware technologies could have facilitated the introduction of competition into an important market. (paragraph 411)

Most harmful of all is the message that Microsoft's actions have conveyed to every enterprise with the potential to innovate in the computer industry. . . . Microsoft's past success in hurting such companies and stifling innovation deters investment in technologies and businesses that exhibit the potential to threaten Microsoft. The ultimate result is that some innovations that would truly benefit consumers never occur for the sole reason that they do not coincide with Microsoft's self-interest. (paragraph 412)

RESOLUTION OF THE CASE?

As this is case study is written, it seems likely that the case has been resolved, and a remedy chosen. The path to a remedy has been circuitous. The appellate court made clear its distaste for a structural remedy that would break up Microsoft into two separate companies—an OS company and an applications company. The case was remanded to the district court, where Judge Colleen Kollar-Kotelly presided over settlement discussions. The U.S. Government and nine of the eighteen states that remain as plaintiffs reached a tentative settlement with Microsoft in which Microsoft would consent to a range of behavioral remedies. However, nine states and the District of Columbia opted not to join the settlement; they objected that the remedies were likely to be ineffective, and pressed for stronger remedies. The court held a remedies hearing in which a broad range of issues were debated.

While emphasizing Microsoft's attempts to thwart competition from Netscape, the Government had argued at the original trial, and continued to argue in its settlement discussions, that there is a broader issue—that Microsoft engaged in anticompetitive acts with the goal of stemming competition from middleware products that threatened its OS monopoly. Seen from this perspective, the issue of what is an appropriate remedy to restore competition and to achieve adequate deterrence remained an open issue at the remedy hearing.

In its original remedy argument post-trial, the Government took the position that behavioral remedies could serve a useful temporary role, but such remedies would likely be difficult and costly to enforce, and could inadequately deter Microsoft's wrongful behavior. Structural remedies, on the other hand, are less regulatory and therefore less subject to extensive intervention by interested parties. The proposed breakup would have divided the company along lines that some would argue are inefficient, and would not by itself guarantee increased operating system competition.

With the decision of the appellate court discouraging structural remedies, and its own skeptical concerns, the Department of Justice (now under the Bush administration) and the nine settling states chose to focus entirely on conduct remedies, and, contrary to the argument just outlined, took structural remedies off the table. Their proposed settlement contained three components. First, it attempted to prohibit Microsoft from foreclosing the OEM channel of distribution by eliminating restrictive licensing agreements, and outlawing retaliatory measures against OEMs by Microsoft. Second, it attempted to keep the ISP distribution channel open by placing limits on Microsoft's ability to discourage others from developing, promoting, or distributing non-Microsoft middleware products. Third, the settlement offered a series of compliance measures whose goal is to enforce the terms of the settlement agreement.

Those states opposing the proposed settlement argued that the proposed behavioral remedy will be largely ineffective. Their primary concern was that the proposed settlement did not prohibit Microsoft from illegally bundling Microsoft middleware into the Windows OS. Absent such a remedy, there is nothing to limit Microsoft from technologically tying non-browser middleware software to the OS, when such software is seen as a potential platform that would compete with Windows. The opposing states also argued that the proposed consent decree will not effectively prohibit retaliatory conduct and restrictive licensing practices, and it will not effectively open the ISP channel of distribution. They also claimed that the proposed settlement would allow Microsoft to withhold vital technical information from developers of rival middleware. Finally, they argued that the proposed enforcement mechanism will be ineffective.

Judge Kollar Kotelly's ruling was generally supportive of the settlement agreement reached between the DOJ and Microsoft. While the court rejected many of the more aggressive remedies proposed by the nine litigating states, the court did offer more aggressive, and potentially more effective, compliance procedures that were sympathetic to issues raised by the litigating states. In a summary of its full opinion, the court suggested that its remedy "is carefully tailored to fit the wrong creating the occasion for the remedy . . . and is forward-looking in the parameters of relief provided. . . . [and] is crafted to foster competition in the monopolized market."[18] Only the future will provide an answer as to whether a settlement that includes a complex set of behavioral remedies will indeed restore competition and effectively deter wrongly anticompetitive conduct.

REFERENCES

Clark, Scott. "Browser Statistics Look Good for IE." http://www.internetnews.com/wd-news/article/0,,???10_4033661,00.html (June 27, 2000).

Evans, David S., and Richard L. Schmalensee. "Be Nice to Your Rivals: How the Government is Selling an Antitrust Case without Consumer Harm in *United States v. Microsoft.*" In *Did Microsoft Harm Consumers?: Two Opposing Views,* edited by Robert W. Hahn and Robert E. Litan, 1–44. Washington, D.C.: A.I. Press, 2000.

Fisher, Franklin M., and Daniel L. Rubinfeld. "*United States v. Microsoft:* An Economic Analysis." In *Did Microsoft Harm Consumers?: Two Opposing Views,* edited by Robert W. Hahn and Robert E. Litan, 45–86. Washington, D.C.: A.I. Press, 2000.

Gilbert, Richard J. "Networks, Standards, and the Use of Market Dominance: Microsoft (1995)." In *The Antitrust Revolution: Economics, Competition, and Policy,* 3rd edition, edited by John E. Kwoka, Jr. and Lawrence J. White, 409–429. New York: Oxford University Press, 1999.

Gilbert, Richard J. and Michael L. Katz. "An Economist's Guide to *U.S. v. Microsoft.*" *Journal of Economic Perspectives* 15 (Spring 2001): 25–44.

Klein, Benjamin. "The Microsoft Case: What Can a Dominant Firm Do to Defend Its Market Position?" *Journal of Economic Perspectives* 15 (Spring 2001): 45–62.

Pindyck, Robert S., and Daniel L. Rubinfeld. *Microeconomics,* 5th edn. Upper Saddle River, N.J.: Prentice-Hall, 2001.

U.S. v. *Microsoft,* Civil Action No. 98-1232 (Antitrust), *Complaint,* U.S. District Court for the District of Columbia.

U.S. v. *Microsoft,* Civil Action No. 98-1232 (TPJ), *Findings of Fact,* U.S. District Court for the District of Columbia, 84 F. Supp. 2d 9 (D.D.C. 1999).

U.S. v. *Microsoft,* Civil Action No. 98-1232 (TPJ), *Conclusions of Law,* U.S. District Court for the District of Columbia, 87 F. Supp. 2d 30 (D.D.C. 2000).

U.S. v. *Microsoft,* Civil Action No. 98-1232 (TPJ), *Final Judgment,* U.S. District Court for the District of Columbia, 97 F. Supp. 2d 59 (D.D.C. 2000).

U.S. v. *Microsoft,* 253 F.3d 34 (D.C. Cir., 2001)(en banc).

U.S. v. *Microsoft,* 231 F. Supp. 2d 144 (D.D.C. 2002).

White, Lawrence J. "Present at the Beginning of a New Era for Antitrust: Reflections on 1982–1983." *Review of Industrial Organization* 16 (March 2000): 131–149.

---

[18]"Executive Summary." http://www.microsoft.com/presspass/trial/nov02/98-1233summary.pdf (November 1, 2002), p. 19. See more generally *U.S.* v. *Microsoft,* 231 F. Supp. 2d 144 (D.D.C. 2002).

The American Airlines Case:
A Chance to Clarify Predation Policy (2001)

Aaron S. Edlin and
Joseph Farrell

INTRODUCTION

Predation occurs when a firm offers consumers favorable deals, usually *in the short run,* that get rid of competition and thereby harm consumers in the long run. Modern economic theory has shown how commitment or collective-action problems among consumers can lead to such paradoxical effects.[1]

But the paradox does signal danger. Too hawkish a policy might ban favorable deals that are not predatory. "It would be ironic indeed if the standards for predatory pricing liability were so low that antitrust suits themselves became a tool for keeping prices high."[2] Predation policy must therefore diagnose the unusual cases where favorable deals harm competition.

Farrell thanks SIEPR for research support through a Cain Fellowship, and Edlin thanks the Alfred P. Sloan foundation for a faculty fellowship. Farrell was Deputy Assistant Attorney General at the Department of Justice in 2000 to 2001. Edlin was senior adviser covering antitrust on the President's Council of Economic Advisers during 1997–1998 and commented on drafts of Department of Transportation (1998). The views here are our own and not those of our former employers; nor can they be attributed to helpful colleagues, who included Severin Borenstein, Craig Shapiro, and Carl Shapiro, and Gregory Werden. This paper is based solely on public information. We thank Charles Clarke for helpful editing.

[1]See Edlin (2002), Bolton, Brodley, and Riordan (2000), and Spector (2001). The relevance of these problems is illustrated in *Barry Wright,* where the collective action problem is limited because there is one large purchaser, Grinnell. Grinnell can presumably choose whether to take favorable deals (even if temporary) or whether to subsidize competition (Barry Wright) for the sake of long-term low prices. Even here, though, too little entry can occur if the buyer cannot commit not to "take the bait" of post-entry discounts.

[2]*Brooke Group,* pp. 226–227, cited in American Airlines' Appellees' Brief at 15.

To this end, courts and commentators have largely defined predation as "sacrifice" followed, at least plausibly, by "recoupment" at consumers' expense. The *American Airlines* case raises difficult questions about this approach.

The Case

American Airlines or "AA" is the dominant carrier at Dallas-Fort Worth International Airport (DFW). As the judge wrote, the case

> arises from competition between American Airlines and several smaller low cost carriers [Vanguard, Western Pacific, and SunJet] on various airline routes centered on Dallas-Fort Worth Airport (DFW) from 1995 to 1997. During this period, these low cost carriers created a new market dynamic, charging markedly lower fares on certain routes. For a certain period (of differing length in each market) consumers of air travel on these routes enjoyed lower prices. The number of passengers also substantially increased. American responded to the low cost carriers by reducing some of its own fares, and increasing the number of flights serving the routes. In each instance, the low fare carrier failed to establish itself as a durable market presence, and eventually moved its operations, or ceased its separate existence entirely. After the low fare carrier ceased operations, American generally resumed its prior marketing strategy, and in certain markets reduced the number of flights and raised its prices, roughly to levels comparable to those prior to the period of low fare competition. (*U.S. v. AMR et al.,* 140 F. Supp. 2d 1141 [2001])

The Department of Justice (DOJ) argued that American's *initial* response to the entry of "low-cost carriers" (LCCs) was to match the entrants' fares on a limited basis. But then American grew concerned that the LCCs might expand and perhaps create a mini-hub at DFW[3]—a prospect that alarmed American after ValuJet's Atlanta mini-hub had cost Delta $232 million in revenue.

American then *shifted* to a more aggressive response, increasing the availability of its low fares, and adding flight frequencies and/or larger aircraft. American also entered a route, DFW-Long Beach (LGB), that it had previously abandoned as unprofitable and that Sun Jet was serving.

The DOJ sued American under Sec. 2 of the Sherman Act for thus monopolizing or attempting to monopolize four DFW routes: Kansas City (twice), Wichita, Colorado Springs, and Long Beach. The DOJ claimed as predatory not American's *prices* alone, nor its initial response to entry, but a "totality" of its subsequent *expansion* of low-fare availability and capacity (including flight schedules).

---

[3]DOJ Appellant's brief, p. 8. As of this writing, redacted versions of the appeals briefs and other key documents are available at www.usdoj.gov/atr/cases/indx199.htm (for the Government-Plaintiff) and at www.aadoj.com.

The DOJ claimed that the expansion made no business sense unless it made the LCCs withdraw or cease to compete so hard. It quoted American's CEO: "If you are not going to get [LCCs] out then no point to diminish profit," and said that this "no business sense but for exclusion" criterion was the essence of predation.

Specifically, the DOJ argued that American knew that an alternative strategy—sticking to its initial response—would have been more profitable, except for the effect of American's actual actions on LCC competition. The DOJ's expert used American's internal decision-support profit measures (discussed below) to run four tests for sacrifice that the DOJ summarized as:

Test 1. Whether incremental cost exceeded incremental revenue;

Test 2. Whether long-run (18-month) AVC [average variable cost] exceeded price;

Test 3. Whether price was below American's 18-month cost measure (persistent negative profitability); and

Test 4. Whether incremental [. . .] cost exceeded price.[4]

The DOJ argued that these tests showed sacrifice (estimated at $41 million),[5] and that American reasonably expected to "recoup" its sacrifice by reducing competition on these and other DFW routes that it dominated and through the development of a reputation for predation.

American responded that its prices were never below route-level average variable cost; that the routes in question remained profitable; that it had at most matched, not undercut, the entrants' prices; and that the DOJ's theory of "recoupment" was speculative. It moved for summary judgment, which the district court granted in April 2001. The court believed that, even if the Government were right about all contestable facts, it would still lose on the law. The DOJ appealed to the Tenth Circuit Court of Appeals; the appellate briefs were filed early in 2002, and oral argument was expected later that year.

Key Questions

The District Court ruled for American on four key issues:

1. Should courts measure "sacrifice" relative to

   a. Maximized profits, or profits from marginally less output;

---

[4]DOJ Reply Brief, p. 4. Not all the tests could be applied to all episodes; see the appeals briefs for discussion.

[5]See District Court Opinion, 140 F. Supp 2d 1141, 1213, hereafter referred to as "Op."

b. Profits after entry, but before the alleged predation; or

c. Reservation profits: profits if the defendant had exited the market (route)?

2. Should the sacrifice benchmark differ when the plaintiff alleges predatory nonpricing conduct—here, the "capacity increase"—rather than low pricing per se?

3. How conclusively must prospective recoupment be proved? Should the evidence focus on financial results or on consumer harm? Must recoupment be in the market where sacrifices are made, or does recoupment in other markets count?

4. If a defendant meets but does not beat its competitor's prices, is this a defense? If so, how should one weigh differences in perceived quality?

The case raises at least two other important questions:

5. Should the test or standard of proof for predation be different for a monopoly than for an oligopoly?

6. Is sacrifice merely *evidence* of predation, or is it a *necessary* element of the offense of monopolization?

We discuss these questions below, but first we consider the economies that American enjoyed from its hub operations in Dallas.

AMERICAN'S HUB OPERATION, DECISION ACCOUNTING, AND MARKET DEFINITION

Paradoxically, major carriers maintain large market shares, even dominant market positions, in their hubs despite higher prices and higher costs than competitors at those hubs. In 1995, American reportedly commanded premiums in DFW of 31 percent and yet served 70 percent of the passengers who originate or terminate nonstop travel in DFW (Borenstein 1992; Edlin 2002, fn 9). Like other majors, American also has high costs per flight, or per available seat-mile (ASM), largely due to union contracts. In 1994, American's cost per ASM was 8.54 cents, while it estimated ValuJet's comparable cost at 4.32 cents.[6] Why, then, don't LCCs easily outcompete the majors?

Much of the answer lies in the countervailing economies of scope and scale not captured in measures of cost per ASM. Economies of scope come largely from hub operation, in particular from the sharing of flights by pas-

---

[6]Op. at 1151. Similarly an internal American document stated that Southwest's labor costs per ASM were 45.8 percent lower than American's in 1993.

sengers who are flying different routes. An AA flight from Wichita to Dallas carries not only passengers traveling from Wichita to Dallas but also those from Wichita to Los Angeles or Miami. Thus, there are economies of scope in service from Wichita to Dallas, to Los Angeles, and to Miami.

Some passengers on the Wichita-Dallas flight will go on to Miami and would likely not fly AA at all if AA didn't serve Wichita-Dallas. The Wichita-Dallas ("upline") flight causes additional traffic and profits on AA's Dallas-Miami ("downline") route. Thus, AA might profitably serve (say) the Wichita-Dallas spoke even at very low fares, because doing so boosts its profits on the Dallas-LA, Dallas-Miami, and similar routes.

American's break-even fare level (or load factor) for the Wichita spoke may be low even though its cost of flying planes (or cost per ASM) is much higher than a smaller airline's. American's competitive advantages thus lie in its hub complementarities. Its decision accounting system did take these complementarities into account, as we discuss next.

American's Decision Accounting Incorporated Complementarities

AA's internal accounting tools for routing and scheduling decisions took account of the hub complementarities discussed above. The DOJ in turn relied on these internal decision accounts.

In particular, AA measured each route's "Fully Allocated Earnings plus Upline/Downline Contribution Net of Costs," or FAUDNC, which includes a measure of the route's net contribution to profits on *other* routes. Thus, when a passenger buys a ticket from Wichita to Miami via Dallas, FAUDNC would attribute a measure of the Downline Contribution (conceptually the price for the Dallas-Miami leg, less its incremental cost) to the Wichita-Dallas route, and would attribute an analogous Upline Contribution to the Dallas-Miami route.

While one might initially be taken aback by the double-counting, in fact this is a sensible way to do route-level *decision* accounts[7] in light of hub complementarities, and both sides in the case used these accounts. FAUDNC, the court found, was "one of the factors American uses when deciding whether to exit a route." It is

> part of a number of profitability measures intended to reflect the economic value of operating a flight, a segment, a hub or the entire system *[sic]*. The company expended a substantial amount of time and money investigating its accounting systems, and in developing decision FAUDNC. Since its development of FAUDNC in 1995, American has continued to modify its methodology to improve route profitability reporting. (Op. at 1175)

---

[7]The double-counting makes FAUDNC and its cousins unfit to measure AA's overall system profitability, or to calculate its tax liability.

On the revenue side the judge believed that even FAUDNC understates the benefits to AA of operating a route. He noted that "FAUDNC does not capture the system benefits . . . [of] enhanced regional presence or origin point presence . . . [such] benefits accrue on other routes and flights.[8]

On the cost side, despite the "Fully Allocated" name and the fact that FAUDNC includes roughly 97–99 percent of AA's total costs, the DOJ's expert found that "FAUDNC cost is conceptually close to long-run average route-level variable cost." But the judge concluded that FAUDNC included too many (fixed) costs, including "certain costs that would not be entirely avoided if AA were to abandon service on a particular DFW route" (Op. at 1176), such as "fixed maintenance expenses" and "fixed overhead expenses." He found that "FAUDNC . . . is a fully allocated earnings measure, not a measure of the variable costs of serving a route."

Economists, like the court, often criticize fully allocated measures as including too many fixed or common costs, and stress that not all accounting costs are economic costs of decisions, especially decisions where exit is not contemplated. Yet, as the judge notes elsewhere, American conducted a "detailed audit" to decide which costs to include. Although it chose to include 97–99 percent of total costs, it apparently felt that this made for the best decision measure with which to "compare the performance of its various routes against each other."

Why might a decision accounting system include costs that seem not to vary with the decisions for which it is designed? One possibility is that some costs are more variable than they look. In particular, variable congestion costs can easily be missed in the short run if the firm makes no extra expenditures. A facility or service such as baggage handling or an airplane will become congested with increased usage. This congestion is a real cost even if the firm spends no money to alleviate congestion in the short run. Indeed, if the firm would in the long run prefer to hire more baggage handlers or add airplanes, rather than inflict congestion on its customers, but can't do so in the short run, then the long-run money cost is a *lower bound* on short-run variable cost, which might thus even exceed FAUDNC cost.[9]

FAUDNC was not the only upline/downline decision accounting system. VAUDNC is a similar measure on the revenue side but includes only "the variable expense categories of costs" (those "categorized as variable over an 18-month planning horizon"); a third measure, VAUDNS, also allows for "spill," the possibility that carrying one passenger displaces another (Op. at 1174). VAUDNC even excludes aircraft costs (surprisingly, only about 7 percent of AA's costs); the judge commented that aircraft costs are not regarded as variable—even though the number of aircraft used on

---

[8]Op. at 1176. For instance, a broader system makes frequent-flyer rewards more valuable.

[9]Short-run costs of expansion may thus exceed short-run cost savings from output reduction. It appears that DOJ did not pursue the congestion argument as sketched here and maintained that FAUDNC cost reasonably measured short-run AVC for American's expansion on the routes.

the route was in fact varied, and aircraft surely have an opportunity cost on other routes, or in other hands—there is a leasing market for planes.[10] The DOJ's expert believed that VAUDNC's cost component was an appropriate measure of short-run route-level AVC if one adds to it aircraft cost, creating VAUDNC-AC.

Market Definition

Antitrust markets are generally defined based on demand-side substitutability, suggesting that markets consist of city-pairs or airport-pairs. Restrictions on service at Dallas' other airport, Love Field (where Southwest operates), plausibly made it an inadequate substitute for DFW. A related empirical question is whether connecting service is an adequate substitute for nonstop service on a route. These conventional questions of demand substitutability were not central on appeal, and we will not pursue them here.

But antitrust markets are sometimes pressed into the role of defining a universe of discourse. Routes are ill-suited for this, since different routes are closely linked as sketched above. AA's extensive and profitable hub operations at DFW made it more profitable for AA to operate any individual DFW spoke, because spokes are complements in hub operation. And the DOJ argued that AA was much more concerned that LCCs might establish DFW hubs than about LCC operations on isolated DFW routes. To understand the case one must thus think across routes, as we will see repeatedly below.

WHY LOOK AT SACRIFICE?

Both sides followed tradition by arguing that the court must assess whether American lost money (sacrificed profit) through its actions. Why?

First, if there is no sacrifice, this might indicate that all is well. In order to eliminate competition, a firm might need to sacrifice short-term profits. But not always: A low-cost monopoly may harm competition (not only competitors) by using its advantages strategically to exclude competitors, with little or no sacrifice, as Edlin (2002) explains.

Second, conscious voluntary sacrifice might indicate that the firm thinks that it can thereby eliminate competition, and thus that harm is indeed in prospect. Sacrifice may be what Bork (1978, p. 145) called "an in-

---

[10] If AA brought planes and other factors from other routes (rather than buying or hiring more), the right measure of their cost is their opportunity cost elsewhere. This opportunity cost presumably includes both upline/downline contributions and broader network benefits. If it is hard to measure, one might gauge it from the long-run equilibrium condition: AA will have tried to ensure that the full gross benefits of these factors *on its marginal routes* will be about equal to their long-run costs.

vestment in monopoly profits." But not always: A firm may have legitimate reasons to sacrifice short-run profits. For example, production today may lower future costs in an industry with learning-by-doing, as Arrow (1962) describes. Or, more to the point, "sacrifice" in one product can be immediately recouped (often quite legitimately) because it boosts profits in a complementary product.[11] Thus, sacrifice of short-run profits is neither necessary nor sufficient for harm, and could be far from both.

Before discussing sacrifice benchmarks in the *American* case, we point out two fallacies to avoid in tests for sacrifice. First, a predator presumably doesn't expect to sacrifice profits *overall*. Profit sacrifice tests compare what is loosely called "short-run" profits—*not counting* the consequent profit from exclusion—against some other benchmark level of profit. If (as we normally assume) the firm is really maximizing its overall profits, then the fear is that the missing element is the effect of reducing competition. Certainly there are many good reasons not to maximize short-run profits at the product level, such as (pro-competitive) penetration pricing and complementarities. But sacrifice of short-run profits at least indicates that something strategic may be going on, and might make it worth looking further to see whether there is a credible theory of anticompetitive effect. In short, testing for an overall failure of profit maximization would catch only irrational predation: the "actual sacrifice fallacy."

Second, entry ordinarily reduces an incumbent's profits even if the incumbent responds optimally. That profit reduction must not be confused with sacrifice; taking *pre-entry* profits as the benchmark would fall into an "involuntary sacrifice fallacy." Tests of profit sacrifice must compare profits (not counting the subsequent rewards from exclusion) against those of some other post-entry option available to the alleged predator.

BENCHMARKS FOR SACRIFICE

The DOJ claimed that American lost money through its capacity expansion, but American responded that the proper legal question was really whether it lost money *overall* on any route in question. The dispute was thus: Relative to what profit benchmark must the plaintiff show losses or sacrifice? Is the relevant comparison exit from the route, as American implicitly contended, or profits absent the capacity expansion, as the DOJ advocated?

Hub complementarities, included (as we saw) in American's decision accounts, make it relatively cheap—in terms of overall profits—for Ameri-

---

[11]See Farrell and Katz (2000, 2001). For example, supermarkets that supply free parking are not normally engaged in predation against commercial parking establishments; rather, they charge through the complement (groceries). Such cases need not be viewed as sacrifice. One might try to redefine revenues to include contributions to complementary products as American does by including "Upstream" and "Downstream" contributions.

can to cut prices and/or expand service on a given spoke (which boosts demand on others), as long as it doesn't do so on too many spokes at once. Indeed, this effect could outweigh its cost-per-ASM disadvantage versus an LCC.

Yet, in part precisely because it can improve its offer to customers if need be, a hub carrier such as American may be able to respond to entry aggressively enough to discourage entry even by a lower-cost carrier—perhaps without much sacrifice or conceivably with none. While aggressive responses are good for consumers in the short run (while the entrant is there), the *prospect* of such a response can deter desirable entry and thus be bad for consumers and perhaps for efficiency. So the question of which sacrifice benchmark to use is central.

Profit Maximization and the Areeda-Turner Test

The DOJ cites Judge Bork as explaining:

> Predation involves aggression against business rivals through the use of business practices that would not be considered profit maximizing except for the expectation that (1) actual rivals will be driven from the market, or . . . (2) rivals will be chastened sufficiently to abandon competitive behavior the predator finds threatening to its realization of monopoly profits.[12]

In Bork's view predation is an investment (a sacrifice) in pursuit of monopoly profits. Figure 20-1 shows a firm's profits, as a function of how good an offer it makes to consumers, with better offers lying to the right.[13] In principle this profit function should incorporate everything except effects on competition, but in practice sacrifice tests often use short-run data, and we will often follow the conventional shorthand of calling it "short-run profits." A firm thus aggressively sacrifices profits if it chooses a point to the right of the peak in Figure 20-1.

There are at least three ways one might test for a sacrifice of short-run profits:

1. Calculate profit-maximizing output or price; then compare actual output or price.

2. Test whether the profit function is downward-sloping at the point that the firm chose.

3. Allow aggressive plaintiffs to pick *any* alternative course of action for the firm (benchmark) and show that *it* would have led to higher profits.

---

[12]*Neumann v. Reinforced Earth Co.*, 786 F.2d 424, 427 (1986).

[13]Thus, one can think of the horizontal axis in Figure 20-1 as showing quality, or quantity; one can also think of it as measuring price but in a right-to-left direction.

FIGURE 20-1 A "P < MC" test is more lenient to an alleged predator than a profit maximization (MR < MC) test because P > MR. If MC exceeds AVC, then a "P < AVC" test is more lenient still.

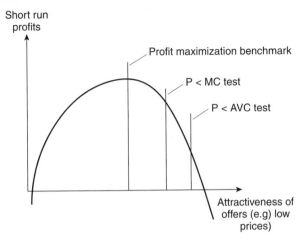

Implementation (1) seems unrealistic; yet (or therefore) it has been the butt of much criticism of sacrifice tests. In the *American* case, the district court said that antitrust does not require profit maximization, and cited a prior decision:

> A rule of predation based on the failure to maximize profits would rob consumers of the benefits of any price reductions by dominant firms facing new competition. . . . In addition, a "profit maximization" rule would require extensive knowledge of *demand* characteristics—thus adding to its complexity and uncertainty.[14]

The court also cited a treatise arguing that the profit-maximizing price is seldom knowable: "It depends not only on the defendant's costs at the moment but also on projections of what those costs would be at higher and lower levels of output."

Implementation (2) compares the firm's marginal revenue (MR) against its marginal cost (MC). If MR < MC, then the profit function is downward-sloping: the firm could have made more money by making a slightly less favorable offer or producing slightly less output.[15]

Suppose for a moment that the firm has little or no static market power: It faces a highly elastic short-run demand curve. Then MR < MC becomes p < MC, the Areeda and Turner (1975) test and a test that the district court

---

[14]Op. at 1201, citing *MCI Communications*. The first sentence of the quote is an odd claim in itself.

[15]When the profit function is single-peaked (as we have drawn in Figure 20-1), MR < MC also implies that the offer is more attractive than the profit-maximizing offer.

seemed to endorse.[16] For a firm without market power, the Areeda-Turner (A-T) test is a profit-maximization test: Any output above the profit-maximizing output will trigger an A-T "sacrifice" alarm.

Usually, of course, an alleged predator faces a downward-sloping demand curve. Then the A-T test is more lenient than profit maximization. In Figure 20-1 the A-T benchmark would be to the right of the peak, allowing a firm to sacrifice *some* profit before the A-T test flags a sacrifice. It could well make sense for a sacrifice test to have some lenience (or margin of error). After all, a firm might be to the right of the peak by accident (no firm can always fully maximize profits); or might wrongly be thought to be to the right of the peak; or (if the curve literally shows short-run profits) might be to the right of the peak for legitimate reasons. But the A-T version seems ad hoc and oddly mixes marginals and averages (price is average revenue). It is most lenient for a firm with the most short-run market power (i.e., whose demand is least elastic)—even though presumably one should worry *more* about predation by such a firm.[17] Nonetheless, many people have come to think that A-T is the ideal test or gold standard.

Other approaches, including both the DOJ's and one reading of American's and the court's, involve comparing profits against certain discrete benchmark alternatives, as we discuss next.

DOJ's Benchmark: Profits but for Challenged Acts

Recall that AA's response to entry on some routes came in two phases. In the first phase, which the DOJ did not challenge, AA matched the entrant's prices on a limited-availability basis. In the second phase, AA increased flight frequency, flew larger planes, and/or increased availability of its lowest fares: an expansion of "capacity" in the DOJ's words. The DOJ's Test 1 therefore assessed sacrifice by comparing AA's profits in the second phase to its profits in the first. This comparison also has the practical virtue that actual profitability data were (in some cases) available.

The DOJ claimed to show that AA's profits would have been higher had AA stuck to its initial response and not shifted to the second phase. American argued, and the court agreed, that this amounted to a profit max-

---

[16]Op. at 1198–1199. Areeda and Turner (1975, p. 716) conclude that "marginal-cost pricing is the economically sound division between acceptable, competitive behavior and 'below-cost' predation." As we will see, they propose average variable cost as a "surrogate" because of "the difficulty of ascertaining a firm's marginal cost."

[17]If the firm's demand elasticity is $e < 0$, then its marginal revenue is $(e + 1)/e$ times price. Thus the A-T test is an MR-MC test with a "fudge factor" of $e/(e + 1)$. To illustrate, consider a Cournot market with market demand elasticity equal to -2. Relative to the stricter, more logical MR-MC test, the A-T test gives a firm with a 10 percent market share (and thus a firm-specific demand elasticity of $-2/0.1 = -20$) a fudge factor of 20/19 or about 1.05, meaning that A-T finds sacrifice only if MR $<$ MC/1.05. A dominant firm with a market share of 80 percent (and thus elasticity of $-2/0.8 = -2.5$) gets a much more generous fudge factor of about 1.67.

imization test. The DOJ claimed that this was not so, and one of its experts urged the court to

> determine whether the incumbent had clear alternatives that the incumbent knew or could reasonably be expected to have known would have made it more money absent any predation profits. Importantly, it is not necessary to compare the alleged predator's actual behavior with its *most* profitable alternative.[18]

If American's initial response was not "short-run" profit maximizing, then the DOJ benchmark is more lenient than a profit-maximization benchmark, and would lie to the right of the profit-maximization benchmark in Figure 20-1. (And, if the initial response was to the left of the peak, then a range of shifts to the right would have passed the DOJ test.)

Did the DOJ unwittingly engage in Implementation (3) of a profit maximization test? We think not, because the alternative it used was presumably very salient in American's decision making. There is no sign that the DOJ creatively or exhaustively searched for a highly profitable alternative to which to compare American's profits, nor that the DOJ used the benefit of hindsight to second-guess what American originally thought would be a profitable strategy.

American's Benchmark: Exit from the Route

American argued that the proper legal test of sacrifice was whether its route-level variable costs (or perhaps its avoidable costs) exceeded its revenues on the routes. This "average variable cost" test has two rationales, each with shaky underpinnings.

Baumol (1996) Rationale

American sometimes followed Baumol (1996), who argued that comparing route-wide revenues with avoidable costs was the right test in principle because it promotes "competition among equally efficient firms, without sheltering less efficient firms from competition on the merits. See *Morgan,* 892 F. 2d at 1363; *Henry,* 809 F. 2d at 1344" (American's Appeals Brief at p. 23). If AVC is close to average avoidable cost, this might justify a price-AVC test. The idea is that if the incumbent's post-entry price satisfies p > AVC, then any firm with equal or lower AVC can profitably enter the route, so only less efficient firms will be excluded. Baumol's argument for marketwide average avoidable cost assumes that successful entry will fully displace the incumbent, and his test effectively amounts to a test of *sacrifice relative to exit* from the market (here, route).

---

[18]Op. at 1180.

But, as a DOJ expert noted, a rival might not fully displace the incumbent, and might be more efficient at serving the increment than the incumbent, yet still be excluded. This can occur if expression (1) holds:

(1)   American's Route-Level AVC < p < Rival's AC
                < American's Incremental cost

We argue below that condition (1) is quite plausible.

A second potential failure is more subtle, and arises because the DOJ tests used American's accounting system, not a literal price-cost comparison. Recall that this accounting system adds to a route's revenues its upline and downline contributions. An entrant on the route who does not have a hub will not capture such "contributions"; thus, even if it can fly more cheaply per seat-mile, it might yet be excluded by American's profitable pricing. If the complementarities are inherently lost to society when the entrant displaces American, then the asymmetry broadly reflects a true difference of product. But if passengers can connect between airlines flying the entrant on one leg and the incumbent on another, or if American could cheaply let them do so, then the complementarities can survive but may not be captured by the entrant. This can produce inefficient incentives.

But if American's hub operation is what handicaps entrants, why would an LCC enter on only a few routes, and then respond to adversity by exit, rather than enter with full-blown hub operations? At the extreme, why didn't Vanguard—one of the LCCs in the *American* case—take advantage of its much lower cost per ASM and simply enter with a full duplication of AA's route structure, including hubs?

The answer is that it can be hard quickly to acquire, and integrate a large number of flight control slots, aircraft, crew, and other inputs; indeed, this is why short-run and long-run costs may differ. Business models often need time to be "shaken down" before they can scale up. Capital markets may more readily finance a toe-dipping strategy than a riskier all-out plunge. Even if neither AA nor the LCCs really thought of the route as the unit of analysis, an LCC practically had to survive a period of being limited to a small number of routes. Such entry could be efficient in the long run even if it would be productively inefficient in the short run for an LCC to enter, then never expand.

Areeda and Turner (1975) Rationale

Areeda and Turner (1975, p. 716) provided the more traditional rationale for comparing price with AVC to gauge sacrifice. They suggested that AVC might be a more readily observed proxy for MC (recall that they argue that MC should in principle be compared with price). This "proxy A-T test" has been highly influential.

However, in the *American* case, route-wide AVC may have importantly underestimated incremental or marginal cost (or AVC for the incre-